Women and the Nazi East

Women and the Nazi East
Agents and Witnesses of Germanization

Elizabeth Harvey

Yale University Press
New Haven and London

For information about this and other Yale University Press publications, please contact:
U.S. Office: sales.press@yale.edu   yalebooks.com
Europe Office: sales@yaleup.co.uk   www.yaleup.co.uk

Set in Walbaum MT by SNP Best-set Typesetter Ltd, Hong Kong
Printed in the United Kingdom at the University Press, Cambridge

Library of Congress Cataloging-in-Publication Data
Harvey, Elizabeth.
  Women and the Nazi East : agents and witnesses of Germanization/
by Elizabeth Harvey.
     p. cm.
Includes bibliographical references and index.
  ISBN 0–300–10040–X (cloth:alk. paper)
   1. National socialism and women—History 2. Poland—History—
    German occupation, 1939–1945. 3. Germany—Politics and
    government—1933–1945. 4. Women—Germany—History—
    20th century. I. Title.
  DD256.7.H37 2003
  305.48′8310438′0904—dc22   2003014727

A catalogue record for this book is available from the British Library.

10 9 8 7 6 5 4 3 2 1

Contents

Illustrations

Plates

Maps

Tables

Preface

.

The support I have received from many individuals and institutions has been crucial to the writing of this book, and it is a pleasure to be able to record my thanks to them here. The research in German and Polish archives was made possible by a grant from the German Academic Exchange Service, a Nuffield Foundation Social Science Research Fellowship and a Research Fellowship awarded by the Alexander von Humboldt Foundation: I am extremely indebted to these institutions for their generous support. A grant from the University of Liverpool Research Development Fund assisted the project in its early stages; the University of Liverpool was also helpful in awarding periods of study leave without which the research for the book could not have been undertaken.

I greatly appreciate the help I received from the staff of the following archives and libraries: the Bundesarchiv (in Koblenz, Potsdam and Berlin), the Nordrhein-Westfälisches Staatsarchiv Münster, the Nordrhein-Westfälisches Staatsarchiv Detmold, the Staatsarchiv Würzburg, the Institut für Zeitgeschichte, the Geheimes Staatsarchiv Preußischer Kulturbesitz and its picture archive, the Landesarchiv Berlin, the Archiv des Diakonischen Werkes, the Deutsches Historisches Museum, the Archiv der deutschen Jugendbewegung, the Polish regional state archives in Poznań, Łódź, Katowice, Gdańsk and Lublin, the Instytut Zachodni in Poznań, the Poznań university archive, and the archive of the Main Commission for the Investigation of Crimes Committed against the Polish People in Warsaw.

I would also like to record my enormous debt of thanks to the women who agreed to be interviewed for this book. In giving so readily of their time, often following up interviews by offering additional information or allowing me access to private material, they provided insights into the topic I could not have gained in any other way.

Many friends and colleagues offered support and advice and shared with me their knowledge of the subject: their generosity made the process of researching the book all the more rewarding. I would like to thank Richard Evans, Richard Bessel, Anthony Nicholls, Reinhard Rürup, Jill Stephenson and Karin Hausen for their interest in and support of the project from its early stages. I would also like to thank Elisabeth Meyer-Renschhausen for her hospitality and kindness, Gabriele Czarnowski for her continuous interest in the project and for sharing her knowledge of occupied Poland and Polish sources, Mathias Niendorf for his very helpful advice and for providing me with sources on the inter-war German–Polish borderlands, and Wendy Lower for making available to me archival sources gathered during her research on occupied Ukraine. Many other people offered advice and ideas, provided me with information and material, and helped me locate sources for the project. I cannot mention them all here, but I would particularly like to thank Michael Alberti, Miriam Yegane Arani, Rebecca Boden, Jo Catling, Deborah Cohen, Andy Davies, Jane Elliott, Karin Friedrich, Johanna Gehmacher, Andreas Gestrich, Geoffrey Giles, Helen Graham, Julia Hallam, Kirsten Heinsohn, Rosaleen Howard, Helen Jones, Jenny Kermode, Jadwiga Kiwerska, Peter Klein, Alan Kramer, Jon Lawrence, Haide Manns, Anthony McElligott, Robert Moeller, Susanne zur Nieden, Susan Pedersen, Jan Piskorski, Janet Price, Dagmar Reese, Mark Roseman, Eve Rosenhaft, Carola Sachse, Joanne Sayner, Claudia Schoppmann, Gudrun Schwarz, Pat Starkey, Matthew Stibbe, Irene Stoehr, Georgina Waylen, Lora Wildenthal, Louise Willmot, Perry Willson and Ortrud Wörner-Heil. Helga Adler, Christoph Bernhardt, Wolfgang Hofmann, Sabine Kock, Johanna Meyer-Lenz, Susanne zur Nieden, Dunja Noack and Karen Schönwälder helped put me in touch with potential interview partners. Robert Wylot and Ewa Maciag-Balmforth assisted by translating and summarizing Polish literature and sources. Sandra Mather drew the maps with care and efficiency.

Special thanks are due to Lynn Abrams for commenting on parts of the manuscript: I have benefited greatly from her suggestions and criticisms. To Karl Christian Führer and Tim Kirk, who read much of the manuscript and discussed the project with me from the start, I owe an outstanding debt of gratitude. Any errors and shortcomings that remain are, of course, entirely my responsibility.

I would also like to thank Robert Baldock of Yale University Press for his support of the project, and Diana Yeh, Candida Brazil and Kevin Brown for their help and advice during the editing process.

Finally, this book would not have been finished without the support of Alison Kraft, whom I would like to thank for her insights and her companionship.

Abbreviations

ANSt	Arbeitsgemeinschaft nationalsozialistischer Studentinnen (Working Group of National Socialist Women Students)
APG	Archiwum Państwowe w Gdańsku
APK	Archiwum Państwowe w Katowicach
APL	Archiwum Państwowe w Łodzi
APLub	Archiwum Państwowe w Lublinie
APP	Archiwum Państwowe w Poznaniu
BA	Bundesarchiv
BDC	Berlin Document Center
BDF	Bund Deutscher Frauenvereine (League of German Women's Associations)
BDM	Bund Deutscher Mädel (League of German Girls)
BDO	Bund Deutscher Osten (League for the German East)
DNVP	Deutschnationale Volkspartei (German National People's Party)
DRK	Deutsches Rotes Kreuz
DVL	Deutsche Volksliste (German Ethnic Register)
EWZ	Einwandererzentralstelle (Immigration Centre)
FRG	Federal Republic of Germany
GDR	German Democratic Republic
GG	Generalgouvernement (General Government)
GKW	Główna Komisja Badania Zbrodni przeciwko Narodowi Polskiemu, Warsaw (Main Commission for the Investigation of Crimes Committed Against the Polish People)
HAG	Hauptarbeitsgebiet (Section)
HJ	Hitler-Jugend (Hitler Youth)
HSSPF	Höherer SS- und Polizeiführer (Higher SS and Police Leader)
IfZ	Institut für Zeitgeschichte
NSDAP	Nationalsozialistische Deutsche Arbeiterpartei (National Socialist German Workers' Party)
NSV	Nationalsozialistische Volkswohlfahrt (National Socialist People's Welfare)
NWStA	Nordrhein-Westfälisches Staatsarchiv
RADwJ	Reichsarbeitsdienst für die weibliche Jugend (Reich Women's Labour Service)
RErzM	Reichsministerium für Wissenschaft, Erziehung und Volksbildung (Reich Ministry of Education)
RFF	Reichsfrauenführung (Reich Women's Leadership)

RKF   Reichskommissar für die Festigung deutschen Volkstums (Reich Commissioner for
           the Strengthening of Germandom)
RM   Reichsmark
RMdI   Reichsministerium des Innern (Reich Interior Ministry)
RSF   Reichsstudentenführung (Reich Student Leadership)
RSH   Reichsstatthalter (Reich Governor)
SSPF   SS- und Polizeiführer (SS and Police Leader)
UAM   Uniwersytet im A. Mickiewicka
UWZ   Umwandererzentralstelle (Relocation Centre)
VDA   Verein (later Volksbund) für das Deutschtum im Ausland (Society for Germandom
           Abroad)
VjZG   *Vierteljahrshefte für Zeitgeschichte*
VoMi   Volksdeutsche Mittelstelle (Ethnic German Liaison Office)

Note on Place Names and Terminology

Where place names have a commonly used English form (Warsaw, Cracow), this is used throughout. Other place names are generally given in the form used by the prevailing political authorities at the time (thus Posen for the pre-1919 period; Poznań for the years 1919 to 1939; Posen for the years 1939 to 1945). Where German place names are used in relation to occupied Poland, Polish names are also given at the first occurrence in each chapter, and in the case of Litzmannstadt/Łódź at subsequent occurrences as well.

For the sake of readability, some German terms and their English equivalents that are associated with National Socialist notions of nationality, ethnicity and geography are used in the book without inverted commas. These include the following: ethnic German (*volksdeutsch, Volksdeutsche/r*), Reich German (*reichsdeutsch, Reichsdeutsche/r*), old Reich (*Altreich*), the East (*der Osten*). The terms *Deutschtum* and *deutsches Volkstum*, with their connotations of a German ethnic community transcending national borders, are not easily rendered in English: equivalents used here include 'Germandom', German ethnicity and Germanness.

Map 1. Germany's eastern provinces and western Poland in the inter-war period.

Map 2. Poland under German and Soviet occupation at the end of 1939.

Map 3. Reichsgau Wartheland and Reichsgau Danzig-Westpreußen.

Map 4. Central and eastern Europe at the end of 1941.

Map 5. Annexed territories and General Government at the end of 1941.

Map 6. Distrikt Lublin and Distrikt Galizien.

Map 7. Zamość area.

Chapter 1

Introduction: Women, 'Germandom' and Nazism

'We felt a bit that we were the "Eastern wall",' a former BDM leader told me, and laughed at the idea. In the 1990s, she could look back ironically at an ideology that had inspired a host of schemes in which German women were to help in making, 'Germandom' (*Deutschtum*) a bulwark against the supposed threat from 'alien' Slavs and Jews in the eastern borderlands of inter-war Germany and subsequently in the territories conquered from Poland in 1939. Rural projects aiming to create a model German peasantry in the eastern regions of the Reich bordering on Poland had, before 1939, provided an outlet for youthful 'borderlands activists'. They were also a model for larger-scale operations in occupied Poland after 1939. As Himmler's resettlement programme brought wave after wave of uprooted ethnic Germans to the conquered territories of Poland, displacing Poles and Jews in the process, German women, predominantly from the Altreich ('old Reich', or Germany in its borders of 1937), were recruited to help make the programme of peasant settlement work. Some of them were enthusiasts inspired by the vision of a 'new East' based on German peasant culture. Some were more pragmatic, sceptical and reluctant, but went nevertheless, sometimes under pressure. Once in occupied Poland, they undertook educational and welfare tasks while inculcating Nazi norms of 'Germanness' into a population defined as the future masters of the East. While focused on the welfare of the ethnic Germans, this 'womanly work' functioned to reinforce the National Socialist hierarchy of nationality and race in which the Jews were destined to have no place and the Poles no rights.

Exploring why German women became involved in implementing Nazi Germanization policies in the East and what they made of their experiences opens up a number of new perspectives on the history of women and Nazism. First, an analysis of how and why ideas about home, family and domestic culture came to be a crucial component of the drive to create the Nazi 'new order' in the East raises questions about women and constructions of

'Germanness' as well as the place of female activism in the Nazi state and its imperialism. Secondly, asking why usually young, typically middle-class women became involved in measures to 'strengthen Germandom' in the East brings one to consider the factors shaping the convictions and aspirations of middle-class German women growing up in the inter-war period and during the Second World War – as well as the constraints imposed upon them by the Nazi regime. Thirdly, an examination of these women's contribution to the occupation regime in Poland and what they witnessed of the regime's treatment of the non-German population raises the broader question of German responses to the Nazi persecution of groups defined as 'racially alien', both within the old Reich (Altreich) and in the occupied territories of eastern Europe. Finally, exploring how women recalled their experiences after 1945 can shed light on some of the factors shaping German memories of the war and its consequences in the decades since the collapse of the 'German East'.

The roots of womanly activism to 'protect Germandom': campaigns in Imperial and Weimar Germany

Long before the rise of National Socialism, German relations with eastern Europe and particularly with Poland were marked by a widely shared view that a cultural gradient existed between West and East and by the notion of a 'civilizing mission' as part of a German 'drive to the East'.[1] The National Socialist version of the 'civilizing mission' in conquered Poland was an exterminatory campaign of 'demographic restructuring' that was, nevertheless, still accompanied by claims to be bringing 'German culture' – frequently presented in terms of order, hygiene and efficiency – to the East. The recasting of the East, as envisaged in blueprints such as the 'General Plan East', entailed the destruction of the Jews, the displacement and decimation of the Poles, and the settlement of the territory with Germans – those, in other words, who fulfilled the regime's notions of Germanness – to ensure permanent domination. These plans, and the immense destruction of human life which took place in the course of attempts to put them into practice, are well documented.[2] Less attention has been paid to the way in which this vision of a new order in the East operated to mould those classed as German into suitable 'settlement material', how they were – in the routines of daily life – set above and apart from other racial and ethnic groupings, and how a gigantic 'pedagogical mission' evolved to lead and cajole ethnic Germans into playing their allotted colonizing role as embodiments of German culture.[3] Monitoring and mobilizing ethnic Germans was a 'total' effort that entailed intervention into the private as well as the public sphere. On the 'ethnic frontier', every German child, every 'German' cookpot and kitchen garden were matters of public concern, bricks in the 'human boundary wall' of 'Germandom', potential weapons in the 'struggle' against 'alien ethnicity' (*fremdes Volkstum*). All of these matters were defined as matters for 'womanly expertise' and demanded womanly intervention. Such intervention, while often focusing on the domestic arena, could also span the private and public spheres, extending beyond the household into the wider community.

Analysing the way in which women were assigned, and in their turn embraced, a place within the colonizing efforts of the Nazi regime in occupied Poland means examining the nature of that role, and tracing the origins of an ideology that simultaneously exalted womanly concerns as national concerns, lauded women's caring energies, and harnessed them to a racist and chauvinistic pan-German vision of expansion and domination. Pre-Nazi campaigns to uphold and strengthen German ethnicity in the East against Slavic peoples helped form this thinking, as did German colonial expansion in Africa, where particular notions of gender in relation to the boundaries of national identity were evoked through the conquest of non-European territories and peoples. However, Nazism and its territorial expansionism was to give a new slant to the idea of womanly tasks, and a 'space' for women, in relation to an enlarged German *Volkstum*, a community transcending the borders of existing states and defined by language, culture and 'blood', inhabiting an expanding *Lebensraum*.

Looking back to the Kaiserreich and tracing the role claimed by, and assigned to, women in those campaigns on behalf of the German cause in contested borderlands or in conquered overseas territories reveals how the 'civilizing mission' – whether directed towards territory inhabited by Slavic or by African peoples – was also interpreted as a mission to 'domesticate' disputed or newly gained frontier zones. Strengthening *Deutschtum* and ensuring its domination at the point where it appeared challenged or compromised by the presence of a rival culture or a colonized people meant ensuring that German home life flourished and conformed to bourgeois notions of thrift, orderliness and cleanliness. These were projects over which women could preside, and in doing so stake their claim to a public role in the nation. Out of a presumed responsibility for the domestic sphere could be constructed women's wider responsibility for building German national identity and defending German claims in relation to other nations and peoples.

However, the female claim to share in the task of nation-building and colonizing had to be fought for: in this, nationalist women in Germany were sharing the experience of patriotic women elsewhere. How the relationship between 'womanly concerns' and 'national concerns' was defined and how women might justify their inclusion in the nation were issues that resonated in bourgeois nationalist movements throughout Europe during this era. As recent studies of gender and nationalism have demonstrated, nationalist ideologies have commonly displayed contradictions in their attempt to reconcile the notion of the homogeneity of a nation, and the equality of those designated for inclusion in its membership, with that of gender difference.[4] On the face of it, nationalism potentially transcended differences of class and sex. It projected the nation as a modern political formation in contrast to dynastically based regimes with their rigid and archaic inequalities: within the national polity or the nationalist movement, 'the people' are supposed to be united and empowered by each member contributing equally to the national whole.[5] At the same time, and in tension with the notion that men and women belonged equally to the nation, models of nationhood have also often depended on ideas of 'natural' gender difference, 'separate spheres', and gender hierarchy. For German women in the Kaiserreich to claim a role in the 'historic' and political task of reclaiming the 'German East' for Germans, or of helping to build a colony of German settlement in South West Africa, was to carve out a space for women in the public sphere at a time when assumptions about a strict separation between a public sphere identified as masculine and a private sphere denoted as feminine were widely held and strongly defended.[6] Typically, their participation in 'national tasks' was justified in terms of special contributions made by women to national life, either as the biological mothers of the next generation, as the guarantors of national culture and customs, as guardians of morality or as specialists in 'womanly' fields of endeavour such as child welfare, educational and charitable work. By defining such fields of activity as essential to the nation, women used nationalist ideology to challenge the construction of a public/private divide. Women's activities, whether focused upon the individual family or on activities within the wider society, could be represented as a seamless continuum of 'maternal' service to the nation, bridging the private and public worlds. Nationalism's claim – that it entailed popular participation in the life of the nation by all its members – could thus be used to challenge conventional 'separate spheres' ideology and provide an opening for women.

In Imperial Germany, where women had no vote and where in the largest *Land*, Prussia, they could not even join political parties until 1908, 'the nation' emerged as a rallying-point for middle-class women's aspirations for a public role in the absence of political equality. While bourgeois feminists combined a patriotic allegiance with a more fundamental challenge to the gender order that deprived women of rights and – in their view – stifled women's potential contribution to the nation, middle-class women who were less inclined to question existing gender roles found outlets for public activism within movements dedicated to the German cause.[7] From the perspective of the conservative establishment of the Kaiserreich, such nationalist engagement did not count as 'political', and the male leaders of nationalist associations were ready to see women swell their ranks and act as propagandists of the national cause. Within such organizations, women argued that their place in national life was based not on any idea of women's rights but on their duties as German women: in defining themselves, notions of proper womanhood and visions of orderly home life were all part of the rhetorical arsenal. 'Without German women there can be no German culture, without them no German land' were slogans to which both male and female devotees of 'Germandom' could subscribe.[8] In adhering to such beliefs and goals, German women gained the prospect of a public role that presupposed no particular expertise and no political insights beyond an exaltation of 'Germanness'.

The duty of nationally conscious German women to defend German *Volkstum* appeared all the more urgent where Germans were compelled to come into contact with 'alien' cultures, such as in the enclaves of 'Germandom abroad', in contested borderlands and in the colonies. This *Volkstum* was conceived as an all-encompassing ethnic whole that spanned national frontiers, uniting the population of the Bismarckian Reich with German-speakers beyond its borders and across the globe. Its bedrock was – so went the argument of *Volkstum* ideologues – a common mother tongue and culture that was transmitted by tightly knit, ethnically conscious families from one generation to the next and could thus remain 'untainted' by foreign influences whatever the environment. This idea formed the basis for the founding of women's groups within the Society for Germandom Abroad (Verein für das Deutschtum im Ausland) from the 1880s onwards, whose members predictably made much of German women's responsibility for the 'mother tongue' in their drive to promote German-language education in areas of German settlement beyond the borders of the Reich.[9] The women's groups in Germany took their cue from the flourishing women's activism within the German Schools Association (Deutscher Schulverein) in the Habsburg Empire, which mobilized nationally minded middle-class German-speaking women to oppose the alleged cultural incursions of Czech-speakers in the Austrian half of the Dual Monarchy.[10]

Just as German-speaking nationalists in Austria-Hungary constructed

Czechs as a threat to the German 'cultural mission' in central Europe, so the lobby of conservative nationalist Germans in the eastern provinces of the Reich who gathered in the Society for the Eastern Marches (Ostmarkenverein) conjured up the Polish menace. This organization saw itself as spearheading the German side in the 'ethnic struggle' that unfolded as Prussian governments sought to suppress the Polish nationalist movement and promote German settlement: to Germanize, in other words, the eastern provinces.[11] From the 1850s and 1860s onwards, the term *Germanisierung* had been routinely used to describe the policies used by the Prussian government to curb Polish cultural self-assertion and economic power, thereby forcing the Polish-speaking minority to assimilate into German culture on German terms, while at the same time expanding the area colonized by German *Volkstum*.[12] These goals were vigorously supported and propagated by the Ostmarkenverein.[13] A year after its founding in 1894, a German Women's Society for the Eastern Marches (Deutscher Frauenverein für die Ostmarken) was set up in Berlin.[14] German women were exhorted to outdo what was presented as the heroic biological and cultural contribution of women to Polish nationalism as mothers, educators and community activists.[15] The local groups of the German Women's Society for the Eastern Marches largely dedicated themselves to classic charitable tasks such as fund-raising for district nursing provision and German kindergartens in the rural East.[16] Some of its activists, however, sounded more combative tones that signalled a desire not to be restricted to domestic and charitable endeavour but to be involved fully on equal terms with men in public campaigning, demanding that women focus their energies less on charity bazaars and more on civic affairs and public speaking.[17] Even in the most reactionary political milieux, women could be found pushing against boundaries drawn by men to limit female activism. Given the all-encompassing nature of the 'struggle' against an ethnic 'foe', they reasoned, nothing less than the all-round involvement of women in the public sphere alongside men would suffice to meet the challenge.

From the 1890s onwards, German colonialism opened up a further space for women's activism in defence of the *Volkstum* as well as inspiring visions and expectations about German territorial expansion and domination that outlasted the history of the colonies themselves. German colonialism was also, of course, imitating the practices of other colonial powers and its enthusiasts echoed in their views on the role of German womanhood and domesticity in the colonies some of the ideas prevailing in the longer-established colonies of Germany's British, French and Dutch rivals. There, European women came to take part in colonial society, enjoying, in Anne McClintock's words, the 'rationed privileges of race', as wives and as single women working as missionaries, nurses and teachers.[18] Their function as European women in the colonies was to help maintain the 'superior' culture, promote the cohesion of colonial society, and enforce the boundaries between the colonizing and the colonized 'race' inside and outside the home.[19] The ideal of bourgeois domesticity – defined in terms of family life and customs and the physical environment of the home – was fundamental to the 'civilizing mission': it was to be lived by example by the colonizers and disseminated to the colonized.[20] In addition to their tasks of model housekeeping, European wives in the colonies had the function of upholding the sexual boundaries between 'white' menfolk and 'native' women and thus 'protecting the race' by preventing miscegenation.[21] The process of 'domesticating' the colonial conquests was, Ann Stoler has argued, not just a matter of 'civilizing' the indigenous people: the 'civilizing mission' was also about policing one's fellow-colonists.[22] If European women in their role as mothers and homemakers, nurses and missionaries were constructed as embodying 'cleanliness, purity and maternal fecundity' as the 'gatekeepers of the nation',[23] they were at one level defining themselves against the supposed standards and habits of the indigenous population, but also acting as models and guarantors of standards within the community of European colonists.[24]

Women who agitated in Wilhelmine Germany through the Women's League of the German Colonial Society for a greater female presence in the German colonies argued, as Roger Chickering has pointed out, that women had a 'particular, gendered civilizing mission' in which 'the domestic sphere was but a metaphor for German culture', standing for 'order, discipline and cleanliness – for civilization in the highest sense'.[25] The presence of German women in the major German colony of settlement, South West Africa (today Namibia) was intended therefore not only to help build family life and domestic culture, but also to uphold the respectability of colonial society, reproduce the 'civilized' norms of cleanliness, thrift and sobriety, and ward off the private and public disorder associated with the 'danger zone' of the frontier, where 'mixing' might occur and the culture of the colonizers degenerate.[26]

The position of the German woman colonizer, like that of other European women colonizers, was fraught with ambiguity, but nevertheless offered a literal and metaphorical space for self-realization, and the possibility of sharing the power of the colonizer.[27] German women were subordinate within colonial society to German men; yet racist doctrines placed them alongside German men as the 'racial superiors' of the colonized population. Germans of both sexes had to play their allotted roles in order to uphold the gender order and the racial hierarchy. If, according to 'imperial feminist' Frieda von Bülow,

German women's freedom and fulfilment in colonial society depended upon racial hierarchies remaining firmly in place, this also required their German male comrades to act the part of colonizer with sufficient vigour.[28]

The women who were active in campaigns to 'protect Germandom' and promote German colonialism in the Wilhelmine period scarcely constituted a mass movement.[29] They were not always listened to by the nationalist men whose efforts they aimed to support and often felt a need to justify the space they sought for themselves as women within nationalist campaigning. Nevertheless, they were not a marginal force in terms of the political and intellectual climate of the time. On the contrary, they were contributing to a powerful legacy of attitudes that comprised arrogance towards neighbouring Slavic peoples, dreams of domination over indigenous peoples overseas, and a conviction that the German *Volkstum* must be defended at all costs against alien influences – convictions that were strengthened by the experience of the First World War.[30]

Defeat and revolution gave this thinking new virulence as Germans faced the loss of Germany's colonies and of substantial territory and population, particularly in the East to the new Polish state. The climate of nationalist ferment, together with the growing political mobilization of women on the Right during the war and afterwards, fuelled female claims to be 'at the heart of the *Volk*' and its 'struggle'.[31] Middle-class nationalist women, enfranchised by the revolutionary government in November 1918, campaigned against the Versailles Treaty, expressing their outrage at the nation's humiliation.[32] Their concerns were shared by much of organized middle-class female opinion in the Weimar period, including bourgeois feminists.[33] Nevertheless, women who were active in the German National People's Party, in organizations dedicated to 'protecting Germandom', or in nationalist groups in the youth movement, were set apart by their overriding focus on the cause of the nation and *Volk*.[34] Many were also increasingly drawn to a strain of *völkisch* thinking whose appeal grew as disillusion with party politics and economic conflict spread.[35] The *völkisch* vision of the future nation was at one level concerned with putting a greater Germany on the map, aligning the state borders more closely with areas of German population in central and eastern Europe in order to gather in greater quantities of German *Volkstum*. Internally, building the nation on *völkisch* lines meant creating a community that would be united and homogeneous, suppress class conflict and exclude aliens: the Jews, the Slavs or other ethnic groups alleged to threaten German interests. It also meant building a society based on the polarity and complementarity of the sexes. For women on the extreme *völkisch* Right, commitment to 'womanly service' to the nation was welded to a vision of racial exclusion and struggle against the nation's enemies.[36]

Nazism and the 'ethnic struggle' in the East: a space for women?

Under Nazism, the ideology of the *Volkstum*, including the role in its cultivation played by domesticity and 'womanly' work and the corresponding function of women as missionaries of Germanness in the East acquired the status of official doctrine and was disseminated more powerfully than ever before. It was gaining new dimensions and implications. Germanness – as ever – began in the home, but with ever more emphasis now given to health and 'racial hygiene' as well as language and beliefs. The corollary of the regime's homage to the domestic sphere was its determination to interfere in it more radically than any previous government: this immediately opened up a rich field for female expertise and intervention. Domestic culture, moulded along Nazi lines, was defined as a bastion against the eugenically unacceptable as well as the ethnically alien. It was also envisaged as a bulwark against the cultural influences of decadent urbanism: the model household of Nazi fantasy was the peasant family centred upon a mother who was as competent in modern housekeeping as she was at cultivating folk tradition.[37]

For *völkisch* and nationalist women, the advent of the Nazi regime appeared to bring the fulfilment of their hopes for a resurgent nation and *Volkstum* as well as securing their place as comrades and 'fellow-fighters' in the new regime. But what sort of space did Nazism provide in practice for womanly activism, and what function did such activism fulfil? Historians have generally agreed that the female Nazis who sought most forcefully to assert women's interests and influence were quickly marginalized. They were replaced by leaders who were more compliant with the Nazi leadership's notions of a place in the public domain for women that was not merely 'complementary', but also subordinate to that of men.[38] More disagreement has arisen over whether the women who supported the regime did nevertheless succeed in carving out for themselves a 'womanly sphere' or 'womanly space' and what this amounted to. Certainly single-sex organizations such as the Bund Deutscher Mädel (League of German Girls), the NS-Frauenschaft/Deutsches Frauenwerk (Nazi Women's Group/German Women's Enterprise) and the women's Labour Service developed a high public profile.[39] But did Nazi claims that they were coordinating and promoting special women's tasks within the Third Reich amount to anything more than propagandistic dressing up of a policy that tended to limit women's professional and political activities to certain fields, assign women to subordinate rather than leading roles, and hold them back from gaining positions of authority except over other women?[40] Or, as has been suggested, did female supporters of the Third Reich create a realm within which they extolled 'motherly' values, with the effect of expanding the female presence in the public arena while affirming women's identification with home and family?[41]

Some general points can be noted about these questions. One is that notions of women's space or a women's sphere that radiated out from family and household into areas of public activity such as education, health and welfare should not be taken too literally. Such images can help illuminate how women and men at the time sought to understand and to prescribe gender roles in the Third Reich. Women could, for instance, use such a notion as the basis for a career within the regime's single-sex organizations.[42] However, this should not obscure the degree to which women were often deployed in their professional or political tasks alongside men, sharing in policy implementation in similar ways – even if not performing identical functions.[43] The second is to keep within view the context of ethnic and racial confrontation out of which *völkisch* thinking on gender emerged. In defining their nature and role as German women, women supporters of the Third Reich were always defining themselves as much against the ethnic or 'racial' enemy as against German men. As women, they might experience constraints dictated by gender norms; as Germans, however, they could claim comradeship in the 'ethnic struggle' (*Volkstumskampf*) in face of a presumed foe, and such comradeship was an important way of challenging rigid gender boundaries. The third is to raise the question of space in a territorial sense, and to ask what difference Nazi expansionism made to the conceptualization of a 'womanly space'. Conquered and annexed territories could appear, like the former colonial territories over-seas, as a blank sheet, a laboratory in which models of racial domination would be developed. This raised the question of how gender and racial boundaries would be organized in such a 'new order'.

With these considerations in mind, looking at the construction of a womanly role in the Nazi *Volkstumskampf* and wartime expansionism in the East may shed light on the space defined for women in the Nazi state and the function it played within the regime overall. The efforts to promote 'Germandom' in the eastern borderlands and after 1939 in occupied Poland exemplified the drive – as outlined above – to create model communities and a model domestic culture as the bedrock of the future Germanic nation. In the pre-war borderlands, women were drawn into 'combating the Polish threat' through social and welfare activities. As has been observed in relation to the women's Labour Service, cultivating 'national consciousness' among border-dwellers helped pave the way psychologically for subsequent imperialist expansion.[44] The proximity to the Polish border and the presence of the Polish minority, together with fears about the physical and cultural resilience of the native German population, all served to legitimize interference by 'missionaries of Germandom' not only in the political and cultural life of the community, but also in the private sphere. Such interference was generally characteristic of National Socialism, but here the efforts to politicize and penetrate the private sphere in the name of saving the nation were undertaken with additional zeal.

The attempt to construct a peasant-based Germanic Reich became immeasurably more ambitious and destructive after 1939 in occupied Poland, where the territories annexed to the Reich were immediately earmarked for Germanization, as were, after 1941, parts of the General Government. National Socialist Germanization was, in theory, based on the notion that the territory, not the people, was to be its object. The process would, accordingly, often be termed *Deutschwerdung* or *Eindeutschung* – the distinction between these terms and *Germanisierung* is lost in translation – to mark it off from the old, supposedly discarded policy of *Germanisierung* based on the repression and assimilation of non-Germans: this distinction was in line with Hitler's declaration in a speech to the Reichstag on 17 May 1933 that 'we do not recognise the concept of *Germanisieren*'.[45] Insofar as the population of the conquered territory could be defined as German, they were to be instructed in German ways: women here embraced a vast mission to stiffen the morale and improve the efficiency of the new ruling caste. With regard to the 'ethnically alien' (*fremdvölkisch*) population, the Jewish and non-Jewish Poles, the Nazi conquerors and colonizers in the East set out not to subdue, assimilate and exploit, but to displace and decimate them. The Polish population remaining was thus not to be an object of pedagogical efforts but the recipient of German commands – commands that could be issued by German women as well as by men.

Nazi women's and girls' leaders were assiduous empire-builders within the limits set them by the Party and state system in the Third Reich.[46] As the territorial boundaries of the Nazi empire began expanding, they embarked on programmes of 'womanly work' in the conquered territories: these were in the west (for instance in Alsace) as well as in Poland, but were pursued with particular ideological fervour in the 'new East'.[47] Analysing their involvement is a chance to probe the link between 'womanly work' within the Nazi regime and women's role in implementing racist policies. German women from the

Reich working with ethnic Germans in occupied Poland participated at the grass roots in a number of processes that reinforced the new 'racial' order there. But it is not certain whether these women were operating in practice in anything like a separate womanly sphere; whether they were routinely working alongside men, perhaps with special responsibilities as women; or whether they were crossing gender boundaries and taking on 'men's jobs'. Tracing detailed examples of women's involvement in maintaining structures of segregation and discrimination is a way of exploring general hypotheses about women's complicity and gendered spheres of action under Nazism. It can shed light on the question of whether it was in carving out a space for 'womanly activism' that women sealed their complicity in the inhumane measures of the regime, or by taking opportunities to cross boundaries conventionally demarcating men's from women's work.[48]

Women with a mission, careerists or conformists?

The focus so far has been on the way key functions were assigned to domesticity and 'womanly concerns' within the Nazi Germanizing project, and the implications of this for female activism in Nazi Germany. Further questions open up when one turns to look more directly at the women – mainly quite young, usually single and with above-average education – who were involved in schemes to 'strengthen Germandom', initially on a small scale in the eastern borderlands before 1939, and then on a much larger scale in the conquered territories of Poland. Policies that were based on ideas of German superiority and domination over 'alien peoples' opened up spaces for women as well as for men. The female pedagogical mission to the countryside sought to promote German culture through influencing mothers, children and indirectly the whole village: it could provide opportunities for a potentially all-round leadership role in which women could represent themselves as model Germans. How much appeal did such opportunities have, for what reasons, and for what sort of women?

The role of 'missionary of Germandom' may have appealed to a core of true believers, but it is worth asking whether the tasks allotted to women under the rubric of policies to 'strengthen Germandom' also appealed to a wider section of younger German women with more diverse motives and aspirations – just as women who in earlier decades had gone out to work in the colonies were attracted by a variety of prospects and opportunities. These questions have been briefly touched on by historians who, in the context of broader studies of girls and women in Nazi Germany, have looked at the mobilization of women for tasks in the East.[49] Other studies have considered the personnel recruited for the civilian administration in occupied eastern Europe – ranging, it has been suggested, from 'Eastern fanatics' to opportunists, those on the make and those escaping stalled careers or other problems back in the Reich – though they say little specifically about the recruitment of women.[50]

Exploring the mentality of the committed core of enthusiasts means looking at women who were typically recruited on the basis of their functions in Party or state organizations for tasks in the East. They may have volunteered to go, or they may have been expected to go because of the position they held: eastern assignments were presented as a test of activists' commitment.[51] Volunteers or not, these were the sort of women who embraced the role of 'female missionaries of Germandom' and who propagated it to others. One of the questions explored in this study is how far this category of enthusiasts reflected upon their role as women in relation to the 'historic tasks' opening up for Germans in the East, and how far they were carried away by the 'intoxication with the East' (*Ostrausch*) – a 'colonizing high' that, it has been argued, swept many Reich Germans as they arrived in occupied Poland.[52] In her study of the Nazi organization of women, Jill Stephenson has suggested that working in the newly occupied territories after 1939 (in the west as well as the East) represented for diehards in the NS-Frauenschaft 'a kind of escapism for fanatics', a chance for some to regain the dynamic momentum experienced during the so-called *Kampfzeit* that seemed to Nazi enthusiasts to have been lost in most parts of Germany since 1933.[53] The BDM activist Melita Maschmann claimed in her often-quoted memoir that being assigned in occupied Poland to what she termed 'a sort of "colonization work" in an "outpost"' helped restore 'the sense of national honour that had been so wounded in our childhood and early youth'.[54]

Some studies, and some participants' memoirs, show that other motives too – ambition, a desire for a wider field of responsibility – may have fuelled activists' willingness to work for the regime in the East. Nazi women students, it has been suggested, developed their programme of rural service in the eastern borderlands in order to assert themselves both in relation to their sometimes dismissive male colleagues and to a largely indifferent mass of female students, and saw it as a project that would accord with their self-image as an elite.[55] Other activists who 'went East' may also have envisaged a longer-term future in Poland, where they might be rewarded for their effort in the Germanization programme with improved prospects for themselves.[56] Some may have been inspired by romantic notions of rural life: a factory welfare worker whose memoir appeared in a 1980s anthology on German women's wartime experiences recalled her dream that a posting as a settlement adviser in the Warthegau would rekindle her 'idealistic' hopes in National Socialism, but also offer 'sun and wind and green fields after the years in the city'.[57]

Newly qualified teachers, kindergarten teachers, plus the rank and file of women students were pressed to take on tasks after 1939 in the annexed territories of Poland. There was a chronic shortage of personnel to govern the newly conquered territories: such postings to the East in turn made the short-age of teaching staff worse back in the Altreich.[58] Women were not regarded as replacements for men, but they were thought fit to plug some gaps, par-ticularly in sectors like schoolteaching. Accordingly, they were pressed into service in the East just as they were pressed into all kinds of compulsory wartime service, and restrictions were placed on those seeking to leave their postings or change their jobs.[59] Compulsion may thus have been the overrid-ing factor when such women, who might be termed willing conformists as opposed to activists, were sent to work with ethnic Germans in Poland. However, other reasons may have predisposed them to go along uncomplain-ingly with the regime's demands. The factors that ignited a blaze of enthu-siasm in a minority of 'believers' may have helped to generate uncritical compliance in others. It is worth asking whether women's reactions to such postings to the East – sometimes positive, sometimes mixed – were also influ-enced by their political socialization in inter-war Germany. Anti-Versailles and anti-Polish propaganda may have particularly influenced young women growing up in Weimar and Nazi Germany who belonged to those sections of German society most disposed to support German nationalism: the Protestant middle classes. Nationalist sympathies were certainly manifest in the outlook of girls in the bourgeois youth movement and Protestant youth and student organizations in the Weimar period, whose notion of a generation-based mission to save the nation was often coupled with xenophobic resentment and fears.[60]

For some young German women, accepting duties in the East may have seemed an opportunity for personal and professional development, even a form of emancipation that was in keeping with aspirations already encouraged by the regime. National Socialism promised young people a new status in society and a new freedom from the constraints of traditional structures of authority embodied in school and family. Such emancipation freed young women from home and family ties only to place them under new constraints of state and Party; nevertheless, the sense of gaining status, freedom and responsibility outside the family and through 'service to the *Volk*' appealed to many.[61] For them, exposure to a barrage of political instruction or compulsory rituals of national commitment may have seemed a price worth paying for the chance to be part of a peer group, with opportunities for sport and travel and developing one's talents in an environment structured by competitiveness and an emphasis on individual performance and efficiency. Young women who had absorbed the messages of the Bund Deutscher Mädel and the women's Labour Service would have been trained to regard a posting to the East as a further challenge, as a chance to prove their adaptability and resilience in an environment far from home and to gain novel and interesting experiences.[62]

For the career-minded, a posting to occupied Poland could also appear advantageous. The National Socialists came to power proclaiming they would reverse the 'unnatural' trends of modern democracy and female emancipation but signalled that women were needed as 'comrades' and 'helpmeets' to build the new 'national community'.[63] After a brief period when it seemed that women's higher education would be restricted, the aspirations of women with educational qualifications and career hopes were once again encouraged – while being channelled towards fields considered appropriate for women.[64] During the Second World War, the demand for women to enter new fields of work and take on new responsibilities was boosted: for many female graduates, as Jill Stephenson has pointed out, the war brought 'unprecedented opportunities'.[65] Some of those opportunities were beyond the borders of the old Reich. A posting to the East in wartime might be the necessary next stage in acquiring qualifications; for others, it could mean a step up on the career ladder that might not have come so quickly in the Altreich.[66]

While asking why women accepted a posting to the East enthusiastically or at least willingly, it is also important to consider how women who were indifferent or sceptical about working in occupied Poland ended up there too. The story of women's involvement with Germanization policies in the East thus raises the issue of how the regime – here as in other spheres – succeeded in securing compliance as well as mobilizing enthusiastic support. One explanation might be that few were prepared to risk possible personal and professional consequences by turning down a posting to Poland. Another might be that a sense of wartime duty overrode a dislike of the regime: that, in Gellately's words, 'once the war came . . . many who might have had second thoughts and grave reservations about Hitler and Nazism now put their country first'.[67]

Agents of segregation – witnesses of persecution?

One aim of this study is to consider the diverse routes by which women ended up on assignments in the eastern borderlands or occupied Poland. It also sets out to identify what functions women fulfilled once they were there, and to explore the different ways in which they responded to their experiences. In occupied Poland, German women were deployed to serve a regime of untrammelled force and brutality. To varying degrees, depending on their particular function, the timing and location of their posting, women could end up assisting in ethnic screening procedures and the selection of 'Germans', in the resettlement of Germans on Polish properties, and in the seizure and redistribution of Polish and Jewish property. Not all women were involved, or involved to the same extent, in all of these processes. The common denominator of that work, however, was that it served to reinforce the privileged status of those designated as ethnic Germans and sought to enforce certain norms of conduct on them. Whatever their views of the regime, women were in their daily routines – as teachers, advisers or organizers – implementing policies of segregation and discrimination.

Women sent to work with ethnic Germans in occupied Poland may thus collectively be considered as agents of regime policies. Whether individual women committed acts that would justify them being termed 'perpetrators' or 'co-perpetrators' is another question.[68] There were other German women living and working in Poland who certainly fell into that category. There were, for instance, women pursuing academic careers in occupied Poland as 'racial experts' in planning offices and 'research institutes'.[69] Others assisted in the forcible 'Germanization' of Polish children spirited away to the Altreich for adoption.[70] To take an extreme example, there were SS wives who chose to get involved in their husbands' work of rounding up and killing Jews or tormenting prisoners.[71] To answer the question of whether any of the women who are the focus of this study – nearly all of whom advised settlers and taught German children – should be considered in any sense perpetrators or co-perpetrators, it is necessary to identify any cases where they can be shown to have been involved in decisions that meant harming or endangering the non-German population, and cases where through obeying orders they assisted in carrying out any such acts.

Whatever the acts of particular individuals or groups, the women who taught, advised, monitored and assisted ethnic Germans in occupied Poland can be regarded as bearing a share of responsibility for helping maintain a system based on injustice. What, then, did women make of their experiences? How did they represent their work at the time, and how did they remember it in later memoirs and interviews? Contemporary accounts, subsequent recollections and interviews are frequently characterized by expressions of enthusiasm for the challenge of meeting the needs and solving the problems of the ethnic Germans: these include expressions of satisfaction at doing something 'worthwhile' and 'rewarding', of feeling needed, of 'being someone' for the first time, or of undertaking hard work under tough conditions. Where women did describe their work so positively, one can ask whether such responses were tempered or outweighed by unease at the consequences of Germanization, or whether their reactions changed over time. Bernhard Chiari, writing about German civilian personnel in occupied Belorussia after 1941, notes that some wrote euphorically of their experiences and cites a report by a BDM leader who described her work as 'the best and most interesting task in my whole life': such reports, in Chiari's words, 'are hard to reconcile with the horrors that could be observed all around'.[72]

Examining accounts written at the time by women working with ethnic Germans in occupied Poland can shed light on how far they replicated the regime's dogma, acknowledging that Germanization measures could be harsh on the non-Germans but legitimizing them with reference to the long-standing German–Polish conflict and alleged Polish crimes against Germans. Others may have sought to draw a veil over the destructive dynamic of 'strengthening Germandom' at the expense of non-Germans. Retrospective accounts offer the chance to explore how far women described their earlier actions in such a way as to defend such actions, exonerate themselves or express a more critical, and self-critical, perspective. Johanna Gehmacher, analysing an interview with an Austrian woman who through a BDM 'eastern assignment' (Osteinsatz) in 1942 ended up teaching in an elementary school in Poland, noted how her respondent took refuge in the view that her – 'womanly' – work was 'unpolitical', in line with a regime ideology which suggested that politics was predominantly the business of men.[73] It is worth exploring how some women may have sought to minimize their complicity – in contrast to others who were more self-critical – and whether notions of gender and 'womanly work' came into play in such self-exonerating accounts.

Their accounts may thus be read at one level for what they tell us about their actions – their role, as I would term it, as 'agents'. However, the women can also be viewed as potential 'witnesses': not in the strict sense of having had direct knowledge as eyewitnesses of specific events,[74] but in the broader sense of having been able to learn about the practices of the occupation regime by virtue of where they were and what they were doing. If they were confronted in Poland to varying degrees with evidence of the regime's exploitation and persecution of the Polish and Jewish population, the question arises as to how they dealt with such knowledge. Were they perturbed, did it change their attitudes to their assignment – or did they banish such impressions to the margins of their consciousness?

Some ways of approaching these questions are suggested by studies of the

old Reich and what Germans there knew about the crimes resulting from
Nazi racial policies. The population of the Altreich, while not confronted in
the same way with the regime's terror against 'alien populations' as Germans
living in occupied Poland or Wehrmacht soldiers on the Eastern Front, could
witness the treatment of Polish and Soviet forced labourers and of concentration camp inmates, whose numbers and visibility in public places grew in
the course of the war.[75] On the basis of how the regime treated its 'enemies'
within the Altreich and of information coming through from Poland and the
Soviet Union, obvious conclusions could be drawn about the treatment of
Jewish and non-Jewish civilians in the occupied East.[76] Those who have inves-
tigated what non-Jewish Germans in the Altreich knew at the time about the
'Final Solution' have concluded that anyone who wanted to know the fate
of the Jews deported eastwards would have been able to find out.[77] Many did
indeed know that the SS and its auxiliary forces were from 1941 onwards systematically murdering Jews, either on the spot or following deportation to
extermination centres. However, it appears that many others sought to shield
themselves from that knowledge by not asking questions and by not thinking
too hard about the clues that were there.[78]

Other questions about women as potential witnesses are raised by studies
of the 'occupation society' constituted by Reich Germans in the eastern territories under Nazi rule including the Soviet territories conquered in 1941.
These studies have highlighted both the level of involvement of civilian
administrators in the implementation of the crimes of the SS and police apparatus, and the spread of knowledge about the Holocaust. Male bureaucrats
in the notoriously corrupt, overstretched and chaotic civilian administration
in the East were fully aware of and often direct accomplices in persecution
and terror.[79] Studies of occupation policies in the General Government have
emphasized that the mass murder of the Jews soon became common
knowledge among the Germans – men and women alike – who were
living and working there.[80] How much German women in occupied Poland
saw and heard about the treatment of the non-German population would
depend partly on their typically subordinate role in the men's world of the
occupation administration, but also on the nature, timing and location of their
assignment.

As far as the women are concerned who were brought in to supervise and
support the ethnic Germans, the degree to which they must have learned, or
could have learned, about the worst crimes of the occupation regime is not
self-evident. Some may have been working hand in glove with SS officers;
others might have spent their entire assignment in the countryside isolated
from other Reich Germans and from the main centres of Party and state

administration. Simply by being in Poland, however, German women would have experienced how the occupation authorities treated the subjugated population, and from 1941–2 onwards it would not have been difficult to find out about the murder of the Jews. On the basis of what they wrote at the time and recounted later, their responses to such knowledge as they did acquire – whether callous, curious or compassionate – can be explored.

Perspectives and sources

This study focuses on German women's involvement, before and during the Second World War, in a range of schemes and initiatives designed to 'strengthen Germandom'. Its depiction of Nazi Germanization policies in occupied Poland is, inevitably, partial. The book seeks to shed light on the implementation of Germanization policies at the grass roots, particularly in the countryside, exploring the relationships between Reich Germans and ethnic Germans, and the devastating impact of Germanization on the non-German population. It does not, however, set out to provide a full picture of the experiences of the Poles and the Jews displaced, dispossessed and persecuted in the course of Germanization measures: that would require another study. The perspective that dominates in this account is that of German women from the Altreich. This does not imply identification with their view of events, but it does enable a more detailed probing of their testimony.

The scope of the study is also affected by other, more accidental factors. Many contemporary sources were destroyed, including most of the records relating to the activities in occupied Poland of the Bund Deutscher Mädel (BDM), the NS-Frauenschaft/Deutsches Frauenwerk, the Nationalsozialistische Volkswohlfahrt (NSV) – the Party welfare organization – and the women's Labour Service (Reichsarbeitsdienst für die weibliche Jugend: RADwJ). Many of these records were deliberately destroyed during the German withdrawal. Other records fill some gaps, but some aspects of the topic remain better documented than others. Sometimes, a cache of reports written at the time turned up unexpectedly; more often, trawls yielded a blank. The study does not, for this reason, aim at equal coverage of all regions where Germanization efforts took place: instead, it examines a range of initiatives in the pre-war eastern borderlands, and subsequently looks in detail at different aspects of 'womanly work' in different parts of occupied Poland, focusing first on the 'annexed territories' (*eingegliederte Gebiete*) and moving on to consider areas within the General Government.

Some comment is called for on the ideologically loaded terms 'East' and 'German East' to be found in Nazi discourse on the borderlands and occupied Poland and which crop up in texts quoted in this study. The pre-war border-lands, together with the annexed territories and the General Government, were all liable to be referred to generally as 'the German East' (*der deutsche Osten*) or 'German eastern territories' (*deutsche Ostgebiete*) as well as simply 'the East' (*der Osten*). Confusion over the concepts that were bandied around as the Nazi empire expanded triggered an official attempt to regulate 'Eastern terminology': the term 'German East' was to denote the old eastern provinces of the Altreich together with the annexed territories of western and northern Poland, while 'the East' could be used to refer to the General Government as well as the occupied Soviet territories and the Baltic states.[81]

As far as the annexed territories are concerned, this study places particular emphasis on the so-called 'Reichsgau Wartheland'.[82] Compared with the other annexed territories, the Reichsgau Wartheland, or Warthegau for short, was characterized by the most extensive measures to displace Poles and to bring in ethnic German settlers in their place. This policy was coupled with a tighter screening of the native ethnic German population than that carried out in 'Reichsgau Danzig-Westpreußen' or in the formerly Polish areas of Upper Silesia that were incorporated into the Reich.[83] The Warthegau is also noto-rious in the history of the Final Solution as the region of occupied Poland where the mass killing of Jews by the use of gas began, in December 1941 at Chełmno.[84]

Where the General Government is concerned, the focus is on the two regions which were targets of Germanization from 1941 onwards: Distrikt Lublin and Distrikt Galizien. Examining German women's involvement in these efforts, particularly with relation to the Zamość lands in Distrikt Lublin, which have been seen as a 'laboratory' of Nazi ethnic policies in Poland, entails – here as elsewhere – examining evidence of their reactions to the actions of the occupation regime, specifically to the genocide of the Jews and the wholesale eradication of Polish villages in the struggle to enforce German settlement in the face of growing Polish resistance.[85]

Where contemporary unpublished sources were found, they are used, together with material from Nazi publications, partly to reconstruct what women's role in constructing the new East was supposed to be and to convey a sense of what Germanization entailed at the grass roots – including the reac-tions of the ethnic Germans to being monitored and drilled by 'missionaries of Germandom'. The aim is also to build up a picture of the expectations, aspirations and outlook of the women concerned on the basis of what they wrote about their professional work or about their 'voluntary' assignments.

Some of these texts were straightforwardly propagandistic and written for publication; others were internal monthly reports written for superiors. In addition to this material, the study draws on published and unpublished memoirs. That of Melita Maschmann is already well known and has been the subject of critical analysis,[86] but other published memoirs have less often been quoted. Some unpublished recollections by women who lived and worked in occupied Poland form part of the extensive collection of personal memoirs gathered by the *Dokumentation der Vertreibung* project sponsored by the West German government in the 1950s, only a proportion of which was selected for publication.[87]

The study also draws on interviews as well as on other forms of personal testimony.[88] The main body of interview material comprises transcripts from sixteen interviews conducted between 1994 and 2001 with women who took part in schemes to reinforce the German presence in the East: other interviews yielded useful additional information, but do not form part of the main body of material analysed. The respondents included two BDM leaders, six elementary school teachers, a kindergarten teacher, a teacher of agriculture, a women's Labour Service participant, a press officer working for the NS-Frauenschaft, a settlement adviser, and three students sent on vacation assignments to the Warthegau. One had been active in East Prussia before and during the war, while all the others had worked in occupied Poland for shorter or longer periods, all but three of them in the Warthegau. All but two had lived in West Germany after the war. Two of them, in addition to being interviewed, also allowed me access to private material they had written dating from the war years. While the respondents are a relatively small sample, they did include women whose motives for going to Poland and whose reactions to their experiences in the East were, to judge from their accounts, very different, and whose views in hindsight of the work they had done there diverged widely. Basic data about their background and activities in relation to the Nazi Germanization of the East are given in the appendix. All respondents have been given fictitious names.

The oral testimony provided at one level further factual information that could be compared with contemporary written sources concerning the process of recruitment, living and working conditions, typical numbers of children looked after or taught, and so on. At another level, the interviews offered the chance to probe how the respondents recalled their reactions at the time to the situation in occupied Poland, and how they reflected on their past actions and responses from the perspective of the present. The respondents' post-war personal and professional lives affected how they interpreted and presented to an outsider the memories of the weeks or years they spent in the East as young women. However, the way they talked about their wartime experiences also reflected their position in relation to controversies about the Nazi past that characterized the old Federal Republic and have continued in united Germany since 1990.[89] As a sense of collective shame and responsibility for the mass murder of the Jews has come to be widely shared and publicly expressed, the fate of non-Jewish Poles under the Nazi regime – not least those deported to the Reich as slave labour – has also become more widely acknowledged amid debates on the issue of restitution to survivors.[90] Insofar as such a process of consciousness-raising has occurred, it is likely to shape German women's memories of occupied Poland and the way they choose to express them, depending on their political standpoint and their degree of self-reflection. Like the published and unpublished memoirs, some of which date back to the 1950s, the interview material offers clues to how memories of the Nazi period have been shaped both by the process of forming an individual life story and by the shifts in German public memory and political culture since the Second World War.

Chapter 2

Weimar Women and the Mission to the Eastern Borderlands

For nationally minded middle-class German women – from activists explic-itly concerned with 'protecting Germandom', to members of Protestant or bourgeois feminist organizations, to the cohorts of young nationalist women in the youth movement – the issue of the eastern borders after the Treaty of Versailles was one that aroused patriotic protests and triggered practical aid initiatives. Coupled with the issue of the German minorities newly created in the territories lost under the Versailles treaty, who were labelled 'border Germans' (*Grenzdeutsche*) as distinct from the 'Germans abroad' (*Auslands-deutsche*) living further afield, the plight of the eastern fringes of the Reich became a focus for womanly national engagement in the wake of the First World War.[1] Out of the Weimar campaigns relating to the 'German East' both within and beyond the new borders emerged key motifs that continued after 1933 to shape ideas about women's role in defending *Deutschtum* in the East and images of the Polish foe.

Germany's eastern borders after Versailles

The creation of successor states at the Paris peace conference of 1919 produced borders that in many cases did not coincide with ethnic boundaries, depriving the defeated powers of territory and population and leaving national minor-ities within the new states. Areas of potential conflict were created and cases where the discontented could argue that the principle of self-determination, proclaimed as guiding the peace settlement, had been flouted. Germany's new borders, laid down in the Treaty of Versailles and in subsequent decisions taken by the Allied powers following plebiscites in selected borderland areas, provoked protests and campaigns in the west and north as well as in the East; however, it was the issue of the eastern borders which in some regions provoked violent clashes and which caused the most intense and lasting resentment.[2] The Versailles Treaty awarded to Poland nearly all of the former Prussian province of Posen – where a Polish uprising in December 1918 secured Polish control in anticipation of the peace settlement – and most of the province of West Prussia, which after 1919 formed what Germans called the 'corridor' giving Poland access to the sea and dividing East Prussia from the rest of the Reich. Danzig, which Poland had hoped to gain, was instead separated from the Reich and given the status of a Free City.[3] The Treaty furthermore ordered plebiscites for ethnically mixed parts of East Prussia (Ermland[4] and Masuria) and for the north-eastern part of the former province of West Prussia. These took place in July 1920 and resulted in overwhelming majorities in favour of the territories remaining German: the borders were then confirmed with some further minor adjustments in favour of Poland.[5] A plebiscite was also set for the eastern part of Upper Silesia to take place in March 1921: in the period up to the plebiscite, the region became the site of violent clashes between German and Polish forces which erupted again in May 1921.[6] On the basis of the plebiscite, Upper Silesia was partitioned, with much of the industrial zone awarded to Poland as a consequence (see Map 1).[7] An additional loss to Germany in the east was the Memel district, a strip of territory which was placed under Allied administration by the 1919 peace settlement and annexed by Lithuania in 1923.

The bitterness of German opposition to the territorial losses in the east was fuelled by the fact that a large German minority remained in the western areas of the new Poland, particularly in the former West Prussia, now the Polish province of Pomorze, though also in the western part of the former province of Posen (Poznania). The size of the minority was reduced by a sub-stantial German exodus to the Reich from Pomorze and Poznania, especially from its towns and cities, between 1919 and 1921. Those who chose to remain became Polish citizens; only a very small number remained while retaining German citizenship.[8] Territorial gains had made Poland, like other 'winners' at the Paris peace conference, notably Romania, an ethnically heterogeneous state. Conversely, territorial losses had made Germany more homogeneous. The large Polish-speaking minority population within pre-First World War Prussia, the target of state repression and attempts at enforced 'Germaniza-tion', had shrunk to a remnant within the new borderlands.[9] Nevertheless, Germans in the inter-war period who remained bitter and outraged by the new borders regarded the Polish minority within the eastern borderlands of the Reich with suspicion and often hostility, associating them with the powerful new Polish state that had been built upon Germany's defeat.[10] Entrenched German anti-Polish stereotypes, dating from the Kaiserreich and earlier, continued to flourish.[11] Fulminating anti-Polish phrases were, however,

coupled with pragmatic policies on the part of the Reich and Prussian authorities that set out to monitor, criticize, curb and weaken Polish minority
organizations in the borderlands rather than smash them. Such caution
derived not least from the need to protect the interests of the German
minority in Poland.[12]

The eastern borderlands of the Reich, shrunken after Versailles, were reorganized administratively by the Reich government in ways that highlighted
the 'amputations' that had taken place. The north-eastern part of West Prussia
that remained with Germany following the 1920 plebiscite was integrated into
the province of East Prussia: it became 'Regierungsbezirk Westpreußen',
its name a reminder of the lost territory, with Marienwerder as the seat of
district government.[13] The eastern part of Silesia that was subjected to the
1921 plebiscite was constituted as a new province of Upper Silesia, shorn of
its eastern fringes after the plebiscite: this status continued until 1938 when
administrative reorganization reabsorbed the territory into the province of
Silesia.[14] The part of the former Prussian province of Posen and the western
remnant of West Prussia that remained with Germany after the Versailles
treaty were amalgamated in July 1922 into a new province, Grenzmark Posen-
Westpreußen (Border Province of Posen-West Prussia), consisting of a single
Regierungsbezirk (Schneidemühl), a government district formed of three dis-
connected parts with a total population of around 330,000 in 1925. Administratively, the new province made little sense, and it was dissolved in 1938,
with the northern part becoming a Regierungsbezirk in the province of
Pomerania, while the middle and southern parts were added to the provinces
of Brandenburg and Silesia respectively. The point about its creation and its
name was that it served as a reminder of the lost provinces: it was territorial
revisionism embodied in an administrative structure.[15]

The eastern borderlands were viewed throughout the inter-war period by
the governments of the Weimar Republic and the National Socialists alike
as a crisis region, warranting subsidies and special measures to combat the
longer-term problems of the decline of agriculture and depopulation, coupled
with the short-term problems caused by the drawing of the new borders –
infrastructure difficulties where rail and road lines had been severed, the loss
of industries in the case of Upper Silesia, and the loss of markets for agricultural products. East Prussia was highlighted in borderlands propaganda as
plagued by its position, cut off from the rest of the Reich by the 'corridor'.
Using Reich and Prussian sources of structural aid to the eastern borderlands
governments, politicians and administrators in the regions sought to ease the
burden of debt on farms and businesses and channel resources into welfare
and education. There was much talk about rural settlement in the border

regions as an answer to depopulation, and some action: nearly 40,000 new
settler holdings were created between 1919 and 1933.[16] For some, rural settlement was seen primarily as a solution to the social question, but frequently
the discussion of social and economic issues was accompanied by the evocation of a Polish threat.[17]

The 'German East', comprising the issue of the lost territories and the condition of the eastern borderlands remaining within the Reich, continued to be
a major public issue throughout the Weimar period and beyond. In the sphere
of foreign relations, Weimar politicians, diplomats and administrators tried for
the most part to avoid confrontation with Poland; governments generally
sought to tackle disputes over minority rights on both sides of the new borders,
while keeping alive the hope of future border revision through negotiation.[18]
At the same time, state funding helped to finance the propaganda of nationalist organizations protesting at the loss of territories in the east and protesting
at alleged violations of the rights of Germans living under Polish rule.[19] Organizations founded during the Kaiserreich to protect and promote 'Germandom'
now had the new eastern borders on their agenda: these included the govern-
ment-subsidized Society for Germandom Abroad (Verein für das Deutschtum
im Ausland or VDA), traditionally concerned with maintaining German-
language schooling in German minority communities abroad.[20] A major new
lobbying organization concerned with the question of the lost eastern territories was a new confederation known as the German Protection League
(Deutscher Schutzbund für das Grenz- und Auslanddeutschtum), founded in
1919 and supported by the German Foreign Office. The German Protection
League sought to coordinate efforts to promote and preserve 'Germandom
wherever it was threatened, whether in the borderlands or abroad':[21] its
affiliated member organizations included older *Deutschtum* organizations
together with newly founded groups representing former inhabitants of the
lost territories.[22] The German Protection League helped organize the German
vote in the plebiscites in East and West Prussia in 1920 and in Upper Silesia
in 1921, chartering ships and trains to take former residents to their old
homelands to vote.[23] Thereafter, it pressured Weimar governments for tougher
action on behalf of German minorities in the territories ceded to Poland and
for more resources to be channelled into the eastern borderlands.[24]

Women, the Volkstumskampf *and the*
'German East'

On the extreme Right of women's borderlands campaigning in the 1920s
was the singular figure of Käthe Schirmacher (1865–1930) (see Plate 1).

Schirmacher had been a campaigner for women's rights within the bourgeois feminist movement, but her national concerns came to predominate over a feminism that linked her to liberal and internationalist political circles. Before the First World War she had already been a vocal advocate of upholding German domination over the Poles in the East, becoming a speaker for the Pan-German League, the Deutscher Ostmarkenverein and its partner organization, the Deutscher Frauenverein für die Ostmarken.[25] After the war, she became active in the DNVP (German National People's Party) and was elected in January 1919 to the National Assembly for the constituency of West Prussia, a seat she held only until the Reichstag elections the following year. Her blistering attacks in articles and speeches on the Allies, on Poles, Jews and alleged enemies focused on atrocities perpetrated against Germany and Germans, and the violation of what she depicted as the helpless, weakened body of the nation. Schirmacher excoriated the (male) cowards and traitors who in her eyes had brought about Germany's downfall, exposing it to 'poison' and 'white fungus', to 'international Jewry' and the 'alien rabble of murderers from red Moscow'.[26] In a ruined, mutilated Germany, 'a rump, a stump, a cripple', women were needed to rebuild national unity and strength, to create a 'rule of both the sexes'; this would mean overcoming the opposition of men who resisted sharing power with women.[27] Schirmacher presented herself as a lonely crusader for Germany's honour, forever 'playing the song of the Ostmark',[28] preserving the memory of wrongs and losses. However, her energies also went into denouncing the marginalization of women in the nationalist movement and into staking German women's claim for an equal place in the national community.

Schirmacher's uninhibitedly *völkisch* and racist language contrasted with the more restrained style of many nationalist women who had been active in campaigns to 'protect Germandom' before the First World War and who now turned their attention to the lost lands in the East and the condition of those remaining on the eastern edges of the Reich. Nevertheless, these women too were quick to denounce the victorious Allies together with the Poles and to dwell on Germany's victimhood, while asserting women's indispensability in the struggle against Germany's enemies that – in their eyes – would determine the nation's future. That nation – as imagined by women in the long-established Society for Germandom Abroad (VDA), in the German Protection League and its affiliated organizations – was a gigantic *Volksgemeinschaft* comprising Germans from the heartlands of the Reich to the borderlands and further afield, bound into a single community by language, culture and 'blood', united across national borders. Such a community promised harmony between the sexes, and the absence of class, confessional and party political conflict. This vision could be read as a counter-model to the political and social order of the unloved Weimar Republic as these women saw it, beset with class conflict, economic miseries for the middle classes, and unsettling new models of womanhood.

While many women in the VDA continued to see their core activity in the 1920s as raising funds to support German communities abroad from Brazil to Transylvania and the Baltic, mobilizing children in VDA school groups in the process, they also concerned themselves with the Polish–German borderlands. Major areas of attention in 1920 and 1921 were the plebiscites in East and West Prussia and in Upper Silesia. Through the German Protection League together with organizations based in the eastern regions, middle-class nationalist women threw themselves into the plebiscite campaigns, caring for German refugees from the areas awarded to Poland and engaging in propaganda work to rouse public opinion across Germany and to draw in other women's organizations to work on behalf of the *Volkstum*.[29] In a brochure appealing for support for Upper Silesian charities, Else Frobenius evoked the fate of east Upper Silesia, overpowered by 'Polish terror':

> Whoever has travelled through Poland knows what happens in a short time to any area under Polish rule: desolate tracts of land, decaying huts, impassable roads, begging, ragged people on the streets and in the squares. A glaring nadir of culture, in harsh contrast to the gilded domes of churches and the faded palaces that rise like citadels out of the general chaos and are symbols of the arbitrary brutality enslaving the people . . . This is the image of Poland that sticks in the mind and it is this which is happening today in Upper Silesia. The Poles are penetrating into areas which under international law belong to Germany. Life and property of the inhabitants are mercilessly destroyed. Destroyed villages, blown up bridges, mutilated corpses mark the route taken by Polish terror. It has descended as if with brimstone upon a flourishing land that will soon be a wasteland as desolate as the rest of Poland.[30]

Else Frobenius (1875–1952) made a career out of 'protecting Germandom'. The sole woman present at the founding of the German Protection League and the first chair of its women's committee, she was a journalist from Latvia who saw her work on behalf of borderlands Germandom as indissolubly connected to her work for German colonialism and German communities across the globe.[31] From 1913 onwards, based in Berlin, she was the secretary of the Women's League of the German Colonial Society. In the 1920s, she travelled in the eastern borderlands and abroad on behalf of the German Protection League and the VDA and turned out a stream of articles for the press. Together with Ludwine von Broecker, a *Volkstum* activist originally from Posen, and the

Prussian *Landtag* deputy Elisabeth Spohr, Frobenius mounted an exhibition of women's propaganda work on behalf of 'Germans in the borderlands and abroad' at the German press exhibition in Cologne in 1928.[32]

Frobenius made her mark not least by coining banal but appealing slogans that sought to sum up the distinctive role of women as nurturers of national identity. As a publicist, her mission was to magnify women's contribution to the German cause across the world. Her voluminous output hammered home variants on a single message: 'Women are the heart of a people. Their love is its love. Their hatred is its hatred. If an idea is to permeate the entire people . . . women must be its custodians.'[33] Wherever she travelled among German-speaking communities, Frobenius would report back confirming this insight.

Such reports from key sites of the 'ethnic struggle' aimed to keep the 'bleeding borders' fresh in the minds of the members and of a wider public and to persuade women in the interior of the Reich to see themselves as fellow combatants. Describing the situation in the German East at the annual conference of women VDA members in Kassel in 1928, Elisabeth Spohr warned her audience about the situation of Danzig, stranded 'like a small island' off the larger 'island' of East Prussia, exposed to Polish designs upon it; meanwhile, she alleged, Polish propaganda was trying to persuade the Masurians in East Prussia that their vote in 1920 had not really been for Germany but for a 'Baltic Switzerland', an East Prussian state independent of the Reich.[34] She declared that the East Prussians were 'holding out' but needed more resources to combat the problem of depopulation and the crisis in agriculture. Spohr ended by declaiming the famous lines by the female bard of East Prussia, Agnes Miegel (1879–1964) (see Plate 2) that opened her pathos-filled hymn, couched as the appeal of the embattled homeland to the 'fatherland' beyond the Vistula: 'Über der Weichsel drüben, Vaterland höre uns an!'[35]

Alongside the battalions of VDA women and organized Protestant women who affirmed their commitment to the cause of Germandom in the borderlands and abroad,[36] bourgeois feminists were also adding their voices. German feminists in the 1920s were torn between affirming international cooperation and putting the German case in the wake of Versailles. For all that, defending German interests in the borderlands was and remained on the feminist agenda: demonstrating their national commitment and seeking to build bridges to new constituencies of organized women, nationally minded bourgeois feminists climbed on the borderlands bandwagon.[37] In 1920 Dorothee von Velsen, the later chairwoman of the German Women Citizens' Association (Allgemeiner Deutscher Frauenverein, later Deutscher

Staatsbürgerinnenverband) reported to the women's committee of the German Protection League on women's organizations in the eastern borderlands; in 1921, the social work pioneer Alice Salomon lent her support to patriotic appeals on behalf of Upper Silesia.[38] The League of German Women's Associations (Bund Deutscher Frauenvereine or BDF) affiliated to the German Protection League and in 1929 set up its own committee on 'nationality questions' (*Volkstumsfragen*). Its chair was Rosa Kempf,[39] who became an active participant in the German Protection League and a member of its working party (*Kleiner Arbeitskreis*) from 1930 onwards. Kempf could strike liberal tones: she spoke of the active woman citizen as a crucial factor in campaigns to protect German rights abroad and of the need for tolerance of ethnic difference and the defence of minority rights against a rising tide of chauvinistic nationalism across Europe.[40] However, she was also concerned to defend the particular rights of Germans and denounce Polish perfidy in stirring up disloyalty among the Polish minority in Germany.[41] Readers of the special issue of the BDF newsletter edited by Kempf on nationality questions were informed in 1931 of the spread of Polish kindergartens in the Grenzmark Posen-Westpreußen and of the need to counterpose the spread of 'alien culture' with efforts to build up 'our own culture' through 'libraries, singing clubs, folk dancing, amateur theatricals, kindergartens, women's clubs and sports clubs'.[42] Another article in the same issue highlighted, from the point of view of 'we women in East Prussia', the problems of the borders and the problems of East Prussia cut off from the rest of the Reich.[43]

Women's borderlands propaganda staked their claim to a distinctive cultural role in defending Germanness. An essay published in 1931 by Ludwine von Broecker, now chairwoman of the women's committee of the German Protection League, brought together several common motifs of this propaganda.[44] Avoiding explicitly revisionist demands, von Broecker conjured up a vision of an organic national community of Germans transcending the 1919 borders to encompass German-speakers throughout central and eastern Europe, to be upheld and celebrated by 'those who suffer even more from the internal fissures within the German *Volk* than from its division and fragmentation externally'.[45] The struggle for Germandom now welded Germans within the Reich to those outside its borders, transcending class and confessional differences, and in this 'struggle to decide the fate of our *Volk* which is being fought out on its borders' women had an 'indispensable' part to play. They would help build the 'spiritual community' of what Broecker called '*Volksdeutschland*' while stemming the 'hostile flood of alien *Volkstum* (*feindliche Flut des fremden Volkstums*)' that threatened Germanness from without. That role was based on 'silent work within the household' that preserved the family as the bedrock of German culture, but also on women's cultural and charitable activities in the wider community.

The evocation of domestic self-sacrifice combined with militancy in von Broecker's rhetoric was characteristic of how women's role in the *Volkstumskampf* was defined and propagated by borderlands campaigners. 'The German woman in the German home is a living fount of German *Volkstum*,' intoned a VDA activist from Essen at the VDA women's congress in 1927.[46] The idea of German motherhood, suggested Else Frobenius, should be at the centre of a 'festival of Germandom' among German-speaking communities abroad.[47] Maternalism would inspire women in the interior of the Reich to care for German women in the borderlands and abroad: acting in the spirit of 'highest spiritual motherhood'[48] women in the Reich would forge links with borderlands women, learning from their experience while 'enriching the bare existence of the sisters out there'.[49] Meanwhile, women in the borderlands would preserve the *Volk* by guarding folk culture and transmitting the 'mother tongue'. Far from being a private matter, remote from the affairs of state and nation, the German home was elevated into the site where the nation was generated and reproduced. Women were the biological guarantors of the *Volkstum* at a time when the birth rate, not least in Germany's eastern border provinces, was becoming a matter of concern: as a sign of the eugenically minded times, the German Protection League set up a committee on population questions in 1925 and the VDA women's newletter began carrying items on population policy.[50] Through its housewives and mothers, German values and German stock would prevail. Such ideas were reinforced by a deep vein of domestic ideology: the norms by which a nationally conscious woman would run her household were those of the model bourgeois housewife.[51] Thrift, order and 'ideological cleanliness' (*gesinnungsmäßige Sauberkeit*) would characterize the home that would act as a bulwark of national identity.[52]

Alongside this rhetoric of 'clean home, German spirit' ran the more militant discourse of women's role in the 'border struggle' (*Grenzkampf*), laced with the imagery of war and violence. Aggressive imagery was plentiful in evocations of the borderlands struggle in the wake of the First World War: in their writings, the 'soldierly men' of the Freikorps used metaphorical bulwarks, dams and the storming of alien-held positions in ways that have been read as reinforcing their embattled sense of masculine identity.[53] However, it was not just a fringe of militarist fanatics who evoked the alien floods threatening to overwhelm heroic border fighters: these motifs were part of the linguistic repertoire of a broader nationalist mainstream and were drawn on by women as well as men. Women in their border propaganda sought to

remind fellow-Germans about the martyrdom of the nation and its outrageous
treatment at the hands of the Allies. Alongside the cosy evocations of the
German housewife keeping faith with her *Volkstum* ran the discourse of
fortresses, warriors and battles together with the imagery of a national body
violated and mutilated, with borders that were 'burning' and 'bleeding'. In
July 1921 the Union of Protestant Women's Organizations wrote to Reich
Chancellor Wirth protesting against the 'outrageous rape of Upper Silesia'.[54]
In similar vein, Schirmacher described Upper Silesia in 1921 as 'burning':
'Burning land needs burning hearts. To the Upper Silesian front, oh burning
hearts of German women!'[55] Beyond the borders, Schirmacher saw barbar-
ians, ogres and rapists lurking: in 1922, she characterized the French as 'degen-
erate' and 'nigger-ridden' (*vernegert*) threatening Germany in the west, with
the Poles in the east as an 'immature people, backward and brutal . . . eating
into us like a hungry wolf';[56] elsewhere, she wrote of 'the Slavs' having
'devoured' the 'German' cities of Cracow and Prague and now 'lusting' after
Danzig.[57] Echoes of the same imagery appear in writings by VDA women.
'The alien fist drives every thorn deeper', wrote a VDA woman about East
Prussia in 1927, noting that the population of southern East Prussia were
sensing a 'voracious greed' emanating from the nearby border.[58] On the basis
of an emotional identification with home and fatherland, threatened by alien
'floods' and 'invasions', nationalist women conjured up the notion of a national
emergency requiring women to look beyond their immediate and 'natural'
sphere of home and family in order to stand shoulder to shoulder in comradeship with the nation's defenders. Luise Scheffen-Döring opened her
account of the work of the women in the German Protection League by citing
a verse by Gertrud von der Brincken evoking the warrior spirit of past generations and declaring that the Baltic Germans would stay put for ever:

> We carry too deeply in blood and gaze
> The long-gone ancestors' warrior fate
> And the same bonds hold us in their sway
> Should distant coasts lure us with glittering hue
> To the land that needs us we stay true
> We will stay – we will stay![59]

The mixture of the militant and the sentimental in depictions of women's
role in the border struggle is also to be found in reports of German women's
journeys to the eastern borderlands in the 1920s and early 1930s.[60] Rallies held
in the eastern borderlands, for instance that of the VDA in Elbing in 1932,
together with patriotric excursions organized by the VDA women's branches,
offered nationalist women from the interior of the Reich the chance to

experience at first hand the 'bleeding border', with its commemorative stones, plaques and crosses. Such excursions, in which participants could be duly horrified by the sight of barriers and border posts 'disfiguring' an otherwise idyllic 'German' landscape, were a chance for outpourings of nationalist mourning and defiance. Accounts of such trips might depict them as a pilgrimage: one Stettin woman described a journey through East Prussia as a 'bitter way of the Cross'.[61] Other accounts dwelt on grateful borderlands-dwelling women, touched by the charitable gestures of their sisters from the 'interior' and their empathy with their 'suffering'. At the same time, such narratives were an opportunity to strike poses of heroic resistance in the spirit of the Teutonic Knights. It was a commonplace to cite the song of the 'riders to the East' – 'Nach Ostland wolln wir reiten / Nach Ostland wolln wir gehn . . .'[62] – and, as Agnes Miegel did in her poem 'Über der Weichsel drüben', to conjure up past triumphs of German colonization in contrast to present humiliations.[63]

Women's agitation on behalf of the German cause during the Weimar years involved a spectrum of conservative nationalists, *völkisch* right-wingers and bourgeois feminists who shared an insistence on the injustices of Versailles and on the continuing threats to Germans inside and outside the borders of the Reich. *Volkstum* propaganda was a vehicle for expressing the vision of an organic national community that transcended state borders, united by the common project of asserting and defending German interests wherever they were threatened: within the nation thus imagined, women would have power and influence both in the private sphere and in community life. This vision may have appealed to those middle-class women who felt little affinity with the parliamentary politics of the Weimar Republic: the simple slogans of *Deutschtum* campaigns could enable women to pretend, by 'putting the nation first', to be 'above politics'. Yet such women still sought a form of public engagement, basing it on claims of female expertise in the household, welfare, health, reproduction, education and the cultivation of folk customs. Thus defined, the womanly work of nationally minded women was then assigned, in a manner typical of nationalist movements, a grand significance. The fighting talk of the nationalist Right and the conjuring up of images of the enemy – above all the Poles – served to frame fund-raising work, folklore exhibitions, mothercraft courses and the cultivation of social contacts between women in the interior of the Reich and women 'on the frontier' in heroic ways: unspectacular tasks were elevated into a historic mission. Simultaneously, eastern borderlands ideology with its emphasis on the German cultural mission in the East and the exemplary resilience of German frontier folk offered German women the opportunity to rehearse a version of a female national identity that was flatteringly superior to the 'foreigner', reassuringly traditional but with a militant and activist edge.[64] Borderlands womanhood would be a model for the rest of the Reich: unparalleled in housewifery, motherly but combative, caring but dauntless.

Meanwhile, a younger generation of women were turning to new ways of boosting 'Germandom' in the East. These women took up the ideology of the 'historic East', the theme of German victimhood and the negative stereotypes of the Poles; they celebrated women's place in the *Volkstumskampf*; sang 'Nach Ostland wolln wir reiten' and recited the verses of Agnes Miegel. However, they placed less emphasis on tea parties, sociability, committees, delegations and fund-raising. Instead, they were more interested in 'going to the peasants', fending off perceived Polish incursions while improving rural conditions: they saw their priority as 'saving the borderlands' from the rural grass roots up.

Saving the borderlands: the 'Polish threat' and the female 'pedagogical mission'

During the Depression years, a type of female borderlands activism became established in the eastern fringes of the Reich as a response to concerns about rural conditions coupled with nationalist anxieties about alleged alien, above all Polish, cultural and political influence. These were initiatives concerned with the borderlands peasantry, aimed at boosting German ways and German culture in poverty-stricken regions. Such activities came to be labelled as ideal work for the model young nationally minded woman, constructed as caring, energetic, tough and fearless: prescriptions aside, however, these tasks clearly had some appeal to some young women during these years. The result was a pedagogical mission typically undertaken by young women through a diverse range of agencies and initiatives: its aim was to activate the farming popu-lation of the borderlands in its allotted role as a bulwark of Germanness. Through a barrage of instruction and advice, these women activists attempted to encourage peasant families to assume orderly habits and unequivocally German loyalties, cultivating an image as comrades and fellow-fighters while highlighting their feminine contribution to the national project. Borderland activism was a chance to demonstrate national commitment combined with womanly devotion to the welfare of the borderlands. Undeterred by the mixed reception they had from the rural population, enthusiasts proclaimed them-selves to be a female vanguard inhabiting 'outposts' and 'citadels', vigilant against imagined incursions while looking ahead to conquest and expansion. In doing so, they created a template of social and nationalist intervention that would later be adopted by organizations for girls and young women under Nazism.

These initiatives were inspired partly by the borderlands agitation of nationalist women's organizations in the 1920s, their concerns with the 'endangered East' and their calls for solidarity with borderlands-dwellers. They also had important roots in the Weimar youth movement (*bündische Jugend*) and its 'discovery' of Germany's eastern borderlands, together with pedagogically inspired initiatives during the Depression to aid farmers' wives and reform rural culture to create a German 'bulwark against the Slavs'.

The youth movement's engagement with the 'problems of the *Volkstum*' had expressed itself since the early 1920s in excursions to experience at first hand the situation of Germans in the borderlands of the Reich and beyond. Trips organized by the *bündische Jugend* to German-speaking settlements in Yugoslavia, Hungary, Romania and Volhynia in eastern Poland gave students rich material for research projects as well as flattering opportunities for posing as envoys of Germanness to fellow-Germans.[65] For several participants in the Volhynia trip, it helped launch academic careers in *Ostforschung* that were to flourish under Nazism.[66] Closer to home, border excursions targeted East Prussia, Upper Silesia and the Border Province of Posen-West Prussia. At one level, these trips were about boosting the morale of the 'natives' through demonstrations of support and solidarity. At another level, they were a narcissistic exercise in which participants self-consciously displayed their dedication to the borderlands cause, enjoying the hospitality of fellow-Germans and the thrill of 'confronting the enemy'. As members of an educated younger generation that saw itself as politically and economically marginalized during the Depression, *bündisch* activists seized upon the 'crisis of the German East' trumpeted by nationalist lobbying groups and amplified by the press as a focus for their brand of nationalist, but socially conscious engagement. In this way, a self-styled generation of youthful pioneers believed that they would make their mark while remaining aloof from the party politics they despised.[67] The notion of being needed as agents of a 'spiritual resettlement' (*geistige Wiederbesiedlung*) in the depleted rural borderlands also had some appeal to educated young men and women facing bleak career prospects in their home towns and cities.[68]

Young men and women in the youth movement embraced the ideology of the *Grenzkampf* with its calls for borderlands defence and for measures to counter the Polish 'threat' with measures to save the economy of the borderlands, stem the outflow of population and invigorate the national consciousness of the Germans who must be persuaded to 'remain at their posts'.[69]

The mission to the borderlands was therefore not just about setting up facilities or institutions that might outbid or undermine Polish minority organizations: it was about drawing sharper lines between 'Poles' and 'Germans', and discouraging an indifference to national questions that might lead German-speakers and Polish-speakers to live in harmony, do business with each other, intermarry and not bother too much about what language their children spoke.

The *Grenzkampf* mentality assumed that where 'Germans' were indifferent, Polish nationalist fanaticism would rush in. In fact, the evidence of Polish subversion in the eastern borderlands was flimsy, whether one looked at the numbers of potential 'Poles' in the borderlands or at the nature and extent of Polish nationalist activity. German government statistics on the eastern borderlands in 1925[70] identified a total of 177,758 inhabitants who spoke only Polish, a figure which fell to 112,574 in 1933. In 1925, a further 478,548 were registered as bilingual or as speaking one of the regional dialects, a figure which also fell in the period up to 1933 to 323,585.[71] Most of those identified either as Polish-speaking, bilingual or dialect-speaking were residents of Upper Silesia; the second biggest group was to be found in the mixed-ethnicity districts of East Prussia (Ermland, Masuria and Regierungsbezirk Westpreußen); in the Border Province of Posen-West Prussia, the combined total in 1933 was around 10,000. In terms of language-use statistics, therefore, the 'problem' of the Polish-speaking minority was hardly overwhelming.

Moreover, language use was not a straightforward predictor of nationalist activity, still less of subversive intent towards the German state. A large spectrum of Polish organizations operated among the minority areas of the eastern borderlands, and they did receive support both from the government in Warsaw and from the Polish Association for the Western Marches. However, for all the paranoia of the German authorities their major concerns were the preservation of the Polish language by the provision of Polish-language instruction in German state schools (following a Prussian government decree in 1928 onwards, private Polish-language schools were also allowed),[72] kindergartens and youth organizations, maintaining Polish as a language of use in Catholic churches, and the promotion of a Polish-language press.[73] Above and beyond these cultural concerns, Polish mutual aid and community institutions such as agricultual cooperatives and banks sought to support the small farmers who constituted much of the borderlands minority population. In addition, the League of Poles in Germany (Bund der Polen in Deutschland, often shortened to Polenbund) which sought to represent the interests of the minority population had at its height had around 50,000 members in Germany as a whole.[74]

Such evidence made little difference to Germans who were determined to construct a Polish threat to Germany's eastern borderlands as grounds for going there, diagnosing problems and offering solutions. For young women in the youth movement, imbued with the tradition of exploring and celebrating the homeland, the eastern borderlands as a cause fitted their agenda neatly. The leader of the girls' section of the Freischar junger Nation (Corps of the Young Nation), one of the larger nationalist *Bünde*, described in May 1932 the rationale of their tour through East Prussia: 'On this excursion we want not only to give, but also to receive. We want to learn what belongs to us in the East and how it is threatened. We want to learn to love it by experiencing it personally and we want to create a strong bond between us and the people there.'[75] Alongside border tourism, practical forms of patriotic 'service' were emerging. In the late 1920s, new forms of borderlands activism for women developed in connection with the Boberhaus in Löwenberg, Lower Silesia. Set up in 1926 by the Silesian section of the Deutsche Freischar (German Corps), the Schlesische Jungmannschaft, the Boberhaus was conceived as a 'borderlands education centre' (*Grenzschulheim*) and gained prominence through its work camps bringing together 'workers, farmers and students'. In the Depression, work camps caught the public imagination as a model for tackling mass youth unemployment, and the Brüning government used the idea as a basis for the state-sponsored Voluntary Labour Service (Freiwilliger Arbeitsdienst) in summer 1931.[76] Women were initially marginal to the work camp movement, but from 1929 onwards Deutsche Freischar women began taking part as helpers in the Boberhaus camps; at the beginning of 1933, they set up their first women-only camp as a Voluntary Labour Service scheme.[77] The work camps run by the Schlesische Jungmannschaft aimed not only to create a model for community-building across the class divide, but also to assert a German presence in the mixed-language border region of Upper Silesia: the assumption that Poland and Polish influence within the borderlands posed a threat to Germany's national interest was a given.[78] Thus a work camp run in Pilchowitz on the Polish border in winter 1932–3 studied a text by Oertzen *Polen an der Arbeit* (Poland at Work), and dispatched a troupe out to tour the villages of the border area, where many spoke the local Upper Silesian Polish dialect, with a programme of amateur dramatics and folk songs. This three-month cultural offensive was intended, in the words of one of the camp participants, Lore Lommel, to 'awaken people's sense of attachment and obligation towards the German language and all things German': it was also, she claimed, bringing a superior form of culture to a mass audience refreshingly unspoilt by tawdry urban distractions: 'We were taking to the people something better than was ever given to them in the city – cinemas and bars – anything in the city that was good was always only for the higher social strata. Only in the countryside was it possible to embark unburdened on an active new cultural policy.[79]

Women in the Deutsche Freischar also took part in 'village weeks' organized by the Boberhaus in Silesian villages near the border. In 1931, fifteen students from the University of Breslau went for ten days to Himmelwitz (near Groß-Strehlitz) in Upper Silesia to undertake 'ethnographic research' among the borderlands-dwellers, staying in farming households, helping with farm work, and preparing presentations for afternoon workshops on themes such as rural settlement and farm economics. Evenings gave participants the chance to chat to their hosts, extract information from them and to write up the data thus gathered in reports on the family's daily routines, genealogy, farm management and 'mentality' ('political and religious views, mental outlook'). Recording her impressions of Silesian village life for the women's newsletter of the Deutsche Freischar, one participant noted the 'characteristic loose jackets' worn by the women in the fields and the 'Polish dumplings' in the soup pot.[80] Following up the 'village weeks', a group of Breslau schoolgirls embarked on a 'Land Service' project in 1932. In the words of one of the male leaders of the Deutsche Freischar, Land Service aimed to educate its participants in the ways of the peasantry and teach them to 'mediate' between the Germans on the periphery and in the heartlands of the Reich, and between the middle classes and the peasantry. It also saw itself as monitoring the borderlands, where 'from the church towers one can look into Poland, where a restless neighbour is arming itself that will not hesitate to seize more German land when the opportunity is favourable'.[81] The Breslau girls' Land Service involved nine schoolgirl members of the Deutsche Freischar between the ages of 16 and 19 spending a fortnight in Petersgrätz, a village in Upper Silesia, helping with the harvest while filling in questionnaires based on those of the Boberhaus village weeks on the political views, income and personal habits of the villagers. The purpose, explained the author of a report on the project for the Deutsche Freischar women's newsletter, was pedagogical in a dual sense: participants would learn about rural Upper Silesia, while the farmers would gain new ideas, 'stimulation' and contact with the urban world. With apparently unreflecting arrogance, she remarked that it was essential for rural folk to adopt a broader view of events and look beyond the narrow concerns of their daily round.

The agenda underlying the young women's investigations emerged in extracts of their reports published in their newsletter. A close eye was kept on the 'national' and political situation of the locality: one of the village families, it was noted, was 'proud to be an island in a Polish sea', regarded

Polish-speaking Catholics of the region as Poles, and was pleased to belong to 'the village with the most Nazis in the whole district'. The visitors also noted carefully how frequently their hosts washed themselves and their children and brushed their teeth, and recounted with satisfaction their assault on dirt and disorder in the local tavern. They were pleasantly surprised that the girls of the village could swim; but tut-tutted, from their perspective of impeccably bourgeois 'good taste', at the village women's adoption of 'modern' style and what they saw as the resulting aesthetic lapses: artificial flowers and garish cushions in the parlour, Sunday best outfits with glass bead necklaces, high heels and hair done with curling tongs. They also reported with concern a tendency to inbreeding in the village: '2% Idioten, Degeneration' noted one schoolgirl expert. Small-scale as it was, this Land Service was part of a trend during the Depression: inquisitive young urbanites headed for the country-side, enthusing about the joys of physical labour, and set about monitoring the political loyalties, the housekeeping standards, taste and bodily health of the borderlands population, using the 'crisis of the East' as legitimation for their investigations.[82]

Like other youth movement groups, notably the extreme right-wing Artamanen,[83] the Schlesische Jungmannschaft thought that the problems of the depopulated and 'endangered' rural East could be solved by rural settle-ment. The ruralizing fantasy that settlement could solve urban unemploy-ment, reverse the long-term trend of east–west migration and build a 'wall of Germans' (*Wall von deutschen Menschen*) against Polish influence in border regions had been a staple of public debate earlier in the 1920s, but gained further momentum in the Depression years.[84] The dream of repopulating the countryside with the urban jobless underlay the thinking behind the Voluntary Labour Service,[85] and promoting rural settlement was to remain, for all the Nazi regime's failure to enable large-scale settlement at the expense of big landowners, part of the agenda of the Reich Labour Service (Reichsarbeitsdienst).

The vision of rural settlement offered women a role as pioneers. Women were needed on the land not only as settler wives, but also as providers of rural cultural and social amenities that would help make settler villages more viable. Such tasks provided opportunities for untrained women volunteers as well as for female professionals. Volunteers without farming experience might lend a hand in farm households and organize village entertainments; meanwhile, women with expertise in farming matters and a background in education and social work would undertake a systematic programme to advise farmers' wives: in so doing, they would reform domestic culture, increase the health and fitness of rural families and build village community life. Such ideas drew on a longer tradition of concern with standards of rural house-keeping that generated a movement to train girls in agriculture and horticul-ture and deploy women agricultural teachers as countrywomen with expertise in advisory roles.[86] However, the Depression with its attendant rise in farm foreclosures and simultaneous calls for rural settlement schemes made the needs of agriculture and the situation of farm women the focus of broader public interest.

By 1932 bourgeois feminist periodicals, social work and educational jour-nals and the press more generally were portraying the woman settlement adviser as a new female professional meeting the needs generated by the upsurge in rural settlement, particularly in eastern Germany. A pilot project was launched in eastern Pomerania.[87] There, on the initiative of Dr Änne Sprengel, an official of the Pomeranian Landwirtschaftskammer (Chamber of Agriculture), twelve settlement advisers (*Siedlungsberaterinnen*) were appointed in spring 1932 to work in the district of Köslin. In Sprengel's vision, the settlement advisers had to address farm women in their roles as mothers, managers and workers simultaneously. Sprengel's ideas found a ready audi-ence in youth movement circles, where they were energetically promoted by the educational reformer Herman Nohl. Nohl, professor of education in Göttingen, who welcomed what he saw as the younger generation's new orientation towards the land and towards the East, had agitated for a plan for a thousand youth centres and kindergartens throughout the eastern border-lands; he had helped mobilize funding for Sprengel's plans, and went on to elaborate the vision of a female pedagogical mission in the East, tackling 'cultural poverty' and building rural communities from the grass roots, to audiences of students and social workers.[88]

Nohl pointed out that the educational reform movement of the early Weimar years had sought to analyse the urban milieux that generated neglect, disease and delinquency: now he exhorted his fellow educational reformers during the Depression years to turn their attention to the poverty and depri-vation of remote rural backwaters where high infant mortality and child neglect lurked unsuspected. The woman settlement adviser, or settlement helper, according to Nohl, was a key to the educational mission in the East, and embodied powerful contemporary trends. In Nohl's diagnosis, these included 'the recognition of the national significance of the East and its endangered position', characterized by depopulation and cultural neglect; the back-to-the-land movement triggered by unemployment; and a trend on the part of women to reject 'old-style women's emancipation' in favour of cele-brating women's 'creative energies within the family and the household'. In tune with the times, enthused Nohl, the settlement adviser would thus combine the reassertion of distinctively womanly values with the unleashing of a new pioneer spirit associated with the land and the East.[89] The settlement adviser could also help to launch kindergartens in rural areas, reinforcing the efforts of local authorities to employ qualified kindergarten teachers in village kindergartens. Nohl and other advocates of rural kindergartens agreed that they would not just relieve the burdens on overstretched housewives but would be a means of transporting new values and new ways into families, exerting an influence upon mothers 'hygienically, educationally and in general human terms'.[90] At the same time, Nohl emphasized, kindergartens in the eastern borderlands would serve 'national political' goals: as the 'living core' of rural welfare, the kindergarten gained particular importance in mixed-language border areas, as it did among German-speaking communities abroad, by ensuring that pre-school children not only spoke the German language but acquired its 'spirit' from earliest youth.[91]

Providing aid to settlers also appeared to give the women's Voluntary Labour Service something substantial to do: the lack of obvious tasks, apart from doing the laundry for men's camps, had plagued the women's schemes from the outset.[92] Proposals published in autumn 1932 by feminists and youth welfare experts envisaged women's Voluntary Labour Service camps in rural areas providing not only help for farmers' wives but a focus for cultural life (laying on 'evening events for the whole village'): these camps would also act as a training ground for women settlers of the future and help overcome what was diagnosed as 'girls' aversion to the occupation of settler'.[93] In the Reich Labour Ministry guidelines on the women's Voluntary Labour Service issued in November 1932, provision of aid to settlers' wives was presented, among other examples, as an appropriate model for such schemes.[94] Youth movement women saw all this as a sign that politicians, administrators and welfare experts were coming round to their point of view. Magdalene Keil-Jacobsen, a Boberhaus activist, wrote early in 1933 about the potential for youth movement projects within the Voluntary Labour Service framework and the need for more camps for women: 'at least here in the East, the most important task [for women's camps], is to assist in the expansion and shaping of settlements'.[95] Youth movement women, she argued, should become more involved in the Voluntary Labour Service: not least, they should make natural camp leaders.

Harnessing the Voluntary Labour Service to assist settler wives was already being tried out in summer 1932 following contacts between Sprengel and Elisabeth Eckert, who ran women's Voluntary Labour Service camps in Pomerania on behalf of the Evangelisch-Soziale Schule (a Protestant social work training college). Their contact led to a link-up between the work of the Pomeranian settlement advisers and the Voluntary Labour Service.[96] Under this arrangement the female Labour Service volunteers supported the settlement advisers by helping with farm and household tasks and organizing kindergartens in the settler villages.

By 1933, small-scale initiatives associated with the youth movement and the women's Voluntary Labour Service had set a pattern of what Nohl termed 'pedagogical aid to the East' (*pädagogische Osthilfe*), a task that appeared particularly suited to women, inspired as it was by a vision of defending the German East through cultural activities and modernizing it through social welfare. For women whose careers in education and social work were blocked by welfare cutbacks during the Depression, working in the rural East could appear as both a refuge and an outlet for their talents.[97] At the same time, schemes to aid settlers offered the potential for absorbing a mass of amateurs: presented to young unemployed working-class women and middle-class students alike as offering new challenges and experiences, they appeared to meet a perceived need to train young women in domestic skills while providing cheap labour for rural households. The idea appealed not least to feminists whose vision of 'shock troops' of young women aiding settler wives was coupled with the idea of a countryside shaped by the pedagogical influence of the female settler adviser and the young woman teacher: such schemes would expand into new fields the 'social mothering' role achieved by women in the caring professions.[98]

The social reforming thrust of such initiatives, from Nohl's vision of an all-encompassing social-pedagogical rural infrastructure and his desire to open up employment opportunities for unemployed young teachers and social workers, to Sprengel's concern for the health of the overworked farmer's wife, was unmistakable. The reforming impetus reflected the belief shared by the youth movement and by liberal and left-wing educational reformers in welfare provision and social pedagogy as the key to moral progress and national cohesion. The 'civilizing mission' they constructed saw the German population of the borderlands as neglected and marginalized: if Germans on the periphery of the Reich were to be bound more firmly into the national community, they needed modern welfare and education facilities together with, in Nohl's words, an infusion of 'intellectual energies' (*geistige Energien*) from all over Germany.[99] Recourse to arguments about defending 'Germandom' against alien forces was, however, never far away: such arguments were tinged with anxieties about Germany's capacity to hold out against future Polish territorial claims that would be backed up by Poland's demographic strength and military might. Thus Sprengel referred to the poor health of German schoolchildren in a settlement 'right by the Polish border', while Nohl cited the comparative birth rates of Poles and Germans in support of his argument that the borderlands were in danger and that the 'wall of German people' had to be strengthened as a defence against the Poles.[100] Depictions of the borderlands-dwellers were tinged with ambivalence: the 'natives' might be celebrated as the stalwart defenders of German culture, but they also needed to be galvanized into performing their allotted role as a bulwark against Polish influence more effectively. Similarly, incoming settlers in the rural East were presented as brave pioneers, but at the same time vulnerable: if they were to play their part in boosting the population and economic strength of the borderlands, they had to be taught how to make their new villages into viable communities. In this mission to teach borderlands Germans to be more efficient and more nationally conscious, women claimed a central role.

Chapter 3

The Nazification of Women's Borderland Activism, 1933–39

The Nazi takeover in 1933 did less initially to sharpen German–Polish tensions than had been expected or feared: the new regime moved carefully.[1] On the face of it, the pact with Poland in 1934 defused tension and even encouraged Polish organizations in the borderlands to assert themselves more strongly in response to Hitler's declaration in 1933 that 'we do not recognize the concept of Germanization', seemingly distancing Nazi policy from the forced assimilation policies of the Kaiserreich and assuring Poles that they would not be forced to become Germans.[2] In practice, however, the German authorities' attempts to undermine and weaken Polish cultural organizations in the borderlands continued after 1933, often copying and imitating successful Polish models in the process.[3] The German aim was to prevent Polish organizations extending their influence to the ethnic 'in-betweens', to isolate a core of committed Poles, and to ensure that National Socialist organizations dominated community life. From 1938 onwards, moreover, the cautious approach began to give way to more overt aggression, and the Polish minority in the eastern borderlands of Germany began to experience new levels of harassment and even assault.[4]

For many women who had been involved in campaigning on behalf of the 'German East' in the Weimar years, National Socialism appeared a promising vehicle. Just as the chairmen of the various *Volkstum* organizations rushed to greet the new regime in 1933, women activists in the German Protection League and the VDA placed themselves at the disposal of the 'national revolution'.[5] For its part, the regime soon brought *Volkstum* groups into line and ended the pluralism of Weimar campaigning. Insofar as bourgeois feminists had sounded more liberal tones on nationality questions, they were no longer to be heard as organized feminism vanished from the scene.[6] Meanwhile, conservative lobbying groups within the eastern borderlands of the Reich were absorbed into the newly created Bund Deutscher Osten (BDO): Ludwine von Broecker emerged as the 'women's leader' of the BDO.[7] The VDA continued in existence under a new leadership, its autonomy radically diminished, while its ostensibly private and unpolitical status made it a convenient cover for Nazi policy in relation to German minorities abroad. VDA women continued their propaganda campaigns and excursions to enlighten German women on border issues.[8] However, they found themselves increasingly competing with, and ultimately subordinated to, the NS-Frauenschaft.[9] The Nazi women's organization, ever eager for new fields to conquer, set up a department on 'borderlands and foreign affairs' and began training its members on *Volkstum* issues, undertaking border excursions, partnership arrangements and donations to Germans abroad.[10] Nazi women leaders lectured each other and their memberships on the 'spirit of the border', the Versailles Treaty (with maps), and the need to counteract Polish cultural offensives with offensives of their own.[11] The impact of this was to keep pushing to willing or captive audiences the notion that women were the heart of the *Volk* and crucial to the *Volkstumskampf*. That message had changed little from the Weimar period, though there was now an insistent emphasis on the biological as well as the cultural foundations of Germanness.[12]

Meanwhile, the initiatives in the rural borderlands that before 1933 had been a minority enthusiasm proliferated and expanded as state and Party organizations took them over and raised their profile. Many of the assumptions underpinning women's activism before 1933 – the notion of a womanly pedagogical mission, the perceptions of the needs and deficiencies of the German borderlands population, and the assumed need for vigilance against a Polish threat – continued to characterize borderlands schemes as they became instrumentalized for National Socialist purposes.[13] Änne Sprengel continued her campaigns for settlement advisers, and in early 1934 Herman Nohl could be found delivering his messages about social pedagogy in the countryside to women's Labour Service recruits in Pomerania. However, changes were afoot as well. The Voluntary Labour Service was taken over by the National Socialists, and new schemes emerged such as the Land Year and the Student Land Service, both giving a high priority to *Volkstumsarbeit* in the eastern borderlands and providing opportunities for girls and women as participants and organizers. Welfare and youth work provision sought to present itself as having a clear 'national-political', i.e. anti-alien mission. Overall, ideology became more sharply anti-Polish; at the same time the mistrust of the Churches' role in the 'ethnic struggle' became more pronounced.

Borderlands activism after 1933 played its part in policing political conformity among the borderlands population: by definition, the right sort of Germans for the borderlands were not just hard-working German-speakers, but loyal National Socialists. Community-building now took place under the banner of Nazi Party organizations, and the levels of local activism and loyalty towards the regime were monitored. Whereas the youth movement activists before 1933 had – in their general suspicion of party politics – diffuse ideas about any political message they were disseminating in the countryside apart from the need for commitment to the German cause, rural activists were now expected to project the Party message, including racial ideology, into farming households. In 1934, alongside Herman Nohl at the Pomeranian women's Labour Service training camp, a Professor Solger lectured the recruits on 'race as an obligation'.[14]

'Ethnic struggle' and empire-building: defining women's tasks and mobilizing resources

The idea of placing women in borderlands villages to help settlers and to run kindergartens and youth groups had an obvious appeal for National Socialists. In its variants – ranging from the deployment of volunteers on short-term assignments to the appointment of kindergarten teachers and youth workers – this formula was taken up and applied by women's and girls' organizations as well as by the state authorities. Those organizing young women under the regime's auspices – to take the examples of the women's Labour Service, the Student Land Service and the girls' Land Year – saw borderlands schemes as a ideal form of 'service'.[15] Participants would learn about rural housekeeping while being exposed to the discipline of community life and 'wholesome' rural ways; the young women would help preach modern hygiene and nutritional wisdom to rural housewives, while promoting children's fitness and discipline through kindergartens and youth activities. This, so went the theory, would improve rural efficiency, which in turn would serve the 'ethnic struggle': the rural housewife would express her German identity in the orderliness of her house and garden, in the tastefulness and authenticity of her dress and décor, in her children's health, habits and fluency in German, and her explicit rejection of Polish language and culture. Aside from the inflated claims, these programmes were a device to provide ideological training while giving participants something practical to do. They reflected the ambitions of organizations that were competing to expand their sphere of action. That expansionist drive also entailed asserting women's interests, securing a niche for women within the 'ethnic struggle' and raising the profile of female activism alongside that of men.

The quest for organizational self-aggrandizement dovetailed with the interests of regional and local authorities in the border provinces, who were also quick to deploy the 'borderlands rationale' when bidding for resources. Pet projects could be justified on the grounds that they affirmed German culture and combated Polish influence: the most banal activities could be presented as having a heightened significance in the context of the *Volkstumskampf.* Keep-fit classes, village sewing circles, mothercraft and cookery classes could all be depicted as counteracting foreign cultural influences; indeed, any initiative which gathered girls and women together as Germans could be presented as a blow against 'alien' organizations and a form of political socialization.

The 'borderlands rationale' featured prominently in the development of the women's Labour Service under Nazism, which in 1936 was renamed Reichsarbeitsdienst für die weibliche Jugend (RADwJ) and brought under the control of Reich Labour Service leader Konstantin Hierl. Hierl and Reich Labour Service representatives used the alleged role of the women's Labour Service in boosting Germanness in borderland communities to raise the profile of the scheme. In April 1938, a deputy of Hierl's, trying to persuade the Reich Ministry of the Interior that new camps in East Prussia should belong to the Labour Service rather than to local authorities, declared that the women's Labour Service 'is deployed in the borderlands primarily in the interests of *Volkstumsarbeit* and will go on being deployed permanently for that reason'.[16] The women's Labour Service in the East fulfilled – in theory – several functions related to the needs of the eastern border regions as defined by the regime: these included combating the shortage of farm labour caused by the flight from the land while excluding Polish migrant labour; combating the flight from the land itself by enhancing the quality of rural life; and bringing the regime and its message to backwaters where Nazism had not yet penetrated.[17] At the 1937 Party Congress, Hierl described women's Labour Service camps as 'citadels in the countryside' (*Burgen im Lande*) in which 'conscious Germandom and practically applied National Socialism can be lived in an exemplary way and from there transmitted into the families'.[18]

The resources of the Labour Service were increasingly channelled towards the eastern provinces.[19] Regional governments in these provinces lobbied hard to reinforce the trend.[20] In spring 1938 the Reich Ministry of the Interior's borderlands fund (*Grenzlandfonds*) granted RM 30,000 for the setting up of twelve borderland camps in East Prussia. A few months later, a district government official from Pomerania asked the Reich Interior Ministry to fund ten new permanent women's Labour Service camps in his province, claiming that the camps would supply labour for small farmers and settlers and boost the morale of the population in remote villages: all this was particularly important, he argued, in districts bordering on Poland.[21] By the end of

December 1938, following a phase of rapid expansion, there were 45 camps in East Prussia, 48 in Pomerania and 56 in Silesia.[22]

Meanwhile, other schemes were emerging that mobilized German youth to aid – and influence – borderlands farmers. Within such schemes, young women were typically expected to provide help to farmers' wives, or run kindergartens and activities for rural youngsters. The Student Land Service set up in 1934 recruited young academic men and women for the task of converting a supposedly 'unpolitical borderlands population' into 'convinced National Socialist Germans'.[23] The participants liked to think of themselves as an elite that would 'provide a living example to the German people of the Eastern idea' (*dem deutschen Volke den Ostgedanken vorleben*).[24] They were certainly in no danger of becoming a mass, given the numbers involved: around 400 in 1934, rising to around 3,000 in 1938–39.[25] Women remained in the minority: in summer 1937, 852 women took part in the Student Land Service, comprising 26 per cent of the 3,263 participants.[26] The students' efforts were mainly focused on Pomerania, Silesia, the Border Province of Posen-West Prussia, and East Prussia.[27] Here, they worked both in new settler villages and in ethnic 'danger zones' where large numbers of Polish-speaking inhabitants were seen as a threat to German domination. While acknowledging that other Party and state organizations were operating in the rural East with the same goal, the students argued that they could act as a vanguard, providing intensive bursts of national-political tuition that would make a difference in areas of Polish 'cultural insurgence'. Participants usually lived and worked for several weeks with farming families in exchange for board and lodging and a nominal wage: the format clearly owed much to the pre-1933 village weeks and the Land Service of the *bündische Jugend* described in the previous chapter. Reich government subsidies to the scheme rose to more than RM 82,000 in 1939: whenever funding was threatened, the student organizers pointed out that the Land Service was not just a way of relieving the shortage of agricultural labour, but a '*volkstumspolitische Maßnahme*', a measure of ethnic policy.[28] Through their work in the house and on the farm, it was argued, students would have a chance to influence their host family's working methods, domestic habits, political consciousness and national identity. Participants were exhorted to 'make people understand what National Socialism is about and get across to them the fact that Poland wants to ruin us'.[29] They were to promote Nazi ideas on race: Land Service students were instructed to go out and raise racial consciousness and to 'listen and watch out for the connections, the linkages, the power of the blood'.[30]

The style of the Student Land Service was often aggressively masculine: 'The Student Land Service demands tough types (*Kerle*) who know how hard and endless it is to struggle and to work for the *Volkstum* . . . who can and want to work as strong farm hands.' Male students presented themselves as a 'cultural assault commando' (*kulturelles Überfallkommando*), or depicted the relationship between the interior of the Reich and the borderlands as that between the rear area and the front line.[31] This self-presentation alienated members of the Nazi women students' organization, the Arbeitsgemeinschaft nationalsozialistischer Studentinnen (ANSt), who felt either ignored altogether by the men, or pressured to fit in with pseudo-military constructions of their role: 'we girls are not soldiers,' one protested.[32] In 1936 Hertha Suadicani, a student organizer in Berlin, took a stance against male objections to women's involvement in borderlands work and among Germans abroad:

> Again and again one hears that girls should not be involved in politics and certainly not in foreign affairs. When will people finally understand that we girls are not trying to design grand political plans for German domestic and foreign policy, and that we are only staking a claim to regard tasks that concern women in particular as belonging to us, and to help with the work of reconstructing Germany?[33]

Some male Land Service organizers did acknowledge that women had a part to play in the scheme and would provide a distinctively feminine element in the campaign to 'remould whole villages'.[34] Ursula Buettner, a woman student organizer who like Suadicani was based in Berlin, also argued that women had a special contribution to make to the 'ethnic struggle': their concerns first and foremost would be with the farmer's wife and her household. Pre-empting any notion on the part of her male colleagues that this contribution might be secondary or subordinate, Buettner contended that it should be seen as 'political':

> We know . . . that academic work and women's work generally must be political, whereby we understand political not in the sense of a thinking that one-sidedly emphasizes the state, but in terms of an understanding that is more strongly rooted in the *Volk* and is thus pedagogical (*nicht das einseitig nur staatlich betonte Denken, sondern das stärker volklich gebundene und damit erzieherische Verstehen*). Particularly for us as women, therefore, practical work for the *Volkstum*, which is not limited to village evenings, folk dancing, folk songs and amateur dramatics but also includes the cultivation of values . . . such as the culture of the home, is in the last instance political action (*politischer Einsatz*).[35]

Through the experience of working in borderlands villages, Buettner claimed, women students would enrich their academic studies, restoring the 'unity between political, cultural and so-called "private life"'. Such grand perspectives elevated a few weeks of labour in a farm household into an experience from which to review woman's place in the national community.[56] Women like Suadicani and Buettner were determined to make a female presence felt in a male-dominated scheme. Defining womanly work as political was part of a strategy of asserting its significance: this entailed widening the concept of the political beyond high politics to the grass roots, and beyond the public arena to encompass the private sphere. With this, the sphere of womanly action was theoretically limitless.

The women students' attempts to grapple with concepts of the political and gendered notions of the public and private spheres were rarely matched by the leaders of other organizations. Their practical agenda, however, had much in common with those of Party and state agencies that sought to deploy girls and young women to spread the Nazi message in the eastern borderlands. Another network of female activists attempting to bring the Nazi message into the villages of the eastern provinces after 1933 were the girls' Land Year leaders. Their work, running eight-month residential camps for 14–15-year-old girls, was one more example of a pedagogical initiative designed to raise 'borderlands consciousness' among the young while promoting and Nazifying village community life. The Land Year (*Landjahr*) had been launched in spring 1934 by the Prussian Ministry of Culture, picking up, like the Labour Service, on ideas of 'back to the land', settlement in the underpopulated East, and education through work.[37] The scheme continued in existence under the control of the Reich Education Ministry until the end of 1944, surviving attempts to wind it down, bids to take it over, and redefinitions of its function and target group. Initially, the Land Year claimed to be rescuing working-class adolescents who were 'at risk' from their environment, and providing them with a 'revolutionary education' along Nazi lines, featuring camp life in spartan accommodation and daily farm work.[38] Soon, however (with discipline problems in the camps helping to prompt the shift) the Land Year was redefined as a reward for an elite to be trained as cadres of the Nazi movement. At the same time, its labour market rationale shifted: from being a method of absorbing surplus juvenile labour from the towns at a time of high youth unemployment, by the late 1930s it was defined as a scheme to encourage youngsters from both urban and rural areas into rural occupations.[39]

The Land Year was thus a scheme in clear need of a purpose. Predictably, its advocates seized upon the argument that the Land Year could be, among other things, a factor in the struggle for the endangered East.[40] It would raise awareness by giving youngsters from the industrialized western provinces experience of the East, while camps in the borderlands stimulated village life, brought spending power to the area, boosted the local Party and counteracted 'confessional influence'.[41] A flurry of activity took place to set up Land Year camps in the eastern border provinces, and the national training school for girls' Land Year leaders was set up in the Grenzmark.[42] By the end of 1935 in the Land Year district encompassing Köslin in Pomerania and Schneidemühl, there were nineteen girls' camps employing a total of 100 female staff; in East Prussia by 1936, there were sixteen Land Year camps for girls.[43] Of the 19,630 boys and 12,870 girls in Land Year camps in Prussia in 1937, about a quarter were placed in camps in the eastern border districts.[44] As the expansion continued, staff shortages began to become a problem: in 1936 the district leader of the girls' Land Year in Köslin/Schneidemühl was concerned about recruiting and retaining staff.[45] However, the BDM, ever keen to expand its field of operations, sprang into the gap: a ruling introduced in 1939 allowed Hitler-Jugend (HJ) and BDM leaders aged 19 and above to enter training as Land Year leaders without going through normal pre-training camp for applicants.[46] Magda Tiedemann mentioned in 1939 that, having got the regional BDM leader and the *Gauleiter* interested in the problem of recruiting female Landjahr leaders, she was now being flooded with applications from BDM members.[47]

Local administrators used the special needs of the borderlands as an argument for maintaining and if possible increasing their complement of camps within the Land Year as a whole. Appealing to the Education Ministry in the light of planned cuts in the Land Year in January 1938, the Schneidemühl provincial government emphasized the importance of the Land Year in the 'nationally disputed Grenzmark': the Land Year had established itself as a crucial factor 'in the defence against the activities of the Polish minority as well as in the ideological training and education carried out by the Party among the rural population'. Negotiations shortly afterwards in Berlin brought success: as the official responsible put it to the women's Land Year district leader, 'our shouting and screaming (*unser Geschrei*) has, by the way, worked. The border areas have been only slightly affected by the cut in Land Year numbers compared to areas in the interior.'[48]

As schemes for helping farmers' wives in eastern border areas proliferated, aiding the borderlands peasantry became a crowded field, particularly in areas seen as flashpoints of the 'ethnic struggle'. A boys' Land Year camp leader expressed concern in August 1936 about the establishment of a women's Labour Service camp in Groß-Dammer/Dąbrówka Wielka in the Grenzmark. This village in Kreis Meseritz was a focal point for Polish-language cultural activism; it was described by a Land Year administrator as being '95 per cent Polish-speaking' and a 'point at which Polish ethnicity has broken through'.[49] The camp leader warned that the arrival of the women's camp would make the position of the boys' Land Year impossible because the Labour Service would try and take over the scarce placements with German settlers.[50]

If schemes trod on each other's toes in organizational terms, there was also much overlap in what they were doing. Whether a farming household took on a women's Labour Service recruit, a girl from a Land Year camp, or a woman student from the Student Land Service, the outcome could be similar: the family would gain the doubtful benefits of an extra pair of untrained hands, sometimes for only a few hours a day, but also find its domestic routine and childcare habits scrutinized at close quarters: in the case of a student, the helper would also be living under the same roof. All the schemes were based on the idea that working in the borderlands would be a mutually educative experience for the incomers and their hosts: that students, Labour Service women and Land Year youngsters would learn political lessons from the embattled East, while farmers' wives would be enlightened and encouraged by the advice and example of their guests. What the schemes also did was to import a mobile mass of young Germans to sing, dance, perform theatricals and provide a focal point for village activities – for short bursts in the case of the student vacation assignments, over the longer term in the case of the Land Year and Labour Service camps – in an attempt to fill a vacuum in community life which might too easily, it was feared, be filled by Polish-sponsored alternatives.

The efforts of the Land Year, Labour Service and Student Land Service women to organize village sport or improvise temporary kindergartens at harvest-time coincided with more systematic plans on the part of the state authorities and the National Socialist Welfare organization (Nationalsozialis-tische Volkswohlfahrt or NSV) to squeeze out Polish provision in the area of kindergarten and youth work. Organizing German kindergartens and Nazi girls' groups thus emerged as a further niche for women who wanted to engage in nationally oriented welfare work in the eastern borderlands, backed by officials and politicians eager to extend the reach of their organization or their region's social provision.

Children between the ages of three and six potentially represented the ultimate captive audience for the Germanizing mission, as long as the Polish kindergarten organizers did not get in first. Kindergarten provision was pre-sented in the eastern border provinces by the public authorities and the NSV as a way of reinforcing the German presence against a supposed Lithuanian threat in northern East Prussia, but above all against the Polish influence in southern East Prussia, Upper Silesia, the Grenzmark and Pomerania. In the words of a BDO official addressing the NS-Frauenschaft in January 1937, 'Against every Polish kindergarten we must set a German one. For if a child has been through a Polish kindergarten, he will never be a German again (*dann wird aus ihm kein Deutscher mehr*).'[51]

The provincial government of the Grenzmark in Schneidemühl requested funds from the Reich Education Ministry in May 1935 to preserve existing kindergartens and set up new ones in the 'endangered areas' of the province. While the application talked also of the social deprivation of the borderland population, it emphasized above all the need to respond to the proliferation of Polish-language kindergartens and schools which might lure children in ethnically mixed areas into the Polish-language camp, a trend noted particularly in Kreis Flatow.[52] The following year, the Schneidemühl government began planning a training school for kindergarten teachers in Kreis Flatow, and in 1937 obtained grants from the Reich Education Ministry and from the 'Reichsgrenzlandfürsorge' fund for the project, which quickly came under the control of the NSV.[53] The school opened in November 1937: its location in Radawnitz, a village with a substantial Polish-speaking minority, highlighted the role it was supposed to play in the ethnic struggle.[54] Students were recruited both locally and from elsewhere in the Reich; the local students were seen as especially important by an official of the Schneidemühl provincial government, who argued that 'in the currently escalating *Volkstumskampf*, the particular role to be played by the woman from this region is a crucial one for the cause of Germandom'.[55] Parallel developments were under way in East Prussia. Although the chair of the BDO, Theodor Oberländer, warned against arguing publicly that kindergartens were a weapon in the national struggle lest the Poles use it as ammunition for anti-German campaigns, the case was routinely put internally for kindergartens being crucial in 'nationally endangered' borderland areas.[56] In August 1935, the NSV in East Prussia met representatives of the state authorities and the HJ and BDM to discuss how to spend RM 380,000 allocated by the Reich Ministry of the Interior for the construction of NSV youth centres in those parts of East Prussia judged to be under 'national threat'. In Gumbinnen, Allenstein and Westpreußen, a number of Kreise were targeted (the Kreis was the state administrative area at the level below the Regierungsbezirk). It was envisaged that the youth centres would ideally house a kindergarten, a district nurse's office and a meeting-hall for the HJ and the BDM, but if plans had to be scaled down priority was to be given to the kindergarten.[57]

Kindergarten provision was also on the agenda of the borderlands office of East Prussia (Gau-Grenzlandamt), which was set up in 1935 to coordinate and subordinate to Party control the various 'borderlands defence' activities in the province.[58] As in the Grenzmark, the East Prussian state authorities and the NSV expressed concern about the supply of kindergarten teachers, emphasizing that politically reliable staff were crucial for kindergartens in border areas. In 1936, the *Gauleiter* and *Oberpräsident* of East Prussia, Erich Koch, announced a plan for creating an NSV-controlled training school for kindergarten teachers in Königsberg by taking over the existing social work school run by the Protestant welfare organization, the Innere Mission. Expanding kindergarten provision and imposing NSV control was a waste of time, he argued, if kindergarten staff continued to be recruited from the training schools run by the Innere Mission in Lötzen and Königsberg and by the Catholic Caritas in Allenstein.[59] The Reich Education Ministry agreed to Koch's proposal: the new NSV school was recognized in November 1936 and by autumn 1937 the Innere Mission's training school in Königsberg was shut down.[60] By 1938, the East Prussian Party and state authorities had the Protestant training school in Lötzen in their sights, with the Party pressing strongly for the training school to be closed sooner rather than later and for all training of kindergarten teachers to be put in the hands of the NSV.[61]

Ever seeking new outlets for its influence, the BDM leadership seized upon the shortage of suitable personnel for borderlands kindergartens as an excuse to intervene. In January 1935, Hanne Albrecht, the BDM official at the Reich Youth Headquarters in charge of its foreign affairs section (whose activities included borderlands affairs) proposed to the Reich Education Ministry that BDM leaders should staff kindergartens in 'nationally threatened' border areas. Their lack of training and qualifications would be remedied by an intensive course following three months' work experience and in the longer term by further training.[62] The plan was backed by the head of the BDO and the Reich Interior Ministry, but met with scepticism in the Education Ministry, which sympathized with the argument of the kindergarten teachers' organization that such a scheme would undermine the employment prospects of properly qualified personnel.[63] The scheme nevertheless went ahead on a one-off basis, with thirty BDM leaders deployed as kindergarten assistants in border areas of East Prussia between April and July 1935. Their task, in Hanne Albrecht's words, was 'to turn borderlands children into Germans capable of holding back the threat of the Polish flood'.[64] They were also expected to involve themselves in the life of the village, organizing the local BDM and Jungmädel groups, taking part in the village choir and helping to arrange village evenings (*Dorfgemeinschaftsabende*) along the lines envisaged by the Gau-Grenzlandamt. Following a three-month course in Weißenberg (Kreis Stuhm), the twenty-one candidates who had successfully completed the placement and the course were taken on by the NSV and posted to children's holiday homes and kindergartens in Silesia, the Bayerische Ostmark, Kurmark, Pomerania and East Prussia.

Youth work in the eastern borderlands, like kindergarten provision for pre-school children – and kindergarten teachers in rural areas often doubled as BDM leaders – was closely linked in the minds of the Hitler Youth/BDM and of the state authorities with Germanizing efforts. One channel through which work with girls was harnessed to the 'ethnic struggle' in the borderlands was the institution of the female regional youth officers (*Bezirksjugendwartinnen*). Regional youth officers were employed under the Nazi regime by the education authorities of the *Länder* and the Prussian provinces to promote sport, recreation and group work with young people: they were the direct successors of the Weimar Republic's *Bezirksjugendpfleger/innen*. From 1933 onwards, their activities overlapped increasingly with those of the Hitler Youth and BDM, so that they became effectively agents of the Hitler Youth or BDM while being employed by the public authorities. Typically, women were only appointed as regional youth officers after being proposed by the regional BDM leadership (Obergau); they were made part of the regional BDM staff and given a function at that level within the BDM hierarchy.[65]

Until 1936, women were employed throughout the Reich as regional youth officers. Following the Hitler Youth Law of December 1936, which asserted the Reich Youth Leadership's responsibility for all youth work outside home and school, the Reich Education Ministry ceased funding the posts. An exception was made, however, for the 'nationally endangered border areas' Gumbinnen, Allenstein, Marienwerder, Schneidemühl, Köslin, Oppeln and Schleswig – all but the last being in the eastern borderlands of the Reich.[66] The Reich Education Ministry decided that 'for the nationally endangered border areas . . . the post of female regional youth officer must be retained under all circumstances', and secured funding for the posts (and for those of the lower-level male and female Kreis youth officers) annually thereafter, which included a contribution from the Reich Interior Ministry.[67] This decision followed submissions by the state authorities in the eastern provinces in defence of the work of the *Bezirksjugendwartinnen*. Arguing in January 1938 for the renewal of the contract of the *Bezirksjugendwartin* and of the male and female Kreis youth officers in Upper Silesia, the district government in Oppeln pointed to the 'ever-growing Polish propaganda activity' and the 'often hostile and at least passive attitude of the population' in mixed-language areas of Upper Silesia as justification for keeping the posts.[68] In his submission in December 1937, Erich Koch justified the retention of the *Bezirksjugend-wartinnen* in his province by pointing out the Polish success in recruiting young Polish-speaking women from border districts of East Prussia for

residential courses at a home economics training school over the border in
Poland near Działdowo (Soldau). These young women, according to Koch,
were not just taught home economics but were trained in '*praktische Volkstumsarbeit*' so that on their return they would act as female borderlands
activists for the Polish side.[69]

Organizational rivalries and empire-building notwithstanding, borderlands
projects and the women involved in them were linked by a common agenda
and by personal ties among the activists and organizers. A kindergarten
teacher in Pomerania described in 1936 how she doubled as BDM leader
in her village, liaising with Hitler Youth and local Party leaders, and at the
same time organized a children's group on behalf of the NS-Frauenschaft.[70]
Meanwhile, women's Labour Service camps, girls' Land Year camps and
Student Land Service women all ran kindergartens as part of their strategy
for getting involved in village life as well as assisting with the activities
of the Jungmädelbund and BDM. Some women's Labour Service and
Student Land Service volunteers later became Land Year leaders, while the
Bezirksjugendwartinnen had constant close ties with the BDM as well as with
the other girls' and women's schemes in the rural borderlands.

A report by the 31-year-old Gertrud Gregutsch on her first months as
Bezirksjugendwartin based in Schneidemühl in the Border Province sheds
further light on how this network of women borderlands activists functioned,
and in particular how the BDM saw itself as a recruiting agency for key borderlands personnel. Between April and October 1935 Gregutsch spent time
lecturing at training courses for the BDM in the district on topics ranging
from 'borderlands work' to first aid; led a 'borderlands excursion' for BDM
girls in the northern part of the Border Province; gave a talk on 'borderlands
work' to Student Land Service volunteers; visited every Land Year camp in
the region and provided women Land Year leaders with materials for their
camps; and liaised with the camps of the women's Labour Service. Furthermore, she spent much time developing kindergarten provision: she lectured to
kindergarten teachers in Kreis Flatow, inspected and advised a large number
of kindergartens in her district, and sought to ensure that 'politically reliable
girls', who would also be able to act as BDM leaders in their localities, were
appointed as kindergarten teachers. Finally, she consulted the regional leadership of the BDM about suitable BDM leaders to appoint as unpaid youth
liaison officers in a number of Kreise, and persuaded the regional government
in Schneidemühl to appoint a paid woman youth liaison officer in Kreis Flatow
'in view of the enormously important work in this Kreis saturated with Polish
minorities (*von polnischen Minderheiten durchsetzt*)'.[71] Her frenetic activity
was rewarded with lavish praise from a Schneidemühl government official in

1937: arguing for her contract to be renewed, he singled out her work with kindergarten teachers in villages with large Polish-speaking minorities, her organization of handicrafts, music and sports courses, her lectures on borderlands issues and her role in liaising with a range of agencies in the field of *Deutschtumspflege*.[72] As one of the few officials employed by the Schneidemühl government who could speak Polish, Gregutsch was also considered useful for monitoring the activities of the Polish-speaking minority. Her post was renewed and her career as a missionary of Germandom continued, with the support of the regional BDM leadership and the Gauleiter of Pomerania Schwede-Coburg, into the war years – even though the conquest of Poland had by this stage turned the borderlands status of Germany's inter-war eastern provinces into a curious fiction.[73]

Participants in borderlands projects 1933–39: tourists, escapists or political enthusiasts?

Women became involved in borderlands projects and initiatives for a variety of reasons, some of them more pragmatic than ideological. Some chose freely to go there, possibly attracted by the nature of the work or the appeal of a rural existence. Others – for instance the prospective students for whom joining the women's Labour Service was a condition of gaining a university place – had a limited say in whether or not they ended up doing a stint of 'service' in borderland farming communities, and may simply have been content to go to Pomerania or East Prussia because they had to go somewhere. Commitment to the *Volkstumskampf* may not have been the dominant factor in many women's willingness to 'go East'. On the other hand, National Socialist slogans about borderlands struggle may have inspired some to see themselves as missionaries of Germandom, and Party and state agencies certainly set out to convince women that this was what they were doing. Those who ended up in the East as Labour Service participants (or *Arbeitsmaiden*, as they were quaintly termed), Student Land Service volunteers, Land Year camp leaders or kindergarten teachers were likely to be exposed to a barrage of instruction designed to reinforce a proper sense of their role. In turn, women who had 'experienced the border' generated further propaganda in which they proclaimed their belief in the borderlands mission and their place as women in it. An unnamed kindergarten teacher writing in the journal of the NSV in 1936 described her responses to her posting the previous autumn to a village in Pomerania: 'I was, as no doubt all young people are who are border-minded (*grenzwillig*) and who are placed in borderlands work, very

happy and full of all the enthusiasm and commitment that one can bring
to such a great cause'. Contrasting her commitment with the attitude of
feeble *Beamte* she had encountered, male bureaucrats who resented their
border posting and longed to return to 'civilization', she asserted her own
toughness in the face of 'hardship' and 'struggle' and declared her commitment to building the 'human wall' ('*Menschen- und Volkheitswall*') on
Germany's eastern border.[74]

Attempts to trace what women felt about working in the East must be ten-
tative. Descriptions of study sessions on border issues and 'Ostland' ceremonies
with recitations and songs about Teutonic Knights can give the impression of
enthusiastic participation, but whether the message about Germany's destiny
in the East was preaching to the converted or meeting with indifference is
hard to tell. On the other hand, it is possible that post-war recollections played
down an enthusiasm which did exist at the time. Women's Labour Service
participants from western parts of Germany, for instance, may have recalled
in the 1970s that their interest in East Prussia was inspired not by propaganda
about the 'endangered East' but by descriptions of its lakes, forests and
beaches. Perhaps this version renders exactly what they felt forty years earlier,
but some may have been tempted to play down ideological motives and play
up their enthusiasm for exploring East Prussia, memories of which could have
been enhanced by the territory's inaccessibility to West Germans during the
Cold War.

For some, work in farming villages in the eastern fringes of the Reich seems
to have been a refuge and an outlet for the 'back to the land' enthusiasms
of the Depression years. In particular, the Voluntary Labour Service in the
eastern provinces attracted a number of women who had been active in
youth movement initiatives before 1933.[75] Elisabeth Eckert, for instance, later
became organizer of the women's Labour Service in Pomerania.[76] While some
of those who made that transition adopted the values of the new regime,
others hoped that their ethos of self-determination would be preserved in
some form under the new system. Initially, such hopes were borne out: the
Nazification of the Labour Service took place unevenly at first at grassroots
level and some nonconformity was tolerated or overlooked. This meant that
the onslaught of political instruction was not experienced by everyone in the
early months. Maria Klein, an East Prussian, joined a camp near Osterode
(East Prussia) in spring 1933 after passing the school-leaving examination
(*Abitur*) that qualified her for university entrance. She recalled a camp leader
who was casual about organizing political instruction, disinclined to arrange
any ceremonies saluting the obligatory swastika flag, and tolerant of camp
singing which, thanks to the presence of a former leader of the East Prussian

Girl Scouts (*Pfadfinderinnen*), had a strong *bündisch* flavour. Klein remembered how she and another ten or so post-*Abitur* girls were joined by around twenty-five unemployed teachers and clerical workers. Most came from the towns and shared with the post-*Abitur* contingent, she recalled, a degree of 'back to the land' idealism. The participants, according to Klein, wanted a fresh start after stuffy schooldays or after a period of unemployment: 'we felt that our lives would be renewed . . . through this peasant way of thinking and we undertook our work with the farmers almost out of conviction'.[77]

The paradox that the women's Labour Service as it burgeoned in the eastern provinces of the Reich during the early months of the regime was, at least for a while, something of a haven for political outcasts – quite at odds with the Nazi aspiration to turn the borderlands into a stamping-ground for fanatical nationalism – was emphasized by the educationalist Elisabeth Siegel in her 1981 memoirs. Siegel (born 1901) had studied with Herman Nohl in Göttingen in the 1920s. During the Depression, while working as a lecturer in teacher training colleges in Stettin and Elbing, she had been taken by Sprengel on a tour of snowbound settlements in Pomerania in March 1932 accompanied by Nohl. After the Nazi takeover, she was dismissed from her lecturing post on political grounds: turning to a new outlet for her pedagogical energies, she volunteered for the women's Voluntary Labour Service in Pomerania, where she found herself in the company of a number of Nohl's former students. She joined a camp in Varchmin near the Baltic coast, working with settlers, helping with the potato harvest and in the settler household. Despite her politically suspect status, she was soon able to embark on a brief career on the land as a Labour Service camp leader.[78] She recalled how for her, an unemployed 32-year-old professional, the Labour Service offered for a while not only the chance of work but a refuge for those who were critical of the Nazi regime.[79]

Other participants in the women's Labour Service in the eastern borderlands claim to have been inspired more by curiosity and the desire to make the best of what for many was an obligation. Although the women's Labour Service was formally voluntary until 1939, girls taking their *Abitur* and intending to study at university had to complete a half-year in the Labour Service first. Having signed up, willingly or unwillingly, participants could then try and make the most of their options by choosing to be sent somewhere that sounded interesting and attractive. One young woman from Saarbrücken who signed up together with a schoolfriend for the Labour Service because they wanted to go on to study, opted for Pomerania 'because', she said later, 'the camps in Pomerania had a good reputation and because we wanted to see lots of things which were new and unknown'.[80] East Prussia inspired

particular curiosity. One woman who had done her *Abitur* in Weimar recalled
that out of nine girls in her class joining the Labour Service, six had put down
East Prussia as their preferred destination.[81] Another *Abiturientin*, this time
from Wuppertal, joined the women's Labour Service in 1938: she and her eight
classmates all wanted to get a place in a camp in East Prussia, but she was the
only one who had her wish granted.[82]

In later recollections, some participants remembered having their hopes of
seeing and exploring the rural East fulfilled. At a reunion thirty years on in
1965 of camp participants from Maszuiken (East Prussia), it was the memories of the countryside round the camp and of excursions to the border (to
Schirwindt, on the eastern border of East Prussia with Lithuania, and to
Tilsit in the north) which were among the most vivid, or at least the most
readily expressed.[83] To one girl joining the Labour Service in 1937, a fishing
village on the East Prussian coast offered a glimpse of a world which was 'like
Grimms' fairy tales come to life'.[84] Another wrote: 'We were so enthusiastic in
those days about the beautiful land of East Prussia and we felt so fortunate to
be able to work and live there.'[85] One recalled the camp in 'an old sheep farm
fifteen minutes from the edge of the town ... This was the rural idyll which
I had dreamed about at school.'[86] Negative impressions of the landscape were
rarer, though one woman described the coastal village of Nemonien in East
Prussia in retrospect as 'the most desolate landscape I had ever seen': it was
only partly redeemed by the occasional appearance of elks.[87]

Among all these recollections of the landscape, it is hard to tell how far
requests to 'go East' on the part of women's Labour Service participants were
influenced by an interest in borderlands issues. One woman who had worked
in a camp in Pomerania recalled later that out of eighteen girls 'only one
had wanted an assignment in the East out of idealism in order to be able to
help there'.[88] One woman who taught sport in the Labour Service from 1934
onwards and made a career in the organization, ending up as a district leader
in the Sudetenland, was inclined to doubt it. She commented in the 1970s that
of the many volunteers from 'the rest of the Reich' who wanted to join a
Labour Service camp in East Prussia, most wanted to be in a camp near the
sea, while others sought a location on one of the Masurian lakes: only the 'very
enlightened' (*ganz einsichtige*) wanted to be in a camp near the border.[89]
Whether or not training sessions convinced the hitherto indifferent of their
political mission is another question. Maria Klein, for one, recalled having had
little interest in politics or border issues on her arrival in East Prussia but was
galvanized by a charismatic instructor at a training camp for Labour Service
leaders in Penken (East Prussia) in 1934:

So Luise Rutta came in, dressed in black with the high-necked black pullover which set off her light-coloured hair and narrow face. She put on a very serious expression and had a book under her arm. We all realized that something very serious was going to be discussed. It was about Versailles. She portrayed it very dramatically, how it looked in the conference room, that Clemenceau [*sic*] stayed sitting and the Germans had to stand and listen to the whole catalogue of wrongs laid at Germany's door. L. kept looking very grim and her voice was deep and cutting and full of outrage, and that of course communicated itself to us. At any rate that was the result of this session: we want to free ourselves from this shame and create a Germany that was respected. That is how I remember it. . . . We learned other things too — Luise Rutta saw to that — but this session on Versailles really stands out in my memory. That lecture was for me the start of becoming a bit more political . . .[90]

A spell in the women's Labour Service camp in the borderlands might have been for some young women a brief port in a storm, a chance to experience rural life, the fulfilment of an obligation or an opportunity for tourism in unfamiliar corners of Germany, or a combination of these things. At the same time, for social workers, kindergarten teachers, youth leaders and teachers prepared to toe the political line, projects in the borderlands offered an alternative career path. The social work training college in Breslau positively nudged its students in these new directions. Hailing rural pedagogy as a new field for social workers under the new regime (in her words: 'in the new state'), its director Luise Besser laid on a special training course in spring 1934 in which social work students would train as Land Year leaders.[91] Young teachers also gravitated towards the Land Year and the Labour Service. Out of a sample of 25 women Land Year leaders in 1934, 20 had either been unemployed or were newly qualified teachers awaiting permanent appointments.[92] Of the 50 women Land Year camp leaders and assistants (*Landjahrführerinnen* or *-erzieherinnen*) in the district of Köslin and Schneidemühl in 1935–6, 25 were aged between 20 and 25, 13 between 25 and 30, and 12 were over 30. Twenty-five were qualified teachers (mostly teachers of crafts and vocational subjects); 15 were qualified social workers or youth workers; 10 had the *Abitur* but no professional qualifications.[93] Such figures suggest that, at a time when the labour market situation was difficult for newly qualified teachers and social workers, some women found opportunities in the borderlands to gain relevant work experience — while they would have been expected to embrace the idea of a borderlands mission at the same time.

If there were women who became involved in borderlands assignments in the East by chance or for pragmatic reasons more than ideological zeal, it is also possible to identify committed borderlands activists. Among them were the women who occupied leading positions as organizers in the Labour Service and the Land Year in the eastern provinces – women like Gerda Walendy and Elisabeth Eckert, district leaders of the women's Labour Service in East Prussia and Pomerania respectively, or Magda Tiedemann and Lotte Dieck in the girls' Land Year in the Border Province and Pomerania – whose careers involved constantly promoting the borderlands cause. Similarly, the regional youth officers appointed in the eastern provinces in the mid- to late 1930s to develop the BDM and other youth work initiatives were women who built careers on a combination of commitment to the borderlands cause, a background in the BDM and experience in educational or welfare work. Anna Stockdreher (born 1895), appointed in Allenstein in April 1938, described herself as a native of the area, daughter of a farmer and as having 'long years of experience as a Kreis youth officer, teacher, and BDM leader' which gave her insight into rural conditions and the political conditions on the border.[94] Frieda Jeschke (born 1897), had led a children's group of the NSF, acted as a social welfare officer for the BDM at Untergau (district) level and worked as a Kreis youth officer in Rummelsburg in Pomerania before her appointment as regional youth officer in Köslin from 1936 to 1939.[95] The *Bezirksjugend-wartin* in Schneidemühl mentioned above, Gertrud Gregutsch, had an impeccable pedigree as a Party stalwart and a native of Germany's lost Eastern territories: she was born in 1904 in Strasburg (Brodnica) in West Prussia, left after the region was awarded to Poland after the First World War, and worked as a volunteer for the Red Cross in a refugee camp in Upper Silesia with other West Prussian refugees in the early 1920s. Her family then moved to Baden, where she joined the NSDAP in 1929. She founded the BDM in Lahr in April 1932, rising to become a district leader (*Untergauführerin*); after the Nazi takeover she was given a post in the youth welfare department in Lahr before taking up her job in the Grenzmark in 1935.[96] Elisabeth Schneider (born 1902), a native of Neisse in Upper Silesia, worked as a *Bezirksjugendwartin* in Upper Silesia from 1935 onwards. She had qualified as an elementary school teacher in the 1920s and worked as a governess on an estate in the Grenzmark before going abroad to teach in the German school in Cairo for several years. As part of the expatriate German community in Cairo, she joined the NSDAP before returning to Germany in 1934 and becoming active in the BDM and as a Kreis youth officer in Neisse. She described her process of political awakening as having been informed by her experiences abroad: 'I saw Germany for the first time through the eyes of Germans abroad and those of foreigners'.[97]

One of the respondents interviewed for this book, Frau Niemann, had also been a *Bezirksjugendwartin* in East Prussia.[98] Born in Tilsit in 1906, she had been a teacher of the deaf and a sports teacher as well as a part-time BDM leader before taking up her post as regional youth officer in Gumbinnen in East Prussia from 1935 to 1938. When appointed, she recalled, she was required to join the Party.[99] She had a vivid sense of being a border-dweller: as a teenager, she had witnessed the Lithuanian annexation of the Memel district in 1923. Asked about how interested she had been in 'ethnic politics' (*Volkstumspolitik*) before being appointed as regional youth officer, she replied: 'We were anyway, because we lived on the border, and because we were separated off by the Polish corridor we were in that respect already sensitized and interested in politics. We kept an eye on what was happening.'[100]

Alongside the professional activists, borderlands enthusiasts – some of whom went on to careers in the eastern provinces or in occupied Poland – can be identified among the women students who volunteered for the Student Land Service. It is true that by the late 1930s in some institutions some pressure began to be exerted on students to 'volunteer'.[101] But on the whole participation in the Student Land Service before 1939 was voluntary, as is evident from the complaints by student organizers about recruitment. One organizer complained that recruiting for the Land Service and Harvest Help (Erntehilfe) schemes was a 'labour of Sisyphus': only in a few universities and training colleges, situated in locations where the 'border problem' made itself felt, was there any awareness of the issues: everywhere else, 'particularly Berlin', universities were 'in a way intellectually out of touch with the border' (*geistig in einer Weise grenzfern*).[102] The willing participants represented a hard core of the 'committed' among an increasingly politically indifferent mass. In 1936, the Land Service organizer for Pomerania warned against the tendency for a Land Service group to become a clique of borderlands fanatics who shut themselves off from the rest of the student body.[103] Volunteering for short stints of service in border villages enabled such enthusiasts to get away from the thankless task of mobilizing their unresponsive fellow-students to an environment where, one suspects, they hoped to win appreciation and wield authority more easily.[104]

Women students who volunteered for the Land Service were therefore a minority within a minority, confronting not only the sexism of their male Land Service 'comrades' but also the apathy of their female contemporaries.[105] For this rather marginal group of enthusiastic Nazi women students, borderlands activism had several attractions. Together with the issues of 'Germandom abroad', which generated trips to encounter German-speaking communities in Yugoslavia and Romania as well as covert visits to agitate in pre-Anschluß Austria, borderlands issues offered a focus for their academic studies and for their activities in the Nazi women students' organization (ANSt).[106] Study groups on border issues, folk culture and the like were an opportunity to bond with like-minded students and show off knowledge. Drawing up plans for village work might include working up topics for discussion evenings with village girls such as 'Women in Communism and Women in National Socialism' and 'The Status of German Women in Past Ages' (choosing materials carefully 'so that the girls do not get bored'), or getting hold of new patterns for traditional costumes that the young women of Silesian border villages would be encouraged to make.[107] Taking part in the Land Service offered fieldwork experience and a source of disser-tation topics: students were encouraged to see such work as preparation for later careers in the East.[108] As Ursula Buettner argued (in her comments quoted earlier), it would encourage an applied approach to their studies. Irmgard Rummel reported on a study group at the University of Halle in 1934 that included those who had been on trips abroad or in the Land Service together with those who were hoping to go; members of the group were also attending a seminar on 'Ethnic Germans' and lectures on 'South-Eastern Europe: Peoples and Cities'.[109] Training camps and newsletters exchanging experiences 'out on the frontier' reinforced participants' identification with their 'mission', and their sense of being a vanguard of experts on rural ways and community life.[110]

Ortrud Krüger, the 24-year-old organizer who had managed to mobilize an unusually large group of women volunteers at the teacher training college in Schneidemühl, wrote with a rare touch of self-mockery how she and her troop of eighty-two students had embarked on their land service at Easter 1937: in her account, 'We were all gripped by a boundless desire for action and by a sense of our "exalted tasks" in relation to the layout of the farmhouses, to culinary matters, clothing and the like!!'[111] Krüger, as a veteran of the women's Labour Service and of an earlier Land Service assignment in 1935, was an old hand. Like her, a number of volunteers went back to the borderlands for a second stint. Returning to Kreis Bütow in Pomerania in 1936, Elfriede Tschiersch declared that having got to know the area and the people she felt it was 'natural' to volunteer again.[112] Another enthusiast returned to the Border Province in 1936 to work in a Land Year camp, having been inspired by her Land Service the previous year in Kreis Flatow. In order to take up the job in the Land Year, she recounted, she had had to 'fight for two months with ministries and other authorities with letters, applications and interviews' until she got the posting in the East that she wanted.[113]

Two of the Berlin ANSt activists in border matters and 'ethnic questions' had careers ahead of them that would within a few years take them to occupied Poland. Hertha Suadicani, born in 1915, was in 1936 the women's organizer in the Berlin students' 'external affairs' office (Außenamt) and, as has been shown above, an eloquent advocate of women's role in borderlands work. Her colleague Luise Fick, born in Innsbruck in 1913, was in 1935 and 1936 putting her energies into developing a programme of agitation focusing on Austria and the Germans of South Tyrol, which she described as 'only one branch of our *Volkstumsarbeit*, but one of the most important'.[114] In 1939, Fick was to publish her dissertation on the history of the youth movement, in which the contribution of the *bündische Jugend* to the all-important projects of borderlands and *Volkstumsarbeit* was critically assessed, not least its role in pioneering the form of Land Service that she saw as paving the way to 'our Land Service today'.[115] A year later, in summer 1940, in what must have seemed a logical progression from her earlier enterprises, she was based in Litzmannstadt/ Łódź in the 'Reichsgau Wartheland' and, under her married name of Dolezalek, mobilizing women students to assist with the resettlement of ethnic Germans (see below, Chapter 6). Meanwhile, her old colleague Hertha Suadicani had taken a similar route and from October 1941 was also to be found working in Litzmannstadt, in the SS resettlement office.[116]

A 'Volkstum *which is not healthy':*
activists encounter the peasantry

By virtue of their supposedly exposed location at the front line of a *Volkstumskampf* directed primarily against 'Polish insurgence', but also against the supposed Czech and Lithuanian threat, peasant families in the eastern borderlands were liable to find themselves playing host to officious young women offering help in the household. Styling themselves as experts in household affairs and cultural matters and their place in the struggle for the *Volkstum*, these Germanizing 'helpers' set about disseminating to farm wives and their families their ideas about how to be 'better Germans' – healthy, efficient and politically reliable. Some sense of these encounters as seen by the young women involved can be gained from letters and recollections of Labour Service participants and reports by Land Year camp leaders, and above all from reports written by women in the Student Land Service. These recount in sometimes voluminous detail missions that – whatever their impact on the farmers – left a vivid impression upon the participants.

A number of obvious pitfalls awaited those who sought to raise ethnic consciousness in the borderlands. The process of monitoring and assisting families was supposed to draw distinct boundaries between German and Pole. However, it was unclear whether this meant inculcating anti-Polish attitudes into those who already defined themselves as German, or, alternatively, changing the ethnic alignment of families identified, typically by local Party officials, as 'uncertain' in their national loyalties. 'Converting' families in this way might mean persuading Polish-speaking and bilingual households to speak German, 'act German' in their lifestyle and habits and demonstrate support for German-language institutions.[117] The attempt in practice to do both generated bewilderment on all sides. In the case of Kashubian, Masurian and Upper Silesian dialect-speakers, contradictions reigned as well: students were told not to brand dialect-speakers as non-German because of their speech, but to encourage them to speak standard German all the same.[118]

Confessional differences posed other dilemmas. The National Socialists sought to counter the Polish nationalist argument that Catholics in border areas of Germany should identify themselves as Poles. The Nazi response was to affirm that nationally conscious Germans could – of course – be Catholics, and that Catholics in border areas should be encouraged to define themselves as Germans: but Catholics all the same should be discouraged from attending mass held by pro-Polish priests and, above all, services held in Polish. From all these arguments, it was clear that for all the ostensible inclusiveness of definitions of Germanness, Polish-speakers and Catholics were regarded by National Socialists in the borderlands as problem categories, potentially untrustworthy: the weaker the Catholic Church, the more that German kindergartens could poach children from Polish-speaking kindergartens, the better.

In theory, the encounter between the 'expert' helpers and their hosts was supposed to be based on the building of trust and mutual respect. If the helpers were expected to bring new ideas into rural backwaters, they were also supposed to be learning from the 'heroic struggle' of Germans in border regions. In the reports they wrote about their experiences, however, there is as much ambivalence about their hosts as admiration. Young women were exhorted to be sensitive and tactful in their mission to 'educate the peasants'. For all that, the language used about the mission to borderlands homes and villages was often that of invasion, penetration and colonization, of 'strong points' and 'crumbling fronts'. What the rural population thought about the visitors can only be guessed at by reading between the lines, but there are indications that relations between the visitors and the objects of their visitation were marked by mistrust and sometimes conflict.

Young women seeking to act as missionaries of the *Volkstumskampf* were told to tread carefully around issues of language and confession, and warned not to drive Catholics and Polish-speakers politically into the Polish camp by disparaging Catholicism or making assumptions about their national loyalties. But they were also expected to act as propagandists for National Socialism and to make it clear to those who saw themselves as German that they should take sides actively against the Poles in the *Volkstumskampf*: in the words of a male student organizer, 'one must make sure that people do not merely opt for one ethnicity, but decide against the other'.[119] Using the family and the household as a recruiting ground for the Party meant encouraging the women to read the Nazi press, join the NS-Frauenschaft, send children to Nazi youth organizations, and shun Polish organizations of any kind.

Apart from the more obvious criteria involved in defining and promoting the German cause in borderland farming households, Germanness was also seen as involving the proper definition of gender boundaries and a proper division of labour between the sexes. In line with the efforts by Änne Sprengel and others since the late 1920s to reform and raise the status of farm wives, campaigners in the *Volkstumskampf* proclaimed that a 'German' farm wife would be identifiable by the way she prioritized her proper and distinct sphere of activity – the care of the household and the children – as opposed to being overburdened by work in the fields. A farm woman, it was said, should assert herself as the mistress of the household, and not be reduced to a general drudge.[120] At the same time, she was to be encouraged to see the connections between her domestic and maternal role and the fate of the nation: this involved inculcating 'racial awareness' and a sense of responsibility for the future of the race. A small band of professional settlement advisers led the way in taking these messages to farm wives, and Labour Service volunteers and student volunteers followed suit: highlighting the importance of womanly work in the farm household fitted neatly with the search by National Socialist women's organizations for a distinctive sphere for their activism.

The farm wife, thus encouraged to reclaim her 'natural' sphere – or rather having been constructed as a bourgeois housewife, but in folk costume with milk churns – was expected to practise 'German' housewifery, defined on the basis of an amalgam of bourgeois hostility to 'superstition', a cult of folk traditions, Nazi racial hygiene and long-standing German stereotypes about 'Polishness'. In the words of Ursula Buettner, the student organizer from Berlin, women students needed to tackle the faults found in households 'out there':

the sometimes surprising disorder in the household, the mistaken approach to childrearing, the often noticeable disintegration of family life, and not

least the kitsch which we encounter, not just in the homes of agricultural
labourers, but those of the peasant farmers, in the furniture, pictures and
the things that can make a room into a real home – all this is the visible
expression of a *Volkstum* which is not healthy.

The women students, Buettner continued, were to forge a domestic culture
which would demarcate Germans from Poles. 'Precisely these values, such as
the style of home décor, distinctive dress, strongly knit family life, are to be
strengthened out here if the German *Volkstum* is to demarcate itself clearly
and consciously from the Polish.' In her view Germans needed their distinctive domestic culture as an anchor of national identity more than Poles did:
Poles' national identity was more robust, she declared, thanks to their strong
ties to the Church.[121]

Buettner was not alone in her dismay at the state of the German peasant
household. Young women recounting their experiences helping farmers' wives
often expressed a degree of culture shock that was hardly surprising given
that many of the volunteers were middle-class youngsters from urban backgrounds. A visceral sense of disgust, particularly relating to eating utensils and
food hygiene, continued to be expressed forty years on by some Labour Service
participants, whose sensibilities had clearly been deeply outraged. Some young
women felt an urge to scour and purge their surroundings. Their accounts of
filth were the prelude to descriptions of frenetic, sometimes aggressive, bouts
of cleansing. Ingeborg Britten, writing to her parents from a Labour Service
camp in Pomerania, described her assignment with a Kashubian family,
'the poorest and dirtiest family in Lowitz', and concluding a long account of
washing and scrubbing floors, walls, clothes and children, declared that 'never
before have I felt so satisfied by my work, never before did it make me so
happy, never before have I been able to work so independently as at the Kw.'s
house'.[122] A woman Land Year leader described a cleaning offensive undertaken by Land Year girls in a border village in Silesia. The village appears in
the report as alien and primitive, 'dirty and untidy'.[123] 'Some of the farmers
left the girls in charge of the house. A great opportunity! A thorough house-
cleaning is embarked on at once'.[124] A Berlin student reporting for the ANSt
newsletter on her work in a settler household in the Grenzmark in 1938
talked of her 'cleaning campaign' (*Reinigungsfeldzug*) throughout the house
'carrying on right into the kitchen cupboards', watched 'in wonderment' by
the farmer's elderly mother.[125]

Meanwhile, in newly established settler villages in the Border Province of
Posen-West Prussia, Ortrud Krüger's troop of students from the teacher training college in Schneidemühl were placed with families selected in consulta-

tion with the BDM district leader (*Untergauführerin*) and the Kreis farmers'
leader (*Kreisbauernführer*): both recommended that students should be placed
not just in places with Polish-speaking minorities, but generally in new settler
villages where Party organizations were establishing themselves.[126] There,
they helped farmers' wives lay out gardens and advised them on how to vary
their menus and manage with less meat. The women students, convinced
of their superior grasp of aesthetic matters, dreamt of transforming rural
domestic culture and persuading rural-dwellers to renounce 'industrialized
and urbanized kitsch'.[127] To promote authentic peasant culture, they offered
advice on dress and identified particular items of room décor as tasteless
(though one report sounded disappointed that there had been less 'kitsch' to
criticize than its writer had expected).[128] One student, deciding that the children of a settler family were getting insufficient attention, introduced songs
and fairy tales and tried to teach the children's mother to sing.[129] Another
reported that she had tried to coach her host family in table manners and
interior décor, lamenting their failure to cultivate a proper domesticity: the
farmer's wife attached no importance to family meals where everyone sat
down together, and her décor, in the student's opinion, lacked taste. However,
the student was optimistic that the farmer's wife now had a 'good understanding of the difference between kitsch and authenticity' and that one day
the farmhouse would, 'with some advice', become 'orderly and attractive'.[130]
While some of the Schneidemühl students professed satisfaction at their cleaning operations or their dispensation of aesthetic advice, some recognized that
they could merely register that, for instance, a farmer's wife simply took orders
from her husband, for whom the state of the household mattered less than
getting on with the work outside; or that another farmer's wife was good at
heavy farm labour but had no real feeling for housework.[131]

Moreover, having been inculcated in their training sessions with notions of
the *Volkstumskampf*, some of the Schneidemühl students wondered what they
were doing in unequivocally German households and in villages where Party
organizations were flourishing. One student took the view that while the overworked new settlers certainly needed practical help, national consciousness-
raising was unnecessary in the settler village where she had stayed, for all
its proximity to the border. As she pointed out, new settlers were carefully
screened politically and racially before they were allowed to take over their
farms:[132] the new village was free of 'alien elements' and posed no problems
politically. Nearly all the women were in the local NS-Frauenschaft group
and attended the monthly meetings. Sending in students to provide political
leadership to these already exemplary settlers was, she argued, pointless.[133]
Such students wondered whether the purpose of the Student Land Service was

to reward model households by providing them with cheap help around the house, or target families seen as politically unreliable on the grounds of their affinity with Poland and the Poles. Acting as farm-hands or household helps to German settlers was not enough for those who sought 'front-line action'. As borderlands activists, they needed antagonists to confirm their identity and justify their efforts.

However, students could run into a brick wall when they arrived as proselytizing lodgers in farming households thought by local Party officials to be politically or 'nationally' unreliable. It was all very well to declare that German should be spoken in 'German' homes, but enforcing this was another matter where German-speakers and Polish-speakers had intermarried and where the main language of the household was Polish. One woman student observed that her hosts in a village in Kreis Stuhm (East Prussia) were prosperous farmers and, thanks to the influence of the German-speaking farmer's Polish-speaking wife, pillars of the local Polish-speaking minority community: irrevocably committed to sending their children and those of their farm employees to Polish-language schools, reading the Polish press, and supporting the Polenbund (The League of Poles in Germany). She did, though, claim to have persuaded some of the children of the village to switch from the 'very good' Polish kindergarten to the (also 'very good') German kindergarten.[134]

Penglitten (population c. 200), near Schönfelde and about 20 kilometres from Allenstein in the Ermland district of East Prussia, became something of a laboratory for the efforts of the Student Land Service to intervene in the domestic sphere of village households as well as the life of the community. Between 1935 and 1938, seventeen students, four women and thirteen men, from Königsberg and from the Rhineland, went there and reported back on how the villagers ran their farm and household, when they went to church, how they raised their children, what newspapers they read and who bought fertilizer from the Polish cooperative. The village was diagnosed as politically labile: while there was little sign of activity on the part of Polish organizations, few of the village's Catholic inhabitants supported the Party, the SA branch had collapsed, and several families were seen as 'sympathetic to Poland' (*polenfreundlich*).[135] Four households were singled out for the students' efforts on the basis of advice from the *Ortsgruppenleiter*.[136] Ortrud Krüger visited one of them in 1935: she found that the farmer was an *Erbhofbauer* (owner of an 'entailed farm' or *Erbhof*) and Party member, but that 'one must count him and his brothers and sisters in the category of those who are indifferent to national-political questions'. She reported that the language of the house was Polish; that the grandfather had enjoyed a free trip to Warsaw 'organized by the Poles'; and that the family attended weekly mass and were indifferent to whether it was held in German or Polish. During her weeks there Krüger tried to get the family talking to her in German.[137] The following year, a male student described the elderly father of the household as 'one of the few *Polenfreunde* in Penglitten', who only spoke German when he was drunk: however, the student observed that the old man had an impressive sense of pride in being a peasant.[138] A year later, another male student placed with the same family reported that they still attended the mass when it was held in Polish, but that some family members did so reluctantly; moreover, the children were answering in German when questioned in Polish: this he put down to the influence of the village schoolteacher and kindergarten teacher.[139] Another family in the village was visited by three different women students in successive years between 1935 and 1937, each of them trying to cajole the family into speaking German.[140] Every year, the women reported the same thing: the farmer's wife and grandmother held out against the students' best efforts. As one noted, the women were adamant: 'Why shouldn't we speak Polish, we are Polish, the whole of Allenstein speaks and is Polish.'[141] Another talked about trying to avoid discussions about religion ('there is no point discussing confessional differences with a Catholic and certainly not with an Ermland peasant'), while attempting to gain the family's trust by attending Protestant church services herself. If the family mistrusted her, they had reason to do so: the student reported that she had 'found in the grandmother's room *hidden* [emphasis in original] some Ermland church magazines that were more reactionary than you could imagine'.[142] The last student to visit them concluded resignedly that her hosts were 'politically completely uninterested', 'absolutely wrapped up in the church', 'would never allow their children to join the HJ', and impervious to efforts to influence them. However, she clutched at some straws: she had got the servant interested in the women's Labour Service, and thanks to the German kindergarten the children were no longer answering in Polish when addressed in Polish.[143] Another woman student, reporting on another Penglitten family in 1936, shared the view that any hope of change in the village lay with the village children: attempts to influence the 'inner political, social or moral attitudes' of adults were doomed to failure and student energies should be concentrated on moulding the next generation.[144]

'Citadels in the countryside'

Land Year camp leaders, Labour Service and Student Land Service participants, kindergarten teachers and BDM organizers working in the eastern borderlands were all schooled in the slogans of border campaigning and the ideology of Germany's mission in the East. To stiffen their resolve, they were told about 'Polish strongholds' such as Buschdorf/Zakrzewo in the Grenzmark, presided over by a priest who was alleged to have bought up properties with his own money to prevent them passing into German hands and to have pressured the 'simple German population' to believe that to be Catholic they had to be Polish.[145] Those enthused by such training sessions anticipated a drama in which they would star alongside local heroes and heroines of the *Grenzkampf*, supporting Party organizations that were 'still in the *Kampfzeit*'[146] and joining forces with local National Socialist stalwarts. As they sought to penetrate the household, so they would colonize the village, aiming to embody a German public presence and inducing the 'politically and nationally uncommitted' to take sides.[147]

Reports on such efforts conjured up the spectre of incoherent communities of hybrid nationality and uncertain loyalties, indifferent to the National Socialist message and swayed by confessional ties. Priests, pastors, nuns and deaconesses were seen as diverting children and young people from the path of the Hitler Youth, and claims made by both confessions were thought to be damaging the National Socialist line on nationality in the borderlands: if Protestantism was viewed as the embodiment of German identity, this alienated Catholics, making them all the more ripe for manipulation by energetic and well-resourced Polish organizations. 'Catholic priests, clergy from the Confessional Front, a multitude of sects and Polish agitation' were accused of hampering the work of the regional youth officer trying to mobilize girls in the district of Allenstein, East Prussia, for 'the ideas of National Socialism and for engagement in the village community'.[148] The girls' Land Year organizer Lotte Dieck reported in July 1934 that the villagers of Sampohl in the Grenzmark were 'to a worrying degree under the influence of the Centre, which in this locality is identical with the Polish cause. The confessional divide seems unbridgeable there and the National Socialist movement is still in its infancy'. It did not help that the Land Year could only rent premises from the Protestant Church, but she declared that a Land Year camp 'under the right conditions and with the right leadership and participants could fulfil a particular national and political task'.[149] BDM organizers in the Grenzmark claimed to be blocked in their efforts both by the Protestant Church, which was reported in 1936 to be organizing lavishly resourced youth camps, and by the youth work of the Polish minority.[150] A Jungmädelbund leader from Neukramzig wrote to the Schneidemühl government pointing out that Neukramzig was a 'stronghold of the Polish minority, which receives all kinds of help and support from the Polish side, particularly in the field of youth work' and listing the equipment she needed for her counter-offensive: a table, chairs, a handball, mouth-organs, recorders.[151] In Upper Silesia, Elisabeth Schneider ascribed the success of Polish organizations partly to Catholics there being alienated by Nazi 'tactlessness' on church issues, but also to the fact that Polish youth organizations charged lower membership dues than the Hitler Youth and BDM and offered other financial benefits and incentives. Schneider had tried to set up sewing groups (*Wäschesparkassen*), but the Marian congregrations, she found, had got in first and were better equipped with sewing machines.[152] Schneider proposed that the state authorities should provide her and her team of *Kreisjugendwartinnen* with cars, the better to monitor the activities of her Polish rivals, but her bid was turned down.[153]

Along with the effort to set up courses, classes and Party organizations, the colonizing drive to establish a German presence entailed events to fill the villages with the sight and sound of Nazism in action: marching down the village street, dancing on the green, singing in the village tavern, speeches and recitations in the village hall. Reports on the activities of the girls' Land Year, the Labour Service and the Student Land Service convey the impression of the village street echoing with Nazi 'battle songs' (*Kampflieder*) and the villagers crowding to watch theatrical sketches or hard-hitting puppet shows featuring a cast of 'peasants, Jews, *ostische Menschen*, urbanites, judges, doctors, Bolsheviks and barons', sometimes performed by mixed groups but sometimes by young women alone.[154] In the description of one Land Year camp leader: 'In a tight column and keeping step fabulously we marched down the village street to the tavern singing', where the girls sang and performed sketches to the tavern clientele.[155] In Buschdorf, Kreis Flatow, the 'Polish village', the women's Labour Service camp held a 'community evening' every Thursday in the meeting-room of the local tavern to boost the morale of the German-speaking minority.[156]

Metaphors of occupation and conquest dominated a report published in the newsletter for Land Year staff on a girls' camp in a village in a mixed-language area of Upper Silesia that had been subject to the 1921 plebiscite. The author, a woman Land Year leader, portrayed the village as strange and primitive, 'dirty and untidy': 'The children surround us, stare at us and chatter to each other in Polish. Women join them, curious and suspicious, in the long "Polack jackets" and full skirts, an infant wrapped in their shawl.'[157] The article portrayed the villagers as having lost touch with their German identity: following the official line of claiming the Upper Silesians for Germany, it depicted them as having been driven into the Polish camp by mistaken efforts to wipe out the Upper Silesian dialect (often called *wasserpolnisch* or Water Polish) and policies that transferred the dregs of officialdom to Upper

Silesia. The Land Year camp set about its task, making the villagers 'see that we are proud to be German, in other words honest, clean, cheerful and efficient' (*gerade, sauber, froh und tüchtig*). The villagers, portrayed as mistrustful, 'as if surrounded by a wall', were described as having been 'conquered' through a 'systematic' offensive of regular community singing and children's games on the village green. 'Even if we can no longer reach the older people, the children will be with us and sing with us. In the kinder-garten we are planting the seed of a decisively German mentality.'[158] Looking to the future, the article's author saw her camp already 'living the new national consciousness' while working for the time when the Geneva agree-ment expired. This was the 1922 convention on the protection of minority rights in both the German and the Polish parts of Upper Silesia, due to expire in 1937.[159]

Such upbeat accounts notwithstanding, in which clean and cheery German girls appear as the victors over disorder and the dark morass of confused ethnic identities, the colonizing effort sometimes left its agents frustrated. In the Land Year camps in the northern Grenzmark in 1935, the effort of imprint-ing the 'German presence' on unresponsive villagers, and the resulting sense of embattlement, was reported to be taking its toll: some of her 'comrades at the front', reported the organizer of the girls' Land Year there, were exhausted and in need of a transfer. She was also concerned that the 'camp world' was turned in on itself: 'Although the camp is part of the village, the Land Year camp remains a closed-off world in which attitudes and values tend to form which cannot hold up "outside"'.[160]

The women students who reported in detail on their community-building and consciousness-raising initiatives during their stints of Land Service liked to claim they had overcome initial mistrust through effort and willpower. Thus a student from Berlin recounted how she had persuaded the girls of Mariendorf in the Grenzmark to embroider a wall frieze portraying the village and its families: its purpose was both to consolidate the work of the BDM and to raise awareness of rural population decline (the small number of children in each family was supposed to leap out at the viewer).[161] Another report from the Grenzmark told of how keep-fit classes for the women of the village had been a roaring success.[162] But while some women students were confident that they were able to mould the countrywoman of the future, equally comfortable in peasant costume and in sports gear, some were less sure that the cultural mission was working. Some thought that if they could not get through to villagers, it was because the folk culture that the Student Land Service thought fit to revive and promote to country-dwellers was irrelevant to them.[163] One (male) student wondered, if villagers preferred the 'modern dancing' that the local NS-Frauenschaft social evening was offering, why force folk dancing upon them instead?[164] A woman student from Berlin thought that making a fuss about traditional costume was likewise a mistake and that sportswear should be the new badge of modern German girls' identity.[165] On the other hand, bringing modern ways to the countryside could backfire too: a male student in Upper Silesia noted that the locals were offended by female students 'going around half naked'.[166] Above all, the students were concerned that their brief visits would leave no lasting impression. Ortrud Krüger, reflecting on her experiences in Penglitten, was sceptical about her and her colleagues' efforts to organize the village youth. Local youngsters, in her opinion, consumed the students' entertainment programme readily enough, but would do nothing to organize things for themselves once the students had left.[167] Where the gulf between the incomers and the local population – even the local Party – was so evident, student activists wondered if the only Germans really fit to play the role of defenders of the borderlands were themselves.

Sometimes, incoming borderlands activists had to contend not just with apathy but aggression. In Deutsch-Fier in Kreis Flatow in the Grenzmark in March 1938, local youths did not take kindly to male students from Berlin attempting to set up a BDM group. The students professed to be shocked that the girls of Deutsch-Fier were not engaged in healthy village pursuits, but drinking and hanging out with the youth from nearby Jastrow. One student's approaches to a village girl he had picked out as a potential BDM leader led to a fight: he was later set upon and fatally injured. The affair was something of an embarrassment for the local NSDAP, since the youth later convicted of the killing was an SA member and his mother headed the local branch of the NS-Frauenschaft. Moves to erect a memorial in the village were dropped on the grounds that it would offend local sensibilities, make future student assignments in the village impossible, and that to publicize the incident would be grist to the mill of the Polish-speaking minority.[168] A fellow-student claimed defiantly that the dead student's memorial would be the village BDM group, now launched and maintained with the help of the local women's Labour Service camp.[169]

No such drastic incidents have come to light involving women, but members of the women's Labour Service in Groß-Dammer/Dąbrówka Wielka reported in 1937 being assaulted and harassed by Polish-speaking locals. Groß-Dammer, in Kreis Meseritz in the Grenzmark, was predominantly Polish-speaking, and it was a centre of Polish community organizations, with a Polish-language school and a Polish kindergarten. It was, inevitably, a prime target for monitoring and counter-measures by the Nazi authorities. It was already the site of a boys' Land Year camp when in August 1936 a women's Labour Service camp was set up there.[170] At the beginning of 1937, an influx of twenty new German settlers arrived, strengthening the German presence in the village and provoking some hostility from the Polish-speaking inhabitants: tensions in the village were generally on the increase in the course of that year.[171] In November 1937, the leader of the women's Labour Service camp in Groß-Dammer reported to the local district police commissioner that, following a series of earlier incidents of harassment by young Polish-speaking men, two members of her camp in the previous week had in separate incidents been pushed from their bicycles and insulted by Polish-speaking boys and a woman: one of the girls had been spat at. Her decision to go to the police, she explained, was 'not because we are afraid, but because I take the view that we must not allow this sort of thing to happen on German soil'.[172] The significance of the incidents, she insisted, had to be grasped in the context of the whole ethnic struggle: 'This is an attack not only upon the honour of the individual girls but upon us as *German* girls and as members of a National Socialist organization, the Reich Labour Service' (emphasis in original). Poles, she argued, were very aware of the symbolic significance of such incidents; over the border in Poland, any such attack by a member of the German minority upon a Pole would be seen as a slight on the honour of the Polish nation and would be 'punished with a prison sentence of several months'. She was convinced that the attacks on the *Arbeitsmaiden* were planned and organized and that boys and women were deliberately being selected to carry them out. 'For this reason I take the view that action must be taken, otherwise the minority will feel itself ever more secure and will regard us as intruders who cannot claim any rights.'[173]

This trivial incident was to have far-reaching consequences. The *Regierungspräsident* in Schneidemühl ordered the police to round up those suspected of assaulting the *Arbeitsmaiden*: if 'a number of false suspects' were caught in the process, this would 'do no harm'. Fifteen-year-old Antoni Kwasnik was hauled in for questioning: he was eventually let go, but his name was clearly on a police list. On 11 September 1939, he was arrested with twenty-eight other members of Groß-Dammer's Polish-speaking community: in 1943, Kwasnik perished in Flossenbürg concentration camp.[174]

By 1938, with Germany gaining territory through threats and ultimatums, and Hitler's plans turning towards further prizes in the East, thoughts of combating alien influences within the borderlands of the Reich were increasingly accompanied by visions of conquest and revenge. Enthusiasts who proclaimed themselves to be a female vanguard of Germanness, inhabiting bastions in the rural East, began to see themselves as positioned on an expanding frontier, lined up ready to support the military strike outwards. In East Prussia, the women's Labour Service organizer Gerda Walendy saw 'her' *Arbeitsmaiden* as a troop ready to be mobilized under her command. In September 1938, during the Sudetenland crisis, she invoked a sense of national emergency to summon 500 Labour Service women who had completed six months' 'service' in East Prussian camps to the castle in Marienburg. There, she called on them to return to their camps for a further fortnight until their successors arrived: men in East Prussia were on the point of being mobilized, and the potato harvest needed to be got in. The 'passionate speech', as one of those who responded to Walendy's appeal recalled it, was compelling enough to persuade around half the women assembled to stay on: nearly forty years later, another who volunteered for the extra stint recounted that 'we felt in our commitment bound to the Sudeten Germans and with the arrogance of youth we called ourselves "Freikorps"'.[175] The following summer, Walendy was organizing women's Labour Service camps in the Memel district that had been annexed by Germany in March 1939; in August 1939, she recalled two years later, troops were massing on the southern border of East Prussia, men were called up, and the women's Labour Service camps came into their own: living up to Hierl's characterization of the women's camps as 'citadels in the countryside' (*Burgen im Lande*), going about their farm work, hoisting their flags, chanting defiant verses by Agnes Miegel, resisting suggestions that they be evacuated to the interior of the Reich. Then, she continued, 'our army was allowed to cross the border and Poland was smashed in a few days and East Prussia was so richly rewarded . . . Just as we were able to experience the Führer that spring in Memel, so we could celebrate him on 19 September in Danzig. Our work on the West Prussian border in Stuhm, Rosenberg, Marienwerder was now fulfilled. The land beyond the Vistula was free and German.'[176]

Chapter 4

The Recruitment Drive: 'Womanly Tasks' and Germanization in Occupied Poland

Nazi occupation policies in Poland set out to eradicate Polish nationhood and to Germanize (*eindeutschen*) the territory through a massive programme of population screening, expulsions and resettlement. Initially focused on the territories of western Poland annexed in 1939 and incorporated into the Reich, this violent programme of population restructuring, conducted under Himmler's aegis as 'Reich Commissioner for the Strengthening of Germandom', began from 1941 onwards to be extended to parts of the General Government as well. The programme entailed the displacement, ghettoization and systematic destruction of Poland's Jewish population. At the same time, the non-Jewish Polish elites were decimated, Polish farming families were uprooted and impoverished, relations between Poles and Germans were torn apart, and ethnic German 'resettlers', brought to Poland from all over eastern Europe from the Baltic to Bessarabia, were turned into pawns in Himmler's strategy.

Occupation policies succeeded in wreaking havoc on Poland, but not in Germanizing it wholesale. Population transfers and creative use of ethnic classifications produced different outcomes for Germanization policies in different parts of Poland, not only between the annexed territories and the General Government but also between different regions within the annexed territories (see Table 1). Within occupied Poland generally and within the annexed territories as a whole, the population designated as German remained a minority. The rulers and planners from the Altreich expected this German population to exert 'mastery' over the non-German population, and they set out to press and cajole the native ethnic Germans (*Volksdeutsche*) and the ethnic German resettlers (*Umsiedler*) into performing this function.

Germanizing Poland was thus a dual process. First, it entailed physically clearing space for Germans: once the population was screened and separated into 'Germans' and 'aliens', the SS resettlement apparatus set about displacing non-Germans and appropriating their land and property. Secondly, it

Table 1: The ethnic composition of the population in occupied Poland, 1944 (annexed territories and General Government)

Composition of population		Reichsgau Wartheland	Reichsgau Danzig-Westpreußen	Annexed territories incorporated into East Prussia	Annexed territories incorporated into Upper Silesia
Germans from the Reich		194,000	50,000	26,000	100,000
Resettled ethnic Germans		245,000	52,000	8,000	38,000
German Ethnic Register (DVL):					
	DVL 1	218,000	113,000	9,000	97,000
	DVL 2	192,000	97,000	22,500	211,000
	DVL 3	64,000	726,000	13,500	976,000
	DVL 4	19,000	2,000	1,500	54,000
Total German Ethnic Register		493,000	938,000	46,500	1,338,000
'Poles and others'		3,450,000	689,000	920,000	1,040,000

Composition of population	General Government
Germans from the Reich	100,000
Resettled ethnic Germans	9,000
Native German population (*eingesessene Deutsche*)	80,000
Population of 'German stock' (*Deutschstämmige*)	50,000
Ukrainians	4,000,000
'Poles and others'	12,800,000

Source: RKF-Kleiner Umsiedlungsspiegel, Jan. 1944. BA Berlin, R49, 87.

involved ensuring that the heterogeneous population of ethnic Germans met the Nazi criteria of Germanness. This dual campaign encompassed the domestic arena as well as the public sphere, and involved German women as its agents as well as men. Women were expected to contribute to the new ethnic and 'racial' order by assisting in the 'cleansing' of the conquered spaces, bringing 'German order' to what was habitually labelled 'Polish chaos' and creating a homely environment for the German colonizers. Their mission was then to ensure the maintenance of order in ethnic German homes and communities: a process of moulding the ethnic Germans into model Germans

which involved influencing private as well as public behaviour, and disciplining bodies as well as minds. Reich German women were assigned the task of
promoting modern hygiene, housewifery and infant care to the ethnic
Germans while propagating faith in Nazism and scorn for Poles. This definition of a female mission to 'strengthen Germandom' drew on the models
developed before 1939 in the context of the *Volkstumskampf* in the eastern
borderlands and described in previous chapters. However, it was now to be
practised on a much vaster scale and associated with much greater coercion
and violence towards the non-German population in the context of war and
the seemingly limitless Nazi drive eastwards.

Women from the Altreich were also needed in occupied Poland to help reinforce the German presence there, and particularly the Reich German presence. It did not matter if women were young, newly qualified or unqualified:
the regime's assumption was that with a little knowledge and the correct
political attitude, any Reich German was competent to lead ethnic Germans
and to uphold the system of domination. 'Every German who goes East is
in the first instance "the master" in relation to the "alien" (*dem Fremdvölkischen*),' as the official bulletin of the NS-Frauenschaft put it.[1] While some
male politicians and planners were critical of the efforts of young women
amateurs, others were quick to make a virtue of necessity: amateurs were celebrated as revolutionaries. For radical Nazis, Poland was to be the laboratory
in which 'pure' Nazi methods and solutions were to be tested and where a
shortage of personnel legitimized unconventional solutions. 'Bureaucratic'
methods were to be shunned in favour of the politically driven, 'can-do'
approach. Insofar as women's organizations pledged to supply flexible, task-
oriented personnel for tasks in the East, their empire-building tendencies coincided with the regime's need for people to maintain its overstretched empire.

There were thus plenty of tasks for German women in Nazi-occupied
Poland: whether and how women could be recruited for them was another
matter. Alongside a core of genuine volunteers, many who actually went from
the Altreich to work for shorter or longer periods during the Second World
War were pressured or obliged to accept assignments there.

The launch of Germanization in the
annexed territories

Nazi Germanization policies in Poland were based on notions of separating
Germans from non-Germans on the basis of 'blood' and on constructing an
'eastern wall' of German settlement.[2] Writing in 1942, Himmler declared that

'Our task is not to Germanize the East in the old sense, i.e. teaching those living there to speak German and to obey German laws, but to ensure that the East will be inhabited only by people of genuine German blood (*wirklich deutschen, germanischen Blutes*).'[3] 'Germanizing the East in the old sense' was a derogatory reference to the Prussian state's attempt before the First World War to Germanize its Polish provinces. Portrayed by Nazis as half-hearted and misconceived, Prussian policies had allegedly settled too few Germans on the soil and had put too much faith in imposing the German language on the Polish-speaking population. Writing in the 1920s, Hitler had insisted that 'the *völkisch* state must under no circumstances annex Poles with the intention of one day making them into Germans'; one option would be to 'seal off' the 'racially alien elements' from those of German blood or 'simply to remove them on the spot and assign the vacated land to one's fellow-countrymen'.[4] At the end of September 1939, German troops having crushed the Polish forces, a campaign of terror was unleashed by SS *Einsatzgruppen* and native ethnic German *Selbstschutz* groups against the Polish elites and against Polish Jews.[5] Hitler, having launched the terror, also quickly signalled the radical goals of Nazi occupation by his rabid outbursts about the inferior 'racial quality' of the Polish population ('a thin Germanic layer, beneath it frightful material. The Jews, the most appalling that one could possibly imagine', etc.), and his appointment on 28 September 1939 of Himmler as Reich Commissioner for the Strengthening of Germandom (Reichskommissar für die Festigung deutschen Volkstums or RKF): this appointment was confirmed by a secret decree of 7 October.[6] Himmler's official brief was to eradicate the 'influence of alien population elements' and to lay the basis for population restructuring through deportation and resettlement.[7] In autumn 1939 it was already becoming clear that Poland was to provide land for German colonization, that its educated classes were to be destroyed and its remaining population deprived of rights.[8]

Nazi planners at first earmarked for Germanization only the annexed territories of western Poland (*eingegliederte Gebiete*); only later did Germanization plans come to encompass additional areas for German settlement in the General Government and further afield. The annexed territories were heterogeneous in history and ethnic composition: they included territories ruled by Germany before 1919 and others which had been under Tsarist rule or part of the former Habsburg Empire. The vast majority of the population, even according to German statistics, was Polish. Estimates of the number of Germans living in the formerly German provinces in the inter-war period varied from one million to 700,000.[9] The non-German population of the territories annexed in 1939 has been estimated at about 8 million, including Poles and Jews. The non-German population of the General Government in 1939 has been estimated at 12 million, including Poles, Jews and Ukrainians, compared with an ethnic German population of less than 100,000.[10]

A crucial source of Germans to colonize the annexed territories began to be tapped in the autumn of 1939 as a consequence of Hitler's U-turn in policy towards German minorities abroad.[11] Before 1939, Nazi policy had sought to support, control and manipulate these minorities as an instrument of its foreign policy.[12] Now, German minority groups were to be uprooted from territories where their security could be represented as being under threat by actual or anticipated Soviet occupation, and brought to Poland as colonists. Transfer arrangements were agreed with the governments concerned, and the ethnic Germans affected were pressed to accept the 'option' of transfer. The first wave of Germans coming 'home to the Reich' were the Baltic Germans from Estonia and Latvia, which fell within the Soviet sphere of influence as agreed in August 1939 in the secret protocol to the Nazi–Soviet pact. The Baltic Germans began arriving in Danzig-Westpreußen in late October and November 1939.[13] They were followed by Germans from Soviet-occupied eastern Poland (western Volhynia, eastern Galicia and the Narew district: see Map 2) in January 1940, accompanied by fanfares of propaganda and images of Volhynian German peasants driving horse-drawn wagons through the snow.[14] Most in fact travelled in unheated trains, and more than a hundred children died as a result of pneumonia and other illnesses as a consequence of the journey.[15] Successive waves of ethnic German 'returners' were to follow in 1940–1 from Bessarabia, Bukovina and Dobrudja as further German minority groups were targeted for transfer.[16]

The urgency of making space for shiploads of incoming Germans from Latvia and Estonia had acted as a catalyst for Himmler's appointment to oversee the resettlement programme. Under Himmler's aegis, SS-staffed agencies answering to the Berlin RKF headquarters were created: one to deal with the incomers (the Einwandererzentrale, or Immigration Centre) and one to carry out the expulsion of Poles and Jews from premises and land confiscated for German use (the Umwandererzentralstelle, or Relocation Centre).[17] Himmler's responsibilities for Germanization policy also anchored the position of the SS in the regional administration in the annexed territories: the executive apparatus of the RKF burgeoned alongside the civilian administration set up in October 1939. While eastern Upper Silesia was incorporated (as Regierungsbezirk Kattowitz) into the existing province of Silesia, and Suwalki and Zichenau (Ciechanów) were incorporated into East Prussia, powerful regional chiefs holding the posts of *Reichsstatthalter* and *Gauleiter* simultaneously – Albert Forster and Arthur Greiser – presided in the new 'Reichsgaue' of Danzig-Westpreußen and the Wartheland over the Party hierarchy and the state administration (see Map 3).[18] Though their methods were to differ, with Forster more inclined to inflate the 'ethnic German' population by coercing ethnic Poles to declare themselves German, both pledged to bring about Germanization of their respective territories with the utmost ruthlessness. Forster boasted of his intention to 'solve the Polish question' and to make Danzig-Westpreußen 'in a short time 100% German', Greiser of waging an 'ethnic struggle' against the Poles that would be 'brutal, hard and once again hard'.[19] Both were to fight to maintain control of the Germanization programme in their respective fiefdoms against the rival power bases created by the Higher SS and Police Leaders in each of the new Reichsgaue. Wilhelm Koppe in the Warthegau and Richard Hildebrandt in Danzig-Westpreußen built up an executive apparatus alongside the Reichsstatthalter administration that among other things carried out tasks relating to the 'strengthening of Germandom' delegated to them by Himmler: deportations of Poles and Jews, the elimination of Polish resistance, the creation of forced labour camps and ghettos, the settlement of ethnic Germans and the creation of ethnic German militias all came within the purview of the SS and police.[20]

The first phase of Germanization policies, up to the summer of 1941, was characterized by a succession of frenetic improvisations. Three intertwined policies were launched simultaneously: the screening of the population of the annexed territories to separate Germans from Poles and create a hierarchy of ethnic Germans; the deportation of 'surplus' Poles and Jews; and the importing of ethnic German 'settlement material' (*Siedlungsmaterial*), in the words of a government official in Kattowitz.[21] In terms of Poles deported and ethnic Germans resettled, the Warthegau outstripped the other annexed territories; this corresponded to Greiser's construction of his Gau as a 'model Gau' and the 'front line' in the 'ethnic struggle'.

Screening the resident population of the annexed territories of Poland began in the Warthegau, then still 'Reichsgau Posen', in October 1939. The categories adopted there came by 1941 to prevail throughout the annexed territories. According to Greiser, the 'German Ethnic Register' (Deutsche Volksliste or DVL), was an instrument that would maintain the memory of the pre-1939 *Volkstumskampf* and demonstrate that the Nazi regime was not setting out to Germanize those of 'alien blood'.[22] The screening of the population gave the state authorities in the annexed territories an instrument to deprive a large part of the population of rights, as well as a means of disciplining and manipulating the population designated as German. Poles who wished to secure their property and escape the draconian laws imposed on those excluded from the DVL had every incentive to apply, though many refused. However, they thereby subjected themselves to the control of the regime, since the privileged status granted by membership of the DVL could be revoked if a person was judged to have engaged in anti-regime activities.[23]

The DVL sought to define ways of separating Germans from Poles using Nazi notions of 'blood'. This meant sifting the population of the annexed territories on the basis of criteria of ancestry (based on names, mother tongue, schooling, religious confession, and so on) and on the basis of 'racial' criteria: 'racial quality' counted all the more where ancestry was doubtful. The stated purpose was to 'reclaim for Germandom' those considered to be of German 'blood' regardless of their chosen national identity: it was argued that 'even an indifferent or a bad German remains a German' (*'Auch ein Gleichgültiger oder gar ein schlechter Deutscher bleibt Deutscher'*).[24] Past activism for the German cause, however, was rewarded with higher status within the DVL's hierarchy. Those judged to be of German blood could fall into one of four categories. Those who had actively participated in German organizations and campaigns before 1939 were awarded category 1 status; those who had 'retained' their German identity without engaging in the 'ethnic struggle' were category 2. Categories 1 and 2 both received German nationality (*deutsche Staatsangehörigkeit*) automatically.[25] Those who were judged to have 'abandoned' their German heritage (demonstrated by speaking Polish, sending children to Polish rather than German schools where German schools existed, joining Polish political organizations, etc.) were category 3; alleged 'renegades' who had actively campaigned in Polish anti-German organizations were category 4. DVL categories 3 and 4 were granted only 'German nationality subject to revocation' (*Staatsangehörigkeit auf Widerruf*): nationality would be revoked if their conduct as Germans proved unsatisfactory.[26] The policy on what to do with the Polish partners in German–Polish marriages was to absorb them into 'Germandom' if they were judged to be of sufficiently 'good racial quality' and if 'German influence' had predominated in the marriage: Polish spouses could thus be included in category 3. The logic of 'separating on the basis of blood' was also challenged by the 'borderline nationalities': the Kaschubians of Danzig-Westpreußen, for example, and the mixed German–Polish population of Upper Silesia were, however, deemed acceptable as category 3 Germans.

The non-Jewish Poles excluded from the DVL were regarded as stateless 'protected members of the German Reich' (so-called *Schutzangehörige*) and were subject to special laws and decrees that ranged from draconian penalties for criminal offences to petty regulations barring Poles from facilities reserved for Germans. Policies designed to segregate, subordinate and exploit the Polish population, developed and practised in all the annexed territories but taken to their utmost extent in the Warthegau, reflected the notion of a continuing 'ethnic struggle'. This assault on all things Polish, based on the conviction that Poles were the enemy, to be kept at a distance while being subjected to the will of Germans in all spheres of daily life, was to be waged even after the Polish state had been erased.[27] At a moment's notice, Poles were liable to be driven from homes and workplaces and deported from the annexed territories, either to be dumped in the General Government or sent to the Reich as forced labourers.[28] Below them, at the bottom of the Nazi ethnic hierarchy, excluded even from the label of *Schutzangehörige*, were the Polish Gypsies and the Polish Jews.[29]

Approximately 600,000 Jews lived in the annexed territories in 1939, around 400,000 of them in the Warthegau. In the first eighteen months of Nazi occupation, the Jews of the annexed territories were either expelled to the General Government or incarcerated in ghettos and labour camps, where they were exploited as slave labour.[30] An initial plan in the winter of 1939–40 foresaw the expulsion of a million Jews and Poles from the annexed territories. In the event, the numbers deported to the General Government never matched the monstrous numbers and tight deadlines originally set by the RKF planners, though the numbers deported to the General Government in this phase of the occupation were still considerable. By January 1941 the number of Jews and Poles expelled from the Warthegau into the General Government had reached 261,500, with a further 63,000 having been deported from Danzig-Westpreußen, Zichenau, and the areas of Upper Silesia annexed in 1939.[31] That the deportations had been scaled down from the earlier plans was partly due to Governor-General Hans Frank's opposition and to logistical problems in the months preceding the German attack on the Soviet Union, and partly due to the realization that Polish labour remained indispensable in the annexed territories: thus in May 1941 Greiser ordered that Poles were no longer to be deported but displaced to other parts of the Warthegau.[32] By the end of 1943, it was estimated that a total of over half a million Poles had been expelled from their homes in the Warthegau alone, of whom around two-thirds had been deported to the General Government.[33] Every new wave of incoming ethnic Germans and the resultant build-up in the transit camps created pressure for a further bout of evictions.

Expulsions of Poles and Jews yielded up farms, businesses, houses and their contents for German use. Ethnic Germans thus became direct beneficiaries of policies that persecuted and terrorized the non-German population.[34] The confiscated property was used to compensate the incoming ethnic Germans for the property they had left behind in their home countries. The Nazi regime, which had ensured that the governments who had taken over that abandoned property paid indemnities to the Reich government for it, therefore profited from the operation. The incoming ethnic Germans, placed in 'observation camps' in the Altreich or in the annexed territories, were tested – in the so-called *Durchschleusung* or 'sluicing' procedure – for racial and political fitness before receiving citizenship and permission to settle in the East (graded 'O' for *Osten*): incomers failing to make the grade were consigned to the Altreich as labourers.[35] Those earmarked for settlement in the East then waited again in different camps until Polish farms and businesses were confiscated for their use. As they waited, they had to be soothed and managed: Himmler himself appeared at one resettler camp in May 1940 to promise the Volhynian and Galician German inmates that they would soon be on their farms and enjoying the full protection and support of the Reich.[36] In the summer of 1940, with some of the first wave of incoming settlers still in resettler camps, SS teams were on their way to Romania to prepare a new series of population transfers. In September 1940 the Reich government reached an agreement with the Soviet Union to remove the Germans from the formerly Romanian territories of Bessarabia and northern Bukovina that since August 1940 had been annexed by the Soviet Union (with Germany's tacit agreement); and in October 1940 a similar agreement was reached with the Romanian government to remove the Germans from southern Bukovina and northern Dobrudja.[37]

The scale of evictions and resettlements varied throughout the annexed territories. Where more elastic criteria were applied by the administrators of the DVL, as was the case in Upper Silesia and in Danzig-Westpreußen, Polish inhabitants were classified, often under duress, as category 3 Germans. Adult men in category 3 were liable for conscription, but category 3 Germans retained their homes and farms. Expanding the pool of 'native Germans' in this way blocked the RKF drive to confiscate land for resettlement and in Danzig-Westpreußen this gave rise to condemnations of Forster's policy by RKF officials.[38] In Greiser's Warthegau, by contrast, an initially restrictive application of the DVL criteria debarred all but a few Poles from registering as Germans, rendering them vulnerable to eviction. Greiser meanwhile ensured that evictions would take place on a large scale by channelling the largest possible share of the incoming resettlers into his Gau. By December 1940, 71,435 ethnic Germans had been settled in the Warthegau.[39] In the other annexed territories, resettlement proceeded at a slower pace: by September 1941, for instance, only around 14,000 Bessarabian Germans had been settled in Danzig-Westpreußen.[40] By August 1943, around 37,000 ethnic Germans had been settled in the annexed territories in Upper Silesia.[41] By January 1944, the total number of ethnic Germans resettled in the different annexed territories had reached 343,000: this included 245,000 settled in the Warthegau, 52,000 in Danzig-Westpreußen, 38,000 in Upper Silesia, and 8,000 in the annexed territories allotted to East Prussia (see Table 1). In March 1944, Greiser sent a telegram to Hitler in which he claimed that the total number of Germans in the Warthegau had reached one million 'as the first success of this genuine process of Germanization' (*als ersten Erfolg dieses echten Verdeutschungs-prozesses*). At the same time, he announced that 'Jewry has apart from a small remnant disappeared altogether (*im gleichen Zuge ist das Judentum bis auf einen ganz geringen Rest verschwunden*) and 'Poledom (*Polentum*) has been pushed back from 4.2 to 3.5 million'.[42]

'Protective walls' and 'helping hands': tasks for German women in the annexed territories

The setting up of a civilian administration in the annexed Polish territories and the implementation of the initial stages of the Germanization programme mobilized Party organizations and Reich ministries across the board. While SS and *Selbstschutz* units were rounding up, imprisoning and killing members of the Polish elite, and the first trainloads of Jews from Łódź were being dispatched to the General Government, Altreich agencies and institutions with their staff and baggage trains were converging upon the new Reichsgaue. In this process, women were drawn into tasks relating to Germanization through a variety of channels. In liaison with the SS officials of the RKF resettlement apparatus, organizations ranging from the NS-Frauenschaft, NSV and women's Labour Service to the student and BDM 'eastern assignment' (Osteinsatz) programmes carved out niches for women's activism.

One major focus for the Nazi women's organization and the Nazi welfare organization (NSV) over the winter of 1939–40 was providing welfare for the incoming Baltic Germans and the Germans from eastern Poland (western Volhynia, eastern Galicia and the Narew district), who on their arrival in the annexed territories were placed in transit camps in Danzig, Posen and Łódź/Litzmannstadt (see Plates 7–11).[43] The NS-Frauenschaft ran the canteens while the NSV handed out emergency supplies and provided health care. Both organizations took the opportunity to recruit women with relevant skills and political background for administrative jobs, and to sign up the new arrivals for mothercraft and housewifery courses.[44] In spring 1940, new tasks emerged in the resettlement areas of the Warthegau, where the first wave of expulsions and resettlements was taking place. Women joined the NSV teams sent in to distribute household goods to the new settlers.[45] The women's

Labour Service and the girls' Land Year reinforced those efforts.[46] Along with the Land Year and the BDM-Osteinsatz, the women's Labour Service established a pattern of operation in which girls and women from the various types of camp (typically set up in confiscated country houses or former schools) were sent in to clean Polish houses following the expulsion of their owners and then provide assistance to the incoming Germans.

Meanwhile, activists from the Altreich, some of them drawn from the pre-1939 eastern borderlands, had been setting up the organizational infrastructure of the BDM and the NS-Frauenschaft/Deutsches Frauenwerk.[47] The NS-Frauenschaft in the Warthegau mobilized 500 new recruits in summer 1940 to help new settlers with the harvest.[48] Local government officials[49] and RKF planners were actively soliciting women's services. In June 1940, the RKF settlement office (Ansiedlungsstab) in Litzmannstadt approached the Warthegau BDM leadership asking that the BDM set up camps in resettler villages.[50] Meanwhile, the same office was recruiting students from all over the Reich for vacation assignments in the Warthegau and urging local SS settlement teams (SS-Arbeitsstäbe) to locate premises for new women's Labour Service camps to be set up in resettler villages.[51]

In parallel with the RKF's resettlement campaign, Party organizations and the state administration in the annexed territories closed down Polish churches and schools, deported teachers and priests, and banned Polish associations.[52] In their place, German institutions and organizations were expanded to provide the infrastructure of German community life. Ethnic German parents were to send children to German kindergartens and schools, teenagers and adults were to be recruited into Party groupings and attend Party courses and community events, while Nazi organizations were to provide welfare, leisure and health provision. To contribute to that provision, and to ensure that it conformed politically to regime goals, the NSV recruited women from the Altreich and from the annexed territories as kindergarten teachers and district nurses, and took over or set up training facilities in Danzig and Posen for various branches of social work.[53] A major recruitment drive was launched to bring teachers from the Altreich. Since male teachers were rapidly being called up, a large proportion of the teachers arriving in the annexed territories were women.

As women established themselves in a range of social and educational tasks in the annexed territories, grandiose propaganda accounts of their work embellished the idea of a historic mission for women in the East in an attempt to persuade others to join them. Before the war, girls and boys in nationalist youth groups and Nazi youth organizations had sung 'Nach Ostland geht unser Ritt' and 'In den Ostwind hebt die Fahnen'. 'In the footsteps of the Teutonic

Knights' had been a slogan used to sell tourist trips to East Prussia (see Plate 6). Now, those venturing East to make their mark in the new project of colonization were encouraged to project themselves into the role of conquering heroes. 'We want to cast ourselves back into the spirit of the *Ordensritter* (Knights of the Teutonic Order)', proclaimed Forster in October 1939.[54] 'The songs that once were only romantic are now a living reality,' wrote a Hitler Youth leader in 1942.[55] Greiser gave a modernizing slant to the motif: 'The German Reich must once again, as it did hundreds of years ago, ring to the cry of "Nach Ostland wollen wir reiten". But now on the modern roads of Adolf Hitler . . . and with the best cars and fastest planes!'[56] The motif was also used to lend a sense of grandeur and history to the work of women: Emmy Poggensee, a 30-year-old from Schleswig-Holstein who had moved to Posen[57] and who wrote a series of articles on women's work in the Warthegau, began a piece for the Nazi women's magazine *NS-Frauenwarte* by quoting 'Nach Ostland . . .' and conjuring up the Teutonic Knights 'as they rode in their white mantles "across the green heathland" to the struggle in the East'. She went on: 'And a burning desire arose in some of us – to go there as well, where youthful strength and readiness for action could help make the wide, vital (*unverbraucht*) land into a German homeland'.[58]

Women also drew on another cliché of Nazi propaganda that had resounded through pre-war borderlands campaigning, that of a human 'boundary wall' (*Ostwall*) or 'a wall of hearts and bodies' (*ein Wall der Herzen und der Leiber*).[59] In the blueprints of Himmler and the RKF planners, the image of the 'wall' pervaded plans to create bulwarks and bridges of German frontier peasants.[60] Such imagery suggested defence against an external military threat, but also against the perceived danger of alien forces seeping from all directions to swamp the German presence. In the words of the national leader of the BDM, writing in 1942 on the tasks of the Hitler Youth Land Service in occupied Poland, 'it is the task of youth to fill this land with German life and to give it a German face. A bulwark must be erected here against all that is alien, made not of concrete but of brave men and courageous women.'[61] The woman working as a settlement adviser in the Warthegau, an article proclaimed in early 1942, 'is helping the National Socialist movement in the Warthegau to construct the living wall in the East which will ensure the future of the Reich and the destiny of the German people'.[62] Giving the 'wall' image a gendered slant, Dr Nausikaa Fischer wrote in the periodical *Wartheland* in 1941 of a 'protective wall of helping hands and ready hearts' that would help to turn the Wartheland into an 'impregnable citadel and treasure-house of the Reich'.[63]

One way in which women constructed a role for themselves in the East was through a notion of domesticity writ large. If one motif in the Germanizing discourse was the notion of raising bulwarks and walls of Germandom, another was that of sweeping away the 'debris' of Polishness and bringing German culture to the supposedly neglected and unformed spaces of the East. The notion of a civilizing mission that would push back the darkness, disease, chaos and backwardness seen as characterizing eastern Europe in the name of health, light, hygiene and modernity had a long tradition. In the exterminatory Nazi version of the German 'cultural mission', the aim was not (ostensibly, at least) to Germanize or assimilate the Poles but to eradicate 'Polishness' and ultimately eliminate the Polish population from 'German soil'. Speaking to students embarking on their Osteinsatz in 1942, Greiser proclamed that 'We must give the land a new face. The lack of culture must vanish . . . Step by step, farm by farm, village by village, town by town, the foreigner must be pushed back, until only Germans remain'.[64] In the words of the Gau women's leader of Danzig-Westpreußen (see Plate 4), writing in 1942, 'One day the Polish language and the last *polnische Wirtschaft* will vanish, and we women want to help that happen!'[65]

A powerful current within the 'civilizing' discourse was that which conjured up a Poland mired in filth and vermin. This discourse had genocidal implications when it came to the decision to 'cleanse' German-occupied Europe of Jews: the Nazi idea that occupying eastern Europe meant eradicating vermin and germs was used to legitimize 'disease-control' measures that segregated and imprisoned the Jews.[66] Stigmatizing Jewish areas as prone to epidemics proved to be a self-fulfilling prophecy: in the overcrowded ghettos, typhus eventually spread, triggering 'solutions' to the problem of overcrowding and disease that led towards genocide.[67] The fear of lice as carriers of typhus was pervasive among the German occupiers and was matched by major disinfection and radical delousing campaigns.[68] Readers of the Nazi women's periodical *NS-Frauenwarte* were invited to share in revulsion at the notion of confiscated Polish houses in Gdynia and in the feeling of reassurance given by the disinfection process: 'gas had to be used to rid them of vermin before German people could be accommodated there'.[69] The concern with health and hygiene meshed with the horror of the alien and translated into a drive to purge living environments of Polishness, continually equated in propaganda with dangerous filth. Women proudly reported the direct and literal contribution of women to the campaign through clearing from Polish properties all traces of their evicted owners. Depictions of 'battalions' and 'commandos' of women deployed in this symbolic act of destruction underlined the message that German housewifery was crucial to transforming Poland down to the last confiscated nook and cranny.[70]

From 1941 onwards: limitless expansion

RKF Germanization plans were behind schedule in the annexed territories even before the German attack on the Soviet Union in June 1941 put all goals, projections and time scales back into the melting pot. While the programme of screening, evictions and resettlement continued on different trajectories in the Warthegau, Danzig-Westpreußen and the other annexed territories, additional 'fronts' of the Germanizing campaign opened up further eastwards, extending south-east into the Ukraine and north-east into the Baltic (see Map 4). Over ever greater tracts of territory, areas of German settlement were to be established, supported and defended amidst the majority non-German population; ethnic German settlers were shuttled between transit camps, on to farms and moved on again. A small stream of fresh colonists trickled into the Reich as new pockets of ethnic German settlers were 'rescued' from south-eastern Europe, from Serbia, Croatia and Bosnia, Bulgaria and Greece.[71] Meanwhile, areas from which Germans had been removed westwards in 1939 saw new resettlement activity: these included the district of Lublin in the General Government, where the SS and Police Leader Globocnik had been pursuing a 'search for German blood' since the end of 1940, and eastern Galicia, occupied by Soviet forces in 1939 but following the German invasion in 1941 absorbed into the General Government (see Map 5). The twists and turns in German resettlement policy were vividly illustrated by the case of the Lithuanian Germans. In early 1941, around 50,000 ethnic Germans from Lithuania had been transferred to the annexed territories, screened and placed in resettlement camps both there and in the Altreich. Only a fraction of these were settled in occupied Poland, mainly in the region of Zichenau that had been incorporated into East Prussia, before Lithuania came under German occupation in summer 1941 and plans began to circulate for sending the Lithuanian Germans who still awaited settlement in the East back to Lithuania. In 1942–3, around 20,000 of those uprooted from Lithuania returned there as resettlers in their former homeland, though in most cases not to their former homes.[72]

From 1943 onwards, the RKF's drive to create new 'belts', 'bulwarks', 'outposts' and 'stepping-stones' of Germandom was flagging: securing and defending existing settlements became a more urgent concern. However, the movements of population continued: in 1943 and 1944, ethnic Germans flooded into occupied Poland from the Ukraine,[73] the Caucasus and Transnistria (the strip of Ukrainian territory assigned to Romanian rule in 1941). The mills of the Einwandererzentralstelle (Immigration Centre) were still grinding as Nazi rule in Poland was beginning to collapse.

The murderous dynamic of population restructuring continued. In the summer of 1941, when unthinkable solutions suddenly became thinkable, the step from the idea of deporting and dumping, and simply killing, was a short one. The mass murder of Soviet Jews that was carried out by SS *Einsatzgruppen* in the summer of 1941 in the wake of the Wehrmacht advance was followed in October by the start of the systematic killing of Jews in Distrikt Galicia in the General Government, and by the preparations for the construction of killing centres using gas at Chełmno (Warthegau) and Bełżec (Distrikt Lublin, General Government).[74] These were fateful stages of escalation in the implementation of the 'Final Solution'.

For Nazi women activists, the expansion eastwards of the Nazi empire meant new fields for women to conquer. If in the summer of 1940 the eastern Warthegau had been seen as a new frontier of Germandom, two years later the sense of a definite frontier had given way to a vision of limitless expansion. In 1942, at the zenith of Nazi conquests, the bulletin of the NS-Frauenschaft celebrated this expanding frontier and conjured up the image of a growing mass of German women helping to fill the spaces opening up behind it:

> The expanses in the East which our troops have traversed, fighting and winning, become ever greater; ever greater are the numbers of Germans who go out into the East (*Ostraum*) with the civilian administration. First it was only the Warthegau and the new territories of East Prussia, Danzig-Westpreußen and Upper Silesia, then it was the General Government too, now too former Soviet territories. The fighting troops are always quickly followed by German women, above all those in social and educational, administrative and commercial occupations.[75]

In the General Government, as the Germanization campaign gained momentum in 1941, women were drawn in both to fill the gaps left by the chronic shortage of German personnel and to undertake the by now well established 'womanly' flanking activities associated with Germanization policies: 'care' (*Betreuung*) of resettlers and of newly Germanized native Poles; setting up kindergartens and village schools; and promoting German community life through social events.[76]

Nor did the expansion of the frontiers of 'womanly work' end there. In 1942 and 1943, women recruited by the NSV and the BDM were carrying out social and educational work with ethnic Germans in the Ukraine, Belorussia and Lithuania.[77] Germanizing efforts in the occupied Soviet territories after 1941 were building on German communities that in many areas had been depleted by Soviet deportation measures. The Soviet authorities had responded to the

Wehrmacht advance in 1941 by deporting ethnic Germans, beginning with adult men, eastward to Siberia. However, deportations were not always begun or completed and German communities, some consisting largely of women and children, remained behind to come under Nazi rule.[78] Policies to 'strengthen Germandom' in 'Reich Commissariat Ostland' and 'Reich Commissariat Ukraine', together with the Romanian-occupied Soviet territory of Transnistria, were put in the hands of the RKF's Volksdeutsche Mittelstelle, which combed through the population to find pockets and remnants of 'German stock' and then called upon organizations in the Altreich to send kindergarten teachers, schoolteachers, nurses and youth leaders to assist with the now routine tasks of *Betreuung*.[79]

The empire-building drive of organizations such as the BDM and the NSV was fed by the frontier ideology current among those who were inspired by the vision of the 'German East'. This dictated that organizations push their operations as far east as possible: the nearer the outer limit of German rule, the greater the prestige. However, this could mean that resources had to be withdrawn from what in 1940 had been the 'new East' – the annexed territories of western Poland – in order to shore up the over-extended empire at its outer edges.[80] As a consequence, regional occupation bosses competed with each other not only for sources of 'settler material' – with Greiser in 1944 gladly seizing upon the consignments of refugees from the evacuated Soviet territories to fill up his still far from Germanized 'model Gau' – but also for German personnel from the Altreich.

Going East: channels and methods of recruitment

The women undertaking social and educational tasks with the ethnic Germans in the occupied East were recruited through a variety of channels, and their responses to being recruited were shaped by a variety of factors. Some were native *Volksdeutsche* employed on their home ground, recruited through Party organizations or by the state authorities. Of the women from outside, coming from the Altreich or from Austria, some came for short assignments of a few weeks, while others were there on longer-term postings. For the organizations such as the BDM, the NS-Frauenschaft and ANSt, mobilizing activists for assignments in Poland was a matter of prestige. In their efforts to generate enthusiasm, they highlighted in their recruitment propaganda the Nazi image of the East, in which occupied Poland appeared as a zone of struggle and heroism, but also of self-fulfilment. While emphasizing the notion of service

and obligation, such propaganda also suggested that the East offered opportunities for personal development and adventure.

In November 1939, the BDM began setting up its organization in the
annexed territories: while recruiting some functionaries from the ranks of the
Volksdeutsche in Poland and the incoming ethnic Germans from Estonia and
Latvia, the two leaders appointed to the top posts in Danzig-Westpreußen
and the Warthegau were Reich Germans, one of whom was an old 'borderland hand', having worked in Upper Silesia since 1936. Their appointment followed a pattern common in the annexed territories in which Reich Germans
were placed in authority over ethnic Germans.[81] In summer 1940, the BDM
launched its Osteinsatz: designed to mobilize activists on a large scale but for
short stints, and serving the purpose of training the participants as well as
assisting the settlers, the 'eastern assignment' began by sending 1,400 BDM
members and leaders from the Altreich to the Warthegau to work with
Volhynian and Galician German settlers. A further 450 volunteers participated
in a Christmas 1940 assignment in the eastern Warthegau;[82] in 1941, the
programme expanded to include a total of around 3,500 participants, the vast
majority again channelled to the Warthegau.[83] The drive to mobilize participants, intensified through the proclamation by the Hitler Youth leadership of
1942 as the year of 'Osteinsatz and Land Service', was accompanied by a lively
campaign in the BDM press.[84] A certain amount of informal pressure was also
applied. Each recruitment drive assigned each region of the Altreich a quota
of recruits to fill.[85] Moreover, prospective BDM functionaries graduating from
courses at the Braunschweig training academy were expected to undertake a
three-month assignment in the East before taking up their full-time post;
those already in post were expected to use their holidays to spend four or
six weeks in Poland.[86] Ordinary BDM members were subject to no such
obligation, but there were incentives: for instance from 1942 onwards, BDM
members affected by the 'Duty Year' (*Pflichtjahr*) regulations could count
their six or twelve months spent in an Osteinsatz camp towards their obligatory year.[87]

The BDM sought to promote the occupied territories as a land of opportunity where its activists could make long-term homes and careers.[88] In 1943,
the BDM leadership introduced an extended Osteinsatz option lasting six
months or a year, targeted at young women who were willing to undergo training or pursue longer-term employment in Poland: in 1943, 1,027 took part in
this in the Warthegau alongside 2,683 in the shorter assignments.[89] One suggested route, promoted by the 'Bauerntum and Ostland' section in the Reich
Youth Leadership, was that of the Hitler Youth Land Service, which was
supposed to prepare girls for careers in agriculture or for the life of a farmer's

wife.[90] The Landdienst became increasingly oriented to occupied Poland, but it never grew into a mass movement: at its peak in 1943 in the Warthegau, 29 Land Service camps for young women were operating (alongside 30 camps for young men), with a total of around 1,500 male and female participants.[91] Meanwhile, the BDM sought to open up teaching careers in the East for BDM leaders lacking academic qualifications: after gaining experience as school assistants, they would have the chance to qualify as elementary school teachers. By July 1941, 141 BDM school assistants were working in village schools in the Warthegau, this figure rising to 199 by February 1942.[92] In 1944, 623 BDM school assistants were working in the Warthegau.[93]

Like the BDM, the NS-Frauenschaft regarded occupied Poland as a training site for its cadres from the Altreich.[94] Appealing to young NS-Frauenschaft officials in the Altreich to volunteer for a six-week period of service in the Warthegau, Helga Thrö (Plate 3), Gau women's leader in the Warthegau, declared the East to be the 'testing-ground for Germany's young talent'.[95] Flattered though they might be, those targeted for assignments in Poland had to be pressured as well: in its search for recruits, the Nazi women's leadership was driven to 'coercing those with positions to aspire to or, perhaps, to lose'.[96] In 1941 and 1942, on Helga Thrö's initiative, younger NS-Frauenschaft functionaries were dispatched to the Warthegau for six-week assignments: salaried officials of the Nazi women's youth section (Jugendgruppen) at Kreis level were required to participate, and the time spent in Poland was taken out of their annual paid holiday. Other paid and unpaid functionaries at the level of the Kreis and the Ortsgruppe were urged to join in, though it was emphasized that ordinary members should participate only if they were of 'leadership' calibre.[97] The response was less than overwhelming: after the announcement in early 1941 that between 400 and 500 would be sent that summer, 320 actually took part; in 1942, fewer than 200 participated.[98] Meanwhile, the NS-Frauenschaft was constantly looking for women who were 'young, fit and without dependants' to go East for longer periods.[99] This did not necessarily mean unmarried: married women with husbands at the front were positively encouraged to go East, and one circular appealing for recruits even suggested 'young war widows' should be targeted.[100] One much-vaunted initiative was the employment of full-time settlement advisers (*Ansiedlerbetreuerinnen*) recruited mainly from the Altreich. The first settlement advisers were appointed in December 1940 in the Warthegau and in March 1941 in Danzig-Westpreußen.[101] By summer 1941 there were 168 settlement advisers in the Warthegau; numbers rose to 221 in 1942, and fell to 190 in 1943.[102]

Further cohorts of young women were recruited for short-term assignments in occupied Poland by the women's Labour Service, for which young women aged 18–19 were conscripted from 1939 onwards. Women's Labour Service camps were set up in the annexed territories from the beginning of the occupation in 1939, and by the end of 1940 thirty camps had been established in the Warthegau and 21 in Danzig-Westpreußen.[103] By June 1944, when the women's Labour Service had expanded to encompass 130,000 young women, it was estimated that 'probably over 10 per cent' were working outside the Altreich in conquered territories (including Poland). A proportion of the young women in Labour Service camps in occupied Poland were recruited from the ranks of ethnic Germans there, but the majority were from the Altreich, and at least in the first years of occupation up to around 1942, the indications are that many of the Altreich recruits had freely opted for a camp in the East.[104]

Women students were another group targeted in the recruitment drive for the East. In the winter of 1939–40, student leaders who styled themselves 'Eastern experts' on the basis of their pre-war Student Land Service experience mobilized several hundred male students as assistants to the RKF apparatus; their work included surveying and selecting Polish farms in the Warthegau to be confiscated for German settlement.[105] Women students followed close behind. In summer 1940, a vacation programme sending women students to the Warthegau was launched by the ANSt in collaboration with the RKF authorities in Posen and Litzmannstadt.[106] The *Facheinsatz Ost* programme of summer 1940 in the Warthegau was replicated in later years in the other annexed territories and beyond.[107] Students in 'relevant' disciplines applied their skills – teacher training students set up village schools (female trainees also set up kindergartens), medical students assisted with health care for settlers – while students from other disciplines carried out general tasks, some of which were defined by gender: male students carried out repairs to settler homes, female students ran kindergartens and carried out home visits to settler families. Although men outnumbered women in the 1940 programme, women came to predominate in subsequent years.[108] Recruitment was assisted by the fact that all students were forced to perform some kind of war work in the summer vacations: participation in the *Facheinsatz Ost* was voluntary only in that students could choose to work with settlers in occupied Poland in preference to working in a factory or on a farm. Several factors might sway the undecided in favour of an assignment in Poland: novelty, the chance of vocational experience, and the living allowance which was set higher than that for factory work or work on the land.[109]

The ANSt had few difficulties in recruiting women for the various forms of Osteinsatz in 1940. A total of 345 women students participated in the summer programme of 1940, of whom 64 ran kindergartens, 203 assisted with 'looking after' settlers (*Siedlerbetreuung*), and 78 teacher training students took part in the programme to set up village schools. In later years, recruitment targets were harder to meet, and the demand for students to fill, in the words of Reich Student Leader Gustav Scheel in January 1944, 'the thin, in places threadbare, carpet of Germans stretched out across the East', was less easy to satisfy.[110]

Many of the women recruited through the BDM, NS-Frauenschaft, women's Labour Service and ANSt were in Poland for relatively short periods – from a few weeks to a few months – after which they returned to their employment or training back in the Reich. The exceptions were the settlement advisers employed by the NS-Frauenschaft, who committed themselves for longer periods, and the BDM and NS-Frauenschaft officials and Labour Service organizers who had longer-term postings. For other categories of recruits, a longer posting was the norm: these included the social workers and kindergarten teachers sent to Poland by the NSV, and the state-employed Land Year leaders and schoolteachers. For these women, a transfer to Poland was a move – sometimes unwelcome and involving informal or formal pressure – that related to their professional development.

The NSV, like other Party organizations, sought to establish its profile in the annexed territories and the General Government; it was also continuing its drive to accumulate responsibilities at the expense of the state authorities and the confessional welfare organizations.[111] A male-run organization, it was nevertheless a major employer of women, who did the work of running the canteens in the transit camps, visiting settlers to distribute household goods, and acting as transmitters of the Nazi message into the domestic sphere.[112] The political agenda of welfare was particularly evident in the NSV campaign to provide kindergartens, where German children would be kept apart from Polish children: here, its efforts coincided with those of the women students on vacation assignments, the BDM Osteinsatz and the women's Labour Service. In eastern Upper Silesia, the NSV was running 350 kindergartens in December 1939.[113] By 1943 in the Warthegau, the NSV was employing 2,500 staff in 459 all-year and 393 summer-only kindergartens.[114] In the German settlement areas of the General Government and the Ukraine, dozens of kindergartens were set up between 1941 and 1943 (see below, Chapter 8).

In attempts to beat staff shortages, the NSV expanded its training provision in Posen and Danzig, where it recruited ethnic Germans as well as Reich Germans and offered them accelerated training courses.[115] What the NSV sought above all, however, was trained personnel from the Altreich, particularly for supervisory positions.[116] NSV Gau and district leaderships in the

Altreich were told to nominate a certain number of staff for posts in the East.[117] Despite the prospect of generous 'eastern bonuses' on top of a salary, or daily living allowances in lieu of a salary of between 8 and 10 Reichsmarks per day, and the likelihood of greater autonomy and responsibility, many requests for staff by the NSV Reich leadership were not met, or not met in full. If no staff volunteered, or if those nominated objected, the NSV administrators sometimes gave up, though some employees were leant on or formally compelled (*dienstverpflichtet*). As the NSV's commitments in the Altreich grew – having taken over confessional welfare facilities, expanded kindergarten provision in response to the mobilization of female labour in the war economy, and set up the children's evacuation programme – administrators in occupied Poland complained bitterly about a 'catastrophic' shortage of trained social workers; as the NSV sought to extend its reach into occupied Soviet territory, some administrators in occupied Poland were declaring that plans to expand facilities had been suspended in the absence of personnel.[118]

Women schoolteachers were another major group of professional women who were drawn into the regime's Germanization efforts in occupied Poland. Schools for German children would serve to separate Germans and Poles, privileging the German children within the ethnic hierarchy. The schools were to educate their pupils into German ways. School teaching, in contrast to kindergarten teaching, was not an exclusively female occupation, and women schoolteachers' work in occupied Poland was not generally presented in terms of 'womanly mission'. On the contrary, some male schools administrators regarded women as less than ideal recruits, especially for schools in remote rural areas. Nevertheless, as male teachers were called up, schools for German children in occupied Poland became an increasingly female domain, a trend reinforced by the 'dilution' of the teaching profession with female school assistants recruited by the BDM and the women's Labour Service.

The schools authorities' preference was for fully qualified teachers from the Altreich. They did appoint teachers both from the local ethnic German population and from among the resettled Germans, particularly from among the Baltic Germans, but reserved the best jobs for Reich Germans and regarded ethnic German teachers, whether from Poland or from elsewere, as problematic.[119] Teachers from the Altreich would, it was thought, guarantee ideological conformity and be familiar with the Nazi school system and teaching methods. In March 1940, the Reich Education Ministry instructed the schools departments of regional governments in the Altreich to fill quotas of teachers to be seconded immediately (*abgeordnet*) to the 'new eastern territories'.[120] Seven hundred teachers were supposed to be nominated under this plan, earmarked for the Warthegau, though fewer actually arrived and some of those that did arrive were deemed unsatisfactory. Meanwhile Danzig-Westpreußen and the formerly Polish district of Kattowitz in Silesia were receiving contingents of teachers posted from the Altreich and hiring lay assistants locally.[121] Other recruits from the Altreich came to the annexed territories straight from the training colleges for elementary school teachers (*Hochschulen für Lehrerbildung*), with a first contingent of 230 arriving in the Warthegau in spring 1940. Of the training college graduates, most were women: out of a contingent sent to the Litzmannstadt district in 1940, 54 were women and 34 were men, and of the men 23 were conscripted almost as soon as they took up their posts. Despite the qualms of the Warthegau school authorities about putting women in charge of single-class elementary schools (*einklassige Volksschulen*) in rural areas, they had little choice. By October 1940, 355 such schools, a third of all elementary schools in the Warthegau, were run single-handedly by a woman teacher.[122]

The teacher shortage was only partly relieved by the recruitment of school assistants, and was exacerbated by attempts to set up German schools in the General Government and occupied Soviet territory, though these plans were never realized on a significant scale. As a result, despite all the initial qualms on the part of school administrators about the preponderance of women teachers among Altreich recruits, qualified women teachers came to be regarded as an essential commodity, to be retained regardless of requests for exemption or transfers back to the Reich. A schools department official in Łódź/Litzmannstadt commented in summer 1941 that a request by a newly graduated teacher to be released from her Warthegau posting was one of many. If such requests were to be granted, he told the Reich Education Ministry, 'no one apart from a few idealists would come to the eastern territories at all'.[123]

'Seeing something of the world': responses to being recruited for work in Poland

Some women expressed spontaneous enthusiasm at the prospect of going East. These included the old 'borderland hands' who relished the anti-Polish struggle from pre-war days and who now sought to move further east. The organizer of the girls' Land Year in Pomerania noted in February 1940 that 'my comrades, who for years have been oriented to the East and the eastern struggle, are understandably pressing for a post in the new Reichsgaue'.[124] Others, new to the East, seemed eager for the great challenges and opportunities portrayed in Nazi propaganda accounts. In summer 1940, the ANSt leader at the University of Cologne reported that the announcement that students could opt for an assignment in the Warthegau had brought a flood of volunteers clamouring to go.[125] Administrators in the annexed territories received unsolicited offers from women wanting to work in the East. A research assistant in Himmler's Ahnenerbe institute in Berlin (for the study of Germany's 'ancestral inheritance') wrote in April 1940 to the Land Year department in the Warthegau enquiring about the possibilities of a more active job in the East. Her desire to join in the work of 'construction' in the Warthegau was, she said, partly inspired by the death of her brother, an SS officer killed in the war against Poland.[126] A student teacher who had volunteered for a 1940 vacation assignment in the Warthegau wrote from her training college in München-Pasing in February 1941 to the schools department in Posen expressing her 'particular wish' to work in the East again – 'I found the work in the German East enjoyable and it has greatly stimulated my interest in Eastern tasks' – and asking the department to allocate her again to the village school she had set up the previous summer.[127] A student at the same training college wrote to the same department a few months later following up an earlier visit she had made to Posen to find out about teaching in the Warthegau, saying that she was about to take her first state examination and was looking forward to working in the Warthegau. Addressing her letter personally to an official she had met earlier in the year, she thanked him for 'opening her eyes to the great tasks there in the East!'[128]

Ideologically fuelled enthusiasm could be mixed with a sense of self-interest. Enthusiasts determined to work in the East had some scope for choosing their posting, and they encountered the flattering scenario that their services were nearly always welcome. Organizations cooperated with each other to offer another post to an applicant who was not qualified for her first choice of job;[129] sometimes there was even competition for their services. Women seeking jobs as camp leaders enquired about promotion prospects and conditions in both the women's Labour Service and the Land Year in the annexed territories before deciding to take a post.[130] Teachers sought to pick and choose where, within the occupied eastern territories, they would be deployed. One teacher put in a request to work further east within the Warthegau so that she could put to good use her skills in teaching German to non-German speakers.[131] A BDM school assistant fresh from the training college in Posen was allowed by the schools officer in Kreis Gostingen (Warthegau) to select her first posting from five different village schools.[132] Two other BDM school assistants requested permission, after completing their training in Posen, to take up a posting in Bialystok district rather than stay on in the Warthegau: when their request was turned down, they went all the same, ignoring the remonstrations of the Warthegau authorities and relying on the support of officials in Białystok.[133] Another decided she would rather work in Rawa Ruska (in Distrikt Galizien in the General Government) than in the Warthegau.[134] Students made sure that if they were going to have to perform some vacation assignment, it would be one of their choosing: in 1943, several students from Vienna offered their services to Dr Franz Stanglica, director of Globocnik's 'research unit' in Lublin, fixed up jobs for their friends and specified what they themselves would prefer to do.[135] One wrote that she was 'already looking forward to Lublin and the interesting work! I wonder what the main task will be? Resettlement, surely? Is Kreis Pulawy next in line according to the plan?'[136] Such undiluted enthusiasm for the radical goals of the regime's resettlement policy may have been unusual. However, the sense that the East offered 'interesting work' was probably less uncommon, and a factor that assisted the regime in its mobilization efforts.

Interviews with women who were recruited for tasks in occupied Poland provide further insights into the degree of enthusiasm as opposed to reluctant conformity involved in the acceptance of such postings, even if such evidence must be read with an awareness of the role of hindsight in shaping such narratives. It is plausible that while some women might be willing to describe the enthusiasm they had felt at the time for the German 'mission' to colonize the East, others might seek in retrospect to play this down, in particular any component of ideological motivation in their readiness to go to Poland, and instead to highlight their lack of choice in the matter. Nevertheless, it is notable that many respondents – even those for whom a posting to Poland was an order rather than a choice – did remember feeling keen and excited at the prospect.

Three of those interviewed were leaders or members of the NS-Frauenschaft or the BDM who were sent to Poland under the aegis of their organization. Such women, whether they were formally posted by their organization to Poland or came forward of their own accord, shared a pre-existing commitment to that organization and to National Socialism. They were, perhaps, the most likely to respond with alacrity to the regime's 'call'. Another group of respondents went to Poland after being drafted into various forms of wartime obligatory service, which could take the form of an assignment in the East. This group includes a woman drafted into the women's Labour Service as a 19-year-old, together with three who were sent on vacation assignments as university or training college students. These young women, while they may have opted for a stint of service in Poland as opposed to working in the Altreich, were potentially less than willing conscripts, though some recalled being pleased at the prospect of working in the East. The third category comprises the elementary school teachers, together with one kindergarten teacher and a teacher of agriculture, who were posted early in their professional careers to jobs in occupied Poland. This group were under some pressure to accept their postings: again, however, some remembered leaping at the opportunity.

The differences in the circumstances of a posting, and the degree of compulsion involved, shaped how women told their stories of being recruited for work in Poland. However, what they said also depended on how they constructed and reflected upon their individual biographies. Some, in self-critical vein, talked about their acceptance of particular ideas or instructions at the time as worthy of comment; others were more inclined to take it for granted that they had not been able to question or go against what was imposed on and inculcated into them. Some women chose to highlight the 'private' dimension rather than the public context of their recruitment. Thus some told stories that emphasized personal and professional aspirations and family relationships as factors that made a posting to Poland welcome or less welcome, while others talked about their reactions to the news of an assignment in Poland in terms of a sense of duty they felt at a time of national need.

One of the three respondents who were posted to Poland as a result of their involvement in the NS-Frauenschaft or the BDM, Frau Danneberg (all names here and in the following are fictitious) was posted to Posen in late 1939. Since 1937, she had been working in the Reich Women's Leadership headquarters in Berlin after gaining a doctorate in history and working for a time as a bookseller. She presented her appointment in the Reich Women's Leadership headquarters as a happy accident, the result of an acquaintance mentioning a job coming up, rather than something she herself had actively sought out. She characterized herself in retrospect as 'not a passionate supporter of Hitler'. However, she talked of 'many young people who were enthusiastic about Hitler in 1933' and stated that she had been profoundly impressed by the 'union with Austria, and the Saarland and everything'. At the Reich Women's Leadership headquarters, Frau Danneberg found herself, to her delight, among like-minded and highly educated female colleagues ('a lot of doctorates'): she remembered it as a 'wonderful community' in which to work. Frau Danneberg described the atmosphere in the Reich Women's Leadership as one in which the ethos was about showing the regime what women could do; in her recollection, the 'Reichsfrauenführerin' Gertrud Scholtz-Klink fended off the 'toughs' of the Party, asserted women's rights, celebrated the legacy of the bourgeois feminist movement which the regime had forced out of existence in 1933, and generally 'stood up for herself and was somebody'. 'Altogether it was was a very fulfilled – and – well, critical life, because there were criticisms, one could talk – but of course one had to stand up for the thing as a whole, that's clear' (*man mußte zu dem Ganzen ja stehen*).

Frau Danneberg's positive memories of working at the Reichsfrauen-führung suggest that her commitment to the organization was strongly established when the order came in autumn 1939 to move from Berlin to Posen to work as a press officer in the Warthegau headquarters of the NS-Frauenschaft under the Gau women's leader Helga Thrö. 'First there was the task for the East, something like a Gau women's leadership had to be built up, and then I was the press and had to build that up.' From Frau Danneberg's account, the move to Posen appears less as a break than a forward move in her career. Having shared in the mood of excitement at successive German foreign policy triumphs in 1938 and 1939, she now had the chance of being part of what she felt at the time to be a promising new beginning. 'The whole new beginning, the mood in the Warthegau was basically positive.' She arrived in Posen in November 1939, coinciding with the arrival of the Baltic German resettlers and just ahead of the subsequent influx of Galician and Volhynian Germans. In her words: 'everything was cold – and everything was full of refugees'.

Just over a year later than Frau Danneberg, Frau Peters, a leader and district organizer of the Jungmädelbund (the junior branch of the BDM), received orders to report in Posen. She arrived there in January 1941, *en route* to Kreis Kalisch, where her job was to set up the Jungmädelbund. Frau Peters's involvement with the Jungmädelbund went back to 1934, when as a 14-year-old she began leading a group of younger girls. After leaving grammar school aged 16, she spent a year at an agricultural college for women and a further period of around a year as a volunteer with the women's Labour Service; returning home, she threw herself again into working unpaid in her spare time for the Jungmädelbund, and from 1938 became a full-time district leader (*Untergauführerin*). Looking back at her political socialization and her attitudes before the war, Frau Peters recalled wanting to join the women's Labour Service not just to gain relevant experience for a later career as a teacher of agriculture, but also: 'the thing with the national community. The girls were to put themselves at the service of the national community, to use the words that were used then.' Later on, as a full-time BDM official, she remembered the comradeship and the sense of 'the tasks'. 'Always the feeling that what you do is important. Not from the point of view of the Party, not necessarily the goals of the NSDAP, the Reich Youth Leadership never emphasized that particularly, I would say it was a German task (*ein deutscher Auftrag*)'. Sixty years on, Frau Peters painted a picture of the BDM and the Reich Youth Leadership as a world that kept itself separate from 'the Party', in which friendship, comradeship, training camps and trips were in the foreground, including a trip to Carinthia on the eve of the war where she encountered the ethos of the 'borderlands struggle' in exchanges with fellow-BDM activists in Austria.

Following years working from choice in the Jungmädelbund, Frau Peters's commitment to the goals and ideals she regarded as being pursued by the Hitler Youth was well established. For all that, she did not recall feeling enthusiastic about her posting to Poland. This was because the move to the Warthegau was a consequence of a 'real blow', namely the reorganization of the Jungmädelbund in late 1940 that eliminated the post of district leaders at Untergau level. Since she regretted the abolition of her old job, it was with mixed feelings that she contemplated the alternatives that the BDM now offered to her, to go to Alsace or to Poland to build up the Jungmädelbund in the occupied territories, where the Untergaue were to be retained as administrative units. In her words:

> As I said, that was autumn 1940, November 1940, one must take the time into consideration, '39 was the Polish campaign, a year later in other words. And I hesitated between Alsace or the East, and I said to myself, I'm always − anyway, I decided on the Wartheland. I can't remember how it was, whether it was the Reich Youth Leadership or the regional leadership (Obergau) that managed it all, anyway I was told to report to the Jungmädel leader in Posen . . . I was 21, my parents weren't happy at all that I was going to Poland, because everything was still very unclear, one wasn't sure − there weren't many Germans there − it wasn't clear what job one was to do.[137]

Whereas Frau Danneberg recalled, along with memories of the harsh climate and uncomfortable quarters in Posen, a sense of positive new beginnings associated with the creation of Party structures in the Warthegau, Frau Peters − arriving a year later − recalled above all impressions of disorganization and a sense of stepping into the unknown. While she had, according to her account, exercised a preference for the Warthegau over Alsace, her willingness to make the move was based on her strong and long-standing commitment to the Jungmädelbund rather than any conviction that she had a role to play as a pioneer in the East. Moreover, her doubts about going to Poland were amplified by the concerns of her parents.

No such doubts entered into the mind of Frau Bauer, a 27-year-old sales assistant and member of the NS-Frauenschaft who grew up in western Germany near the border with Belgium. She stood out from all other respondents for having been in the strictest sense a volunteer. Her training and occupation would not otherwise have taken her to Poland: the initiative to go there was entirely her own, and she was eager to tell the story of how she took the decision. She remembered responding as an ordinary member of the NS-Frauenschaft to a recruitment drive for settlement advisers for the Warthegau: when in January 1941 the Kreis leader of the NS-Frauenschaft spoke at a local branch meeting about 'The German East and its People' and finished with a call to 'young women and girls who were independent and who wanted to help people and be of service to them', Frau Bauer knew immediately that this was for her.[138] She presented it as a sort of annunciation: 'It was a call, somehow from above, from the stars, I must do this and this is what I have to do with my life'.

EH: No hesitation?

B: No, it was a call and there was no going back. I was single and free, my mother had recovered from a serious illness and could do without me at home and so that was for me the call that was meant for my heart. . . . It was completely new territory. We only knew that these are German people who have come to Germany and we had to help them find a homeland.[139]

Whereas for Frau Danneberg and Frau Peters, both already full-time employees of their respective organizations, the posting to the Warthegau entailed a degree of continuity in their work, Frau Bauer embarked on something completely new. Several factors emerged from her recollections as having contributed to this 'out of the blue' decision. Born in 1914, Frau Bauer's commitment to the German cause appears to have been strengthened by her early memories as a young schoolgirl of the occupation of the Rhineland by British and French troops and of their withdrawal in 1928; moreover, she recalled how after 1933 her consciousness of the Versailles treaty had been further raised by the Nazi regime's emphasis on the issue: in a remark spoken off tape, she talked about 'inwardly resisting' the Treaty. She had complete faith in the regime: 'we believed everything word for word'. Her enthusiastic response to the *Kreisfrauenschaftsleiterin*'s appeal came across in the interview as having arisen out of her conviction that the Warthegau was indeed 'Germany's new land' and that energetic young people from the Altreich had a mission to fulfil there. At the same time, personal factors helped determine her decision. Some time before the January 1941 meeting she had given up her job as a sales assistant to look after her mother: by then, with her mother recovered, she felt free to leave home. By May 1941 she was in the Warthegau attending a brief training course; by the end of May she was working as a full-time employee of the NS-Frauenschaft as a settlement adviser in Kreis Samter. It was a move which in retrospect she regarded as the best she could have made, one which led to 'the precious time that was the best in my life so far'.[140]

If one compares the circumstances surrounding the recruitment for work in Poland of the three respondents who portrayed themselves as having been committed to their respective organizations and to the regime, it seems likely that this commitment was for all of them a factor in their willingness to work in Poland. Frau Danneberg, the NS-Frauenschaft press officer, remembered the comradeship of the Reichsfrauenführung, excitement at German foreign policy triumphs and early optimism about Nazi plans for the Germanization and resettlement of conquered Poland. Frau Peters, the Jungmädelbund leader, conveyed in her recollections a sense of her commitment to the BDM as an organization as well as her memory of feeling dedicated within the Hitler Youth to 'German tasks'. Frau Bauer, the settlement adviser, recalled an overwhelming conviction that she had to respond to the call of the NS-Frauenschaft to serve the ethnic Germans: decades afterwards, she was still pleased at her decision, and proud to recount that she had for a long time been the only woman from her home Kreis to volunteer for the Warthegau. Personal factors were also mentioned by two of these 'committed' respondents as having shaped their reactions to a posting to Poland. Frau Peters's parents voiced a concern that reinforced her own doubts about the assignment, even though it did not change her mind about going; for Frau Bauer, by contrast, family considerations worked only in favour of her decision to volunteer: the fact that she was not working and that her mother could now do without her at home meant that she was 'single and free' and could respond to the NS-Frauenschaft's appeal for volunteers. In addition, Frau Bauer, whose narrative stressed so strongly her sense of mission to go and help the ethnic Germans find their 'new home' in the Warthegau, also mentioned that she was a keen traveller, and when questioned admitted that this might also have played a role in her eagerness to go to the Warthegau.[141]

Turning to the respondents who were drafted into assignments in occupied Poland through the Labour Service and the organization of women students, some were more willing conscripts than others. Frau Holz emphasized how she had been pleased to be conscripted in 1942 to the Labour Service and eager to go to Poland. She recalled how on the outbreak of war, a year into her apprenticeship with a bookseller in a small town in north Germany, she had worried that the war would be over before she had had the chance to do her bit. Her enthusiasm for the Nazi cause, reflected in her joining the Jungmädelbund in 1933, remained undimmed. On being drafted into the Labour Service as a 19-year-old, she saw it as a chance to realize her personal wishes: inspired by the propaganda about the East, and encouraged by her cousin's positive reports on a Labour Service camp in Kreis Wollstein in the Warthegau, she requested a posting to that particular camp and was sent there accordingly. The way she told her story was not to play down the ideological dimension of her enthusiasm at the time, but to highlight it in order to wonder at her credulous youthful self caught up in the fantasy of a Poland populated by 'soldier peasant' families.

EH: So you came to this camp in Wollstein – motivated by –

H: Yes, through a cousin and: as far away as possible . . . and then that non-sense (*dieser Quatsch*) where one wanted to go as far to the east as possible, because that was the land of the future, and after this time in the Labour Service and in the apprenticeship to become a *Wehrbäuerin* (female frontier peasant) in the East and bear six children for the Führer.

Going 'as far away as possible' may have referred to getting away from home, though Frau Holz did not mention this particularly as a motive, but it also appeared to refer to the notion that the farther east one went, the more one showed one's commitment: as she elaborated, 'right out there (*j.w.d*) – because the East was supposed to become totally German – that was our view'.[142]

Frau Holz's seven-month Labour Service in the Warthegau led to a further two years as a school assistant in a village school in the same Kreis: taken as a whole, her experiences in Poland constituted a major part of her wartime experience. By contrast, the short assignments undertaken by the women students were brief episodes rather than turning-points in the respondents' lives, and the memories of how the assignment had come about were less clearly etched in their minds. As a result, it was not always easy to reconstruct the degree of compulsion involved: did they recall opting for the Osteinsatz as one of a limited choice of vacation assignments on offer, or were they simply told to go? Frau Fischer, 19 years old in 1940, was in her first year at a training college for elementary school teachers in her home town in western Germany when she heard that she had been assigned to vacation duties in the Warthegau. She could not remember a campaign to recruit volunteers for the Osteinsatz; all she recalled was a hasty announcement that she and two others from the training college had been 'selected' for the Warthegau and were required to leave almost at once for Litzmannstadt. Reconstructing her responses to this news, she recalled having felt no particular impulse to go East. She was an only child and felt close ties to her family: she expected to feel homesick so far from home. She had no previous connections to the East and no real knowledge of Poland: she dimly recalled that there had been talk just before the outbreak of war of Polish measures directed at the ethnic German minority, but said that she had only begun to take an interest in the history of German–Polish relations after the end of the war. At the time, in her words, Poland 'was alien to me actually. It was alien to me. And it was the only time I went there. The furthest east I went after that was Berlin.'[143] Alongside her reluctance, Frau Fischer did also recall a feeling of patriotic duty: she remembered believing that it was important that those who went to Poland from the Altreich fulfilled the expectations placed in them: 'One felt the obligation to give assistance, and to set an example'.[144] She went on, however, to ponder those feelings of duty and to examine critically her former devotion to the fatherland. Looking back at the degree to which she had been caught up in the nationalism of the time, she talked of a 'mystification of the concept of Germany', criticized the manipulativeness of the organizers of 'eastern assignments', and praised her good fortune that after her brief 1940 assignment in the Warthegau she had been able to steer clear of anything to do with the occupied East.

The cohort of women students recruited in the summer of 1940 for the 'Studentischer Facheinsatz Ost' in the Warthegau also included another respondent, Frau Winter, who was at that time a 21-year-old student of interior design at an art college in southern Germany. Frau Winter recalled little of how she and one other fellow-student from her college came to volunteer or be put forward for the Warthegau assignment in 1940. Like Frau Fischer, she spoke of feeling a sense of duty: 'We were needed, and so any question of being critical was irrelevant.'[145] She recalled the argument being used that 'You have the good fortune to be studying: that means that you have to do your bit the best you can and provide help so that the mothers can have their children well looked after.' However, Frau Winter's willingness to go East appears to have been increased by personal factors and preferences. Already in 1938, when required to perform the six months of Labour Service demanded of girls planning to go on to higher education, she had on her own request joined the Labour Service in East Prussia (see above, Chapter 3). Moreover, her family had connections in Posen and Westpreußen, including one member who owned an estate in the Posen area. While Frau Fischer, after her Warthegau assignment in 1940, was glad to find herself the following year on an assignment in north Germany, Frau Winter, having enjoyed her time in Kreis Sieradz, volunteered for a second stint in the Warthegau in summer 1941.

Frau Winter's cousin, Frau Mahnke, had a clearer memory of being given a choice of vacation assignments. Encouraged by Frau Winter's example, she opted for the Warthegau when in 1942 as a student of archaeology she was faced with having to do vacation work. Like the other respondents who had been on eastern assignments, however, she recalled few details of the mechanisms of recruitment and suspected that there may have been talk of the Osteinsatz in ANSt meetings. Frau Mahnke presented herself as in many respects critical of the regime and incidentally told vivid stories of contacts to wartime student resistance circles. Although she admitted that she had at one stage before the war been enthusiastic enough about Hitler to travel to Cologne in order to cheer him when he visited the city, she insisted that she had felt fundamentally dubious about the prospects for Nazi plans to colonize the East, citing a teacher at her grammar school who had convinced her that the historical movement of population on the European continent from East to West was long-standing, natural and irreversible by any Nazi 'drive to the East'. Such doubts did not, however, put her off an eastern assignment in preference to factory work or helping with the harvest.[146]

As in the case of the 'committed' respondents sent to Poland by the NS-Frauenschaft and BDM, a combination of personal and political factors shaped the reactions of women drafted for Labour Service and student assignments in Poland. Willingness to go might be boosted by previous experiences, positive reports by family members or other family connections with the East, or on the other hand dampened by the prospect of being far away from home and family. It was also assisted by a general sense of patriotic duty. However, there were differences in the degree to which the three former student 'volunteers' emphasized the element of compulsion in their recruitment: Frau Fischer, whose narrative had a particularly critical, and self-critical edge, emphasized it strongly, while Frau Mahnke and Frau Winter presented their eastern assignment more as an acceptable option within a framework of wartime duties.

Eight respondents – a teacher of agriculture, six elementary school teachers and a kindergarten teacher – were posted to occupied Poland in a professional capacity early in their careers. These women, on receiving their postings, knew they could be there for the duration of the war. With the implications of such a posting being potentially so far-reaching, respondents often remembered vividly how it had come about and their reactions to the prospect of working in the East.

Frau Hagen, the teacher of agriculture, had already been teaching in a colonial women's school in north Germany for one year when in 1942 she received her 'call' to Distrikt Lublin in the General Government. When interviewed, she recalled her enthusiasm for the colonial idea and her childhood dream of becoming a farmer's wife in Africa: as a child she had read Hans Grimm's bestselling novel of German colonialism *Volk ohne Raum*, and had been delighted at the colonial women's school to have the chance – while teaching her own agricultural subjects – of joining other students in learning 'colonial subjects', including an African language. In 1942, however, it was announced at the school that 'our colonies no longer lie in Africa but in the East', and later that year Frau Hagen was approached – she recalls that it was because she was the 'only young and active' member of staff at the school – to take on the job of setting up and running a school for village advisers in Distrikt Lublin under the auspices of the Nazi women's organization in the General Government. Asked about how she had reacted to this proposal, she remembered thinking that this was a chance to experience something new, and on the other hand that 'one did not have much say in the matter'.[147] She could have turned the post down – it was not, in contrast to the elementary school teachers' postings to Poland, an order from the state authorities – but nevertheless she felt some pressure to accept it, though she stressed that there had been no pressure to join the Party, which she had already refused to join several years earlier. Her espousal of the colonial ideal was a given: what she thought specifically about the German colonization of Poland is harder to reconstruct. Her account of her responses to her posting to the East focused on her personal aspirations and career plans: this was the case both in retrospect in the interview and in what she wrote in her diary at the time. In her entry for New Year 1943, she expressed both a sense of anticipation and some apprehension: 'The new year begins with snow and a slight chill in the air: what will it bring me, will real fulfilment lie in the East?'

For freshly qualified elementary school teachers, who had trained with the aim of entering the public service as a lifelong career, there seemed even less choice in the matter of a posting to Poland than was available to Frau Hagen: to have refused a posting would have jeopardized their future prospects of civil servant status. Yet several of the elementary school teachers did feel reasonably happy at the prospect of working in Poland. In 1943, Frau Ullmann was posted as a newly qualified elementary school teacher at the age of 21 to Kreis Rawitsch, where she was to stay until January 1945. Immediately after taking her first qualifying examination at training college, Frau Ullmann was told that all who had just qualified except those with aged or sick parents to care for would be sent to the 'new territories' in the East. In the interview, she was asked how she felt about this:

Yes, well, (a) with all the stress of the bombing around Hamburg, not a bad thing at all. It wasn't bad. Secondly from a purely private angle: my two brothers, the one after me had a very difficult development even as a small child . . . I went to school in C——, and my brother failed his second year of school and these 'wonderful' neighbours said: what's the girl doing at secondary school, shouldn't she be looking after the brother, in those days boys counted more than girls, boys have to become something, don't they. So this conflict, I could escape it, and another thing: the others were all going, why shouldn't I? And my favourite subject at school was actually geography, I actually wanted to see something of the world as well, and the boys got to go as soldiers – wherever, to France or to Finland or to Norway, and that wasn't on offer for us, but this way – I was happy to get to know somewhere new.[148]

Frau Ullmann thus recalled going to Poland willingly; yet she went on immediately to recount an episode in 1935 when her father was briefly arrested by the Gestapo. The purpose of the story was to demonstrate to me the constraints imposed by the regime and the sense that one had no alternative but to do what was demanded. Later on in the interview, she added that she felt she was obliged to do her bit as everyone else was in the war: 'It was so instilled into me, everyone has to do their best and work as hard as they could'. Overall, her story conveyed the impression that for her the posting to Poland had compensating factors, but one obeyed orders anyway.

Like Frau Ullmann, Frau Geyer was posted to Poland straight out of teacher training college. She recounted how all the students in her year, graduating in 1941 – 90 per cent of them women, by this stage – knew in advance that they were going to be posted East, probably to the Warthegau. Theoretically, she explained, one could express a preference to be posted somewhere in the Altreich, but it made no difference: Frau Geyer couldn't remember anyone whose wishes had been respected. She described her response to her posting as follows:

I was idealistic. I didn't mind – I thought, oh well, so that's where you're going. I grew up in a village, village life wasn't hard for me. I didn't see it as a political task. I wasn't against Hitler, I was very enthusiastic about the youth movement, but – I believed, he's on the right lines, something like that . . . That's where I'm needed, and that's where you'll go.[149]

Frau Geyer presented herself, in retrospect self-critically, as someone who as a 20-year-old had been 'pretty uncritical' of things taught at training college such as 'racial theory'. 'I took everything in that was presented to me, and what was, had to be.' She remembered her enthusiasm for the BDM and portrayed herself as someone who 'wasn't against Hitler': she saw her willingness to teach in Poland partly as 'idealism' and a conviction that she was needed, and partly in terms of feeling she would cope: having grown up in Lower Silesia, the western Warthegau was not so far from home. Coming from a farming family, she was accustomed to village life, and her father, who had grown up on the border with Poland, was 'not unsympathetic' to her going to the Warthegau. However, she recalled knowing too little about Poland and about what to expect: 'I knew about the history, about the Corridor after the First World War, how the country was divided and then how Poland was recreated, that there are many Germans there, but I didn't know more than that.'

Some women were dismayed at the prospect of working in occupied Poland, and protested. Frau Andreas, graduating from a two-year training college course for kindergarten teachers in Königsberg in 1944, said that she and her fellow-students received a form to fill in expressing a preference for where they should be posted: the tutor, however, ordered them not to fill it in. Frau Andreas was convinced that the rule ordering newly qualified kindergarten teachers to go wherever they were sent applied only to those receiving state grants; her fees, however, had been paid by her father and she was determined to express a preference for a posting in southern Germany. As she told the story, she was punished for this by being sent to the annexed Polish territory of Suwalki.

> My father paid, so I was not obliged, neither to the National Socialist authorities nor to anyone else, and so we got shortly before our examinations a letter from the labour office where one could tick – personal details, where one would like to work and so on, and I wrote down 'South Germany', and the tutor came in and said 'Don't fill that in, you have to cross all that out.' And I said 'But why, my father paid everything' – so I put it down. And that was why I ended up way out East. I'd never been to south Germany.[150]

Having grown up in a household with a father who was a Labour Front and later a Party official, Frau Andreas was not fundamentally opposed to National Socialism: only after the war, she said, had she undergone what she called a 'difficult process' of grasping, in her words, the 'criminal' nature of the regime and the 'senseless' waste of life it had caused. However, she recounted how as a young woman she had gained a reputation for being outspoken. She added later that the director had 'not sent her favourite people to Suwalki' and had singled out her and her friend Agnes for the posting: no one else had been 'sent abroad'.

Other respondents, too, were less than happy at the news of a posting to the East. Frau Keller, having left grammar school in 1932, had qualified as an elementary schoolteacher in 1937. She told her story as one of finding herself repeatedly 'going against the grain' in Nazi Germany: 'I was never in any Party organization, neither BDM nor anything else'. She remembered hating a brief enforced spell in the women's Labour Service because of the 'real Nazi' camp leader, and resenting compulsory shooting practice that was part of the university sports curriculum ('I always missed, and they put it down to my bad eyesight!'). After qualifying, Frau Keller taught in a village in her home region of Thüringen. Following a dispute there when she refused to stop teaching religious education as part of the curriculum, she decided to try and get out of Germany altogether and applied to the Foreign Office for a place in a German school abroad: 'I thought maybe the Nazis there wouldn't be so strict'. Nothing happened immediately with her application, and instead one day in early 1940 the *Schulrat* called on her to tell her that she was being sent to Danzig-Westpreußen, along with a hundred or so other teachers from Thüringen (in her words: 'one had to be young, single and have done well in the examination'). She recounted her reaction:

> K: I was of course shocked, because I was very attached to my home and family. And I knew I wouldn't be able to get home for a while. We all stuck together very closely.
>
> EH: But you wanted to go abroad.
>
> K: Yes, certainly.
>
> EH: But not there?
>
> K: Yes, that's right![151]

Frau Keller wanted to go and teach abroad in order to escape the political pressures to which she felt exposed, rather than to get away from her family home, which was strongly Christian and anti-Nazi and to which she was strongly attached. A posting to Poland was for her a posting in entirely the wrong direction; her dismay was all the greater since it was clear that the posting could last as long as the war continued.

Frau Eckhard, aged only 18 when she graduated in spring 1942 from a teacher training course that had been compressed into an intensive nine-month programme, also received news of her posting to the East with dismay. However, the reasons for her reaction were different from those that determined Frau Keller's negative response. 'I just remember that I lay in bed at night and wept because of the wolves there!' Frau Eckhard had been brought up by her father always to obey orders: 'my father was an officer and what is ordered gets done, from the top downwards'. However, on this occasion her parents backed her appeal against the posting to a school near Posen on the grounds that her father was serving in the Wehrmacht and she was needed nearer home:

No, I didn't want to go there because of the wolves. And my parents said I'd be better off staying in the Reich. It would be nearer – and I could have gone home, Saturday or Sunday, whatever. But that was turned down and so I got the order, Kreis Sieradz, and that was where I had to report.[152]

Even if Frau Eckhard had experienced conflicts within her family, she preferred to stay nearer home than go to Poland. However, as she explained, the outcome of her unsuccessful appeal was that she was posted even further east, to Kreis Sieradz instead of Posen. Frau Eckhard spoke of her posting to Poland in terms of her own fears of the unknown and her relationships with her family: considerations of wartime duty, professional ambition or commitment to the German cause did not enter into her narrative at all. Unusually among the respondents, she told her story as something of a comedy, playing up her imaginings of Poland as a dark and terrible place populated by wolves. But what she conveyed along with the comic narrative was a memory of strong antipathy to her posting, as well as less explicit hints of ambivalence about remaining close to home or getting away.

Frau Eckhard's experience contrasted with that of her friend Frau Vogel, interviewed on the same occasion in a conversation in which their very different experiences teaching in the Warthegau emerged. Frau Vogel remembered not even waiting to be posted but volunteering, together with a fellow-student from her university teacher training course, to go to the Warthegau: 'I know that we already said in Jena, we'll go to Poland voluntarily'. She and her friend got a posting to Kreis Welun in the spring of 1942; on arrival they insisted on being sent to the same village. They stayed there until January 1945. Frau Vogel explained her readiness to go to Poland as resulting from feeling 'shut in' and unable to travel abroad during the years of National Socialist rule. Her family had been used to travelling and had contacts overseas, including relatives in the United States:

Uncles and aunts and cousins visit, why can't we go to America too – later on, that was one of the reasons that I really went travelling around the world with my husband, because we simply had the need – perhaps it's in my blood a little bit, one never knows – anyway it was a reason for me and for my friend as well, that we said: we can't go anywhere, now we can go somewhere different, somewhere we don't know.[153]

However, Frau Vogel said that while she and her friend were happy to go to Poland, above all if they were going to be able to teach in the same place, other fellow-students she knew had been compelled to go against their will:

V: I know of two, I know for certain that they were made to go. They were told 'You're going there' – if you want to be a teacher and whatever – in those days you simply couldn't say 'I don't want to do that', that just wasn't possible.

EH: Do you know of any of your fellow-students who refused to go?

V: One of them was from a family of Jesuits, she refused and they told her, 'You're going there or something will happen.' And because people from her family had been arrested because they were Jesuits, she didn't dare, but later on she was always – she was absolutely miserable. I can still see her in my mind's eye, a bit older than us, a really pious Catholic – her brother was a Jesuit. It was awful. She didn't want to.

Frau Vogel's story about the Catholic forced against her will to go and teach in Poland provided a sombre counterpoint to her generally cheerful narrative of how she and her friend from university had seized the opportunity of getting to see 'somewhere different, somewhere we don't know'.

The last respondent, Frau Teplitz, who graduated from teacher training college in spring 1943, was quite willing to go to the Warthegau for her first job, and recalled, like Frau Vogel, actually volunteering to go. She told her story as follows:

After my examination – I lived in Hamburg, we were totally bombed out, had very poor sleeping quarters, a very poor flat – and I volunteered to go to the East. I hate the big city, I like the countryside, where one can have personal relationships with people, in the city it is completely impersonal. We only got to know the other tenants in our apartment block in the air raid shelter during the bombing. And so it was my first job, away from the family, where I hadn't had it particularly easy. And I had no idea what was to await me.

Frau Teplitz spoke of her move to the Warthegau as representing a long-awaited move towards independence. She recounted how she had qualified as an elementary school teacher at the age of 27, after several years of frustrated career plans and false starts, including initially being turned down for teacher training after doing her *Abitur* in 1935 on the grounds that she was the only one in the class not in the BDM. At the same time, she had experienced conflicts and difficulties at home. The prospect of her first job in the East outweighed all other considerations: Frau Teplitz recalled how she had, as a committed Christian, been involved in the Confessing Church, but had otherwise been 'quite unpolitical' and ignorant of what the East would be like. She simply looked forward to the escape from bombs and overcrowding, the complete change of scene and the greater scope for self-determination that her first job as a village schoolteacher seemed to promise.

Reviewing the accounts by those sent in their professional capacity to teach in Poland, it emerges that most were formally posted. Frau Hagen, the agricultural teacher, was the exception in that she was given the option. Of the elementary school teachers, only two, Frau Vogel and Frau Teplitz, put themselves forward of their own accord. Responses to the prospect of having to work in Poland varied: Frau Geyer recalled being willing and Frau Ullmann remembered being quite eager to go. Three, by contrast, were reluctant: the schoolteachers Frau Eckhard and Frau Keller, together with the kindergarten teacher Frau Andreas, were unhappy about their postings to the Warthegau, Danzig-Westpreußen and Suwalki respectively.

Family ties and a desire to stay close to home made some reluctant to go: this emerged from the accounts of Frau Keller and Frau Eckhard. By contrast, Frau Ullmann and Frau Teplitz welcomed the chance of getting free of families with whom they had difficult relationships. Others placed their accounts of being sent to work in Poland within the context of their overall attitudes to National Socialism and to the regime's wartime demands on individuals. Frau Ullmann and Frau Geyer, for instance, remembered feeling a general sense of patriotic duty and a willingness to 'do their bit' in wartime, given that everyone else was doing so as well. Frau Keller, by contrast, the committed Christian teacher who had come into conflict with the school authorities in Thüringen, described feeling dismayed at the prospect of working in occupied Poland, particularly since she had hoped to escape from living under Nazi rule by leaving Germany altogether. However, a critical stance towards the regime could also, paradoxically, go hand in hand with an enthusiastic response to a posting to Poland. Frau Teplitz was, like Frau Keller, a committed Christian and someone who had kept her distance from all Nazi organizations, but she was happy to go and work in Poland for personal and professional reasons.

One consideration mentioned by several was the notion of 'seeing the world'. Frau Hagen recalled her response to the proposal that she go to Distrikt Lublin as being shaped by her eagerness to experience something new. Frau Vogel presented the desire to see beyond the borders of the Reich as her primary motive for her volunteering to teach in the Warthegau: if she couldn't get to the United States, at least she could explore foreign parts closer to hand in Poland. Frau Ullmann, who was concerned to get away from the bombing in her home town as well as from family conflicts, also mentioned her desire to 'see something of the world', just like the men did when they joined the Wehrmacht, as one factor in her positive response to her posting to Kreis Rawitsch. Finally Frau Andreas, although she resented the posting to Suwalki and thought it a spiteful act on the part of her training college director, mentioned her hopes at the time of getting to go somewhere away from home: 'one wanted to get to know the world, and during the war it was quite possible for us to go somewhere'.[154]

Propaganda depictions of women's work with ethnic Germans in occupied Poland conveyed the impression of youthful volunteers surging eastwards to offer their womanly services to the cause of Germandom. Such accounts emphasized the feminine capacities that the women recruited would bring to the tasks of assisting ethnic German women and children, but also their energy, authority and capacity for improvising and solving problems on the ground. It was an image representing a deliberate antithesis to rule-bound bureaucracy. In some accounts, for instance depictions of school assistants, there was a positive cult of youth and of the amateur and a disparagement of 'traditional' approaches to educational practice. What they lacked in training and experience, young women would, it was suggested, make up in energy, enthusiasm and the authority derived from their Reich German identity: they would through the force of their personality carry the Nazi message into German homes and generate a momentum of community-building among the ethnic Germans. Such images were constructs designed to flatter and to boost recruitment of the categories of women most easy to mobilize for the regime's goals: young, single women.

The regime did manage to mobilize several thousand women from the Altreich for educational and welfare tasks in the annexed territories of western Poland and later in the General Government and the occupied Soviet territories, even though many spent only a short time in the East and the number of recruits never sufficed to meet the occupation authorities' demand for Reich German personnel. Clearly some of those who went East were genuine volunteers. Inspired by the Nazi vision of a Germanized East, by a sense of wartime duty, or by the prospect of 'interesting work' and of travel to unfamiliar places, some responded unprompted to the regime's recruitment campaigns. However, the lack of personnel to run the Nazi empire in eastern Europe made it impossible to depend on genuine volunteers alone. Informal and formal pressures operated to induce women to 'volunteer' for shorter or longer-term assignments, and formal sanctions could be applied to enforce postings to occupied Poland. Activists and leaders in the BDM or NS-Frauenschaft were expected and sometimes required to accept a short-term assignment in Poland, depending on their place in the organizational hierarchy. Those drafted for student vacation assignments and the Labour Service might express a preference for the East when obliged to undertake a form of service anyway, but such a desire to go East has to be seen in the context of what may have seemed more unpalatable alternatives. Trainee teachers came to assume that they would be posted straight to Poland after their first state examination, and knew that refusal put in jeopardy their later appointment as civil servants. Women who were posted there unwillingly, or who changed their mind having volunteered, found it difficult to get away: once they were there the authorities were reluctant to let them go.

Yet, even taking into account the pressures that contributed to women accepting an assignment in Poland, many women seem to have been intrigued and pleased by the prospect when it was presented to them and to have regarded it as an opportunity to prove themselves. The regime could not depend on deploying only those who were totally committed to its goals: the women who volunteered to go East on the basis of their enthusiasm for National Socialism and their sense of mission as a female vanguard were a minority. However, the regime could rely on the readiness of a wider spectrum of young middle-class women to conform to its demands upon them. In accepting such tasks, these women sought to demonstrate their competence, and their self-reliance away from their families, and to gain responsibilities, status and new experiences.

Chapter 5

'Uncanny Space' or 'German Homeland'?
German Women's Constructions of the 'East'

Were German women natural colonizers? Karin von Schulmann, the Estonian German who headed the Nazi women's organization's section for 'Border and Foreign Affairs' asked this question in October 1942 in a speech to a Party meeting on racial and national issues. Her speech was delivered in the context of recruitment efforts by the Nazi women's organization aimed at persuading women to go East. Schulmann began by painting a picture of the German people as a domesticated nation of homebodies:

> We Germans love confined spaces, the German feeling of cosiness and homeliness (*die deutsche Traulichkeit und Heimelichkeit*). When we go East we have to break with this confinement of which we are so fond. . . . The touchstone of whether a person is spiritually fitted for settlement in the East is a portrayal of space on a grand scale with all the beautiful and the burdensome things that the *Ostraum* has to offer. If this image of *Raum*, this uncanny space (*unheimliche Weite*) appeals to people, that is a sign that the colonizing spirit is still there. The average woman in Germany loves homely things. The East is *unheimlich*. This inclination towards confined spaces clings like a sticky mass to the German people and must be overcome. The spaces of the East must be embraced inwardly, only then can this conquered land become a homeland (*Heimat*) for Germans.[1]

Von Schulmann in her speech hovered between celebrating what she presented as the 'German' qualities of loving homeland and homeliness, and praising 'exceptional' Germans who overcame their alleged attachment to the familiar world of the homeland in order to become colonizers. Her final sentence, however, sought to resolve that tension. The spaces in the East, she declared, which would be held and colonized successfully only if German women played their part alongside men, would in turn become a 'homeland' for Germans: the *unheimliche Weite* would be transformed into *Heimat*. Her speech provides a point of departure for looking at how German women

working in occupied Poland depicted the East, the ideas of space and homeland. This entails exploring the racism, the notions of 'German' and 'foreign',
and the assumptions about gender that underlay these depictions, and it raises
the question of whether German women writing about Poland used similar
images and clichés to portray the land and its people as men did.

Following the conquest and occupation of Poland, the Nazi propaganda
machine swung into action to portray the 'new East' as a future German
homeland. Party activists were encouraged to visit and report back to the
Reich; those posted to occupied Poland were exhorted to return home and
counteract images of the East as a place to which Germans from the Reich
would be posted only as a punishment. Areas such as eastern Upper Silesia,
West Prussia and Posen, which had been under German rule in the recent
past, were presented as being 'restored' to their true identity, while territories
further east that were formerly under Russian domination, such as the eastern
part of the Warthegau, were described as manifesting traces of German
settlement. The Germanization campaign was thus presented as stripping
away and building bulwarks against the 'alien', excavating and retrieving the
'hidden beauties' of the land, exploiting its 'untapped wealth', and restoring
'German culture'.[2]

German women visiting occupied Poland, together with women working
with ethnic Germans in the annexed territories and in the General Government, contributed to the body of writing on the Nazi East when they set down
their impressions – sometimes cursory, sometimes detailed – of the towns, the
countryside and their inhabitants. Such texts ranged from pieces by professional journalists and propagandists to accounts written by students, BDM
leaders, schoolteachers and kindergarten teachers. Some were written for
publication, others as reports for the eyes of leaders, organizers and superiors.
Some of the latter reached a wider circle of readers back in the Altreich as
they were reproduced in edited form in internal newsletters and bulletins as
recruitment propaganda. It was understood that women would put a positive
gloss on their reports. BDM leaders working in Alt-Sandez in Distrikt Krakau
in the General Government in 1943 were told by a Party official to go home
and convey the correct message about the East: 'in the Reich there is in many
quarters a completely false picture of the German East', something the BDM
leaders were expected to 'combat vigorously'.[3] While there is nothing remarkable in finding the Nazi line on Poland and its Polish and Jewish population
reproduced in reports written for the press, for officialdom or for dissemina-
tion within regime organizations, it is still worth noting the way in which
these sentiments were expressed.

Diaries and letters written at the time give some indication of how far regime propaganda about Poland may have influenced women's more personal responses to the East. German soldiers and male civilians in Poland often reproduced in private letters stereotypes of Poles and Polish Jews that appear to have been fuelled by Nazi racism: such prejudices were manifest in the indifference and malice to be found in descriptions of encounters with Polish poverty and the degradation of the Polish Jews.[4] This prompts the question of whether women, too, expressed anti-Polish and anti-semitic sentiments in private documents. It is also worth exploring how far the official rhetoric about turning Poland into a German homeland was reflected in private comments about whether the conquered land was indeed 'just like home', a space to be appropriated unproblematically by Germans, or an 'uncanny space' with the power to unsettle them. If Germans found occupied Poland uncanny, what provoked the fear, unease or even disgust associated with such a sensation?[5]

The impressions recorded by German women travelling or working in occupied Poland can also be compared with descriptions of encounters with the foreign or 'alien' in other contexts. Narratives of such cross-cultural encounters reveal frequent use of gendered metaphors by those identifying with their own nation against the foreign, or describing the relationship between colonizers and colonized.[6] They also point to the different ways in which men and women have placed themselves in relation to the nation beyond the border, the frontier landscape or the colonized territory.[7] In a colonial or frontier context, 'white women' shared in the privileges of the colonizer in relation to the 'natives', even though within their own society they were subordinate to men.[8] Women, it has been argued, could thus share in the prejudices and the perspective of the 'master'. All the same, women may have adopted a distinctively feminine perspective on colonized lands and their inhabitants. They may have displayed a particular concern with domestic order within colonial society as a way of securing boundaries against the natives,[9] or a desire to turn conquered space into a bounded and ordered domain: laying out gardens could represent a way of taming a frontier territory.[10] Texts written by German women at the time can be explored in the light of such parallels with colonial or frontier societies to discover how far women expressed a stance of 'mastery' over the conquered native population, and how far they reflected a female perspective on German rule in Poland.

Oral testimony provides a further source of women's impressions of the East, albeit filtered through hindsight. Several respondents recalled seeing ghettos in Polish towns and cities. For some, this seems to have been a sight to pass over and not dwell on, while others recalled it as a turning-point in their experiences in Poland. Comparing these memories with the impressions recorded at the time may give some indication of how German women imagined Germanness and Polishness, 'homeland' and 'otherness'. It may also shed light on what they saw and how they perceived the discrimination, persecution and violence against the subjugated Jewish and non-Jewish population of Poland.

Male encounters with the East: the colonizing gaze

In January 1940, the 34-year-old novelist and dramatist Felix Lützkendorf joined a delegation of a dozen journalists and cameramen travelling to Poland to document the 'homecoming' to the Reich of ethnic Germans from Soviet-occupied eastern Poland. His report from the East, published later that year, encapsulated in literary form a whole spectrum of Nazi clichés about Poland and the East. It was striking for its use of gendered imagery to represent nationhood and national identity. This is how Lützkendorf describes Warsaw:

> Life in the destroyed city has long since returned to normal. Lavish window displays in the shops. A large number of very fashionable shops in Parisian style. Very many hairdressers and shops selling perfume. The population is generally well dressed. Many sumptuous, well-made fur coats. We encounter a striking number of beautiful blonde women. Dressed with the elegance that models itself on Paris. It is not the attractive, tasteful but functional look (*Sachlichkeit*) of the Berlin woman. Here, the extravagance and showiness is already to be found in the little messenger girls. Generally, in this land, in this city, the women are more impressive than the men. One remembers the great women of Polish history. This history, this present: truly, one could call Poland a feminine state. Feminine entirely in the Slavic sense. Everything is glitter. Moods instead of deeds; mendacity instead of alliances, fantasies in place of political reality, prattle in place of hard work, and always the desire to be kept by someone. The whole state a whore's existence. On top of that, cruel towards the weak, pitiless towards the poor, but pious in the plentiful churches. This is the eternal Poland.[11]

Warsaw appears in this passage as a city of women in a feminized Poland. The gaze of the male reporter/flâneur, who sees Warsaw through the eyes of the conqueror and colonizer, is both fascinated and repelled. The city, with its luxurious shops, appears seductive, as do the women who walk its streets; yet it is artificial and showy, in contrast to the authentic, tasteful, but less elegant 'Berlin woman'. In a strange sequence of images, Polish women appear 'impressive' and even to embody greatness in Polish history, but immediately the positive images are cancelled: Poland is presented as a glittering whore, incapable and unworthy of an independent existence as a state.

The technique of representing the foreign as unmanly, feminine or feminized pervades Lützkendorf's text. In a description of young Polish men imprisoned in Lublin, he contrasts their 'feverish, boastful delight in hearing and being intoxicated by the very name of Poland' to the 'masculine feeling of quiet patriotism that is so singularly German'.[12] In his account of the Warsaw ghetto, his anti-semitic imaginings conjure up 'thick-lipped' Jewish men and 'obese oriental "Mammes" with fat gold-ringed fingers'.[13] Fighting his way, as he describes it, through the crowds of Jews in the narrow streets, he seeks to flee through a side street, but finds it closed, so he has to return 'once again through this crowd, whose exhalations, whose gazes, whose language make one physically sick'. It is a classic description of disgust, while his account of getting lost and retracing his steps through the 'hellish street' adds to Lützkendorf's evocation of losing control, of being in a nightmare.[14]

In contrast with the evocation of shrill artificiality and gender ambivalence in relation to Poland and Polishness, Lützkendorf's portrayal of the Volhynian and Galician Germans arriving as colonizers of the annexed territories of western Poland functions in the text as a reassuring vision of 'normality'. It features the classic peasant family of Nazi ruralist dreams: tall, taciturn bearded men, proud women in headscarves and tough, healthy children. In their wagons, on the move or drawn up in camp, Lützkendorf presents them as re-enacting historic treks of the past, those of the ancient Germanic tribes or the Great Trek of the Boers. Located in a great chain of Germanic peasants trekking away from oppression towards new lands, the marching columns of ethnic Germans fill up the Polish landscape, a landscape depicted by Lützkendorf as formless, featureless, bound by ice and mud.[15]

Lützkendorf's text can be read in the context of German nationalist writing about Poland that drew on a tradition of German anti-Polish and anti-semitic stereotypes and on the notion of German cultural superiority. As a piece of Nazi wartime propaganda, it revels in the recent victory over Poland, seen as reversing two decades of perceived German humiliation. At the same time, in its use of gendered imagery, Lützkendorf's text has features that have been identified as typical by writers on gender, nationalism and colonialism: for instance the image of the nation as family-writ-large under patriarchal leadership or as a band of brothers, and the representation of women as 'boundary markers', embodying the cultural heritage in their dress, appearance and gestures. In Lützkendorf's text, the wagon train of Volhynian German families led by rugged patriarchs is likened to German nationhood on its march through history. Meanwhile, in his representations of Poland, Warsaw women are seen as embodying Polish nationality, displaying in their 'Paris fashions' the alleged showiness, artificiality (and Francophilia) of the Polish nation. The supposed authenticity and solidity of German nationhood are by contrast evoked in the image of the smart but sensibly attired 'Berlin woman'.

Lützkendorf draws heavily on the notion of German cultural superiority and of a German 'civilizing mission' in eastern Europe. To Lützkendorf, Poland bears the marks of a German heritage waiting to be restored: the old market square in Warsaw suggests to him that he is 'in the middle of Germany, in the market place of a medieval town'. But Poland is also portrayed as uncanny and threatening: the deserted night-time streets of Cholm are silent apart from a 'hellish chorus' of dogs barking: it is an *unheimlich-tote Stadt* in which a German's insecurity is heightened by fear of snipers. At another level, the text can be seen as displaying features of colonial discourse in its arrogant gaze upon the subjugated population, conjuring up a procession of stereotypes ranging from seductive Polish women and loquacious and excitable Polish men to bejewelled Jewish women and unmanly Jewish men. It also echoes colonial discourse in the way that it depicts the landscape. As Mary Louise Pratt and others have shown, the colonized landscape in colonial or frontier texts is often seen either as virgin territory to be opened up and tamed, or dead and featureless land waiting to be penetrated and fertilized by the male colonizer.[16] Lützkendorf emphasizes the harshness of the Polish landscape (highlighted by the below-zero temperatures of a Polish January) but also its featurelessness and chaos: it is presented as awaiting a structuring and ordering drive based on Prussian military virtues that will make it hospitable to Germans: 'Prussian-German order and honour, cleanliness and clarity are beginning to reshape this East from the bottom up'.[17]

Lützkendorf's gendered imagery of Poles, Jews, the Polish landscape and the German colonizing drive echoed in different ways through other descriptions of Poland written by male journalists, propaganda officials and Party functionaries. Such pieces appeared, for example, in *Das Reich*, the newspaper with literary pretensions that targeted an educated readership; *Das Schwarze Korps*, the SS journal that liked to mock 'bourgeois' thinking in the name of radical Nazism; *Die Bewegung*, the newspaper of the Nazi student organization, and periodicals of the Nazi welfare organization NSV. They were written to stir up interest in the East among readers in the Altreich, to legitimize the regime's racial policy and to present the East as an exciting land of challenges and opportunities for Germans.[18]

Some authors invoked an eroticized vision of the East in classic colonialist terms as a kind of dark continent.[19] In a piece in *Das Reich* in November 1941, a male reporter recounting a journey to the General Government portrayed the East as a magical, alluring expanse that cast a spell more powerful than that of the lands to Germany's south. The land is seen as dark, heavy and fertile: 'People speak of the Germans' longing for the south. But the ties are stronger, deeper and more mysterious that bind Germans to the East. It stretches by our side, darker, wider and more limitless than the sunlit land beyond the Alps to which we are bound by the simple tie of friendship.'[20]

The East might inspire a 'colonizing high', something that in Nazi circles at the time was termed the *Ostrausch* (intoxication with the East).[21] On the other hand, the territory's perceived flatness and wetness, its 'melancholy' and 'monotony'[22] could also trigger fear and revulsion alongside the urge to impose discipline and structure upon it. 'Slavic-Asiatic' lethargy was blamed for allowing structuring features of the landscape created by former generations of German settlers to sink into the 'morass'.[23] Accounts insisted on the need to erect boundaries and fences in a desolate landscape of formless villages and roads that turned to mud.[24] Himmler in his blueprints for the East was obsessed with overcoming the 'monotony' and 'emptiness' of the annexed territories with hedges and shelter belts.[25]

A standard repertoire of images shaped Nazi accounts of Polish townscapes as well as those of the countryside. If, to Nazi eyes, *Kultur* manifested itself in landscape through a rational organization of agricultural cultivation, a neat ordering of farm buildings and villages and a modern road network, in towns the hallmarks of German influence were to be found in historic monuments, in the style of buildings and the layout of streets and parks. The identification of disorder and disharmony in the ordering of space with Polishness also pervaded Nazi descriptions of the towns, cities and infrastructure of conquered Poland. Having visited Gdynia in autumn 1939 to inspect arrangements for the reception of the Baltic Germans there, Dr Richard Csaki of the Deutsches Auslands-Institut (Institute for Foreign Affairs) pronounced the modern architecture of the new port city to be 'gigantomanic' and American-influenced.[26] An unnamed small town in the Warthegau was depicted by the writer Gerd Gaiser[27] in *Das Reich* in 1941 as characterized by low, 'half-sunken' houses on 'crooked little alleys', contrasting with 'pretentious' and 'barbaric' public buildings.[28] Towns such as Bromberg (Bydgoszcz) and Posen which had been part of Prussia before 1919 were presented as being in the process of recovering their German character as they obliterated alleged Polish architectural and planning monstrosities: such were the products, according to these vindictive polemics, of the 'outrageous Polish state', out to undermine with its 'bestial Satanism' the German cultural heritage in western Poland.[29]

Łódź/Litzmannstadt was conventionally dismissed as 'grotesque' and 'inorganic': any buildings of quality spotted there, wrote a propaganda official from the Wartheland, were bound to be German.[30] Its layout, according to the introduction to a volume of German artists' impressions of the Warthegau, resembled not so much an 'organically constructed *Heimatraum*' as a 'sea of houses stretching out without a clear shoreline into the equally unstructured endlessness of the mindlessly deforested surroundings'.[31]

Gazing at the towns of occupied Poland, German visitors might notice and comment on the existence of ghettos. Descriptions of ghettos were sometimes curt: Gerd Gaiser in his sketch of the small town in the Warthegau merely noted, 'Over there a rectangle of streets: fenced off and made into a ghetto: 1,300 Jews'.[32] Other authors gave full vent to anti-semitism in images designed to 'enlighten' readers about the 'Jewish problem' in the East. In a brochure on the work of the NSV in Poland, one reporter wrote of 'degenerate Jewish parasites', 'subhumanity' and 'criminal visages' encountered in the ghetto in Łódź: 'one literally feels sick'.[33] Another piece, from *Das Reich* in 1941, portrayed the Warsaw ghetto: 'There surely cannot be a place on the continent that offers such a graphic cross-section of the chaos and degeneracy of the Semitic mass. At a glance one can take in the enormous, repellent variety of all the Jewish types of the East: a gathering of the asocial, it floods out of dirty houses and greasy shops, up and down the streets, and behind the windows the series of bearded, spectacled rabbinical faces continues – a dreadful panorama.'[34]

As the descriptions of the 'wild East' proliferated, odd notes of criticism were voiced in some quarters of the Party and its press: it was feared that exaggerated portrayals of backwardness, quaintness, disease and danger might make Germans back in the Reich wonder how such a land could possibly offer a homeland to future German generations. In summer 1941, for instance, the NSDAP Kreis leadership in Zawiercie-Blachownia in eastern Upper Silesia urged the Gau Party authorities to get press reporting on violent crime in Upper Silesia toned down in the rest of the Reich. 'The impression is always being conveyed in the Reich that things are like the Wild West here.'[35] The criticism of 'sensationalist' images of the 'new East' was that such exotic images swamped the crucial propaganda message about the success of Nazi colonization. Instead, Poland under Nazi rule should be depicted as a land from which Polishness was being rapidly stripped away: soon, modernity and German order would prevail. Adopting this anti-sensationalist tack, an anonymous contributor declared in August 1940 in the student newspaper *Die Bewegung* that 'This land with its wells and windmills, with its wide sandy roads through the villages that simply reflect the

expanse of the countryside, with its thatched farmhouses half hidden
behind trees – somehow it has been alienated from us by all the reports
and descriptions that depend for their effect on a cheap romanticization.'[36]
The East was no place, he insisted, for adventurers or for 'wild-west-
romantic' accounts: instead, he urged, the Polish landscape should be demys-
tified and seen for what it was: rural life went on and cattle grazed in meadows
little different from those back home. With a similar agenda of 'normalizing'
the images of Poland in order to emphasize the smooth integration of the
annexed territories into the Reich, the Gau authorities in the Wartheland
organized an exhibition in the spring of 1941 entitled 'The Eastern
Wartheland'. Its declared intent was to display the formally Congress Polish
part of the Warthegau not as primitive, alien and a 'vermin Dorado', but as
shaped by an allegedly deep-rooted German heritage.[37] In February 1941, *Das
Schwarze Korps* ran an item mocking the 'foolish prejudices' that saw the East
as a quasi-Siberian steppe, and parodying descriptions of 'roads lost in the
morass', 'melancholy huts', and 'wolves in the night howling their wilderness
yowl'.[38]

However, appeals for more sober representations of the East remained
in tension with exterminatory fantasies and intoxicated visions of limitless
power. The supposedly 'sober' anonymous critic in *Die Bewegung* condemned
those who 'romanticized' the backwardness of the Polish rural landscape only
to move on to his own technocratic fantasy of boundless domination: 'At the
moment when one realizes the enormous scale of the work that is to be
done to take this expanse in hand in such a way that every square metre is
harnessed to its proper purpose, one can experience a sort of intoxication . . .
it is in such a feeling that one may find a deeper and more justified core
of romanticism.'[39] *Das Schwarze Korps*, too, continued to purvey its own range
of stereotypes about occupied Poland. Within weeks of its demolition of
eastern 'myths', it published an article with lyrical descriptions of rugged
Volhynian peasants 'straight out of a painting by Thoma'[40] as well as a 'day
in the life' piece on an SS officer policing villages in the General Government
that set out to conjure up images of disorder and chaos kept in check by
German security forces. The reporter described the villages of Cykow-Stary
and Izbica as being inhabited by 'obsequious' Poles' and 'lying' Jews and
policed by determined SS men who drank after their day's duties in the 'Wild
West Bar'.[41] In 1941, when that account was published, Izbica was a village
where Polish Jews were concentrated. From 1942 onwards it also became a
holding place for German Jews from the Reich before they were deported to
the death camps.[42]

Lützkendorf's text and others give us insights into the way in which gender, national identity and colonial fantasies interacted in the minds of the Nazi colonizers of wartime Poland. Responses to the East are shaped by a mixture of unease, fear and excitement. Some are dominated by what could be read as the unease of the male fascist about being flooded and submerged by an unbounded and female Other, and the corresponding compulsion to erect dams and bulwarks against it.[43] History, in these polemics, is told in terms of monuments of German cultural achievement set against the 'sluggish flood of Slavic living and being'.[44] The clichéd metaphors that talked of the 'German East' as a 'wall of hearts and bodies' were a fundamental element of this discourse.[45] Others place in the foreground the pleasure at the spectacle of space awaiting the hand of the colonizer, who will eradicate the traces of the alien culture and population and put a new order in its place. In these texts, the expanse of territory and the alien, subjugated population constituted a backdrop for the new wave of German colonists, 'the civil servants, the Hitler boys, the soldiers and Labour Service girls, the *Feldjäger*, the estate managers and the solid fair-haired BDM leaders from the Reich'.[46] The Germans were depicted as having a 'taut bearing and clear, forward-directed gaze';[47] German soldiers and police were described striding through Polish cities, embodying 'the ordering principle that represents the dominant power over this space' and filling the air with the sound of military bands.[48] And German order was declared to be coming to 'ugly' Łódź/Litzmannstadt: 'The street names, signs, the traffic, the façades of buildings and the shop fronts, the maintenance of public transport, the complete removal of the Jews (*die völlige Ausschaltung der Juden*), all this is rapidly accomplished with German thoroughness'.[49]

Polish towns and Jewish ghettos through German women's eyes

The texts quoted so far could be described as examples of masculinist colonizing rhetoric. But did women write about Poland in similar terms? Women's accounts of Polish townscapes written at the time for publication or for official consumption reflected the curiosity of *Reichsdeutsche* generally about the unfamiliar urban territories of the East, and their eagerness to retail their impressions. Many also gave expression to the flattering sense of 'mastery' that Reich Germans felt in occupied Poland by lamenting that towns looked 'grey' and uncared for,[50] sneering at the shortcomings of Polish architecture and planning, and casting pitying or scornful glances at the native Poles and Jews. Writing in the BDM periodical in June 1940, an unnamed

BDM official recounted a visit to eastern Upper Silesia, accompanying the leader of the BDM, 'Reichsreferentin' Jutta Rüdiger. 'The villages and towns bear the stamp of "Polish culture" . . . . A glance into Polish huts and workers' flats, a drive through the ghetto in Bendzin showed us what worlds our girls had to deal with in the long years of Polish rule'.[51] Margarete Blasche, a trainee teacher of rural housekeeping at the training college at Schneidemühl, submitted her impressions of a 'study tour' undertaken with fellow-students in summer 1940 to the Party periodical for rural women *Die deutsche Landfrau*. The tour followed the traditions of the pre-war border excursion in combining political training with sightseeing; it began with a dutiful visit to Marienwerder, the old border town, now liberated from its 'border' status, before moving on to the new East, the Reichsgau Danzig-Westpreußen. She dismissed Gdynia (now 'Gotenhafen'), in what was becoming a German ritual insult,[52] as a product of 'capitalist spirit' and soulless internationalism: she contrasted its flat-roofed concrete buildings with the architectural glories of the German past in Danzig.[53]

Blasche, like other female zealots who wove atrocity stories about Polish attacks on ethnic Germans into their writing on the 'new East', embellished her portrayal of occupied Poland with portentous references to the blood of the *Volksdeutsche* spilt in the 'ethnic struggle'.[54] Several thousand ethnic Germans were murdered or perished as a result of internment by the Polish authorities during the German campaign in September 1939.[55] Some of the worst excesses took place on so-called Bloody Sunday in Bromberg (Bydgoszcz) in West Prussia on 3 September 1939, when at least a hundred ethnic German residents of the town were killed.[56] Nazi propaganda quickly inflated the total of German victims during the German invasion to 58,000, and a spate of accounts of German 'martyrdom' sought to whip up anti-Polish feeling back in the Altreich and among Germans in occupied Poland.[57] A 1940 text targeted at a BDM audience entitled *Deutsche Mädel im Osten* (German Girls in the East), celebrating the 'struggle' of the ethnic German minority in pre-war Poland, culminated in depicting scenes of Polish brutality in September 1939, quickly succeeded by German 'liberation'.[58] In May 1940, the Reichsstatthalter authorities in Posen instructed the regional governments in the Warthegau to disseminate a new publication entitled *Documents of Polish Cruelty*, declaring that 'every German in the Warthegau should possess a copy' to remind them of 'the bestial atrocities of Polish sub-humanity' (*die tierischen Greueltaten polnischen Untermenschentums*) perpetrated against the ethnic German community, and recommending it particularly to 'those from the Altreich assisting in the work of construction in the eastern territories'.[59]

Blasche, in her account of her tour of Danzig-Westpreußen, was thus elaborating a well-worn theme when she dwelt on the 'massacre' of *Volksdeutsche* in Bromberg. She presented the town's parks as the symbolic site of German–Polish confrontation:

> Bromberg has many extensive green spaces. About 100 gardeners at the edge of town looked after them. On Bloody Sunday, ninety of these gardeners laid down their lives: proof that they were Germans. Once again we listened shocked to the report on the events of Bloody Sunday. It is understandable that it is still very fresh in the minds of people living there. People are convinced that Bromberg will soon have shaken off its Polish features and that it will soon be a lively and elegant German town once again.[60]

Whatever the truth of the atrocity story – certainly the number of victims can be queried, given the likely total of Germans killed on Bloody Sunday – it functioned neatly to identify the murdered gardeners and the parks they looked after with Bromberg's once threatened but now salvaged German identity. Łódź/Litzmannstadt, the biggest city in Greiser's Warthegau and a key target for Germanization, offered prime material for women as well as men to evoke scenarios of alien menace, climaxing in portrayals of the city's Jewish population which were drenched in racist fantasy. The BDM periodical *Das deutsche Mädel* carried on two occasions, in 1940 and again in 1941, descriptions of the Łódź ghetto designed to instil the anti-semitic message into its readers. In the March 1940 issue, a woman journalist used the motif of the nightmare to frame her monstrous images of Łódź's Jewish quarter: in the 'unreal city' of the Jews, manically gesticulating figures in 'greasy kaftans' swarmed in the streets, people and dwellings alike mired in pestilential filth.[61] In the April 1941 issue, a piece by an anonymous author was framed with photos of ghetto scenes; she described a visit to the Łódź ghetto using the established clichés of dirt and menace.[62]

While a trainee teacher who did her teaching practice in Łódź found herself pleasantly surprised by the city ('everything had been painted in too black a colour'), many accounts of Łódź written for superiors or organizers of 'eastern assignments' by women from the Altreich echoed the standard propaganda images of jarring, hybrid architecture and alien population. In the words of a woman student viewing the 'reconquered, or rather newly conquered' city for the first time:

> Houses that look like building bricks with chimneys stuck on them, with hacked-off walls – one next to the other – a large bleak stone building next

to small wooden huts. Not a tree or bush in sight; just one small patch
of grass looking lost in the great mass of grey stone. . . . In this city many
soldiers, Germans, representatives of party and state – and many Poles. A
conquered or reconquered city like this has a strange character. You
can't describe it, only feel it. – There are Germans, they have an open,
determined look, creeping Poles and the ghetto.[63]

Placing herself here in relation to the city, this student identified herself with
the German men she sees as dominating the streets – 'soldiers, Germans, representatives of party and state' – while elevating them into heroic Nazi types
with the 'open, determined look' cultivated in Nazi iconography; she noted as
a passing contrast the other inhabitants of the city: the 'creeping Poles' and
'the ghetto'.

During the first months of 1940 the Jews remaining in Łódź/
Litzmannstadt were concentrated in an area designated as the ghetto, which
on 1 May was sealed off from the rest of the city.[64] The ghetto quickly became
a sightseeing stop for Germans from the Altreich and, to judge from the fre-
quency with which it was mentioned, an object of considerable interest for a
number of the women writing accounts of the city. German sightseers could
look into the ghetto through high fences on both sides of a road leading out
of town: Jews crossed the road by wooden bridges.[65] Liselotte Purper, an ambitious young photojournalist, captured a 'typical' German view of the ghetto
from the road in a photo taken in 1940 (Plate 32).[66] Some of the young
German women who visited the same spot and who stared at the Jews through
the fence seem to have shared the gaze not only of the conqueror and colonizer but of the voyeur. After her visit in the summer of 1940, a trainee teacher
from Hamburg noted: 'Something that made a big impression on us was the
ghetto (the fenced-in Jewish quarter). Here we saw the real greasy Eastern
Jews who were standing around among their shabby and dilapidated houses.'[67]
Another student recorded her impressions in her 'letter to a friend':

The most shocking sight in this town (where until last year only about 10%
of the 750,000 population were Germans) is the ghetto, an enormous district fenced off with barbed wire, where the streets and squares swarm with
Jews roaming around, many of them truly criminal types. Just what are we
to do with this rabble? (*Was wir bloß mit diesem Pack anfangen?*)[68]

The dominant feature of these students' reports of 'shocking sights' is their
voyeurism and spite. Mobile themselves, and enjoying the freedom to roam
through the spaces of the city, they witnessed in passing – with apparent satisfaction – the immobilization, marginalization and degradation of Łódź's

Jews. Feeling themselves to be venturing on to the 'front line' of the struggle
for Germandom, they were gripped by the spectacle of 'real' Jews: Jews who
must have seemed closer to the familiar stereotypes of Nazi propaganda than
the Jews of the Altreich. Having seen what films, books and Party training
courses conditioned them to see, they then reproduced the stereotypes exactly
in their reports.

The student reports contain further examples of how the young women's
pleasure of strolling through a strange town as a tourist was enhanced by their
sense of authority and superiority conferred by membership of the colonizing 'race'. The same student who wrote in the extract quoted above of the 'real
greasy Jews' of Łódź also described 'a great experience' later on during her
assignment when she and several fellow-students went on a 'study trip' to
Warsaw. In a carefully euphemistic account of destruction wrought by the
Wehrmacht, she noted:

> Looking at the heavily bombarded city and the completely destroyed
> citadel gave us a real sense of the destructive power of war. We walked for
> several hours through the quarter that is sealed off because of the epidemic
> danger (the Jewish residential quarter) and gained a good insight into the
> life and doings (*Leben und Treiben*) of the Warsaw Jews. I could describe
> many other pleasant and interesting experiences but that would take too
> long.[69]

Another woman student, together with three other women students from
Heidelberg, described an enjoyable visit to the town of Leslau (Włocławek) in
the eastern Warthegau in the summer of 1940.

> Lots of German shops had been opened and had surprisingly good window
> displays. At other shops people were busy renovating. The town was
> working so hard at its German appearance that it was a joy to behold. Par-
> ticularly novel for us four from the Altreich was the treatment of the Jews.
> While in Litzmannstadt and Kutno we had looked with a certain revulsion
> at the ghettos where the members of this crooked-nosed race were gath-
> ered, it struck us here in Leslau that the Jews could walk freely in all the
> streets, though not on the pavement but only on the thoroughfare, and each
> wears a yellow triangle on their back. We often came upon a Jewess wad-
> dling along the road with her Polish woman friend walking beside her on
> the pavement. But when we reached the Vistula we forgot all Jews and Poles
> and enjoyed the wonderful view that presented itself: the broad flowing
> Vistula, behind us the town with the cathedral and the beautiful park, in
> front of us the Vistula hills.[70]

For this student, watching a Jewish woman 'waddle' along the street while her Polish friend walks alongside her on pavement apparently provided an interesting, even amusing, spectacle for 'us four from the Altreich'. It was one sight among others for a group of young women whose pleasure in viewing the city, with its emerging 'German face' and panorama of the Vistula, was at its most intense when Poles and Jews were obliterated from their minds. Particularly striking is the explicit gesture of 'forgetting' 'Jews and Poles' and of looking away from the more curious but unsettling sights of Leslau towards the aspects of the town that were more reassuring to German eyes.

These reports did not merely toe the line but embraced and reproduced anti-semitic thinking with a positive zeal. Nevertheless, while their malice is striking, it is worth remembering that any who did not share such views had little scope for expressing dissent. Private accounts such as diaries or letters may give some clues about the extent to which women gave a different version of their impressions of Polish cities and of the ghettos when they were not writing reports for public scrutiny. To what extent were these accounts also coloured by National Socialist views of Poland and of the 'Jewish question'? If they did express a degree of genuine shock at the poverty or misery they encountered, how hard did they reflect about its causes? Liselotte Purper, the photographer, stayed in Welun (Wieluń) in the southern Warthegau in October 1940 and recorded her impressions in her diary:

> Everything here is caked in dirt. Desolation. . . . The Jews − each with their star − are only allowed to walk in the roadway. Polish women wrapped in their big woollen shawls drag their feet through the town. Wild-looking urchins stand around everywhere gazing at the world going by. Desperate poverty! Dull despair in every metre of this filthy hole (*Drecknest*) into which a 'dear God' has probably never looked.[71]

While Purper's words might be read as containing some element of pity, they evoked above all her distaste for and alienation from the poverty and the filth she perceived.

In her diary of 1943, the agricultural teacher Frau Hagen gave the briefest impression of the ruins of the ghetto in Lublin a year after its inhabitants were deported and murdered in March/April 1942.[72] This ghetto clearance, involving mass shootings of Jews within the city itself as well as deportations to Bełżec, had left the non-Jewish residents of the city in no doubt about the fate of the Jews. After the clearing of the Lublin ghetto, knowledge of the 'Final Solution' had spread quickly among the population of the General Government.[73] Frau Hagen, who arrived in Lublin too late to witness any of this directly, merely saw what remained of the buildings of the ghetto. 'This morning', she wrote on 8 May 1943, 'I was already walking at 6 o'clock through the freshly sprinkled, really clean streets, took B. to the station and wandered aimlessly through the streets. – To the ghetto, where all the houses with cellars, sometimes 3 storeys deep in the ground, were being demolished. What illicit goods (*Schleichwaren*) lay there hidden all those years – even animals: rabbits, hens, cows! were kept by the Jews down there in the ground.' It is a strange comment, even taking into account her interest in all things to do with livestock keeping. She was presumably recording a story she had been told by other Germans since her arrival in Lublin a few days earlier. Even if it was true, and even if she was struck by the notion of such remarkable feats of hoarding, it is still notable that she reproduces in a private document an image of the Jews, in their struggle for survival, as illicit traders. The impression here, as with Purper, is of a rather matter-of-fact, unreflecting registering of the existence – or former existence – of the Jews.

Oral testimony provides further evidence about what German women may have thought at the time about what they saw around them in occupied Poland. For instance, several women recalling their impressions of the towns and cities they saw as they travelled through Poland described feeling anxious or unnerved. Such memories are suggestive, but hard to interpret. It is impossible to be certain whether respondents were reconstructing their reactions accurately, or projecting into their remembered responses an unease based on later knowledge. Even assuming that their recollections are accurate, one wonders whether unease felt at the time derived from internalized stereotypes of Polish cities as 'alien' spaces (and hence ripe for Germanization), or from concern at the regime's treatment of the 'alien' population.

Some of the stories women told about glimpses of the ghettos and camps in the cities of Poland still seemed coloured by National Socialist clichés as well as informed by hindsight. One BDM leader from East Prussia, touring Zichenau and the Warthegau with a group of other BDM leaders, recalled that her first impression of Łódź/Litzmannstadt was that it was 'ugly', though on being told that Agnes Miegel had called it an 'industrious city' (*eine fleißige Stadt*) she had tried to see it in a more positive light. Of ghettos, she had very little recollection, and commented only that on visiting Sichelberg (Sierpc) in Zichenau she had been told by another BDM leader, 'when we want coffee there's always some in the ghetto'. It was the alleged ingenuity of the Jews in obtaining goods, rather than the fact of their persecution, that seemed to be in the foreground even in her recollections: 'You imagine they were guarded all the time but you have to remember how sharp (*spitzfindig*) the Jews are or were and all the things they managed to do.'[74] Her memories of a visit to Białystok were more disturbing. She recalled the *Kreisleiter* there taking her to see a concentration camp: 'I saw these Jews, that doesn't exactly leave you cold', and she recounted a strange sense of panic in a hotel room in Białystok that seemed in her account to be linked to what she saw that day in the camp as well as a sense of insecurity in the hotel itself: she described it as 'for the first time in my life a real nightmare (*Alpdruck*) as if someone was sitting on top of me'.[75] One could speculate that this direct glimpse of the regime's treatment of the Jews might have manifested itself in the feeling of paralysis and panic that she remembered.

Other respondents recounted their memories of ghettos and camps for Jews in occupied Poland in different ways. The one-time press officer for the NS-Frauenschaft in Posen, Frau Danneberg, responded as follows when asked about her impressions of different towns she had visited in the Warthegau, particularly Lodz (as I called it, using its common form in German) and Posen:

> For a start Posen was western and Lodz [Łódź] was more eastern, very eastern. And there it began already in Lodz with the Jews, Jewish camps in Lodz. That was terrible. I was in Cracow too, Cracow was very Polish. And the smaller places were to our way of thinking unimaginably primitive.

There are echoes here of the propaganda images of the eastern Warthegau – the part of the 'Reichsgau Wartheland' that had been under Tsarist rule before the emergence of independent Poland – as being a world apart from Posen where she was based. However, hindsight was surely shaping this account as well: for Frau Danneberg, the memory of Łódź being 'eastern' – alien to her compared with 'western' Posen – was bound up with her knowledge, more complete now than it could have been then, of the murder of the Jews ('And there it began already in Lodz with the Jews. . . . That was terrible').

Frau Danneberg's passing and uneasy allusion to 'Jewish camps' in Łódź contrasted with the vivid recollection of Frau Teplitz, who recalled the sight of the ghetto there as a devastating shock: its significance, embodying Nazi inhumanity towards the Jews, was, as she recalled it, obvious to her at once. She had gone to the city in early 1943 on a teaching practice organized by her Hamburg teacher training college that lasted a few weeks. It was characteristic of Frau Teplitz's recollections, which were driven by her condemnation of Nazi policies in Poland, that in answer to the first question, about how she came to teach in the Warthegau, she chose to focus straight away on the ghetto:

> There is not much to say about the teaching practice, since we had no contact with the population. – It was the icy winter, the most shattering experience was the tram ride right through the middle of the ghetto. Ghetto to the right and to the left, empty windows without glass in them,

and the freezing, starving people, figures of misery, no smoke coming from the chimneys. We had no idea. I had no idea about concentration camps and the like. We weren't prepared for anything.

Frau Teplitz's account managed, in a few sentences, to convey both the human misery of the ghetto and her shocked reaction: here, she presented herself as an innocent suddenly confronted with the consequences of Nazi anti-semitism: it was a revelation to her. From the intensity and fluency of the description, the listener got the impression that Frau Teplitz had revisited this memory many times, and it had probably been amplified over time through her reading and thinking about the fate of the Poles and the Jews. The image was a pivotal one for her whole experience of Poland.

Hindsight was also very evident, along with rather unspecific memories of what she had actually seen, in the account given by Frau Winter, the art student, of a brief visit to Łódź/Litzmannstadt during her vacation assignment in the summer of 1940. The visit lasted only a few hours, and her memories were more of hearing about the ghetto rather than seeing it. However, in recounting these memories she combined them with more recent insights and images:

> What I remember about Litzmannstadt is that as we were wandering around, the ghetto was, so to speak, observed. It wasn't closed off, and they went, could move around, people said – we didn't meet any inhabitants of the ghetto, and it was three hours that we had to wait in Litzmannstadt before we were taken home to Sieradz or near Sieradz. It is most odd (*zu komisch*) that I cannot remember the actual locality there at all. But I remember walking through Litzmannstadt, those hours until we were collected again, and that the ghetto as a part that was closed off, or less accessible, was mentioned. It was something that we knew about from the Middle Ages, that there had been ghettos in German cities, but that there was one in Litzmannstadt was something that I realized only then for the first time, and all further consequences that then take place in *Schindler's List*, that was all completely unthinkable then. '40, '41, that was very early in the act of violence (*Gewalttat*) against the Polish Jews.

Frau Winter's memories were vague, and not quite consistent on the point of whether the ghetto had been closed off or not. Asked specifically whether she remembered being on a road that bisected the ghetto, she said she did not: indeed, she retorted 'you know that from the literature', implying that I should not bother asking if I knew it all already. A striking feature of her comments was her reference to the murder of the Jews as the 'further consequences that then take place in *Schindler's List*. Perhaps this was just a euphemistic turn of phrase. However, it did also suggest that Frau Winter's vague or absent personal memories relating to the fate of the Polish Jews – a vagueness or absence that could be the result of her not wanting to look at what was there when she was in Litzmannstadt – have been replaced or overlaid by the heightened, intensified and dramatized images of Cracow in Spielberg's film.

Splendid views: exotic and familiar landscapes

Vistas of the Polish landscape figured prominently not only in the accounts German women wrote for public and for semi-public consumption, but also in descriptions they wrote privately for themselves or others. Much of this material is about the Warthegau, but some texts record impressions of other parts of occupied Poland, in particular the General Government. At one level the descriptions are merely that: drawing on a standard repertoire of motifs, they depict the 'big sky', the flat or rolling countryside, the cornfields, patches of woodland, unmade roads, scattered farmhouses and villages. But some of these texts are also emotionally laden, expressing the viewer's excitement, curiosity and occasionally discomfort. Some women were impressed by the 'exotic' strangeness of the scenery. Others sought and found elements in the landscape that reminded them of home and might make them feel more at home in a strange and remote place.[76] Some descriptions featured the aesthetic judgements of the pleasure-seeking tourist; others self-consciously adopted the perspective of the colonizer, enjoying the sense of boundless horizons and boundless possibilities, and imagining the reshaped landscape of the future.

The idea of 'boundless expanse' (*grenzenlose Weite*)[77] was a recurrent motif in women's descriptions of the landscape. Press reports on travels in Poland conventionally began with the view from the train window of endless fields stretching towards the horizon.[78] In a 'letter to a friend' by a woman student on an 'eastern assignment' in the Warthegau in 1940 (the format seems to be a device to frame the report required by the organizers of the Osteinsatz), the contrast between the constricted, crowded south-west of Germany and the limitless spaces of the East was highlighted as a revelation:

You were in East Prussia, so you will know what a wide-open landscape of fields and meadows is like. For us from Swabia where the villages are crowded up against each other it is new. At least for me it is only now that I have grasped what 'space' means – and that the whole question of the

East is simply a life-and-death question for the German people. You travel from Berlin to Litzmannstadt for hours through the broad plain of meadows and fields and as you travel the scattered farmsteads look more and more Polish.[79]

While some commented matter-of-factly on long journeys across a rain-soaked plain or 'an endless sandy desert',[80] other women sought to evoke images of the wide open spaces in a self-consciously lyrical prose. One contributor to the periodical *Die deutsche Landfrau* conjured up summer 1940 in the Warthegau: 'A still, boundless wide flat land, clear into the farthest distance. A dusty, hot sandy track, cows grazing at its edge. Ripe golden corn on both sides and the swishing sound of scythes'.[81] A Labour Service member described how she had been part of a theatre troupe consisting of thirty young women travelling through the annexed territory of Suwalki (Sudauen) in summer 1943 to entertain ethnic German villagers; writing about the tour, she depicted their column of bicycles moving slowly through 'golden-yellow ripe cornfields' on what she called their 'great trek', and described an instant where the troupe stood, feeling apparently like monarchs of all they surveyed, 'high on a hill, singing out our Sudauen song over the valley below: indeed, it was not just singing, it was shouting with joy'.[82]

When women wrote about boundless spaces or used the caption 'endless expanses' under a photo of the Polish countryside in their photograph album, it is conceivable that they were simply describing flat countryside in Poland with its wide horizons. One woman interviewed in 1999 about her vacation assignment in the Warthegau in 1940 took issue with my inter-pretation of women's descriptions of the landscape as being characterized by a 'colonizing gaze' – she insisted that such accounts were straightforward landscape descriptions, just as she might choose to describe landscapes in the USA as wide open spaces without any intention of colonizing them. For all that, it is hard in some cases to avoid the impression that perceptions of the wide open spaces of conquered Poland were inseparable from images of struggle and domination. This passage, for instance, is from a private letter written by Frau Peters, the BDM leader on a temporary assignment in the eastern Warthegau in 1942, describing her impressions of the landscape in Kreis Lentschütz:

I so enjoy travelling through the countryside. I am always one who cannot live without mountains – but the East just is a plain of a special kind. The land has something peculiar about it that is impossible to express, it doesn't let you go. Maybe it really is like it says in the Baumann song 'So many

have shed their blood for it/ That is why the soil does not remain silent!'?
Kreis Lentschütz particularly saw a lot of action in the Polish war
[*Polenkrieg*]. The battle of Kutno was fought here, and through it runs the
road to Lowitz. A military cemetery is just near here.[83]

The idea of a landscape that 'spoke' of history was a continuation of the
'border excursion' narratives of the inter-war period, when visitors to
the border used a vision of the landscape to recall past struggles and losses.
The reference here to the battle of Kutno was to a successful Polish counter-
attack during the German assault on Poland; and the 'road to Lowitz' is an
evocation of the 'martyrdom' of ethnic Germans following their internment
by the Polish authorities in September 1939: a group of detainees had been
driven from western Poland eastwards, ending up at Łowicz.[84] Other accounts
also noted the reminders of war in the Polish landscape, tending to talk of
'the war' as an impersonal force and sometimes assigning to the Germans the
role of victims. A woman student on a vacation assignment in Kreis
Welun in the Warthegau in summer 1943 described in her activity report the
area where she was working: 'Leading one into the lonely, gently rolling land
of the East, the road takes us to the badly destroyed village of Dilltal,
near the border. But the bright woodlands and the river Warthe shimmering
through them let us forget what the war destroyed here'.[85] Gertrud Kapp,
the head of the women's Labour Service in the Warthegau, had arrived
there in late 1939 and noted bridges destroyed and farm buildings burned out,
using such observations as a point of departure for her anecdotes alleging
Polish aggression and German victimhood.[86] And Frau Hagen, the teacher of
agriculture working near Zamość in the summer of 1943, described in a
letter to her parents how she had stood on the River Bug looking over the
border of the General Government into occupied Ukraine: 'here is where the
war began two years ago – today the meadows and fields look peaceful and
only the border posts are a reminder that this is where the endless expanse of
Russia begins.'[87]

Some women stressed how their surroundings in occupied Poland seemed
German and reminded them reassuringly of home. A teacher in a school in
the south-west corner of the Warthegau, Frau Ullmann, recalled her surroundings as 'quite near to the border, not so strange, almost German'.[88] Given
that this was a part of the annexed territories that had indeed been part of
Germany until the end of the First World War, this sense of a familiar landscape might not seem so surprising. However, women also made such remarks
about further-flung areas of occupied Poland that had not been part of the

post-1870 German Empire. A school assistant in the eastern Warthegau in 1944 wrote: 'Here I am in the eastern corner of the Wartheland, 12 kilometres from the GG [General Government] but in a lovely area. Waldrode has beautiful scenery, lots of woodlands, meadows and low hills, if the houses were a little different parts of it could almost be Swabia.'[89] If that part of the eastern Warthegau could conjure up Swabia, an area further south struck another observer as like north Germany: writing to the mayor of Litzmannstadt to express appreciation of their stay in the city, a trainee teacher from Hamburg described a tour of nearby countryside with her fellow-students organized by a schools official to mark the end of their teaching practice:[90]

> We drove in vehicles decorated with birch leaves through the cornfields and woodlands and could survey the lovely endless rolling landscape. And it confirmed for us that − just as was the case with Litzmannstadt − everything had been painted in far too black a colour. We had heard about a desolate flat landscape without trees and woods and were pleasantly surprised again and again that even this part of the 'East' has a similar aspect to our north German homeland. But the landscape here is more beautiful because it is without any constricting borders. (*Noch schöner ist das Land, weil ihm jede engen Grenzen fehlen.*)

She celebrates the limitlessness of the land while enjoying its surprising feel of familiarity: a reminder of home which she, like other travellers in other times and places, may have been looking out for.[91]

Other descriptions of rural Poland, by contrast, emphasized its strangeness, remoteness and backwardness. A kindergarten teacher in Distrikt Galizien referred to her village 'at the back of beyond' (*hinter dem Mond*): 'I can now imagine the life of primeval mankind (*das Leben der ersten Menschen*).'[92] A BDM school assistant in the Warthegau talked of having 'landed on the moon' and the journey to her village as having seemed like a 'rocket flight to the moon'.[93] The confusing encounter with both familiar and alien elements in the landscape comes across vividly in Frau Hagen's diary. In June 1943, a few weeks after her arrival to work in Kreis Zamosc in the General Government, she saw the countryside as both alien and 'homely': 'Sometimes one can believe one is travelling through Schleswig-Holstein − a solitary farm, livestock on the meadows, trees and hedges surrounding an estate − but it is only a reminder and it still remains a foreign place (*Fremde*) − the air that surrounds everything here is different and remembering is somehow painful.'[94] For her, the impression of familiarity turned out to be deceptive and only underlined the alien quality of her surroundings: the feeling of homeliness seemed to her to be an illusion.

Housewifely colonizers and the domesticated environment

The idea of creating German homeliness, embodied in domestic environments, as the basis of a German homeland in the new East gave a distinctively feminine slant to propaganda accounts by women of the Germanization
campaign in Poland. Women journalists and political functionaries writing in
the Nazi press put women in the foreground as agents of Germanization, and
they typically emphasized the 'ordering', 'cleansing' and 'domesticating'
dimension of the colonizing process, while concealing the fact that such ordering and cleansing also entailed the killing of what the National Socialists
decided were 'surplus' population. Renate von Stieda, writing in the *NS-
Frauenwarte* about the conversion of a psychiatric hospital in Schwetz
(Świecie) into a home for elderly Baltic Germans, made no mention of the
700 mentally ill Polish patients transferred out of the hospital in September
or October 1939, of whom perhaps 300 were shot immediately. This empty-
ing of the institution had the effect of creating space for incoming Baltic
Germans, even if the mass murder may not necessarily have been carried out
with that in mind.[95] Von Stieda noted only with approval how 'busy tradesmen's hands have removed the traces of "Polish chaos", the rooms are bright
and welcoming, flowers bloom in the park and in the vegetable garden,
from which one has a splendid view of the Vistula and the old castle of the
Teutonic Order'.[96] A report on a visit to the Warthegau in the farm women's
magazine *Die deutsche Landfrau* in 1940 was similarly typical in its emphasis on the 'busy, never-tiring hands that are working without rest to build up
a German homeland': 'We are visiting the Baltic and Volhynian German settlers who are now together with the [native] ethnic Germans filling this land
cleansed of Poles with new German life. . . . It is wonderful to behold how a
German land allows the debris of foreignness to be cast off, how it
blossoms into order and beauty.'[97]

An organizer of the women students' Osteinsatz, Herta Miedzinski, looked
back in the student newspaper in 1940 at the summer assignments in the
annexed territories:

> On Sunday trips into the countryside, whose spaciousness we learned to
> love, we experienced now from the other side the necessity of a large-scale
> settlement with Germans. Wide stretches of fertile land still bore the traces
> of the Polish era; they demand an ordering hand – and it became clear to
> us what the wide space of the German East means, for we all came from
> densely populated regions where everyone is constantly bumping into each

other – here land and more land, hour after hour no villages or farms, and where we did find them they offered a picture of unimaginable poverty which stood in contrast to the richly fertile land. The villages are unforgettable – a collection of mud-brick huts without a single right angle among them, without trees or straight roads, without gardens and flowers.[98]

The focus on the tidy home and garden and the 'freshly cleaned window-panes' as embodying the visible display of German identity – making Poland, in Miedzinski's words, 'spotlessly German' (*fleckenlos deutsch*) – is something that is typical of women writing accounts of the colonizing drive in Poland.

Against images of supposedly featureless, empty landscapes, women pro-pagandists painted a German colonizing enterprise that was embodied in womanly activism. Dr Suse Harms, writing in the BDM periodical *Das deutsche Mädel* in spring 1940, depicted an empty rural landscape, punctuated by an occasional peasant 'half sunk into the straw of his horse-cart', before going on to portray women helping in a thriving camp for resettled ethnic Germans in Łódź.[99] The same motifs recurred in an article by another woman journalist, Ilse Urbach, in *Das Reich*, describing a visit to the eastern Warthegau in the winter of 1940: she reiterated the common image of the Polish population as bowed, cowed figures submerged in the landscape and of the Jews as swarming, teeming, scarcely human creatures:

We crossed the border which separated the German Empire from Russia before the war. Here the earth has become the master of man. The wooden huts crouch into the ground under the heavy thatched roofs. There is no marketplace, no architectural planning which could make the towns and villages relieve the monotony of the landscape. They seep away like the marshes and rivulets all around. The roads wind away as lethargically as the man with the fur cap sits on his horse-cart; the people are slow, uncer-tain and apathetic. Part of the landscape, serfs of the ice-sheet covering it. We reach Wielun, town of the Jews. They still walk around here freely, shuddering we turn from the swarming mass of yellow stars on backs and chests. Schwarzgrund camp is like a salvation, here there is order and clean-liness, freshness and a determination to get on with the job.[100]

The narrative here seems to be building up to a point at which erect, heroic 'Germanic' figures must stride across and master this 'passive' landscape of flatness and floods. They duly appear, and they turn out to be female. The location representing deliverance from Poles and Jews is Schwarzgrund, a women's Labour Service camp. Imposing order might thus be a task for (male) conquerors and technocrats; but it was also – this text implies – a mission for competent young women creating cleanliness and domestic comfort in the midst of a wasteland. A similar motif occurs in a description by a Nazi woman student functionary of a women students' assignment helping German settlers: 'One sees at a glance that German settlers have been creating order. What a difference compared to the neglected, falling-down Polish huts that still remind us of the past era of a decaying pseudo-state. And suddenly a Munich woman student stands before us, pleased and smiling she strides towards us in her big heavy knee boots'.[101]

The nationalist poet Maria Kahle was sent to Poland in 1940 to report on German settlers who had emigrated to the then province of Posen from her homeland of Westphalia in the late nineteenth century. In her book there are echoes of Lützkendorf's portrayal of a Poland dominated by the flashy and the insubstantial, embodied in the figures of Polish women. Travelling through a Polish village in the Warthegau, Kahle notes scornfully her impressions of 'Polish girls garishly decked out in their Sunday best, dressed as if for the city, standing in front of decrepit thatched huts'.[102] Such figures act as a foil for the heroines and martyrs of her narrative, the German women settlers, notably the 'tall, blonde, strong' Frau N., widow of a settler 'murdered by marauding Poles' twenty years before: depicted in her spotless kitchen baking bread, Kahle portrays her as mistress (*Herrin*) of the farm as well as the household.[103] Set against their Polish antitheses, the idealized stereotypes of German womanhood in these narratives combine housewifely efficiency with the mastery required of the frontier German facing the Polish enemy.

German domestic culture, presided over by ever-energetic German women, was counterposed in contemporary accounts both to the 'culturelessness' of Polish peasant life and to the alien culture of the Polish landowning gentry ousted and decimated by the Nazi occupiers. But was the process of taking possession of the spaces of conquered Poland always so unproblematic? Across occupied Poland, and particularly in the annexed territories, groups of German women were 'setting up house' in premises expropriated from the Polish state, Polish landowners and from the Church. Even in relentlessly enthusiastic accounts of women's role in 'building the new East', a sense of the strangeness of this situation comes across. Miedzinski, the student organizer, wrote of students living in a former nunnery: 'In this strange environment they led their merry routine and filled the rooms from 4.30 in the mornings to 10 in the evenings with their cheerfulness, which stood out oddly against the silent face of the building (*Fröhlichkeit, die merkwürdig abstach von dem lautlosen Gesicht des Hauses)'.*[104] This sense of another culture being overwritten but not obliterated was more explicit in the article quoted above by the journalist Ilse Urbach, who described the 'most beautiful Women's Labour Service camp in the Wartheland' in Baschkow in a bizarre evocation of a new German order, complete with singing Labour Service girls and 'peasant furniture', taking shape within a confiscated aristocratic mansion, the 'fairytale castle' which had been the property of the Zatoriski family:

> The taste of the Polish aristocracy has stayed alive in its rooms. Garish wall-paper goes oddly with the dark-panelled rooms, the stairwell of grey stone is slightly cold and uncanny (*unheimlich*), hidden compartments in the walls heighten the sense of ghostliness (*das Spukhafte*). Then there are cheerful salons in the French style with gracious chandeliers and charm-ing flowered wall-coverings. In front of the fireplace in the spacious hall the *Maiden* have taken up position. They sing us a German folk song as a greeting. It fills with cheerful life the strange rooms where plain cupboards and peasant-style chairs now stand.[105]

What is uncanny here is, it could be argued, the sense of a powerful aristo-cratic tradition being forcefully overlaid by the present community of Labour Service girls. The text evokes in macabre fashion the 'ghosts' of the former life of the mansion in order to banish them again through the voices of the *Arbeitsmaiden*: their singing, filling the 'strange' space, represents the colo-nizing force of sound.

Committed female supporters of the regime writing about Poland appro-priated the discourse of conquest and colonization, emphasizing how the spaces of conquered Poland were filling with bustling womanly activism. They presented models of German womanhood that were constructed in opposition to the stereotype of Polish womanhood as weak, decadent and sexu-alized: the effect was to celebrate not only the dedicated housewife, but also the more androgenous figure, boots and all, of the fearless female comrade. 'Our women are strong women', as a recurrent phrase in an article in the Nazi women's organization journal about ethnic Germans in occupied Poland put it.[106] This model of housewifely colonization was dutifully repeated in many of the reports written at the time by women working to build up Labour Service camps, kindergartens, schools, training schools and Land Year camps in occupied Poland. However, even a committed believer in the colonization project might question the clichés that such accounts purveyed about Poland as empty and chaotic, awaiting the ordering hand of German men and German women and destined – through the efforts of pioneering Germans like herself – to become a German land. Frau Peters, the BDM leader who

went to Kreis Lentschütz in the Warthegau in 1942 in charge of a group of
girls assisting ethnic German settlers, wrote in July 1942 in a private letter
that some of her preconceptions had been wrong. 'The very well cultivated
vegetable fields and the orderly houses, including Polish houses astonished us.
We had expected a fairly desolate area.' There were, she wrote, very few
German settlers in the area, but the fields looked in good shape thanks to the
abundance of Polish labour. A few days later, she wrote once again, this time
reporting enthusiastically that German children were being born every day,
but sounded a note of understandable, if uncharacteristic doubt: 'When one
travels through the countryside and one only hears Polish, one could become
anxious whether we will really manage one day to make this land completely
German. – But if all these children become good farmers, then we will
manage it after all.'[107]

Were German women 'natural colonizers'? Certainly the regime was never
able to recruit enough female personnel for the East without using compulsion: to that extent, Karin von Schulmann and her colleagues in the NS-
Frauenschaft were correct when they assumed that enthusiasm was limited
among the mass of German women for 'colonial tasks' in the 'new East'.
Nevertheless, there were women who were ready to embrace such a role. Influenced by Nazi propaganda and long-standing German notions about the East,
and motivated by a thirst for new experiences and wartime adventure, they
wrote with enthusiasm – even in private – about colonizing a space without
boundaries, evoking a territory whose existing non-German population,
together with its culture and traditions, could be ignored or stripped away.
Such women, like men, were viewing Poland through the eyes of colonizers
and 'masters', sharing the perspective of the Nazi planners who sized up the
conquered territory as something to be appropriated, reorganized and repopu-
lated. Sometimes they recorded their impressions as if they were tourists,
consciously seeking out and enjoying novel sights and experiences. They
were taking the opportunities given to them by Nazi expansionism to 'see the
world', and as – for the most part – middle-class educated women, perhaps
having read articles in the press about the cities and scenery of Poland, they
were keen to inspect and reflect upon the sights it had to offer. They revelled
in the open vistas and distant horizons that for writers on the East provided
so many gratifying metaphors of boundless possibilities and challenges. The
enthusiasm was not always unclouded: some expressed privately at the time,
or recalled later, a sense of insecurity or alienation in the expanse of the conquered East, or unease about the treatment of Poland's population. However,
there were others who adopted wholeheartedly the 'tough' stance of the

colonizer in recording their impressions of the territory, its inhabitants and their customs. Such reports could be as viciously racist, and as full of the condescension of modern urbanites towards 'backward' or 'primitive' ways, as those of their male peers.

How distinctive was the role of the female colonizer? Women might write from the point of view of the master, but they were also prone to giving Nazi clichés a distinctively 'feminine' dimension. While at one level women's visions of an emerging 'German order' triumphing over 'Polish chaos' (*polnische Wirtschaft*) were those which dominated all Nazi propaganda about the East, one sometimes also finds what could be read as a housewifely emphasis on tidying, ordering and purging the conquered environment. If male publicists wrote about the 'hard men' who were needed to impose themselves on the dark, mysterious expanse of the colonized territory, women were likely to conjure up housewifely activists tidying, scouring and laying out gardens. Womanly work in the colonization of the East could thus seem to confirm boundaries between gender roles, but it could also subvert them, as the following chapters on the practice of women's work with ethnic Germans at the grass roots in different parts of occupied Poland will show.

Chapter 6

Motherliness and Mastery: Making Model Germans in the Annexed Territories

In mid-December 1940, 172 women students from universities in the Altreich arrived in the western Warthegau to stage a 'German Christmas'.[1] The German Christmas was part of the battle for ethnic German hearts and minds and an attempt to impose upon villages in occupied Poland the German character evoked in Nazi blueprints. It was an assignment planned, according to a report in the student newspaper *Die Bewegung*, in the belief 'that the resettlers and also the ethnic Germans and Reich Germans of the Wartheland, who are celebrating the festival in the new homeland for the first time, will find the fulfilment of their searching and striving hitherto in a great return home (*Heimkehr*) to German ways and German life'.[2]

The Christmas 1940 assignment was a piece of improvisation characteristic of the way the SS officials of the RKF apparatus ran the settlement programme in the annexed territories, and arose out of the cosy relationship between the Reich Student Leadership and the RKF that had developed in the course of 1940. It also reflected the women students' bid to play a key role in the Germanization campaign alongside the BDM, the NS-Frauenschaft and the women's Labour Service, who were all by this stage pitching in with their own initiatives in 'looking after' settlers (*Siedlerbetreuung*). On 3 December 1940, Ilse Behrens, the organizer of the women students' Osteinsatz, was summoned to Posen from the Reich Student Leadership headquarters in Munich following an order from the Higher SS and Police Chief in the Warthegau, Wilhelm Koppe.[3] On arriving in Posen, Behrens learned from an employee of the settlement office, Dr Erna Hager, that Koppe wished that the settlers' Christmas be organized and managed, and that a hundred women students should perform this task for the western part of the Warthegau. The BDM, she learned, was also involved, and had already recruited 450 volunteers, but since it had already 'occupied' (as she reported the words of the BDM representative) the eastern Warthegau, the BDM was happy to leave the western part to the students. Having tracked down Alexander Dolezalek, coordinator of student assignments and now a planning official with the RKF apparatus, Behrens agreed that the women students should be mobilized: 'firstly for propagandistic reasons, and because the resettled Hauländer (Erna Hager's problem child!) are in particular need of it and not least because Koppe has explicitly requested it'.[4] As she reasoned in a note to 'Renatsche' (presumably Renate Kalb, then organizer of political training for women students at the Reich Student Leadership), the women students would get paid for it, and have a 'good time', and 'moreover we can use them forwards, backwards and upside down in the press for our purposes' (*Außerdem lassen wir sie von hinten, vorn, oben und unten pressemäßig ausnützen*). Behrens went on: 'I was bursting with rage yesterday but I have realized meanwhile that it would be very unwise to fall out with all the agencies in charge of the money. On the contrary: one good turn deserves another. . . . The rest I will tell you in person. See you on Saturday morning at Frau Heissmeier's, Nürnberger Hof.'[5]

This last comment referred to 'Reichsfrauenführerin' Gertrud Scholtz-Klink, who had married her third husband, the SS officer August Heißmeyer, a few days previously.[6] On 14 December, Scholtz-Klink received at the Reich Women's Leadership headquarters in Berlin a delegation of women students involved in the Osteinsatz, congratulated them and bestowed upon them a sum of money with which to fulfil 'legitimate Christmas wishes' of the settlers. Her organization, meanwhile, was beginning to deploy full-time women advisers to steer the ethnic Germans towards performing their colonizing role effectively. At the beginning of December 1940, the first thirty full-time women settlement advisers (*Ansiedlerbetreuerinnen*) appointed by the NS-Frauenschaft took up their posts in the Warthegau (see Plates 16–21).[7]

The students' Christmas assignment and the appointment of the women settlement advisers followed months in which the SS settlement teams of the RKF had overseen the settlement of the Baltic Germans, Germans from Soviet-occupied eastern Poland and from the General Government, and were preparing the next major wave of activity to settle Germans from Bessarabia, Bukovina and Dobrudja. The bulk of settlement activity in 1940 had focused on the Warthegau, and it was here that overlapping and sometimes competing initiatives to 'look after' the newly settled were launched. 'Settlers who did not want to stay, who wanted to move to another farm, grumblers, etc.' were already in the spring of 1940, according to Luise Dolezalek's account written two years later, emerging as an obstacle to the smooth operation of the resettlement programme. It was her idea, she claimed, to recruit women to combat the settlers' 'insecurity and disappointment', and she obtained backing for her plan from the RKF in the person of Hitler's old associate, SS-Obersturmbannführer Sepp Dietrich.[8] The women would help out in settler households, organize or assist with a kindergarten, conduct surveys of what the settlers lacked in their households, perhaps even set up and run a village school until such time as qualified teachers were deployed[9] – the expectation being that these educated young women would be flexible and capable of turning their hand to anything. 'Apart from the lack of men due to the war', she wrote, 'it is clear that only women are suited to this work of *Betreuung* within the family and the village'.[10] As she recounted it, the pioneering efforts of the women students she helped to mobilize in the summer of 1940, together with BDM leaders participating in their Osteinsatz, had shown the way forward and had inspired the creation of a 'new profession' for women, that of settlement adviser. 'Today', she wrote, 'there are five settlement advisers working in every Kreis – exactly as I had originally proposed'.[11] The NS-Frauenschaft, by contrast, presented the decision to appoint full-time settlement advisers as the initiative of the Gau women's leader (*Gaufrauenschaftsleiterin*) Helga Thrö.[12] Whatever its inspiration, the appointment of full-time settlement advisers also reflected Greiser's drive to make the Party rather than the RKF responsible for the care of settlers, as well as the efforts of the Gau women's leader to expand the role of her organization. Over the following years, several hundred full-time settlement advisers were employed in the Warthegau and the other annexed territories (see map 3).

By summer 1942, Luise Dolezalek commented that the field of *Siedlerbetreuung* was now occupied by a plethora of women's organizations and agencies 'looking after' settlers in the countryside.[13] The growing volume of women's activities was in addition to the monitoring of settlers undertaken by the Party, the RKF teams at Kreis level (SS-Arbeitsstäbe), male agricultural advisers and local police forces. As women's initiatives expanded, the organizations involved generated flattering propaganda portrayals of the women from the Reich who were allegedly helping to create a 'home' for Germans in occupied Poland. More illuminating details of how 'looking after' ethnic Germans worked in practice, and the power relations involved in the process, emerge from unpublished activity reports written by women at the time. Most of the surviving reports are by women students and settlement advisers: the evidence on *Siedlerbetreuung* as practised by the BDM and women's Labour Service in the annexed territories is more fragmentary, and if internal reports were systematically collected they appear to have been destroyed or lost along with the bulk of those organizations' records. The students wrote reports for their assignment organizers, and those which have been preserved document above all the summer and winter assignments of 1940 in the Warthegau: many reflected some of the more grandiose visions of the East circulating in Nazi student circles, fuelled by the sense of victory widespread among the German population in the summer of 1940.[14] The settlement advisers wrote monthly reports for the Party leadership in their Kreis, some of which were collected by the RKF 'settlement research unit' for planning purposes. In them, the settlement advisers described the mood in the countryside and their interactions with grateful, stubborn or needy ethnic Germans. Dating mainly from 1942 and 1943, mainly from the Warthegau but also from Danzig-Westpreußen, they also provide insight into the efforts made to maintain morale during the months when the war turned against Germany.

Many of the reports radiated a sense of authority and conviction in the Germanizing mission, together with a scorn for the Poles. This is not surprising since they were written for the eyes of superiors, but some show a surplus of zeal that give some indication of their authors' mentality. Moreover, the reports provide clues about the place of this 'womanly work' within the colonizing enterprise and how it functioned to secure Polish property for ethnic German settlers and to drill the incoming Germans into their colonizing duties. For one thing, they confirm that women engaged in the task of *Betreuung* were drawn into the operations to 'clear' Polish homes of their inhabitants to make way for Germans.

The reports also betray the widespread arrogance and manipulativeness of the colonizing Reich Germans towards the ethnic German settlers and the native ethnic Germans: this was something about which ethnic Germans complained bitterly at the time. In line with the visions of Konrad Meyer and the technocratic planners of the RKF, 'looking after' settlers was part of the drive to make the ethnic Germans efficient, resilient, and obedient to the regime's demands. Ethnic German settlers, together with the native ethnic German population, had to be taught to shun Poles and all that was classed as Polish; they were to be encouraged to cultivate 'authentic' folk traditions while letting go of 'superstitious' or religious ideas. Women involved in *Siedlerbetreuung* sought out ethnic German women and children as the particular, though not sole, target for this Germanizing and modernizing message: ethnic German women were to display 'German identity' in the domestic sphere and follow prescribed norms in their clothing, diet, furnishings and bodily habits; and girls and women were to be coaxed into participating in community events run on Nazi lines.

The authority of Reich German women in relation to the Poles and the Germans was constructed in a way that crossed conventional demarcations of gender. Towards the Poles, Reich German women presented themselves in the guise of masters, displaying the 'unsentimental' attitude to the non-German population that was supposed to be an attribute of the Germans colonizing the East. As German women, they were to suppress 'womanly' impulses: they were to show no sympathy for Poles expelled to make way for Germans, and to discourage sympathy in others. In relation to the ethnic Germans, however, the women engaged in their 'care' presented themselves both as 'model masters' embodying the correct attitude towards the Poles, and also in terms of their feminine identity, using the rhetoric of maternalism. As 'leaders' but also 'mothers' to the ethnic Germans, women involved in *Siedlerbetreuung* presented themselves as authority figures in relation to 'their' ethnic Germans, in particular women and children, defending them from the threat of the alien. The task of the settlement adviser was defined as combining emotional work, 'motherly' care for the settlers' well-being and womanly attention to the condition of settlers' homes, with the political task of integrating settlers into the national community.[15] Renate Kalb, the women students' training organizer, described the woman student engaged in *Siedlerbetreuung* as needing to act 'like a mother in the family: she must be aware of and take responsibility for the impact and potential of all her actions, her advice, her educational measures, however slight. For her, the settlement villages are like big families in which again and again the fulfilling task of woman falls to her to build and protect the community.'[16] This racist brand of maternalism also involved enforcing the boundaries of the community and dispensing discipline to its members. While the settlement advisers joined forces with those who provided material welfare and benefits to the ethnic Germans, particularly to the settlers, they were also part of a monitoring and policing system that 'de-settled' those seen to be deviating from Nazi norms of conduct. Ten Volhynian German families were reported in October 1940 to have been removed from their farms in Kreis Gostynin (later known as Kreis Waldrode) and sent back to the resettler camp for having a history of siding with the Poles. At the end of 1940, eight Volhynian German families were sent back to the resettler camp for 'failing generally' and 'never being satisfied'. In Kreis Welun, families were evicted for 'not fitting in' and belonging to 'sects'.[17]

How did the visions of mastery coupled with motherliness translate into practice? Up to a point, the reports by women students and settlement advisers confirm that Reich German women did indeed exercise, and seemingly relished, a form of womanly authority that extended into both the private and public spheres. This authority was facilitated by the scarcity of Reich German personnel in Poland and sustained by the ethnic and 'racial' hierarchy imposed by the National Socialist occupation regime that placed Reich Germans above ethnic Germans, graded ethnic Germans into different categories, and relegated the Poles and Jews to the position of serfs and outcasts. At the same time, the reports also reveal how women's authority could be challenged and compromised in practice by recalcitrant ethnic Germans and dismissive male colleagues: colonizing zeal could give way to frustration and even doubts about the long-term prospects of the Germanizing project.

Post-war recollections and recent oral testimony in which women reflect upon their assignments 'looking after' ethnic Germans provide some confirmation, as well as some blurring, of the picture drawn by the reports at the time of the relationship between Reich Germans, ethnic Germans and Poles. Such recollections were usually from a perspective in which the positive memories of a busy routine working with grateful ethnic Germans and of a pleasing sense of being needed and respected were mixed with uneasy recollections concerning the oppression of the Polish population. Comparing the texts of the time with the more critical recollections from decades later raises again the question of how much unease existed at the time and how much is a product of hindsight.

Displacing the Poles

The seizure of Polish houses and farms and the expulsion of their inhabitants was the method by which the Nazi authorities in occupied Poland provided properties on which to place the ethnic German *Umsiedler*: the forcible expulsions were typically carried out at night.[18] Police reports give some impression of what was involved. Families selected for expulsion by the SS-Arbeitsstab at Kreis level – the first households to be selected tended to be, in the words of one SS report, the 'most valuable and efficient' farmers, so that the best farms would be made available for the incoming settlers – were ordered to leave their homes a few hours before the new German owners were due to arrive.[19] Those expelled in this way in the early stages of the resettlement programme were deported to the General Government or deported directly to the Altreich as forced labourers; later they might end up staying in the area, crowding into whatever accommodation could be found. The expulsions were carried out on the orders of the SS-Arbeitsstab, usually by local police (Gendarmerie). In the words of the commander of the local police forces in Posen, 'The Poles did not always leave voluntarily, in many cases it was necessary to intervene. It was also necessary to protect the house contents from removal until the settlers arrived, and to clean up the farms.'[20]

German women from the Altreich involved in *Siedlerbetreuung* and other work with ethnic Germans in Poland would often have been aware of expulsions going on in their locality. They might even determine who was to be expelled. One woman student participating in the Osteinsatz of summer 1940 arrived in the village of Krzywa Gora near Leslau and began by locating premises for a kindergarten. She described considering and rejecting a number of potentially suitable houses belonging to Poles, who, she recounted, watched her with 'frightened eyes' as she went through their houses: the houses were, she decided, too vermin-ridden, and a former tavern turned out to be preferable.[21]

How commonly women were on the scene and actively involved in the act of expulsion is not easy to establish.[22] Post-1945 written recollections, in which former functionaries of National Socialist women's organizations working in occupied Poland have presented contradictory versions of women's involvement in the expulsion of Poles, have done little to clarify the picture. Melita Maschmann, a former BDM official who also worked for some time as leader of a women's Labour Service camp in the Warthegau, recounted in her 1963 memoir that she had during her time in the women's Labour Service directly participated in 'evacuation' operations, on one occasion taking over the function of the police in driving out the Poles. She recalled her resentment at the time at having to take on this 'men's work'.[23] Maschmann chose – as part of her sometimes convoluted attempt to address the question of her involvement in the regime – to highlight her role in the expulsions.[24] By contrast Hildegard Friese, a former BDM leader who had worked for two and a half years as an organizer of BDM 'eastern assignments' in the Warthegau, insisted in 1964 that expulsions had lain 'outside her sphere of competence' and that she had learned of their taking place 'by chance, if at all'. Only once, she claimed, had one of 'her' BDM girls been present when Polish families were being expelled: Friese asserted that she had not known that this young woman had been ordered to be present and protested about it afterwards. Implausibly Friese added that the young woman had been summoned to be present at the expulsion 'in order to help the Polish mothers with their children prior to their being transported to the General Government'.[25] A similarly self-exonerating line was taken by the former leader of the NS-Frauenschaft in the Warthegau, Helga Thrö, who wrote in a letter in 1984 that her organization had had 'nothing to do' with the forcible expulsions. By this she meant that the decisions on expulsions lay in the hands of Himmler's RKF apparatus and the actual expulsions were carried out by SS and local police forces. She did admit that local officials of the NS-Frauenschaft had been called upon to get the vacated houses cleaned in the hours after their owners had been deported.[26]

Margarete Gerlach, a women's Labour Service camp leader in the Warthegau early in the war, remembered SS men discouraging her from asking too many questions about what they were doing in the Polish countryside. In the 1970s, in a short manuscript submitted for a planned chronicle documenting the history of the women's Labour Service and entitled 'May I speak after thirty years?', she recalled SS men on several occasions arriving at her camp in the early morning, requesting breakfast but refusing to answer the women's questions, enquiring if they could come again but warning the women not to press them about their activities. In Gerlach's account, she and her Labour Service colleagues got used to their visits and became accustomed to not asking questions: 'the questioning lost, as so often in times of war, its justification'. Finally, on a last visit before being posted elsewhere, one of the three men told the women that they had been carrying out expulsions of Polish farmers. After a night spent driving families from their homes they came to the women's Labour Service camp in search of solace after such disagreeable duties: Gerlach recalled the men telling her that the camp offered them an 'oasis of orderly life and a sense of home'. As Gerlach's title 'May I speak . . . ?' indicates, her narrative set out to defy post-1945 taboos and to defend the SS men she had encountered. The story she told highlighted their 'human' reactions to their 'distressing' work, and the fact that until their final visit they had spared the women who willingly ministered to them with coffee and sympathy the details of what they had been doing.[27] The fate of the Poles mattered less to her than what she viewed as unwarranted slurs on the reputation of the SS.

Gerlach's memory is of a tacit convention that men did not talk and women did not ask about forced expulsions, and of a notion that expulsions were 'men's work' in which women had no part to play. However, her recollection is directly contradicted by a great deal of evidence that, far from being banished or 'shielded' from the process, women were regularly present alongside SS officers and local police during forced evictions. The head of the women's Labour Service in Danzig-Westpreußen published an article in 1942 that described how whenever a 'resettlement action' took place a team of about fifty Labour Service women would be deployed to assist, together with four Labour Service leaders. Her text makes it clear that the women were there during the expulsions, not merely in their wake:

Around four leaders and fifty *Arbeitsmaiden* are always deployed in a resettlement camp during an action (up to 10 days). Some welcome the resettler families who arrive by special train and see to catering and accommodation. The majority goes out with the men of the SS to the villages. When the Poles are transported away, all the rubbish is burned with the help of Polish women workers and the farm is cleaned. Around seven in the morning the resettlers arrive. . . . Thus for example in Kreis Dirschau with 50 *Arbeitsmaiden* and around the same number of SS men, a hundred Bessarabian German families were settled in the course of a week.[28]

Similarly, Labour Service women from two camps at Marysin and Rzadka Wola in Kreis Leslau in the Warthegau played a key role in expulsion/resettlement operations in 1941, as an internal SS report recounted:

> Thanks to the great interest of both camp leaders in the work of the SS-Arbeitsstab, the *Maiden* of these camps became virtually full-time co-workers (*nahezu ständige Mitarbeiter*) of the SS-Arbeitsstab on resettlement days. In the absence of male colleagues, the assistance of the *Arbeitsmaiden* for the SS-Arbeitsstab was particularly valuable. With great enthusiasm, pleasure in the work and exemplary discipline the *Maiden* set to work on behalf of the resettlers. On resettlement days they ensured that the evicted Poles did not take everything with them, but left the necessary items behind for the settlers. They cleaned the farm and the house of the often atrocious filth (*verheerendem Dreck*), decorated the table with flowers to welcome the settlers, and cooked a meal so that the settlers would quickly feel at ease in their new home. In view of the various 'broken-down shacks', the friendly welcome by the *Maiden* was particularly valuable for the mood of the settlers.[29]

In 1940 a woman student wrote about having taken part, along with several others, in an 'evacuation' operation near Alexandrowo in Kreis Hermannsbad in the Warthegau after cajoling the SS officer in charge to let her and the other women students accompany the police teams carrying out the nocturnal raid. Here, however, there were signs that some sort of taboo was in operation: while other SS officers clearly came to see it as perfectly routine to involve young women as 'co-workers' on resettlement days, this one seemed to be more reluctant. The student wrote that the SS officer had been unwilling to take them along on the grounds that 'women would not be able to understand the tough measures necessary in such an operation', but had eventually agreed. In her report, in which she emphasized how fully she had indeed 'understood' and identified with the 'tough measures', she portrayed the Polish families as subhuman creatures whose dispossession was only deserved. Observing them after their eviction, packed together into a shed, she professed herself shocked by the Poles' passivity. Their apparent lack of reaction rendered them, in her eyes, 'incomprehensible':

> Sympathy with these creatures? – No, at most I felt quietly appalled that such people exist, people who are in their very being so infinitely alien and incomprehensible to us that there is no way to reach them. For the

first time in our lives people whose life or death is a matter of indifference (*Zum ersten Mal in unserem Leben Menschen deren Leben oder Tod gleichgültig ist*).[30]

The report ended with night passing, and with it the fate of the Polish farmers fading, as she saw it, into insignificance: 'The new day already belonged to the Volhynians, who a few hours later took over their new property.'[31]

If women were not always directly involved in expulsions, they were routinely called upon afterwards to secure the household contents and see to the cleaning of the houses. Students reported how they had helped ensure that Polish property was retained to maximize the welfare of German families. One student recounted collecting furniture from houses left empty after their Polish owners had been evicted and distributing it to settlers.[32] Another reported how she had warned ethnic German villagers not to tell their Polish neighbours about the imminent 'evacuation' operation, lest the Poles remove 'everything that was not nailed down' and leave nothing for incoming settlers; she had also sent for the police to retrieve property that had been taken by Poles from formerly Polish farms.[33]

Settlement advisers employed by the NS-Frauenschaft were also involved in the process of expulsion and resettlement, either organizing teams of women from the locality to prepare the houses for the settlers to move in, or actually helping the police to evict the Poles.[34] One settlement adviser working in the Warthegau welcomed the opportunity to take part in such an operation in September 1942: she observed that, since she had not experienced one before, it was for her a 'very interesting task'. She justified the eviction by alleging that the Poles were smuggling goods over the border to the General Government. Describing the eviction briefly, she remarked that 'in some of the houses there was a lot of screaming and shouting, others were quite calm'.[35] Grete St., working near Łódź/Litzmannstadt in autumn 1942, described how in one of the villages in her area 35 Polish families were driven out to make way for 14 families from Dobrudja. Together with a male colleague she met up before dawn with the police and SS settlement team and drove out to the village of Polik: 'There was screaming and wailing, the Poles had no inkling. It was a lot of work before the Poles were ready. Then at 10 o'clock the settlers were already arriving in two large buses. Then the settlers were led to their farms.'[36]

Like the students, the settlement advisers saw it as their job, in line with their responsibility for the domestic well-being of the ethnic German settlers, to stop Poles taking possessions with them that could be used by settlers. Meta K., working in Kreis Konin, recorded that when she had been present during evictions she had always managed to make the Poles leave behind more of their goods for the settlers.[37] If there was no one else to clean the houses, the settlement adviser would do that too, as Elfriede B. described, writing in August 1942: 'I had the good fortune of being able to help with the settlement of the Dobrudja Germans in the village of Tkaczek'. At four in the morning, she and other young NS-Frauenschaft women on various summer assignments were driven out to the different villages. From her report, it seems that in this case the women were even taking the lead in driving out the Poles: 'First of all we made sure that the Poles left the houses, the police helped with this. Then we got down to the cleaning. We fetched the usable furniture from the farms that were to be added on,[38] put flowers on the table and cooked a meal. When the settlers arrived, the house looked quite nice.'[39]

Model homes and model communities

Ethnic German settlers may have been relieved to be out of the resettler camps. However, their expectations of what would await them once they were out, fuelled by the promises and assurances of the officials dealing with them, were often disappointed. While some settlers were satisfied with the size and quality of the farms they had been allotted, others were dismayed.[40] In August 1940, a couple of resettlers in Kreis Ostrowo (Warthegau) organized a demonstration in which twenty-five resettlers tried to refuse to take over the farms they had been allotted: the alleged ringleaders were arrested and sent to the Altreich to work as agricultural labourers.[41] Elsewhere in the Warthegau, Galician German settlers in Kreis Krotoschin were reported in September 1940 to be deserting their newly allocated farms and heading back to the resettler camp in Łódź/Litzmannstadt.[42] Many settlers were alarmed to have been placed in Polish houses and farms that showed signs of the forced eviction of their owners. Moreover, their community and neighbourhood networks from the homes they had left behind were broken up, sometimes deliberately when National Socialist planners decided to remove the alleged danger of inbreeding.[43] Frequently living scattered among Polish neighbours and native ethnic Germans, the incoming settlers now had their performance as colonists placed under scrutiny.

The relationship between the Reich Germans and the ethnic Germans whom they saw as their charges was fraught with contradictions. The incoming ethnic German settlers were said to be the unspoilt raw material out of which a peasant culture fit for the East was to be constructed. In the words of Alexander Dolezalek from the planning department in Posen, who was clearly pursuing — now in a much larger and seemingly more promising context — the cultural fantasies of the Student Land Service of the 1930s:

> In the Warthegau there is the unique opportunity of forming the entire *Volkstum* in the sense of an authentically German culture (*das gesamte Volkstum im Sinne einer artdeutschen Kultur zu durchformen*), to promote German songs and customs and the culture of the home (*Haus- und Wohnkultur*), and to keep at a distance all urban and western (*westlerisch*) influence. It will after all not be a matter of firstly having to overcome things that are familiar and that people are fond of, say the dancing associated with the city, instead it will be possible from the outset to bring in and cultivate the new. The fact that we have such thoroughly receptive ground to work on does, however, oblige us to ensure that in the camps there are no more cabaret performances but that instead the cultivation of folk songs etc. begins as early as possible.[44]

This might be read as confirming the cultural authenticity of the ethnic German settlers waiting in the transit camps: less alienated from folk traditions than other Germans, they would therefore be more receptive to the drive to mould them as bearers of a renewed German culture. However, Reich Germans saw the identity of the ethnic German settlers from Volhynia, Galicia, Bessarabia and Bukovina as problematic (the Baltic Germans were less often singled out for criticism).[45] While any of these categories might be perceived as fulfilling Reich German norms in some respects, they might deviate in others and thus come to be regarded as not quite — or not yet — 'proper Germans'. Whether it was their way of speaking German, their practices with regard to hygiene, housekeeping and childcare, their attachment to religious beliefs and to the Christian Churches, their taste and customs, or their tolerance of 'alien' ethnic groups, the different groups of settlers found themselves the target of Reich German fault-finding and of corresponding efforts to enforce conformity to the norms of the *Volksgemeinschaft*. Using as much of the property of the evicted owners as had been forcibly retained, settlers were expected to display the German nature of their home in its outward and inner appearance and to purge traces of Polishness in the decor.[46] As farmers, they were supposed to adapt quickly to what were sometimes completely new soil and climate conditions, and to command their Polish labourers with assurance. Outside the home, they were expected to be part of a 'village community' that was supposed to bond on the basis of a shared German identity and to hold itself aloof from the remaining Poles. Settlers were also supposed to accept that religion would no longer serve as a focal point of community life.[47] Under Greiser, who was determined not only to

destroy any foundations of Polish identity in the Warthegau but also to blaze
a trail for the rest of the Reich in his destruction of Church life, hundreds of
Polish Catholic priests were imprisoned, deported to the General Government
or sent to concentration camps: by October 1941, seventy-four priests from the
archdiocese of Posen alone had been shot or had died in concentration camps.
Most Catholic churches were closed down, leaving behind only a remnant to
minister – separately – to German and Polish Catholics. The Catholic and
Protestant Churches alike were declared to exist in the Warthegau only as
private associations; religious instruction in schools was banned and confessional welfare associations effectively dissolved. Protestant Church life was
pared down to the minimum: the holding of religious services – and even
these were liable to be disrupted and restricted at local level by Party zealots.[48]
Religious sects – Baptists, Adventists and others – whose adherents included
settlers from Bessarabia, Galicia, Bukovina, Dobrudja and Volhynia – were the
target for surveillance and suppression.[49]

In being exposed to a barrage of Nazi propaganda and 'training', ethnic
German settlers were no different from Germans in the Altreich, who were
constantly exhorted to learn the lessons of racial hygiene, distance themselves
from 'alien' races, pursue body culture, apply modern hygiene and rational
housekeeping, and embrace substitutes for religious rituals. However, the
ethnic German settlers in the annexed territories were particularly accessible
targets for propaganda, interference and surveillance by Party and state agencies. Insecure in their new environment, knowing that their tenure of the
property that had been allotted to them was conditional on their good behaviour, they were also heavily dependent upon the assistance of the Party and
state authorities to supply their initial needs and provide protection, welfare
and assistance. All this undermined settlers' ability to resist incursions by
advisers and 'experts' into their affairs, though they sometimes tried to fend
them off. Party and state agencies were thus in a position to penetrate the
private sphere and shape community life to a much greater extent than in the
Altreich.

Women employed as settlement advisers or students and Labour Service
women deployed to 'look after' settlers in the annexed territories of Poland
made it their particular business to target women settlers and to oversee the
reproduction of Germanness in the private sphere. In the words of one
student, 'We must be clear that all these people who hitherto have lived only
among Poles and Russians are not used to the German work tempo and also
are not fully familiar with German order and cleanliness. Much educational
work has to be done and we students are making a start.'[50] Women students
wrote of their drive to revolutionize the ethnic German women's cooking

techniques, childrearing and infant care. They claimed to have persuaded ethnic German mothers to give their babies more light and air, and to have a secular naming ceremony instead of a Christian baptism.[51] Settlement advisers and students alike policed women settlers' décor, denounced kitsch as Polish and enforced their notions of German taste (nothing too garish) by replacing paper flowers with fir twigs.[52] Polish images of saints were vanishing from the houses she visited, commented a settlement adviser in Upper Silesia: 'one can really call that progress'.[53] Portraits of Hitler were given out as substitutes.[54] However, expectations that the women would have brought with them pleasing folk art and craftwork to decorate their houses were often disappointed. Settlement advisers, always delighted to find anything embroidered or handmade, were still quick to criticize designs and colours as vulgar.[55] One settlement adviser reported: 'I have noticed no folk art, but a lot of tasteless handicrafts . . . landscapes, pictures of stags etc. appallingly painted in impossible colours.'[56] Another noted with dismay that a Christmas tree was decorated 'very brightly, even with crepe paper flowers'.[57]

If the Bessarabian Germans were singled out for being houseproud, other groups were castigated as being 'little better than the Poles'. The Volhynian Germans were a frequent target of comments like that in the following report from Kreis Kempen in the Warthegau in April 1943: 'My Volhynians . . . still remain my problem children. They have too many Polish habits and their language is still very poor as they make no effort to learn German. They still cannot get used to keeping order in the household and the farmyard. In some families you can wear yourself out telling them, and even if you lend a hand yourself it makes no difference, as you find the same filthy mess (*Sauwirtschaft*) next time you visit.'[58] Settlement advisers complained that some women sought to keep them out altogether: 'some just leave me standing in front of their door', reported one who worked in Kreis Lask.[59] Other settlement advisers admitted that they made little headway: 'It is like talking into the wind', commented one, noting that she was going to report one individual to the local Party women's group leader, who would take it up with the district nurse.[60] Another wrote that the 'indifference that some women show regarding their households could make one despair.'[61] Arguments that hygiene was essential to health met with the response that 'my children will grow well enough even if they're not completely clean'.[62]

Modern ways were German ways, old ways were Polish ways: this was the general lesson being promoted and enforced with some vigour both inside and outside the home. Settlement advisers were impatient with settlers' wives who ignored or criticized the prescribed regime of hygiene and vitamins and who said their children were thriving anyway. Encountering what they saw as passivity and fatalism in face of illnesses and infections, they simply intervened. In one case, a settlement adviser sent a sick child into hospital against its parents' protests and coolly braved out their bitter recriminations when the child died there.[63] Another case where a settlement adviser insisted on sending a child to hospital ended happily, and the adviser reported that her authority with that particular family was now unshakeable: 'everything I said to them was for them almost like a religion'.[64]

In the case of modern medicine, science and attitudes to the body, settlement advisers had little difficulty in identifying and condemning 'superstition' and old-fashioned notions. Prudery was to be condemned: Bessarabian German mothers were instructed to tell their daughters the facts of life.[65] One settlement adviser noted with disbelief how a settler from Bukovina had removed the illustration of a nude sculpture from a Nazi propaganda booklet so that his 10-year-old daughter would not see it.[66] This was all straightforward enough, but in other cases it was harder to distinguish 'backwardness' (equated with 'Polishness') from 'authentic' German folk ways. In matters of dress, for instance, there was confusion over the question of whether modern or traditional styles were to be favoured. Those who wore traditional peasant clothing might be regarded as preserving the German heritage, but ran the risk of looking 'Polish' all the same. One settlement adviser instructed by the cultural department of the NS-Frauenschaft to look out for folk crafts and traditional costume reported that she had found nothing except the characteristic headscarves worn by Bessarabian German women, and that these were, regrettably, likely to disappear because they were mocked by the locals as 'Polish'.[67] Another, by contrast, was a committed modernizer who set out herself to eradicate the headscarf. She recorded that

> my settlers are willing to learn modern ways if one explains to them that they belong to us and they should adapt themselves, so that when they go to town they won't be spotted a mile off as resettlers. If you say this to them they are very proud. Several women opened their wardrobes and asked me to look at all their dresses, and asked me how they could make them look nicer. I was astonished that they really followed every piece of advice. If you tell them that the headscarf makes them look older, they take it off, because they'd rather not hear such a thing.[68]

Where Germans formed in practice anything but a homogeneous group, and often had much in common with those classified as Poles, visible markers of national identity were crucial. However, as the headscarf issue shows, such markers were not always easy to agree on.

The annexed territories were supposed to be a melting-pot of Germandom. Detached from the Poles, detached from the Churches which could divide Germans but draw Poles and Germans together, detached even from identification with past homelands in the Baltic, eastern Poland or Romania, the deracinated settlers were meant to blend with native ethnic Germans and incoming Reich Germans into a homogeneous bloc under the guidance of the Party. If resettled and native ethnic Germans in the countryside often lived scattered among the Polish majority population, marooned by poor roads and lack of transport, it was all the more important that women 'looking after' settlers should carry through a programme of village activities and entertainments to fill up the evenings and weekends and conjure up community spirit. Recalling the alleged successes achieved by the women's Labour Service in the eastern borderlands before 1939, Alexander Dolezalek put the case to the SS teams at Kreis level in autumn 1940 for more women's camps in the Warthegau: 'the organizing of free time that the camps achieve contributes much to the formation of the village community'.[69]

Groups of young women living in BDM or women's Labour Service camps easily served as ready-made troupes of entertainers, even if their programmes largely consisted of little more than singing. Frau Peters, the BDM leader of an Osteinsatz camp, described in a letter in summer 1942 how she was looking forward to organizing a 'morning ceremony' for the settlers in the village's newly created 'German house' and – as a climax at the close of their assignment – a 'big village community evening'. She and her troupe of young women were even called upon to organize a birthday celebration for one of the villagers: not even birthdays, it seemed, could do without some form of festive Nazi ritual.[70] A group of eight students from the newly founded 'Reich University of Posen' spent five weeks in the village of Penskowo in Kreis Scharnikau (Warthegau) in 1943.[71] There, they tried to overcome the villagers' suspicions of yet another influx of young women volunteers by particular efforts to organize village events, carefully designed and staged to engineer the appropriate responses, which the leader of the group, the ANSt leader for the University of Posen, proudly recounted:

We gathered together with our farmers for a morning ceremony that we opened with the hoisting of our flag. In the course of the ceremony we focused particularly on the suffering of the ethnic Germans in Poland and on the resettlement. To finish with we portrayed our task in the German East and ended with a reference to the Reich. By contrast, in our 'variety afternoon' (*bunten Nachmittag*), which doubled as our farewell celebration, we offered a light-hearted programme and created a carefree and cheerful mood. We ended the afternoon in more contemplative mood and finished with a nice song with everyone joining in.[72]

Such rituals were also intended to fill the gap left by organized religion. 'If only we had a church where our children could pray and hear the word of God!' was a typical lament heard among women settlers.[73] Such laments were reported, but they were of no consequence: settlement advisers were to promote German communities while ruling out traditional forms of community life based on a church or sect.[74] This was the thinking that lay behind Higher SS and Police Chief Koppe's launching of the 'first German Christmas in the Warthegau' in 1940. In Kreis Kutno, the SS resettlement team expressed the hope that, in view of the problems with (unspecified) 'sects' as well as with Catholics, the BDM's efforts during the weeks running up to Christmas 1940 would 'divert settlers from such religious gatherings'.[75] However, tensions could arise about the style and content of the ersatz Christmas ceremonies. Women students arrived in villages to find festivities planned that did not accord with their vision of how things were to be done, and sought to intervene and stage alternatives. Some were in their eyes overly religious, with bible readings and trombone chorales. Others were too strident politically, with too much emphasis on pagan symbolism: the latter included one ceremony organized by a newly appointed settlement adviser.[76]

While there were some aggressive secularizers – one settlement adviser attending a Catholic funeral pointedly gave a Hitler salute at the graveside[77] – others sought an element of compromise in their efforts to provide uplifting alternatives to familiar church rites and festivals.[78] 'The settlers can best be influenced through music and cheerful singing, because their mute day-to-day existence makes them sentimental and they look for consolation and cheer in the church or the sect', remarked one settlement adviser.[79] 'We must offer them something, a room that can be their favourite meeting-place in the evenings, and where they might come together on a Sunday. People need something for their souls.'[80] The quasi-religious elements in the staging of Nazi rituals were unmistakable, sometimes to the point where organizers seemed to lose sight of their ideological mission altogether. The women's Labour Service in Baschkow ('the most beautiful women's Labour Service camp in the Wartheland')[81] used their mansion and parkland setting to stage a Mothers' Day in 1942 for the Bessarabian women settlers. The guests were invited along to sit 'in a semicircle round the picture of the Führer' and to listen to a programme of songs and recitations. These included Hitler quotations glorifying maternity as well as a song 'Lobet der Berge leuchtende Firne', ('Praise the mountains' shimmering snows')[82] whose opening line evoked the

Lutheran hymn 'Lobet den Herren' but which praised nature and Germany rather than God. This was followed by coffee and cakes served at tables set up in the grounds. The camp leader who described the day in minute detail concluded by noting that one of the Bessarabian German women had congratulated them on creating an atmosphere that was 'really pious' (*so richtig fromm*).[83] Strangely, she had not noticed or had chosen to ignore the nonreligious nature of the ceremony. Even more bizarrely, the camp leader appeared quite satisfied with this as a compliment.

Students and settlement advisers tried to intervene in village life by organizing youth groups and trying to stimulate villagers into community activities.[84] One student claimed to have transformed a group of silent village girls into a disciplined troop of singing young sportswomen in BDM uniform: such was the power of sport, she enthused, that they were now 'scarcely distinguishable from their comrades in the Altreich'.[85] Not all the students claimed such dramatic successes. A student reporting on her assignment in the village of Kelpin in Kreis Tuchel in Danzig-Westpreußen in summer 1942 sounded a more pessimistic note. Adelheid K. reviewed the ethnic composition of the village where she was posted and described her efforts to identify potential 'leadership material' among the locals. The village had, she explained, been almost entirely Polish before 1939: following the implementation of the German Ethnic Register (DVL), only one family had been recognized as ethnic German (by this she meant DVL group 1 or 2) and had been rewarded by being given the post office to run. The student was scornful about those in the village who had been classified, under the criteria applied in Danzig-Westpreußen, as DVL group 3. According to her, 'those belonging to group 3 do not stand out in any way from the Poles and speak just as much or as little German as the Poles. One could even say that those of more valuable character have stayed Polish.' An ethnic German from another area had come to the village to manage two confiscated farms and was acting as the local village leader (*Ortsvorsteher*) and farmers' leader (*Ortsbauernführer*); a nearby ethnic German estate owner acted as the mayor for the area (*Amtskommissar*): the student described him as 'completely inaccessible both in private and in his public function'. Further tensions had arisen since Bessarabian settlers arrived in May 1942. All but one family came from the same village in Bessarabia: they socialized with each other but shunned the family who came from elsewhere, and had no contact with the local village leader. The student noted that the settlers were living in bleak surroundings and many wanted to return to Bessarabia. They were worried about the coming winter and fearful of the Poles, following attacks on the settlers and in view of the fact that the Poles who had been expelled from their homes were still in the area and trying to fetch possessions from their farms. Summing up the situation as far as the 'German community' was concerned, she observed that there was none to speak of. Party formations were non-existent: she named two women she thought suited to lead local women's or youth groups if and when they were set up. Overall, she remarked, there was no focal point for the Germans of the village: 'Such a focal point is needed as a counterweight to the Polish focal point, which is the tavern'.[86]

Settlement advisers trying to steer the dynamics of village life into the correct channels drew a vivid picture of conflicts, jealousies and rivalries plaguing the villages where settlers were living. Such anecdotes served to reinforce the settlement adviser's self-image as wise mediator: those who engaged in conflicts and quarrels were portrayed as childish, selfish and short-sighted. Conflicts were reported between different groups of settlers[87] and between settlers, the native ethnic Germans and Reich Germans. Settlement advisers depicted Bessarabian German children fighting local *Volksdeutsche* children.[88] Native ethnic Germans were portrayed complaining that everything was done for the incoming settlers but nothing for them, and murmuring that if the settlers hadn't come, they would have got all the confiscated Polish land for themselves.[89] One settlement adviser reported that the local ethnic Germans called the settlers from Bukovina 'gypsies'; Bukovina Germans hit back by calling the local ethnic Germans 'Poles'.[90] In Danzig-Westpreußen, local ethnic Germans were reported to be calling the Lithuanian Germans 'Communists'.[91] Settlement advisers were also quick to criticize fellow Reich Germans, usually men, for arrogance towards the *Volksdeutsche*. One told the story of a settler's wife from Bukovina who forgot to wear the badge showing she was German and was thrown out of the post office, where she was trying to post parcels to her son at the front, by a Reich German man who hit her in the face.[92]

With men away at the front, the 'community of Germans' being targeted by the women settlement advisers was increasingly a female one. Settlement advisers may have hoped that this might favour their community-building efforts. One reported that now the men were called up, neighbourliness was beginning to flourish.[93] On the other hand, observed another, the more the men were called up, the more the women wanted to go to church.[94] One settlement adviser recorded that Party events were indeed helping the different groups of Germans to get on with each other: at a festivity organized by a local NSDAP branch she saw 'mixed' groups of Bessarabian Germans, local ethnic Germans and Galician Germans sitting together, 'and the focal point of these mixed grouplets was often a settlement adviser'.[95] Other reports were less optimistic: one noted that the native ethnic Germans were particularly reluctant to attend village events; another commented that when local ethnic German women did come they only insulted the women settlers.[96] Efforts to encourage settlers' wives to attend meetings of the Deutsches Frauenwerk[97] were met by objections that the meetings were too far away or that folk singing and dancing were 'unworthy and godless'.[98]

Reading between the lines of the settlement advisers' and students' reports provides some indication of the responses of the ethnic German women settlers to the experts who descended upon them. Women settlers' own accounts of these encounters are harder to find, but one such account from the perspective of those being 'looked after' is given in a fictionalized memoir by the Bessarabian German Fred Michaelsohn, published in 1965 in a periodical for Bessarabian Germans in West Germany.[99] Recalling the time he and his family were learning to farm in the Warthegau with the help of Polish workers, some of whom had been the former owners of the properties allotted to him, Michaelsohn described his wife's antipathy towards the women who invaded her privacy as a semi-comic stand-off between traditional and modern gender norms:

> She could not get on with the women here. She could not stand the women advisers who came into the house on official business. She knew how to conduct herself and she did not need to be told how to deal with the Poles. We had lived among Russians, Bulgarians and Moldovans and had still remained German. These advisers should mind their own business. One day a lady drove up in a car who had been sent by a research organization in Berlin to study the family life of the newly settled ethnic Germans. She talked to me for a long time about our Bessarabian community: she had already visited a number of families from that community. She was surprised that so many were so dissatisfied. I was able to enlighten her on a number of points. At the table at lunch we carried on our conversation, my wife said little and remained very reserved. When the lady drove off, my wife hissed: 'I cannot stand women who behave so insolently like men. This witch drives around the place like a man! They call themselves German women!?'

Michaelsohn implied that he had fewer difficulties with such women than his wife, whom he presented as stubbornly set in her ways and irrationally suspicious of the 'emancipated' lady from Berlin. His narrative was one of stoicism: he and his family had, in the end, managed to adapt to life in the Warthegau up to the time the signal came to evacuate westwards in January 1945. Nevertheless, as he told it, the process of adaptation was fraught with tensions and misunderstandings with the authorities in the Warthegau, of which his wife's conflict with the settlement advisers and the woman researcher from Berlin was one example.

Instilling Herrenbewußtsein

Some of the women involved in *Siedlerbetreuung* were full of praise for the settlers' commitment to Germany and to National Socialism. Frau Peters wrote in a letter from her Osteinsatz camp in Kreis Lentschütz in summer 1942 how impressed she was by the attitude of the Volhynian and Galician German settlers: 'They are all people who have been through a lot but have such a strong belief in the Führer and in Germany, which helps them through everything. The Reich is something that is extraordinarily exalted to them, and that we have come to them from the Reich seems to them sometimes beyond comprehension.' A woman student wrote in her report about the fearlessness of the settlers she encountered: 'where most Reich Germans would simply turn tail, these settlers pick up an axe and gradually give their farms a German look, and at night they stand guard against any Poles who might be wandering around'.[100] Other women, however, dwelt on the alleged deficiencies of the ethnic Germans: one student was particularly critical of the Volhynian Germans, whom she described as 'not Germans any more as we understand the term' (*deutsche Menschen in unserem Sinn sind das wohl nicht mehr*).[101] Another talked of 'shaking up' the entire mentality of Volhynian German settlers, who appeared 'alien' to her: they had, she argued, to learn the demands of the collective and the goals of the state and to be 'awoken' into self-reflection and self-criticism. 'We must turn the Volhynians into a new race of people,' she concluded.[102]

Training the ethnic Germans to be committed colonizers meant breaking the social bonds between them and the Poles. In the instructions issued to students on vacation assignments in the Warthegau in summer 1940, those visiting ethnic German settlers were urged to banish any sympathy that might be shown for Poles, who had after all, according to Nazi atrocity propaganda, shown no mercy towards tens of thousands of Germans in Bromberg and elsewhere at the beginning of the war: 'Do not allow any sympathy to develop! Explain what the Poles did in West Prussia and what bad farmers they are.'[103] Women students attending a training course in June 1943 in Kreis Birnbaum (Warthegau) were instructed by a Party official that the correct German way to treat the Poles was 'tough but fair' (*hart aber gerecht*).[104]

Whatever the influence of such training sessions, some women engaged in *Siedlerbetreuung* were clearly wary of the Poles. The BDM leader Frau Peters

wrote about the Volhynian and Galician German settlers, 'who only speak
broken German', and the Poles she had encountered:

> The Poles are frightfully polite, take their hats off and sweep them to the
> ground – but of course they would like to do all sorts of things to us, you
> see that in their eyes. The settlers have friendly exchanges with them, for
> after all they have lived with them all these years. It will be very hard to
> bring them away from these friendly relationships. The Polish children
> have no school instruction, hang around all day on the streets if one does
> not somehow get them to work. They are as cheeky as anything and stare
> at us as if we were wonders of the world.[105]

Her concern about the Poles and about German–Polish friendships, here
expressed not for the eyes of officialdom but in a private letter, is striking.

Several students wrote in their assignment reports about how they had
approached the task of undermining the social bonds between Germans and
Poles. One wrote: 'It is our task as *Betreuerin* to make it clear to people: "If
Poland had won, what would have become of Germany and what would have
become of you?" '[106] Another stressed the need to 'destroy the sense of affinity and being drawn to the Poles that is felt by the native ethnic Germans and
the Volhynians', complaining that the ethnic Germans were still forced to
employ non-Germans: 'How can one badger the Volhynian or the ethnic
German into keeping apart from the Poles, taking pride in his Germanness and being conscious of his mastery (*Abstand von Polen, Stolz auf sein
Deutschtum und Herrenbewußtsein einschimpfen*) when he is forced to have
work done by Poles or even by Jews, simply because there are no German
tradesmen?'[107] The same student despaired of the entire older generation of
Germans currently in occupied Poland. Reich Germans and ethnic Germans
alike, in her view, needed re-educating by the 'clearer-sighted' student generation. At the same time, she adopted a high moral tone in relation to German
men's lax sexual morals:

> It has become clear that the current generation of adults living in the
> Warthegau, which has not been socialized into our world view, is to a certain
> degree incapable of preserving the correct distance from the Pole and of
> living in accordance with the correct hierarchy. There are instances of
> Reich German schools officials suggesting a common school for German
> and Polish children; of ethnic German assistant policemen, even Reich
> German men too, having relationships with Polish women; it is very
> common for Germans to make careless remarks in front of Poles and thus
> feed the Poles' boundless sense of confidence.[108]

In their reports, the women students demonstrated their identification with the project of colonization and their conviction that they, with their academic training, political commitment and inherent sense of mastery (*Herren-bewußtsein*), were naturally equipped to lead and educate the ethnic Germans. Unconcerned by their lack of practical experience or expertise, they saw their task as 'simply being Germans willing to help', or embodying 'a piece of the German fatherland' for the settlers.[109] Styling themselves as models for ethnic German adults, they took the gratitude and deference of ethnic Germans for granted, though they complained if their advice was ignored or resisted. Some were hugely flattered by their new status: 'One feels like a demi-god here,' commented one student after spending a summer in the Warthegau in 1940. 'In the village you have no one above you but God himself.'[110] Another, describing how she took her leave of the Volhynian settlers at the end of her assignment, wrote as if she had been a prophet addressing her disciples: 'Once more I spoke to them, as so many times before, of how they were here as Germans and as peasants on the border of the Reich, and I asked them, even when no Reich German was with them any more, to follow the path that I have tried to show them, that of being faithful, fearless Germans.'[111] The students took themselves seriously as researchers and investigators, seeing their assignments as fieldwork contributing to the overall planning and development of the East and making confident predictions in their reports about the prospects of moulding the current and future generations of Germans in the East to the colonization tasks.

Like the students, the settlement advisers set out to strengthen ethnic German settlers' commitment to colonizing occupied Poland and to discourage nostalgia for their homelands. Some, it seemed, needed little encouragement: Volhynian Germans were reported to believe that the regime had rescued them from 'torments' suffered at the hands of the Russians and the Poles, Bukovina Germans were said to be shocked by Russian atrocities in their former homeland.[112] While some of the Bessarabian Germans were reported, following the German attack on the Soviet Union, to be hoping for a quick return to their homelands,[113] by early 1943 settlement advisers noted that settlers were talking less of going back home again.[114] Settlement advisers were at any rate quick to discourage those who mentioned the possibility of a return home. After a male settler in Danzig-Westpreußen declared to a settlement adviser that 'once the war is over wild horses won't keep me here, I'm going back to where I come from', she lectured him to the point where, she predicted, he would never say it again.[115] If Dobrudja Germans failed to grasp 'why and to what purpose they are here', if Bessarabian German women 'have eyes only for themselves and their own inferior farm and forget that there are more important things', settlement advisers took pains to enlighten them.[116] If lectures failed to bring malcontents into line, there was always the sanction of expelling the settlers from their farms and sending them back to the transit camp, or to the Altreich. In September 1942, Ilse H. in Kreis Grätz (Warthegau) reported that most of the settlers were getting on well enough, but that there were some trouble-makers (*Stänkerer*) 'whom we are dealing with firmly and threatening to move them to the Altreich as labourers, which often works wonders'.[117]

Some settlement advisers, however, struck less confident tones. They were less quick to sweep aside the settlers' complaints, admitting the difficulty of persuading them that one day their farms in 'Siberia' would flourish and their homes would be comfortable.[118] Several reported suicides among the settlers.[119] Galician and North Bukovina families in eastern Upper Silesia were reported to be short of bread and potatoes and going hungry: in Kreis Saybusch in October 1941 'the people look thin and exhausted. The children almost all have a rash. Many look pale and thin.'[120] A report from Danzig-Westpreußen in February 1943 portrayed settlers 'who have a cold and miserable house and who live completely isolated among the fields. With a small amount of petroleum for the long dark nights, with broken lamps which are hard to replace, without any radio, and if a blizzard sets in no newspaper either'.[121] From the southern Warthegau in March 1943, a settlement adviser commented: 'In these three villages things really are bad, I have to admit to myself that they are right, they really cannot make a living, the land cannot support them'.[122]

Generally, however, settlement advisers gave accounts of their exchanges with settlers in which they portrayed themselves in heroic mode, battling against 'sentimentality', self-pity and defeatism. One noted loftily in June 1942 that 'I always try and explain the world-historical importance of this military conflict, but one notices that they are not really following; they sometimes read something else into what the newspapers report. It is hardly to be expected given their total lack of knowledge of history.'[123] From late 1942 onwards, when the German advance across the Soviet Union was halted at Stalingrad and the Allies gained the upper hand in North Africa, the settlers' anxieties had to be managed all the more vigorously. If the settlers expressed disbelief in newspaper reports about the war, settlement advisers told them not to listen to Polish rumours and hammered home the official version of military events.[124] Women settlers whose sons and husbands had been called up were, not surprisingly, reported to be pessimistic and anxious. In Kreis Warthbrücken in November 1942, Volhynian German women were alleged to be saying 'I wish I had stayed in Volhynia, at least I'd be with my husband,

even if I was dead'.[125] Bessarabian Germans, wrote settlement advisers, complained that their sons were being killed in disproportionate numbers.[126]
Already in the summer of 1942 Volhynian German women were said to be
trying to get their husbands exempted from call-up, getting pregnant in the
mistaken hope that this would enable exemption to be granted.[127]

Settlement advisers poured scorn on defeatists. One, writing in May 1943,
praised the toughness of the younger generation while commenting causti-
cally on the 'softness' of the older men and women: 'I've even seen men
weeping'.[128] The gloom of the settlers about the future, according to one settlement adviser, was not only due to rumours spread by Poles, but due also to the
cynicism of bureaucrats posted from the Altreich. 'Doubts about victory are
widespread. And there are some from the Altreich, spineless creatures who
have some insignificant job here, who make the mood of the settlers worse.'[129]
Nevertheless, after Stalingrad, convincing settlers that a German victory
was certain became an uphill task. 'After Stalingrad the settlers were very
depressed,' reported a settlement adviser from Kreis Zempelburg in Danzig-
Westpreußen.[130] The news of the defeat 'hit the settlers like a bomb', reported
another, who claimed to have restored morale: 'Sometimes the conversation
lasted for hours but every time it ended with the settlers' eyes lighting up once
more and their heads held high again.'[131] Nevertheless, the effect of such
reassurances must have been limited at a time when the Polish government
in exile was already extracting promises from Allied leaders about the evacuation of Germans from a restored post-war Poland.

The settlement advisers, encouraged to lead by example, expressed in their
reports their own sense of mastery over the Poles and their disdain for any
ethnic Germans who dared to doubt a German victory and sought to stay on
the right side of the Poles just in case. Reporting on Kreis Ostrowo in January
1943, Else R. observed that the settlers 'have fearful anxiety, they tremble and
think the Russians will soon be here because the Poles are so buoyant. They
calm down when one says they will never get this far. One has to talk to them
like one does to children.'[132]

Where Poles had not been deported following eviction, or, having fled their
homes before the eviction teams arrived, were still living and working in the
area, settlers were reported to feel nervous, fearing that the Polish owners
would return to claim their goods. A settlement adviser in Schrimm described
how Poles were taking from their former homes a pig, bedding and clothing.
One had left a note behind with the words: 'All of this is my property. I know
that I am not allowed to take it but I am in need.'[133] A settlement adviser
in Kreis Litzmannstadt, bordering on the General Government, recounted
in March 1943 how the Polish owners were returning from the General

Government, staying with their neighbours, and meeting up with Poles who were working for German settlers: this was reported to be worrying settlers' wives in particular.[134] Where settlers' wives were left on their own to run the farm using Polish labour when their husbands went to the front, settlement advisers encouraged them, 'woman to woman', to toughen up, insisting that German women must be the masters of Polish men and women.[135] Some found that the settlers' wives adapted quickly and praised their courage and efficiency. 'Recently I have begun to notice a much greater self-reliance in most of these women,' commented one.[136] Another thought that some of the settlers' farms were being run better by the wives in their husbands' absence.[137] Others portrayed the women struggling to impose their authority on their Polish employees. 'Particularly where the men are at the front, the Poles think they can give the women the run-around. Of course these are the women one has to stand by and support most of all,' observed a settlement adviser from Kreis Warthbrücken in November 1942.[138] Responding to women settlers who, left on their own, expressed their fears of the Poles, one settlement adviser declared her fearlessness. 'When I tell them that I know no fear etc. then they admire me. On the whole it's the older women who are anxious, the younger ones are different, I can be proud of them.'[139] Another found women slow to grasp that they were the masters now their husbands were away; she blamed the husbands for not teaching their wives enough about the farm, but criticized the wives for not being more active managers. 'They have been told that they are the masters and now they live as the masters on their farm and still they have not grasped that mastery, even if it is appropriate, sometimes means leading the workers oneself.'[140]

Settlement advisers presented themselves as models of unsentimentality towards 'troublesome' Poles. One who was working near Graudenz in late 1942 demonstrated this by reporting to the police and the employment office a Polish farm servant who had allegedly injured her hand on purpose: she noted that 'the girl is being sent to a camp'.[141] Another, based in the northern Warthegau, noted in March 1943 that '[t]he Poles have recently been getting very obstinate again and I often send the police out to people's houses, then they work better again for a short while'.[142] An adviser working in Kreis Krotoschin reported to the local Party leader a Polish maidservant who had allegedly in the course of a quarrel with her employer said to the Volhynian German farmer's wife that 'if all Poles thought as she did, all the Germans would have to be killed': once notified, the local Party leader 'went with the police straight out to the village and restored order'.[143] The outcome of this incident is not known, but the result of incidents where Poles were accused of threatening Germans could be drastic. In April 1942, Ilse Knauer, a BDM

1. A right-wing nationalist propagandist of the 'German East' in the Weimar Republic: Käthe Schirmacher (shown on left, with Klara Schleker, 1917).

2. The female bard of East Prussia: Agnes Miegel.

3. The leader of the Nazi women's organization in the Warthegau: *Gaufrauenschaftsleiterin* Helga Thrö.

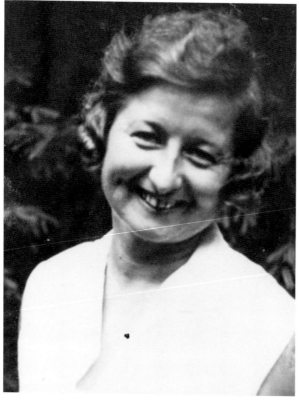

4. The leader of the Nazi women's organization in Danzig-West Prussia: *Gaufrauenschaftsleiterin* Frieda Balcerek.

5. Anti-Versailles propaganda: poster for 1922 exhibition 'Deutschland und der Friedensvertrag' ('Germany and the Peace Treaty').

6. Teutonic Knight as marketing tool: a tourism advertisement for East Prussia (1938).

7. Baltic Germans arriving in Stettin, November 1939.

8. Baltic German woman in Stettin with NS-Frauenschaft official, November 1939.

9. Volhynian German resettlers.

10. Dobrudja German resettlers in transit camp in Semlin, near Belgrade, 1940.

11. *Gaufrauenschaftsleiterin* Helga Thrö visiting Bessarabian Germans' resettler camp in the Warthegau.

12. 'Resettlement day': German resettlers heading for their new homes.

13. Resettlement, 1941: cleaning up after forced evictions.

14. Resettlers arrive on the farm.

15. Resettlers inside the farmhouse.

NSDAP Gauleitung Wartheland
NS-Frauenschaft   **Deutsche Frau!**   **Deutsches Mädel!**

Der Osten braucht Dich!

Werde **Ansiedlungsbetreuerin** im Gau Wartheland!

Photo: Liselotte Dueper

Anmeldungen jederzeit an die eigene Gaufrauenschaftsleitung oder an die Gaufrauenschaftsleitung Wartheland, Posen, Robert-Koch-Straße 18

Vorbedingungen: Einsatzbereitschaft, politisch und weltanschaulich einwandfreie Haltung, Gesundheit und körperliche Leistungsfähigkeit, wenn möglich haus- und landwirtschaftliche Vorkenntnisse. Alter: 25 bis 45 Jahre

Unterlagen: Lebenslauf, Lichtbild, Zeugnisabschriften, politisches Führungszeugnis

16. 'Der Osten braucht dich!' ('The East needs You!'): title page of recruitment brochure for settlement advisers.

17. Deputy Gauleiter Schmalz (Warthegau) addressing settlement advisers at training course, May 1941.

18. Settlement adviser with map of Landkreis Litzmannstadt, Warthegau.

19. Settlement adviser with settler couple.

20. Settlement adviser with settler.

21. Settlement adviser with settler.

22. Popularizing the resettlement programme: Volhynian German child on the title page of the magazine *Koralle*, 31 July 1940.

23. Christmas gifts for Volhynian Germans.

24 a and b. Puppet show for Volhynian German children.

25. Women's Labour Service leaders with *Gauleiter* Arthur Greiser (left).

26. Official visit to women's Labour Service camp in the Warthegau.

27. Women's Labour Service participants dancing, Baschkow, Warthegau.

28. BDM coffee party in park, Łódź, Warthegau, 1940.

29. School garden in the Warthegau (photograph taken by a village school-teacher).

30. Village street in the Warthegau (photograph taken by a student during her *Osteinsatz*).

31. Ghetto in Stryków, Warthegau.

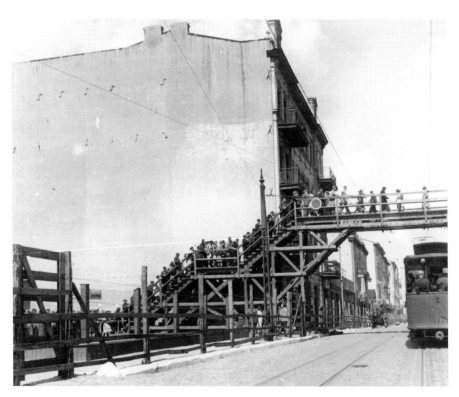

32. Ghetto in Łódź.

33. School for village advisers, Sitno, Distrikt Lublin: in winter (from Frau Hagen's diary).

34. Garden in Sitno (from Frau Hagen's diary).

35. Polish woman in village street (from Frau Hagen's diary).

36. Landscape near Sitno (from Frau Hagen's diary).

girl working with German settlers in Kreis Krotoschin, reported Franz Matysiak, a Polish agricultural labourer, to the police for having shouted at her that Germans were pigs and threatened her with a stick. Matysiak was convicted of 'anti-German behaviour' and sentenced to five years' imprisonment in a penal camp.[144] In another case tried a few days earlier in Posen, Agnes Drzewiecki, a Polish domestic servant employed by German resettlers, was sentenced to death for shouting at and pushing and shoving the woman she was working for.[145]

The ethnic Germans had to be trained not to be fearful of the Poles, but on the other hand not to be too casual or friendly towards them: distance and separation were to be the rule. Even if, given the shifting yardsticks of Germanization policy, yesterday's 'Pole' might be tomorrow's 'German', today's boundaries had to be policed rigorously. The Nazi obsession with racial purity made sexual contact between Germans and Poles an area of particular concern, and a number of settlement advisers reported informing the local Party or the SS settlement team about ethnic German men and women who had sexual relationships with Poles (often Polish farm servants with whom they lived and worked).[146] But ordinary friendships and neighbourly relations were also grounds for intervention. The exaggerated statistics of ethnic Germans killed in Polish reprisals during September 1939 were used to justify the ban on contact with Poles: one settlement adviser expressed surprise that Germans who had lived in Poland before the war persisted in socializing with Poles, as if they had forgotten 'how many German brothers and sisters had perished bestially at the hands of Polish murderers'.[147]

Such stories and memories must have had a limited impact: repeatedly, settlement advisers had to remind ethnic Germans of the need to draw boundaries in daily life, to ban Polish servants from sleeping in the same room as Germans, to stop sharing a table at meals or allowing German and Polish children to play together. The reported responses were sometimes defiant: 'You can do with me what you like,' answered a settler's wife who shared the bedroom with her children and her Polish employee while her husband was at the front.[148] A woman settler who entrusted her child to a Polish childminder refused point blank to send it to the German kindergarten; she was duly reported to the district office of the NSV.[149] Reprimanded for receiving Polish visitors, a Bessarabian German woman was said to have remarked that '[t]he Poles are not that bad at all and it is wrong to treat them so coldly'.[150] Enforcing German as the language of daily use in the home and the neighbourhood was a battle in itself. Although the Germans from the Baltic, from Bessarabia, Bukovina and Dobrudja spoke German, there were German resettlers from eastern Poland, together with some of the resident population

of the annexed territories who had been 'Germanized' through the German
Ethnic Register, who were more used to speaking Polish. One settlement
adviser was irritated always to be greeted by the cry of 'prosze!' when she
knocked at a particular house.[151] Another was so disoriented when she encountered not only the settlers but also local village functionaries speaking to local
Poles in Polish that she wondered whether she had misunderstood her brief
and sought confirmation: was Polish really to be discouraged? She thought it
was, but 'I'm not sure if my opinion is correct here!'[152]

Combating 'sentimentality' and excessively 'Christian' feelings was crucial
when it came to supervising settlers' dealings with Poles. One adviser reported
that women settlers had given the Polish workers who had helped with the
harvest 'too much pay' and had baked cake for them as well. 'When I pointed
out that after all our soldiers at the front only have black bread to eat, they
excuse themselves by saying that the local village officials bake cake for the
Poles too.'[153] Another intervened to stop settler families from Dobrudja
taking meals together with their Polish farm workers: 'Most Dobrudja
Germans think that eating separately from the Poles is a sin and they say
that Poles are human beings too, if you work alongside them all day then
surely you mustn't make the distinction at mealtimes. But if you tell them
what the Pole is like and what he can be like, then they are in complete agreement with you.'[154]

Asserting women's expertise against men

In their reports, the settlement advisers were expected to highlight successes,
record difficulties and convey a sense of the mood at the grass roots for
the benefit of planners and policy-makers. The reports allowed settlement
advisers to portray the inefficiency or short-sightedness of the ethnic
Germans as a foil for their own dedication and political vision. However, they
were also a vehicle for criticizing regime policies from the perspective of the
ethnic Germans' advocate. In the role of settlers' advocates, but also in the
guise of experts who really knew how to manage the settlers, settlement advisers blamed other agencies, and particularly men, for letting down the settlers
and jeopardizing the project of Germanization.

Settlement advisers depicted agencies and colleagues who professed to be
ministering to the needs of the settlers but made things worse through broken
pledges and clumsy interventions. One described 'gentlemen from Posen'
who descended upon the villages with talk of organizing this or supplying
that, demanding butter or the odd duck as a favour but never delivering

on their promises.[155] A settlement adviser in Kreis Krotoschin in summer 1942 reported Party meetings at which Bessarabian Germans were criticized, told to work more and spend less time driving around in their wagons: the settlers, she pointed out, had to drive around to get the things they needed, and such meetings damaged morale.[156] A colleague of hers in Kreis Krotoschin protested after a similar meeting where Party representatives harangued the settlers: 'they hadn't been brought here to live in castles, they should buckle down and work harder, etc.', thereby alienating the settlers and widening the gulf between them and the other Germans that she had been trying to bridge.[157]

Others expressed the view that there were simply too many agencies monitoring the settlers. One or two settlement advisers noted that the settlers mistrusted them along with all the others who called in to investigate their progress. 'It's as if they want to say to me: "What are you doing here? So many have already been and held us up from our work and talk a lot and do nothing".'[158] Given that there was so much home visiting already going on, some settlement advisers thought their own energies might be better channelled elsewhere: one remarked that she could use her time better running a school for the settlers' children.[159] Another thought that the native ethnic Germans would get on all right 'even without our *Betreuung*'.[160] More usually, settlement advisers thought their own work essential but that of others superfluous. While some praised the help given by the temporary Osteinsatz activists from the Altreich, others found them a burden. 'We had a lot of different assignments here in the summer, there was all sorts wandering around the district,' commented one, noting that one visiting activist had told settlers that their houses were unfit for human habitation, undermining the settlement adviser's efforts to make the settlers accept their lot.[161]

Sometimes criticisms were levelled at more fundamental aspects of the Germanization programme: settlement advisers, finding themselves trying to justify to the settlers measures they could not understand or disagreed with themselves, vented their frustration in their reports. Resettlers were being kept in camps in the Altreich a long time, noted one: was this, she wondered, because they were useful labour for the war economy?[162] German families from Lithuania assigned to work on farms in the Altreich rather than getting a farm of their own in the East asked the settlement adviser why: she had no answer.[163] Men living in camps for resettlers and sent to work on farms went on strike over the level of wages paid by the Ostland, the state holding company running confiscated estates: the settlement adviser commented that the wages paid by the Ostland really were too low.[164] Settlers in the western Warthegau district of Birnbaum asked in 1943 'why Poles were being given

German nationality': the settlement adviser, equally mystified by the policy of selecting 'racially valuable' Poles for Germanization, asked 'are we really helping build the Fatherland by doing this?'[165] Settlers were also sensitive to rumours that Nazi planners were going to uproot them again, from Upper Silesia to the Warthegau, or from the Warthegau to the Ukraine, either immediately or after the war: settlement advisers noted the impact such rumours had on morale.[166]

A number of settlement advisers complained about male colleagues who denigrated or ignored their efforts. 'Many of the men seem to think our work is pointless,' noted one adviser working in Kreis Saybusch in Upper Silesia in 1941. 'I am not complaining, merely stating a fact.' Settlement advisers, she went on, were not being told by the SS settlement team when and where resettlement was taking place, and requests on behalf of particular settlers were ignored: 'I now have the feeling that if it is me asking for something, it makes it all the more certain that the request will get turned down.'[167] A settlement adviser in Danzig-Westpreußen complained in a series of reports that the district agricultural officer employed by the Reich Food Estate (Reichsnährstand) was insulting her, asking her what she did to earn her salary. 'It is unbelievable that a German and a political functionary to boot can have so much malice in him.'[168] Another, working in Rippin (Danzig-Westpreußen), reported in August 1943 on how she had refused to be intimidated by male colleagues who had questioned her competence on agricultural matters. 'One even dared to tell me to keep to "women's affairs". Others started joining in as well but as the only woman among fifteen men I didn't let myself be pushed around. I said once more that I shall carry on going into the sheds and barns and looking into every corner just as I do inside the farmhouses.'[169]

If women settlement advisers had a sense of self-importance in relation to their 'historic' mission with the ethnic Germans, they probably felt all the more affronted by any disrespect shown them by male 'comrades'. Such affronts must have been common enough, for the problem was taken up publicly at the annual gathering of the settlement advisers from the Warthegau in December 1942 in Posen. Hertha Koschowitz, the Gau coordinator of the settlement advisers, addressing an audience that included *Gauleiter* Arthur Greiser, demanded greater support for the work of the settlement advisers, and more acknowledgement of the women settlers who were increasingly the target of *Betreuung*. Koschowitz's complaint was partly directed at the Reich Food Estate: she depicted a situation in which farms were increasingly being run by women, conscription was cutting the numbers of male agricultural advisers, women settlers were talking to women settlement advisers about supplies of seed and repairs to farm buildings, and yet male Reich Food Estate officials were still telling women settlement advisers not to meddle in farm affairs. Secondly, Koschowitz criticized male officials of the occupation administration more generally for snubbing settlement advisers: if their requests appeared to be fuelled by womanly sympathy for the settlers rather than respect for the rules, such requests should still not be dismissed as pestering. Women's emotional engagement, implied Koschowitz, served the regime and its aims better than the male bureaucrat's respect for regulations: an argument likely, and probably calculated, to appeal to the *Gauleiter* sitting in front of her. Thirdly, Koschowitz pointed out while farm women were celebrated in the regime's propaganda as never before, ethnic German farm women were often treated brusquely by the authorities with whom they came into contact, sometimes, she alleged darkly, because positions in the administration were being given to Poles. Greiser's 'Gau of front soldiers', concluded Koschowitz, should look after its soldiers' wives and mothers better.[170] Koschowitz's language and arguments revealed the peculiar blend of impulses that underlay the work of the NS-Frauenschaft and its settlement advisers: a 'tough' chauvinism directed at the Polish foe, a self-consciously 'motherly' attitude that patronized, but also sought to protect, the ethnic Germans, and a prickly rivalry with obstructive male colleagues in the occupation administration. Her intervention triggered a sharp warning from Greiser to the authorities in the Warthegau, including the RKF settlement teams and the Reichsnährstand, instructing officials to receive settlement advisers 'politely' and to deal with their requests.[171]

'Race', gender and authority

The women 'looking after' ethnic Germans in the annexed territories performed a number of functions. They were there to stabilize the settlement programme and maintain the morale of settlers in the face of their personal losses, hostile conditions and, from 1943 at the latest, a growing sense of military vulnerability. Women, it was argued, would fulfil a useful task particularly with relation to struggling settlers' wives; they would also fill the gaps left in the ranks of Reich German personnel generally, as more and more men were called up. At the same time, 'looking after' the ethnic Germans meant making them fit Nazi norms of Germanness: in other words, Germanizing the ethnic Germans. 'Germanness' was defined on the one hand in terms of differentiation from what was constructed as the alien: 'German ways' were 'rational' norms of individual efficiency and competence, especially but not only in relation to the womanly sphere of housewifery and childcare.

On the other hand, Germanness was also defined in terms of the relationship between ethnic Germans and the Nazi regime. Germanness meant loyalty to Nazism: it was counterposed to the 'materialistic individualism' or 'selfishness' of the 'unenlightened' peasant farmer and presented as unquestioning subordination to the demands of the collective as defined by the Party.

Germanizing the ethnic Germans also implied promoting new gender norms. Just as Nazi women's organizations, and in particular the BDM, sought to promote a 'modern' conception of womanhood in which individual self-reliance and competence were stressed alongside the more traditional womanly virtues of motherliness and self-sacrifice, so the settlement advisers and students – setting themselves up as role models for their protégées – endeavoured to 'modernize', 'enlighten' and 'broaden the horizons' of ethnic German girls and women. This project could be clothed in the language of emancipation and empowerment: settlement advisers praised girls and women who stood on their own feet, who demonstrated their competence and their toughness, who overcame silence and shyness and stepped confidently into the public domain. Settlement advisers might or might not regard traditional headscarves as suitable markers of German womanhood, but the wearing of BDM gym kit could be welcomed unequivocally as a sign of girls progressing towards full integration into the national community. Two things stand out regarding this project of enhancing the status of ethnic German women. First, although it might imply enhancing women's status in relation to their menfolk, it was also specifically in relation to and at the expense of the non-German population: ethnic German women had to be taught to be the masters of the Poles. Secondly, any profession of intent to boost ethnic German women's status took place in a context which presupposed the absolute subordination of women and men alike to the dictates of the Party and state authorities.

The reports written by the women students and the settlement advisers reveal the complex ways in which these often young women legitimized their authority – as 'mothers' of the ethnic Germans, but also as 'comrades' of men, and 'masters' over the non-Germans – within the hierarchies of gender and nationality/'race' that characterized Nazi rule in Poland. The discourse of maternalism was prevalent and powerful. In its racist Nazi version, maternalism assigned Nazi women a role that implied educating and caring for members of the *Volksgemeinschaft* at the expense of those excluded from the national community. When the role of the women students was constructed as one of mothering the ethnic Germans, when women students talked about 'my children', when settlement advisers were described as 'the mother of the settlers who have returned to the Reich', talked about their 'little flock' (*meine*

Leutchen) or referred to ethnic Germans as 'like little children', they echoed a widely used trope that patronized and infantilized the ethnic Germans and presented them as vulnerable, needy and trusting.[172] Up to a point, the 'motherly' discourse correlated with a 'fatherly' discourse on the part of the SS: an RKF planner argued that the leader of the district SS settlement teams should regard himself as the 'father of the settlers'.[173] Familial metaphors generally, in particular the loaded images of motherhood, sentimentalized the relationship between Nazi mentors and the ethnic Germans who were the targets of their efforts. The notion of mothering the ethnic Germans implied an affective bond and a task of caring and helping that was 'instinctive': it served to justify intervention in matters private, physical and intimate as well as those relating to the community at large. Such language disguised the situation of the ethnic Germans, who were subjected to crude and direct pressure by the agencies of the RKF to shut up and stay put.[174]

If the discourse of maternalism was pervaded by the sentimental vocabulary of 'helping hearts and hands',[175] that of comradeship and mastery enabled women to identify with the system of 'unsentimental' domination over the non-Germans. Racist maternalism helped to legitimize a particular womanly mission within the project of colonizing Poland; claiming a role as comrades and masters also enabled women to assert their capacity to serve the regime alongside men, to substitute for men in the latter's absence, share in the power of the Reich Germans and to cross on occasion the boundaries demarcating men's from women's work. Women portrayed themselves as ready to regard all business as their business if the cause of the settlers and the destiny of Germandom appeared to warrant it. Contrasting themselves to rule-bound bureaucrats, students and settlement advisers claimed competence in matters from infant health to the construction of potato silos and signalled their readiness to get their hands dirty in all senses: if Poles had to be evicted to make way for ethnic Germans, women would help the police drive out the Poles and clear out the houses afterwards as well.

The reports written by the women students and the monthly reports of the settlement advisers did not only recount incidents portraying their exercise of authority over the ethnic Germans and over the Poles. As texts submitted to Party agencies and the RKF planners, they were in themselves instruments of mastery that 'fixed' the ethnic Germans as objects of scrutiny, presenting them as needy, grateful, misguided or anxious, denigrated the Poles as idle or aggressive, and constantly reiterated and confirmed the notion of separating Germans from Poles. Settlers were not unaware of the power of reporting. Villagers in Penskowo in Kreis Scharnikau in summer 1943 had become wise to the phenomenon of eager 'assignment girls' writing uncomplimentary bulletins about them, and the issue turned into a conflict between women students and a local NSV official. The latter protested on behalf of the villagers. Reports, he declared, that had repeatedly alleged the settlers to be 'filthy and ridden with disease' harmed them far more than any *Einsatz* had ever helped them.[176]

The reports were shaped by a dominant narrative: that of the successful pedagogical mission in which the confidence and persuasiveness of the woman adviser carries all before her. As such, their accounts of the relations between Germans and Poles and between different groups of Germans in occupied Poland, and of the ethnic Germans' responses to the pedagogical efforts of women students and settlement advisers conform to a set of typical patterns. Sometimes, however, the reports recounted conflicts, and even doubts on the part of the settlement advisers themselves, in a way that hinted at more complex and unresolved stories, in which ethnic Germans despite all persuasion refused to accept their lot, and Reich German male colleagues refused to accept the authority of the women settlement advisers.

Other sources, meanwhile, gave versions that cut across the women's accounts of their interaction with ethnic Germans. Internal SD reports mentioned scepticism in the Warthegau about the value of the women students' *Einsatz*, comparing their ability to communicate with the farming population unfavourably with that of the BDM.[177] A policeman reported that ethnic German farmers had no respect for the settlement adviser – small wonder, he commented, since she had no relevant expertise and came from Berlin.[178] A memoir by a Reich German schools administrator in the Warthegau recalled encountering women settlers in the villages who – far from being ignorant of modern medical care – came to local meetings of the NS-Frauenschaft to express their anger at the inadequate medical provision in their villages: they could not get hold of doctors or get children suffering from diphtheria and scarlet fever transported to hospital. That narrative, written after the war, provides a telling counterpoint to the typical accounts of 'backward' ethnic Germans having to be persuaded to appreciate the benefits of modernity.[179]

Women's recollections of working with ethnic Germans in the annexed territories

Contemporary sources indicate that women sent by the BDM, NS-Frauenschaft, women's Labour Service or ANSt to work with ethnic Germans in occupied Poland were told to see themselves as emissaries of the Reich and representatives of the regime. However, women interviewed about their work with resettled and native ethnic Germans in the annexed territories gave a variety of responses when asked whether this was something they had been called upon to do. Some remembered that they had willingly embraced a 'missionary' role; others could not recall even being expected to play such a role.

Two women who had been on student vacation assignments in the Warthegau played down the extent to which they had been 'schooled' for this dimension of their duties. Frau Winter recalled no political instructions relating to her assignment at all, either at college in Stuttgart or when she arrived in Łódź/Litzmannstadt to be assigned to her posting. Frau Mahnke, who went to the Warthegau in 1942, remembered being lectured to in Posen before being sent on her assignment, but said that she had no recollection of what was said, and wouldn't have been inclined to listen anyway: 'we were so tired of them we didn't listen any more'. The two women, who were cousins, were interviewed together and both declared that they did not understand their assignment to have represented any sort of political mission:

> *EH*: Surely there was some sort of instruction coming from above, political training
>
> *W*: No, nothing
>
> *EH*: – about how you should view your task, your 'mission'?
>
> *M*: We had no political mission.
>
> *EH*: No political mission?
>
> *W*: Absolutely not. It was the personal, human component that they were looking for.[180]

Frau Fischer, who took part as a student in an Osteinsatz in a village near Posen in 1940, did recall participants being encouraged at the introductory camp to see themselves as role models for the ethnic Germans: 'We were made aware that we as *Reichsdeutsche* had to set an example and that we represented hope to these people there – that applied especially to people sent to work with the Volhynian Germans.' She recalled being shocked subsequently at those whose boorishness contravened this notion of Reich German behaviour in Poland. She thus acknowledged that Reich Germans were expected to play a role in public that would set an example to other Germans in Poland, though she did not recall performing any particular role in the village beyond her duties in the kindergarten, which she ran for several weeks. [181] Frau Holz, working as an *Arbeitsmaid* in Wollstein in 1942, had more explicit memories of being called on to act as a propagandist of National Socialism to the *Volksdeutsche*. Assigned a group of five young boys from local families who had been categorized as ethnic Germans, she remembered her task as *Betreu-ung* in the sense of providing them with political instruction. Asked what that entailed, she replied 'Tell them what a wonderful person Hitler was, more or less – and other things too.' The idea, she remembered, was 'you had to guide them on the right path. And when they got home they were told quite different things.' In her self-critical narrative, she portrayed herself as having been a true believer in those days, completely immersed in Nazi ways of thinking, who only came to rethink her values after the war.[182]

These differences in the recollections of a 'mission' could be explained in various ways. Respondents who portrayed themselves as having been politically indifferent or critical of the regime may genuinely have blocked out at the time this dimension of their work, since it was something they did not wish to hear and did not wish to be part of. They may genuinely have sat through political instruction sessions about their mission in the East, letting everything wash over them. On the other hand, they may have blocked out such memories later in order to preserve a view of their work in Poland as being a matter of simply 'helping' the ethnic Germans, without any sense of having acted as representatives of the Reich, the regime and its ideology. It was as if they could render their 'womanly' work unpolitical because they could not recall having understood it as anything else. Conversely, it is possible that Frau Holz remembered the notion of a Germanizing mission particularly clearly because she had been willing at the time to embrace it. She was also less likely to deny it in retrospect, having arrived at a critical view of her past self and her involvement in implementing Nazi policy in Poland.

Frau Bauer, the former settlement adviser, remembered embracing the mission of Germanizing the East with great enthusiasm. She recounted her experiences working for the NS-Frauenschaft as a settlement adviser in the Warthegau as a story of finding comradeship with like-minded women, all inspired by the goal of transforming the conquered territory into a 'German homeland'. In her words, 'whoever wasn't committed to it in their hearts was no good'. Frau Bauer described her work in terms reminiscent of the images put out by the NS-Frauenschaft at the time of a distinctive 'female mission in the East'. For all that, she assured me that her task had not been political. It was, instead, about women, children, home and family, in line with the lectures at the introductory training course on health issues, housekeeping and 'culture and education'. She had not been responsible for organizing the settlers politically, she insisted: the Party was responsible for that. She had only 'explained concepts', and only in private, never at public meetings: 'We only knew that these are German people who have come again to Germany, and we have to help them find a homeland. We had the homeland within us, and we had to get that across to them, everyone more or less tried to do that, with the heart, not just with the head.' Nor had the women settlement advisers concerned themselves with technical farming matters: that had been left to male farm advisers. 'We women were there for the family, for the house, for the housekeeping, family things, health and so on, that was what we were there for.'[183]

However they understood their tasks in Poland, a number of respondents did remember a sense of 'being somebody' when they were working there. That feeling stemmed partly from the authority which Reich Germans could command among ethnic Germans, particularly among some resettlers. Moreover, some respondents recalled ethnic German settlers showing affection and gratitude to the often educated young women from the Reich who were sent to monitor and assist them. Frau Peters, on her BDM assignment in summer 1942 in Kreis Lentschütz, recalled the Volhynian and Bessarabian settlers there wanting the girls on the assignment, mainly older schoolgirls from grammar schools, above all to tell them about 'the Reich'. The settlers, she recalled were 'delighted and grateful' that young women from the Reich had come with the promise of helping them. Frau Peters was possibly all the more pleased to record such gratifying responses given her hastily abandoned assignment in the Warthegau eighteen months earlier, when she had been posted to be a Jungmädelbund leader at Untergau level. Nevertheless, her descriptions were echoed by other respondents. Frau Winter recalled ethnic German settlers showing the same striking respect for everything associated with the Reich. Lodging with an ethnic German settler family on her first Warthegau assignment in 1940, she recalled being singled out for particular respect 'as a student and Fräulein from the Reich': she was brought meals in her room so that she would eat separately from her hosts. The ethnic Germans, as she described them, were 'incredibly obsequious':

It was completely new for me coming from the West. They kissed one's wrist, they kissed the hem of your skirt, not every day, but Sundays or when one went away for a weekend. There was an incredibly friendly affection and respect. It was very moving. It just was like that. And they insisted on this status, even when I said – I thought of myself as a modern student – please, please don't. But no, that was their way of doing things.[184]

Such behaviour may have been 'incredible' and even embarrassing, but overall to Frau Winter the encounter with the ethnic German settlers in 1940 was a revelation, a 'wonderful coming together of people'. Her second assignment, a year later in Kreis Wollstein, was disappointing compared with her experiences in the summer of 1940 because she had far less contact with the families of the kindergarten children: it was an assignment 'without real intensity'.

Frau Bauer, the settlement adviser, remembered being 'treated like a queen' when she arrived on visits to the settlers. The settlers from Volhynia and Bessarabia were, in her words, 'very, very grateful'. Any 'cares and worries' paled in Frau Bauer's recollections beside her abiding memories of tireless settlement advisers to whom grateful settlers 'opened their hearts'. The sense of being needed and welcomed appealed strongly to her: it gave her self-esteem, and she missed it intensely after leaving the Warthegau. More than any other respondent, Frau Bauer talked about her work in the Warthegau as a watershed in her personal and working life. After having given up the job and returned to her home in western Germany in 1943 to have a child, she dreamed of returning to Poland and was on the way there at the beginning of 1945 when she was forced to turn back and join the tide of refugees; she narrowly survived, with her child, the bombing of Dresden. After the war she worked once again as a shop assistant, living with the friend whom she had met in the Warthegau and keeping in touch with other former settlement advisers. In Frau Bauer's narrative the years of working in Poland appear as a high point: they were the 'best years of her life' and something she clung to in the post-war years to blot out her worst experience: Germany's defeat.

The women sent from the Altreich to 'look after' ethnic Germans were instructed at the time to enforce the boundaries between German and Pole, to banish feelings of sympathy for the Poles in themselves and discourage it in others, and to treat Poles with aloofness: there was to be no socializing or friendly interchange with the Polish population. To what extent did the women involved accept these instructions? How much notice did they take of the Poles in their locality and the way they lived? Did they reflect upon the way the Poles were being treated, or did they try not to think about it? If they did reflect upon it, did they feel that it was unjust? Reconstructing German attitudes at the time towards Poles in occupied Poland from subsequent rec-ollections and from oral testimony is fraught with difficulty. Memories of the treatment of the Poles in a specific locality and a particular situation might be made more vivid by a hindsight informed by subsequent knowledge of the fate of the Polish people in general. On the other hand, the same hindsight might lead to the erasure of memories – for instance of forced expulsions – too uncomfortable for some to confront. It is thus possible to guess at the dif-ferent ways hindsight may affect women's memories; ultimately, however, it is not possible to determine where gaps in memory are due to selective per-ception and 'blocking out' at the time, or selective recall since.

From her testimony, it seemed that Frau Bauer had either noticed little about the situation of the Poles at the time or had forgotten it. Her perceptions at the time and her memories appeared to be entirely taken up with the German settlers for whom she felt responsible. She was aware of where the Poles were in each village, but what mattered was where the Germans lived. It was only with some prompting that she recalled anything about the Poles:

EH: The settlers could probably speak Polish, some of them?

B: Some. Yes, those from the Lublin and Cholm area, they could.

EH: They'd lived among Poles.

B: They'd had to. They'd been neighbours.

EH: And there were surely still Poles as neighbours in the villages.

B: Who were often working in plants, in factories, not on farms. Yes. Factories and plants and craft trades, the trades in which they had worked.

EH: And Polish farm-hands?

B: They all had Polish farm-hands, yes. And they could all speak German. That wasn't a problem. And the women servants, if the families could maintain a servant, that was a Polish girl, but – that was all no problem.[185]

Frau Bauer recalled the Poles merely as posing 'no problem' from the point of view of the German settlers: they could speak German, they fulfilled their functions as workers, craftsmen and farm servants and that, as far as she was concerned, was that. Her narrative did not denigrate or criticize the Poles so much as obliterate them from the picture. Frau Winter, working as a student in Kreis Sieradz in the summer of 1940, also presented a bland picture of relations between Poles and Germans that downplayed any tensions and difficulties. Frau Winter remembered the Poles and the incoming ethnic German settlers 'helping each other out now and then', and Poles and Germans alike came to her if they needed first aid or advice 'and they repaid the favour with vodka'. As her detailed sketch-map of the village showed – she had drawn it at the time in the notebook where she recorded her comments on the ethnic German families she visited – ethnic German settlers and Poles lived alongside each other in the houses on the main street. Recalling relations between the Germans and the Poles, Frau Winter recalled: 'Friendly would be putting it too strongly, but the respect between the incomers and the normal Polish population in K. never gave any cause for concern.' Although she recalled expulsions of Polish families going on during the weeks she was there, as will be seen below, Frau Winter still chose to paint a picture of village life in which mutual respect and assistance between Polish and German neighbours were in the foreground. Such an unproblematic version matched her positive recollections of her enjoyable first assignment in the Warthegau.[186]

Frau Danneberg, the press officer who witnessed the arrival of ethnic German resettlers from the Baltic states and from Galicia and Volhynia in resettler camps in Posen during the winter of 1939–40, was much more eager than Frau Bauer and Frau Winter to address the issue of German–Polish conflict. She was also combative: prepared to acknowledge the oppression of the Poles by the German occupiers, but also more inclined to excuse anti-Polish actions. Acknowledging that Poles were harshly treated – 'they were oppressed, no doubt about it (*sie wurden eben unterdrückt doch*),' she was also quick to cite Polish aggression towards Germans as evidence that the Poles 'weren't all that refined either (*Die Polen sind ja auch nicht sehr vornehm gewesen*).' Referring to a colleague who had narrowly escaped the violence against German civilians in Bromberg in September 1939, she went on: 'Bloody Sunday, Bromberg Bloody Sunday, that was a fact after all. She only escaped being killed, the Germans arrived ... Otherwise the Poles just bumped the Germans off in the cellars (*Sonst haben die Polen in den Kellern die Deutschen einfach abgemurkst*).' In contrast to her pleasant memories of sociability with the Baltic Germans with their wit and conviviality, and of the resettlers generally and their admirable outlook ('*fantastische Haltung*'), Frau Danneberg recollected cool or non-existent contacts with Poles and, while admitting that she 'was not entirely objective', projected a view of Poland that was coloured by mistrust and disdain.[187]

Frau Fischer recalled from a more critical perspective than that of Frau Danneberg how tales of Polish atrocities during the German invasion were used to justify the treatment of the Poles. She remembered an incident in summer 1940, which she described in an internal report for the organizers of her student assignment, in which a little Polish girl ('not at all the usual shifty Polish type') had tried to join her kindergarten group. Feeling regret at excluding her, Frau Fischer had spoken to the district nurse in the village. The nurse, according to Frau Fischer's 1940 report, came from Bromberg and her father had been among the German victims in September 1939: this, Frau Fischer wrote at the time, had served to stifle any sympathy she felt. Looking back at the report nearly sixty years later, Frau Fischer recalled feeling anxious at the time about even admitting to any sympathy for Poles, explaining that the only way to do so was to end her report by showing how the sympathy had been 'correctly' suppressed in the face of evidence of Polish brutality. She was, however, shocked to encounter the phrase 'not at all the usual shifty Polish type'. Unprompted, she asked herself how she had come to use it: 'I ought to have, if I had thought about it, known better. . . . It is completely untenable, something like that. But – perhaps it contains an element of apology, yes the little Polish girl, first of all she was blond, and I had sympathy with her, but she wasn't, she didn't embody this type, something like that.'[188]

Frau Fischer also described feeling uneasy at the time about obtaining a kitchen cupboard for the kindergarten that she selected from a stock of goods taken from families deported from the area:

> And you will certainly now ask how I felt about that: firstly an astonishment, as far as I can remember, that one had taken these really quite shabby things away from poor people, that one confiscated such things at all. And subliminally also perhaps a certain unease (*Und unterschwellig auch vielleicht ein gewisses Unbehagen*).[189]

Frau Fischer's critical engagement with the past and her own past self meant that, while she wanted to highlight the impulses of sympathy for the Poles and unease about German actions that she had felt at the time, she was also ready to acknowledge and condemn certain attitudes that she had held as a young woman and which she now found quite unacceptable.

Another participant in a student Osteinsatz also recalled her unease at the time about the way the Poles were being treated. Frau Mahnke, who ran a kindergarten in Kreis Kolmar in the Warthegau in summer 1942, said she had had an uncomfortable feeling about the assignment in the East from the start. She was particularly disturbed when she discovered that the kindergarten, in her words a 'National Socialist facility', was occupying a building where the local Catholic chaplain had lived. Thinking that from the point of view of the Poles it would be less offensive if the kindergarten were located somewhere else, she wondered about moving to different premises:

> I was naïve, and I thought this place where the chaplain had lived was not suitable for the kindergarten, and I thought the kindergarten should be moved to some small house. Then I was sent by the *Ortsgruppenleiter*, or maybe someone from Kolmar, I don't remember, to look at a little house. And then I realized that the Poles would have been thrown out so that I could move in there with the kindergarten. And immediately I went back and said, no, that place is not suitable.[190]

Frau Mahnke's attempt to undo what she saw as an affront to Polish sensibilities misfired, and she was compelled to stay where she was in the chaplain's house.

With their references to the confiscation of premises and the seizure of household goods, Frau Fischer and Frau Mahnke raised the question of the forced expulsions of Poles, though neither recalled any taking place in their localities when they were there. Frau Winter, however, mentioned that expulsions took place in her village in Kreis Sieradz in summer 1940.

> I heard it at night. It was in total darkness, no lights, it was, as we would put it, a *Nacht- und Nebelaktion* [lit. 'night-and-fog action']. It wasn't supposed to be public. Not much was said, sometimes on the German side they would tell people off if it didn't happen fast enough. It had to be done within a certain time. And where they had got the permit that we thought they would have needed to do this, to clear out the farms, that was never clear to me, and I couldn't find out in the village. . . . They didn't talk about it.[191]

Frau Winter, by her own admission, 'preferred not to look' when expulsions were taking place and emphasized more than once that 'no one talked about it'. Another respondent who seems to have kept her knowledge about the forced expulsions to a minimum was Frau Bauer, the former settlement adviser. When asked whether she had experienced the operations to evict the Poles and resettle the Germans in the vacated farms, she responded hesitantly. She remembered resettlers arriving 'mostly in the evening, or as night was falling', but insisted that she had never been there herself. However, this topic set Frau Bauer reflecting upon what she had not known about or thought about sufficiently when she was working in the Warthegau and how 'one believed too readily what one was told (*man war gläubig*).' In her words, 'One accepted everything at face value. . . . After the war, then one was a lot wiser. During the war one took everything to be the truth, just as one knew nothing about concentration camps. One only knew about that after the war.'[192] Earlier in the interview, Frau Bauer had said that she had believed the displaced Poles were being given farms in the General Government in exchange. This was at most true for some involved in an 'exchange' with Germans brought from the Lublin and Cholm areas of the General Government in autumn 1940, and it did not apply to those displaced to make way for Bessarabian Germans, whom Frau Bauer also remembered being in the villages she visited. My assertion that most evicted Poles were not given farms elsewere evidently unsettled her; however, she seemed to be containing her unease again as soon as she had voiced it by switching to the question of what 'one' knew about the 'concentration camps'. Whether she meant the concentration camps generally, or specifically the murder of the Jews, she connected her youthful lack of awareness about the situation in the Warthegau with the larger issue of many Germans' failure at the time to grasp what crimes the regime was committing. This enabled her to identify herself with a wider German public, whose

exact level of knowledge about the Holocaust still remains disputed. Consciously or not, she diverted the conversation from what she surely should have
known about the treatment of Poles in the Warthegau to what she believed
she did not and could not know about the 'concentration camps'.

Frau Danneberg, in contrast to Frau Bauer, needed no prompting to talk
about forced expulsions. 'That was the upsetting thing (*das Bedrückende*) –
that a large part of the old [inhabitants? inaudible on tape] were taken to the
General Government by force, in trains which – God, yes, had straw in them,
were heated, I saw it myself, they had food, but what happened then?' Later
in the conversation, talking about the settlement advisers, she returned to
the topic: 'Basically it was dreadfully hard, in came the newcomers from
Volhynia or elsewhere in at the front and the Poles out the back.' Asked
whether this had been much talked about, she responded:

> *D*: One said little and one knew it. It was awful. It was really awful, but –
> something had – they had to go somewhere.
>
> *EH*: 'They had to go somewhere'? – did you experience that yourself?
>
> *D*: Experience it? Yes. Yes. But – God, it happened to us later on, didn't it?
> In Silesia. *C'est la vie*.[193]

On the one hand Frau Danneberg called the forced expulsions 'awful', 'upsetting' and 'dreadfully hard'. Yet by adding 'they had to go somewhere',
then by talking about how Germans in the end suffered expulsion too and
observing 'that's life', she tended to undercut her more troubled and critical
memories of the expulsion policy.

Frau Holz, the women's Labour Service participant in Kreis Wollstein who
was sent from her Labour Service camp to help teach in the nearby village
school, was the only respondent to recall being drawn into the process of
expelling the Poles. Together with a group of Labour Service women, she was
called on to clean and prepare the houses for Bessarabian German incomers
in 1943. She remembered more vividly than Frau Bauer what it had meant
for the Poles. Asked if she had known any of those who had been expelled
from their homes, she replied that she had: 'After all, they hadn't gone. They
moved in with relatives. And you saw them around, maybe had a few words
with them.' (At this stage of the resettlement programme, the RKF authorities were no longer trying to deport those expelled to the General Government.) Frau Holz's account of her role in the expulsions was driven by her
determination to acknowledge her failure at the time to grasp the injustice of
the process: 'We didn't think about it'; 'We did it without thinking about it
and that is what I cannot understand today.' If she had felt no unease at the

time, she felt it acutely in retrospect. She also recalled feeling disappointed at the Bessarabian Germans' reaction: 'They were very unhappy. And we thought they will be pleased when they arrive and have flowers on the table. Nothing like that.'[194]

The line always used by the RKF and by Party organizations to persuade women to assist in the resettlement programme was that the alleged misdeeds of the Poles and the needs of the incoming ethnic German settlers justified the displacement and dispossession of the Poles, and that the reward of working with settlers was their gratitude.[195] This may have led to some, if not all, blocking out the human cost of the resettlement programme. However, if the incoming ethnic German settlers were not grateful for what was allegedly being done for them, the comforting legitimation on which the regime relied to mobilize young women for their 'constructive' tasks in the East looked all the more threadbare.

Moulding the Next Generation: Village Schoolteachers in the 'Reichsgau Wartheland'

In May 1943, Gauleiter Arthur Greiser outlined to an audience of BDM school assistants (*Schulhelferinnen*) in Posen his vision of school education and the 'ethnic struggle'. Addressing them as 'my dear young comrades', he depicted the encounter between BDM school assistants from the Reich and the resettled ethnic Germans as a *völkisch* epiphany in which the young women's 'idealism' found its counterpart in the pent-up longings of the resettled ethnic Germans.

> The resettlers and particularly the children came to us with great hopes and a great longing for the Reich (*Sehnsucht nach dem Reich*). In the school assistant, the girl who concerned herself with them, many of them experienced their first contact with the people who represent for them the realization of their longing for the Reich. Thus the contact with the school and the BDM leader, who was to transmit knowledge to them, was in fact the first contact with the new homeland and thus with Greater Germany. It is particularly in this respect that I see the deployment of BDM leaders in schools as such a great realization of ideals (*ideellen Erfolg*), because the longing of the one, the resettlers and their children, merged with the idealism of the other to achieve a common form (*mit dem Idealismus des anderen Teils zusammenfand zu der gemeinsamen Form*).[1]

The BDM school assistants were according to Greiser 'an expression of National Socialist-revolutionary outlook' who would bring a radical approach to teaching and overcome the prejudices of 'those state authorities who would make the deployment of a woman teacher dependent on the passing of an examination'. Hitler, claimed Greiser, was '100 per cent in favour' of the programme to put BDM leaders into schools. Greiser reassured his audience that their deployment was not just a wartime expedient due to the absence of male teachers. Even after victory, he declared, the *Volkstumskampf* would continue and with it the need for village school teachers with leadership skills.[2]

In the Warthegau, as in the other annexed territories, elementary schools formed a key element in the policy of 'consolidating Germandom', and school-teachers were portrayed as engaged on the front line of the *Volkstumskampf*. Schools had traditionally been a battleground in German–Polish conflicts: under German rule in pre-1914 Posen, they had been state-sponsored instruments of Germanization; in inter-war Poland, the effort to protect German-language schooling became a focus for German cultural self-assertion. In the annexed territories after 1939, the Nazi authorities wasted little time in closing down Polish schools and reopening them for Germans only. Himmler himself had signalled in his memorandum of May 1940 on the 'treatment of the ethnically alien in the East' (*Denkschrift über die Behandlung der Fremd-völkischen im Osten*), distributed to the *Gauleiters* of the annexed territories as well as Governor General Hans Frank, that education for the 'alien population of the East' should consist of four years of elementary schooling where all that would be taught would be 'simple sums up to 500, writing one's name, and the lesson that it is a divine law to obey the Germans and to be honest, hard-working and well-behaved'.[3] Such thoughts were grist to Greiser's mill: in schooling, just as in other areas of policy, Greiser envisaged his Gau as a laboratory of Nazism, a 'model Gau' where the *Volkstumskampf* would be waged with exemplary ferocity.[4] Here, above all, German schools and qualified teaching staff were to be reserved for 'only unquestionably German children', while Polish children would be taught, if at all, by less qualified German staff, to understand and obey German. A schools official in the Reichsstatthalter government in Posen declared in July 1940 that schools policy in the Warthegau should contribute in due course to the eradication of Polish culture and language (*Ausmerzung der polnischen Kultur und Sprache*) as well as the influence of Polish Catholic priests.[5] Meanwhile, Greiser had ambitions, as is clear from his speech to the BDM school assistants, to ensure that the German children in his Gau would be educated on lines more radically Nazified and by teachers more 'revolutionary' in their outlook than in the Altreich.

Greiser and the schools department of the Reichsstatthalter administration may have argued that elementary schools for German children in the Warthegau should be staffed by a band of fanatic Germanizers whose teaching qualifications and experience counted for less than their political zeal. Such a policy had the merit of sounding radically Nazi: at the same time, it meshed neatly with the need for teaching personnel of any kind, particularly in the countryside. In practice, schools policy in the Warthegau prioritized the towns over the countryside, and in so doing prioritized the schooling of the children of Reich German officials, who tended to be concentrated in the towns, over provision for the children of farmers and settlers out in the villages.[6] Here once again, the ethnic hierarchy served to subordinate the ethnic Germans as well as exclude those of 'alien ethnicity': Reich German privileges were protected at the expense of rural ethnic Germans.

A policy that allowed unqualified young women to set up and run village schools meant that women students on vacation assignments, BDM leaders and women's Labour Service leaders could all be included in the campaign to put every German child into some sort of German school. The less 'revolutionary' school authorities in the Regierungsbezirke of the Warthegau (Posen, Hohensalza and Litzmannstadt) together with the school inspectors at Kreis level (*Kreisschulräte*) expressed more reservations about the use of unqualified staff, even if they had no alternative but to employ them. Consequently, they went to some lengths to secure qualified elementary school teachers and teaching probationers (*Lehramtsanwärterinnen*) fresh out of training colleges in the Altreich. As has been shown in Chapter 4, many of these recruits had no choice about a posting to the Warthegau, even if many were open to the prospect of a challenge and an adventure as well as the opportunity to gain professional experience. However, any who did not want to go in the first place, or who tried to leave, had to confront schools administrators who were determined to get them to the Warthegau and keep them there.

The women recruited to teach in village schools in the Warthegau — ranging from students on vacation assignments to BDM leaders and qualified schoolteachers — came to their tasks with very different experiences and attitudes. They also encountered conflicting expectations on the part of the state and Party authorities about their professional and political functions. Something of their outlook and experiences can be deduced from the activity reports written at the time for official consumption by student teachers working on short-term summer teaching assignments and by BDM school assistants; the experiences of the qualified schoolteachers are illuminated by the records of the Warthegau school authorities, by teachers' published and unpublished recollections, together with the recent oral testimony of five teachers, all of whom were posted to the Warthegau immediately after completing their college or university training. The diversity of the experiences recorded at the time and since reveal some of the typical contradictions and ambivalences inherent in the situation of female village schoolteachers in occupied Poland. The status of village schoolteacher potentially brought with it a sense of 'being somebody', in which they gained the respect of children and parents and enjoyed a degree of professional autonomy. On the other hand, they might feel isolated from ethnic Germans and Poles alike. Some teachers were pressured by zealous and overbearing Party officials and Kreis school inspectors, and scrutinized in their private lives; others remembered being left alone to get on with the job and depicted their time in the Warthegau as a respite not only from the bombings but also from the political pressures of the Altreich.

As in the case of the women involved in *Siedlerbetreuung*, the non-German population of the Warthegau figured only marginally in contemporary reports as well as in some of the recollections and oral testimony: however, some of the written recollections and oral testimony spoke more eloquently about what women teachers had witnessed and known about at the time of the fate of the Jews and of the Polish population of the Warthegau. Here, as elsewhere, women's testimony poses the conundrum of how the more disturbing memories related to what many summed up in retrospect as a 'good' time.

Elementary schools in the Warthegau and the Volkstumskampf

The most basic function of elementary schools in the Warthegau was to create a physical separation between children classified as 'ethnic German' and those categorized as Polish. Wherever even a handful of 'German' children were to be found, a 'German school' was to be set up for them. The schools department of the Reichsstatthalter administration in Posen emphasized that providing at least minimal schooling for German children was a political imperative. As the department commented in July 1941, the employment of BDM school assistants to help plug the gaps inevitably meant cutting corners on teaching standards: 'It is clear that these staff will hardly achieve adequate results in terms of schooling. But that is not decisive; what is important here is the task of supervision in the sense that the children of the resettled Germans living among the numerically far greater Polish population are gathered together in a German school and at least have their German consciousness reinforced.'[7] In October 1941, supporting the Warthegau BDM leadership's request for funding to train more BDM school assistants, the department again upheld the policy of bringing in BDM leaders as teaching personnel: in the absence of properly trained teachers, it was the only way to run German schools throughout the Warthegau to cater for the scattered German communities. 'The employment of BDM leaders as auxiliary teaching staff was a necessity of ethnic policy (*eine volkstumspolitische Notwendigkeit*). It was essential that every village, even one with only a few German children of school age, got a German school in which the

German children were brought together and thus set apart from the Polish children.[8]

In October 1943 the official Gau newspaper proclaimed that the goal had been fulfilled in the Warthegau of placing 'the very last German child under German supervision at a German school'.[9] By April 1944, the number of elementary schools for German children in the Warthegau had grown from 59 existing schools at the time of the German invasion, all of them in the administrative district of Posen, to 2,032 schools. Of these, 1,439, or 71 per cent, were single-class schools in which all age groups were taught together: this represented a slight fall from 1940, when the proportion of single-class schools had been 80 per cent. Thanks to resettlement measures, ethnic 'sifting' and the expansion of facilities, the number of pupils in German elementary schools had risen from 4,000 to over 144,000, and the number of teaching staff in elementary schools in April 1944 was 3,628. Of these 3,628 teachers (men and women were not counted separately), 2,375, or 65.5 per cent, were qualified (this figure included the probationers fresh from training college) and 1,253, or 34.5 per cent, were 'school assistants' and 'auxiliary personnel' without teaching qualifications.[10] However, as has been shown in Chapter 4, women formed both a high proportion of the qualified personnel arriving directly from the training colleges and the bulk of the untrained 'school assistants'. Already in 1940, a third of the elementary schools in the Warthegau were being run single-handedly by a woman teacher,[11] and as more schools were set up and more male teachers were conscripted, more gaps were left to be filled by qualified and unqualified women.

Polish children received minimal or no education. Where schools for Polish children were set up – this varied in practice in different parts of the Warthegau – their function was less to educate than to contain (and to drill pupils in basic German).[12] Basic elementary schooling thus remained a privilege for German children. It served to create a cultural gap between Germans and Poles and equip Germans to fulfil their future function as employers and supervisors of Polish workers and servants. If German children grasped their privileged status relative to the Poles at an early age, so much the better. Schools administrators were clear that schooling was to be provided for Poles only as a measure of social control, and forbidden to Jews even as a measure of social control. Lieselotte Gumpert, who worked as a schools administrator in the schools department in Łódź/Litzmannstadt in 1942–3 and later in the Reichsstatthalter education department from October 1943 until Easter 1944, recalled her reactions and those of her colleagues when, in the last months of her posting, German schools began to be closed down again under pressure from the Wehrmacht in its search for premises:

The confiscation of school premises by the Wehrmacht was seen as sense-less, because it meant breaking off the work of construction. The contra-dictory nature of the measures [to shut down German schools] was doubly clear when one recalled that originally the possibility of orderly school instruction was conceived precisely as a privilege of the Germans; elemen-tary school classes were only organized for Poles as far as was feasible when the devastating effects of not providing any teaching became apparent; and the Jews in the Litzmannstadt ghetto were granted no permission to set up schooling – in order to curb delinquency – even in response to the urgent requests of the Council of Elders.[13]

Her recollection was concerned with the failure of the Warthegau authorities to carry through consistently its policy of ethnic differentiation in education; even in retrospect, she did not comment on its morality, and it was the only time she mentioned the Jews at all in her account.

Beyond these basic political goals, the goals of German elementary school-ing in the Warthegau were less clear, and there were differences of opinion about the nature and standard of teaching required. Some administrators expected professional competence and experience and were less convinced than Greiser of the merits of youth and political enthusiasm: such differences usually emerged in the context of discussions of the BDM school assistants and other stopgap or auxiliary staff. Resorting to such staff to tackle the teacher shortage put into question the goal originally proclaimed in 1939 by the Warthegau authorities of bringing elementary schools up to Altreich stan-dards as a symbol of the complete integration of the annexed territories into the Reich. This goal was later dropped from official propaganda as the empha-sis shifted to simply putting every German child into a German school. Though it was agreed that all teachers should be able to convey basic skills and to remedy language deficiencies in their pupils, disagreements remained about how much more than this should be expected. The 'revolutionary' view espoused by Greiser, the BDM leadership and Reichsstatthalter schools administration in Posen was that in the frontier situation of the Warthegau the overriding priority was to turn out 'conscious, healthy Germans'. An article in the National Socialist Student League newspaper also took the line that the priority for schooling in the Warthegau was the creation of a younger gener-ation that 'feels German, thinks German, writes German, reads German and speaks German' and that this was better achieved by students with 'modern' attitudes than by professional teachers from the older generation.[14]

An account for the BDM periodical *Das deutsche Mädel* gives an insight into the BDM model of village school teaching: having gathered the children of the village together, she 'told them about the Führer' on the first day, and began on the second day to teach arithmetic to the mixed age group: 'when I made mistakes in the calculations they were all delighted'. She was also determined to turn the children into 'proper Germans':

> I knew from the start that I had not only to get across knowledge to the children but also educate them into being fit German people. As a first priority I undertook to teach them outward cleanliness. . . . Little by little the children begin to notice that dirt is ugly, and above all they are now saying to every little dirty-paws (*Schmierfink*) 'You must be Polish'.[15]

Schools officials in the district administrations of the Warthegau were less impressed by BDM success stories and more inclined to apply Altreich standards regarding the level of knowledge to be communicated and to be correspondingly wary of inadequately trained enthusiasts. Though they had little alternative but to employ such staff, they continued to warn against overestimating what they could do. Thus an official in the schools department in Litzmannstadt declared that the teaching performance of most BDM school assistants 'falls short by a long way'; they just about managed in their own way to teach the children reading, writing and basic arithmetic, but were unable to progress much further, leading to frustration on their part and failure on the part of the pupils.[16] The Posen schools department agreed that the BDM school assistants were often unsatisfactory. The Hohensalza schools department, slightly more optimistic, pointed out that in the rare cases where BDM school assistants were employed under supervision in larger schools they could progress from a form of teaching that was mostly play to something which could be taken more seriously.[17] Likewise, the Kreis school inspector (*Schulrat*) in Kreis Scharnikau often noted in his inspection reports the BDM school assistants' lack of 'methodological training' and criticized one who for all her reported popularity in the village and her commitment to the pupils taught haphazardly and spent too much time on sport. Conversely, he explicitly praised an experienced teacher seconded from the Altreich who 'knew what teaching and education is all about'.[18]

Further differences of opinion surfaced in relation to the nature of the 'special political task' of the 'educator in the East'. Schools officials conceived of the task in academic terms: 'frontier consciousness' and Nazi values were to be instilled through a curriculum tailored to the East in which history, geography and science lessons would focus on the 'ethnic struggle' and the battle for 'living space': to wage these struggles, in other words, one had to know one's historical and geographical facts. However, unqualified staff were said to be unable to convey such material effectively:[19] again, this provided

grounds on which to challenge the deployment of BDM school assistants, certainly in the longer term. For Greiser and the BDM leadership, by contrast
waging the *Volkstumskampf* was understood more in terms of village activism
and mobilizing children and youngsters for sports, singing and other practical forms of performing and enacting German community spirit. The BDM
leadership described the tasks of BDM school assistants in terms of teaching
basic skills, accustoming the children to 'cleanliness, discipline and order' and
to 'physical exercise, singing and fun in a community with other children'.[20]

Overwhelming demands or freedom to manoeuvre?

With single-class village schools comprising around three-quarters of the elementary schools in the Warthegau, the majority of the women recruited from
the Altreich to teach in Warthegau schools were sent to rural areas, where
they were typically in charge of a village school. Experienced teachers from
the Altreich confronted unfamiliar teaching situations; the inexperienced
young teachers who comprised an ever larger proportion of the Warthegau's
elementary school staff were thrown in at the deep end. All were expected to
perform feats of practical improvisation in terms of premises and equipment
to create an acceptably German school environment, manage pupils of all ages
and mixed educational backgrounds, establish their authority with parents
and more widely in the village, attend weekend professional training sessions,
and take full part in community events and political life outside the classroom.
Women teachers from the Altreich, who unlike men rarely had spouses or
children living with them, were expected to sacrifice private life for the
literally boundless tasks of the 'ethnic struggle'. In return, there were bonus
payments for working in the East and the flattering propaganda portrayals of
the endlessly willing and endlessly competent village schoolteacher or school
assistant.

Sometimes, premises and facilities were not a problem at all. They might
merely be Polish: many of the schools for German children were set up in the
Polish village schools which had been closed down by the Nazi authorities at
the end of 1939. A BDM school assistant reported finding old German textbooks dating from the Kaiserreich in the unused spare classroom of her school,
a discovery that presumably confirmed for her how legitimate the reappro-
priation of the premises in 1939 had been.[21] A student from Hamburg arriving in the village of Druzbice in Kreis Lask for her summer assignment
in 1940 expected – presumably on the basis of assumptions about Polish
'backwardness' – that she would have to set up school in a tavern or similar

accommodation; having relished the prospect of dramatic improvisation, she reported that she was 'pleasantly disappointed' to find, simply, the empty Polish school premises with two furnished and equipped classrooms and the empty teacher's apartment.[22] Whether she wondered what had happened to the Polish teacher is not known. In Mixstadt, Kreis Ostrowo, a BDM school assistant who took up her teaching post in April 1943 found that the school for forty-four German children was housed in premises which had clearly been a much larger Polish school with four classrooms, of which she only needed one.[23] In the village of Gultsch in Kreis Scharnikau, where Gabriele Hornung (née Rusch) was posted in May 1942, the school building was far too big for the thirty-six children allowed to attend it: even after the classification of mixed German–Polish families as ethnic Germans and the influx of Bessarabian German settlers, the German population numbered around 200 compared to a Polish population of 700. The Polish children of the village, as Hornung recalled in her 1985 memoir, were taught reading and writing twice a week in a neighbouring village by a retired German teacher 'from the time before 1939'. What seemed to disturb her most about all this was the wasted space in the school building in Gultsch.[24]

In some villages in the western Warthegau, schools catering for the German minority had existed before 1939 and only needed continuing or reviving. A newly qualified teacher arriving in 1941 in a village near Wittingen (Kreis Gnesen) found the school building – a German school that had been closed down in 1938 and reopened under Nazi rule in 1940 – equipped with German textbooks, maps and some equipment for biology teaching.[25] In other cases, women were setting up from scratch. One BDM school assistant reported that her school premises, built originally as a school, had 'in Polish times' been a shop with a dance hall on the second floor.[26] Another BDM school assistant found that the school she was posted to in the summer of 1943 was a small wooden building that had formerly been someone's dwelling: here too, one wonders whether she thought about how it had come to be uninhabited.[27] A classic triumph of improvisation was reported proudly by a student on a summer assignment in 1943: she set up a school for twenty-two children in the second-class waiting room of the station in Dilltal in Kreis Welun.[28]

The students and the BDM school assistants boasted in their reports of their successes in assembling equipment, getting the school refurbished and, in the case of previously Polish schools, purging them of Polish features. Thus the student in Druzbice set about removing Polish pictures, flags and notices, 'restoring cleanliness and order'. She stamped a new German identity on the premises by putting up portraits of Hitler. She also turned round the maps of

Poland on the classroom wall and stuck maps of Germany on the back.[29] Gabriele Hornung recalled in her memoir of teaching in Gultsch finding another use for the maps: having been tipped off by fellow-teachers in other villages, she soaked the fabric off the back of a map of inter-war Poland that had been dumped in a corner and got her Polish servant to make a blouse for her out of it.[30]

On the whole, resources for refurbishment seem to have been plentiful, at least in the early years of the occupation. Women Land Year leaders visiting village schools near Posen in January and February 1943 as part of a 'national-political' training course reported that the formerly Polish school in Jägerslust had been totally renovated and re-equipped and was now a 'clean, distinct building which stands out in the village and represents German ways'; similarly, a school in Rautendorf was praised for its new furniture and its general air of comfort.[31] These schools may have been showcases selected for the Land Year leaders to visit, and there are indications from other sources of draughty, unrenovated premises with defective stoves and uncompleted repairs.[32] Nevertheless, the schools administrator Lieselotte Gumpert confirmed in her post-war account that resources for converting and equipping schools in the Warthegau had in the early years of the war been 'most generous'; only from 1943 onwards did the money run out.[33]

The nature of the intake into elementary schools varied from one part of the Warthegau to another, and even from one village to the next, and it also changed over time as the resettlement programme brought in successive waves of ethnic Germans. Overall, however, contemporary accounts and later recollections highlighted the patchy and interrupted educational background of the pupils and the difficulties of those for whom German was not their first language. Thus while teachers in the administrative district of Posen might find schools dominated by local ethnic Germans who spoke only German, elsewhere in the same Regierungsbezirk there were village schools where the pupils, whether local *Volksdeutsche* or resettlers, spoke better Polish than German.[34] In the districts of Hohensalza and Litzmannstadt, the native ethnic German population was sparser and a correspondingly greater proportion of the pupils were the children of resettlers; some of these – though by no means all – spoke German with difficulty.

Although the number of staff employed overall in the Warthegau rose, teachers reported their workloads increasing as Greiser's policies to boost the German population in the Warthegau at any price took effect. In particular, the large influx of Black Sea German refugees in 1944 brought sudden increases in class sizes. BDM school assistants reported the difficulties of squeezing the newcomers into existing classes and their solution, which was to lay on additional sessions for them. One reported how she had to teach her 72 pupils in two shifts per day in a classroom designed for 30: in her words 'I would never have thought that they would have let so many children loose on me, the "new girl". But it is fun, though it is lots and lots of work.'[35]

Nazi propaganda tended to present local 'ethnic German' and resettler children as well-behaved, eager to learn and grateful; initially shy, but straightforward and 'unspoilt' (*unverfälscht*). Reports by women students on eastern assignments and by BDM school assistants often reproduced these images and fed them in turn: some of the women students' accounts were judged suitable for use as propaganda and extracts from them were published in the student newspaper. BDM school assistants' letters to their training college director in Posen were similarly edited and circulated in the newsletter for ex-students who were now teaching in Warthegau schools. In an extract from a diary by Hedi K., a student teaching on an eastern assignment in summer 1940, which was reproduced in the student newspaper, she wrote that 'the children are very nice, clean and tidy. One can see at once that they are German children. They like coming to school, and they are eager to learn and hard-working. They speak very good German, and their Pfalz dialect is genuine and undistorted. They have preserved the characteristics of their ethnic group (*ihre Stammes-eigenart*) and after they have overcome their initial shyness they are very lively.'[36] A BDM school assistant, writing at the beginning of February 1943 from Märzdorf, enthused about children and parents alike: 'It is simply wonderful here! The people are frightfully nice and the children really sweet! (*Es ist einfach herrlich hier! Die Leute sind furchtbar nett und die Kinder goldig!*)'[37] The student with the school in the Dilltal station waiting room wrote that her twenty-two pupils 'learn with that eagerness that one only finds in these Germans in the East'.[38] A BDM school assistant described how some of her older girl pupils came to her in the afternoons for extra coaching in geometry and arithmetic so that they could keep up with the two boys in their age group.[39]

Ethnic German children and their parents were represented as being easily impressed by anything unfamiliar and modern and by all things associated with the Reich. An article in a student newspaper in August 1940 told how a young Hamburg student teaching in Kreis Turek rewarded her class for performing a German song to the visiting reporter by giving them rides in the reporter's car: 'the first ride in a car in their lives'.[40] Some accounts of the 'quaint' habits of the children and their parents have the knowing tone of the colonial describing 'the natives': thus Gertraud von M. reported how on her arrival the whole village turned out to witness the 'fabulous beast', the new teacher; 'Young lads and old women stood around in my room and stared placidly as I unpacked my suitcase. Now and then they offered expert advice on how I could fit everything into the cupboard. Only when I told them that I was very tired from the long journey did they gradually leave. . . .'[41] Another student described her surprise when on the first day of school the children came not on their own but accompanied by their parents, all dressed in their Sunday best, as a mark of (in the student's eyes excessive, but touching) respect for the German school.[42]

A teacher training student from Swabia in October 1940 reporting about her summer assignment in a Warthegau school described the children as 'so receptive and generally so harmless and unspoilt that one enjoys working with them'. Moreover, she admitted, the fact '[t]hat my children are not yet terribly learned is very pleasant for me; it means that my wisdom is accepted almost without question and one doesn't need to write out long preparations since the main thing is practising reading, writing, speaking German and arithmetic'.[43] Occasionally, contemporary accounts portray pupils who were less of a joy to teach: thus a BDM school assistant who had been moved from her original posting at an 'ideal little school' to one where she was 'counting the days' until she could move on again, complained of her 'dreadfully delinquent' pupils;[44] another described her pupils as a 'rather unruly lot' (eine arg verwilderte Bande) and said that she was struggling to keep order without resorting to the cane.[45] However, one teacher writing recollections after the war of teaching Volhynian settlers' children in a village school in Kreis Kutno echoed the most positive of the contemporary accounts, remembering the pupils as the most rewarding children she had ever taught – better than those she taught later in the war in the town of Kutno, and better than those she taught after the war in West Germany.[46]

One key function which teachers in Warthegau elementary schools were supposed to perform was to instil into ethnic German children love of the fatherland, loyalty to the regime and faith in Hitler. This was to take place both in formal lessons, through rituals and performances inside and outside school, and through leisure activities organized – if no one else was doing it – by the teacher. Whatever problems might be entailed in transmitting the basic skills, the schools departments of the district administrations and the Kreis schools inspectors also expected teachers to deliver an elementary school curriculum tailored to the political imperatives of the 'eastern struggle' and framed in-service training sessions accordingly. In January 1943, twenty-eight BDM school assistants employed in the Hohensalza district assembled in Hermannsbad for ten days for a course of lectures on curriculum planning entitled 'Cultivation of the Volkstum as the Principal Task of the Educator in the East'. Here, they were instructed how to devise geography lessons 'with contemporary relevance' which would show the 'struggle of the German *Volkstum* for living space' and the 'heroic struggle of the German *Volkstum* for existence in alien living space'. Biology lessons were to be built around the concepts of 'Volk und Rasse'. As part of a process to 'educate the politically thinking person' (*Erziehung zum politischen Menschen*), history lessons were to help bridge the divide separating the different groups of Germans – resettlers, local ethnic Germans, Reich Germans – inhabiting the East.[47]

A flavour of what was expected in lessons oriented to the 'struggle in the East' is given by a plan of a history lesson presented at a workshop in February 1942 organized by the *Schulrat* in Kreis Scharnikau for twelve *Lehramtsanwärterinnen* (teaching probationers, i.e. those who had completed the college-based part of their training and had gained the first part of their elementary school teaching qualification but had not yet taken their second and final examination) and five school assistants. The plan, circulated in advance by one of the participants, Hildegard G., a probationer who had been teaching in the single-class village school in Grützendorf since September 1941 and was reported following the *Schulrat*'s inspection in July 1942 to be working 'conscientiously and successfully',[48] took as its theme 'The World War: The Struggle on the Eastern Front in the Year 1914' and was designed for years 5 to 8 of the elementary school:

> Aim of lesson: to show what danger threatened in the East. The achievements of the troops and of the military leaders. Tannenberg, the battle of liberation, which saved German land from the Russian-Asiatic destruction.
>
> Method: At the beginning of the lesson the song 'Sacred Fatherland' is sung. After a short recapitulation of the battles on the Western Front we turn to the East. Here in accordance with the Schlieffen Plan only weak forces faced the enormous Russian army. The Russians descend upon East Prussia plundering and murdering. Parallels may be drawn here to earlier invasions e.g. Mongol invasion in 13th century. . . .

The model lesson continued with further military narrative ranging via Frederick the Great back to Hindenburg, the battle of Tannenberg and the salvation of East Prussia, ending with the victory led by General Litzmann near Łódź. To bring home East Prussia's 'suffering' and 'salvation', the lesson plan included the recitation of two poems, one by Frida Jung ('Ostpreußenart') and the other by the ubiquitous Agnes Miegel ('Hindenburg'). As a blend of militarism and sentimentality with a strongly anti-Russian slant, the plan was no doubt fully in line with the regime's propaganda requirements at that stage of the war: its conclusion was to be 'to point out

that through these battles Germany and with it Europe was saved from
Russian destruction, just as today through the struggle of our soldiers in the
East a new Russian invasion is being prevented'.[49]

Lesson plans did not necessarily reflect day-to-day classroom reality, but
they show what sort of lessons teachers in the Warthegau were trained to
devise. Another lesson plan, again for history, was submitted by the probationer Herta M. in October 1942; she had been teaching in the village school
in Lubasch since May 1942.[50] Her outline focused on the conflict between the
Huns and the Germanic people:

> Aim of lesson: The children should learn to identify the Germans and the
> Huns as two racially different peoples with different appearance and behav-
> iour and should learn that the strength of a people lies in its unity and its
> leadership. Teaching materials: map, and poem by Börries von Münch-
> hausen 'Hunnenzug'.

Following an introductory recapitulation on the Germanic peoples, the lesson
introduced its new material: 'The Huns, their characteristics, way of life and
origins. 2. The Huns invade Europe striking fear and terror everywhere they
go. Repetition of points 1 and 2. Recitation of poem: Hunnenzug. Conclusion:
One People, one Reich, one Leader. Song at start of lesson: "Lasset im Winde
die Fahne", and last week's slogan of the week: "Faithlessness once defeated
our people, faith will one day again redeem us": Adolf Hitler.'[51]

The use of 'slogans of the week', portraits of Hitler and regime symbols in
the school building contributed to an atmosphere intended to instil loyalty and
conformity in the pupils: they could also be used as props to instil respect for
the school into parents and children. Thus on the first day at a newly opened
village school in August 1940, the two women students running the school
improvised an opening ritual by borrowing from the village mayor a swastika
flag and a portrait of Hitler and displaying them, arranged with a bouquet of
wild flowers, at the front of the class. One of the students greeted parents and
children with a short speech and 'at the end we sang the national anthem and
the Horst Wessel song'.[52] Last days of term also offered the opportunity for
staging a ritual aimed at binding the pupils to the regime, as in the example
of the BDM school assistant in summer 1944: 'When we held our end of term
ceremony on the 30th and I said to them once more quite particularly that we
must always ask ourselves whether our behaviour is such that we can hold our
heads up before our soldiers without shame, I noticed by the way the children
listened and were involved that all the education up to now has not in the end
passed them by without trace.'[53]

The impression gained from the records of the school departments, from the contemporary accounts by women teaching staff and from post-war recollections is that the pressures from Party and state authorities upon women teaching in the typical one-class rural elementary schools in the Warthegau could be considerable: they were expected to manage large numbers of pupils, sometimes with faulty German, cope with sudden influxes when settlers arrived, and take on community duties such as running the BDM group or language classes for adults. But in practice – if they were the only teacher in a school – they did have a degree of freedom to organize things as they pleased. This clearly suited some women. One BDM school assistant described her satisfaction at having built up her school as well as her work with her BDM group: 'I couldn't have had it better anywhere – here I can build things up in the way I want.'[54] Another BDM school assistant recorded how disappointed she had been when, after having been prepared at the Posen training college for running a single-class school, she was initially posted to an 'ordinary' elementary school in Schieratz (Sieradz) with several classes where she worked alongside other staff. She was pleased when a few months later she was transferred to a single-class village school where she was in charge of forty-three Volhynian resettler children.[55] Moreover, although teachers were required to attend weekend seminars and meetings, inspection visits were infrequent. Kreis school inspectors complained that excessive paperwork and transport difficulties meant they could not get round to inspect and supervise inexperienced teachers working in village schools as often as they wished. In May 1944, the school inspectors in the Posen district demanded extra clerical assistance and a higher petrol allowance, pointing out how urgent inspection visits were if school standards were not to 'collapse totally' in face of the high turnover of staff and the influx of school assistants, women's Labour Service and Auxiliary War Service recruits, women training college graduates and, most recently, hundreds of Black Sea German teachers.[56]

'One really has scarcely time to think': public tasks and private life

Schools officials in the Litzmannstadt district administration regarded women teachers seconded from the Altreich as ill qualified to take on the village schoolteacher's role as a focal point of community life,[57] but other authorities took it for granted that the women appointed to Warthegau village schools – whether seconded from the Altreich, training college graduates, or BDM school assistants – would play a central role in binding together the Germans in their locality politically and socially. The BDM school assistants in

particular were expected to compensate for their lesser degree of competence
in the classroom by their presumed ability to lead and galvanize the community. Far from being a poor substitute for a male teacher, the BDM school
assistant was portrayed by the BDM leadership as a figure of authority whose
field of activity would extend beyond that of any male counterpart:

> In their free time they naturally do their utmost for their village. The school
> assistant places herself at the disposal of the mayor and local Party leader,
> she is the leader of one or of several Party organizations, she joins in the
> monitoring of settlers and helps the NSV. Often she is the organizer of adult
> education within the framework of the *Volksfortbildungswerk*,[58] she gets the
> cultural life of the village under way and functions as a source of advice
> and practical help in health care.[59]

From the BDM's point of view, BDM cadres made ideal village leaders: qualified politically to deputize for local functionaries, but equipped on the basis
of their womanly competence to diagnose villagers' needs and to play a special
role in welfare, cultural life and health care. The BDM school assistants were
accordingly expected to engage in a political 'mission': if they did not, they
risked being barred from the final qualifying course at that institution for
zealots, the Posen training college. The Warthegau leadership of the BDM
drew up a list in October 1943 of several such undesirables: two were reported
to 'have no interest in working in the Hitler Youth'; one 'is not a member of
the Hitler Youth and has never been active in the Hitler Youth'; Lieselotte R.
'is not active in Hitler Youth work and is unsuited to being a BDM leader, has
also rejected all political engagement (NS-Frauenschaft), strong Church ties.'[60]

   In the case of the teachers seconded from the Altreich and the probationers posted from teacher training colleges, there was a similar expectation
that they would take on community functions, though it was formulated less
forcefully than in the case of the BDM school assistants. From the inspection
reports by the Kreis school inspector (*Schulrat*) in Scharnikau, it appears that
teachers tended to be 'requested' to take on a particular job. Still, it is likely
they had a certain amount of choice in the matter. Out of 43 qualified
teachers and probationers inspected by the *Schulrat* during the years 1941 and
1944, 29 were recorded as having some political or other function in the
locality, whether organizing the BDM, teaching German language courses for
adults, organizing NS-Frauenschaft children's groups, acting as 'press and propaganda officer' for the local NS-Frauenschaft, or participating in the
Deutsches Frauenwerk. Twelve were reported to have 'not yet been requested'
to take on any function, while two, both fully qualified teachers, were noted
as having refused: an older teacher who was unhappy about being posted to

the Warthegau after '30 years in Berlin' refused to take on the function of leading the local NS-Frauenschaft branch on the grounds that her nerves would not stand it. Another refused on the grounds that her health was poor due to the climate; in an earlier posting, the *Schulrat* had noted that 'she has no contact with the village community and does not seek it either'.[61]

Thus not all teachers were in practice compelled to take on a wider public role in their local communities. Of those who did, some probably did so under some pressure, while others embraced it enthusiastically. Looking more closely at the public role of women who taught in elementary schools in the Warthegau, it is worth considering at how they portrayed such engagement. This also raises the question of what sources of authority they drew on, how a form of 'female public authority' might have been constituted, and how this public role was played out both in village meetings and events, and within German villagers' homes.

Given the gendered nature of Nazi Party life, the role of women teachers in 'building up the work of the Party' at village level meant above all gathering youngsters into the Hitler Youth and helping to organize adult women in the NS-Frauenschaft/Deutsches Frauenwerk: as 'Reich Germans', they were obvious candidates for tasks which entailed replicating organizational structures and activities that were well established in the Altreich, and as women their authority was most easily exercised over other women and young people. A number of the BDM school assistants whose letters appeared in *Der Ruf* reported on such efforts. One described how she had got the girls and boys organized in the Hitler Youth; she was also summoning their mothers to a meeting and her next move was to 'try her luck with the Deutsches Frauenwerk'.[62] Male Party functionaries meanwhile retained responsibility for running political meetings and delivering political speeches addressed to the adult population of the whole village. Women might, however, substitute for men in that role. Angela G., a woman student participating in the Lehrereinsatz in 1940, reported that she came to the rescue at a village political meeting when the *Kreisleiter* failed to turn up and the *Ortsgruppenleiter* could not or would not improvise the required speech. Stepping in with the *Ortsgruppenleiter*'s agreement, she appealed to the audience to support the work of the German school by speaking only German at home, led a session of singing and finally, in place of the speaker, improvised a short speech on 'Germany's recovery'.[63]

Women teachers also exercised their authority at village level by leading celebrations and ceremonies intended to stimulate loyalty and boost morale. A BDM school assistant reported how on Whit Sunday 1944 she had organized, with the help of 'her girls', a village afternoon social: the

Ortsgruppenleiter had been present, and the farmers who had attended were, she reported, 'very enthusiastic'.[64] Another came up with a novel ritual: when a child was born in the village, she mustered the older pupils from her school, together with reinforcements from her BDM group, to serenade the new mother outside her window and deliver flowers.[65]

Probably aware that BDM school assistants would be tempted to stick to what they were best at – running games and singing with youngsters – a member of staff at the Posen training college urged them: 'Do concern your-selves with the adults in your village as well. I know it is often difficult to get talking to the people, but you bear a large part of the responsibility for the mood of the whole village.'[66] Home visits were an opportunity to stage within the private sphere an encounter between Reich German and ethnic German. A student in the 1940 Osteinsatz reported: 'This evening I sat for a long time with the farmers. They described to me their experiences with the Poles and their journey back to the Reich. I told them about the Führer and showed them newspapers and books which I had brought with me.'[67] For the student teaching in Dilltal in the summer of 1943, social calls in the village were laden with significance:

> The Germanness that is hidden within them has to be awakened. How often it has happened that a father or a mother joined in a folk song that I was singing as I sat with them on the bench in front of their house. How nice it is to talk and to sing for a while like that in the evenings. The people tell me their worries and I have to tell them about the Reich, how things look there.

This young woman had no doubts at all about her role as leader for the settlers and the 'Germanized' locals (*Eingedeutschte*) in Kreis Welun. For her, the only real Germans around were the Reich Germans:

> It is a great task that awaits one here: leading people towards Germandom, whether it is through the school, through courses or – best of all – through one's own example. In my 'assignment village' in a few years' time, the local agriculture officer and I won't be the only Germans any more: no, there will be German settlers and *Eingedeutschte* creating a German village together. Helping in this: what a task![68]

Dispensing advice was another part of the 'community work' which some of the students and BDM school assistants in their reports and letters claimed to engage in. A student on her Osteinsatz in 1940 reported that the villagers solicited her help in writing letters or dealing with requests for information about their farms; they also asked her advice about the care of livestock. The student working in Dilltal found that, as a Reich German, she was asked advice on matters ranging from cooking to growing vegetables; she was proud at being able to rise to this: 'A girl from the Reich has to know about farming matters, even when she comes from Cologne and has studied at university!' But after all, she added, given that she had spent a year in the Labour Service and was currently lodging with the local agriculture officer, she ought to have sufficient knowledge to advise with confidence.[69] As the Eastern Front crumbled, 'looking after the community' also meant getting involved in civil defence: a school assistant reported in the summer of 1944 that on top of organizing both the younger and older girls' groups in her own village and the next village, she was acting as an instructor for the Reich Air Protection League (Reichsluftschutzbund); the next commitment she could see coming her way was working for the Red Cross.[70]

In the enthusiastic reports quoted above, the relationships between teachers and villagers are presented as thriving, with their authors recording admiration for the ethnic Germans. The student teaching in Dilltal also noted their 'racial' qualities: 'her' villagers looked 'like North Germans, really light blond hair, blue eyes, long skulls'.[71] The women's perceptions of what they were doing and their impact on 'their' village were no doubt fed by political training sessions and by images in the Nazi press of benevolent, efficient Reich Germans and deferential, grateful ethnic Germans. By writing such accounts which were circulated through the student press and the BDM school assistants' newsletter, they fuelled the myths in turn. However, as we have already seen, there were women teachers and school assistants who avoided the role of political missionary and 'mother of the village' altogether, and there are indications in contemporary as well as later accounts of how problematic such tasks could prove.

Some reports pointed to mistrust between ethnic German villagers and the Reich German teacher. In January 1943, as part of a training programme, Land Year camp leaders went to visit village schools near Posen, and wrote up their impressions as unpublished reports for their training supervisors. One such report hinted at resentments felt by ethnic German settlers which affected relations with the young village schoolteacher from the Reich, Fräulein B., who had been there since the summer of 1941. After observing Fräulein B.'s teaching, the Land Year women walked through the village with her. 'We did not visit individual farms, because there are a lot of resettlers from many different parts of the world here and they haven't really developed contact with each other, and because Frl. B. as a "Reich German" has found it particularly difficult to establish proper contact with the families. Frl. B. told us that a Bessarabian German woman had said to her: "Oh, for you it's completely different, after all you're not staying here for ever." '[72] Tensions between ethnic Germans and Reich German women teachers also arose out of an excess of (in one case literally) missionary zeal. The Kreis school inspector in Kreis Scharnikau reported in June 1942 on an unqualified teaching assistant working on her own in the village school in Penskowo: he noted that she had previously studied two years of medicine and been employed on 'mission work' in East Africa, and observed that she had 'set herself a very ambitious goal in her pedagogical efforts towards the villagers. However, she lacks the necessary tact.'[73] Theodora Sch., a probationer teaching in Slugi, a village in Kreis Lentschütz in the eastern Warthegau, did not get on with the people in her village either. Her sister, applying on Theodora's behalf for her to be transferred away from Slugi, gave an account of this that was disputed by the Kreis school inspector. According to Theodora's sister, 'Slugi is a small, very dirty village with mainly Polish population. The German population, mostly Galician German resettlers, sympathize very much with the Poles and are not well disposed towards my sister, since she as a German teacher cannot of course approve of their attitude towards the Poles.'[74] The inspector, critical of the resettlers himself – he described the ethnic German settlers in Slugi as 'without exception obstinate Catholic Galicians' – nevertheless saw the conflicts between Theodora Sch. and the resettlers as largely due to her inept attempts to convert them from Catholicism to her own views as a '*Gottgläubige*' (a term used of National Socialists who renounced Church affiliations) – something she had allegedly been warned against.[75] Although teachers in the Warthegau were pressed by Kreis school inspectors to renounce church membership,[76] and although the provision of German schools and teachers who were free of religious ties was thought to be an antidote to settlers' traditional loyalties to the Churches,[77] teachers were not meant to engage in aggressive agitation which would put villagers' backs up: the campaign against the Churches was supposed to be more subtle.

In a report for the *Dokumentation der Vertreibung* project in the 1950s, Annelies Regenstein, a probationer teaching in Kreis Kutno, recalled her growing desire to avoid a public role within the village. She depicted this withdrawal as having been motivated by a desire to distance herself from Party functionaries and state officials and a reluctance to act as a mouthpiece for the regime:

I went to the Warthegau full of idealism. But because I was so much thrown on to my own resources in my remote teaching jobs I kept myself very much to myself. I did visit the families of my pupils. But the behaviour of trustees[78] and Party leaders often created impossible situations, so that as a young person one felt bewildered by these machinations. Particularly in the final months before we fled, I was often asked by parents what I thought about our long-term future in the East. It was expected of us as leaders (*Führungskräfte*) that we would have our own opinion, but what opinion were we supposed to have? Were we not merely degraded to being the mouthpiece of the Party and State doctrine? The feeling of being a means to an end, without having any accurate picture of all the circumstances, became stronger from year to year and made me in the end very indifferent. I did my work in school and took part in youth work only to the extent of doing sport.[79]

Regenstein's account gives political disillusion as a reason for wishing to withdraw from her public duties. Even without the factor of political disaffection, a number of women teachers appear to have felt the need to defend their private sphere against the encroachments of public tasks. Lieselotte Gumpert recalled that the constant demands made her want to protect her private life all the more.[80]

What sort of private life did women village schoolteachers have? Anneliese Schober, teaching in Urbach, was thrilled about sharing living quarters with another BDM school assistant:

The best thing of all is that I can share a house with Friedl. Imagine a nice little schoolhouse, no bigger than a farmhouse, with a little flower garden and a little birch wood outside the window. Inside we've made ourselves a comfortable home. Everything's still quite primitive – for instance we made ourselves a couch out of bricks, bed slats and mattresses. . . . We are proud of it and show it to every visitor. The only thing we don't have is pictures for the walls. . . . A few days ago we acquired a radio: we were pleased as anything about that.[81]

She went on to describe how she explored the countryside together with Friedl, learning to ride horses and motorbikes. The student working in Dilltal in 1943 also mentioned hikes, bicycle rides and bathing trips to the River Warthe. Other teachers, by contrast, complained that they had virtually no leisure at all or no means of enjoying it. For probationers and BDM school assistants, weekends were often taken up with training sessions, and a BDM school assistant complained that her supposedly free afternoons were taken up with answering requests from villagers for advice and help: 'One really has scarcely time to think.'[82] Even if teachers did have time, sources of entertainment were limited. Teachers' obligations to monitor and 'look after' villagers could prevent normal socializing, even if the teachers were inclined to try. Some were not so inclined, for example Theodora Sch. in Slugi.

According to Theodora's sister, 'neither in Slugi nor in the surrounding area are there any Germans with whom my sister could socialize, where she could find entertainment and stimulation'. She was described as often sitting alone in her schoolhouse, with her radio broken and without any light because her supplies of petroleum were too meagre to last the winter.[83]

Strict boundaries were set regarding female teachers' behaviour. Apart from the outright ban on social contacts with Poles, relationships with German men in the vicinity could be risky as well. Sexual relationships were regarded as compromising a woman teacher's public standing in the locality, and such relationships were subject to sanctions that contrasted with the way in which the promiscuity of Reich German men in Poland was tolerated. This, according to Gabriele Hornung's memoir, had been particularly obvious at the outset before their families had arrived: 'The male civil servants . . . had more or less all seized the moment and the fresh air of the East for a bout of happy hunting. In their eyes, all those young women teachers out on their own in the villages were fair game.'[84] A teaching inspection report on Käthe R., an auxiliary teacher in charge of a village school in Kreis Scharnikau, depicted a woman whose 'suspect' past alone gave grounds for questioning her capacity to fulfil her function as a teacher and figure of authority in the village. 'Turbulent past. Taught (among other jobs) in Spain. Twice divorced. Very nervous and superficial. Teaches in a cold and unventilated classroom. The door of the stove is open, the stove has already gone cold. A rootless urbanite, lacking a sense of calm, care and empathy. Inclines to flirtations (*Liebeleien*). Requires firm management, needs a constant check on her preparation, her teaching and her lifestyle.'[85] If Gabriele Hornung's memoir is to be believed, the Kreis school inspector writing this report was the very embodiment of the double standard that condemned women for doing what men did with impunity. This man, according to Hornung, had ordered the transfer of Hornung's predecessor for having conducted an affair with the *Landrat* too openly, while he himself was at the time having an affair with a village schoolteacher in his own Kreis.[86]

Cases where young women teachers became pregnant as the result of affairs in the Warthegau villages where they were teaching triggered investigations by their schools departments. Around Christmas 1941, a teacher in the village of L., Kreis Konin (Hohensalza district) began an affair with the headmaster of the school where she was working, a *Volksdeutscher*, and became pregnant in the spring of 1943. She applied for and obtained a transfer away from Kreis Konin, and was permitted to transfer to Thuringia. The headmaster stayed at his post, despite being denounced, in a dispute over maintenance payments, as a womanizer who had also had an affair with the 22-year-old kindergarten teacher in the village.[87] In another case in the Posen area, a probationer became involved with a forester in the same village, and the latter's marriage broke down as a consequence. In January 1944, the schools authorities attempted to resolve the teacher's future: the district administration in Posen, anxious not to lose any staff, wanted her transferred to another Kreis in the Warthegau, and was happy for her to take her final qualifying exams with the prospect of teaching again once the child was born. Local schools and Party officials agreed, and only the Gau women's leader Helga Thrö was against this solution, insisting instead that the teacher be transferred to the Altreich, which was presumably intended as a punishment.[88]

This discussion prompted a search for guidelines to deal with such cases: allegedly, 'moral lapses' among young women teachers were on the increase. 'The general loosening of morals, the early departure of the young women teachers from their parental home and their transplantation into isolated regions must be seen as the cause of this.' It was recommended that such cases should generally be treated more seriously than hitherto, with dismissal a possibility, and that to pre-empt such 'lapses' the NS-Frauenschaft should keep a check on unmarried women teachers and find families for them to have contact with.[89] In practice, such guidelines, designed to appease the NS-Frauenschaft, seem to have remained on paper. However, the conflict inherent in the proposal between placing young women teachers under such tutelage and requiring them to exercise public authority within their villages appears to have gone unnoticed.

Maintaining ethnic boundaries

Women teachers assisted the policy of separating those labelled as ethnic Germans from the Polish population in the Warthegau first of all simply through their work of teaching German children in separate German schools, while other less qualified (or, in some cases, even less qualified) German staff – usually ethnic Germans – were hired to teach Polish children, if schools for Polish children existed at all. The hierarchy of personnel was intended to mirror the relative status of the schools. However inadequate village schools for German children were, schools for Polish children were designed to be worse. Sometimes, however, this racist logic began to collapse in the face of practicalities. In Kreis Scharnikau, where in summer 1941 only a fifth of Polish children of school age had schools of any sort to go to, pressure was building to get more of the Polish children off the streets. In response to a request by the *Amtskommissar* of Filehne-Land, the *Schulrat* agreed to allow

Polish children in the village of Penskowo to attend classes in the same school premises as the German children. Separation would still be guaranteed, however: the Polish children would have different teachers and a separate school entrance and playground.[90]

Women Land Year leaders who visited rural schools near Posen in early 1943 recorded their impressions of Polish children. In the village of Konradsaue, where 62 out of the 400 inhabitants were classed as German, the women first visited the school for the German children, finding the children 'alert and fresh'. They then decided to look at the school for the Polish children, where they found all their preconceptions about 'Polish filth' and 'Polish danger' confirmed: 'The difference between the Polish school and the German school was very marked. The children looked completely ragged and disorderly, the boys in particular looked as if they were the offspring of criminals. Which, when we asked, turned out to be true.' Another Land Year leader reported visiting a school for 735 Polish children and watching a German-language class where everyday vocabulary was being taught, with the children chanting the words in unison.[91]

In a more general way, the Reich German women working in Warthegau elementary schools were expected to maintain ethnic boundaries by conforming to the Nazi ban on socializing with Poles. Contravening this ban could be grounds for dismissal: Emma L., an ethnic German woman teacher from the Łódź/Litzmannstadt area, was arrested by the Gestapo in 1942 for maintaining friendly relations with Poles. The Litzmannstadt schools department was more inclined to leniency than the personnel section of the Warthegau NSDAP, which demanded her dismissal from teaching altogether, on the grounds that ethnic Germans had been accustomed before 1939 to socializing with Poles and that old habits died hard. The department recommended that Emma L. not be dismissed but transferred from the Warthegau to the Altreich, a decision queried by the more ideologically zealous Reichsstatthalter schools administration in Posen but upheld by the Reich Education Ministry. All the authorities were in agreement, however, that she could not be retained as a teacher in the Warthegau.[92]

If contemporary accounts written for official consumption referred to Poles at all, which was rare, they did so only in terms that confirmed the authors' conformity – even super-conformity – to the Nazi notion of the racial hierarchy in the East. The Swabian student quoted above, who found her German pupils so receptive and easy to teach, expressed a sense of power and superiority towards the Poles in her village which, as she knew, rested on Nazi military domination. She described how she got her meals at the police station, where 'a Polish woman cooks for us very cheaply' and how in the shadow of the police station one feels oneself able to measure up to any Poles or obstinate *Amtskommissare*. Most Poles immediately become very timid when they hear the word 'gendarme'; they are and remain a nation of serfs (*ein Knechtvolk*), regardless of whether they happen to have their feelings whipped up by the English or whether they cringe before the Germans. The point is that English agitation can do nothing here in the Warthegau in face of German weapons. Often enough one still has people staring at one – looks that would kill if they could.[93]

Some of the recollections written in the 1950s by women teachers who had worked in the Warthegau highlighted how Nazi policies sought – not always successfully – to drive a wedge between ethnic Germans and Poles. Annelies Regenstein, teaching in Laningen in Kreis Kutno, remembered how the resettled ethnic Germans were constantly being told to think of themselves as superior to the Poles and how this created a 'crass polarization' between Germans and Poles; Poles, she recalled, were regarded as indispensable labourers, a necessary evil, but not as human beings.[94] Hildegard Grabe, also teaching in Kreis Kutno near Zychlin, noted how much cultural common ground remained between the Poles and the Volhynian Germans, for all the Nazi attempts to drive them apart: 'They talked to each other in Polish, the schoolchildren too could speak Polish and Russian, though among themselves the Volhynians spoke German, mixing in Polish and Russian words and using odd word order in sentences.' The Reich Germans, she remembered, looked down on the Volhynian Germans because of their friendly relations with the Poles and their faulty German.[95]

Both these memoirs also touched on the murder of the Warthegau's Jews. Plans to deport the Jews wholesale from the Warthegau to the General Government had been shelved in 1940, leaving the main ghetto in Łódź/Litzmannstadt and smaller ghettos in other towns in existence for longer than originally envisaged by the Nazi authorities in the Warthegau.[96] Eager to rid the areas under their command of Jews, Warthegau Nazis were thus all the more resentful in the autumn of 1941 when Himmler ordered Greiser to accommodate within the ghetto in Łódź a new influx of Jews from the Altreich, Vienna and the 'Protectorate of Bohemia and Moravia', together with 5,000 Gypsies.[97] The sought-for 'solution' to the resulting intensification of overcrowding in the Łódź ghetto was, however, already being devised at the highest level: mass murder by means of gassing.[98] This was initiated in a specially constructed extermination centre in Chełmno/Kulmhof in December 1941, earlier than anywhere else in Nazi-occupied Poland. In this, Greiser's Warthegau once again practised first what was to be implemented elsewhere.[99]

In the course of 1942, Jews labelled 'unfit for work' were deported to Chełmno from the ghetto in Łódź and from the smaller ghettos of the Warthegau.[100] In June 1942, the Gestapo in Łódź reported that more than 44,000 Polish Jews, together with more than 10,000 German, Austrian and Czech Jews, had been deported from the Łódź ghetto and murdered. The same report noted how the Kreise of the Warthegau were being emptied of Jews by turn: the Jews living in Kreis Lentschütz and Landkreis Litzmannstadt had already been deported, either to the ghetto in Łódź or directly to their deaths in Chełmno.[101] The Jews from other Kreise were to follow: Gestapo records of August 1942 explicitly mentioned Kreis Welun and Kreis Sieradz as having just become 'free of Jews', and in October 1942 it was confirmed that deportations of Jews from the rural Kreise of the Warthegau had been completed that August.[102] In early 1943, the killings in Chełmno were suspended and in March 1943 the camp was wound up and its premises destroyed. Its function as a killing centre was restored for several weeks in June/July 1944.[103]

The accounts given by Regenstein and Grabe suggest that the fate of the Jews in the Warthegau was widely guessed at by the Germans living there. This state of semi-knowledge may have left some uneasy – and probably not wanting to know any more – but others indifferent. As Annelies Regenstein wrote:

> I saw nothing more of the Jewish population of what had been Poland. In 1940 I travelled on one occasion through the ghetto in Litzmannstadt, a dark area of the city fenced off with barbed wire in which thousands of Jews were herded together and left to vegetate. Something of the terrible fate of these people probably seeped into the population. But anti-semitic propaganda and a hostile attitude on the part of the resettled Germans towards the Jews made them indifferent.[104]

She did not spell out her own reactions at the time to the knowledge that was 'probably seeping' into German consciousness.

Hildegard Grabe, referring back to earlier comments in her report about feeling mortified about using furniture that had been confiscated from Poles, recalled what happened to the Jews of Zychlin and Kutno:

> The Jews who had lived in the ghetto in Zychlin and Kutno disappeared one day (I can't remember when that was, perhaps 1942). People whispered to each other that they had been loaded into lorries and gassed (*Sie wären in Autos geladen und vergast, wurde genuschelt*). These rumours affected me even more painfully than the notion that I was using confis-cated furniture.[105]

Kreis Kutno, where Grabe and Regenstein both taught, bordered on Kreis Warthbrücken, where Chełmno was situated. Gas vans were the method of killing used in Chełmno, and according to a report in May 1942 these were becoming well known among the civilian population, who 'openly referred to them as the "death trucks" (*Todeswagen*)'.[106] Grabe's recollection is unusual in explicitly mentioning the method of killing, but it confirms that a degree of knowledge about the specific manner in which the Jews of the Warthegau perished was current among German civilians that went beyond the general awareness of mass murder that Regenstein described.

Ways out of teaching in the Warthegau

For some teachers, working in the Warthegau was intolerable. It was clear to most, however, that in view of the teacher shortage in the East a request to work in the Altreich instead was unlikely to be granted, and that simply leaving one's job was likely to incur penalties. Regulations on the employment of teachers during the Second World War meant that women teaching in the Warthegau had no freedom of mobility. If they simply left their jobs, as did one school assistant in the summer of 1944 following the rejection of her application for a transfer,[107] the Reich Education Ministry could bar them from employment in schools in the Altreich in the future. Only if they were prepared to risk their professional future under the Nazi regime was 'desertion' an option: the effect of such a deterrent might admittedly have been wearing off by summer 1944.

Teachers did seek to be released from their postings in the Warthegau on a number of grounds and with mixed results. Some of the older teachers seconded from the Altreich complained that they were unable to settle in a village environment. Responding to such complaints, the Kreis school inspector in Scharnikau in at least one instance was sympathetic and noted that the secondment of the teacher concerned should be terminated;[108] in another case, where the 48-year-old teacher from Berlin complained of isolation but was considered to be carrying out her duties satisfactorily, the *Schulrat* noted that he could not support her transfer back to the Altreich.[109]

A number of probationers asked to be released from teaching in order to upgrade their qualifications and study at university. The Litzmannstadt authorities, commenting on the case of an ethnic German woman who had worked her way up through school assistant training and subsequently taken her *Abitur*, and in October 1942 – after a year teaching at a school in Kreis Sieradz – applied to go to university in order to qualify as a teacher for middle schools (*Mittelschullehrerin*), pointed out that 'recently there have been a number of applications from probationers seeking release from teaching duties in order to go and study at university and that all such applications have at the insistence of the Reich Education Ministry been turned down for the duration of the war'.[110]

Applications such as that of Barbara Sch. on behalf of her sister Theodora for a transfer away from her village school in Kreis Lentschütz on the grounds that the villagers were unfriendly, the countryside inhospitable, transport non-existent and the accommodation uninhabitable, were likely to get a brisk rejection – in this case, the *Schulrat* of Kreis Lentschütz dismissed Theodora Sch. as a problem personality suffering from an 'acute attack of Eastern blues' (*akuter Ostkoller*). Declaring her to be 'manic depressive' and unsuited to work in the East, he nevertheless did not recommend that she be allowed a transfer. At odds with the villagers or not, 'manic depressive' or not, 'unsuited to the East' or not, Theodora Sch. was still teaching in Slugi two years later in December 1944.[111]

Family circumstances might offer a route out of a teaching post in the Warthegau. Getting married in itself was not an automatic reason for leaving one's post; pregnant women were expected to teach until their maternity leave began, though not to carry on teaching in the Warthegau after giving birth. Pregnancy as a result of an extra-marital affair, as we have seen above, was likely to bring about a transfer to the Altreich; it was designed as a penalty, but some may have seen such a transfer as a reward. One application for a transfer back to the Altreich which was more sympathetically regarded than most was from a young woman who had been posted to the Warthegau after completing her teacher training in Dortmund in October 1941. After several changes of school she had taken over a school in the village of Sorge (Kreis Grätz) in the summer of 1942; in January 1943, she married an estate inspector from neighbouring Neustadt who was killed in action two months later. After her marriage she had continued teaching. In the summer of 1943 she requested a transfer back to Gelsenkirchen: 'My wish to return home is surely understandable, since all my relatives live in Gelsenkirchen-Buer. Being with them will make it easier to bear my sorrow. Living in solitude in Sorge, where the memories of my husband are so strong, would be enormously difficult.' The schools department of the district administration in Posen agreed that this was a strong case, but insisted – given the inability of the authorities in Münster to provide a replacement – that she could be transferred only when a substitute was recruited from a teaching training college.[112]

Later in the war, schools departments began to look more favourably on some requests for transfers back to the Altreich in view of the fact that some of the applicants had been in the Warthegau for nearly four years. Thus in May 1944 a probationer from Bavaria who had been working in Kreis Gnesen since July 1940 was allowed to transfer back home. However, her fellow-applicant, another Bavarian, was turned down since she had only been working in the Warthegau since April 1942. 'I cannot support your request to return so soon in order to study, since this would represent granting you preferential treatment compared with not a few *Kameradinnen* who want to do the same but have worked here longer.' The Reichsstatthalter schools department claimed to be concerned about what it saw as 'psychological distress' (*seelische Not*) among the probationers who had been in the Warthegau for too long.[113] Such a claim bolstered yet another attempt to persuade Altreich schools administrators to send fresh supplies of teachers; however, it pointed to conditions which the typically glowing accounts by BDM school assistants and by students of teaching in the Warthegau conceal.

Going against the grain? Women's memories of teaching village schools in the Warthegau

Five former teachers were interviewed between 1996 and 1999 about their experiences teaching in the Warthegau (Table 2).

These women were typical of their generation of trainee elementary schoolteachers in that they were all posted directly to the Warthegau after their first qualifying examination at the end of their college or university training, which gave them the status of probationers (*Lehramtsanwärter-innen*). All but Frau Vogel were given sole charge of a village school: Frau Vogel had negotiated with the Kreis school inspector in Welun on her arrival that she and a friend from university would be assigned a larger village school to run between them.

Table 2: Five former teachers interviewed between 1996 and 1999 about their experiences teaching in the Warthegau

Name	Year of birth	Period spent teaching in Warthegau	Kreis
Frau Teplitz	1916	Spring 1943–January 1945	Kempen
Frau Geyer	1921	Summer 1941–summer 1944	Gnesen
Frau Ullmann	1922	April 1943–January 1945	Rawitsch
Frau Vogel	1922	May 1942–January 1945	Welun
Frau Eckhard	1923	April 1942–January 1945	Sieradz, Lask

Several of the women emphasized that teaching in the Warthegau had been a formative experience, both personally and professionally. For some, it was the first time that they recalled enjoying such respect and recognition. Not seeing their work in terms of the 'ethnic struggle', some teachers nevertheless felt that their work had provided a focal point of village life: while not everyone told this sort of story about feeling appreciated and important, it was a recurrent theme. Frau Vogel remembered that she and her fellow-teacher had felt 'special', enjoying an authority that derived both from their class background and education and from their status as Reich Germans.[114] She spoke of the local *Amtskommissar*, a Party man from Upper Silesia, as being intimidated by their education, while the ethnic Germans were glad to have two teachers sent to them from the Reich:

V: The *Amtskommissar* was a bit stupid, a Party man, certainly, SS member before 1933, but neither an intellectual nor specially bright, he was just one of these – well, he was an idiot, a Party idiot, but he didn't try and indoctrinate us, he didn't try that. And that may be because he felt inferior to us – I sometimes had the feeling that he didn't dare . . .

EH: So this status as a teacher, been to university –

V: That really was something special for people – at home it wasn't anything special at all, but that's right, it was something special there, and the people were very proud that they had two teachers that came to them from the Reich. As I said, they came and said: please read us out this letter, can you write a letter to my husband, then they told us what they wanted saying and so forth. That was a real relationship of trust with the people from the village – and when I see today, those that are still alive and whom we've met up with again – you still feel that today, that it was nice for them when we arrived.[115]

In the words of Frau Teplitz, remembering how she found her feet as the village schoolteacher in Kreis Kempen and enjoyed a sense of making her mark in a small community, 'I was somebody for the first time'. She described how she had met the challenge of a village school with 110 children. Taking all the classes from year 3 to year 8 in one large room, she described how she had organized her teaching, sometimes giving two dictations at the same time: 'you would think it's impossible, but it worked'. She remembered proudly how two of her pupils had reached the standard for entering secondary school. In her words, 'I took my profession very seriously, I was married to my profession'. Even though she had switched profession after the war to become a pastor in the Protestant Church, it seemed that the confidence she had built up as a village teacher in rural Poland had laid the foundations for her post-war work. It also laid the basis for the emancipation from her family: back home, she had always been treated as her mother's daughter, but when her mother arrived as an evacuee to stay with her daughter in Kreis Kempen, 'she was the mother of the teacher'.[116]

Like Frau Teplitz, Frau Geyer, in charge of a small school in Kreis Gnesen in an area where the pre-war population had been largely German, emphasized her determination to demonstrate her competence: 'The pupils were friendly and nice, the parents were very nice too. It was a very big job, twenty-five youngsters, and I was pretty conscientious, I wanted to teach them something!' Throughout the interview, Frau Geyer came across as a dedicated professional. She described finding, after a phase of isolation, friends and a social network in the village, but above all she presented her three years in Poland as laying the basis for her teaching career. She traced for me her qualifications and salary awards as well as recounting memories of her efforts to raise the children's levels of achievement to something nearer that achieved in the Reich. 'They were very difficult to teach. I wanted to teach them much more — and I had to make a *lot* of compromises.' When German refugees arrived from the Black Sea in February 1944, Frau Geyer suddenly had an influx of a further eighty pupils, 'not very intelligent', much more deficient in their education and accompanied by a teacher she recalled as incompetent and whom she had to instruct step by step.[117]

Frau Ullmann, teaching in Kreis Rawitsch, had positive memories both of her teaching and of the social life in the village, where she was the only Reich German and was regarded, she recalled, as 'our Fräulein'. The neighbours were friendly, the schoolchildren she taught were 'nice, good children' who gave her presents on her birthday, and mastering the art of teaching different age groups in one class gave her satisfaction. Frau Ullmann's teaching performance impressed her superiors sufficiently for her to be inspected as a potential nominee for the War Cross of Merit (*Kriegsverdienstkreuz*), though in the end she was not nominated. Despite that disappointment, she regarded the experience of teaching in the Warthegau as very satisfying: 'When you start something and immediately you have to cope with enormous problems, afterwards you feel happy that you have managed it somehow.' As it had for Frau Geyer, teaching in the Warthegau represented for Frau Ullmann the start of what was to be a longer career in the post-war period that she combined with marriage and motherhood.[118]

Frau Eckhard, teaching in two different parts of the Warthegau between 1943 and January 1945, did recall the time as something of a personal water-shed, but — in contrast to a number of the other narratives — not as a time when she felt particularly important or appreciated. Asked to compare her experiences as a teacher there with those recounted by Frau Vogel, with whom she was interviewed, she recalled few social contacts in the places she lived and taught:[119]

> *EH*: Did you also have that feeling of being a focal point?
>
> *E*: No, I can't really say that I did.
>
> . . .
>
> *EH*: Did you want to be part of the village, or did you prefer to be on your own, out and about?
>
> *E*: Yes, actually – more on my own, out and about. I wasn't really so keen on integrating myself into the village.

Her story was of 'getting through' a posting to Poland that had been unwelcome from the beginning and had not been made easier by familial interference: at one point, she recalled, her father had learned that she was involved with someone. 'I was living my own life, and I had a boyfriend as well.' Putting paid to this, her father turned up during one of his army leaves and insisted that his daughter be posted elsewhere. For Frau Eckhard, the memory of teaching in Poland was of struggling as a new teacher without sufficient support or guidance, establishing an independent life for herself away from her family, and making the best of things in her free time by getting away to the cinema as much as she could. Her stories were not of grateful ethnic German parents and village sociability, but of isolation. In retirement, Frau Eckhard could look back at a successful career lasting more than four decades in which she had ended up as a primary school head teacher, but her stories of the Warthegau underlined, sometimes with a touch of bitter comedy, the hard beginnings of that career and her feeling of being thrown in at the deep end.

Three of the teachers were drawn into running the BDM in their village, though with varying degrees of enthusiasm and without any desire to assume any political leadership role. Frau Ullmann replied in the negative when asked whether she felt under pressure as a Reich German to play a political role in her village in Kreis Rawitsch. On the contrary, she presented a picture of village life and teaching in Poland as a politics-free zone: there was virtually no Party life, nor any pressure upon her to provide political leadership or instruction. She recalled leading the village BDM group, but described this as organizing games and playing the recorder; when sent propaganda brochures for political training sessions with the girls, she put them away in a cupboard and left them there. She explained that the villagers 'were Germans anyway and didn't need to be converted or trained', and added later: 'I wasn't given the task of being a missionary and I never felt myself to be a missionary, absolutely not'.[120]

Frau Geyer, describing her village in Kreis Gnesen, similarly insisted that there was no pressure to take on political duties outside school:

G: I undertook no sort of social or political duties there. To begin with I was in the BDM but I couldn't manage it. My school – I wasn't asked, either.

EH: Sometimes there seems to have been some pressure on teachers that they got things like that going in the village.

G: They couldn't have got me to. I was too far away. It was too isolated.[121]

Frau Eckhard and Frau Vogel, however, did recall some pressure to play a wider role in the village community. Frau Eckhard generally kept herself to herself in the village, getting on with her job but avoiding wider involvement. In a report she wrote in 1947 for the school authorities in the American zone, to whom she was applying for re-employment as a teacher, she recounted how at Christmas 1944, after she had held a successful celebration in the school, she was approached by a local Party official with the demand that the celebration be repeated for the whole village community: this would have meant that she could not have gone home for Christmas. She refused, and travelled home as planned.[122] Frau Vogel also recalled pressure to take on extra-curricular duties in the village. Her Kreis school inspector warned her that she should take on some sort of political function, otherwise she would not be able to keep her job after the war: her response was to become a leader, 'lowest rank', of the Jungmädelbund: 'you had to get the children together and tell them some sort of nonsense (*irgendwelchen Mumpitz erzählen*) that I can't remember any more.' Otherwise, recalled Frau Vogel, there was little political pressure exerted on her: they were, she said, 'very lucky' in this respect.

Alongside their mainly positive memories of living and teaching in villages in the Warthegau, the teachers also spoke of having witnessed the subjugation and persecution of the Jewish and Polish population. Not all, admittedly, had memories relating to the Jews. Frau Ullmann, for instance, who only arrived in April 1943 in Kreis Rawitsch in the western Warthegau, had no recollection of encountering Jews. By this time most Jews who had been living in ghettos in the smaller towns in the Warthegau had been deported and killed in Chełmno or incarcerated in the ghetto in Łódź, where 80,000 Jews were still working in spring 1943.[123] By contrast both Frau Eckhard and Frau Vogel, who arrived in spring 1942, remembered seeing Jews at the beginning of their postings in the Warthegau in Kreis Sieradz and Kreis Welun respectively, though only rarely and only when they were visiting the local town. Frau Eckhard saw Jews in Sieradz wearing the star: 'and they weren't allowed to walk on the pavement, and I remember I was coming from the station, going into town, I saw a group of Jews – walking towards me along the road. And later on I was surprised (*habe ich mich gewundert*), I never saw any again.' She went on: 'I asked myself, where have they gone? Everyone from our generation can confirm that we didn't know what was taking place in the concentration camps (*in den KZs*).' Frau Eckhard presented what she had witnessed in the Warthegau as significant, not because she had seen scenes of violence, but because she had seen Jews in Sieradz and then stopped seeing them. The immediate comment she added to this, underlining that she had not known at the time what was going on, suggested that she had revisited this memory in the interim and had thought about it. Perhaps this was to reassure herself that she had been perceptive enough to notice the Jews' disappearance and be troubled by it, even though she had failed to grasp what was happening to them. In this, however, Frau Eckhard felt that she was no different from the rest of her generation.[124]

Frau Vogel, too, was concerned to pinpoint what she had known about the fate of the Jews in her part of the Warthegau at the time. She, like Frau Eckhard, remembered the stigmatization of the Jews when she saw them in the streets of Welun: 'they walked in the gutter and they wore these caps. But when were we in Welun – only a handful of times. In the village we had nothing to do with these things, there was nothing.' She also told a story of Nazi terror against the Jews that she had only avoided witnessing directly at her own insistence: her local *Amtskommissar* ordered her, together with her fellow-teacher, to go to Welun to attend a public execution of five Jews condemned to death for allegedly carrying out ritual slaughter. 'The *Amtskommissar* wanted us all to go there and I said "I won't do that. I can't do that, I'll feel sick". And my friend said, "No, please leave us out".' The two women did not go. Frau Vogel then went on to describe witnessing the deportation of Jews from Welun, which took place shortly after the execution she did not witness:

> After that we were there once more, there they were being loaded on to lorries, and it was said that they're being sent to Warsaw to the ghetto. But no one could confirm that, that was just what was said. But we were so rarely in Welun. It wasn't the same thing, living in the town or in the countryside. Where we were it was peaceful.[125]

Frau Vogel underlined the sense of uncertainty and rumour surrounding the Jews' destination, suggesting that even at the time it was hard to be sure that the destination was Warsaw. (The destination is, in fact, more likely to have been the death camp at Chełmno or the ghetto in Łódź.) She then reverted to emphasizing what she had already stressed before: that within the village community where she was working, she had been spared greater direct confrontation with the events which were taking place in Welun. Her narrative suggests how fortunate she had been to have been protected by living where she was from worse pressures and worse sights.

When asked about the situation of the Poles in their locality, and if they knew of expulsions having happened before or during their time in the Warthegau, the teachers' responses ranged from the vague to the vivid. Frau Ullmann recalled the Poles in her village in the western Warthegau rather vaguely.[126] She chose to highlight how Poles and Germans worked together harmoniously and recalled the expulsion of three of the village's Polish families as farms being 'exchanged'. She did not dwell on what sort of 'little huts' the remaining Poles inhabited, and moved on swiftly to a light-hearted anecdote about surprising a Polish labourer with her competence at milking. Asked later on in the interview about experiences outside the village, she remembered feeling secure and never having had a dispute with a Pole; generally, she insisted that she had witnessed only Germans and Poles getting on amicably as they had always done. 'People over the years had always got on with each other. This hatred of Poles, it was whipped up artificially before the war. The people there, they lived alongside each other quite peacefully. In my area nothing happened at all.' It would be hard to verify or challenge Frau Ullmann's account of life in her village. However, it is conceivable that she recalled a benign version of Polish–German relations that accorded with her memory of her stay in Poland as a time when she felt at ease. She had been sent there but had gone willingly; once there, she had felt protected not only from bombs but also from political pressures. She had enjoyed the respect of the village and liked the status of being 'unser Fräulein'. Seeing the village as a place that was free of 'fanatics', where Germans and Poles ate together and worked together, was another important element in her comfortable, and probably comforting, recollections.

For other respondents, pleasant memories of German–Polish neighbourliness were coupled with others: of Germans victimizing Poles, and of Poles who were cowed and fearful, or embittered and hostile. Some respondents mentioned being shocked by the behaviour of their fellow-Germans. Ethnic Germans figured in some of these anecdotes: Frau Eckhard, for instance, recalled being horrified at the behaviour of her predecessor's wife, a *Volksdeutsche*, who carried on living in the village when her husband was called up. Frau Eckhard witnessed this woman beating and pulling the hair of her Polish maid: 'I just couldn't grasp it, couldn't understand it at all'.[127] In other

cases, respondents singled out Reich Germans whose behaviour had shocked
them, and in two cases respondents compared the Reich Germans in Poland
with West Germans who went east to the new *Bundesländer* after 1990: the
recent images of the *Besserwessis* triggered memories and comparisons with
Germans who went east and threw their weight about there, towards the
ethnic German settlers but also towards the Poles. Frau Teplitz told many
stories of the arrogance and brutality of the Germans she encountered in
Kreis Kempen, particularly the Reich Germans, but singled out the local
Amtskommissar, who 'shot at the Poles if they hadn't got the shade of paint
exactly right'.[128]

Several respondents told of how they had been slow to grasp certain features of Nazi rule in occupied Poland and its impact on the Poles, accompanying such stories with comments such as 'I was naïve...' 'I didn't
realize until later...'. Frau Eckhard recalled an occasion when, dragging a
heavy suitcase, she had asked two young Polish men to help her and they
had refused: 'I thought − "how rude" − only afterwards did I think − if I'd
been Polish I wouldn't have either. ... I wouldn't have helped someone
who was here to occupy me and re-educate me. But I was too naïve in
those days.'[129] Frau Geyer arrived in the Warthegau in summer 1941: scram-
bling with her luggage on to a tiny train taking her from the town of
Gnesen to the village where she was to teach, she found herself in a com-
partment full of Poles who looked 'grim' and 'not friendly': 'Then the
conductor came and said "come with me" and fetched me out. There were
separate carriages for Germans and for Poles. That was my first encounter.
And of course that remained very clear in my memory.' Arriving in the village,
she found the population dominated by long-resident ethnic Germans,
together with a few Baltic German settler families and a number of Polish
families who had been allowed to stay in the village. It had, however, taken
her several weeks to realize that so many Poles were still living there 'because
I only ever saw the German parents of my pupils'. The Poles included a black-
smith, whose wife, and then daughter, came to clean for her: 'that's the family
where I saw that there was embitterment there on the part of the Poles'. She
subsequently learned about the events of autumn 1939: that German villagers
had been interned, injured and killed, that Polish families had been expelled,
making way for the Baltic Germans. As far as expulsions and resettlement
were concerned, therefore, 'When I got there it had all happened already.' She
remembered that there had been a school somewhere in the area for Polish
children where they were taught German, but that the children 'didn't go'.
As the war turned against Germany and partisan activity in some areas
increased, some women remembered feeling insecure travelling alone, but

Frau Geyer remembered having had no fear of the Poles: this, she recalled, was because she had realized that no Pole would dare harm a German because of the fearful reprisals that would ensue. Frau Geyer's account of the situation of the Poles was matter-of-fact rather than dramatic, but she made it clear that she saw the situation in which she was living and working as one of repression, where Poles were embittered but fearful, and those *Volksdeutsche* who were sympathetic towards the Poles on the basis of pre-war friendships and neighbourly networks feared saying anything against the anti-Polish reprisals.[130]

Two of the teachers recalled expulsions of Polish farming families going on in their locality while they were there. Frau Vogel, teaching in Kreis Welun in 1942, remembered the SS carrying out expulsions, though the local police commander warned her to stay inside and not look out when they were happening.[131] She recalled feelings of fear and unease, shared with her friend and fellow-teacher: 'We often wondered what it meant that the Poles had to leave their farms and the Volhynians came and were ensconced there. If that will work out, if that will work. . . . And when the expulsions took place, when the SS came, one felt very uneasy – perhaps they were feelings of fear, not for oneself but about the whole situation.' Frau Vogel recalled the few Poles who remained in the village living in poor conditions – 'they got no ration cards, they only got a tiny piece of butter now and then, they didn't have – they only had what they . . . and the land didn't belong to them any more.' The Volhynian German settlers 'didn't let the Poles starve': however, the poverty of the Poles was brought home to her when – despite the German district nurse's warnings – they ate infected poultry after an outbreak of poultry disease. She also remembered a Polish watchmaker who turned out to be involved in the resistance ('he had a transmitter') but managed to elude arrest. Whatever positive memories Frau Vogel had of her teaching job, the sense of being needed and appreciated by the ethnic Germans, and idyllic memories of summer outings with the children in the local countryside, coexisted jarringly with memories of pity for the Poles scraping by on the margins of the village and anxiety that the police might arrest the resistance activist with the transmitter.[132]

Frau Teplitz, in Kreis Kempen from spring 1943, also recalled expulsions of Poles taking place to make way for incoming Volhynian German settlers.

T: The lorries came at night, they sent the mayor, the ethnic German mayor, a nice man, he had to go ahead and knock at the houses at night, had to say, here is the mayor, I have to talk to you about something. Then as soon as they opened the door, in went the SS, put the men on one lorry

and the women on another and the young people on the third and off they
went. . . .

EH: Did you see that happening yourself, the expulsion of the Poles?

T: The lorries drove past where I lived. The school was directly on the street
and there was a lot of noise in the village. It was so horrible (*Es war so
schaurig*).

Frau Teplitz's account underlined the deception involved in the SS sending
the mayor, whom the Poles trusted, to get them to open the door. She also
depicted the mean-spiritedness of the Volhynian German incomers, who set
the dogs on former inhabitants who had evaded deportation and then come
back to the village to beg for some of their belongings, 'a quilt for the sick
grandmother'. As in the rest of Frau Teplitz's narrative, her stories impressed
upon the listener her sense of shame at German meanness and duplicity and
her sense of outrage at the injustices done to the Poles.[133]

Most respondents had some memories of Poles with whom they were able
to forge friendly relations and of how they had gone against the grain of Nazi
policy by ignoring strictures about not eating at the same table as Poles, or
maintaining other social contacts with them. Frau Geyer talked about how she
had cooked meals and eaten with the Polish girl who came and cleaned the
apartment and the school premises. Frau Vogel showed me photographs of the
young Polish woman who had cleaned and cooked for her and her colleague:
the two German women had become friendly with her, and recent photos of
a visit to Poland documented how all three had kept up the friendship until
the present day. For Frau Teplitz, determination to subvert the regime's policy
of excluding Polish children from German schools was the central experience
of her eighteen months teaching in the Warthegau and the main theme of
her recollections in the interview. Explaining why she had refused to toe the
line and taken risks in order to help the local Poles, she emphasized the part
played by her Christian convictions. Although, as we have seen above in
Chapters 4 and 5, she had gone to the Warthegau willingly, she was immediately shocked on her arrival in Poland by the sight of the ghetto in Łódź.
Arriving at her posting in Kreis Kempen, she immediately had a showdown
with the local Nazi boss over her commitment to the Church: the *Amtskommissar*, 'who'd made himself at home in the vicarage', demanded that she and
the two teacher colleagues who had arrived at the same time leave the Church,
in line with Greiser's policy in the Warthegau. The other two, as Frau Teplitz
recalled, assented, but Frau Teplitz refused. From this point onwards, as she
recalled, her efforts to counteract and subvert the orders of the Nazi occupation authorities began, which subsequently led her to encourage the Polish

children of the village to attend her school (where she was the only teacher).
She recorded their names on a separate register which she kept hidden.

> It was forbidden to teach the Polish children. But I did it, I slipped the
> separate list of pupils each morning into the register and after I read out
> the names I took it out again and put it in my bag. That was my risk. But
> the Poles thanked me for it. And I can't tell you how helpful and friendly
> they were. That made me really glad.

Remarkably, her actions had no negative consequences: either she was shielded
by the sympathetic *Schulrat* or simply regarded as indispensable. She remembered feeling secure in the knowledge that the authorities could ill afford
to lose teachers: in her words, 'they really needed us!' (*sie brauchten uns ja
dringend!*)'.[134] Possibly her actions went completely undetected, but this is
unlikely, since one of Frau Teplitz's most vivid and painful memories was
of the 1944 school Christmas party at which a woman teacher from the
neighbouring village whose Nazi views were known to Frau Teplitz turned
up uninvited:

> And she shouted 'Who are the Poles here?' And a few put their hands up,
> and then a few more, and – 'Get out, you've no business here, this here is
> only for German children'. And I apologized to the parents afterwards
> because I felt so bad about it. How can children help it if the politics is so
> stupid?

This and other incidents were recounted by Frau Teplitz to drive home to me
her point about the stupidity and brutality of the Reich Germans – men and
women – that was shown in their treatment of the Poles. Arriving as a Reich
German, and realizing that, in her words, the Poles 'hated the Reich Germans',
Frau Teplitz was resolved to assist the Poles wherever she could. Where other
respondents talked warmly about feeling appreciated by the ethnic Germans
in the villages where they were working, Frau Teplitz talked much less about
the ethnic Germans than about the Poles. Although she had some good memories of the ethnic German resettlers, particularly of the Bessarabian Germans
('I could work fabulously with them above all'), what gladdened her most was
the gratitude and appreciation shown to her by the Polish children and their
parents. The experience of working in Poland had meant that she had 'felt
somebody' for the first time, but this was about more than feeling needed: it
meant that she had acted on her convictions and gained the respect of the
Poles for it. Where other Reich Germans were hated by the Poles, she had
experienced respect and affection 'because they knew that I was on their side,
and that I thought it was unjust what was being done to the Poles, and said

that sometimes. It was the recklessness of youth, or maybe Christian courage, whatever (*Es war noch jugendlicher Leichtsinn – vielleicht auch christlicher Mut, je nachdem*).' Frau Teplitz's positive memories of working in Poland and her pride in having withstood pressures to toe the Nazi line acted as a powerful spur to her in the post-war years, when she lived in East Germany and became ordained as a pastor in the Protestant Church, to keep visiting Poland, to learn Polish and to think about ways of bridging the historic divisions separating Germans and Poles. To her delight, on one of her visits she managed to re-establish contact with a former Polish pupil.[135]

On the basis of reports from the time, memoirs and recent oral testimonies, it seems that many young women, whether qualified teachers or untrained school assistants, found that by teaching in village schools in the Warthegau they could enjoy the status and authority of a Reich German and a teacher while gaining rewarding experience. The illusion of rural peace could also be beguiling: one BDM school assistant went so far as to describe teaching in a remote Warthegau village as like being 'on an island of happiness in the midst of the harsh, pitiless war (*wie auf einer Insel des Frohsinns mitten im rauhen, harten Krieg*)'.[136] For probationers, being thrown in at the deep end in a single-class village school was a professional challenge: some when interviewed insisted that the experience had stood them in good stead in later careers. There were, however, exceptions, as the cases of women who had been posted unwillingly and who applied to go back to the Altreich demonstrate.

Along with the freedom, responsibility and rewarding work with children came the obligations and pressures to act as exponents and representatives of the regime and of its *Volkstumspolitik*. There were some enthusiasts – at least so it seems from the reports they wrote – who gladly embraced the role of, to use Greiser's phrase, 'living representatives of the National Socialist idea'.[137] However, it seems that the qualified teachers who were not necessarily there from choice or out of political conviction were less likely to do so. Some recalled difficulties with local Party representatives as a consequence; nevertheless, as Reich Germans and as professionals working in remote areas, they remembered having some room for manoeuvre. While BDM school assistants and enthusiastic students could use their freedom of action to invent political ceremonies and deliver speeches invoking the Führer, those who were willing to conform to the regime's demands upon them as teachers but had no interest in being propagandists for Nazism had some chance of running the school in their own way.

For all that, every village schoolteacher in the Warthegau simply by doing her job was playing a part in the occupation regime's apparatus of discrimi-

nation and oppression. This was true even if many teachers felt at the time —
as they said in retrospect that they did — a sense of injustice about the situation of the Poles and the policy of segregating Germans from non-Germans.
Some also tried to reconstruct what they had known about the fate of the Jews.
Some recounted that they were not only disturbed or outraged by the
systematic suppression of the Poles and the brutality and arrogance of
individual Reich Germans and *Volksdeutsche*, but also that they had tried —
in minor or more far-reaching ways — to work against the grain of Nazi policy
and to subvert Nazi measures of discrimination and exclusion. These were
memories which may have served to counterbalance the more uneasy recollections about being part of an unjust order.

Chapter 8

Childcare and Colonization: Kindergartens on the Frontiers of the Nazi Empire

Wherever National Socialist plans for Germanization were put into action in the occupied East, kindergartens were part of the programme. According to an article in the journal of the Nationalsozialistische Volkswohlfahrt (NSV) in 1941, the arrival of a NSV kindergarten teacher or children's nurse in a Polish-dominated village at an early stage of German settlement would have an important psychological impact: 'it will be clear not only to one's own compatriots but also to the alien population (*fremdes Volkstum*) that we do not see the new German *Ostraum* as a grain reservoir but want to make it into a land of children; that we do not merely come to use the economic resources of the land but to settle ourselves here permanently'.[1] Running kindergartens was presented by the regime as a political task, to be kept out of the hands of church organizations and assigned instead primarily to the NSV as a Party organization. Like schools, kindergartens fulfilled a number of functions within the Germanization programme. They were to keep children classified as German separate from the non-Germans, to teach them 'German habits' of cleanliness and punctuality; where necessary, to introduce them to the German language; and to lay foundations for political indoctrination. Like the elementary schools, kindergartens were also supposed to function as a focal point for emerging German communities, and the kindergarten teachers were expected to play the role of community leaders, imparting the regime's values and goals to the ethnic Germans. Moreover, kindergartens were seen as entry points into the home: kindergarten teachers were expected to enlighten mothers as well as teach children about bodily hygiene and healthy nutrition.

Kindergarten teaching, unlike school teaching, was an exclusively female occupation. If women teachers were seen by some school authorities in occupied Poland as less than ideal substitutes for men, it was taken for granted that kindergartens were needed in remote rural areas and that women should be running them. Although men held most positions of authority in the NSV, kindergarten organization was an area where women gained footholds in the hierarchy up to district, Gau and Reich level. At one level, kindergarten teaching was regarded as a professional job for which qualifications obtained at training colleges were necessary. At another level, it was perceived as a 'natural' activity, growing out of experience within the family, to which women were assumed to bring their maternal skills and instincts. The assumption that energetic young women who enjoyed playing with children would be naturally equipped to run a rudimentary kindergarten meant that here, as in elementary schoolteaching, the BDM as enterprising amateurs would seize their chance to fill gaps in the Germanization programme.

It is striking that a field of activity so clearly feminized and at first sight so peripheral to the dominant concerns of military and economic policy was considered important enough for provision to be made in the farthest reaches of the fragile Nazi empire. Kindergartens for ethnic German children were set up across Nazi-controlled territory, not only in the annexed territories but also in the General Government and occupied Soviet territories. As in the case of schools, personnel shortages made for some pressure on qualified Reich German women to take up appointments in the East: freshly qualified kindergarten teachers just out of college were posted immediately to run kindergartens in the annexed Polish territories.[2] At the same time, demands were made on unqualified students and BDM leaders to improvise facilities where necessary: thus women students and BDM leaders on vacation assignments in the Warthegau in 1940 and 1941 were asked to set up temporary summer kindergartens. Kindergarten teachers willing to work in the East enjoyed swift upward mobility: qualified Reich German women were at a premium and were often sent in to train and supervise locally recruited ethnic German staff.

Records that have survived on kindergartens in parts of the General Government make it possible to shed light on women's involvement in Germanizing campaigns that took place far into the Nazi-controlled East in areas not originally earmarked as sites for the 'consolidation of Germandom'. In the General Government, where the proportion of the population that could plausibly be regarded as German was even smaller than in the annexed territories, the initial policy towards ethnic Germans was on the contrary to transfer them out and send them westwards to fill up the spaces of the Warthegau, though initiatives were launched soon afterwards to 'trawl for German blood' among the remaining population of the General Government. From 1941 onwards, with the attack on the Soviet Union, new visions of the Nazi East took root, the place of the General Government in Nazi planning changed, and more rapid and ambitious Germanization plans were adopted, entailing mass deportations of Poles and Ukrainians and the resettlement of ethnic

Germans above all in the 'pilot' region of Distrikt Lublin (see Maps 5 and 6). The decision to implement these plans reflected the burgeoning power of the SS/police apparatus, which the Governor General Hans Frank was unable to contain, and they were set to unfold fully at the point when most of the Jews of the General Government had been murdered.

Exploring the role of women working as kindergarten teachers in these regions entails asking what function they carried out in the regime's policies of persecution and destruction simply by being there and doing their jobs – which, as elsewhere, entailed using for the benefit of the ethnic Germans the possessions of deported and murdered Jews. Moreover, given that some of these women were working there at the time when Jews were being either deported or, as happened in many places in the General Government, killed in the locality, it also raises the question whether, and in what terms, they referred to the fate of the Jews in what they wrote at the time.

From 'trawling for German blood' to mass resettlement plans: Germanization policy in the General Government

Nazi planning for the General Government combined imprecision about the long-term strategy for the territory with brutal cynicism about the fate of its non-German inhabitants. One 'solution' was to use the territory as a reservoir of labour for the Reich and as a dumping ground for unwanted population (Poles and Jews) evicted from the annexed territories; this, however, conflicted with the notion that the General Government should be organized as an economically productive entity. Notwithstanding Hitler's reluctance to see any form of 'orderly' administration in the General Government, Hans Frank sought to create conventional administrative structures and to pursue a degree of stabilization. This meant opposing a limitless dumping of population from other territories. However, Frank's attempt to control policy in the General Government collided with the aspirations of the SS and police apparatus to carve out an empire for itself there.

Whether the General Government was to become an area for German settlement was initially unclear. Only a small proportion of the population of the General Government as constituted in 1939 could be regarded as being of German ethnicity: estimates put the number at between 60,000 and 100,000 (less than 1 per cent)[3] out of a total population of over 12 million, compared to 9.9 million Poles, 700,000 Ukrainians and 1.4 million Jews.[4] Nazi policies in the first phase of the occupation reduced the size of the German minority still further: in the autumn of 1940, 24,500 people identified as *Volksdeutsche* were transferred out of the Lublin–Cholm–Hrubieszów area of Distrikt Lublin into the Warthegau. This has been seen as a belated consequence of the plans of the previous winter to clear an area around Lublin to create a Jewish reservation there: the Jewish reservation plan was abandoned but the removal of the ethnic Germans went ahead.[5] The transfer also dovetailed with the then prevailing policy of concentrating Germanization efforts in the annexed territories. In a process of 'exchange', around 20,000 Poles who had been driven from their homes in the Warthegau, together with several hundred Ukrainian families who had been evacuated from Volhynia to the Warthegau with ethnic Germans in late 1939–40, were sent to the General Government.[6] In theory, the incomers were to be settled on the farms of the departing ethnic Germans; in practice, it was reported, by no means all of the outgoing ethnic Germans had been rural-dwellers, still less owned farms.[7]

The idea of using the General Government as a dumping ground for the 'surplus' population of the annexed territories was at odds with the notion of building up a German presence there. However, a parallel Nazi logic was at work that sought to drive the non-German population ever further eastwards: as the borders of 'Germandom' were flung ever wider, the General Government emerged as a possible area for Germanization.[8] This prospect appeared distant during the early stages of German occupation, and some of Frank's statements from the early phase of the war implied that a policy of Germanization would be embarked upon only after the war.[9] Himmler's RKF agents pressed for a faster tempo: indeed, no sooner had consignments of ethnic Germans from Distrikt Lublin departed for the Warthegau in the autumn of 1940 than the ambitious SS and Police Leader in Distrikt Lublin, Odilo Globocnik, embarked on a campaign to uncover supposedly 'German villages' in the area around Zamość and Biłgoraj and to 'reclaim' these Polish-speaking villagers for Germandom.[10] Frank himself signalled in March 1941 – in other words before the launch of the attack on the Soviet Union – a turn towards a policy of Germanization. The goal, it was declared, would be an entirely German land within fifteen to twenty years, entailing the removal of the Polish and Jewish population.[11]

The General Government was enlarged when, following the launch of the war against the Soviet Union on 22 June 1941, German troops quickly overran the territory of eastern Galicia, alternatively known as western Ukraine, which had until 1939 been part of Poland. Before the founding of independent Poland, the territory had been part of the Habsburg Monarchy. In the years after the First World War, it had been the site of fierce struggles between Polish, Ukrainian and Soviet forces before becoming part of the newly constituted Polish state. In autumn 1939 the territory was occupied by Soviet forces and incorporated into Soviet Ukraine.[12] Even before the Nazi attack on the Soviet Union, Governor General Hans Frank had set his sights upon eastern Galicia. On 1 August, Frank marked the incorporation of the territory into the General Government as 'Distrikt Galizien', the fifth district of the General Government, with a ceremony in the district capital of Lemberg (Lwów/L'viv) (see Maps 5 and 6).[13] At this time, as has been noted in Chapter 4, the notion of Germanizing the General Government was gaining ground. However, like the rest of the General Government, Distrikt Galizien in 1941 had a very small native ethnic German population. This was not least because many of the ethnic Germans who had been living there before the war had been transferred to the annexed territories of western Poland in the winter of 1939–40: around 60,000 had been uprooted following the Soviet occupation of the territory and transported to the Warthegau as part of the agreement between the Nazi and Soviet regimes. In returning 'home to the Reich', the ethnic Germans of eastern Galicia abandoned long-established settlements, some dating back to the eighteenth century.[14]

With the new orientation towards Germanization established, the authorities in the General Government embarked on a new 'trawl for German blood' (*Fahndung nach deutschem Blut*) for native ethnic Germans using looser definitions than before. This fresh screening of the population was ostensibly to identify those who – though not fulfilling enough conditions to be classed as ethnic Germans (*Volksdeutsche*) – could be categorized as being of German ancestry (*Deutschstämmige*). In fact, the aim was less to retrieve 'lost' Germans than to neutralize a section of the local population for the duration of the war, using a mixture of incentives and coercion: it was a policy of divide and rule. The Higher SS and Police Leader in the General Government, Friedrich Krüger, acknowledged that only a small proportion of the *Deutschstämmige* would 'genuinely and inwardly' be 'won back' for Germandom while the war continued: he observed that 'as far as the great majority is concerned, it is only a matter of separating them from the Poles'.[15]

Although Globocnik as SS and Police Leader in Distrikt Lublin had already embarked on the search for *Deutschstämmige* at the end of 1940, the new policy was only officially initiated for the General Government as a whole when in October 1941 Frank issued a decree introducing identity cards for *Deutschstämmige*.[16] The local authorities undertook an initial survey; the final screening was undertaken by mobile teams of the Einwandererzentralstelle. Some recruits signed up for the new status of *Deutschstämmige* voluntarily.

Those whose previous applications for the identity card for *Volksdeutsche* had been rejected were reassessed under the new criteria: such people could be assumed to be willing candidates. However, many were coerced: Poles who were labelled by the Nazi authorities as being of German ancestry but rejected that label were at risk of being sent to concentration camps, with their children being removed to Nazi boarding-schools in the Reich.[17]

The process of registering the *Deutschstämmige* in the General Government had parallels with the operation of the German Ethnic Register (*Deutsche Volksliste* or DVL) in the annexed territories: at least some of those identified as *deutschstämmig* could be regarded as the equivalent of those placed in groups 3 and 4 of the DVL. In contrast to those registered in the DVL, where even those classified in groups 3 and 4 were given German nationality 'subject to revocation' ('*Staatsangehörige auf Widerruf*'), those categorized as *Deutschstämmige* were not awarded the status of German nationals.[18] Nevertheless, the wholesale signing up of people in the General Government with minimal evidence of 'German ancestry' on the basis of where they lived, their supposedly German names, or their 'racial' qualities and apparent economic usefulness aroused some protests from those such as Greiser who took definitions of German blood on the basis of nationality more seriously.[19] Advocates of the campaign to register *Deutschstämmige* in the General Government defended the strategy by drawing distinctions between it and the operation of the DVL in the annexed territories: the DVL was intended to draw final distinctions between Germans and Poles, the *Deutschstämmige* campaign was to make a provisional identification of all those who in terms of their 'value' as well as their ancestry were potentially Germanizable.[20] Moreover, the formal distinction was preserved. Although the introduction of the DVL was mooted, and some in the General Government received identity cards for *Volksdeutsche* rather than identity cards for *Deutschstämmige*, the DVL was never formally introduced in the General Government.

Germanizing the General Government from the autumn of 1941 onwards entailed finding sources of ethnic Germans with which to populate it, removing 'superfluous' population from the territory, and using the resources plundered from the latter to supply the needs of the former. This policy developed as one strand of the radical Nazi planning for eastern Europe that was outlined in the different drafts of the 'General Plan East' (Generalplan Ost) produced by the Reich Security Head Office from the end of 1941 onwards. The drafts of the General Plan East presumed that an area of Germanic settlement would eventually extend far into Russian territory. The plan assumed that the non-Jewish peoples of eastern Europe would be subject to mass deportations, and that the Jewish population would be eradicated in its totality.[21]

The drive to Germanize eastern Europe was thus linked both ideologically and practically with the regime's drive to destroy the Jews. While Hitler had already established the regime's disposition to use murderous violence against the Jews, the moves towards the systematic policy of genocide, and the signals that were consequently given out from the centres of regime policy-making to confirm and promote local initiatives to kill the Jews, were made in the context of ever more radical wartime planning that encompassed the agenda of Germanizing eastern Europe. The murder of the Jews also provided a precedent for the displacement and destruction of other populations. As the goal of 'clearing' the Jews from the conquered territories of the East became not only thinkable but a reality, Nazi planners turned towards policies to displace and decimate the non-Jewish 'alien' population as well.

Assisting in the 'laboratory of Germanization': BDM activists and kindergarten teachers in Distrikt Lublin

Immediately following the transfer of ethnic Germans westwards from areas around Lublin and Cholm in autumn 1940, Globocnik launched a policy to Germanize, or 're-Germanize', his district though a coercive policy of ethnic reprogramming, rural planning and expulsions. The campaign centred on the south-eastern region of Distrikt Lublin, focusing on villages in the area bounded by Zamość, Biłgoraj, Tomaszów and Hrubieszów (see Map 7). Globocnik was determined to raise his profile as a pace-setter in *Volkstums-politik*, and the first moves in this campaign pre-dated by some months Frank's declarations of intent in the spring of 1941 to promote Germanization in the General Government. The initial stage entailed 'rediscovering' and concentrating the *Deutschstämmige* in compact communities.[22] In November 1940, Hitler Youth functionaries travelled through the villages accompanied by ethnic German auxiliary police acting as interpreters. They compiled a provisional register of *Deutschstämmige* using questionnaires, a process that was continued in 1941 by teams of BDM leaders.[23] This 'trawling for German blood' was merely a first step. In October 1941, Globocnik was, in the words of an approving SS officer, 'full of far-reaching and good plans': 'for instance he believes that the gradual cleansing of the whole G.G. of Jews and also of Poles will be necessary in order to secure the eastern territories'.[24] In the short term, Globocnik embarked on expanding the number of Germans in his district by 'topping up' the recently 'discovered' *Deutschstämmige* with ethnic

Germans from elsewhere, for whom space would be cleared by evacuating Polish villages. In November 1941, an 'experimental' evacuation of around 2,000 Polish villagers took place from seven villages north of Zamość. The expulsions enabled the settlement of a hundred ethnic German families from the neighbouring Distrikt Radom.[25] The Germanization by stages of Distrikt Lublin would serve, in Globocnik's vision, to create a 'bridge' between the Baltic and Transylvania, both envisaged as areas of German settlement. The consequence would be to 'hem in' the remaining Polish population and 'gradually to crush them economically and biologically' (*allmählich wirtschaftlich und biologisch erdrücken*).[26]

This move against the Poles to make way for German settlement coincided with, and in Globocnik's planning was fundamentally connected with the decision taken in autumn 1941, probably in October, to murder all the Jews in Distrikt Lublin. This was a decision in which Globocnik played a central initiating role.[27] In the course of 1942, nearly the entire Jewish population of Distrikt Lublin was killed, leaving only around 20,000 surviving at the beginning of 1943.[28] Meanwhile, the decision to eradicate the Jews was extended from Distrikt Lublin to the rest of the General Government.[29]

In the midst of this mass murder, Himmler gave the signal that presaged an onslaught upon Polish communities as well. In the summer of 1942, Himmler visited Lublin and indicated to Globocnik that Kreis Zamosc would be declared an area for settlement and resettlement.[30] In November 1942, Himmler confirmed that Kreis Zamosc was to be 'the first German area of settlement' in the General Government, prompting Globocnik to unleash a series of mass evacuations of Polish villagers to make way for incoming German resettlers from Bessarabia, Croatia and Bosnia.[31] The intention was to divide the deported Poles into categories. Some families would be selected for Germanization, a small proportion of whom were to be allotted model farms in so-called 'Z villages'; those not selected for Germanization were, if over 14 and able-bodied, deployed as forced labour. Children, together with those too old to work, were to be concentrated in so-called *Rentendörfer*.[32] The campaign turned the region into a war zone, racked by the occupiers' terror against the population and, as those driven from their homes or threatened by expulsion took refuge with partisan groups, a growing number of Polish reprisals against ethnic Germans. Partly due to the scale of Polish resistance, partly due to the tide turning against Germany in the war, the resettlement programme in Kreis Zamosc was never realised on the scale envisaged. By August 1943, the settlement programme in Kreis Zamosc, together with areas in the neighbouring Kreis Bilgoraj and Kreis Hrubieszow, had turned 107 Polish villages, 46 hamlets and 60 further scattered groups of dwellings into

126 'German villages'.[33] By April 1943, the number of German settlers brought into the region had reached 9,000, while more than 40,000 Poles and around 7,000 Ukrainians had been displaced.[34] In the summer of 1943, German reprisals against partisans were combined with a new wave of evacuations.[35] In the course of the whole process, entire villages were razed to the ground and their inhabitants killed wholesale in German retribution for partisan attacks; over 4,000 Polish children from the Zamość area were transported to the Reich to be 'Germanized', and tens of thousands of Poles were sent to concentration camps in Poland or deported to the Altreich as slave labour. Of those sent to camps, around 16,000 were sent to Majdanek and 2,000 to Auschwitz.[36]

Throughout Globocnik's Germanizing efforts in Kreis Zamosc, as they escalated from registering the *Deutschstämmige* in 1940–1 into the mass deportation and resettlement measures that began in November 1942, the customary instructions went out that ethnic Germans were to be 'looked after' and German communities consolidated.[37] Once again, young German women from the Altreich were brought in to assist. Kindergartens were from the outset a basic element of the campaign, and setting up kindergartens had been one of the tasks assigned to the BDM leaders who descended on the 'German' villages in 1941.[38] Following the Hitler Youth's mission at the end of 1940, BDM leaders from the Reich were sent from January 1941 onwards to carry on registering those of German descent and, having identified them, to introduce 'those of German descent to German thinking and German ways by means of close personal interaction' (*in engster persönlicher Fühlungnahme*). In March and April 1941, around 20 BDM leaders were arriving each month for four-week assignments, located in 11 villages; this rose to around 30 per month in July and August 1941, now spread across 16 villages. Their tasks included home visiting, advising women on housekeeping, childcare and hygiene, holding evening classes for adults to teach them German and explain their obligations as newly recruited members of the *Volk*; organizing community events and promoting sociability among the Germans; and running schools and kindergartens.[39] In May 1941, an official from the Zamość welfare department complained to his superior in Lublin that the BDM leaders were unreliable judges of who should be recruited to Germandom:

The BDM leaders are inclined to recommend the issue of identity cards (*Kennkarten*) for *Deutschstämmige* with the sole justification that the applicants have such-and-such a percentage of German stock, without the applicants having given a clear commitment to Germandom (*Bekenntnis zum Deutschtum*). They are doing this in order to allow the applicants to obtain the benefits available to those with identity cards and thus drum up more interest in the campaign. I try to convince the girls in such cases of the significance of the identity card. . . ."[40]

From spring 1941, the BDM activists were joined by kindergarten teachers appointed by the Lublin district government's welfare department. The official coordinating the district's kindergarten provision was the 28-year-old Strasbourg-born Marie-Luise Gilgenmann, a qualified kindergarten teacher, former BDM activist and Party member since 1933, who had arrived in Lublin in July 1940.[41] By October 1941 Gilgenmann had supervised the setting up of nine village kindergartens.[42] While some BDM leaders carried on running kindergartens, increasingly a division of labour took place which left the kindergarten work to the kindergarten teachers while the BDM leaders concentrated on running school classes for older children and evening courses for adults.

Besides the pedagogical input of young women at the grass roots, the campaign to marshal a more or less willing population of *Deutschstämmige* into the Nazi fold entailed, from April 1941 onwards, the distribution of bilingual newsletters in German and Polish entitled *Kolonistenbriefe/Listy Kolonistów.*[43] Edited by SS-Untersturmführer Lothar von Seltmann 'on behalf of the SS and Police Leader in Distrikt Lublin', the newsletter was designed as a propaganda tool and language teaching aid. A triumph of Nazi fantasy, the newsletter projected images of contented communities joined by bonds of recently excavated heritage and the sense of a grandiose future within the expanding Reich. More chillingly, by August 1942 it was presenting to the 'reclaimed' ethnic Germans in an article entitled 'The Polish Jew' an image of their homeland 'freed' from the 'burden' of the Jews.[44]

We have every reason to thank providence and thank our Führer Adolf Hitler that we are rid of a burden (*eine Bürde losgeworden sind*), a vile 'companion' that accompanied us at every step. With his cunning, shifty eyes we often saw him pressing up at us, casting greedy glances at our property, into the house, into the barn, into the stable, whenever it was a matter of seizing hold of our hard-won goods gained through arduous effort. All the German readers of these pages will guess at once whom we mean. It is the Jew. . . .

The BDM activists and kindergarten teachers distributed the newsletter and initially provided much of its content as well. Young women from the Reich figured prominently in its pages as smiling missionaries of Germandom, rising early 'fresh and ready to conquer this new world', in the words of one of the first young women to arrive in Białobrzegi in January 1941.[45] Their tales (couched in German suitable for older and younger learners) of community-building efforts, placed alongside photographs of schools, kindergartens, village get-togethers and processions, helped fill up the early numbers. In these accounts, the villagers – old and young alike – were represented as childlike, simple souls who spoke and understood little but sang along valiantly when encouraged and listened respectfully to the homilies of BDM leaders or visiting Party and SS officials on such occasions as Hitler's birthday or the 'Day of National Labour'.[46] The newsletters also chronicled the visits of SS dignitaries to their pet project. In June 1941, Globocnik visited Huszczka; a month later, he accompanied Himmler on a visit to the village of Horyszow. In July 1942, Himmler returned to Zamość to inspect villages where ethnic Germans had been settled the previous November.[47] On such occasions, auxiliary policemen, BDM leaders bearing bouquets and kinder-garten teachers marshalling groups of singing and reciting children were depicted as providing a festive framework for the visit. Such visits were also occasions for villagers to be reminded of their duties as loyal and productive Germans: these messages would be summarized in the *Kolonistenbriefe* in Polish as well as German to ensure they hit home.[48]

Unsurprisingly, internal reports written by kindergarten teachers and organizers gave a different version of Germanizing efforts on the ground in Distrikt Lublin to that of the propaganda of the *Kolonistenbriefe*. Kindergarten teachers told stories of improvised, draughty premises with broken stoves and inadequate washing facilities, and of low attendance due to bad weather and the children's poor clothing.[49] One noted that the children 'had not been brought up to speak German'.[50] If a kindergarten teacher became discouraged and sought distractions, however, she risked being noticed: in October 1941, a pair of BDM leaders self-righteously wrote to the authorities in Lublin denouncing Hertha G., the kindergarten teacher in Dorbozy, for allegedly lacking interest in her work, staying out late and being 'mad about men' (*männertoll*). Hertha G. was transferred to another kindergarten.[51]

Some reports were resolutely upbeat. 'The children are nice, so is working with the parents, and I enjoy the work very much,' wrote Henriette L. from Kolonie Rogóźno near Tomaszów in October 1941, reporting how she had handed out toothbrushes, helped the children make kites and told them to speak only German at home; she had also carried out home visits with the BDM *Einsatzmädel* in order 'to get the parents to the point that we are edu-cating the children on a common basis'.[52] Hertha Z., running the kindergarten in Groß-Brody, declared in September 1941 that 'I am very satisfied with my work. When the work brings as much success as one hopes, one is glad to work.' Her satisfaction was boosted by her progress in finding items to decorate the kindergarten: 'I have organized a portrait of the Führer, admittedly it is not very big but better than nothing I think until we get a new one it will do'.[53] Others sounded more dispirited. Mathilde S., the kindergarten teacher in Huszczka, wrote in August 1941 to Gilgenmann complaining that it was raining constantly, so that she could not go outside in her ordinary shoes; moreover, the children were all ill. She requested knee-boots and blankets and asked when she was going to be paid. In November 1941 she wrote again, this time to the head of the Lublin welfare department, pleading for a break (it is not known whether she got one):

> Wish to request holiday from 20 December because I have been working since 1 May and have had no holiday. I was 6 weeks in Rogozno in Kreis Tomaszow, then 4 weeks in a kindergarten course in Tschenstochau. Since 13 July I have been here as kindergarten teacher in Huszczka. Request immediate answer please if I may go and how long I can have holiday. Also I have not opened the kindergarten this week, the children have no proper clothes, also there is no wood to burn in the stove. I don't know what to do it is so cold I have no children coming to kindergarten. Have tried to ring Herr Jakob today and ask for advice but Herr Jakob is ill. Please give me an answer immediately. Greetings to everybody from the kindergarten teacher in Huszczka Mathilde S.[54]

The internal reports also shed light on the 'triumphs of improvisation' that conjured kindergartens into being where none had existed before. In the process, the young women themselves became involved in confiscating the property of persons defined as superfluous to the 'German' communities they saw themselves as creating. Where kindergarten premises were lacking, Gilgenmann and her kindergarten teachers participated in decisions to seize private houses for the purpose. A member of the Sonderdienst – an ethnic German 'special auxiliary' force deployed in the General Government for local administrative and security tasks – was then called on to undertake the eviction.[55] Following a visit to the village of Freifeld (Zukowo), Gilgenmann noted

> at the time of our visit in Freifeld no premises were available. We inspected the house of a Jewess (consisting of one room and a kitchen), the house is to be vacated by the Jewess. The man from the Sonderdienst was instructed to carry this out.[56]

The sequel to this incident was reported in September 1941 by the Freifeld kindergarten teacher herself, Ottilie D.: it appeared that the house confiscated from the Jewish woman was not good enough after all:

Unfortunately the kindergarten does not meet the requirements, it is firstly too small and secondly cannot be heated. After communicating with the Kreis authorities in Tomaszow, the mayor was given permission to have an empty Jewish house in Plazow dismantled and re-erected in Freifeld. The conversion work is currently under way and will soon be completed.[57]

In another village, Antoniowka, Gilgenmann reported after a visit in October 1941 that no premises were available for the kindergarten yet, but that 'we inspected a room which will be vacated by the family concerned. The mayor was to ensure that the eviction took place; it will be necessary to check whether this has been done.'[58] Meanwhile, plans were under way to transform the village of Sitaniec, north of Zamość, where a German kindergarten had been operating since July 1941. Gilgenmann commented in her report:

> The village is very difficult, since too many Poles live among the people. The plan is to remove the Poles from there and to relocate the settlements of Dorbozy and Rauchersdorf to Sitaniec. (In addition to this there are also eight Jewish families in Sitaniec who are to be resettled (*ausgesiedelt*) as quickly as possible.)[59]

The matter-of-fact tone of such reports underlines how mundane for those involved in the Germanization process the matter of seizure and eviction had become. If one tries to reconstruct the mentalities fostered by such circumstances in those working for the occupation regime, one could suggest that as these acts became normalized, it became ever more unproblematic – for the regime authorities and for the women themselves – that young women were involved in them. Moreover, since the BDM women and the kindergarten teachers had got used to getting things done with the aid of the Sonderdienst, it would have seemed all the more straightforward to call on one of its local members to 'free up' premises where needed. What the reports do not tell us is what the young women knew about what happened to the Poles and the Jews who were displaced. Gilgenmann's use of the term *ausgesiedelt*, referring in autumn 1941 to Jewish families who were to be expelled from Sitaniec, is striking, given that this was exactly the time when the word 'resettle' (*aussiedeln, umsiedeln*), used in relation to the Jews, was becoming a term to camouflage murder.

The surviving kindergarten reports from Kreis Zamosc do not cover the period of the mass evictions and resultant upsurge in Polish partisan activity from the end of 1942 onwards. However, they convey the sense of personal insecurity even in 1941. In Białobrzegi, for example, Gilgenmann noted that tensions were high: it was a mixed German and Polish village, and the Poles were 'time and again spreading their counter-propaganda'. One of the BDM leaders in Białobrzegi had been attacked twice.[60] How far BDM leaders and kindergarten teachers were caught up in the violence sweeping the villages in early 1943 is hard to gauge. Ilse Wilhelm was one who did. Wilhelm was a BDM-*Bannführerin* from St Goarshausen (Hessen-Nassau) whose activities in the Zamość area began with an initial assignment in October 1941 in Antoniowka. She was mentioned eighteen months later in the Hitler Youth bulletin for having helped fight fires and rescue German settlers following a partisan attack on the village of Cieszyn in January 1943 in which thirty Germans were killed.[61] In June 1943, as will be seen in Chapter 9, a kindergarten teacher was killed during a partisan raid on the village of Siedliska.

The *Kolonistenbriefe* together with the unpublished reports convey the sense of the rough-and-ready improvisation that pervaded the Zamość experiment. The young women involved in Germanization measures in Distrikt Lublin were encouraged to regard the achievement of their tasks as a matter of willpower and single-mindedness, whether they were acting under the auspices of the BDM or the district government. As representatives of the regime and often the only Reich Germans in the villages, they were expected to be self-reliant, but also to remain in close touch with the district government: the reports testify to the contacts that took place through inspection visits and correspondence with the authorities in Lublin. They also cooperated on a day-to-day basis with the men of the Sonderdienst stationed in the villages targeted for Germanization.

Even at the start of the Germanization programme in 1941, well before the mass evictions of Polish villages and the escalation of Polish resistance, it was clear that the 'constructive' task of running kindergartens was inseparable from the policies of eviction and deportation of the non-German inhabitants of the villages earmarked for Germanization. From the outset, the 'frontier style' politics of the General Government and the outlook of Globocnik's SS team in Lublin in particular made for an atmosphere of matter-of-fact ruthlessness in which brutality became the norm. The cases where Polish and Jewish homes were seized to serve the kindergarten programme are examples of how women became cogs, albeit minor ones, in the machinery of ethnic expulsion. At the same time, the way in which Gilgenmann and the Freifeld kindergarten teacher reported such decisions is suggestive of their outlook. Whatever their previous attitudes to Poles and Jews, they were now displaying, in an environment where the fates of others were so casually decided, a 'can-do' mentality which took it for granted that the non-German population could be exploited and removed to make way for Germans.

Setting up kindergartens in Distrikt Galizien

Distrikt Galizien, conquered from its Soviet occupiers and incorporated into the General Government in the summer of 1941, soon became scheduled for German settlement (see Map 6). In the 'Generalplan Ost', a belt of Germanic settlement was envisaged encompassing the western Ukraine, including Distrikt Galizien as well as settlements further east in Zhitomir and beyond; the plan assumed expulsions on a vast scale of the native Polish and Ukrainian population.[62] Throughout 1942, it seemed that expulsions and resettlement measures with the aim of increasing and consolidating the German population would be imminent throughout the General Government, including Distrikt Galizien.[63] This was in line with the goal of total Germanization of the territory and the short-term pressure of finding a place to settle ethnic Germans still marooned in transit camps.[64]

However, a number of factors put a brake on such measures with the result that in the end Distrikt Galizien was, in Robert Koehl's words, 'not the scene of any avid settlement activities'.[65] For one thing, the district had no Globocnik, determined to set the pace in Germanization policies and dedicated to making 'his' Zamość a testing-ground for the realization of the 'General Plan East'.[66] Himmler's decision to concentrate resettlement efforts on Distrikt Lublin and to postpone them in Distrikt Galizien has also been ascribed to the fact that the murder of the Jews was by the end of 1942 less far advanced in Distrikt Galizien than Himmler expected, and less far advanced than in neighbouring Lublin.[67] By 1943, moreover, Globocnik's large-scale expulsion of Polish villagers in the Zamość area to make way for German resettlement had triggered intense Polish resistance and led to reprisals against German settlers. The whole operation was proving so damaging to German security interests that it was scaled down in Distrikt Lublin and not replicated on any comparable scale in Distrikt Galizien: mass expulsions of Ukrainians and Poles there were thus avoided.

By 1943 the programme was slowing down, as Himmler lost interest in it and security questions loomed ever larger. Distrikt Galizien did nevertheless witness expulsions and resettlements in 1943. First, more than 5,000 Polish and Ukrainian families were expelled from their homes in the Rawa Ruska area in January 1943 in an attempt to weaken centres of resistance there.[68] Secondly, in summer 1943 Greifelt ordered the resettlement in Distrikt Galizien of around 1,500 Volhynian Germans together with 200 Bosnian German families.[69] However, the biggest influx of new settlers resulted from the Wehrmacht's retreat in the East. From May 1943 onwards, around 12,000 ethnic German refugees from the Volga, Caucasus and Donetz regions of the

Soviet Union were resettled in Distrikt Galizien.[70] As in the annexed territories, the resettlers were moved into houses whose occupants were evicted to
make way for them.[71] Some resettlers, it is true, were moved into houses and
farms vacated by departing Galician Germans in winter 1939–40: some of the
'Russian Germans', for example, were settled in Ugartsberg, a settlement
dating back to the days of the colonization undertaken by the Habsburg ruler
Joseph II in the 1780s.[72] However, even in these areas of former German settlement, some of the vacant properties had just been assigned to Ukrainians
expelled from the Rawa Ruska area in January 1943. To make way for the
German newcomers, these Ukrainians appear to have been moved on again,
this time to premises vacated by some of the last surviving Jews of Distrikt
Galizien. The arrival of ethnic Germans thus triggered in some instances a
chain reaction that accelerated the liquidation of ghettos and Jewish forced
labour camps.[73]

Meanwhile, the registration of *Deutschstämmige* in Distrikt Galizien had
been under way since autumn 1941. By January 1942, 23,000 persons of
'German ancestry' had been issued with provisional identity cards.[74] The
initial trawl was followed up from June 1942 onwards by a mobile EWZ
screening team with around 70 staff. By August 1943, out of a total number
of 30,000 people examined, 3,000 had been confirmed as *Volksdeutsche* and
just over 19,000 as *Deutschstämmige*.[75] Further screenings continued into 1944
and were still going on when orders came to evacuate the German population
westwards.[76]

In Distrikt Lublin, Germanization efforts from late 1940 onwards had
entailed setting up kindergartens alongside other welfare and educational
measures. The same process was repeated in Distrikt Galizien a year later; and,
since fuller records are available, its kindergarten programme there can be
analysed over a longer time span. In autumn 1941, as the registration of the
Deutschstämmige in Distrikt Galizien began, the NSV in its General Government guise of 'Arbeitsbereich NSDAP – Hauptarbeitsgebiet Volkswohlfahrt'
(HAG Volkswohlfahrt for short) launched a kindergarten programme there.[77]
As in Distrikt Lublin, the BDM were deployed in the early stages as 'pioneers'.
Ursula Graefe, a full-time BDM leader, Party member and qualified kindergarten teacher, was put in charge. Within five months she had overseen
the opening of four kindergartens and the planning of six others, all staffed
by BDM leaders on eastern assignments.[78] These kindergartens, like those
in Distrikt Lublin, began to figure in the pages of *Kolonistenbriefe*, whose
remit expanded in January 1942 to target the 'recovered' Germans of Distrikt
Galizien as well.[79] It reported, for example, the opening on 20 January
1942 of the German kindergarten in Żółkiew, a small town north of

Lwów/Lemberg. Two BDM leaders from the Reich had taken over the formerly Polish kindergarten there, advertised the new opening with posters around the town and visited ethnic Germans in their homes, urging them to send their children along: about twenty children arrived on the first day.[80]

In spring 1942, the HAG Volkswohlfahrt appointed a new district kindergarten organizer, 27-year-old Herta Jeschonneck from Essen, a qualified kindergarten teacher and Party member since 1939.[81] She arrived in Lemberg in May 1942 and set about staffing existing kindergartens with NSV personnel from the Reich, recruiting additional local ethnic German helpers, and opening new facilities.[82] Over the following eighteen months she achieved a modest expansion: by September 1942, ten kindergartens were in operation, catering for nearly 400 children.[83] Further expansion followed the influx of ethnic German refugees from the East in spring and summer 1943. By August 1943 twenty-nine kindergartens were operating with 1,200 children attending, and a further fifteen opened by the end of November that year.[84]

Jeschonneck and her colleagues in Lemberg wanted to put responsibility for running kindergartens in the hands of qualified personnel from the Reich, helped by the less qualified and the ethnic Germans. The assumption of the superior competence of Reich Germans was a given. As one organizer put it, 'we can make good use of the ethnic German girls across the board as assistants'; she added that if they proved 'sufficiently self-reliant' they could be put in charge of kindergartens in smaller villages.[85] In the event, out of seventeen kindergartens operating in January 1943 only eight were headed by fully qualified staff from the Reich; the other *Kindergartenleiterinnen*, four Reich Germans and five ethnic Germans, had only completed preliminary training.[86] The women heading kindergartens were young, usually in their early twenties, and their assistants even younger. An age breakdown shows that out of seven Reich German *Kindergartenleiterinnen* whose date of birth is known, six were born between 1920 and 1922; of ten kindergarten assistants whose ages are known, eight were born after 1923. The youngest kindergarten assistant, appointed in 1944, was only 15 years old.[87]

Songs, games and make-believe: community-building in Distrikt Galizien

The detailed monthly reports sent to Jeschonneck in Lemberg by the kindergarten teachers from their villages across Distrikt Galizien provide insights into the typical routines involved in equipping kindergartens and the methods used to inculcate German ways into the pupils and their parents. As elsewhere

where schools and kindergartens were set up in occupied Poland, premises
were found and if necessary confiscated from their owners; furniture, kitchen
equipment and heating fuel had to be purchased or 'organized'; medical
inspections had to be set up, preferably employing a German rather than
Polish or Ukrainian doctor. As elsewhere, the kindergarten teachers were
expected to operate in very basic conditions, often isolated, without transport,
electricity, running water or radio. They encountered extremes of rural
poverty, illiteracy, poor hygiene and ill health that some found shocking.
'However poor the people in the Reich may be, surely one rarely sees such dirt
as I have seen on my visits,' remarked the kindergarten teacher in Żółkiew
in March 1943 after a round of home visits.[88] Many reports portrayed ill-
nourished, lice-infested children who failed to appear at kindergarten in the
winter because they had no winter clothes or shoes.

Such evident neediness appears to have heightened the kindergarten
teachers' sense of working against the odds, engaged in a righteous struggle
– sometimes against hostile officialdom – to provide for 'their' children. In
their monthly reports, they chronicled their encounters with the RKF officials
overseeing the Germanization process in the localities: the so-called village
leaders or settlement leaders (*Dorfführer*, *Siedlungsführer*, *Hauptdorfführer*)
and the representatives of the *Volksdeutsche Mittelstelle*, all of whom concerned themselves with monitoring and mobilizing the newly placed settlers
and the newly 'trawled' *Deutschstämmige*.[89] Most mentioned the local RKF
officials only in order to complain about the latter's failure to organize repairs
or obtain requested items for the kindergarten. Such reports came in from
kindergarten teachers across the district, ranging from Dornfeld: 'I don't get
on at all with the Vomi (*Hauptdorfführer*)'; to Josefsberg: 'I have often quar-
relled with the *Dorfführer* and the agricultural officer about the kindergarten';
and Brigidau: 'all pleas to the *Dorfführer* to deal with problems fell on deaf
ears'. By contrast, the kindergarten teacher in Machliniec praised the helpfulness of a fatherly *Dorfführer*; she found his immediate superior more
obstructive, though after she complained to more senior SS officers the
troublesome *Siedlungsführer* was transferred elsewhere.[90]

Besides recording their frustrations and conflicts with male officialdom, the
kindergarten teachers used their reports to recount their achievements,
whether these entailed scrubbing and delousing their pupils, distributing cod
liver oil and vitamin C tablets or monitoring the children's weight gain, teaching them German songs and games and introducing them to gymnastics.[91] At
the same time, they recounted how they turned their kindergartens into a
setting for Nazi ceremonial. The tenth anniversary of the Nazi takeover of
power was celebrated, by order from General Government headquarters in

Cracow, on 30 January 1943: in Stanislau, the kindergarten children sang the
Horst Wessel song and 'Deutschland, Deutschland über alles' and each was
given a small flag to take home; in Sambor, Ursula Graefe used the occasion
to 'talk about Hitler and look at the book *The Führer in his Homeland*.[92] On
9 November 1943, commemorating the 'fallen' of the Nazi movement, the
kindergarten teacher in Stryj gathered children ranging in age from two and
a half to eleven for a ceremony:

> The portrait of the Führer stood on the table, framed with flowers and
> flags. On each side a boy stood with a flag. We sat in a semicircle facing
> them. First we sang 'Singend wollen wir marschieren'. I explained to the
> children the significance of the day and showed them pictures from the life
> of the Führer. At the end we sang the Deutschlandlied. Then we served
> cake and coffee.[93]

Such ceremonies were also occasions to draw the children's parents into more
general celebrations of German solidarity. Adult villagers were expected to
play at most a passive role, listening, applauding, and consuming refreshments.
Designing events along these lines was all the more necessary since the kindergarten teachers were confronted with parents, particularly the *Deutschstämmige*, with whom they could often scarcely communicate. The teachers'
reports mentioned few individual encounters with local Germans, and
Jeschonneck observed that 'most kindergarten teachers have a certain reluctance about making home visits'.[94] Instead, they played up in their reports the
contacts with the population that took the form of events involving ethnic
German adults as a group and entailing more spectacle than participation.

Kindergarten organizers had great ambitions to orchestrate Christmas for
the ethnic Germans in the General Government along National Socialist lines:
this meant playing down Christian content and replacing the traditional
message of peace with tougher slogans. At the training course for kindergarten
teachers in November 1943, Jeschonneck gave her staff precise instructions:
Christian symbolism was to be muted, while runes, pagan symbols and references to nature were to be in the foreground.[95] The kindergarten teachers were
told to submit their Christmas plans to the kindergartens department in
Cracow beforehand and to report on the events afterwards.[96] Those reports
suggested that some followed Jeschonneck's guidelines, though Jeschonneck
was put out to discover that not all had. She commented that some 'found it
difficult to let go of the Christmas festivities of the past and align themselves
with us wholeheartedly'.[97] From the kindergarten teachers' reports, the celebrations come across as a strange mixture of pagan and militaristic elements

with touches of pantomime and an occasional note of Christianity. In Brigidau, a BDM girl dressed up for the children as 'Knight Ruprecht' of traditional folklore.[98] In Machliniec, the parents of the kindergarten children sang 'Silent Night', were invited to ponder the meaning of the Advent wreath and treated to a reading on 'A Soldier's Christmas at the Front'. In Oblisku, the kindergarten teacher included a Nazi carol on the children's party programme and told the children 'about the winter solstice, about the Führer and the soldiers'; the party ended with a lullaby and 'a greeting to the Führer'.[99]

In these and other reports, the kindergarten teachers presented themselves as producing and starring in a Christmas programme in which the ethnic German adults and children were assigned the role of appreciative audience. To gauge from the reports, audience reactions varied. At the Christmas party for *deutschstämmige* mothers in Lubaczow, the language barrier proved insuperable: the mothers knew no German carols and could not follow the kindergarten teacher's speech.[100] Some kindergarten teachers, however, had no doubts about having dazzled their clientele. Elfriede I. from Schleswig-Holstein, for instance, described the Christmas party she had organized for thirty-eight mothers in Dornfeld. Following welcoming speeches,

> biscuits were nibbled and recipes given out and semolina pudding eaten, the women were delighted. Then at the end Santa Claus arrived and gave out the presents that we had wrapped individually for the children, the women really came out of themselves then. Santa Claus a 22-year-old SS man from the next village was really excellent in his role. . . . This Christmas celebration was a great experience for all these people, they haven't been able to celebrate Christmas for so long. And for me too it was an experience, because the mothers and children were much more excited than in the Reich, they didn't know what to expect.[101]

The reports on Christmas parties confirmed that kindergarten teachers tended to infantilize ethnic German adults and to regard the whole village as a kindergarten. Perceived as being 'backward', cut off from the mainstream of Reich German culture or hindered by their lack of fluency in the language, ethnic Germans could conveniently be treated by the teachers just like their pupils: easily cheered by sweets, puddings, candlelight and carol-singing. The ethnic German parents may have willingly played their part in the make-believe of 'Christmas in the new German homeland', and their motives for doing so are understandable. What they actually thought about their situation and prospects at Christmas 1943 is harder to fathom.

*Naïve or indifferent witnesses? Kindergarten
teachers and the fate of the Jews in
Distrikt Galizien*

Distrikt Galizien was at the time of the Nazi invasion the site of one of the highest concentrations of Jewish population in eastern Europe. It became correspondingly one of the major centres of the Nazi persecution and murder of the Jews, who were either killed in the locality by the security police and their auxiliaries or transported to the extermination camp at Bełżec on the border between Distrikt Galizien and Distrikt Lublin. The civilian administration was closely involved in selecting victims and preparing deportations, and knowledge of the fate of those deported appears to have spread quickly in spring 1942 among the surviving Jews, among the Germans in the administration and among the general public.[102]

Before looking at how far the deportation and murder of the Jews and the appropriation of their property were mentioned by the kindergarten teachers in their reports, it is necessary to recall how many of them had arrived in the district during the main phase of the killing programme. Those who were working in Distrikt Galizien from spring 1942 onwards had arrived as the deportations to Bełżec reached their first peak.[103] A proportion of the Jews who were defined as fit for work were held back from deportation in 1942; they were confined to ghettos and forced labour camps.[104] In autumn and winter 1942–3, these Jewish workers began to be arrested and murdered: some were shot in the locality, some deported to extermination camps. Pohl estimates that by the beginning of 1943, two-thirds of the original Jewish population of eastern Galicia had been killed; the rest, around 161,000, were still living in the district.[105] During the first half of 1943, the remaining ghettos in the district were destroyed and their inhabitants killed. Many were shot locally, the killings in some cases scarcely hidden from public view.[106] This phase of the genocide coincided with the arrival of ethnic Germans fleeing the Soviet advance on the eastern front from spring 1943 onwards and the expulsions of Polish and Ukrainian farming families to make way for their resettlement in the district. After the clearance of the last ghettos by the end of June 1943, the number of Jews surviving in Distrikt Galizien had fallen to 20,000: these Jews were living in forced labour camps. The women who were working in kindergartens in the district in the period between the end of 1941 and the end of June 1943 – around thirty staff, including Reich Germans and ethnic Germans – could have witnessed or heard at the time about deportations and acts of violence against the Jews taking place close at hand. This is less likely to have been the case for those appointed later.

From their reports, it is impossible to tell what the kindergarten teachers saw or heard of persecution, deportations and killings, and still less what they thought. The reports rarely mentioned Jews at all, and when they did the references were fleeting. The BDM leader who, describing in the *Kolonistenbriefe* how she and a colleague set up the German kindergarten in Żółkiew, was unusual in even mentioning seeing Jews on the streets:

> We were a little worried when we saw only Jews (*nur lauter Juden*) standing in front of our nice red posters: '*Volksdeutsche*, send your children to the German kindergarten. Starting on Monday 20 January!' Lore had visited all the parents, but whether the children would come – after all what with 20 degrees outside and a sleigh ride of 2 km out to Lemberger Straße 48. . . .[107]

The report went on to note that the *Volksdeutsche* had seen the poster as well, and that the kindergarten was well attended when it opened. But several things here are striking: the writer's surprise that anyone apart from the ethnic Germans might see and read the poster; the brevity of the reference to the Jews, and the speed with which the report moves on to other matters. The thought that the Jews in January 1942 had good reason to read German posters carefully is something that occurs immediately to today's reader, but there is no way of knowing what may or may not have crossed her mind. Nor is it possible to tell whether she learned that a few weeks later, in mid-March 1942, 700 Jews were deported from Żółkiew to their deaths in Bełżec.[108]

A similarly brief comment, in this case indicating the existence of Jews and a 'Jewish quarter' in the town of Sambor, was made in a report by Ursula Graefe, who after her original assignment in late 1941 stayed on as kindergarten teacher in Sambor and organizer for Kreis Drohobycz. In December 1942 she reported that her handbag, containing money, ration cards, passport, NSDAP and BDM membership cards, had been stolen as she waited in the left luggage queue at Sambor station. Writing to Herta Jeschonneck about the incident, she professed to know where her papers had got to: 'I'm certain that my passport is being sold right now in the Jewish quarter for some fantastic price.' The ghetto in Sambor was still in existence in spring 1943: the Jews surviving there were killed over a period of three days in May 1943 by security police.[109]

Some references to the Jews were concerned with the delays to the repair and renovation of kindergarten premises caused by the deportation and murder of Jewish tradesmen. The kindergarten teacher in Grodek, reporting

on the month of January 1943, remarked that 'they have finally sent the stove-
fitter, but there are no workers available to assist him, the Jews were got rid
of (*weggeschafft*) on Tuesday 26th, and until the labour office sends people
another few days will go by'.[110] Similarly casual were Herta Jeschonneck's
remarks in her report on the whole district for the month of May 1943. The
renovation of the kindergartens was delayed, she noted, both in Lemberg and
in Stryj. 'Since the firms carrying out the work use Jewish tradesmen and
labourers, who at short intervals keep going away (*die in kurzen Abständen
immer wieder fortkommen*), the work keeps getting interrupted and not
finished on time', was her comment on Lemberg. In relation to Stryj, she
observed that 'completion of the renovation works is very slow because it is
always being interrupted by the workers (Jews) dropping out'.[111]

More frequently, kindergarten teachers and organizers mentioned quite
straightforwardly how they had got hold of items taken from the Jews in order
to equip 'their' kindergarten and supply the needs of 'their' ethnic Germans.
Such actions were in line with the instructions issued in summer 1942 by
Friedrich Katzmann, SS and Police Leader in Distrikt Galizien from 1941 to
1943, that clothing belonging to murdered Jews and household goods removed
from their vacated dwellings should be distributed via the Volksdeutsche
Mittelstelle and the NSV to the ethnic Germans of the district.[112] A local NSV
official in Złochów reported in December 1942 that 'furniture and also items
of clothing from confiscated former Jewish property have been distributed to
the neediest ethnic Germans'.[113] Herta Jeschonneck complained in September
that none of the kindergartens were adequately supplied with textiles, except
in Stanislau where she had obtained for the kindergarten 'hand towels confiscated in the *Judenaktion*, some of them already worn out'.[114] Gerda Hoseur,
a Kreis kindergarten organizer, noted on an inspection visit to the kindergarten
in Żółkiew in January 1944 that 'the rooms of the kindergarten teacher and
her assistant are still equipped with Jewish furniture', suggesting it was time
this was replaced.[115]

A number of reports by kindergarten teachers give the impression that
acquiring Jewish property involved minimal bureaucracy: the young women
could take the initiative themselves to find what they needed. The kindergarten teacher in Grodek who had noted in her January 1943 report her problems getting the stove repaired wrote a month later that a solution had been
found: 'Last week I went with the stove-tiler to the ghetto, we had permission
to select two tiled stoves, they will be transported to the kindergarten and set
up there.'[116] The kindergarten teacher in Machliniec, praised by a visiting
organizer for her tireless searching out of opportunities to equip and supply
her kindergarten, stated simply in her report for August 1943 that what she

needed, she confiscated. Among various items she had 'organized' was a doll's pram ('I found that in the ghetto').[117] Two kindergarten teachers working in different villages near Drohobycz in summer 1943 mentioned getting goods from a depot of Jewish goods set up in the synagogue there. Ruth A., working in Ugartsberg from June 1943, first described getting the house she wanted confiscated on her behalf by the *Dorfführer*; she then set about equipping it from supplies of confiscated Jewish goods: 'We fetched the items of inventory that we lacked and the crockery from the synagogue in Drohobycz'.[118] Another kindergarten teacher, working in Mindorf, noted that 'I would like to start soon with cooking but I have no big saucepans I think that there will soon again be some to be got from the Jewish church in Drohobycz'.[119] In the Dornfeld kindergarten, some of the cutlery had been obtained from 'Jewish supplies' (*aus Judenbeständen*), as the kindergarten teacher there recounted:

Recently we had an amusing incident in the kindergarten. We have two sorts of spoons, aluminium ones from the Lemberg office and brass ones from Jewish supplies. We are sitting at table, have our soup in our bowls and have sung our mealtime song. Little Alexander, three years old, doesn't touch his spoon or his soup, so I say, come on now Alexander, eat up. He says: I want a Germany-spoon – he means the shiny aluminium spoon.[120]

The kindergarten teachers' accounts shed some revealing light on the climate of occupation rule in Distrikt Galizien. The casual way in which the kindergarten teachers talked about property confiscated from the Jews suggested that obtaining such items was an everyday occurrence, one which merited little comment. Indeed, in terms of the gravity of crimes committed against the Jews, theft was low down the scale; moreover, the act of taking, with a permit, items from deserted houses or stockpiles kept in a synagogue was probably felt to be not theft or plunder but a normal, everyday and 'legal' act. The acts of violence and terror involved in the confinement, enslavement and finally murder of the Jews remain outside the picture of everyday life and work as portrayed in the kindergarten teachers' accounts; nevertheless, those actions were the necessary condition for some of the triumphs of organization and improvisation that they were proud to report. This does not make the kindergarten teachers and organizers into perpetrators in the sense of persons who were directly or indirectly involved in the policies of selection, deportation and murder.[121] Their involvement was restricted to their appropriation of confiscated property: they knew the provenance of the property, even if one cannot be certain that they knew the fate of its rightful owners. This was a

pattern that corresponded to a gendered division of labour here as elsewhere
in the Nazi-occupied East. The tasks of selecting, rounding up, deporting and
killing were carried out only by men. Women were involved in utilizing the
goods taken from the victims, a procedure they sought to legitimize with reference to the neediness of the ethnic Germans. Whether they were simply
naïve, or just indifferent, about what might have happened to the original
owners of the doll's pram, the cooking pots, crockery and brass spoons, is
impossible to tell.

Ethnic boundaries and loyalties in Distrikt Galizien: from 'consolidation' to retreat

As elsewhere in occupied Poland, kindergartens in Distrikt Galizien were
intended to 'consolidate Germandom' in a situation where boundaries between
Germans and non-Germans were fluid and unstable, and differences between
various categories of Germans were marked. In Distrikt Galizien, a latecomer
to the Germanization programme, the process of classifying and 'consolidating' was particularly confused. Gradations of Germanness were constantly
under scrutiny as kindergarten teachers tried to make sense of the ethnic
boundaries drawn by the SS screening process, and Reich Germans in positions of authority monitored the behaviour of ethnic German staff to check
their suitability as agents of Germanization. Issues of ancestry and 'blood'
might have counted in the screening process, but in 1943–4 it was the demonstration of loyalty to the German cause that became an increasingly crucial
measure of Germanness. The question posed itself ever more sharply: of what
value had 'consolidation' measures been in creating solidarity among the
Germans and securing the German presence against external threat?

In the autumn and winter 1943–4, kindergarten teachers witnessed the
screening teams of the EWZ pass through their villages, overturning in some
cases the decisions on persons graded in an earlier trawl as *Deutschstämmige*.
Children who had been coaxed along to kindergarten to learn German ways
were now unceremoniously thrown out. 'A number of children have had to be
barred from attending kindergarten because their parents have fallen back
into *Polentum* as a result of the renewed screening,' commented Jeschonneck
in February 1944, noting that the kindergarten teachers were upset at seeing
their pupils go.[122] Other reports described the impact of the screening procedures on the 'winners': the kindergarten teacher in Gelsendorf recounted how
a five-year-old boy had told her proudly: 'Now we are proper Germans, we
have got an identity card and we can go to Germany now': her response to

this, she reported, had been to 'explain how naturalization worked', presumably to dampen the child's expectations.[123]

Witnessing the screening teams pass through their localities may have encouraged kindergarten teachers to frame judgements of their own, coloured by Nazi notions of 'blood' and ancestry, on the Germanness of the people they encountered. As far as the kindergarten teacher in Boryslaw was concerned, the good news was that the children were all 'clean' and that 'most are blond and blue-eyed': however, she went on, 'unfortunately only two of them speak any German'.[124] A district kindergarten organizer described ethnic German families from the Soviet Union who had been resettled in the village of Nowe Siolo: 'The families there and above all the children are not so absolutely German as the population of the other villages of Russian Germans, first of all purely in terms of blood and then in terms of their outlook. It is extremely difficult to make contact with the people in this village, some of whom speak no German at all. Still, the screening programme undertaken by the "Vo-Mi" will clarify these matters in the foreseeable future.'[125] The kindergarten teacher in Grodek, an ethnic German herself, described the German families she had visited in her village: 'Of the 17 families I visited, three of the mothers and two of the fathers speak German. But they seem to be descended from good Swabians.'[126] The kindergarten teacher in Rawa Ruska reported in January 1944 that some families were refusing to send their children to the kindergarten: 'These are cases where the mother is Polish, the father *volksdeutsch*. I reported these cases to the Volksdeutsche Mittelstelle.'[127]

Conformity to norms of Germanness was also policed within the ranks of the kindergarten teachers. The tension between Reich Germans and ethnic Germans over their relative status comes through the reports clearly. A number of Reich Germans criticized the work discipline, pedagogical efficiency and linguistic competence of their ethnic German colleagues and subordinates, who were locals from eastern Galicia or incomers from Ukraine, the Caucasus or Romania. One organizer commented on an ethnic German kindergarten helper Helene S., who after two years working in the kindergarten in Grodek had acquired full German nationality. Now promoted to the status of 'Reich German, Helene S. was reported to be 'still speaking Polish and mixing with Poles' while demanding a pay rise in line with her new nationality status.[128] Ursula Graefe, who was working from late 1942 in Sambor, criticized other Reich German kindergarten teachers for being arrogant towards their ethnic German colleagues,[129] but herself complained that the kindergarten children were learning faulty German from her ethnic German assistants.[130] The Reich German kindergarten teacher in Żółkiew, another BDM leader, complained in January 1943 that her *volksdeutsch*

assistant Steffi F. was intimidating the kindergarten children with her unenlightened approach to discipline (Steffi F. had allegedly threatened to lock
disobedient children in the lavatory).[131] Ethnic Germans, too, were ready to
criticize fellow ethnic Germans for not coming up to scratch. The ethnic
German *Kindergartenleiterin* in Grodek wrote an outraged report about her
ethnic German cook, who had recently been granted the green identity card
giving her the status of a *Volksdeutsche*, but who in the eyes of her boss was
already letting the German side down by selling her ration cards to Poles. 'I
wanted to go to the mayor to get him to take away her identity card but I am
ashamed to tell him that we have such Germans in the kindergarten and I
would rather that the kindergarten department do something about it'.[132] By
contrast, the ethnic German kindergarten teacher in Slawitz responded
sharply to what she saw as constant carping at the ethnic Germans. Having
been reprimanded by Jeschonneck in January 1944 for not running her kindergarten properly, failing to enforce attendance and allowing Polish to be spoken
there,[133] Gertrud G. argued that 'the VD [*Volksdeutsche*] have never done anything wrong and are always treated differently'. No kindergarten in the
Kolomea area, she wrote, was being run properly; kindergarten teachers, she
alleged, were frequently failing to turn up for work, but it was only the ethnic
German staff who were singled out for criticism.[134]

From summer 1943 onwards the threats to areas of German settlement
from partisans grew, with an upsurge of activity initially in summer 1943 in
the Kolomea area followed by more widespread threats to German villages
across the district in winter 1943–4. The kindergarten teachers, who were
exhorted at their training course in November 1943 to assume the correct attitude in face of military setbacks, reacted in a variety of ways to the deterio-
rating security situation.[135] Some admitted feeling nervous both in their living
quarters following attempted break-ins and when out on home visits.[136] Some
described the growing security measures, one mentioning that the police ('our
friend and helper') had set up quarters on the kindergarten premises.[137]
One or two clearly wanted to pack their bags: the kindergarten teacher in
Reichenbach, for example, was rebuked in April 1944 by Jeschonneck for
having closed the kindergarten down on her own initiative and was ordered
to open it again immediately.[138]

By contrast, others toughed it out, belittling the dangers while ridiculing
the fears of the ethnic German villagers and the ethnic German staff.
Genuine Germans, they implied, would stay at their posts even if some of the
ethnic Germans lost their nerve. In November 1943, the kindergarten teacher
in Kranzberg, a village near Sambor, complained that her two ethnic German
assistants were trying to get out of working at the kindergarten 'out of fear

of the partisans', who had attacked a property a couple of miles away the previous week; the villagers too, she reported, had become anxious and were
pleading with her to remove the NSV sign from the kindergarten that advertised all too clearly that Kranzberg was a German village.[139] In Rawa Ruska,
the Reich German kindergarten teacher Martha G. reported in March 1944
that her ethnic German assistant Eugenie P. had absconded, taking bed
linen with her and referring to the danger from partisans. Martha G., who
was having none of this, reported the woman to the police for theft. Once
arrested, Eugenie P. was stripped of her German identity card 'on grounds of
unworthiness'.[140]

In March 1944 the evacuation of Distrikt Galizien began, though the Soviet
conquest of the territory took several months.[141] In the area around Sambor
an order to evacuate was issued in March but the German kindergarten in
Sambor was back in action in June; that same month, however, the HAG
Volkswohlfahrt in Lemberg reported that all its facilities in Stryj, south-east
of Sambor, were 'lost'.[142] By mid-September 1944, all German kindergartens
in the General Government had closed and kindergarten staff from the Reich
were being ordered back to their home Gau for further duties.[143]

Up to the final phase of the occupation of eastern Galicia, most kindergarten teachers appear to have fulfilled their role as propagandists and self-
styled models of 'German fortitude'. It was reported in January 1944 that some
of the kindergarten teachers had turned down the Lemberg administration's
offer to get their personal belongings sent to Cracow as a precaution.[144] While
the Reichenbach kindergarten teacher was admonished for closing the kindergarten too soon, another disobeyed orders in March 1944 to 'leave her post'.[145]
Those who sought to 'hold out' may have believed that they were acting, in
the face of the 'Bolshevik danger' in the best interests of the ethnic Germans.
Whether the ethnic Germans saw things the same way is another question.
In one telling account, the kindergarten teacher in Kamionka Strumilova
described what happened on 22 March 1944, the day when the order to
evacuate was given and the villagers were told to assemble for departure in
goods trucks. While all the resettled ethnic Germans from the Soviet Union
appeared as instructed, most of the *Deutschstämmige* failed to turn up: when
the kindergarten teacher rushed round to their houses to persuade them to
pack and leave, she was confronted by refusals: some insisted that the
Russians would do them no harm. She commented: 'At any rate one realized
clearly once again that these people, at such a moment, have not yet achieved
the "right" fusion with Germandom after all.'[146] Nevertheless, her report
ended on a positive note. On the rail transport westwards with the ethnic
Germans who had obeyed the evacuation order, she had managed to secure

heating for the goods trucks and seen to the needs of the women and the children. After this, she noted, she had reported in Cracow for a new assignment: remaining part of the Nazi apparatus, and seemingly driven by her sense of duty and her 'womanly' attention to others' needs.

In their reports, kindergarten teachers often referred to their determination to prove themselves professionally and personally, and their pleasure at being given responsibility. They were, it seemed, often ready to devote great energy and effort to 'their' kindergarten — and this included a drive to get hold of and use for 'their' children the property of deported Jews. Their participation in this act of institutionalized plunder was legitimized for them by the 'higher cause' of aiding the ethnic Germans. Those kindergarten teachers who were working in Distrikt Galizien at the time of the deportation and murder of the Jews recorded little trace of these events in their reports: only occasional scattered references indicate that the Jews were noticed at all. What took up the foreground of the reports, and probably most of the attention of the kindergarten teachers, was the 'normal' daily routine in the German kindergarten, from which all non-German children were banished and in which children labelled 'German' could eat from spoons 'from Jewish stocks'.[147]

The kindergarten teachers were implicated in the criminal acts of the occupation regime, even if the level of their involvement was minor compared to other, mainly male members of the occupation apparatus. The division of labour between German men and women nevertheless produced what one could term specifically 'feminine' forms of complicity which arise out of the gender-specific tasks and duties assigned to women. Thus their involvement in the use and distribution of Jewish property arose out of their obligation to supply 'their' kindergarten with furniture, toys and textiles. At the same time, through their efforts dedicated to the education of ethnic German children, the kindergarten teachers helped to 'consolidate Germandom' at the expense of those classified as non-German, and possibly also combat demoralization and disaffection among some, if not all of the ethnic Germans. This, too, was a 'feminine' contribution to the stabilization of the occupation regime.

Chapter 9

___

Building on the Volcano: Training Village Advisers in Kreis Zamosc

On 1 December 1943, a group of Nazi dignitaries accompanied by journalists drove with difficulty along muddy lanes to a formerly Polish manor house in Sitno, 7 kilometres to the north-east of the town of Zamość in Distrikt Lublin (see map 7). For the final stretch, they were forced to abandon their cars and climb on to horse-drawn wagons. They were attending the opening ceremony of a school for women village advisers (*Dorfberaterinnen*) run by the Nazi women's organization in the General Government. The official invitations highlighted the pioneering character of the school, 'the first of its kind in the General Government and in the Greater German Reich as a whole'.[1] Its mission was described as providing all-round training for the village advisers, who, like the *Ansiedlerbetreuerinnen* in the annexed territories, were given the task of instructing and influencing settlers' wives on matters ranging from poultry-keeping and gardening to cooking and infant care. At the school, young women from the Altreich were to be trained in agriculture and horticulture, hygiene and nutrition; they were also to receive political training, so that they could give a political lead to the settlers and their families.[2]

Frieda Hagen (as she will be called here), the school director, a 29-year-old agricultural teacher from Thüringen, went unmentioned amid the roll-call of VIPs. However, since she kept a diary and some of her letters home have been preserved, the story of the short-lived school for village advisers can be reconstructed in some detail. What she wrote about her work at the time helps to shed further light on the resettlement programme launched by Globocnik in Kreis Zamosc, outlined in the previous chapter, which eventually displaced more than 100,000 Poles from 300 villages and turned the region into a major centre of partisan resistance to Nazi rule.[3] Frau Hagen's account shows how women were drawn into the effort to 'domesticate the frontier', but also to stabilize German settlements in the face of partisan attacks. It also documents her dilemmas: how she sought to reconcile her delight in her surroundings and her work with her ambivalence about the East and her sense of unease; how she tried to preserve her belief in Germany and the German cause while becoming increasingly outraged by the occupation regime and its Party and SS representatives; and how she carried on believing that her work was worthwhile when the military situation was turning her rural refuge into an outpost under siege.

'A German home for the East'

In summer 1942 Himmler had given the signal to Globocnik as SS leader in Distrikt Lublin to embark on creating an area of German settlement within the district (see above, Chapter 8). Following early 'experimental' clearances of Polish villages, in November 1942 a full-scale campaign was launched to evacuate Poles *en masse* from villages in Kreis Zamosc and in Kreis Bilgoraj that had been designated areas of German settlement. In their place, German settlers, mainly from Bessarabia, Croatia and Bosnia, were brought in as colonists, after often lengthy stays in resettler camps. As the evacuations proceeded, ever more Polish villagers vanished into the forests to join the partisan movement. The ethnic German settlers quickly found themselves exposed to partisan attacks, which in turn triggered vicious reprisals from the police.

Globocnik's order of 22 November 1942 detailing the operations necessary to create an area of German settlement in Kreis Zamosc had included plans for leading, organizing and supervising the ethnic Germans once resettled in the vacated Polish villages. 'NSV, Frauenschaft, HJ and BDM' were to be involved in the 'political and educational *Betreuung* of the settlers'.[4] Every group of villages was to have its complement of functionaries under overall SS leadership, and the functionaries were to include a female village adviser. 'Suitable' ethnic German women were also to be deployed at village level as advisers. The drive to put a female 'village helper' (*Dorfhelferin*) or 'village adviser' (*Dorfberaterin*) in every German settler village was the responsibility of the NS-Frauenschaft, or 'Hauptarbeitsgebiet Fraueneinsatz' as it was known in the General Government, and it was the 'Hauptarbeitsgebiet Fraueneinsatz' which at the beginning of 1943 appointed Frieda Hagen to train women for that task in a 'school for female village advisers' to be set up in Kreis Zamosc.

On arriving in Lublin in May 1943, Frau Hagen's initial impressions had been mixed: curiosity about Poland and delight at the 'really German' appearance of Lublin were mixed with alarm at the sinister presence of the SS, at the talk among colleagues of the suppression of the ghetto uprising in Warsaw and at rumours of the 'bandit threat'. The insecurity of the situation was clear, and made her worry all the more about her brother serving in the army ('I hope G. comes out of hospital back to the Reich'). After a week, sitting unhappily in a hotel room in Zamość, she wrote that she 'did not feel at home' and that the East seemed 'uncanny and threatening' (16 May 1943). Her worries seemed partly inspired by doubts about the task that awaited her. On her arrival in Lublin, she had written optimistically that 'The East is calling me to work, I can help German farmers again, help build up the settlement in Kreis Zamosc with all the resettlers from the different German *Sprachinseln* [German-speaking exclaves]' (8 May 1943). However, after days in an office in Zamość sorting through files and trying to ensure sufficient supplies of chicks for the settlers, she sounded less assured: 'The village advisers come with queries and now and then I hear about the settlers, the people for whom I have come here and who are still so remote from me. What am I doing here? If only I could be a village adviser and really help the settlers.' Having seen what was to be her new place of work, she was impressed but still concerned: 'On Wednesday we were in Sitno, where a big manor house is to be turned into a school for village advisers and for local farm women's leaders (*Ortsbäuerinnen*).[5] It is still completely empty; high, bright rooms with a beautiful view of the park where the lilac is blossoming and of the wide open eastern countryside (*das weite ostische Land*). Will I be able to feel happy here, will I be able to work properly here?' But the worries about work were accompanied by other causes for anxiety. In the same entry (16 May) she commented on the military situation, using her diary, as she did from time to time, to record events on the various fronts. Her thoughts at this point were on Africa: on 13 May the last German forces had surrendered in Tunisia, and German power in Africa, the focus and dream of Frau Hagen and her colleagues and students at the 'colonial women's school', had once again been broken: 'A year ago Tobruk was taken by Rommel, today we are giving up Africa' (16 May 1943). Germany's eastern European conquests scarcely looked more secure: this knowledge hung over Frau Hagen's assignment in Kreis Zamosc from the very outset. There was other knowledge that troubled her as well. She noted her shock at having seen, sitting at the same table as her the previous night, an SS man 'with such oversized hands that I was afraid to look at them; how many people has he already helped "resettle", he is said to be the "hangman" here' (16 May 1943). Within days of her arrival in Poland, the prospect of her productive work with farm women, gardening and raising livestock, was overshadowed by signs of the occupation regime's brutality.

A few days later, the mood of anxiety had given way to a new resolve: having received her confirmation from the 'Hauptarbeitsgebiet Fraueneinsatz'

in Cracow that she was now 'mistress of Sitno', Frau Hagen celebrated with
colleagues in Zamość, and wrote in her diary: '. . . the empty house is waiting
for me. I am glad, and also anxious, and I am – soon it'll all be with "eastern
calm" – going to let things happen' (19 May 1943). In a letter home written
on 30 May 1943, she reflected on the task ahead:

> I won't be staying long in the East, setting up the school appeals to me since
> I can learn so much from it, but I don't think they will allow me as a non-
> Party member to stay long as school director. Still, I don't want to come
> back to the Reich at the moment, I want to struggle through here (*ich will
> mich hier durchbeißen*), get to know the sort of people here and perhaps
> through this I will be all the more true to my Christian beliefs and value
> them more than I would if I were in the Reich.[6]

In the following months, Frau Hagen's diary recorded her commitment to creating the school while assisting the Bessarabian and Croatian German settlers
who had been transplanted to Kreis Zamosc as well as the indigenous
Deutschstämmige identified in Globocnik's earlier 'trawls for German blood'.
Working with the village advisers and with the ethnic Germans in the villages, she was inspired by a vision of German homes and gardens flourishing
in the East. She travelled round the villages, sharing her expertise on rural
housewifery from cooking and gardening to poultry-keeping. Writing in
her diary on 3 June 1943, she described enjoying a cookery session with
Bessarabian German women, noting that the women liked to cultivate rhubarb
as a flowering plant for their gardens but did not know the stalks were edible.
'I always feel as if I belong among these ordinary people – not among departments and offices making abstract plans – and it is from them I get back my
strength and belief in Germandom (*Glauben an das Deutschtum*).' A few
weeks later, Frau Hagen went with two colleagues to visit a woman settler in
Golkie, where they admired 'the beginning of an ideal German peasant
garden' (22 June 1943). At the same time she set about creating – in the form
of the school itself – the model of such a household and garden. By late
summer a core of staff and helpers was assembling, by October furniture was
being delivered and in mid-November the first students arrived – a cohort of
seventeen young women – to begin training as village advisers. Following the
grand opening with its attendant dignitaries on 1 December 1943, Frau Hagen
looked back at the preparations:

> It is Sunday. All the girls have gone to invite the farmers' wives to the
> course in baking – after weeks a quiet day – the advent wreath hangs in
> the entrance hall as a foretaste of Christmas. Our house is finished, really

finished after such long preparations. I could hardly believe it when I walked with V. on 30 November in the evening through all the rooms and brought flowers and mats for the tables. Long work days lay behind us, we were sewing cushions for the chairs into the night, scrubbing and cleaning. The day before the opening 10 geese arrived from Lublin and our plans had been for pea soup – now we had to organize cutlery in Zamosc and pots and pans – but we managed it.... Frl. Aldinger is satisfied and I am full of heartfelt gratitude and glad that things have gone well and a really German home for the East has been created: may all the people who come be happy and feel comfortable here. (5 December 1943)

Creating 'a really German home for the East' was a matter of professional pride: restoring order to the house and garden displayed Frau Hagen's mastery of rural household management. At the same time, Sitno also promised to help realize the grander scheme of colonizing the East: it had its part to play in the 'new homeland', the idea at the heart of ruralizing propaganda about the German East and of the promise held out to the ethnic German settlers whom the village advisers were employed to instruct and support. Despite the warning signs that were accumulating in 1943, Frau Hagen still held to this vision of colonizing the East with a German peasantry gathered from far-flung corners of Europe. It corresponded to her love of rural life and her dreams of the land and opportunities once represented by Africa. In working with the ethnic German villagers to construct a rural homeland in the East, she was fulfilling a mission for which her training had prepared her and which she supported personally. Her professional pride and her identification with an ideal of Germany and Germanness also meant that she saw herself as having to protect the ethnic Germans against what she considered the irresponsibility of the occupation authorities.

Protecting the ethnic Germans

The 'German' population of the villages designated for German settlement in Kreis Zamosc was made up partly of *Deutschstämmige*, or *'Stammdeutsche'* as they were also known: these were the indigenous residents of the district who had – often under pressure – been categorized as being of German descent even if they had 'lost touch with' their alleged German roots and the German language. Alongside the *Stammdeutsche* were the resettled ethnic Germans, who were predominantly from Croatia, Bosnia and Bessarabia. For Frau Hagen, as for many other German women from the Reich working in the East, the resettlers were the object of sympathy and admiration, mixed with surprise or concern at the 'otherness' of their ways. While the *Stammdeutsche* seemed to her somewhat alien, not least because they tended to speak little German, and were reported not to be regarded as 'proper Germans' by the resettlers,[7] the resettlers from Bessarabia and Croatia often seemed to her like model Germans. She described them as hard-working and community-minded, particularly when compared with the 'irresponsibility' she saw among Reich Germans in Poland. Frau Hagen's affinity and sympathy with the settlers from Bessarabia were increased by the stories of the 'land flowing with milk and honey' that they had left behind as well as their memories of German pastors there.[8] After talking to a Croatian German who had told her of the good farms they had given up in Croatia, she wrote that

> the great sacrifice – and the great disappointment of the resettlers becomes clear to me. The Führer called them, and they came with such faith in their hearts. And now? It is not just the East and the primitive conditions that disappoint them, they take all that on, it is we Reich Germans who make promises and keep none of them. Why are the settlers treated as second-class people? Why aren't they given the necessary protection so that they can work in peace? The gentlemen in: (this is in ascending order) Lublin – Cracow – Berlin do not see the misery, and when they do come they are shown the good things, or they do not want to see – because they only think themselves of what they can bag (*hamstern*) for themselves. (8 June 1943)

This anger at the way the regime generally, and individual Reich German officials particularly, betrayed their promises to the ethnic Germans became a dominant motif in Frau Hagen's letters and diaries. To her it was 'shaming' that for settlers 'the Reich German has sunk from an ideal role model to a person for whom one has no respect' (3 July 1943). The situation, she felt, obliged her to try and redeem the image of the Reich Germans in the ethnic Germans' eyes.

These concerns seem to have been crystallized by the escalation of violence in the area and the regime's evident failure to protect the settlers. In one incident in Siedliska, a village not far from Sitno, twelve German settlers were killed, along with a kindergarten teacher, in a partisan raid on the night of 5–6 June 1943. This followed a German attack on the village of Sochy on 1 June, in which the German forces had set fire to the village and bombarded it from the air: 183 Polish villagers were killed on the spot and seven more died later.[9] In response to the destruction of Sochy, members of the

Polish Home Army (Armia Krajowa) attacked Siedliska.[10] The news of the raid on Siedliska travelled fast. On 6 June, Zygmunt Klukowski, a doctor in the town of Szczebrzeszyn in neighbouring Kreis Bilgoraj, recorded the raid in his diary:

> Today the village of Siedliska, near Zamosc, was burned down. In the past the inhabitants were mainly Orthodox, having their own nice church, a very well-organized parish, but in 1942 all were evacuated and German settlers took over. The assault on the village was coordinated by a unit of the Home Army in retaliation for the slaughter in Suchy [sic]. Several Germans were killed. From the village some livestock and produce were taken to supply the forest kitchen.[11]

In Sitno, 11 kilometres from the site of the attack, Frau Hagen was also recording the incident in her diary:

> Out of 47 houses 38 have been burned down and plundered. They took 3 horses and carts with them, loaded livestock on to them and food. The kindergarten teacher is dead, murdered with a bayonet, 12 settlers, women and children, and 3 Poles. The bandits surrounded the villages, held up the people with machine guns and were long gone when the German soldiers from Zamosc finally came to their aid. They took their own dead with them, they covered all their tracks, the hiding places in the woods and cornfields cannot be found. A note has been found saying that it is revenge because the Poles have so little to eat and are treated badly. In this way the innocent settlers have to suffer on account of a government that has not handled the Polish question correctly from the outset. We need the Poles as workers, but they must have clothing and food. A Pole is virtually forced to steal and to get food through the black market. In 1939/40 when only a few Germans were here and when justice prevailed there were no bandits. And now? If only one could change things, but the SS has the matter in its control and 'the SS and the Lord God are always right'.[12]

Klukowski saw that the attack on Siedliska was a direct response to the massacre in Sochy (or Suchy); Frau Hagen did not. On the other hand, it is notable that she immediately blamed the regime, and particularly the SS, for a policy of starving and impoverishing the Poles, thereby generally provoking the attack on settlers; in her view the regime then let the settlers down further by failing to provide aid in time. In taking this critical view of a policy that had unleashed massive Polish resistance, Frau Hagen was, though she was probably unaware of it, in agreement with criticisms increasingly levelled during the first half of 1943 by Hans Frank and others at

Globocnik and the RKF more generally in relation to resettlement policies in Distrikt Lublin.[13]

Frau Hagen's disillusion with the authorities was compounded by the way officialdom in Distrikt Lublin handled the funeral of the settlers on 9 June. She described the assembled crowd of around a thousand settlers from Siedliska and neighbouring villages waiting with anticipation for 'the Gruppenführer'. Who this was is not clear: Globocnik held the rank of SS-Gruppenführer, but it could have been General Willi Moser, the army commander in Distrikt Lublin (*Oberfeldkommandant*), who was a Gruppenführer in the SS, and who had been urged in May 1943 to reinforce the army units in Distrikt Lublin in order to combat the partisan danger.[14] For Frau Hagen, 'the Gruppenführer' held the key to reassuring the settlers: 'only he can now help, send in military and console them'. The ceremony, to her disgust, was staged as a political demonstration and consisted of an SS officer reading a speech full of clichés, the Hitler Youth singing one verse of 'Ich hatt' einen Kameraden', and a silent laying of wreaths by the Gruppenführer and other dignitaries. Frau Hagen's anger was fired by the crassness of the secular ceremony and by the apparent satisfaction on the faces of Polish workers filling in the mass grave, but most of all by the failure of the SS leaders to provide words of comfort or to undertake to protect the villagers better in future. This anger exploded into her diary entry:

> The cars drive off, heavily armed – for the settlers the day-to-day struggle for their lives goes on. Left without protection or rights at the mercy of the bandits. Why does no one do anything, why are the settlers left exposed and the Reichskom [RKF officials] carry on with no sense of responsibility. Isn't it like this in Russia? But we are Germans![15]

When the authorities did act, it was only with further vain efforts at 'pacification'. On 9 June (the day of the funeral) Klukowski noted in his diary that 'in retaliation for the attack on Siedlisko [*sic*] the Germans arrested most of the men in Wieprzyc and Szewnia. Some escaped into the forest and joined partisan groups. In this way the underground received more recruits.'[16] Later in June it was reported in the Polish underground press that – still as a reprisal for Siedliska – the Nazi authorities had undertaken wholesale expulsions in other villages nearby and that those expelled were transported in three goods trains to Majdanek.[17]

In the face of a situation in the southern part of Distrikt Lublin that was becoming ungovernable for the regime, the programme of systematic deportation of Poles for the purpose of German resettlement was abandoned in

July 1943.[18] Globocnik's career in Distrikt Lublin was soon to be over and his successor as SSPF Jakob Sporrenberg was appointed in July 1943; Sporrenberg took full command of the district a few weeks later.[19] Meanwhile, partisan activity continued, as did retaliation by the Germans.[20] In late July Frau Hagen remarked that '50 bandits' were rumoured to be in the next Polish village and that in neighbouring Kreis Bilgoraj the Kreishauptmann and the Kreis agricultural officer together with a secretary had been shot dead in their car 'in full daylight on the open road';[21] Klukowski noted the same incident, commenting that the driver, a man who had formerly worked for him as a driver, had also been shot.[22]

In this situation Frau Hagen saw her efforts to advise and instruct women settlers in housewifery as all the more important as a way of boosting their morale, distracting them from their anxieties, and showing them that she at least – as a Reich German – was not going to abandon them. Afer a cookery class in Laziska in late June 1943 she expressed the hope that 'perhaps in these few hours these women will really have forgotten their worries and their daily work, and the never-ending fear of the bandits as well, and will have gone home a little happier and with some new ways of cooking' (22 June 1943). Social events and ceremonies were intended – here as throughout the occupied East – to bind together the embattled German settlers. At the Christmas celebration in 1943, Frau Hagen and her students invited the women settlers to Sitno for a ceremony where candles were lit, carols sung, a puppet play performed, and Frau Hagen read a Christmas story by Walter Flex (12 December 1943). Frau Hagen's commitment to her rural base and 'her' settlers was matched by her sense of being a marginal figure in relation to the 'urbanites' of the 'Frauenein-satz' in Lublin and Cracow (13 June 1943). Following a training course in Cracow in August 1943 she remarked that she and the other agricultural teach-ers representing the farm women's section had been 'real outsiders', not least because they wore no uniform.[23] Sitno could represent an escape from towns thronged with uniformed Nazi officials flaunting their power and from types such as the wife of the commander of the security police (*Sicherheitspolizei*) in Lublin with her ostentatious leather coat. In the process, it seemed as if what she was seeking to construct was a rural niche in which she would work with women settlers, students and instructors while steering clear of the sort of rep-resentatives of the 'occupation society', both male and female, that she could not abide. It constituted a smaller world over which she did have some control. However, in its mission to create a protected niche and support network for German settlers, the world of Sitno could not ultimately be separated from, or be spared the consequences of, the Nazi drive to undermine and destroy Jewish and Polish life in Distrikt Lublin: this unsettling insight was something with which Frau Hagen was grappling from her arrival.

'One is not allowed to feel sympathy': the fate of the Jews and Poles

Arriving in Lublin in May 1943, all that Frau Hagen could witness of what had been its Jewish community were the remains of the ghetto, where she saw the cellars of Jewish houses being destroyed. She seemed intrigued by tales of 'illicit goods – even animals: rabbits, hens, cows!' that the Jews were supposed to have hidden while they lived there (see above, Chapter 5). That she soon became aware, if not in detail, of the fate of the Jews seems clear both from her comment, quoted earlier, about the 'hangman' she encountered at her table a week later in Zamość, and from a remark in a letter home on 30 May where she commented that some of the clothes distributed by the village advisers to the ethnic German settlers were 'dreadful, often still dirty, bloodstained from the ghetto and originating from Jews'.

Like the kindergarten teachers in Distrikt Galizien, the village advisers in Kreis Zamosc were regularly using and recycling what was left of Jewish property for German settlers. Himmler had instructed in October 1942 that the settlers in Lublin should be supplied at Christmas with clothing, suitcases and bedding taken from the 'warehouses in Lublin and Auschwitz'.[24] In Zamość, the so-called Siedlerwirtschaftsgemeinschaft (SWG), an organization run as a limited company (Globocnik was a shareholder) with more than 300 employees by late 1943, administered giant warehouses full of goods abandoned by deported Poles and Jews, ranging from furniture, crockery, agricultural tools and machinery to shoes and clothes.[25] A week before the grand opening of the school in December 1943, Frau Hagen noted that she had been 'racing around' in Zamość trying to obtain scarce goods: 'In the SWG we organize old saucepans from the ruined houses (*Schutthäusern*) and our wagon is full to bursting' (25 November 1943). Demolished houses were recycled too: soon after her arrival in Sitno, Frau Hagen and her colleagues were chopping 'old building timbers' taken from 'destroyed Jewish and Polish houses' for the stove (23 May 1943).

Apart from these comments, the fate of the Jews remained an absence in Frau Hagen's record of her time in Kreis Zamosc. The Poles, who in Globocnik's planning were the next target of exterminatory policies once the mass murder of the Jews had been carried out, figured much larger. This is perhaps not surprising given that it was at the height of the mass expulsions of Polish villagers to make way for German settlement and the upsurge in partisan activity that Frau Hagen took up her posting. It may also be because she had much more chance to observe Polish life and to get to know Poles, and had a clearer view of what their place in the German-colonized East should be. That said, her comments on the Poles were full of ambivalence: pity and sympathy alternated with irritation, but also with admiration and envy.

In some of her comments Frau Hagen expressed commonly held negative German stereotypes about Poland and the Poles. Poles were clever traders and got the better of the Germans, she complained in October 1943, frustrated in her efforts to organize supplies for the renovation of Sitno. 'This trading is awful and why can no one do anything about it?' (13 October 1943). Like so many other German observers of the Polish countryside, Frau Hagen saw Poland as a backward land with primitive agriculture, needing German management to modernize it and make it more productive. As she travelled to Lublin in May 1943, she glimpsed out of the train window 'tiny wooden houses with thatch (*Holzstrohhäuser*), ragged children, undernourished animals grazing on common meadows and by the wayside. Small field strips, one metre wide and arching up in the middle, with weeds and thinly sown, tell of undrained soil and the most primitive land cultivation' (8 May 1943). A few months later, driving through the Zamość countryside, she noticed 'small Polish villages with miserable houses – you can see where the settlers have been living for a while, it is more orderly, the gardens are fenced in and the children greet you with the German greeting [i.e. the Hitler salute]' (30 September 1943). But sometimes she found evidence that contradicted her preconceptions: on 1 May 1944, she noted that she had seen in Szopinek 'Polish farms which were very orderly and looked better than the settler farms – unfortunately'. And for all her enthusiasm for modern agricultural methods, she felt in one respect a powerful affinity with Polish ways of doing things: 'Poland is the land of horses. . . . Every Pole loves horses and the motor will never be able to take the place of horses here.' Having ventured to a Polish horse fair and haggled successfully in order to purchase a pair of horses and a wagon, Frau Hagen pronounced herself 'proud as a king' (2 November 1943).

In other ways too, Frau Hagen was fascinated and attracted by what she saw of Polish culture, sometimes contrasting what seemed to her to be the strengths of Polish nationhood to the weaknesses and flaws of the Germans. On arriving in Lublin in May 1943, she had gone to a small German Protestant church service where the congregation had been small; the same afternoon, she looked into the German Catholic church, where mass was well attended. But it was the Polish churches and their congregations that fascinated her most, causing her to conjure up in her diary a vision of Polish nationhood inspired by Catholic faith:

> The Poles fill their churches at every mass: the tall cathedral, the Dominican church with its ornate baroque altars are probably for all a refuge from poverty and misery. Here they all belong together and I believe that the Church represents a powerful force for its Polish members. A child with bare feet kneels next to a woman with a lot of makeup, a civil servant next to a mother with hungry eyes, wrapped in a big shawl. God is there for all of them and the Virgin Mary prays too for the Poles, all this allows them to forget oppression and hunger. (8 May 1943)

For Frau Hagen, who felt outraged by the Nazi destruction of religious feeling – as the outburst in her diary over the brusquely secular funeral at Siedliska a month later was to show – the way in which Poles, suffering 'oppression and hunger', had their national identity reinforced by Catholicism must have been all the more impressive. A year later, Frau Hagen was once again expressing envy and admiration for the Poles. Polish workers on the farm were celebrating a May festival:

> every other evening they sing a hymn of 28 verses, meanwhile they have a picture of the Virgin Mary on the table, 2 candles in front of it and green birch twigs behind it. . . . There is so much authentic spirit and national strength among Poles in the countryside that one could envy Poland for it. Today there was a smallpox vaccination and all the children here – such healthy, attractive and numerous children who have grown up in the most primitive surroundings. One could become envious and sad because our nation doesn't have this biological strength to the same degree any more. (15 May 1944)

In expressing this admiration for the 'biological strength' of the Poles, Frau Hagen was echoing a long-held view among German *Volkstum* campaigners that Polish motherhood was the foundation of Polish self-assertion against German domination.[26]

How did Frau Hagen reconcile her sympathy, admiration and fascination with aspects of Polish life and culture with her involvement in an occupation regime that subordinated and oppressed the Poles? Ultimately, it seems to me that she could not and that this fundamental contradiction underpinning her work in Sitno remained unresolved. It is true that she had a vision of how Germans and Poles would coexist in a German-dominated East, in which Germans would rule and manage and Poles would provide the essential labour and in return be treated decently. One model for how she thought this could work was the farm of the 'Spanish German' Herr T., who had acquired his farm in neighbouring Jaroslawiec in February 1943: in Frau Hagen's eyes, Herr T. was a good farmer, 'a man here at last who has his heart in the right place', and a good employer, whose Polish workers, she wrote, respected him. In June 1943 Frau Hagen provided a snapshot of the potential idyll of harmony and mutual respect between German employer and Polish workers when she attended, with Herr T., the wedding party of the daughter of one of his employees. First of all they drank a vodka at the bride's home, then the wedding party moved on to Herr T'.s house. 'The farm band, 3 fiddles and a drum struck up and people began dancing on the big open veranda'. However, even this brief idyll was destroyed by the arrival of uninvited guests: three SS men and their female companions, all of them drunk, who then had to be got rid of by Herr T. 'T. called them "locusts" – but what do the Polish workers say in the face of such "masters"?', she commented (14 June 1943). In her account of this incident, Frau Hagen encapsulated her view of the relationship of Germans and Poles in occupied Poland. The Germans had to earn the respect of the Poles through their hard work and efficiency and by demonstrating moral integrity. There were decent Germans who strove to create a viable relationship with the colonized population, but the regime, embodied above all in the SS, vandalized and destroyed the basis of such relationships, starving and oppressing the Poles and driving them – as she observed after the raid on Siedliska – to attack German villagers.

If Frau Hagen still strove to maintain in her mind this vision of a benign colonialism in which respect and decent treatment could integrate Poles as workers into a stable new order in the East, this thinking tended to steer around the knowledge that the German settlers in Kreis Zamosc had obtained their farms because the SS had prior to their arrival violently evicted the Polish owners and dispatched them, sometimes to work as forced labourers in the Reich, sometimes to their deaths in concentration camps. This was brought home very vividly to Frau Hagen in July 1943. It is at this point in her diary that she articulates the injustices perpetrated against the Poles most clearly. In doing so she expresses the deep contradiction of her position, without offering any resolution:

Since Wednesday things have been on full alert, campaigns against bandits, evacuation of Polish villages. The Poles are driven like animals through the town, to their left and right heavily armed police, men, children, women – often they are walking with difficulty and what awaits them in the crowded camps? But one is not allowed to have sympathy, one is supposed to think in national terms and one knows all the same that many innocents are among them. – In the empty villages the animals are wandering around and now Germans are going to be placed there by the Reichskommissar. (3 July 1943)

In showing kindness and respect to her Polish workers, who clearly regarded Frau Hagen with affection – in her diary for January 1944 is stuck a birthday card with greetings and wishes for a long life from her two Polish servants – Frau Hagen could still not ultimately solve the dilemma of believing in the colonizing project while finding the regime that was implementing it repugnant.

Putting on trousers and becoming a soldier

At New Year 1944, writing from a Christmas break back with her family 'in the Reich', Frau Hagen speculated on what the year would bring and wondered whether it would bring peace: she listed the military setbacks of the previous year 'from Stalingrad, to Africa, Italy's betrayal up to the great retreat in Russia. Stalingrad to Schitomir, 1200 km, already the front is nearing the Polish Reich [*sic*], but I cannot believe that our settlers will once again be overrun by war' (1 January 1944).

The following months found Frau Hagen working uninterruptedly in Sitno but increasingly aware that her project was doomed. No sooner had the first cohort of students settled into their course than a delegation appeared in February 1944 to review the function of the school in the light of the Soviet advance. One of its members was Dr Änne Sprengel, the original driving force behind appointing women settlement advisers in Pomerania in the Depression years (see above, Chapter 2). Just as Frau Hagen had created a 'home' in Sitno and had begun to feel at home there herself – as she had remarked in late January 1944 – it looked as if it was sure to be lost: the only question was when the signal to evacuate westwards would be given. Gradually, the function of Sitno changed: as the military situation worsened, students began to leave, the last in March 1944. Meanwhile, a unit of German and Ukrainian troops was quartered in the house. They were gone within a fortnight, but police were then stationed permanently to guard the house. In this situation, Frau Hagen seems to have reasoned that the harder she worked, the more she would maintain her sense of purpose and fend off thoughts that all the effort might be for nothing. As she wrote in her diary: 'Work leaves no time to think and that is good' (21 March 1944). If this was a pragmatic way of coping, there also seemed to be a dimension of patriotric optimism in this strategy of ceaseless effort: at some level she wanted to believe that hard work could even at this stage save the German cause. In the same entry, she reported a conversation with a settler couple from the village in March 1944, packing to leave:

> For a year, said Herr M., I have been building for the settlers, sheds for live-stock and houses, nothing was too much trouble, and now? But it is touch-ing that Frau M. says: look at all that you have done for us: getting furniture and tools, chicks, seeds, preserving jars – all that the Führer has done for us and now we have to give everything up for the sake of the Russians, I want to work, she went on, whether in a factory or working for a farmer in the fields – then we will win and everything will be all right again. – Yes, working, that is the best thing today.

As the sense of the military threat to Sitno grew, Frau Hagen began to depict herself, probably half-jokingly, in quasi-military images. In late February 1944, she had written that 'I am to stay here in any case until the last and I am glad that I am going to be allowed to keep watch as captain'; in keeping with the naval metaphors, her housekeeper Frau M. was designated as her 'helmsman'. Believing that she was about to be called on to trek westwards with the settlers in March 1944, Frau Hagen wrote that she was 'glad that I can support the settlers and that I can travel with them, in a small way one is becoming a soldier – a childhood dream is being fulfilled and I feel great strength and confidence within me'.[27] With the world of Sitno changing from a predominantly female community to more of a military camp inhabited by soldiers and policemen, Frau Hagen seemed to be positioning herself increas-ingly as their comrade by the use of this sort of language.

Frau Hagen wanted to carry on working and not to abandon Sitno until she was convinced there was no alternative. She was also determined to continue acting as advocate for the settlers' interests, which to her mind were being betrayed yet again by those in power. During the final week of March 1944 confusion reigned between the RKF and the army command. Orders to evacuate the Germans in Kreis Zamosc were issued, then countermanded as it was heard that the German forces were fighting their way out of Soviet encirclement at Kowel, and then countermanded again by an order that women and children at least should be evacuated immediately.[28] Frau Hagen, obeying the latest order, arrived in Zamość by horse and wagon with German settler women and children on 26 March. Encountering an official who denounced the decision to evacuate, she decided to request permission from the *Kreishauptmann* to return and stay put in Sitno after all. Finding herself breaking in on a meeting at the *Kreishauptmann's* headquarters, and encouraged by a female employee in the office to 'speak her mind to those bureaucrats' (*d.[en] Herren am grünen Tisch meine Meinung sagen*) she decided impulsively to tell the assembled company, which included District Governor Wendler, what she thought. Exactly what she said is not quite clear: as she remembered the incident in 1999, she complained generally about the 'inhuman' treatment of the settlers, taken from their original homelands, penned up in a transit camp in Nuremberg, then eventually settled in Kreis Zamosc, and now sent in what was still effectively winter to trek back westwards.[29] Her diary records that in her confrontation with the authorities she spoke of 'the impact of the orders and the mood of the settlers', suggesting that her outspoken criticism that day focused on the confusing and demoralizing effect of orders and counter-orders. 'Some of it is unpleasant for them to hear, that is clear, but it is ridiculous to hear how none of them now wants to be responsible for issuing the first order. But the settler is the one to suffer and that is what embitters me.' She reported the district governor's response to her outburst, which was rather remarkable given her diary entry a few days earlier about 'becoming a soldier': 'The governor dismisses me and says: put trousers on, become a soldier and look after the male settlers, we need you – the Kreish.[auptman]n says outside that I am brave – but actually I feel very empty inside' (26 March 1944).

The upshot was that Frau Hagen with some of her colleagues stayed put in Sitno. The German women and children from the settler villages in Kreis Zamosc went on to Łódź/Litzmannstadt, while the men were transported back to their farms to fulfil the role of peasant-soldiers (*Wehrbauern*) that had always inspired Himmler's plans for German settlement. Sporrenberg, SS and Police Leader in Lublin since the previous September, issued a proclamation to the (male) settlers in Kreis Zamosc: 'You have come as settlers and *Wehrbauern* into this land and as such you must defend and hold this territory which has been assigned to you with all means at your disposal and with your lives.' They were instructed to fight back against partisan bands and not give up 'an inch' of German-settled soil to the enemy. How they were to do this was another matter. As District Governor Wendler complained to Sporrenberg in April 1944, a third of this improvised defence force had no weapons.[30] Frau Hagen also doubted the settlers' ability as soldiers. Perhaps influenced by her conversations with army officers billeted in Sitno, she began to make disparaging comments about their courage and fighting potential. After reporting a 'bandit attack' on the village of Horyszow on 12 April 1944, Frau Hagen declared that 'if it comes down to it we Reich Germans will have to defend ourselves' (13 April 1944). She expressed mistrust particularly of the *Stammdeutsche*, who were reported in March 1944 to be 'deserting' to the Polish side – the same thing that was being reported by some of the kindergarten teachers in Distrikt Galizien at around the same time. 'Today another 7 *Stammdeutsche* absconded, even Kr., who was such a bright spark and who had a new farm built for him last summer, speaks good German and yet decides now for Poland' (30 March 1944).

In the following three months, Frau Hagen, with the aid of her German housekeeper and her Polish servants and farm workers, tended the garden and fields while maintaining the manor house as quarters for military personnel passing through and as a night-time refuge for the male settlers. Her doubt about the purpose of what she was doing is clear from her response to being asked to raise 600 chicks for the settlers: 'Glad as I am to do it – but is there any point? One is working for such an uncertain future,' she noted on 30 March 1944. A week later, however, she was conquering her doubts again: 'I believe in the military administration and in staying here, otherwise raising the chicks would make no sense' (7 April 1944). At some level, the doubts remained: her diary entries during these months evoked a sense of how she and her fellow-Germans were clinging on to what they saw as an idyll, experiencing it all the more intensely given the likelihood that it would soon end. Lyrical depictions of riding into the red glow of sunset or by moonlight seem intended to capture impressions of the landscape as familiar, timeless and untouched by conflict. Similarly, descriptions of the garden, the flowers and the onset of summer seem to be an intentional evocation of a 'paradise' suspended in time. On 1 May 1944, she described a drive through the countryside with her neighbour Herr H.: 'The storks were on the meadows and the lapwings were calling, high clouds passed across the sun and the land was wide and beautiful and full of promise of the future (*weit und schön und voller Zukunft*).'

In many passages, the diary descriptions juxtaposed the portrayal of 'paradise' and the 'peaceful island' of Sitno with the looming 'threat to the Reich'. Following military developments at the front ever more intently, Frau Hagen recorded both the advance of the Red Army and the continuing attacks on German settler villages by partisans such as that at Michałow on 2 May: 'All horses, cows taken away – 3 wagons full of sugar, the owner robbed of everything down to his shirt – had to load the sugar himself at gunpoint' (2 May 1943). Writing his diary on the same day, Klukowski also recorded the partisans seizing wagons of sugar, though he specified that this had occurred at the sugar refinery at Klemensow; he also noted that in Michałow '14 horses, ten cows and several large pigs were taken. The horses and cows were taken because they were to be shipped to Germany the next day.'[31]

More and more, military events figured in Frau Hagen's chronicle, including the bombing of German cities and the continuing saga of the struggle for

Kowel: 'near Kowel a mass of Soviet troops are poised to attack,' she reported on 12 May 1944. A few days before the Soviet offensive on the Belorussian front was launched in late June 1944, she noted rather nervously that 'the Russians are strangely quiet'. At the same time she was seemingly trying to persuade herself that all was not lost. Having already wondered in March when the 'new weapon, the "moon rocket" which will be remote-controlled and will be able to destroy everything in England' would be put into action,[32] she responded positively, like many other Germans at the time, to announcements on 16 June 1944 that the regime was now hitting back with its new V-1 flying bombs, dubbed *Vergeltungswaffen* (retaliation weapons).[33] She wrote on 17 June that 'since yesterday, retaliation with the new weapon against London and southern England has begun – people speak of remote-controlled explosive missiles that must have a devastating effect'.

Frau Hagen's diary in the early summer of 1944 combined elements of pastorale, evoking the seemingly timeless idyll of Sitno, while chronicling, newsreel-style, the spate of events which were to shatter it. Once again in Sitno after a holiday 'back in the Reich', she wrote on 6 June 1944 – D-Day – :

> I am back in my 'realm' and I am so happy here! . . . In the school we have people quartered again, this time so far only four men, but things are livened up straight away. – On the first evening we drove with H.'s '9-seater' through the village. The moon shone brightly and only in the distance a Polish village was burning and a great cloud of smoke hung in the sky. Yesterday in Laziska the village leader, the mayor and 1 settler were murdered in their houses [*im Zimmer*]. But tonight I have been out riding with Oberfeldw. L. on moonlit tracks and one could really forget all one's worries, – yes, cares? – in this paradise with flowers and horses they are only in the background, but the worry about the Reich is still within us somehow. The invasion – the much-discussed – began today with the landing of troops near Le Havre and Cherbourg. Fighting now on 3 fronts! Rome has been given up in the south – and heavy bombers are flying continually to Kowel. Will our *Volk* stand firm, inwardly and outwardly, in this last great defensive struggle? One must simply believe in victory.

The sense of unreality arising from the illusion of peace even at this stage of the war persisted when – in July 1944 – Frau Hagen briefly left Sitno for Württemberg. There, she attended a course on 'folk art' intended to instil into its hundred young women participants a sense of 'demarcation' between what was German and what was 'alien' in interior décor and the celebration of festivals and ceremonies. Even Frau Hagen felt there was something bizarre about lessons in woodwork and flower-arranging at this stage of the war. 'Heavy fighting in the West – Kowel and Lida abandoned – and yet we carry on working peacefully – it is almost unnatural and rewarding at the same time. The woodwork is finished and we are now doing knotting [*Knüpfen*] and are carving animal figures and little dolls' (11 July 1944). It was no great surprise to her when she was summoned back to Sitno before the end of the week's course to find Zamość once again in 'evacuation mood'. In the early hours of 19 July, Frau Hagen recorded in her diary that the order had gone out during the previous evening that 'the settlement area is terminated'. She paused to reflect on the failure of the German settlement project:

> What verdict lies in this phrase – more than just our complete defeat – politically and militarily – it avenges the guilt of our arrogance of our peace work, carried out in wartime in confidence of victory, built upon the volcano (*auf dem Vulkan aufgebaut*). – 1000s of people have had a home and lose it today, the work of all the people had no meaning and the war is worse than ever. We talked of 'total war' and celebrated, where we should only have been working quietly at home in the Reich.

For someone who had not pushed for the posting to Sitno, but had embraced it as the fulfilment of certain hopes and ambitions and had thrown herself into the task to which she had been assigned, to realize that 'the work of all the people had no meaning' was to gain a bitter – if one-sided – insight into the consequences of the Zamość experiment and its collapse. Central to her diagnosis of the Germans' failure was a notion of hubris: the colonizing work of peacetime had been begun prematurely in the complacent expectation of victory. The Poles were now the victors in that they were reclaiming the land: however, Frau Hagen predicted, their triumph would be short-lived. Here, her anti-Soviet sentiments came through more strongly than any anti-Polish feelings: it was Soviet revenge against Germany that dominated the scenario she painted of the future: 'What forces will now break over Sitno? – Poles and Ukrainians will cheat each other of the land – the Russians will reap the harvest and press the Poles and Ukraine into its thrall – everything against us – until we cannot breathe.'[34] Twelve hours later, at midday on 19 July, in the midst of packing up for the final departure, Frau Hagen found time to record developments in her diary. Her dawning realization that 'all was in vain' and her speculation about 'what will come after us' were mixed with an unmistakable air of excitement: 'Now it really is a matter of "putting on trousers and becoming a soldier", the Russians [*der Russe*] are pressing very close, have already crossed the Bug near Hrubieszow and the message is: make haste.'

Retreat

Frau Hagen noted on 19 July that 'the Poles are extraordinarily quiet'; on the 20th, looking back at her departure at first light from Sitno, she reported that her Polish servants stood weeping as the wagons left.[35] If the young Polish women who had worked for Frau Hagen and serenaded her on her birthday were sorry to see her leave, different reactions on the part of the Poles were recorded by Zygmunt Klukowski in Szczebrzeszyn. Writing in his diary on 19 July, he noted that all the German civilian employees had left Szczebrzeszyn that afternoon, though the German military presence was increasing; that the Kreis administration had left Zamość, and that 'the Zamosc evacuation is in full operation'. He described the Poles' reaction as suppressed glee – 'while walking you must be careful not to show your delight at the German depar- ture,' he noted – mixed with uncertainty as to what the future would bring: 'Despite the happiness caused by the Germans' departure people are still very tense'.[36] Walter Lippert, a Polish resistance activist whose cover was working for the Germans in Zamość, recalled the moment when his boss departed, and the latter's surprise when some of the Polish employees refused to leave with him.[37] However, the danger was not over for the Polish resistance: partisans were still being captured and prisoners executed even as the Germans were in retreat.[38]

Meanwhile, Frau Hagen had adapted to her new role on the road with the settlers from Zamość, providing first aid for injured settlers and attending to the horses and wagons. 'I am the settler in trousers and M. [the housekeeper from Sitno] is the woman', she wrote on 20 July, seemingly in high spirits. The diary turned into the chronicle of an adventure during the eight days' trek to Litzmannstadt, each entry recording glimpses of familiar faces passing 'as if in a dream' and scenes of drama and danger. At Stary Zamość the trek came under fire and she witnessed a partisan being ' "wiped out" [*"umgelegt"*] – yes, that is the only way to put it', shot down as he ran through a cornfield.[39] The next day they were bombed and shot at by Soviet planes, which killed settlers and soldiers nearby; in the wagon behind Frau Hagen's, a settler was shot in the leg. Having regrouped and driven on to Lublin, they heard the news from SS officers of the failed assassination attempt upon Hitler the pre- vious day. Frau Hagen's reaction, seemingly shared by many Germans, was one of shock. She wondered in her diary – presumably sincerely, since she would not have needed to mention or comment on the plot if she had felt dif- ferently – 'whether the officer corps is really mutinying now at the hardest moment of decision?'[40] Her suspicions of the officer corps could be read as being of a piece with her view, fuelled by experiences in Kreis Zamosc, that those in positions of responsibility in the regime were letting down the rank and file: the Reich Germans had let down the settlers, now officers were letting down their men. Commenting on the tales told by soldiers encountered in Pulawy, she noted: 'time and again you hear that it is the officers who are the first to abscond [*türmen*]'.[41]

The physical effort, the intense encounters and moments of drama during the trek appeared to heighten Frau Hagen's pleasure and satisfaction in snatched moments of rest and contemplation. Perhaps, like many living through dangerous times during the war, her mood of well-being was fuelled by the euphoria of surviving perils unscathed and hearing of perils elsewhere: on the day after they left Lublin, soldiers brought news that Soviet forces had now entered the city. Thus, amidst the record of problems and obstacles, her diary still conveyed that she was glad to be out in the open and on the move in the countryside, with her beloved horses and the settlers who needed her. Resting in Przysucha, to the west of Radom, on the fourth evening of the trek, with the wagons parked on a marshy meadow, Frau Hagen described 'the horses grazing'. She went on: 'I have all sorts of bandages to put on and tablets to give out, one sees across the wide space many old faces and the mutual ties are stronger than ever.'[42] The following night, having reached Opoczno, all the settlers from the Zamość area drew up their wagons in a cornfield in a giant ring and Frau Hagen surveyed the scene, '600–700 wagons with well over 1000 horses. I sit on my wagon and look across over the ground at all the people. The horses are eating their fodder, the pigs are squealing the men are drying their wet clothes and it is a cheerful picture.'[43] Yet there were also some signs of wishful thinking in her diary about the meaning of the experience: perhaps Frau Hagen was imagining that even if the land was lost the vision of a German community welded together by a common purpose was still intact, a nation in miniature on the march to a new homeland, its solidarity experienced all the more intently in the face of danger. 'What cares are there other than this one, that *Germany* must not pass away,' she wrote on the day they arrived in Litzmannstadt.[44]

If such thoughts could flourish in the world of the trek, with its solidarity between officials, settlers and soldiers and its straightforward focus upon a single goal, they dissipated on arrival in Litzmannstadt as the normality of Nazi bureaucracy reasserted itself. While officials clustered around the RKF headquarters, the settlers were dispatched to the transit camp to be reunited with their wives and children. Frau Hagen was gladdened by the scenes of family reunion, and by the fact that some of her Sitno chicks, now young chickens, had made it as far as Litzmannstadt. However, she was dismayed once again to find the settlers poorly treated – 'they are only numbers, they are not allowed to do anything on their own initiative, and instead have to put up with being shouted at and obeying in silence,' she wrote angrily (31 July 1944). With these dispiriting thoughts of the settlers' future, and her sadness at parting from her two horses, the 'final little piece of the Sitno paradise', Frau Hagen headed for the railway station on 31 July 1944 to catch a train home.

Chapter 10

Leaving the East Behind

The experience of Reich German kindergarten teachers in Distrikt Galizien and the village advisers in Lublin as they hastened westwards in the summer of 1944 foreshadowed events in the annexed territories of Poland and in the eastern borderlands of the Altreich. On 22 January 1945, the leader of the Reich Labour Service wrote a postcard to the women's Labour Service leader in the Warthegau, Gertrud Kapp, addressing it to the Kurmark where he knew she was heading:[1]

> Dear Fräulein Kapp! An adverse fate has decreed that today, when I would wish to thank you for your New Year wishes and the good book 'Arbeits-maiden im Osten', your district is being overwhelmed by the Bolshevik flood. But now more than ever we must strive to hold our heads high! This card will − I hope − reach you in your reception district. I hope that you will have brought your camp units (*Lagereinheiten*) back without losses. Do go on helping your camp leaders to keep the *Arbeitsmaiden* well in hand and to give an example of quiet resolve and confidence. No good deed and no achievement is ever lost (*geht verloren*). Your work in the Warthegau too was not in vain. I hope that you will take it up once again when we have fought and won for ourselves an honourable peace. Heil Hitler. Yours Hierl.

Even in retreat, myths of the great German 'achievements' in the construction of the 'new East' and of a German future there continued to circulate as a prop to those committed to the Nazi cause, whose numbers by the beginning of 1945 were dwindling but whose power was not yet broken. Whether they shared such visions or not, German women who had been posted to the East to support the Germanization programme were expected to continue 'at their post' in exemplary fashion until the last possible moment, sustaining the morale of the population, and in retreat to uphold the fiction that the with-drawal was temporary.

In 1943 the retreat from the eastern fringes of the Nazi empire had begun: as German forces retreated in the face of the Soviet advance, successive evacuations had taken place in which ethnic German civilians were pulled back from the front line, on the assumption that Soviet forces would enact retribution upon German civilians in the territories they conquered.[2] Initially, such evacuations transferred ethnic Germans to points further west within occupied Soviet and Polish territories, thus relocating them in places that a few months later would be given up in turn.[3] In the spring and summer of 1944, as we have seen in Chapters 8 and 9, German civilians were evacuated from Distrikt Galizien and Distrikt Lublin in the General Government. By the end of 1944, German forces had been driven from Soviet territory altogether as well as from the eastern General Government, and Soviet forces were controlling the eastern parts of East Prussia. At the beginning of 1945, German forces were still in control of the western part of the General Government including Cracow, and the annexed territories of Danzig-Westpreußen and the Warthegau, but all these territories were soon to be overrun. In the final, chaotic mass retreat from January 1945 onwards, Germans scrambled to escape from occupied Poland altogether and from East Prussia as well. They fled to the main part of the Altreich, though the Soviet advance continued and soon swept across those borders too.

Reports by women who during the early retreats from the East accompanied 'their' ethnic Germans on the trek westwards gave a foretaste of the conditions that would characterize the later mass exodus. As ever, the ethnic Germans were pawns in the schemes of the SS planners. As their security became increasingly precarious, the German women deployed to assist them were often quick to embrace the role of their advocate and protector. This could mean confronting male authority, as when a district nurse employed by the NSV who travelled with ethnic Germans evacuated from the 'Hegewald' settlement area in the Ukraine in late 1943 wrote to the SS officer responsible for the settlers to highlight the mortality rate during the trek and the dangerously insanitary conditions prevailing afterwards in the reception camp.[4] Women who chose the stance of 'protector' also tended to assume a hierarchy of competence in which *Volksdeutsche* appeared passive, childlike and full of gratitude for what was done for them by Reich Germans in authority. A kindergarten organizer writing in early 1944 described how she had accompanied 'her' ethnic Germans from villages in the Nikolayev region of southern Ukraine on a trek starting in October 1943 that took them to presumed safety in Volhynia, still within the 'Reichskommissariat Ukraine' but nearer the border with the General Government. The 'Reich Germans' were more reluctant than the ethnic Germans to abandon the conquered territory, she declared, and she recorded her particular regret at leaving behind 'my 21 kindergartens, which I had built up with so much care and so much trouble'. The ethnic Germans, by contrast, 'were pleased to move a few hundred kilometres closer to the old German homeland'. This – to her – puzzling willingness to relocate, however convenient for Nazi purposes, moved her to comment critically that the ethnic Germans' sense of being rooted to the soil had been 'buried' by collectivization and 'the years of Bolshevik terror'. Her report portrayed the trek northwards as a triumph of Party organization, willpower and psychological management: 'Our ethnic Germans are like children. An understanding look, an encouraging word and giving a hand oneself helps them over the most difficult situations.' By the end of the trek, she judged the ethnic Germans to have proven themselves worthy of all the trouble: they had, she observed, 'conducted themselves bravely and decently' and 'demonstrated that they remain German in their innermost being'.[5]

Other accounts written during wartime for official consumption or propaganda purposes also sought to turn the story of enforced withdrawal from territories which had been conquered and exploited by German occupying forces into a well-organized mission of salvation, an operation to thwart the 'Bolshevik menace'.[6] 'Trek of the 350 000: Ethnic Germans rescued from Bolshevism' read a newspaper headline from August 1944, describing how the 'rescue' of the ethnic Germans was organized 'with meticulous attention to detail' as successive areas of occupied territory in eastern Europe were reconquered by Soviet forces, a process disguised in the report as 'shortening the front lines'.[7] At the end of January 1945, back in the Altreich, Gertrud Kapp compiled a report on how women's Labour Service participants had been successfully 'led back' from the Warthegau. Kapp put a positive gloss on the sudden and chaotic evacuation, playing up instead the degree of planning, foresight and communication between herself and the Party leadership in the Warthegau. When Greiser's categorical reassurance about the military situation issued on 18 January was followed two days later by the order to complete the evacuation of the Warthegau at once, Kapp tried to turn the story of last-minute orders into one of initiative and inspired improvisation:

That day – 20 January 1945 – left us scarcely time to breathe! (*hielt uns alle in Atem!*) The telephone never stopped ringing. . . . At 16.30 we learned by chance through a phone call with the post office that the evacuation of Posen and the western part of the Warthegau had just been ordered. . . . At 16.45 the order to retreat was announced – at 18.00 we had to set off. How it was possible in that short space of time to burn the most important files, pack the material that was to be taken with us, go home to fetch one's own baggage and prepare the bicycles, that is something I cannot fathom even now.

In fact, Kapp escaped from Posen by car, passing by those who were trudging through the freezing night on foot or by horse wagon: 'It was bitter', she commented, 'not to be able to help those fleeing'. Her mission had been to take marching orders to camps in the western Warthegau, though she admitted in the report that after reaching one or two camps her car was running out of fuel so that she had ended up driving directly to Frankfurt an der Oder by the quickest route.[8]

Kapp was concerned at the time and later to defend her actions in the final phase of the occupation as well as generally presenting the role of the women's Labour Service in the best possible light — not least against allegations made in a 1982 memoir that large numbers of *Arbeitsmaiden* had been killed in the course of the retreat.[9] Other women who had been leaders within National Socialist organizations also wrote after the war about the flight westward as a heroic endeavour in which their discipline and devotion to the German cause were tested and proven. In a report written in 1954 for the *Dokumentation der Vertreibung* project, Ute Timm, who in 1943 had been posted by the BDM to Kreis Zempelburg in Danzig-Westpreußen as a *Bannmädelführerin* (district leader), described the days before the signal to evacuate in January 1945 as a time of 'exemplary' efforts: 'On 20 January we had the first refugees from Bromberg arriving in Zempelburg. For us, in other words for my *Führerinnen*, my colleagues, the boys and girls and for myself, this was the beginning of the last great assignment on behalf of our compatriots (*Volksgenossen*), and of the bitter end.' On 25 January the population of Zempelburg was already fleeing, though no order had yet been given: 'Last meeting with the *Kreisleiter*. I receive the task of reassuring any inhabitants of Zempelburg wherever I meet them, and to tell the refugees in the town to leave.' On the following day the order to evacuate the town 'temporarily' was finally given. Looking back, Timm did not dwell on the fact that the Party leadership in her Kreis had delayed the order to evacuate so long. On the contrary, she set out to correct what she saw as a widespread view that Party and state officials had left the rest of the population in the lurch: 'During our flight and afterwards in Pomerania we heard over and over again that the highest Party leaders and state officials had vanished into the blue (*das Weite gesucht*) and left the population that had been entrusted to them to their fate. That cannot be said of our Kreis. Everyone tried to do his duty as long as possible.'[10]

The purpose of Timm's account, like that of Kapp, was to praise the Party and state authorities and celebrate the dedication of 'her' organization during its 'last assignment'. Similarly, Frieda Balcerek, a native of West Prussia who became *Gaufrauenschaftsleiterin* in Danzig-Westpreußen, gave in her 1953 account for the *Dokumentation der Vertreibung* a glowing depiction of the work of the NS-Frauenschaft/Deutsches Frauenwerk during the last weeks of German rule in West Prussia. Their soup kitchens fed refugees from East Prussia until finally, in March 1945, they were handing out provisions to those now fleeing Danzig and Gotenhafen for their voyage: 'What was achieved by our women in the mass canteens in Gotenhafen was overwhelming.'[11]

By contrast, other women recounted in memoirs and interviews how the dawning realization of defeat, the prospect of evacuation and the questions raised by others around them began to disrupt some of their earlier assumptions. Looking back, some mocked their own naïvety in believing for so long the regime's reassurances about a 'final victory' just around the corner. Frau Geyer, who left her teaching post in the Warthegau in summer 1944 shortly before the birth of her first child, remembered her father having a sharper sense than she did that defeat was imminent: 'My father was very pessimistic, I hadn't got that far . . . we were all a bit oblivious to what was going on (*hatten alle ein bißchen ein Brett vor dem Kopf*)'.[12] Frau Andreas, the kindergarten teacher who worked in Suwalki, remembered in an interview how soldiers had 'laughed at me, none of them believed any more in the final victory – whereas I always thought the Führer had a miracle weapon. What that was we did not know.'[13]

Frau Andreas was evacuated twice: once from Suwalki in summer 1944 and again from her new kindergarten posting near Lötzen in East Prussia in January 1945. Like a number of schoolteachers who told the story of their evacuation from the Warthegau and Danzig-Westpreußen in 1945, she presented the way in which local Party and state officials handled the evacuation as undermining any faith she had left in the regime. Having experienced the disorderly retreat from Suwalki ('the leadership was the first to flee') she nevertheless trusted her NSV superiors in Lötzen, who told her to wait for a signal in the case of emergency, when she was to send the children home and make the kindergarten ready to take in the wounded. Her story emphasized her naïvety in staying dutifully at her post until the bitter end:

And there I am running my kindergarten all obediently (*treu und brav*), and along comes this friend Hanni . . . who worked in Lötzen in an office somewhere, Hanni comes home and says: 'Are you crazy? Still doing the kindergarten? Where do you think the *Kreisleiter* is? Where do you think your NSV-*Leiter* is? Empty! Empty! They all left long ago. Taken the

last car and off they went! The offices are all empty, the whole Nazi
bureaucracy has long gone and you sit here!' I said, 'They were going to
phone me.'[14]

Together with the mayor and the district nurse, Frau Andreas then tried to
organize the evacuation of the village, telling all the farming families to
appear the following morning with horse and wagon so that the sick, the old,
the pregnant and the small children could be allocated berths. Once again,
Frau Andreas learned that she had been too trusting, and that any authority
previously invested in her and the other 'leading figures' of the village now
counted for little: 'During the flight I learned a lot about human nature, I am
not so naïve any more – the next morning there was just one single wagon
standing on the village green.' All the rest, she added, had packed up straight
away and gone.

Many other accounts supported the view that the chaos involved in the
flight westwards occurred because the Party and state authorities were too
slow to order the evacuation.[15] This point was made in memoirs and interviews by several schoolteachers who were part of the mass flight from the
annexed territories of western Poland in January 1945. Their narratives were
marked by anecdotes of women battling against obtuse male colleagues
and superiors. Frau Vogel, following instructions to return to Kreis Welun
after the Christmas break to resume teaching, arrived there on 16 January
with her female colleague to discover anti-tank trenches being dug and the
villagers packing. She recalled that the resettled Volhynian Germans, having
gone through the process only five years earlier when leaving Volhynia, 'knew
exactly what to pack'. Two days later, the village was ordered to evacuate,
and Frau Vogel found herself arguing with the local farmer's leader (*Ortsbauernführer*), who wanted to load the village records on to the wagon on
which she was travelling. 'I put up a fight and he threatened me with all sorts
of consequences upon our return (after the victory!).' The papers were left
behind.[16]

Hildegard Grabe, teaching in Kreis Kutno in the eastern Warthegau,
remembered that mothers with children, and the wives of male officials, were
evacuated in reasonable time by train, but that she and other women
teachers were made to stay until the last minute. Only on 22 January 1945 did
the order come through to evacuate. She set off on foot with another woman
teacher, begged lifts from army vehicles, and finally picked up a goods train
going westwards packed with refugees. Some male official vaguely instructed
them – presumably as women without dependants – to 'look after' the refugees
in the train, but the instruction was senseless: 'We could not prevent infants

and the elderly falling sick or freezing to death while the open rail cars stopped somewhere for hours on end.'[17]

Annelies Regenstein, another teacher working in Kreis Kutno who recorded her memories for the *Dokumentation der Vertreibung* project, remembered a signals unit being billeted in the school from June 1944 onwards. As they got increasingly busy that autumn laying cables and setting up telephone installations, she became aware of the front coming closer. Despite that awareness, and despite her father's objections, in January 1945 she returned to Kreis Kutno from her parental home in the Niederlausitz after the Christmas break. In her words, she 'did not want to leave my school community in the lurch'; moreover, the situation in the Warthegau did not seem to her at that time immediately dangerous. However, witnessing the stream of German cars coming westwards from the General Government brought it home to her that the front was advancing quickly. The school authorities summoned the women teachers on 16 January to a meeting in Kutno, where Regenstein realized that rail traffic was already breaking down completely. That night her village was ordered to evacuate: 'the night sky was blood-red and Litzmannstadt was in flames, and the Russians were hard on our heels'. Regenstein was ordered to accompany the trek and told to assist the district nurse. In her view the order to evacuate 'destroyed the last link between the Party and the population': the mass of the population, she felt, had been kept in the dark until the last minute and had then been abandoned to its own devices. The trek soon ran into difficulties and was eventually overtaken by Soviet forces as it tried to cross the Netze river: 'The Russians hauled us off the wagons and so began our road into captivity.'[18] She was to spend a year in Soviet captivity: the fate of many German civilians overtaken by the Soviet advance in early 1945. According to the *Dokumentation der Vertreibung*, the West German government-sponsored publication documenting the expulsions, more than 218,000 German civilians from the eastern provinces of the Reich and from the former annexed territories of wartime Poland were deported to the Soviet Union at the end of the war.[19]

Women, exhorted to act selflessly in caring for others, remembered their outrage at being let down by officialdom. Mary von Bremen, teaching in a girls' boarding-school in Wreschen, recalled in 1956 that her headmistress requested from the Posen school authorities at the start of January 1945 permission to postpone the start of term. The response was negative 'since the front is standing firm'. And yet, von Bremen observed, 'the cars and lorries of the troops flooding back from the front were rumbling past our windows day and night, always from east to west. Thus 200 girls arrived back at school at the beginning of January. Then came the collapse at the front.'[20] If in many of the women teachers' narratives there is a sense of their identification with a predominantly female population against (male) authorities, this was no doubt reinforced by the drafting of the remaining male population – from teenage boys to men of 60 – into the ill-starred *Volkssturm*, the home defence force set up in September 1944. This call-up often left women and children coping alone at the moment of evacuation. Gabriele Hornung's memoir of teaching in the Warthegau described the 'top people' (*die 'Oberen'*) of the town and of the Kreis decamping at high speed from Scharnikau after the order to evacuate on 20 January 1945, leaving the women teachers to work out for themselves how they would get out. The *Schulrat*, she claimed, abandoned all responsibility for 'his' teachers in the town and out in the villages and seemed glad to take refuge in a call-up to the *Volkssturm*.[21]

One of the women interviewed for this book, Frau Eckhard, wrote a report in 1947 about her experience teaching in Kreis Sieradz and Kreis Lask in the Warthegau, in which she observed that the fate of women teachers had counted for little with Nazi officials busy saving their own skins. During the summer of 1944 she and other teachers had been forbidden by the *Schulrat* in Kreis Lask to send their possessions westwards 'because we were supposed to be role models'. In January 1945, she went on, they were assured again at a teachers' meeting that they would get plenty of warning if they needed to get out. 'But nothing of the sort occurred. My superiors drove past me in a car without even a sideways glance.'[22]

Some of the women who looked back at the withdrawal from occupied Poland commented on the attitude of their Polish neighbours and employees at that time. Some thought that Poles were beginning to show resentment of the Germans more openly. However, it was more commonly noted that the Poles refrained from acts of hostility against the Germans and sometimes opted to trek with their German employers.[23] Barbara Besig, who as a newly qualified grammar school teacher had been posted from Essen to Leipe (Danzig-Westpreußen) in 1940, was still there in January 1945. After the war, she remembered that 'even on the day of evacuation' she had noticed no 'change of mood' among the Poles: 'on the day the mothers and children were evacuated my domestic help was as usual willing and friendly', while a Polish removal man helped pack and carry heavy items 'although I thought that he would refuse'. She went on: 'I would never have believed that we would get out of these predominantly Polish areas unscathed. Probably our military might still seemed sufficient to deter them from an uprising.'[24] Annelies Regenstein also recalled Poles who helped those who were fleeing and even drove some of the wagons, though she noted that some – concerned to be with their own families when the Soviet troops arrived – vanished during the trek

and headed back eastwards.[25] Anecdotes about the helpfulness of Poles also
served to show up the arrogance and irresponsibility of German officialdom.
Mary von Bremen, recalling the hasty evacuation of the girls' school in
Wreschen, noted that the Polish staff were 'tireless' in their assistance,
whereas the Party organizations let them down: although the Kreis Party
leader stayed long enough to help, 'the *Ortsgruppenleiter* and the NSV were
the first to vanish'.[26]

The 'German East' was lost − irrevocably so, for all the hopes of refugee
and expellee lobbies in post-war West Germany.[27] For the women who experienced the flight from the East, and for others who had worked in occupied
Poland earlier in the war but had not stayed until the final withdrawal, what
they made of their time in Poland, and the extent to which they sought to
celebrate it, distance themselves from it or otherwise reflect upon it, became
bound up in the post-war period with their particular perspectives on the Nazi
era, on German–Polish relations and on German history since 1945. For some,
their assignment in the East had been an episode of limited significance in
their subsequent biographies. For other women, memories of the East seemed
to play a more important role in their lives after the war: in that sense, they
did not simply 'leave the East behind'.

Some women took their wartime work in Poland as a starting point for
informing themselves about the history of Poland and Polish–German relations. At some level, this may have reflected a desire to make amends. For a
women's Labour Service volunteer who then worked as a village schoolteacher
in the Warthegau, learning about Poland and its heritage of Jewish culture
formed part of a process of rethinking and reflecting on her own past.[28] As
was mentioned in Chapter 7, one teacher living in West Germany after the
war took the opportunity of easier travel to the former eastern bloc after 1990
to vist Poland and seek out a Polish woman who had worked for her during
the war.[29] Another, living in the former GDR, was already travelling to Poland
in the 1960s and 1970s to make contact with a former Polish pupil to whom
she had covertly given lessons. She looked back with pride on her efforts while
in the Warthegau to subvert the social segregation of Germans and Poles.
Those efforts formed a basis for her endeavour after the war to 'build bridges'
between Germans and Poles: learning Polish and visiting Poland grew out of
an empathy with the subjugated population that had developed when she was
an employee of the occupying regime.[30]

For others, exploring memories of the East had more to do with reliving
the past than subjecting it to critical scrutiny. For some who had worked in
the East and who lived after the war in West Germany, their activities before
and during the war provided a focus for post-war reunions, the cultivation of

old affinities and the exchange of recollections. Former BDM leaders gathered round the elderly poet Agnes Miegel until her death in 1964, and after her death continued to meet up in regular commemoration gatherings.[51] In the 1970s, one-time women's Labour Service organizers set about assembling material documenting their work in East Prussia before and during the war and in the annexed territories of occupied Poland.[52] A group of settlement advisers who had worked in the Warthegau met up in the 1970s, choosing as their venue a place near the border between West Germany and the GDR where they could – just as nationalist women had done in post-Versailles Germany – use a 'border excursion' to remind themselves of where the enemy lay.[53] Some of the former settlement advisers also maintained links with their former protégés, ethnic Germans who had been resettlers in the Warthegau and were now resettled in south-western Germany. A former BDM Land Service camp leader, Hildegard Fritsch, described in her memoir meeting up at a celebratory reunion in 1979 with other BDM-Landdienst participants and some of 'their' former Bessarabian German settlers, now living in Württemberg. The language of wartime 'activity reports' was resurrected in her description of the hearty welcome from the Bessarabian Germans, the idyllic rural surroundings and her rosy vision of authentic German peasant culture having survived flight and resettlement in West Germany.[54]

Documenting memories could help to sustain old networks, but also have the purpose of joining in a more public debate about recent German history. In the 1950s, when public discussion in West Germany about the loss of the eastern territories was at its height, some of those who submitted their stories to the *Dokumentation der Vertreibung* project not only stressed the victimhood of Germans driven from their homelands in the East – this was after all the overall thrust of the government-sponsored project – but also explicitly regretted the destruction of German wartime 'construction' and 'achievements' in the East.[55] Writing in 1953, a woman who had taught near Danzig during the war accused 'the Poles' of appropriating, in the process of reconstruction, 'German achievements' as their own: 'After everything that German willpower and German industriousness has created in the East has been destroyed, it is easy for the Poles to present under the world's spotlight that which they are rebuilding as *their* culture.'[56] Frieda Balcerek, the former Gau women's leader of Danzig-Westpreußen, also mourned the destruction of her wartime labours and expressed the hope that one day 'those who come after us will reconstruct the land with the same devotion, the same love of the homeland, perhaps within the framework of an enlarged, peaceful Europe'.[57]

Later interventions sought to influence perceptions in West Germany of the nature and role of the BDM and the women's Labour Service, including their assignments in occupied Poland. In some cases, favourable accounts of these organizations and of their work in the East were solicited, encouraged and recommended by the former head of the BDM, Jutta Rüdiger.[38] Until her death in 2001 aged 90, Rüdiger engaged in a decades-long campaign to counter what she regarded as slurs on the reputation of Nazi organizations for young women in general and the BDM in particular.[39]

Those who sought a public forum for their recollections of working in the East were a minority, and it is unlikely that many outside the circle of former BDM leaders had a great deal of interest in Rüdiger's views after 1945. However, even for those who had no stake in defending their old organizations and dissociating them from the crimes committed by the Nazi regime in Poland, recalling work in Poland often conjured up positive memories of being young and enterprising, 'being someone', fulfilled in work, and developing skills which they felt had stood them in good stead in later life – including, in the words of one, 'learning to get her way'. In common with many others of their generation, they emerged from their war experiences trained to be 'hard-working, resilient and unselfish'.[40] Overall, however, the legacy of their experiences in the East was fraught with complexity. To varying degrees, the memory of enjoying freedom and responsibility as young women coexisted and was sometimes outweighed by unsettling and disturbing memories of Poles humiliated and degraded, Jews stigmatized and persecuted, and by a sense of having been complicit in a system which elevated them as Reich Germans to positions of authority over 'alien races' as well as over the ethnic Germans.

Chapter 11

Conclusion

For some women working in the pre-war eastern borderlands and later on in occupied Poland, the 'German East' was from start to finish a site for female missionary work. The construction of that mission drew on the legacy of Imperial Germany's overseas colonialism, Germanization efforts in the Prussian East, and 'protection work' on behalf of German minorities abroad. These, together with the more recent experiences of defeat and class divisions within Weimar democracy, shaped the definition of a female role in defending 'Germandom' against Slavic and Jewish 'aliens'. To be capable of mastering the territory, Germans on the ethnic frontier had to be loyal, disciplined, efficient, and attuned to modern farming and housekeeping techniques. This logic dictated attempts to influence rural family and village life in the eastern borderlands of the Reich before 1939, attempts which were training grounds for the larger-scale efforts to Germanize conquered Poland after 1939. For women who embraced both the Nazi exaltation of the domestic sphere and the colonizing drive to the East, such activism was based on attractively simple propositions – righting German wrongs, promoting the welfare of mothers and children – that could be represented as 'unpolitical' service to the nation. Straightforward 'womanly' tasks were imbued with grand historical significance, and the German communities who were the targets of this attention could be presented as endangered, needy and grateful.

The appeal of the womanly mission explains the willingness of some recruits to take part in borderlands projects and later to work in occupied Poland. Working in the East gave women the chance to play a flatteringly high-profile role, much celebrated in regime propaganda; it might even appear a substitute for the lost colonial dream that had been focused on Africa. A core of leaders and 'true believers' in the colonizing project were inspired by the propaganda to leap on the bandwagon of projects in the East. But a large number of young, single, mobile and mostly middle-class women – for instance newly qualified schoolteachers – willingly cooperated in tasks that

contributed to the consolidation of German power in the East without necessarily sharing such colonizing zeal. The analysis of their motives and responses
sheds some light on a generation that had been brought up with a sense that
the Versailles Treaty was unjust, who had been socialized through the BDM
and the women's Labour Service into an ethos of hard work and service to the
'national community'; but who had also been encouraged, as educated middle-
class girls, to aspire to a career and to welcome experiences that would serve
their personal development. Conversely, their socialization would not have
encouraged these young women to challenge prevalent German and National
Socialist prejudices against the Poles and 'Polishness'. When posted to the 'new
eastern territories' after 1939, few seem to have considered the situation of the
Polish population as a factor in how they responded to the prospect of working
there. To judge from the accounts of women who were willing participants in
pre-war borderlands projects and in the colonizing efforts in occupied Poland,
going East could be an adventure and a change from routine. Some young
women who were unfamiliar with rural life craved the idyll of Nazi ruralist
propaganda; others, increasingly accustomed to the idea of tourism as something pleasurable and instructive, wanted to discover remote corners of the
'fatherland' and – after 1939 – 'see something of the world' by heading into
the new territories of Poland. Some were pleased at the prospect of professional experience and the responsibility of running a school single-handedly,
or being in charge of a kindergarten and supervising other staff. Others
relished the personal challenge of living far from home, or the comradeship
with colleagues.

Women's expectations of what an assignment in the East might bring were
sometimes confirmed, but also confounded. Students and women's Labour
Service volunteers working in villages in the eastern borderlands before 1939
were sometimes shocked by rural poverty and disconcerted by ambiguous
ethnic identities that failed to match the notion of drawing clear boundaries
between Germans and Poles. From reading between the lines of contemporary reports, it seems that borderlands inhabitants were not always grateful
when outside 'experts' told them how to be proper Germans, how to conduct
themselves in the 'ethnic struggle' and how to run their households. When
faced with such reactions, zealots claimed they redoubled their efforts: only a
few seemed inclined to express doubt about the purpose of borderlands
activism in the light of their experiences.

The conquest of Poland expanded the scope for a womanly mission to
'strengthen Germandom' in the East while transforming its conditions: now,
it was not a case of taking sides against an active Polish-speaking minority
within the borders of the Reich during peacetime, but of creating a new order

in which the defeated and conquered majority population was systematically
deprived of rights. The responses of women from the Altreich to the conditions they found in wartime Poland and to their work with ethnic Germans
in occupied Poland were diverse and not always predictable. At one extreme,
some conveyed the feeling of a 'colonizing high' fuelled by a sense of unlim-
ited power and boundless possibilities for Germany and the Germans in the
East: this was where a young woman could feel like a 'demi-god', where
students could stroll through the streets of a Polish town, share the colonizer's
gaze on the subjugated Poles and Jews and gloat. Others felt threatened and
insecure on entering what felt to them like a war zone. Some remembered
that they had experienced the segregation of Germans and non-Germans as
a shock and that witnessing the treatment of Poles and Jews had triggered
feelings of unease and shame.

Working with ethnic German settlers in the Polish countryside, some
women found their prejudices about Polish 'filth' and 'backwardness' confirmed; others were more struck by the efficiency of Polish farmers, not least
compared with some of the German settlers and those classified as being of
German ancestry, who were after all supposed to be the new masters. Often,
the encounters with the ethnic Germans triggered reactions among Reich
German women that ranged from sympathy and solidarity to frustration and
hostility. The women's sometimes bewildered, sometimes arrogant comments
revealed them grappling with concepts of national identity and with the
regime's opportunistic practices of ethnic classification. If these *Volksdeutsche*
and *Deutschstämmige* really were 'Germans', yet seemed so alien, doubts were
cast on the regime's criteria of Germanness. And if to be German was to have
an outlook that was both 'modern' and Nazi, as the RKF authorities demanded,
what would it take to make true colonizers out of ethnic Germans who could
appear as backward, superstitious and friendly to Poles? Such doubts and questions reverberated through reports written at the time, together with expressions of frustration at bureaucratic inefficiency and poor organization. It could
lead some to wonder about the whole basis of the colonizing project: whether
there would ever be enough Germans to maintain their power over the Poles,
whether the situation of the settlers would ever be secure.

Absorbed in their tasks with the ethnic Germans, Reich German women
in Poland often tended to blot out the existence of the non-German population in the accounts they wrote of their work at the time, and even in later
recollections. Self-censorship may have been one factor shaping the contemporary accounts: paying too much attention to the presence of the 'ethnically
alien' might have been read as inappropriate stirrings of sympathy. The silence
in contemporary accounts and in later recollections may also have stemmed

from the fact that women's daily tasks did indeed focus upon the population categorized as German, whose aim was to weld together a homogeneously German community and keep it separate from the Poles or Jews. Some women clearly remembered taking an interest in the Poles in their locality and could recount stories that can be read as indicating a concern they had felt at the time, but others' memories were remarkably vague. It seems plausible that a tendency not to register the presence of the non-German population, or to register it only peripherally, reflected a common desire not to reflect too hard about those at whose expense the Germans were being privileged. Perhaps, too, it indicated a tendency to take refuge in a belief that the 'constructive' womanly work with ethnic Germans was unpolitical and had nothing to do with the measures of discrimination and persecution against the non-German population.

This brings one back to considering women as agents and witnesses of the regime's policies in occupied Poland and how a gendered division of labour may have influenced the nature of female complicity in the oppression of the non-German population. Assessing such complicity has to take into account the ambiguities in the role and status of Reich German women in Poland. These ambiguities arose from the way in which gender roles were structured by conflicting notions of the role and behaviour appropriate for women and men, as well as by the hierarchy of 'race' and ethnicity.

There was a gendered slant to women's tasks with the ethnic Germans in Poland. Female settlement advisers were assigned responsibility for the domestic sphere and for tasks relating to the welfare of mothers and children; kindergarten teachers were to use their work with German children as a basis for community-building efforts with the mothers of the kindergarten pupils; women schoolteachers were urged to get involved in extra-curricular activities that might mean organizing village girls in a BDM group or getting involved with the local branch of the NS-Frauenschaft. For all that, Reich German women in Poland were also expected to take on duties that extended beyond what could clearly be labelled a 'womanly sphere'. The 'colonial' situation and the shortage of personnel to run the Nazi empire in the East demanded that women use their position as Reich Germans to represent the occupation regime, give orders and get things done, and to act as figures of authority in relation to the local ethnic German population as a whole. That population included men, even if women began to predominate as men were called up. Cases where Reich German women found themselves in conflict with men who disputed or undermined their authority and how they dealt with it are revealing. They show that women – in crossing conventional gender boundaries, for instance involving themselves in general farm matters rather than restricting themselves to 'womanly' issues of housekeeping and child-care, or challenging male authority on general questions regarding the ethnic Germans – were conscious of their 'transgression', and of men's suspicious responses to it, but prepared to justify their actions on the basis of an obliga-tion to their ethnic German protégés.

Women were not, therefore, operating in a rigidly demarcated womanly sphere, and in many situations their status as Reich Germans allowed them a latitude to cross conventional demarcations of gender more easily than would have been the case in the Altreich. Nevertheless, the idea that men and women had different tasks and responsibilities retained significance both for women's involvement in and knowledge of regime measures against the non-German population, and for their perceptions of that involvement.

First, it provided the basis for an image of 'unpolitical' womanly work as separate from the male world of politics, coercion and violence: this image was used by some women as a way of minimizing their knowledge and respon-sibility. Some Reich German women working with ethnic Germans in Poland seem to have been living out a fantasy of an 'intact' 'idyllic' world, remote, as long as the Eastern front held, from the events of the war and from all things political. The descriptions used – 'an island of happiness in the midst of the harsh, pitiless war', as a school assistant in the Warthegau put it, or the 'fairy-tale castle' of the women's Labour Service camp in Baschkow, or the 'paradise' of the estate garden in Sitno – all seem products of the same vision of an intact home for Germans in the East, a haven where young women worked for the community, children would play and learn and mothers would be looked after. In the accounts of these islands or havens, Reich German men might figure as occasional guests: as visiting dignitaries being served coffee and cakes, as an SS man invited along to the kindergarten party to play Father Christmas.

The experience of a haven of peaceful and constructive work with women and children could be a genuine one, though one might judge someone naïve and blinkered who ignored the conditions on which it was based. However, it is clear that the 'haven' created by 'womanly hands' – the clean, pleasant sur-roundings of a women's Labour Service or Land Year camp, the kindergarten decorated for Christmas, providing hospitality and refreshments – was also deliberately staged as a morale-boosting exercise for the ethnic Germans. Moreover, such facilities could also provide recreation for members of secu-rity forces stationed nearby, or visiting Party and state officials. In the latter case, one could ask whether women were creating an institutional form of the homely 'refuge' represented more obviously by the private homes kept by the dutiful wives of male perpetrators. It is possible that the kindergarten teacher who invited the SS man from the neighbouring village to play Father Christmas at her kindergarten party was providing him with a pleasant respite from normal duties, and it is clear that the Labour Service women who served breakfast on repeated occasions to SS men while refraining, as requested, from asking questions about what they had been doing, were enabling such men to recuperate from their 'work' expelling Poles from their homes. A 'homely' environment for Germans, in the midst of a world where non-Germans were persecuted and impoverished, could function in a number of different ways, and one of those functions might be to offer recuperation and a sense of normality for men whose everyday acts were by any standards of humanity and justice abnormal. To that extent, one could indeed speak of a form of female complicity with male crimes that arose out of women's cultivation of an environment 'just like home'. But it is also important to recognize that where women were cultivating and celebrating 'havens' in the midst of occupied Poland, it was above all for themselves – either individually, or as in the case of 'idyllic' women's Labour Service camps, collectively. It was, one suspects, a way of reinforcing their own sense of normality and creating a barrier against an outside world for which they, too, were responsible.

The notion of a separate female world cushioned and isolated from the harshness of the world of occupation politics and warfare was a myth. On the contrary, women's particular tasks and responsibilities in relation to the ethnic Germans were the basis for a specifically female type of complicity and involvement in the measures taken by the occupation regime to deprive non-Germans of their property and their rights. For instance, women's responsibility for ensuring the welfare of incoming ethnic German settlers could dictate their becoming directly involved in the eviction of Polish families: not merely cleaning up in the wake of expulsions, but actively intervening to make sure that the evicted owners left behind household goods that were essential to their well-being, but which had to be handed over to the incomers, whose needs were given priority. While it may have been relatively unusual for women to be so directly involved in depriving people of their possessions, it was virtually unavoidable that women working with ethnic Germans in occupied Poland should end up using premises and goods, and distributing clothing and furniture, that had been taken from the Poles and the Jews. Contemporary reports and later recollections show that women knew whose premises they were living or teaching in and where the furniture, clothes and household equipment they might be using or distributing came from. The classic womanly task of equipping and furnishing homes, schools and kindergartens, making the 'homely environment' for themselves and for ethnic Germans, inevitably involved Reich German women in knowingly using the goods of the dispossessed.

A further dimension of women's complicity as agents and witnesses of regime policies may also be identified. The pedagogical mission to children and women, but also more generally to ethnic Germans was part of the regime's propaganda that aimed to keep ethnic Germans loyal, counteract defeatism, and secure the chaotic and unstable system of domination being erected in occupied Poland. To ethnic Germans, the energetic women 'from the Reich' may indeed have seemed the least unacceptable face of a regime which had broken most of its promises to them. Women's awareness that they might have gained the trust and raised the expectations of the ethnic Germans only tended to increase their commitment – if not to the regime, then to the people with whom they were working – and to make them determined to improve the ethnic Germans' lot. This might entail protesting against injustices done to ethnic Germans by bureaucrats in the offices of the occupation authorities. However, it also might entail finding better premises or resources for them, or encouraging ethnic Germans to make Poles work harder for them.

When women used such energy on the ethnic Germans' behalf, it was for some also perhaps a way of forgetting injustices done to the non-German population. What women actually witnessed, for instance whether they saw Poles being expelled or Jews rounded up and deported, could be a matter of the location and timing of their posting. Sometimes their function could determine what they witnessed, for instance when a BDM regional leader was invited by a *Kreisleiter* to view a concentration camp. Individual decisions could also play a role, as when women teachers refused to obey orders to attend a public execution. However, Reich German women were all in a position, as they travelled through Poland and went about their work, to see for themselves how Poles were treated. Not everyone would have directly witnessed how Jews were treated, but many visited Łódź/Litzmannstadt and saw the ghetto from the outside. How far Reich German women working in Poland heard of executions, deportations and mass killing at the time is hard to say, but some evidence from the General Government in 1943–4 supports the view that the murder of the Jews did become common knowledge among the German 'occupation society' there.

This study has not only been about what women did and what women witnessed in the East, and above all in occupied Poland after 1939, but how they interpreted it at the time and in retrospect. Without taking either contemporary accounts or retrospective testimonies at face value, it is nevertheless possible to categorize certain versions as representing women's work in the East in a particular way. In some cases, it seems as if the passage of time has changed little. Some of the narratives of the post-war period – in the form of published or unpublished memoirs or oral testimony – replicate to a perhaps surprising extent the uncritical and self-righteous stance of the most enthusiastic reports from the time. At the opposite end of the spectrum, women sometimes claimed in post-war testimony that they had felt a strong sense of unease and injustice at the time. Their current critical stance towards the past confirmed, according to their account, what they had felt all along. More often, however, women in their post-war recollections were trying to reconcile their dominant memories of a formative and fulfilling experience with more recently acquired insights into the nature of the regime for which they had been working, a dilemma resolved in different ways by different respondents. Some claimed to have known and seen very little at the time of what was going on, thereby begging the question of whether this was a case of 'wilful ignorance'. Others offered a more self-critical examination of their past actions, wondering why they had not been more aware of what they were involved in at the time. Such narratives stressed an individual process of rethinking. Their testimonies, whether more or less self-critical, are indicative of the continuing debates about German involvement in Hitler's war in the East and the loss of the 'German East' as its consequence. This book has sought to show how German women are part of that story.

Appendix: Biographical Data on Respondents

Frau Andreas

b. 1924; elementary school (*Volksschule*); 1942–4 kindergarten training; 1944 posted to Suwalki, then East Prussia. Occupation after 1945: recitation artist, housewife; initially in Soviet zone/GDR, later in FRG.

Frau Bauer

b. 1914; elementary school; sales apprentice, sales assistant; 1941–December 1942 settlement adviser in Warthegau. Occupation after 1945: agricultural settler in Soviet zone, later factory worker and shop assistant in western Germany/FRG.

Frau Danneberg

b. 1905; university degree and doctorate; bookseller; 1937–9 working in Reichsfrauenführung, Berlin; 1939–42 press officer for NS-Frauenschaft in Warthegau. Occupation after 1945: bookseller, Soviet zone (until 1947), then western Germany, later teacher in secondary and adult education in FRG.

Frau Eckhard

b. 1923; grammar school (*Gymnasium*), school leaving certificate (*Abitur*) 1941; teacher training college; teaching in village schools in Warthegau 1942–5. Occupation after 1945: primary school teacher, later head teacher in western Germany/FRG.

Frau Fischer

b. 1919; *Abitur* 1939; Labour Service; teacher training college. Vacation assignment in Warthegau 1940. Further university study during wartime. Occupation after 1945: grammar school teacher in western Germany/FRG.

Frau Geyer

b. 1921; *Abitur* 1939; 1939–40 home economics college; 1940–1 teacher training college; teaching in village school in Warthegau 1941–summer 1944. Occupation after 1945: primary school teacher; initially in Soviet zone, later in western Germany/FRG.

Frau Hagen

b. 1915; school until 16 (qualification: *mittlere Reife*); 1932–8 women's agricultural college; 1941 teacher in women's colonial school; 1943–4 director of school for village advisers, General Government. Occupation after 1945: agricultural teacher in western Germany/FRG.

Frau Holz

b. 1923; girls' secondary school (*Lyzeum*); 1938–9 bookseller's apprentice; 1942 Labour Service in Warthegau; 1942–5 school assistant, then auxiliary teacher in village school in Warthegau. Occupation after 1945: bookseller, farmer's wife in western Germany/FRG.

Frau Keller

b. 1913; 1932 *Abitur*; 1934 Labour Service (left early); 1934–7 study at University of Jena; 1937–40 primary school teacher; 1940 teaching village school in Danzig-Westpreußen; 1940–4 teacher in German School in Brussels. Occupation after 1945: teacher; until 1947 in Soviet zone, then in western Germany/FRG.

Frau Mahnke

b. 1920; *Abitur*; women's agricultural college; 1939 Labour Service; university studies (Egyptology); 1942 vacation assignment Warthegau. After 1945 living in western Germany/FRG.

Frau Niemann

b. 1906; school until 16; 1929–35 gymnastics and sports teacher at school for the deaf; 1935–8 Bezirksjugendwartin in Gumbinnen district, East Prussia; 1938–44 full-time BDM leader (later Obergauführerin/ Gebietsmädelführerin). Occupation after 1945: teacher in private schools in western Germany/FRG.

Frau Peters

b. 1920; grammar school (*Real-Reformgymnasium*) until 16; 1936–7 women's agricultural school; 1937–8 Labour Service; 1938–40 BDM district leader;

Jan. 1941 BDM posting to Warthegau (resigned); summer 1942 BDM assignment in Warthegau. Occupation after 1945: helping in family business; Soviet zone/GDR.

Frau Teplitz

b. 1916; 1935 *Abitur*; 1942–3 teacher training college; 1943–5 teaching in village school in Warthegau. Occupation after 1945: pastor (ordained 1959), Soviet zone/GDR.

Frau Ullmann

b. 1922; *Abitur*; teacher training college 1942–3; 1943–5 teaching in village school in Warthegau. Occupation after 1945: primary school teacher in western Germany/FRG.

Frau Vogel

b. 1922; 1941 *Abitur*; teacher training, University of Jena; teaching in village school in Warthegau 1942–5. Occupation after 1945: primary school teacher in western Germany/FRG.

Frau Winter

b. 1919; 1937 *Abitur*; 1938 Labour Service; student of interior design at art college. Vacation assignments in Warthegau 1940 and 1941. Occupation after 1945: housewife in western Germany/FRG.

Notes

Chapter 1 Introduction: Women, 'Germandom' and Nazism

1. Michael Burleigh, *Germany Turns Eastwards: A Study of Ostforschung in the Third Reich* (Cambridge, 1988), pp. 3–8; Wolfgang Wippermann, *Der 'deutsche Drang nach Osten': Ideologie und Wirklichkeit eines politischen Schlagwortes* (Darmstadt, 1981); Hubert Orlowski, *'Polnische Wirtschaft': Zum deutschen Polendiskurs der Neuzeit* (Wiesbaden, 1996); Larry Wolff, *Inventing Eastern Europe* (Stanford, 1994) pp. 332–55; on the tradition of Polish and Czech critiques of the notion of a German 'civilizing mission', see Jan M. Piskorski, 'The Historiography of the So-called "East Colonization" and the Current State of Research', in Balazs Nagy and Marcell Sebok, eds, . . . *The Man of Many Devices, Who Wandered Full Many Ways . . . : Festschrift in Honor of Janos M. Bak* (Budapest, 1999), pp. 654–67, esp. pp. 655–6.
2. Martin Broszat, *Nationalsozialistische Polenpolitik 1939–1945* (Stuttgart, 1961); Robert L. Koehl, *RKFDV: German Resettlement and Population Policy 1939–1945* (Cambridge, Mass., 1957); Czesław Madajczyk, *Die Okkupationspolitik Nazideutschlands in Polen 1939–1945* (Cologne, 1988); Czesław Madajczyk, ed., *Vom Generalplan Ost zum Generalsiedlungsplan* (Munich, 1994); Mechthild Rössler and Sabine Schleiermacher, eds, *Der 'Generalplan Ost': Hauptlinien der nationalsozialistischen Planungs- und Vernichtungspolitik* (Berlin, 1993); Joseph B. Schechtman, *European Population Transfers 1939–1945* (New York, 1946); Götz Aly, *'Endlösung': Völkerverschiebung und der Mord an den europäischen Juden* (Frankfurt am Main, 1995); Wolfgang Schneider, ed., *'Vernichtungspolitik': Eine Debatte über den Zusammenhang von Sozialpolitik und Genozid im nationalsozialistischen Deutschland* (Hamburg, 1991); Götz Aly and Susanne Heim, *Vordenker der Vernichtung: Auschwitz und die deutschen Pläne für eine neue europäische Ordnung* (Frankfurt am Main, 1993).
3. On the role allotted to the ethnic Germans in Nazi-occupied Poland and their responses to the occupation regime, see Doris Bergen, 'The Nazi Concept of "Volksdeutsche" and the Exacerbation of Anti-Semitism in Eastern Europe, 1939–1945,' *Journal of Contemporary History* 29 (1994), pp. 569–82; idem, 'The "Volksdeutschen" of Eastern Europe, World War II and the Holocaust: Constructed Ethnicity, Real Genocide', *Yearbook of European Studies* 13 (1999), pp. 70–93.
4. See for example Nira Yuval-Davis, *Gender and Nation* (London, 1997); Anne McClintock, *Imperial Leather: Race, Gender and Sexuality in the Colonial Contest* (New York and London, 1995).
5. Johanna Gehmacher, *'Völkische Frauenbewegung': Deutschnationale und nationalsozialistische Geschlechterpolitik in Österreich* (Vienna, 1998), p. 25.

6. Ute Frevert, ' "Unser Staat ist männlichen Geschlechts": Zur politischen Topographie der Geschlechter vom 18. bis frühen 20. Jahrhundert', in *'Mann und Weib, und Weib und Mann': Geschlechter-Differenzen in der Moderne* (Munich, 1995), pp. 61–132.

7. Ute Planert, 'Antifeminismus im Kaiserreich: Indikator einer Gesellschaft in Bewegung', *Archiv für Sozialgeschichte* 38 (1998), pp. 93–118; Roger Chickering, ' "Casting Their Gaze More Broadly": Women's Patriotic Activism in Imperial Germany, *Past and Present* 118 (1988), pp. 156–85. For general accounts of bourgeois feminism in the Kaiserreich, see Richard Evans, *The Feminist Movement in Germany, 1894–1933* (London, 1976) and Barbara Greven-Aschoff, *Die bürgerliche Frauenbewegung in Deutschland 1894–1933* (Göttingen, 1981).

8. Planert, 'Antifeminismus', p. 110.

9. Erwin Barta and Karl Bell, *Geschichte der Schutzarbeit am deutschen Volkstum* (Berlin, 1930), pp. 275–84.

10. On women in the German Schools Association in the Habsburg Monarchy, see Pieter Judson, *Exclusive Revolutionaries: Liberal Politics, Social Experience and National Identity in the Austrian Empire, 1848–1914* (Ann Arbor, Michigan, 1996), pp. 211–14; idem, 'Inventing Germanness: Class, Ethnicity and Colonial Fantasy at the Margins of the Habsburg Monarchy', *Social Analysis* 33 (1993), pp. 47–67; idem, 'The Gendered Politics of German Nationalism in Austria, 1880–1990', in David F. Good, Margarete Grandner and Mary Jo Maynes, eds, *Austrian Women in the Nineteenth and Twentieth Centuries: Cross-Disciplinary Perspectives* (Providence and Oxford, 1996), pp. 1–17.

11. William W. Hagen, *Germans, Poles and Jews: The Nationality Conflict in the Prussian East, 1772–1914* (Chicago and London, 1980), pp. 174–6.

12. Ibid., pp. 118–36, 166–207.

13. On the Ostmarkenverein, see Adam Galos, F. H. Gentzen and Witold Jakobczyk, *Die Hakatisten. Der deutsche Ostmarkenverein 1894–1933* (Berlin, 1966).

14. Chickering, ' "Casting Their Gaze More Broadly" ', p. 167; Elizabeth Drummond, ' "Durch Liebe stark, deutsch bis ins Mark": Weiblicher Kulturimperialismus und der Deutsche Frauenverein für die Ostmarken', in Ute Planert, ed., *Nation, Politik und Geschlecht: Frauenbewegungen und Nationalismus in der Moderne* (Frankfurt and New York, 2000), pp. 147–59, here p. 147.

15. Drummond, ' "Durch Liebe stark" ', pp. 150–2.

16. Ibid., pp. 154–5; Chickering, ' "Casting Their Gaze More Broadly" ', p. 167.

17. Chickering, ' "Casting Their Gaze More Broadly" ', p. 169; Drummond, ' "Durch Liebe stark" ', pp. 157–8.

18. McClintock, *Imperial Leather*, p. 6. On British nurses sent to British colonies, see Dea Birkett, 'The "White Woman's Burden" in the "White Man's Grave": The Introduction of British Nurses in Colonial West Africa', in Nupur Chaudhuri and Margaret Strobel, eds, *Western Women and Imperialism: Complicity and Resistance* (Bloomington and Indianapolis, 1992), pp. 177–88.

19. Ann L. Stoler, 'Making Empire Respectable: The Politics of Race and Sexual Morality in 20th-century Colonial Cultures', *American Ethnologist* 16, no. 4 (Nov. 1989), pp. 634–60, here p. 640.

20. Jean and John L. Comaroff, 'Home-Made Hegemony: Modernity, Domesticity and Colonialism in South Africa', in Karen Tranberg Hansen, ed., *African Encounters with Domesticity* (New Brunswick, NJ, 1992), pp. 37–74.

21. Stoler, 'Making Empire Respectable', pp. 636–9.

22. Ann Laura Stoler, 'Bourgeois Bodies and Racial Selves', in Catherine Hall, ed., *Cultures of Empire: Colonizers in Britain and the Empire in the Nineteenth and Twentieth Centuries* (Manchester, 2000), pp. 88–119, esp. pp. 93–5.

23. McClintock, *Imperial Leather*, p. 378.

24. On the notion of German housewifery as a marker of national identity, see Nancy Reagin, 'The Imagined *Hausfrau*: National Identity, Domesticity and Colonialism in Imperial Germany', *Journal of Modern History* 73 (March 2001), pp. 54–86.

25. Chickering, ' "Casting Their Gaze More Broadly" ', p. 179.

26. Ibid., p. 180.

27. Friederike Eigler, 'Engendering German Nationalism: Gender and Race in Frieda von Bülow's Colonial Writings', in Sara Friedrichsmeyer, Sara Lennox and Susanne Zantop, eds, *The Imperialist Imagination: German Colonialism and Its Legacy* (Ann Arbor, Michigan, 1998), pp. 69–85, here pp. 78–9.

28. Lora Wildenthal, ' "When Men Are Weak": The Imperial Feminism of Frieda von Bülow', *Gender and History* 10, no. 1 (1998), pp. 53–77, here p. 55. On women's role in German colonialism generally, see Lora Wildenthal, *German Women for Empire, 1884–1945* (Durham and London, 2001).

29. In 1903 the Women's Society for the Eastern Marches had around 1,600 members, in 1910 the Women's League of the German Colonial Society had 7,000 members, and in 1912 the women's groups of the Society for Germandom Abroad had 8,200 members: Chickering, ' "Casting Their Gaze More Broadly" ', p. 167, 174; Barta and Bell, *Geschichte der Schutzarbeit*, p. 278.

30. The short-lived extreme right-wing Vaterlandspartei was notably successful in mobilizing women, who comprised around a third of the membership: Heinz Hagenlücke, *Deutsche Vaterlandspartei: Die nationale Rechte am Ende des Kaiserreiches* (Düsseldorf, 1997), pp. 184–5; Matthew Stibbe, 'Anti-Feminism, Nationalism and the German Right, 1914–1920', *German History* 20, no. 2 (2002), pp. 185–210.

31. Stibbe, 'Anti-Feminism, Nationalism and the German Right'; Raffael Scheck, 'German Conservatives and Female Political Activism in the Early Weimar Republic', *German History* 15, no. 1 (1997), pp. 34–55.

32. Andrea Süchting-Hänger, 'Die Anti-Versailles-Propaganda konservativer Frauen in der Weimarer Republik – Eine weibliche Dankesschuld?', in Gerd Krumeich with Silke Fehlemann, eds, *Versailles 1919 – Ziele – Wirkung – Wahrnehmung* (Cologne, 2001), pp. 302–13.

33. Raffael Scheck, 'Women against Versailles: Maternalism and Nationalism of Female Bourgeois Politicians in the Early Weimar Republic', *German Studies Review* 22 (1999), pp. 21–42; Nancy R. Reagin, *A German Women's Movement: Class and Gender in Hanover, 1880–1933* (Chapel Hill and London, 1995), p. 246.

34. Scheck, 'German Conservatives and Female Political Activism'.

35. Kirsten Heinsohn, 'Negotiating Equality and Difference: The Politics of Extreme Right Women in Germany', in Kevin Passmore, ed., *Women and the Extreme Right in Europe* (Oxford, forthcoming).

36. On women in the *völkisch* movement in Austria, see Johanna Gehmacher, *'Völkische Frauenbewegung'*.

37. Claudia Koonz, *Mothers in the Fatherland: Women, the Family and Nazi Politics* (London, 1987), pp. 177–8; Daniela Münkel, ' "Du, Deutsche Landfrau bist verantwortlich!" Bauer und Bäuerin im Nationalsozialismus', *Archiv für Sozialgeschichte* 38 (1998), pp. 141–64, here pp. 143–7.

38. Jill Stephenson, *The Nazi Organisation of Women* (London, 1981), pp. 97–115; Koonz, *Mothers in the Fatherland*, pp. 127–74.

39. On the Bund Deutscher Mädel, see Dagmar Reese, *Straff, aber nicht stramm; herb, aber nicht derb: Zur Vergesellschaftung der Mädchen durch den Bund Deutscher Mädel im sozialkulturellen Vergleich zweier Milieus* (Weinheim, 1989); Louise Willmot, 'National

Socialist Organisations for Girls: A Contribution to the Social and Political History of the Third Reich', D.Phil. thesis, Oxford, 1980; on the NS-Frauenschaft and Deutsches Frauenwerk, see Stephenson, *Nazi Organisation of Women*; on the women's Labour Service, see Dagmar Morgan, *Weiblicher Arbeitsdienst in Deutschland* (Darmstadt, 1978), and Willmot, see above.

40. Jill Stephenson, *Women in Nazi Germany* (London, 2001), pp. 18–20.

41. Koonz, *Mothers in the Fatherland*, pp. 5–6, 13–14, 218, 389.

42. Dagmar Reese, 'Verstrickung und Verantwortung: Weibliche Jugendliche in der Führung des Bundes Deutscher Mädel', in Kirsten Heinsohn, Barbara Vogel and Ulrike Weckel, eds, *Zwischen Karriere und Verfolgung: Handlungsräume von Frauen im national-sozialistischen Deutschland* (Frankfurt am Main, 1997), pp. 206–22; Andrea Böltken, *Führerinnen im 'Führerstaat': Gertrud Scholtz-Klink, Trude Mohr, Jutta Rüdiger und Inge Viermetz* (Pfaffenweiler, 1995), pp. 134–5.

43. Stephenson, *Women in Nazi Germany*, p. 128.

44. Morgan, *Weiblicher Arbeitsdienst*, pp. 277–8.

45. Max Domarus, ed., *Hitler: Reden und Proklamationen 1932–1945*, vol. 1 (Würzburg, 1962), p. 273.

46. Stephenson, *Women in Nazi Germany*, pp. 90–3.

47. Ibid., pp. 104–5; idem, *Nazi Organisation of Women*, pp. 190–9.

48. Gisela Bock has argued that '[f]emale perpetrators acted in much the same way as male perpetrators': Gisela Bock, 'Ordinary Women in Nazi Germany: Perpetrators, Victims, Followers, and Bystanders', in Dalia Ofer and Lenore J. Weitzman, eds, *Women in the Holocaust* (New Haven and London, 1998), pp. 85–100, here p. 94.

49. Stephenson, *Women in Nazi Germany*, pp. 104–5; idem, *Nazi Organisation of Women*, pp. 190–9; Morgan, *Weiblicher Arbeitsdienst*, pp. 381–90; Dagmar Reese, 'Bund Deutscher Mädel – Zur Geschichte der weiblichen deutschen Jugend im Dritten Reich', in Frauengruppe Faschismusforschung, ed., *Mutterkreuz und Arbeitsbuch: Zur Geschichte der Frauen in der Weimarer Republik und im Nationalsozialismus* (Frankfurt am Main, 1981), pp. 163–87, here pp. 180–4; Willmot, 'National Socialist Youth Organisations for Girls', 242–6, 329–36; Haide Manns, *Frauen für den Nationalsozialismus: Nationalsozialistische Studentinnen und Akademikerinnen in der Weimarer Republik und im Dritten Reich* (Opladen, 1997), pp. 233–7.

50. On recruitment to the civilian administration in the GG, see Bogdan Musial, *Deutsche Zivilverwaltung und Judenverfolgung im Generalgouvernement* (Wiesbaden, 1999), pp. 80–6. On Belorussia, see Bernhard Chiari, *Alltag hinter der Front: Besatzung, Kollabora-tion und Widerstand in Weißrußland 1941–1944* (Düsseldorf 1998), pp. 62–72.

51. Manns, *Frauen für den Nationalsozialismus*, pp. 198–209; Stephenson, *Nazi Organisation of Women*, pp. 198–9.

52. S. Holler, introduction to Alexander von Hohenstein, *Wartheländisches Tagebuch 1941/2* (Stuttgart, 1961), p. 11.

53. Stephenson, *Nazi Organisation of Women*, pp. 178, 191.

54. *'Daß wir nun dort "auf vorgeschobenen Posten" eine Art "Kolonisationsarbeit" verrichten durften, heilte das in unserer Kindheit und frühen Jugend so sehr verletzte nationale Ehrge-fühl'*, Melita Maschmann, *Fazit: Mein Weg in der Hitler-Jugend* (Munich, 1979), p. 77.

55. Manns, *Frauen für den Nationalsozialismus*, pp. 60–2, 233–7.

56. For the case of a young Austrian woman who went to teach in occupied Poland, see Johanna Gehmacher, 'Zukunft, die nicht vergehen will. Jugenderfahrungen in NS-Organisationen und Lebensentwürfe österreichischer Frauen', in Christina Benninghaus and Kerstin Kohtz, eds, *'Sag mir, wo die Mädchen sind': Beiträge zur Geschlechtergeschichte der Jugend* (Cologne, Weimar and Vienna, 1999), pp. 261–74.

57. 'Vom Ende, das ein Anfang wurde: Aus dem Tagebuch von Herta Sch.', in Gerda Szepansky, ed., *'Blitzmädel', 'Heldenmutter', 'Kriegerwitwe': Frauenleben im Zweiten Weltkrieg* (Frankfurt am Main, 1986), pp. 216–31.

58. On problems recruiting personnel for the occupied Soviet territories, see Alexander Dallin, *German Rule in Russia, 1941–1945: A Study of Occupation Policies*, 2nd edition (London, 1981), pp. 102–3; Chiari, *Alltag hinter der Front*, pp. 59–62.

59. Dörte Winkler, *Frauenarbeit im 'Dritten Reich'* (Hamburg, 1977), esp. pp. 129–33; Stephenson, *Women in Nazi Germany*, p. 58; Louise Willmot, 'The Debate on the Introduction of an Auxiliary Military Service Law for Women in the Third Reich and its Consequences', *German History* 2 (1985), pp. 10–20; Elizabeth D. Heineman, *What Difference Does a Husband Make? Women and Marital Status in Nazi and Postwar Germany* (Berkeley, Los Angeles and London, 1999), pp. 59–71.

60. Elizabeth Harvey, 'Gender, Generation and Politics: Young Protestant Women in the Final Years of the Weimar Republic', in Mark Roseman, ed., *Generations in Conflict: Youth Revolt and Generation Formation in Germany 1770–1968* (Cambridge, 1995), pp. 184–209; Christiana Hilpert-Fröhlich, *'Vorwärts geht es, aber auf den Knien: Die Geschichte der christlichen Studentinnen- und Akademikerinnenbewegung in Deutschland 1905–1938* (Pfaffenweiler, 1996), pp. 124–9, 136–8, 143–4; Heinsohn, 'Negotiating Equality and Difference'.

61. Reese, *Straff, aber nicht stramm*, esp. pp. 58–9.

62. Dagmar Reese, 'The BDM Generation: A Female Generation in Transition from Dictatorship to Democracy', in Roseman, ed., *Generations in Conflict*, pp. 227–46, esp. p. 239.

63. Winkler, *Frauenarbeit im 'Dritten Reich'*, pp. 28–33; Stephenson, *Women in Nazi Germany*, pp. 16–20.

64. On women's higher education in Nazi Germany, see Jacques R. Pauwels, *Women, Nazis and Universities: Female University Students in the Third Reich, 1933–1945* (Westport and London, 1984); Jill Stephenson, 'Girls' Higher Education in the 1930s', *Journal of Contemporary History* 10, no. 1 (1975), pp. 41–69; Manns, *Frauen für den Nationalsozialismus*; Michael Grüttner, *Studenten im Dritten Reich* (Paderborn, 1995), pp. 109–26.

65. Stephenson, *Women in Nazi Germany*, p. 65.

66. Lutz Niethammer, ed., *Die volkseigene Erfahrung: Eine Archäologie des Lebens in der Industrieprovinz der DDR* (Berlin, 1991), pp. 570–85.

67. Robert Gellately, *Backing Hitler: Consent and Coercion in Nazi Germany* (Oxford, 2001), p. 260.

68. Angelika Ebbinghaus, ed., *Opfer und Täterinnen: Frauenbiographien des Nationalsozialismus* (Nördlingen, 1987); Gudrun Schwarz, 'Verdrängte Täterinnen: Frauen im Apparat der SS (1939–45)', in Therese Wobbe, ed., *Nach Osten: Verdeckte Spuren nationalsozialistischer Verbrechen* (Frankfurt am Main, 1992), pp. 197–223; Dagmar Reese and Carola Sachse, 'Frauenforschung zum Nationalsozialismus: Eine Bilanz', in Lerke Gravenhorst and Carmen Tatschmurat, eds, *Töchter-Fragen: NS-Frauengeschichte* (Freiburg im Breisgau, 1990), pp. 73–106.

69. On women 'racial experts' working in the Institut für Deutsche Ostarbeit in Cracow, see Burleigh, *Germany Turns Eastwards*, pp. 267–70; Aly and Heim, *Vordenker der Vernichtung*, pp. 198–202.

70. Böltken, *Führerinnen im 'Führerstaat'*, pp. 105–29 (on Inge Viermetz).

71. Gudrun Schwarz, *Eine Frau an seiner Seite: Ehefrauen in der 'SS-Sippengemeinschaft'* (Hamburg, 1997).

72. Chiari, *Alltag hinter der Front*, p. 72.

73. Gehmacher, 'Zukunft, die nicht vergehen will', p. 270.

74. On the bystanders and eyewitnesses of the mass murder of Jews, see Ernst Klee,

Willi Dreßen and Volker Rieß, eds, 'Schöne Zeiten': Judenmord aus der Sicht der Täter und Gaffer (Frankfurt am Main, 1998).

75. Gellately, Backing Hitler, pp. 151–82, 204–23.

76. Marlis G. Steinert, Hitler's War and the Germans: Public Mood and Attitude during the Second World War (Athens, Ohio, 1977), pp. 132–47.

77. David Bankier, The Germans and the Final Solution: Public Opinion under Nazism (Oxford, 1992) pp.101–15; Gellately, Backing Hitler, pp. 145–50.

78. Bankier, Germans and the Final Solution, p. 115.

79. On the quality of personnel in the administration of the occupied Soviet territories generally, see Dallin, German Rule in Russia, pp. 101–3; on civilian personnel in Nazi-occupied Belorussia, see Chiari, Alltag hinter der Front, pp. 72–80 and Christian Gerlach, Kalkulierte Morde: Die deutsche Wirtschafts- und Vernichtungspolitik in Weißrußland 1941 bis 1944 (Hamburg, 1999), pp. 170–3. On the involvement of the civilian administration in the General Government and in Belorussia in the Holocaust, see Musial, Deutsche Zivilverwaltung; Dieter Pohl, Nationalsozialistische Judenverfolgung in Ostgalizien, 1941–44: Organisation und Durchführung eines staatlichen Massenverbrechens (Munich, 1996), pp. 75–83; Chiari, Alltag hinter der Front, pp. 243–7.

80. According to Musial, the mass murder of the Jews became a 'general topic of conversation' among Germans in the General Government, including female employees of the civilian administration. Musial, Deutsche Zivilverwaltung, p. 325.

81. Der Reichsminister für die besetzten Ostgebiete, Abteilung Press und Aufklärung, 'Liste der häufigsten Ostbegriffe' [undated, c. 1942], BA Berlin, R6, 192/Fiche 1.

82. Broszat, Nationalsozialistische Polenpolitik; Madajczyk, Okkupationspolitik; Jerzy Marczewski, Hitlerowska koncepcja polityki kolonizacyjno-wysiedlenczej i jej realizacja w 'Okręgu Warty' (Poznań, 1979).

83. Martin Broszat, Zweihundert Jahre deutscher Polenpolitik (Frankfurt am Main, 1972), pp. 288–90; on Danzig-Westpreußen, see Dieter Schenk, Hitlers Mann in Danzig. Albert Forster und die NS-Verbrechen in Danzig-Westpreußen (Bonn, 2000); on Upper Silesia, see Andrzej Szefer, 'Die deutschen Umsiedler in der Provinz Oberschlesien in den Jahren 1939–1945', in Joachim Hütter, Reinhard Meyers and Dietrich Papenfuß, eds, Tradition und Neubeginn. Internationale Forschungen zur deutschen Geschichte im 20. Jahrhundert (Cologne, 1976), pp. 345–54.

84. Raul Hilberg, The Destruction of the European Jews (New York, 1985), vol. 2, p. 484 and vol. 3, pp. 871, 893, 969–70; Adalbert Rückerl, ed., NS-Vernichtungslager im Spiegel deutscher Strafprozesse: Belzec, Sobibor, Treblinka, Chelmno (Munich, 1977), pp. 243–304, esp. pp. 262–74; Ian Kershaw, 'Arthur Greiser – ein Motor der "Endlösung"', in Ronald Smelser, E. Syring and Rainer Zitelmann, eds, Die braune Elite II: 21 weitere biographische Skizzen (Darmstadt, 1993), pp. 116–27.

85. On Germanization efforts in the General Government, see Broszat, Zweihundert Jahre deutscher Polenpolitik, pp. 298–300; Koehl, RKFDV, pp. 150–60; on the Zamosc 'experiment', see Czesław Madajczyk, ed., Zamojszczyzna – Sonderlaboratorium SS. Zbiór dokumentów polskich i niemieckich z okresu okupacji hitlerowskiej (2 vols) (Warsaw, 1977).

86. For an analysis of Maschmann's autobiography, see Joanne Sayner, 'Depictions of Fascism in Women's Autobiographies in German', Ph.D. thesis, University of Cardiff, 2002.

87. Bundesministerium für Vertriebene, ed., Dokumentation der Vertreibung der Deutschen aus Ost-Mitteleuropa, vol. 1/1: Die Vertreibung der deutschen Bevölkerung aus den Gebieten östlich der Oder-Neiße (Wolfenbüttel, n.d. = 1954) is the part of the multi-volume Dokumentation most relevant to this study. See Mathias Beer, 'Im Spannungsfeld von Politik und Zeitgeschichte: Das Großforschungsprojekt "Dokumentation der Vertreibung der Deutschen aus Ost-Mitteleuropa', VjZG 46, no. 3 (1998), pp. 345–89; Robert G. Moeller,

War Stories: The Search for a Usable Past in the Federal Republic of Germany (Berkeley and Los Angeles, 2001), pp. 51–87.

88. Szepansky, *'Blitzmädel', 'Heldenmutter', 'Kriegerwitwe'*; Reese, *Straff, aber nicht stramm*; Susanne zur Nieden, *Alltag im Ausnahmezustand: Frauentagebücher im zerstörten Deutschland 1943 bis 1945* (Berlin, 1993); Alison Owings, *Frauen: German Women Recall the Third Reich* (New Brunswick, NJ, 1993); Susanne Watzke-Otte, *'Ich war ein einsatzbereites Glied in der Gemeinschaft': Vorgehensweise und Wirkungsmechanismen nationalsozialisticher Erziehung am Beispiel des weiblichen Arbeitsdienstes* (Frankfurt am Main, 1999); Renate Strien, *Mädchenerziehung und-sozialisation in der Zeit des Nationalsozialismus und ihre lebensgeschichtliche Bedeutung: Lehrerinnen erinnern sich an ihre Jugend während des Dritten Reiches* (Opladen, 2000).

89. Richard J. Evans, *In Hitler's Shadow: West German Historians and the Attempt to Escape from the Nazi Past* (London, 1989); Eve Rosenhaft, 'Facing up to the Past – Again? "Crimes of the Wehrmacht"', *Debatte* 5, no. 1 (1997), pp. 105–18; Mary Fulbrook, *German National Identity after the Holocaust* (Cambridge, 1999); Moeller, *War Stories*.

90. Ulrich Herbert, *Fremdarbeiter. Politik und Praxis des 'Ausländer-Einsatzes' in der Kriegswirtschaft des Dritten Reiches* (Bonn, 1985); Annekatrein Mendel, *Zwangsarbeit im Kinderzimmer: 'Ostarbeiterinnen' in deutschen Familien von 1939 bis 1945: Gespräche mit Polinnen und Deutschen* (Frankfurt, 1994); Mark Spoerer, 'NS-Zwangsarbeiter im Deutschen Reich: Eine Statistik vom 30. September 1944 nach Arbeitsamtsbezirken', *VjZG* 49, no. 4 (2001), pp. 665–84.

Chapter 2 Weimar Women and the Mission to the Eastern Borderlands

1. On women's protests against the Versailles treaty, see Scheck, 'Women against Versailles', and Süchting-Hänger, 'Die Anti-Versailles-Propaganda konservativer Frauen in der Weimarer Republik'. On women's activism on behalf of 'Germandom' in the borderlands and abroad in the Weimar period, see Angelika Schaser, 'Das Engagement des Bundes Deutscher Frauenvereine für das "Auslandsdeutschtum": Weibliche "Kulturaufgabe" und nationale Politik vom Ersten Weltkrieg bis 1933', in Ute Planert, ed., *Nation, Politik und Geschlecht: Frauenbewegungen und Nationalismus in der Moderne* (Frankfurt and New York, 2000), pp. 254–74.

2. Rudolf Jaworski, 'Die polnische Grenzminderheit in Deutschland 1920–1939', in Rudolf Jaworski and Marian Wojciechowski, eds, with Mathias Niendorf and Przemysław Hauser, *Deutsche und Polen zwischen den Kriegen. Minderheitenstatus und 'Volkstumskampf' im Grenzgebiet. Amtliche Berichterstattung aus beiden Ländern 1920–1939* (Munich, New Providence, London and Paris, 1997), pp. 49–69, here p. 50; Peter Fischer, *Die deutsche Publizistik als Faktor der deutsch-polnischen Beziehungen 1919–1933* (Wiesbaden, 1991), pp. 11–17; Guntram Hendrik Herb, *Under the Map of Germany: Nationalism and Propaganda 1919–1945* (London and New York, 1997), p. 33.

3. Christoph Kimmich, *The Free City: Danzig and German Foreign Policy 1919–1934* (New Haven and London, 1968), pp. 1–22.

4. Ermland is also known in English as Warmia.

5. Mathias Niendorf, 'Die Provinz Ostpreußen und ihre polnische Bevölkerung', in Jaworski and Wojciechowski, eds, *Deutsche und Polen zwischen den Kriegen*, pp. 159–63, here p. 159.

6. On the plebiscite and the May 1921 uprising, see T. Hunt Tooley, *National Identity and Weimar Germany: Upper Silesia and the Eastern Border, 1918–1922* (Lincoln, Nebraska

and London, 1997), pp. 234–58; see also Richard Blanke, 'Upper Silesia, 1921: The Case for Subjective Nationality', *Canadian Review of Studies in Nationalism* 2 (1975), pp. 241–60.

7. Richard Blanke, *Orphans of Versailles: The Germans in Western Poland 1918–1939* (Kentucky, 1993), pp. 29–30; Mathias Niendorf, 'Die Provinz Oberschlesien und ihre polnische Bevölkerung', in Jaworski and Wojciechowski, eds, *Deutsche und Polen zwischen den Kriegen*, pp. 811–16, here p. 812.

8. Blanke, *Orphans of Versailles*, pp. 32–53.

9. On Prussian anti-Polish policies and the Germanizing drive of the Deutscher Verein für die Ostmarken during the Kaiserreich, see Hagen, *Germans, Poles and Jews*, pp. 118–287; Roland Baier, *Der deutsche Osten als soziale Frage. Eine Studie zur preußischen und deutschen Siedlungs- und Polenpolitik in den Ostprovinzen während des Kaiserreichs und der Weimarer Republik* (Cologne and Vienna, 1970), pp. 2–94; Richard Wonser Tims, *Germanizing Prussian Poland: The H-K-T Society and the Struggle for the Eastern Marches in the German Empire, 1894–1919* (New York, 1941). On the size of the post-war Polish minority in Germany, see Jaworski, 'Die polnische Grenzminderheit', pp. 51–2.

10. Jaworski, 'Die polnische Grenzminderheit', p. 51.

11. Karol Fiedor, Janusz Sobczak and Wojciech Wrzesinski, 'The Image of the Poles in Germany and of the Germans in Poland in the Inter-war Years and its Role in Shaping the Relations between the Two States', *Polish Western Affairs* 19 (1978), pp. 202–28.

12. Martin Broszat, 'Außen- und innenpolitische Aspekte der preußisch-deutschen Minderheitenpolitik in der Ära Stresemann', in Kurt Kluxen and Wolfgang J. Mommsen, eds, *Politische Ideologien und nationalstaatliche Ordnung. Studien zur Geschichte des 19. und 20. Jahrhunderts* (Munich and Vienna, 1968), pp. 393–445.

13. Niendorf, 'Die Provinz Ostpreussen und ihre polnische Bevölkerung', p. 159.

14. Ibid., pp. 811–12.

15. Ibid., pp. 453–7; see also Ian F. D. Morrow and L. M. Sieveking, *The Peace Settlement in the German-Polish Borderlands. A Study of Conditions Today in the Pre-war Prussian Provinces of East and West Prussia* (Oxford, 1936), pp. 386–9.

16. Baier, *Der deutsche Osten als soziale Frage*, p. 386.

17. Ibid., pp. 380–1; Jaworski, 'Die polnische Grenzminderheit', pp. 62–3; Mathias Niendorf, *Minderheiten an der Grenze: Deutsche und Polen in den Kreisen Flatow (Złotów) und Zempelburg (Sępolno Krajenskie), 1900–1939* (Wiesbaden, 1997), pp. 383–92.

18. On negotiations between the governments of Weimar Germany and Poland concerning minority issues, see Blanke, *Orphans of Versailles*, pp. 121–62.

19. Fischer, *Die deutsche Publizistik*, pp. 56–9.

20. On the Society for Germandom Abroad, see Gerhard Weidenfeller, *VDA: Verein für das Deutschtum im Ausland* (Frankfurt am Main, 1976) and Allen Cronenberg, *Volksbund für das Deutschtum im Ausland* (Ann Arbor, Michigan, 1978).

21. K. C. von Loesch and Fr. von Unger, 'Zehn Jahre Deutscher Schutzbund', in *Zehn Jahre Deutscher Schutzbund 1919–1929* (Berlin, 1929), pp. 10–12.

22. Fischer, *Die deutsche Publizistik*, p. 45. The Deutscher Ostbund was formed in September 1920 as a merger of the Reichsverband Ostschutz and the Deutscher Heimatbund Posener Flüchtlinge: it represented the interests of refugees from the former German eastern provinces. In 1922 it also absorbed the Deutscher Verein für die Ostmarken.

23. Blanke, *Orphans of Versailles*, pp. 17–31; Tooley, *National Identity and Weimar Germany*, pp. 234–6.

24. Fischer, *Die deutsche Publizistik*, p. 56.

25. On Käthe Schirmacher, see Anke Walzer, *Käthe Schirmacher. Eine deutsche Frauenrechtlerin auf dem Wege vom Liberalismus zum konservativen Nationalismus* (Pfaffenweiler,

1991); Johanna Gehmacher, 'Der andere Ort der Welt. Käthe Schirmachers Auto/ Biographie der Nation', in Sophia Kemlein, ed., *Geschlecht und Nationalismus in Mittel- und Osteuropa, 1848–1918* (Osnabrück, 2000). On the Deutscher Frauenverein für die Ostmarken, see Drummond, '"Durch Liebe stark, deutsch bis ins Mark", pp. 147–59.

26. Käthe Schirmacher, 'Was sie uns antun', *Deutschlands Erneuerung* (Munich, 1922), pp. 486–93, 542–7; Käthe Schirmacher, 'Landsend', in *Um Deutschland. Nachgelassene Schriften* (Berlin-Nowawes, 1932), pp. 47–50, here p. 48.

27. Schirmacher, 'Landsend', pp. 49–50.

28. Käthe Schirmacher, *Flammen. Erinnerungen aus meinem Leben* (Leipzig, 1921), p. 94.

29. 'Frauenausschuß', *Das Vereinsleben. Mitteilungsblätter des Deutschen Schutzbundes* 1, no. 7 (1920), p. 11.

30. Else Frobenius, 'Notgemeinschaft', in Hauptgeschäftsstelle des Oberschlesier-Hilfswerks, ed., *Oberschlesiens Not* (Berlin, n.d.[= 1921]), pp. 12–14.

31. Lora Wildenthal, 'Mass-Marketing Colonialism and Nationalism: The Career of Else Frobenius in the "Weimarer Republik" and Nazi Germany', in Planert, ed., *Nation, Politik und Geschlecht*, pp. 328–43.

32. *Jahresbericht des Deutschen Schutzbundes über Berichtszeit vom 1. Mai 1928 bis 30. April 1929* (Berlin, undated) pp. 10–11.

33. Wildenthal, 'Mass-Marketing Colonialism and Nationalism', pp. 339–40.

34. Elisabeth Spohr, 'Kulturnot und Frauenaufgaben im deutschen Osten', *Frauendienst am Auslanddeutschtum* 4, no. 47 (1928), pp. 165–7.

35. 'Frauensitzung in Kassel vom 27. Oktober, Sitzungsbericht', *Frauendienst am Ausland-deutschtum* 4, no. 47 (1928), pp. 170–1. Miegel's poem begins: 'Über der Weichsel drüben, Vaterland, höre uns an!/ Wir sinken, wie Pferde und Wagen versinken im Dünensand/ Recke aus deine Hand, die allein uns helfen kann:/ Deutschland, heiliges Land!': see Agnes Miegel, *Gesammelte Gedichte* (Düsseldorf, 1952), pp. 154–7.

36. The German Protestant Women's League (Deutsch-Evangelischer Frauenbund) held its 1929 congress on the theme of 'Grenz- und Auslanddeutschtum'. 'Die 30-Jahr-Feier des Deutsch-Evangelischen Frauenbundes vom 18. bis 22. September 1929 in Marburg', *Frauendienst am Auslanddeutschtum* no. 58/59 (Oct./Nov. 1929), p. 173.

37. Angelika Schaser, 'Das Engagement des Bundes Deutscher Frauenvereine für das "Aus-landsdeutschtum"', pp. 254–69; Irene Stoehr, *Emanzipation zum Staat? Der Allgemeine Deutsche Frauenverein – Deutscher Staatsbürgerinnenverband (1893–1933)* (Pfaffenweiler, 1990), pp. 125–31. On BDF bridge-building efforts: Rundschreiben no. 8 an die Mitglieder des Ausschusses für Volkstumsfragen, 30 Apr. 1932. Landesarchiv Berlin, Helene Lange Archiv, BDF 6 – 29/6.

38. For von Velsen, see 'Frauenausschuß', *Das Vereinsleben. Mitteilungsblätter des Deutschen Schutzbundes* 1, no. 7 (1920), p. 11; Alice Salomon, 'Was bedeutet Oberschlesien für die deutschen Frauen', in Hauptgeschäftsstelle des Oberschlesier-Hilfswerks, ed., *Oberschle-siens Not*, pp. 14–16.

39. On Rosa Kempf's interest in German minorities abroad, see Schaser, 'Das Engagement des Bundes Deutscher Frauenvereine', p. 267.

40. Rosa Kempf, 'Der Ausschuß für Volkstumsfragen', *Nachrichtenblatt des Bundes Deutscher Frauenvereine* 12, no. 6 (1932), pp. 39–40.

41. Rosa Kempf, 'Die Loyalität des Auslandspolentums gegen den polnischen Staat', *Nachrichtenblatt des Bundes Deutscher Frauenvereine* 12, no. 6 (1932), pp. 40–1.

42. Anon., 'Grenzlandnot und deutsche Frauen', *Nachrichtenblatt des Bundes Deutscher Frauenvereine* 12, no. 6 (1932), p. 43.

43. Margarete Skrodzki, 'Ostpreussen und Memel', *Nachrichtenblatt des Bundes Deutscher Frauenvereine* 12, no. 6 (1932), p. 43.

44. Ludwine v. Broecker, 'Die Frau in der Volkstumsbewegung', in Ada Schmidt-Beil, ed., *Die Kultur der Frau* (Berlin, 1931), pp. 384–7.

45. Ibid., p. 384.

46. Hilde Bamler, quoted in 'Frauentagung des VDA 1927 in Goslar', *Frauendienst am Auslanddeutschtum* no. 31/32 (July/Aug. 1927), pp. 352–62, here p. 353.

47. Else Frobenius, 'Der deutsche Muttertag', *Frauendienst am Auslanddeutschtum* 4, no. 40 (April 1928), p. 50.

48. Bertha Kipfmüller, 'Probleme', *Frauendienst am Auslanddeutschtum* 8, no. 91 (1932), pp. 89–91, here p. 90.

49. Von Broecker, 'Die Frau in der Volkstumsbewegung', p. 387.

50. *Jahresbericht des Deutschen Schutzbundes 1928–1929*, p. 8; Helene Fock, 'Die Wichtigkeit des bevölkerungspolitischen Problems für die Grenzländer', *Frauendienst am Auslanddeutschtum* 5, no. 58/59 (1929), pp. 161–6.

51. On the notion of the nationally conscious model German housewife, see Reagin, 'The Imagined *Hausfrau*'.

52. Von Broecker, 'Die Frau in der Volkstumsbewegung', p. 386.

53. Klaus Theweleit, *Männerphantasien, vol. 1: Frauen, Fluten, Körper, Geschichte* (Frankfurt am Main, 1977), pp. 308–12.

54. Doris Kaufmann, *Frauen zwischen Aufbruch und Reaktion. Protestantische Frauenbewegung in der ersten Hälfte des 20. Jahrhunderts* (Munich, 1988), p. 66.

55. Käthe Schirmacher, 'Brennende Herzen', in *Grenzmarkgeist* (Berlin and Leipzig, 1929), pp. 52–4.

56. Käthe Schirmacher, *Die Geknechteten (Die reichsdeutsche Irredenta)* (Berlin, 1922), p. 122.

57. Käthe Schirmacher, 'Danzig', *Alldeutsche Blätter* 32, no. 15 (1922), p. 126, cited in Angela Koch, 'Von männlichen Tätern und weiblichen Räumen. Geschlechtercodes in antipolnischen Diskursen nach dem Ersten Weltkrieg', in Johanna Gehmacher, Elizabeth Harvey and Sophia Kemlein, eds, *Zwischen Kriegen. Nationen, Nationalismen und Geschlechterpolitik in Ost-und Mitteleuropa 1918–1939*, forthcoming.

58. Gertrud M. Hübner, 'Ostmarkenfahrt', *Frauendienst am Auslanddeutschtum*, no. 25 (Jan. 1927), pp. 262–4.

59. Luise Scheffen-Döring, 'Zehn Jahre Frauenarbeit im Deutschen Schutzbund', in *Zehn Jahre Deutscher Schutzbund* (Berlin, 1929) p. 44. The original reads: 'Wir tragen zu tief in Blut und Blick/Erloschener Geschlechter Kämpfergeschick/Und mußten auch uns ihm verschreiben./ – Lockt auch Fernlands Küste flimmerumhaucht/Wir bleiben dem Lande getreu, das uns braucht – /Wir bleiben – wir bleiben!'

60. For a more detailed discussion of these 'borderland excursions', see Elizabeth Harvey, 'Pilgrimages to the "Bleeding Border": Gender and Rituals of Nationalist Protest in Germany, 1919–39', *Women's History Review* 9, no. 2 (2000), pp. 201–28.

61. Hübner, 'Ostmarkenfahrt', p. 264.

62. On the (originally Flemish) song of the *Ostlandfahrer*, see Wolfgang Wippermann, *Der 'deutsche Drang nach Osten'*, p. 12.

63. Ibid.; Henny Pleimes, 'Blick über die Weichsel', *Frauendienst am Auslanddeutschtum* 8, no. 91 (1932), pp. 91–3.

64. On the ideology of Germany's 'cultural mission' in the East, see Wippermann, *Der 'deutsche Drang nach Osten'* and Burleigh, *Germany Turns Eastwards*.

65. 'Grenzlandfahrten und Auslandsbeziehungen der bündischen Jugend', in Werner Kindt, ed., *Die deutsche Jugendbewegung 1920 bis 1933: Die bündische Zeit* (Cologne, 1974), pp. 1529–46. Young women in the Freischar undertook an exchange with young German-speaking women from Yugoslavia: Rundbrief der Mädchen der deutschen Freischar, Gau Sachsen, 31. Dezember 1931. Archiv der deutschen Jugendbewegung Ludwigstein, A2–22/3.

66. Hans Frhr. von Rosen, 'Wir entdecken Wolhynien', *Jahrbuch Weichsel-Warthe*, 1984, pp. 108–14. On the Volhynia trip and the later careers of the participants, see Burleigh, *Germany Turns Eastwards*, pp. 107–15, 176–83.

67. On the youth movement in its *bündisch* phase, see Walter Laqueur, *Young Germany: A History of the German Youth Movement*, 2nd edition (New Brunswick, NJ, 1984), pp. 133–87. For a sample of youth movement views on politics in the Depression, see Helmuth Kittel, 'Politische Kolonne auf der Leuchtenburg, 17. bis 24. Oktober 1931', *Deutsche Freischar* 4 (1931), pp. 110–11.

68. The phrase is that of Georg Götsch, quoted by Herman Nohl, 'Die pädagogische Osthilfe', *Die Erziehung* 7, no. 8 (1931–2), pp. 449–61, here p. 454.

69. On the ideology of 'border struggle', see Fischer, *Die deutsche Publizistik*, pp. 41–3.

70. Jaworski, 'Die polnische Grenzminderheit', p. 52.

71. The 1939 figures showed a sharp decrease in Polish- and dialect-speakers, but escalating discrimination and harassment of the Polish-speaking minority may by 1939 have deterred many from identifying themselves as Polish.

72. On this decree, see Broszat, 'Außen- und innenpolitische Aspekte'.

73. Jaworski, 'Die polnische Grenzminderheit', pp. 55–9.

74. Ibid., p. 56; Wojciech Wrzesinski, 'The Union of Poles in Germany and its Attitude to Problems of Consciousness of Nationality (1922–1939)', *Acta Poloniae Historica* 20 (1969), pp. 52–74.

75. Gertrud Ruhfus, Freischar junger Nation, an die Dienstpflichtigen, Mai 1932. Archiv der deutschen Jugendbewegung, A2–55/3.

76. 'Die Arbeitslagerbewegung' in Kindt, ed., *Die deutsche Jugendbewegung 1920 bis 1933*, pp. 1521–27.

77. On the Boberhaus, the Schlesische Jungmannschaft and the work camp movement, see Peter Dudek, *Erziehung durch Arbeit: Arbeitslagerbewegung und freiwilliger Arbeitsdienst 1920–1935* (Opladen, 1988), pp. 118–68; see also Dagmar Morgan, *Weiblicher Arbeitsdienst in Deutschland* (Darmstadt, 1978) pp. 20–5. On women and the Schlesische Jungmannschaft camps, see Lieselotte Klose-Stiller, *Arbeitsdienst für die weibliche Jugend in Schlesien* (Garmisch-Partenkirchen, 1978), pp. 20–39, and reports by Magdalene Keil and Lore Lommel in *Der Boberhauskreis. Rundbrief* no. 5 (Dec. 1972), pp. 7–10.

78. For an example of these assumptions see for instance Hermann Kügler, 'Landdienst', *Deutsche Freischar* 4, no. 2 (1931–2), pp. 83–6.

79. Lore Lommel, cited in Klose-Stiller, *Arbeitsdienst für die weibliche Jugend*, pp. 36–9, here p. 37.

80. Gertrud Slotty, 'Dorfwoche in Himmelwitz', *Mädchen*, 1932, no. 1 (Feb.), pp. 11–12.

81. Kügler, 'Landdienst', p. 85.

82. Gau Schlesien, 'Landdienst für Mädchen', *Mädchen*, 1932, no. 5 (Nov.), pp. 66–71.

83. Michael H. Kater, 'Die Artamanen – völkische Jugend in der Weimarer Republik', *Historische Zeitschrift* 213 (1971) pp. 577–638.

84. Udo Wengst, 'Schlange-Schöningen, Ostsiedlung und die Demission der Regierung Brüning', *Geschichte in Wissenschaft und Unterricht* 30 no. 9 (1979), pp. 538–51. The expression 'Wall von deutschen Menschen' is found in Herman Nohl, 'Landbewegung, Osthilfe und die nationale Aufgabe der Pädagogik', *Die Erziehung* 7, no. 2 (1931–2), pp. 65–76, here p. 67.

85. Elizabeth Harvey, *Youth and the Welfare State in Weimar Germany* (Oxford, 1993), pp. 136–47.

86. On women's agricultural training schools run by the Reifensteiner Verband, see Ortrud Wörner-Heil, *Frauenschulen auf dem Lande. Reifensteiner Verband (1897–1997)* (Kassel, 1997).

87. Änne Sprengel, 'Ländliche Siedlungspflege in Pommern', *Soziale Berufsarbeit* 12, no. 8 (1932), pp. 88–92; idem, 'Gedanken über die Siedlerfrauenberatung', *Land und Frau* 16, no. 47 (1932), p. 781; idem, 'Der Beruf der Siedlungshelferin', *Land und Frau* 16, no. 41 (1932), p. 685; Frau von Strantz, 'Beratung auch für die Siedlerfrau!', *Archiv für innere Kolonisation* 24 (1932), pp. 133–5; Hermann Schultz, 'Bedeutung und Aufgaben der Frau in der Siedlung', radio broadcast 2 Jan. 1933. Archiv des Diakonischen Werkes, ESD 298.

88. Nohl, 'Landbewegung, Osthilfe und die nationale Aufgabe der Pädagogik'; idem, 'Die pädagogische Osthilfe', *Die Erziehung* 7, no. 8 (1931–2), pp. 459–61; idem, 'Die Siedlungshelferin', *Soziale Berufsarbeit* 12, no. 6 (1932), pp. 57–63. On Nohl and his influence, see Elisabeth Blochmann, *Herman Nohl in der pädagogischen Bewegung seiner Zeit 1879–1960* (Göttingen, 1969), pp. 123–9; Morgan, *Weiblicher Arbeitsdienst in Deutschland*, p. 48. Hans-Christian Harten also identifies Nohl as a formulator of an idea which found its realization in the Student Land Service after 1933 and during the Second World War in BDM projects in Poland, but he overlooks Nohl's connection with Sprengel and more generally the reception of Nohl's ideas by women's organizations in the 1930s: Hans-Christian Harten, *De-Kulturation und Germanisierung: Die nationalsozialistische Rassen- und Erziehungspolitik in Polen 1939–1945* (Frankfurt and New York, 1996), pp. 54–7, 273.

89. Nohl, 'Die Siedlungshelferin', p. 60.

90. Nohl, 'Landbewegung, Osthilfe und die nationale Aufgabe der Pädagogik', p. 74.

91. Nohl, 'Die sozialpädagogische und nationalpolitische Bedeutung der Kinderfürsorge auf dem Lande', *Kindergarten* 73, no. 7/8 (July/Aug. 1932), pp. 168–71, here p. 171; Erna Rosenberg-Schmidt, 'Die Hilfskräfte im Osten', *Kindergarten* 73, no. 7/8 (July/Aug. 1932), pp. 188–92.

92. Harvey, *Youth and the Welfare State*, pp. 136–47; Morgan, *Weiblicher Arbeitsdienst in Deutschland*, pp. 46–52.

93. Der Freiwillige Arbeitsdienst für Mädchen. Eine Denkschrift, bearbeitet vom Deutschen Archiv für Jugendwohlfahrt und der Deutschen Akademie für soziale und pädagogische Frauenarbeit (September 1932). Hamburger Kirchenarchiv, Kirchliches Jugendamt/M 1.

94. 'Freiwilliger Arbeitsdienst der weiblichen Jugend. Erlaß des Reichskommissars für den freiwilligen Arbeitsdienst vom 10. November 1932', *Beilage zum Reichs-Arbeitsmarkt-Anzeiger* no. 22 (22 Nov. 1932).

95. Gau Schlesien [= Magdalene Keil-Jacobsen], 'Mädchen im Freiwilligen Arbeitsdienst', *Mädchen*, 1933, no. 2–3; see also Klose-Stiller, *Arbeitsdienst für die weibliche Jugend*, p. 32.

96. Morgan, *Weiblicher Arbeitsdienst in Deutschland*, pp. 49–50.

97. Hella von Kries, 'Die stellenlose Wohlfahrtspflegerin im Dienste der östlichen Landarbeit', *Soziale Berufsarbeit* 13, no. 3 (1933), pp. 28–30.

98. Hilde Lion, 'Freiwilliger Arbeitsdienst der Frau', *Die Frau* 40, no. 1 (1932–3), pp. 1–9, here pp. 7–8.

99. Nohl, 'Landbewegung, Osthilfe und die nationale Aufgabe der Pädagogik', p. 72.

100. Ibid., p. 67; idem, 'Die pädagogische Osthilfe', p. 450; Sprengel, 'Gedanken über die Siedlerfrauenberatung', p. 781.

Chapter 3 The Nazification of Women's Borderland Activism, 1933–39

1. Rudolf Jaworski, 'Die polnische Grenzminderheit in Deutschland 1920–1939', in Rudolf Jaworski and Marian Wojciechowski, eds, with Mathias Niendorf and Przemyslaw

Hauser, *Deutsche und Polen zwischen den Kriegen: Minderheitenstatus und 'Volkstums-kampf' im Grenzgebiet. Amtliche Berichterstattung aus beiden Ländern 1920–1939* (Munich, New Providence, London and Paris, 1997), p. 67.

2. Ibid.

3. Niendorf, *Minderheiten an der Grenze*, pp. 360–6.

4. Jaworski, 'Die polnische Grenzminderheit', p. 69; Niendorf, *Minderheiten an der Grenze*, pp. 348–52; Wojciech Wrzesinski, 'Die Politik der nationalsozialistischen Machthaber gegenüber der polnischen Minderheit in Deutschland (1933–45)', in Ernst Hinrichs, ed., *Deutschland und Polen von der nationalsozialistischen Machtergreifung bis zum Ende des zweiten Weltkriegs* (Braunschweig, 1986), pp. 85–92.

5. Hans-Adolf Jacobsen, *Nationalsozialistische Außenpolitik* (Frankfurt am Main, 1968), pp. 167–9; Bericht über die Frauentagung des VDA in Passau, 3.6.1933. BA Koblenz, R57/DAI 675.

6. On the fate of the bourgeois feminist movement in 1933, see Evans, *The Feminist Movement in Germany*, pp. 256–9; Koonz, *Mothers in the Fatherland*, pp. 143–9.

7. These organizations included the Deutscher Ostmarkenverein. Ludwine von Broecker, 'Worin bestehen die Aufgaben der deutschen Frau im Bund Deutscher Osten?', *Ostland* 4 Aug. 1933.

8. On the VDA under Nazism, see Cronenberg, *The Volksbund für das Deutschtum im Ausland*, pp. 113–97; Jacobsen, *Nationalsozialistische Außenpolitik*, pp. 175–206.

9. Dr M. Unger, Grenz- und Auslandsabteilung, Reichsfrauenführung, to Gaufrauenschafts-leitung Westfalen-Nord, Abteilung Grenz- und Ausland, 20 Dec. 1937. NWStA Münster, NS-Frauenschaft, Gau Westfalen-Nord, 530.

10. Protokoll über die Wochenendschulung der Abtlg. Grenz- u. Ausland vom 23–25 Jan. 1937 in der Gauschule Hans Botzlar. NWStA Münster, NS-Frauenschaft, Gau Westfalen-Nord, 127.

11. Ibid. On the Grenz/Ausland department of the Reichsfrauenführung, see Stephenson, *The Nazi Organisation of Women*, p. 157.

12. Marie Rabl, 'Volksdeutsche Schulung der Frauen', *Frauendienst am Auslanddeutschtum* 107/108 (Nov–Dec. 1933), pp. 237–8.

13. On the legacy of the Boberhaus for the RADwJ, see Lilli Marawske-Birkner, *Der weibliche Arbeitsdienst* (Leipzig, 1942), p. 177.

14. G.H., 'Arbeit im Arbeitslager und in der Führerschulung', *Vereins-Zeitung der ehem. Pestalozzi-Fröbel-Haus Schülerinnen* 187 (Mar. 1934), pp. 9–11.

15. The BDM Land Service (Landdienst), formed in 1936, could be included in the list of initiatives organizing girls to help settlers, but no detailed information has come to light on pre-war BDM Landdienst camps. On the pre-war Landdienst generally, see Reichsjugendführung, ed., *Wir schaffen: Jahrbuch des BDM 1938* (Munich, 1938), pp. 189–91; idem ed., *Wir schaffen: Jahrbuch des BDM 1940* (Munich, 1940), p. 175.

16. Reichsarbeitsführer an Ministerialdirektor Dr Vollert (RMdI) betr. Übereignung der zu erstellenden 12 Lager des RADwJ in Ostpreußen, 5 Apr. 1938. BA Berlin, R2, 4562.

17. Local functionaries of the Reichsnährstand in Silesia and Prussia continued to press for Polish migrant labour to be allowed into the border regions of the Reich: Reichs-bauernführer an den Reichsminister für Ernährung und Landwirtschaft betr. Zuteilung von ausländischen landwirtschaftlichen Arbeitskräften, 21 Mar. 1939; Vermerk über Besprechung bei Staatssek. Neumann im Preuß. Staatsministerium, 6 Apr. 1939. BA Berlin, 36.01, 1995.

18. Hierl, speech at 1937 Party Congress, quoted by Dagmar Morgan, *Weiblicher Arbeitsdienst in Deutschland*, p. 279.

19. Morgan, *Weiblicher Arbeitsdienst in Deutschland*, p. 278.

20. Willmot, 'National Socialist Youth Organisations', p. 300.

21. Der Oberpräsident der Provinz Pommern (Stettin) an den Reichsminister des Innern (= RmdI) betr. Neueinrichtung von Arbeitsdienstlagern für die weibliche Jugend in der Provinz Pommern, 9 July 1938. BA Berlin, 36.01, 1849.

22. Willmot, 'National Socialist Youth Organisations', p. 301.

23. Hans-Werner Wiebe, Bericht über studentischen Landdienst Frühjahr 1936, May 1936. StA Würzburg, RSF II, 324. On the elitism, see 'Landdienstgruppenarbeit an der Hochschule', *Landdienst-Pommern-Rundbrief* 1 (1936), pp. 16–17.

24. Einsatzreferent Kurmark an die Reichsstudentenführung, Amt für Politische Erziehung, Hauptstelle Studentischer Einsatz, 29 Jan. 1938. StA Würzburg, RSF II, 347.

25. Participants (both sexes): 1934: 420; 1936: 1620; 1938–9: *c*. 3,000. RMdI an Göning, Reichsministerium für Wissenschaft, Erziehung und Volksbildung (= RErzM) betr. Stud. Landdienst, 14 Apr. 1939. BA Berlin, 36.01, 1708. Slightly different figures are given in Grüttner, *Studenten im Dritten Reich*, p. 342.

26. The 1937 figures are from Landdienst organizers' questionnaires, 10 June 1938. St A Würzburg, RSF II, 347. Figures for the students sent to the Border Province and Pomerania 1934: 143 women, 200 men; 1935, 442 women, 619 men. Studentischer Landdienst: Gebietsreferat Grenzmark-Pommern. Organisation, Arbeit und Zielsetzung, undated report (= 1936). StA Würzburg, RSF II, 324.

27. Deutsche Studentenschaft, Amt Landdienst, Rundschreiben Nr. 3/LD, 19 Nov. 1935. StA Würzburg, RSF II, 313. Landdienst students also worked in the Bayerische Ostmark on the German–Czech border.

28. The scheme was subsidized by the Ministry of the Interior, the Education Ministry, the Reich Food Estate and the Reich Working Group for Regional Planning (Reichsarbeitsgemeinschaft für Raumforschung). Vorschlag der Vermögensverwaltung der Abteilung 'Studentischer Einsatz' im Amt 'Politische Erziehung', 1 Jan. 1937–31 Mar. 1937. StA Würzburg, RSF II, 328; Hauptstelle Studentischer Einsatz an die Reichsarbeitsgemeinschaft für Raumforschung, 8 July 1937. StA Würzburg, RSF II, 324; G. Mähner, 'Reisebericht über die Reise nach Berlin am 10. März 1938'. StA Würzburg, RSF II, 294; for figures on subsidies: Hauptstelle Studentischer Einsatz an den Reichsstudentenführer, 26 Apr. 1939. StA Würzburg, RSF II, 364; for the 'borderlands rationale' used in bids for funding, see Leiter des Amtes Politische Erziehung an den Präsidenten der Reichsanstalt für Arbeitsvermittlung und Arbeitsversicherung, 8 Mar. 1938. StA Würzburg, RSF II, 346.

29. Protokoll des ANSt-Lagers Rithmarschen, 15–27 Sept. 1936. StA Würzburg, RSF II, 300.

30. Hans Endres, Gebietsreferent Bayerisch. Ostmark, 1. Landdienstrundschreiben, Pasing, 2 Jan. 1936, StA Würzburg, RSF II, 296.

31. Ibid. ('Kerle'); Walter Nietzsch, Jena, April 1936, Notizen uber Reichslanddienstlager, 1–3 Mar. 1936. StA Würzburg, RSF II, 324 ('kulturelles Überfallkommando'); D. von Oppen, 'Aufbau!', *Mitteilungen Studentischer Landdienst* 3 (Jan. 1936), p. 2 ('Etappe'/'Front').

32. Barbara Wernick, 'Die Haltung der Mädels', *Junger Osten* 25 (17 Nov. 1936), p. 13.

33. Hertha Suadacani, Bericht über die Arbeit im Außenamt der Studentenschaft der Universität Berlin Mädelreferat, 27 Feb. 1936. StA Würzburg, RSF II, 535.

34. Grenzpolitischer Dorfdienst des NSDStB Gau Franken in Verbindung mit dem NSDStB Gau Bayerische Ostmark, undated (= 1937). StA Würzburg, RSF II, 324.

35. Ursula Buettner, Einsatz- und Kulturreferentin im Gau Berlin, Bericht über die Mädelarbeit im Sommereinsatz 1937. StA Würzburg, RSF II, 343.

36. Ibid.

37. On the Land Year generally, see Edith Niehuis, *Das Landjahr: Eine Jugenderziehungseinrichtung in der Zeit des Nationalsozialismus* (Nörten-Hardenberg, 1984).

38. Ibid., pp. 40–1.

39. Ibid., p. 145.

40. *Landjahr-Schulungsbriefe* 2, no. 6 (1937) was a special issue on the borderlands.

41. Jugendführer des Deutschen Reichs betr: Übernahme des Landjahrs in den Geschäftsbereich des Jugendführers des Deutschen Reichs und Stellungnahme zu dem Beschluß, das Landjahr aufzulösen, 20 Aug. 1937. BA Berlin, R2, 12893; Reg.präs. Schneidemühl an die NSDAP Gauleitung Kurmark, 21 June 1938. Archiwum Państwowe w Poznaniu (APP), Reg. Schneidemühl, 2322.

42. Hanna Fischer, 'Reichsführerinnenschule-Landjahr: Behle-Netzekreis', *Landjahr-Schulungsbriefe* 2, no. 6 (1937) pp. 137–9.

43. Figures for Köslin and Schneidemühl: Erfahrungsbericht der Landjahrbezirksführerin Magda Tiedemann in Köslin bis zum 10. Oktober 1935. APP, Regierung Schneidemühl, 2322; figures on East Prussia, Liste der Mädel- und Jungenlager (May 1936). Geheimes Staatsarchiv Preußischer Kulturbesitz (GStAPK), XX. HA, Rep. 240, B12d.

44. Of these, 5,480 boys (28% of the total boys) were in camps in the eastern border districts of Königsberg, Gumbinnen, Allenstein/Marienwerder, Köslin, Schneidemühl and Breslau/Liegnitz/Oppeln; and 3,060 girls (24% of the total girls) were in camps in the eastern border districts of Königsberg/Allenstein, Köslin/Schneidemühl and Breslau/Liegnitz/Oppeln. 'Übersicht über die preußischen Landjahrbezirke 1937', *Landjahr-Schulungsbriefe* 2, no. 1 (1937), p. 25. Niehuis, *Landjahr*, p. 67, has a different figure for 1937.

45. Erfahrungsbericht Magda Tiedemann (see note 43); Bericht über das Praktikantinnen-Abschlußlager in Klannin, Kreis Köslin, 12 June 1936. APP, Reg. Schneidemühl, 2329; cf. Niehuis, *Landjahr*, p. 73.

46. *Reichsbefehl der Reichsjugendführung* 16, no. 4 (28 Apr. 1939), pp. 305–6 betr. Landjahrführer.

47. M. Tiedemann an die Schulleiterin Lotte Dieck, Reichsführerinnenschule Landjahr in Behle betr. Zuweisungen von Praktikantinnen, 3 May 1939. APP, Reg. Schneidemühl, 2329.

48. Reg.präs. Schneidemühl (Abt. Landjahr) an das RErzM betr. Finanzierung des Ausbaus und der Einrichtung von Landjahrlagern in der Provinz Grenzmark Posen-Westpreußen, Jan. 1938; Reg.- Ass. Baron von Ceumern-Lindenstjerna (Abt. Landjahr, Reg. Schneidemühl) an Landjahrbezirksführerin M. Tiedemann, Köslin, 10 Jan. 1938. APP, Reg. Schneidemühl, 2326.

49. Vierteljahresbericht des Landjahrbezirksführers Schubert, Reg.-Bez. Frankfurt/Oder und Grenzmark-Süd, betr. die Lager in Grenzmark-Süd, 1 Oct. 1935. APP, Regierung Schneidemühl, 2322. On Groß-Dammer/Dąbrówka Wielka, see Wiktor Lemiesz, *Dąbrówka Wielka. A Contribution to the History of the Polish Indigenous Population* (Poznań, 1961), and Jaworski and Wojciechowski, eds, *Deutsche und Polen zwischen den Kriegen*, vol. 1, pp. 472–5.

50. Landjahrlager Groß-Dammer an den Landjahrbezirksführer Geuß (Schneidemühl), 19 Aug. 1936. APP, Reg. Schneidemühl, 2326.

51. Protokoll über die Wochenendschulung der Abteilung Grenz- und Ausland vom 23–25 Jan. 1937 in der Gauschule Haus Botzlar. NWStA Münster, NS-Frauenschaft, Gau Westfalen Nord, 127.

52. Reg.präs. Schneidemühl an das RErzM betr. Bereitstellung von Mitteln für Kindergärten in den nationalpolitisch gefährdeten Gebieten der Grenzmark, May 1935. APP, Reg. Schneidemühl, 8035.

53. Reg.-Dir. Cornberg, Schneidemühl, an Frau Förster, RErzM, 16 Apr. 1936; Reg.präs. Schneidemühl an das RMdI betr: Seminar für Kindergärtnerinnen in Radawnitz

(Kreis Flatow), 13 Apr. 1937; RErzM an Reg.präs. Schneidemühl, 2 June 1937; Vermerk (Reg.präs. Schneidemühl), 22 July 1937. BA Berlin, 49.01, 10575/123.

54. Reg.präs. Schneidemühl an das RErzM betr. Genehmigung und Anerkennung der Fachschule für Kindergärtnerinnen in Radawnitz, Kreis Flatow, 4 Nov. 1944. BA Berlin, 49.01, 10575/123.

55. Reg.präs. Schneidemühl an das RMdI betr. Seminar für Kindergärtnerinnen in Radawnitz (Kreis Flatow), 13 Apr. 1937. BA Berlin, 49.01, 10575/123.

56. Theodor Oberländer to Landrat Franz, Stuhm, 21 Oct. 1935. GStAPK, XX HA Rep. 240, B 30 b. Oberländer had become head of the BDO in 1934: see Burleigh, *Germany Turns Eastwards*, p. 145.

57. Protokoll der Besprechung über den Bau, die Einrichtung und laufende Unterhaltung von NSV-Jugendhäusern in den nationalpolitisch gefährdeten Gebieten am 10. August 1935 im Oberpräsidium. GStAPK, XX. HA, Rep. 240, B20b.

58. Protokoll über die Sitzung des Gau-Grenzlandamtes am 29. Januar 1936. GStAPK, XX. HA, Rep. 240, B20b.

59. Oberpräs. der Provinz Ostpreußen an das RErzM betr. Errichtung eines nationalsozialistischen sozialpädagogischen Seminars in Königsberg, 17 Mar. 1936. BA Berlin, 49.01, 10608.

60. RErzM an den Oberpräs. Königsberg, 15 May 1936; Amt für Volkswohlfahrt, Gau Ostpreußen an den Reg.präs. Königsberg, 9 June 1936. BA Berlin, 49.01, 10608; Ostpreußische Frauenschule für Volkspflege an das RErzM, 9 Oct. 1937. BA Berlin, 49.01, 10603.

61. Der Oberpräs. der Provinz Ostpreußen, Abt. für höheres Schulwesen, an die Leitung des NS-Sozialpädagogischen Seminars Königsberg-Ratslinden, 18 May 1938; Gau-Organisationsleiter Dargel an Vizepräsident Dr Bethke, 24 May 1938. GStAPK, XX. HA, Rep. 240, B12a.

62. RMdI an das RErzM, 17 Jan. 1935; Hanne Albrecht, Gauführerin, Reichsjugendführung Abteilung 'Ausland', an das RErzM, 20 Feb. 1935. BA Berlin, 49.01, 10575/94.

63. Fachgruppe der Kindergärtnerinnen, Hortnerinnen und Jugendleiterinnen an die Reichsreferentin des BDM Gertrud Mohr betr. Helferinnen-Ausbildung in Grenzkindergärten, 28 Jan. 1935; RErzM an das RMdI, 13 Feb. 1935. BA Berlin, 49.01, 10575/94.

64. Hanne Albrecht, Plan für die theoretische, dreimonatliche Ausbildung der Kindergartenhelferinnen in Weissenberg (1935). BA Berlin, 49.01, 10575/94.

65. Elisabeth Schneider, Tätigkeitsbericht über meine sechsmonatliche Probezeit vom 1. April bis 1. Oktober 1936 als kommissarische Bezirksjugendwartin für den Regierungsbezirk Oppeln. BA Berlin, 49.01, 3300/7.

66. RErzM an den Staatssekretär und Chef der Reichskanzlei betr. Hitlerjugend, 15 Mar. 1937. BA Berlin, 49.01, 11845.

67. Reg.präs. Oppeln an das RErzM betr. hauptamtliche Kräfte für die Volkstumsarbeit in den deutschtumsgefährdeten Kreisen Oberschlesiens, 12 Mar. 1937; RMdI an den Reg.präs. in Oppeln, 31 Mar. 1937. BA Berlin, 49.01, 3300/7; Vermerk Tschernin, RErzM, 3 Dec. 1937. BA Berlin, 49.01, 3300/8.

68. Reg.präs. Oppeln an das RErzM und an das Preuß. Finanzmin. 10 Jan. 1938; Reg.präs. Oppeln an das RErzM, betr. Erhaltung der Kreisjugendwarte und -jugendwartinnen in 8 oberschlesischen Grenzkreisen im Rechnungsjahre 1938/9, 28 Jan. 1938. BA Berlin, 49.01, 3300/7.

69. Oberpräs. der Provinz Ostpreußen an das RErzM, 17 Dec.1937. BA Berlin, R43 II, 515.

70. Anon., 'Grenzlandarbeit in NSV-Kindergärten: Gau Pommern', *Nationalsozialistischer Volksdienst* 3, no. 10 (1935–6), pp. 145–6.

71. Gertrud Gregutsch, komm. Bezirksjugendwartin für den Regierungsbezirk Schneidemühl, Tätigkeitsbericht vom 1.4.35 bis 30.9.35, 1 Oct. 1935. BA Berlin, 49.01, 3300/3.

72. Reg.präs. Schneidemühl an das RErzM, 3 Mar. 1937. Ibid.

73. Lieselotte Schmidt, komm. Obergauführerin Obergau Pommern an das RErzM, 5 Mar. 1940; RErzM an die Obergauführerin BDM, Stettin, 21 Mar. 1940. Ibid.

74. 'Grenzlandarbeit in NSV-Kindergärten: Gau Pommern' (see note 70).

75. See Morgan, *Weiblicher Arbeitsdienst in Deutschland*, p. 25, for examples of women active in the *bündische Jugend* who made careers in the women's Labour Service under the Nazi regime; another example is Hanna Wolf, formerly involved in the Boberhaus and later *Landesstellenleiterin* for the women's Labour Service in the Nordmark. List of *Landesstellenleiterinnen* in 'Neugestaltung des weiblichen Arbeitsdienstes', *Weibliche Jugend* 43, no. 3 (1934), pp. 75–6; Klose-Stiller, *Arbeitsdienst für die weibliche Jugend*, p. 30.

76. 'Neugestaltung des weiblichen Arbeitsdienstes', pp. 75–6. In the 1970s Eckert published a documentation of the women's Labour Service: Elisabeth Eckert, *Arbeitsdienst für die weibliche Jugend: Antworten nach 40 Jahren. Befragung ehemaliger Arbeitsdienstführerinnen* (Bad Honnef, 1978).

77. Maria Klein, 'Lager Frögenau Kreis Osterode' (undated) BA Berlin, Zsg 145, 19.

78. Elisabeth Siegel, *Dafür und dagegen. Ein Leben für die Sozialpädagogik* (Stuttgart, 1981), pp. 96–105.

79. Ibid., pp. 103–4.

80. Ingeborg Britten, ' "Fängt euer Handwerk fröhlich an!" Briefe einer Arbeitsmaid aus Pommern ins Saarland 1936' (1987, ms.), p. ii. BA Berlin, Zsg 145, 51.

81. Annelotte Hundrieser, letter to Sibylle Burghardt, 8 Feb. 1982 recalling Labour Service in Rinderort bei Labiau. Ibid., 17.

82. Interview with Frau Winter, 27 Oct. 1999.

83. Ilse Seele to Sybille Burghardt, undated. BA Berlin, Zsg 145, 17.

84. Annelotte Hundrieser to Sibylle Burghardt, 8 Feb. 1982. Ibid.

85. Ilse Seele to Sybille Burghardt, undated. Ibid.

86. Annemarie Ruback, geb. Trossert, 'Lager Lehrhof, Kreis Tilsit-Ragnit, 1938' (undated). Ibid.

87. Elsa Stopfel to Sibylle Burghardt, 14 Mar. 1982. Ibid.

88. Ingeborg Britten, 'Fängt Euer Handwerk fröhlich an!', p. iv.

89. Lotte Hartmann-Vennewitz, 'Vor 40 Jahren' (May 1974). BA Berlin, Zsg 145, 16.

90. Maria Klein, 'Führerinnenschulung in Penken-Seeben 1934'. BA Berlin, Zsg 145, 25.

91. Luise Besser, Sozialpädagogische Frauenschule Breslau, an Frau Förster, RErzM, 10 Feb. 1934. BA Berlin, 49.01, 10654.

92. Verzeichnis der Landjahrheime (August 1934). BA Berlin, R2, 12893.

93. Landjahrbezirksführerin Tiedemann, Köslin, Arbeitsbericht über die Arbeit in dem Landjahrführerbezirk Ostpommern/Grenzmark für die Zeit vom Oktober bis Dezember 1935, 9 Jan. 1936. APP, Reg. Schneidemühl, 2322. On qualifications and background of female Land Year staff, see also Niehuis, *Landjahr*, pp. 104–5.

94. Lebenslauf Anna Stockdreher; Tätigkeitsbericht der Bezirksjugendwartin Anna Stockdreher für die Zeit vom 1.4. bis 15.9.1938. BA Berlin, 49.01, 3300/6.

95. Lebenslauf Frieda Jeschke. BA Berlin, 49.01, 3300/1.

96. Gertrud Gregutsch, Lebenslauf (1935). BA Berlin, 49.01, 3300/3.

97. Lebenslauf Elisabeth Schneider (1935). BA Berlin, 49.01, 3300/7.

98. She is given a fictitious name in accordance with my practice concerning all interview respondents, and to protect her anonymity elsewhere in this book.

99. Interview with Frau Niemann, 14 Sept. 1996.

100. Ibid.

101. Gerhard Mähner an die Studentenführung der HfL Dresden, 19 May 1937. StA Würzburg, RSF V, 3 p. 597. On Erntehilfe, see Grüttner, *Studenten*, p. 341.

102. Ralf Link, Gaueinsatzreferat Kurmark, Sommereinsatz 1937. StA Würzburg, RSF II, 343.

103. Gaureferent des NSDStB Gau Pommern, 'Landdienstgruppenarbeit an der Hochschule', *Landdienst Pommern Rundbrief* 1 (1936), pp. 16–17.

104. On the dwindling enthusiasm of university students for active engagement in Nazi student organizations and activities, see Grüttner, *Studenten*, p. 479.

105. M. Cremer, Hauptamtsleiterin VI, Universität Berlin, an Inge Wolff, Berlin, betr. Arbeits-berichte WS 1935/6, 29 Feb. 1936; Elsbeth Kuhn, Referentin fur Arbeitsdienst, Bericht über Land- und Arbeitsdienst im SS 1935; Hauptamtsleiterin VI, Universität Hamburg, Studentenschaft an die Reichsreferentin fur Studentinnen in der Deutschen Studenten-schaft, Semesterbericht, 7 July 1935. StA Würzburg, RSF II, 535.

106. On women students' visits to Yugoslavia, Romania, South Tyrol and Austria, see Hertha Suadicani, Bericht über die Arbeit im Aussenamt der Studentenschaft der Universität Berlin: Mädelreferat, 27 Feb. 1936. StA Würzburg, RSF II, 535.

107. Irmtraut Karnuth, 'Liebe Kameradinnen', in Studentischer Einsatz Gau Schlesien, Merkblatt für den Frühjahrseinsatz, 4 Feb. 1937. StA Würzburg, RSF II, 313.

108. G. Mähner, Bericht über die Dienstreise des Leiters des Amtes Politische Erziehung am 11. und 12. Mai 1938 nach Berlin. StA Würzburg, RSF II, 294.

109. Irmgard Rummel, Hauptamt für Studentinnen, Martin-Luther-Universität Halle, Tätigkeitsbericht für November 1934. StA Würzburg, RSF II, 533.

110. Bulletins appeared under various titles including *Studentische Landdienst-Mitteilungen* and *Junger Osten: Mitteilungen des studentischen Landdienstes*.

111. Ortrud Krüger, Bericht über den Landdienst vom 1. April–14. April 1937 in Minnenrode und Annenfelde bei Dobrin (Kreis Flatow). StA Würzburg, RSF Vi, 7 g 619/2.

112. Elfriede Tschiersch, 'Als Kindergärtnerin im Kreise Bütow (Pommern)', *Junger Osten* 14 (12 June 1936), p. 12.

113. 'Eine Landdienstlerin im Landjahr schreibt uns' [Grete Finke], *Junger Osten* 13 (29 May 1936), p. 11.

114. Akte Luise Dolezalek, BA Berlin, ehemaliges BDC; Plan der Südtirolarbeit aufgestellt von Luis [*sic*] Fick u. Fred Kuzmany, Berlin, 20 Feb. 1936. StA Würzburg, RSF II, 535; Luis Fick to Lieselotte Machwirth, 15 Oct. 1935, StA Würzburg, RSF II, 550.

115. Luise Fick, *Die deutsche Jugendbewegung* (Jena, 1939), pp. 179–89.

116. Akte Hertha Suadicani, BA Berlin, ehemaliges BDC.

117. H.-W. Wiebe, Gebietsreferent Landdienst Ostpreußen, Sommersemester-Bericht 1936, 11 June 1936. StA Würzburg, RSF II, 327.

118. For a Student Land Service view on Upper Silesian dialect-speakers, see for instance Rudi Brodack, HfL Esslingen, Bericht über den Frühjahrseinsatz 1938 in Grieslienen. StA Würzburg, RSF II, 360.

119. Ralf Link, Gaueinsatzreferat Kurmark, Sommereinsatz 1937. StA Würzburg, RSF II, 343.

120. Luise Essig, 'Unsere Ziele für die Mädchen und Frauen des Landvolks', in Konrad Meyer et al., *Landvolk im Werden: Material zum ländlichen Aufbau in den neuen Ostgebieten und zur Gestaltung des dörflichen Lebens*, 2nd edition (Berlin, 1942), pp. 150–1.

121. Ursula Buettner, Einsatz- und Kulturreferentin im Gau Berlin, Bericht über die Mädelarbeit im Sommereinsatz 1937. StA Würzburg, RSF II, 343.

122. Britten, 'Fangt Euer Handwerk fröhlich an!', pp. 23–4.

123. Herbst-Reichelt, 'Das Lager an der Grenze', *Landjahr-Schulungsbriefe* 1, no. 2/3 (1936–7), pp. 2–4. (This is probably Ruth Reichelt: see Niehuis, *Landjahr*, p. 119 n. 80.)

124. Ibid.

125. 'Berliner Kameradinnen in der Grenzmark', *Die ANSt-Gruppe* 5 (30 June 1939), pp. 30–5, here p. 32.

126. Erika Schwarz, BDM-Untergauführerin, an Ortrud Krüger, Schneidemühl, 5 July 1937.

StA Würzburg, RSF V, 7 g 619/2; D. v. Oppen, Studentischer Landdienst Flatow an die HfL Schneidemühl, Studentinnenführerin, 21 Mar. 1937. StA Würzburg, RSF V, 7 g 619/1.

127. Johanna Schötzau, Referentin für Studentinnen im Kreis Deutsch-Krone [Sommerbericht 1937]. StA Würzburg, RSF II, 343.

128. Erika Scholz, Bericht über meine Arbeit im Frühjahrseinsatz 1937; Grete Nitschke, Der Landdienst, undated (=1937). StA Würzburg, RSF V, 7 g 619/2.

129. Hildegard Kuby, Landdienstbericht 27 Apr. 1937. Einsatz vom 1.4–14.4. in Ammenfeld bei Preußisch Friedland. Ibid.

130. Landdienst-Bericht on family H. [unsigned], Schneidemühl 2 May 1937. Ibid.

131. Landdienst-Bericht, 2 May 1937 (see previous note); Gerda Nitschke, Der Landdienst. Ibid.

132. Since the Nazi agricultural settlement programme in the pre-war period was so modest in scale – despite the grand promises made by the Party's agrarian experts – the number of applicants for settler places exceeded demand; and the number of settlers screened and approved exceeded again the number actually settled on farms. It was conquest in the East which promised to provide land for large-scale settlement. On Nazi agricultural settlement policy, see Gustavo Corni, *Hitler and the Peasants: Agrarian Policy of the Third Reich, 1930–1939* (New York, Oxford and Munich, 1990), ch. 6; John Farquharson, *The Plough and the Swastika: The NSDAP and Agriculture in Germany 1928–1945* (London and Beverly Hills, 1976), ch. 10.

133. Anneliese Nider, Bericht über meine Landdienstzeit vom 1. IV–14. IV. 1937 in der Mustersiedlung Minnenrode bei Dobrin, 1 May 1937. StA Würzburg, RSF V, 7 g 619/2.

134. Hildegard Busse, Bericht über den Landdiensteinsatz in Altmark Kreis Stuhm (1938). StA Würzburg, RSF II, 360.

135. Dorfbericht: Einsatz im Sommer 1936 in Penglitten (Kr. Allenstein) [unsigned]; Albert Münzing, Königsberg, April 1937, Dorfbericht über das Dorf Penglitten. Frühjahrseinsatz 1937 Kreis Allenstein. StA Würzburg, RSF II, 327.

136. G. Grau, Einsatzbericht, undated (=1937). Ibid.

137. Ortrud Krüger, Landdienst im Ermland (=1935). Ibid. On 'entailed farm' legislation, see Farquharson, *Plough and the Swastika.* pp. 63–6.

138. Helmut Häber, Einsatz: Sommer 1936 bei Q., Penglitten (Kr. Allenstein). Ibid.

139. Albert Münzing, Königsberg, April 1937, Dorfbericht über das Dorf Penglitten. Frühjahrseinsatz 1937 Kreis Allenstein. Ibid.

140. Inge Grade, Bericht über meine Landdienstzeit (1935); Gertrud Mallmann, Landdienstbericht (1936), Traude Seydlitz, Landdienstbericht vom Frühjahrseinsatz 1937. Ibid.

141. Gertrud Mallmann, Landdienstbericht (1935). Ibid.

142. Inge Grade, Bericht über meine Landdienstzeit (1935). Ibid.

143. Traude Seydlitz, Landdienstbericht. Ibid.

144. Gretel Onken, Landdienstbericht (1936), Ibid.

145. Protokoll, ANSt Lager Rithmarschen, 15–27 Sept. 1936. StA Würzburg, RSF II, 300.

146. Bericht über den Landdiensteinsatz, Sommersemester 1937. StA Würzburg, RSF II, 343.

147. 'Der weibliche Arbeitsdienst in Ostpreussen' (anon.) (=1940). BA Berlin, Zsg 145, 16.

148. Tätigkeitsbericht der Bezirksjugendwartin Anna Stockdreher für die Zeit vom 1 Apr. bis 15 Sept. 1938. BA Berlin, 49.01, 3300/6.

149. Lotte Dieck, Erfahrungsbericht für den Monat Juli 1934 der Landjahrführerin für den Regierungsbezirk Köslin und Grenzmark Nord. APP, Reg. Schneidemühl, 2322.

150. Ibid.

151. Luzia Engler, Neukramzig, an den Reg.präs. Schneidemühl (undated). APP, Reg. Schneidemühl, 7994.

152. Elisabeth Schneider, Tätigkeitsbericht. BA Berlin, 49.01, 3300/7.

153. Reg.präs. Oppeln, an das RErzM betr. Bezirksjugendwartin, 20 Oct. 1936. Ibid.

154. Franz Schall, 'Arbeitsbericht aus Jena', *Ostmarken-Landdienst-Mitteilungen* 1 (Jan. 1935) [should read: 1936], pp. 10–11.

155. Bericht über das Treffen der 6 Mädellandjahrheime der Grenzmark-Süd in Groß-Dreusen am 23. und 24.7.1934. Berichterstatterin Wally Mings, Heimleiterin. APP, Reg. Schneidemühl, 2322.

156. H. Schmidt-Vanderheyden, *Arbeitsmaiden in Pommern. Ein Rückblick* (Göttingen, 1975), p. 30.

157. Herbst-Reichelt, 'Das Lager an der Grenze', *Landjahr-Schulungsbriefe* 1, no. 2/3 (1936–7), pp. 2–4.

158. Ibid.

159. Blanke, *Orphans of Versailles*, pp. 30–1, 195.

160. Landjahrbezirksführerin Tiedemann, Arbeitsbericht über die Arbeit in dem Landjahrführerbezirk Ostpommern/Grenzmark für die Zeit vom Oktober bis Dezember 1935. APP, Reg. Schneidemühl, 2322.

161. Charlotte Hamsch, Berlin, 'Unser Dorf. Ein Wandfries für das BDM-Heim in Mariendorf-Netzekreis', *Studentischer Landdienst – Mitteilungen* 6 (22 Feb. 1936), pp. 10–11.

162. Erika Zenk, 'Turnabende im Dorf', *Der junge Osten* 11 (29 Apr. 1936), p. 9.

163. Rosemarie Groeper, 'Volkstumsarbeit in der Hamburger Landdienstgruppe', *Der junge Osten* 11 (29 Apr. 1936), pp. 10–11.

164. NSDStB Kameradschaft 9, 28 Mar. 1938, Hannover, Bericht über das studentische Landeinsatzlager des Gaues Pommern. StA Würzburg, RSF II, 360.

165. Annelore Bock, 'Sport – Brauchtum? Etwas für Praktiker', *Junger Osten – Mitteilungen des studentischen Landdienstes* 21 (21 Sept. 1936), pp. 13–14.

166. Gerhard Binder, Erfahrungen im Landdienst (1938). StA Würzburg, RSF II, 360.

167. Ortrud Krüger, Landdienst im Ermland. StA Würzburg, RSF II, 327.

168. Landrat des Kreises Flatow an Karl Kracke, Reichsstudentenführung betr. Errichtung eines Gedenksteines in Dt. Fier, 17 May 1936; Trumpf, Aktenvermerk über Besprechung zwischen Gauleiter Stellvertreter der Kurmark, SA-Brigadeführer Wegener und dem Leiter des Verbindungsamtes Berlin, SA-Standartenführer Trumpf (undated). StA Würzburg, RSF II, 347.

169. Schmielau, 'Bericht über die Ermordung des Studenten Siegfried Paul', 2 May 1938. Ibid., p. 10.

170. Landjahrlager Groß-Dammer an den Landjahrbezirksführer Geuß (Schneidemühl), 19 Aug. 1936. APP, Reg. Schneidemühl, 2326.

171. Der Distriktskommissar in Kuschten an den Landrat in Meseritz. Minderheiten-Lagebericht, 16 Nov. 1937, in Jaworski and Wojciechowski, eds, *Deutsche und Polen zwischen den Kriegen*, vol. 1, pp. 575–8.

172. Bericht über zwei Überfälle von Angehörigen der polnischen Minderheit auf mehrere Arbeitsmaiden des Lagers 5/41, Groß-Dammer, Arbeitsdienst f.d.weibliche Jugend, reproduced in Wiktor Lemiesz, *Dąbrówka Wielka: przyczynek do dziejów polskiej ludności rodzimej* (Warsaw, 1959), p. 47; see also the account in Wiktor Lemiesz, *Dąbrówka pod okiem hitlerowskiego żandarma (1935–39)* (Poznań, 1954), pp. 122–31. I am indebted to Mathias Niendorf for these references.

173. Lemiesz, *Dąbrówka Wielka*, p. 47.

174. Ibid., pp. 33–4, and appendix (documents), p. 48.

175. Interview with Frau Winter, 27 Oct. 1999; Eva Endl, 'So entstand das "Kartoffelfreikorps": Aus dem Tagebuch einer freiwilligen Arbeitsmaid, Ostpreußen im Herbst 1938'. BA Berlin, Zsg 145, 22.

176. Gerda Walendy, 'Unsere Arbeit', Bezirk I Ostpreußen Nord, Juli 1942, pp. 3–4. BA Berlin, Zsg 145, 16.

Chapter 4 The Recruitment Drive: 'Womanly Tasks' and Germanization in Occupied Poland

1. Anon., 'Der Auftrag der Frau im Osten', *Nachrichtendienst der Reichsfrauenführung* (= RFF) 11, no. 10 (1942), p. 143.

2. Hans-Erich Volkmann, 'Zur Ansiedlung der Deutschbalten im "Warthegau"', *Zeitschrift für Ostforschung* 30, no. 4 (1981), pp. 527–58.

3. Heinrich Himmler, 'Geleitwort', *Deutsche Arbeit* 42, no. 6/7 (1942), p. 157.

4. Cited in Volkmann, 'Zur Ansiedlung der Deutschbalten', pp. 527–8.

5. Ruth Bettina Birn, *Die Höheren SS- und Polizeiführer: Himmlers Vertreter im Reich und in den besetzten Gebieten* (Düsseldorf, 1986), pp. 186–9; Christian Jansen and Arno Weckbecker, *Der 'Volksdeutsche Selbstschutz' in Polen 1939/40* (Düsseldorf, 1992), pp. 94–159.

6. Jansen and Weckbecker, *Der 'Volksdeutsche Selbstschutz'*, pp. 31–2.

7. Broszat, *Zweihundert Jahre deutscher Polenpolitik*, p. 277.

8. Helmut Krausnick, 'Denkschrift Himmlers über die Behandlung der Fremdvölkischen im Osten (Mai 1940)', *VjZG* 5 (1957), pp. 194–8.

9. Schechtman, *European Population Transfers*, pp. 258–63.

10. The 1939 figure for Polish population in annexed territories estimated at 8 million (including Jews): Broszat, *Nationalsozialistische Polenpolitik*, p. 86, and Aly, *'Endlösung'*, p. 15. For the figure of 12 million, including 1.5 million Jews, for General Government as constituted 1939, see Aly, *'Endlösung'*, p. 15.

11. Koehl, *RKFDV*, pp. 47–9.

12. Ibid., p. 36.

13. H. v. Rimscha, 'Zur Umsiedlung der Deutschen aus den Baltischen Staaten während des Zweiten Weltkrieges', *Osteuropa* 11 (1961), pp. 134–6; Jürgen von Hehn, *Die Umsiedlung der baltischen Deutschen – das letzte Kapitel baltischdeutscher Geschichte* (Marburg/Lahn, 1982), pp. 75–135; Valdis O. Lumans, *Himmler's Auxiliaries: the Volksdeutsche Mittelstelle and the German National Minorities of Europe, 1933–1945* (Chapel Hill and London, 1993), pp. 101–6.

14. Examples of propaganda portrayals at the time and later: 'Die Heimkehr der Wolhyniendeutschen', *Nationalsozialistische Monatshefte* 11, no. 120 (Mar. 1940), pp. 40–3; Alfred Kleindienst and Kurt Lück, *Die Wolhyniendeutschen kehren heim ins Reich* (Leipzig, 1940); Kurt Lück and Alfred Lattermann, *Die Heimkehr der Galiziendeutschen* (Leipzig, 1940); Helmut Sommer, *Völkerwanderung im 20. Jahrhundert. Die große Heimkehr der Volksdeutschen ins Reich* (Berlin, 1940); *Der Treck der Volksdeutschen aus Wolhynien, Galizien und dem Narewgebiet* mit einem Geleitwort von Werner Lorenz und mit einer Einführung von Wilfrid Bade (Berlin, 1943). See also Lumans, *Himmler's Auxiliaries*, pp. 17–19.

15. A DRK report noted that 400 seriously ill children were treated in a temporary hospital in Kalisch in February 1940, and that 'many more than half' of them were saved. Honisch, DRK-Hauptführer, 15 Mar. 1940. BA Berlin, R49, 3055.

16. Dirk Jachomowski, *Die Umsiedlung der Bessarabien-, Bukowina- und Dobrudjadeutschen: Von der Volksgruppe in Rumänien zur 'Siedlungsbrücke' an der Reichsgrenze* (Munich, 1984).

17. Volkmann, 'Zur Ansiedlung der Deutschbalten', p. 531.
18. The Reichsgau Wartheland was originally designated 'Reichsgau Posen' and acquired the name 'Wartheland' in January 1940. On Arthur Greiser, see Kershaw, 'Arthur Greiser', pp. 116–26. On Albert Forster, see Dieter Schenk, *Hitlers Mann in Danzig.*
19. Schenk, *Hitlers Mann in Danzig*, p. 144; Kershaw, 'Arthur Greiser', p. 123.
20. Broszat, *Nationalsozialistische Polenpolitik*, pp. 59–62; Birn, *Die Höheren SS- und Polizeiführer*, pp. 188–97.
21. Oberpräs. in Kattowitz an den Präsidenten des Landesarbeitsamtes in Breslau betr. Arbeitseinsatz von Volksdeutschen aus der Ukraine in der Landwirtschaft, 7 Oct. 1939. Archiwum Państwowe w Katowicach (APK), Oberpräsidium Kattowitz, 826.
22. Hanns-Hermann Berger, 'Die Deutsche Volksliste in den eingegliederten Ostgebieten', *Deutsche Verwaltung. Organ der Verwaltungsrechtswahrer des NS-Rechtswahrerbundes* 18 (1941), pp. 327–31. See Broszat, *Nationalsozialistische Polenpolitik*, pp. 125–35. Codification of the DVL took place in March 1941 and January 1942: Verordnung über die Deutsche Volksliste und die deutsche Staatsangehörigkeit in den eingegliederten Ostgebieten vom 4. März 1941 in der Fassung der VO vom 31. Januar 1942, in Karol Marian Pospieszalski, *Hitlerowskie 'prawo' okupacyjne w Polsce, Część I: Ziemie 'Wcielone'* [= *Documenta Occupationis V*] (Poznań, 1952), pp. 119–22.
23. Diemut Majer, *'Fremdvölkische' im Dritten Reich: Ein Beitrag zur nationalsozialistischen Rechtsetzung und Rechtspraxis in Verwaltung und Justiz unter besonderer Berücksichtigung der eingegliederten Ostgebiete und des Generalgouvernements* (Boppard am Rhein, 1981), pp. 219–20. For an example of such 'disciplining', see Bergen, 'The "Volksdeutschen" of Eastern Europe', p. 81.
24. RMdI, Rundschreiben betr. Erwerb der deutschen Staatsangehörigkeit durch ehemalige polnische und Danziger Staatsangehörige, 13 Mar. 1941. BA Berlin, R49, 71.
25. Verordnung über die Deutsche Volksliste vom 4. März 1941, paragraph 3. (See note 22.)
26. Ibid., paragraphs 5 and 6. On the formal distinction made between the nationality status of persons in DVL category 3 and category 4, the latter gaining the status of 'Staatsangehörigkeit auf Widerruf' only following individual naturalization (*Einbürgerung*), see Majer, *'Fremdvölkische' im Dritten Reich*, pp. 218, 421.
27. Majer, *'Fremdvölkische' im Dritten Reich*, pp. 317–42.
28. Ibid., pp. 215–18.
29. Ibid., pp. 216, 421. On the fate of Polish Gypsies from the annexed territories and in the General Government, see Michael Zimmermann, *Rassenutopie und Genozid: Die nationalsozialistische 'Lösung der Zigeunerfrage'* (Hamburg, 1996), pp. 277–83.
30. Hilberg, *The Destruction of the European Jews*, pp. 194–5, 206–7, 221–3.
31. Broszat, *Nationalsozialistische Polenpolitik*, pp. 85–6; for a detailed analysis of the planning and implementation of expulsions from the annexed territories up to 1941 see Aly, *'Endlösung'*: figures quoted here are on pp. 89–90; Der HSSFP Posen, betr. Abschiebung von Juden und Polen aus dem Reichsgau Wartheland, 12 Nov. 1939. IfZ, MA 225/ 9569–9572.
32. Abschlußbericht über die Aussiedlungen im Rahmen der Ansetzung der Bessarabiendeutschen (3. Nahplan) vom 21.1.1941 – 20.1.1942 im Reichsgau Wartheland. Archiwum Głównej Komisji Badania Zbrodni Przeciwko Narodowi Polskiemu, Warsaw (GKW), Bestand 62, 45.
33. Broszat, *Nationalsozialistische Polenpolitik*, p. 101.
34. Bergen, 'The "Volksdeutschen" of Eastern Europe', pp. 76–7.
35. Organisation und Leistung der Dienststelle des Sonderbeauftragten für die Umsiedlung, 21 Aug. 1940. BA Berlin, NS37, 1069.
36. HSSPF Ansiedlungsstab Litzmannstadt an die Führer der Arbeitsstäbe im Bereich des

Ansiedlungsstabes, betr. Ausführungen des Reichsführers SS, 21 May 1940. BA Berlin, R49, 20.

37. Jachomowski, *Umsiedlung der Bessarabien-, Bukowina- und Dobrudjadeutschen*, pp. 68–9, 93–5; Lumans, *Himmler's Auxiliaries*, pp. 171–5.

38. SS-Obergruppenführer Reinhard to Petri, 20 July 1942. BA Berlin, NS19, 1748.

39. 'Die Ansiedlungen in den einzelnen Kreisen des Warthegaus'. BA Berlin, R49, 3042.

40. Niederschrift über die Tagung der Führer der Kreisansiedlungsstäbe im Ansiedlungsstab am 16. September 1941. Archiwum Państwowe w Gdansku (APG), Bestand 265, 4492.

41. Szefer, 'Die deutschen Umsiedler in der Provinz Oberschlesien', pp. 345–54.

42. Text of the telegram to Hitler in Der Gauleiter und Reichsstatthalter im Reichsgau Wartheland an Reichsführer-SS Heinrich Himmler 7 Mar. 1944. IfZ, MA 303/9332.

43. 'Der Führer ruft in den deutschen Osten', *NS-Frauenwarte* 8, no. 17 (1940), pp. 354–8; 'NS-Frauenschaft betreut Baltendeutsche', *Nachrichtendienst der RFF* 8, no. 16 (1939), p. 519; 'Das Deutsche Frauenwerk im Warthegau', *Nachrichtendienst der RFF* 9, no. 2 (1940), pp. 19–20.

44. Irmgard von Maltzahn, 'Heimat bereiten – Aufgabe der Frau', *Der Gauring: Mitteilungs-blatt des Gauringes Danzig-Westpreußen der NSDAP* 1, no. 7 (1942), p. 3.

45. 'Organisation und Leistung der Dienststelle des Sonderbeauftragten für die Umsiedlung', 21 Aug. 1940. BA Berlin, NS37, 1069.

46. The organizer of the women's Labour Service in East Prussia extended her operations to the newly annexed district of Zichenau. Gerda Walendy, 'Unsere Arbeit: Bezirk I Ostpreußen Nord, Juli 1942'. BA Berlin, Zsg 145, 16; on the women's Labour Service in the Warthegau, see Bezirksleitung RADwJ Bezirk XXVI Wartheland (Chronik von G. Kapp). BA Koblenz, Zsg 145, 49.

47. Lieselotte Vohdin (b. 1914), from Jan. 1940 BDM leader in Warthegau, had been district leader in Upper Silesia; Gertrud Fischer (b. 1911), appointed in 1940 to set up the BDM in the district of Zichenau, had been a BDM district leader in Heilsberg (East Prussia) since 1936. Frieda Balcerek (b. 1897), *Gaufrauenschaftsleiterin* of Danzig-Westpreußen, had been a Party activist since spring 1932 in Deutsch-Eylau (East Prussia). BA Berlin, BDC-PK Lieselotte Vohdin; Lebenslauf Gertrud Fischer, in APP, RSH Wartheland/2415. Frieda Balcerek, 'Aus der Frauenarbeit in Westpreußen von 1939 bis 1945', BA Koblenz, Ost-Dok 8/1; NSDAP registration card, BA Berlin, BDC.

48. 'Schicksalsgemeinschaft im Wartheland. Jugendgruppen des Deutschen Frauenwerkes im Erntehilfslager', *NS-Gaudienst für den Reichsgau Wartheland*, 13 Aug. 1940. BA Berlin, Bestand PL-116.

49. Landrat Kosten an den RADwJ in Posen betr. Arbeitsdienstlager in Schänkendorf, Kreis Kosten, 8 Nov. 1940. APP, Landratsamt Kosten, 67.

50. Lieselotte Vohdin, 'Bewährung des BDM', *Das junge Deutschland* 35, no. 7 (1941), pp. 183–4.

51. A. Dolezalek, Planungsabteilung, Ansiedlungsstab Posen, an die SS-Arbeitsstäbe im Bereich des SS-Ansiedlungsstabes Posen, 12 Sept. 1940; same letter sent on same day by Spaarmann, Leiter des Ansiedlungsstabs Litzmannstadt to SS-Arbeitsstäbe there. BA Berlin, R49, 3065.

52. Majer, *'Fremdvölkische im Dritten Reich'*, pp. 386–94.

53. Reg.präs. Danzig an das RErzMin betr. Sonderlehrgang für Volkspflegerinnen an der NS-Frauenschule für Volkspflege in Danzig-Langfuhr, 19 Aug. 1941. BA Berlin, 49.01, 10749; Edith Zude (Direktorin, NS-Kindergärtnerinnenseminar, Posen) an das RErzMin, 4 Sept. 1941. BA Berlin, 49.01, 10748.

54. Cited in Schenk, *Hitlers Mann in Danzig*, p. 144.

55. Otto Schroeder, 'Landdienst und Siedlung im Osten', *Das junge Deutschland* 36, no. 1 (1942), pp. 10–11.

56. Cited in Richard Nitschke, *Die deutschen Ostgebiete an Warthe und Weichsel* (Breslau, 1940), p. 14.

57. File card for Emmy Poggensee, BA Berlin, BDC.

58. Emmy Poggensee, 'Junge Führerinnen beim Osteinsatz im Gau Wartheland', *NS-Frauenwarte* 10, no. 8 (1941–2), p. 115.

59. Herbert Müller, 'Der Osten des Warthelandes', *Die Bewegung* 9, no. 8 (1941), p. 4.

60. Bericht eines Vertrauensmanns, 'Der Aufbau des deutschen Volkswalles im Osten', Ende Oktober 1940. BA Berlin, R58, 243.

61. Jutta Rüdiger, untitled preface, *Das deutsche Mädel* (May 1942), pp. 1–3; see also Dr Christel Otto, 'Was weißt Du vom deutschen Osten?', *NS-Frauenwarte* 9, no. 8 (1940–1), p. 113.

62. 'Der Beruf der Ansiedlerbetreuerin hat sich bewährt', *Neues Bauerntum* 34 (1942), p. 4.

63. Dr Nausikaa Fischer, 'Einsatz der helfenden Hände und Herzen', *Wartheland* 1, no. 8 (1941), pp. 7–8.

64. A. Greiser, 'Der deutsche Osten ein Land des Kampfes. Grundlegende Ausführungen des Gauleiters zum studentischen Einsatz in Posen', *Litzmannstädter Zeitung*, 2 Aug. 1942.

65. Frieda Balcerek, 'Die deutsche Frau in der Volkstumsarbeit', *Der Gauring. Mitteilungsblatt des Gauringes Danzig-Westpreußen der NSDAP* 1, no. 7 (1942).

66. Paul Weindling, *Epidemics and Genocide in Eastern Europe, 1890–1945* (Oxford, 2000), pp. 259–63, 271–7.

67. Ibid., pp. 273–4.

68. Ibid., pp. 271–5.

69. Renate von Stieda, 'Fahrt durch die befreiten Ostgebiete', *NS-Frauenwarte* 9, no. 8 (1940–1), pp. 113–16.

70. 'Aufbruch und Weisung. Ein Jahr Frauenarbeit im befreiten Gebiet des Gaues Danzig-Westpreußen', *NS-Frauenwarte* 9, no. 8 (1940–1), p. 117; 'Scheuerfest für die Umsiedler', *Danziger Neueste Nachrichten*, 31 Oct. 1940.

71. Lumans, *Himmler's Auxiliaries*, pp. 175–9.

72. Der Generalkommissar in Kauen an den Reichsminister für die besetzten Ostgebiete betr. Stand der litauendeutschen Ansiedlung, 24 Mar. 1943. BA Berlin, R6, 118. See Harry Stossun, *Die Umsiedlungen der Deutschen aus Litauen während des Zweiten Weltkrieges: Untersuchungen zum Schicksal einer deutschen Volksgruppe im Osten* (Hamburg, 1990), pp. 106, 149–225.

73. Correspondence re evacuation of ethnic Germans from Zhitomir to the Warthegau in late 1943: BA Berlin, R6, 117.

74. Christopher Browning, 'The Decision Concerning the Final Solution', in *Fateful Months: Essays on the Emergence of the Final Solution*, revised edition (New York and London, 1991), esp. pp. 29–38; on Distrikt Galizien, see Pohl, *Nationalsozialistische Judenverfolgung in Ostgalizien*, pp. 139–47.

75. 'Der Auftrag der Frau im Osten', *Nachrichtendienst der RFF* 11, no. 10 (1942), pp. 142–4.

76. 'BDM-Osteinsatz im Generalgouvernement', *Reichsbefehl der Reichsjugendführung* 132/42 (15 June 1942), p. 146; 'Mädel aus dem Reich im Generalgouvernement', *Deutsche Gemeinschaft. Wochenschrift für die Siedlungsdeutschen im Generalgouvernement* 2, no. 21 (1943), p. 4.

77. Alfred Falkenberg, 'Aufbauarbeit im Ostland', *NS-Volksdienst* 10, no. 5 (1943), pp. 105–10; 'Osteinsatz in Litauen. Meldung von Führerinnen als Helferinnen in den Schulen', *Reichsbefehl der RJF* 22/43 (29 Jan. 1943), p. 37; Gebietskommissar Shitomir, Hauptabteilung IIk Abt. Fürsorge u. Volkswohlfahrt an das Reichsmin. für die besetzten Ostgebiete, 12

Mar. 1942. Kiev AOR/fund 3206, folder 255. I would like to thank Wendy Lower for this reference.

78. Ingeborg Fleischhauer, '"Operation Barbarossa" and the Deportations', in Ingeborg Fleischhauer and Benjamin Pinkus, eds, *The Soviet Germans Past and Present* (London, 1986), pp. 66–91.

79. Robert Herzog, 'Besatzungsverwaltung in den besetzten Ostgebieten – Abteilung Jugend', Tübingen 1960 (ms).

80. 'BDM-Osteinsatz im Generalgouvernement', *Reichsbefehl der RJF* 22/43 (29 Jan. 1943), p. 37.

81. *Reichsbefehl der RJF* 11/K (10 Nov. 1939), p. 1: 'Organisation der HJ in den ehemals polnischen Gebieten'. On the appointment of ethnic Germans to posts in the BDM, see Volksdeutsche Mittelstelle, Abt. Jugend u. Studentenschaft, Bericht vom 25. November 1939. APP, Volksdeutsche Mittelstelle/118. The two Obergau leaders appointed in January 1940 were Ingeborg Niekerke (b. 1915) in Danzig-Westpreußen, and Lieselotte Vohdin (b. 1914) in the Wartheland: both were born in Hamburg. Vohdin had worked in Beuthen since 1936. BA Berlin, BDC-PK Niekerke and PK Vohdin.

82. Aktenvermerk (= Ilse Behrens), 9 Dec. 1940. BA Berlin, BDC, 'Research' Ordner 'Wartheland' 'Neu', pp. 9–10.

83. 'Mädeleinsatz im Osten' (1941); Liselotte Freimann, 'Osteinsatz des BDM in der HJ im Wartheland 1941'. BA Berlin, NS28, 36.

84. Artur Axmann, 'Parole: Osteinsatz und Landdienst!', *Das junge Deutschland* 36, no. 1 (1942), pp. 1–3; Jutta Rüdiger, 'Die Ostaufgabe der Mädel', *Das junge Deutschland* 36, no. 1 (1942), pp. 3–5.

85. For instance *Reichsbefehl der RJF* 36/41 K (1 Oct. 1941), 'Führerinneneinsatz in den Ostgebieten'.

86. 'Einsatz im Osten – Pflicht jeder Führerin', *Das deutsche Mädel*, June 1941, pp. 6–7.

87. 'Wieder 800 Mädel im Osteinsatz', *Das deutsche Mädel*, May 1942, inside cover.

88. Rüdiger, 'Die Ostaufgabe der Mädel', p. 5.

89. *Reichsbefehl der RJF* 22/2 (13 Oct. 1942), betr. BDM-Osteinsatz; Leistungsbericht der NSDAP Gauleitung Wartheland 1942–3. IfZ Archiv, Fa 88/Fasz. 162.

90. Luise Essig, 'Unsere Ziele für die Mädchen und Frauen des Landvolks', in Meyer et al., *Landvolk im Werden.* pp. 139–60; Otto Schroeder, 'Landdienst und Siedlung im Osten', *Das junge Deutschland* 36, no. 1 (1942), pp. 10–11.

91. Leistungsbericht der NSDAP Gauleitung Wartheland 1942–3. IfZ Archiv, Fa 88/Fasz. 162, p. 3: participants included 'Germanic' youth volunteers from the Netherlands and Norway.

92. Gebietsmädelführung Wartheland, 'BDM-Schulhelferinnen: Erfahrungen und Vorschläge' (c. March 1942). APP, RSH im Wartheland, 2414.

93. *Der Ruf* 2 (June 1943), p. 10; no. 3 (Oct. 1943), p. 10; no. 4 (Apr. 1944), p. 14; and no. 5 (Oct. 1944), p. 14; Leistungsbericht der NSDAP-Gauleitung Wartheland 1943–4, p. 32. IfZ Archiv, Fa 88/Fasz. 162.

94. 'NSDAP Gau Westfalen-Nord, NS-Frauenschaft, Rundschreiben an alle Kreisfrauen-schaftsleiterinnen, 11 May 1942. NWStA Detmold, M15/53.

95. Helga Thrö, manuscript for *Arbeitsblätter für die Jugendgruppen* 6 (July 1941). BA Berlin, R49, 3046.

96. Stephenson, *The Nazi Organisation of Women*, p. 199.

97. NSDAP Gau Westfalen-Nord, NS-Frauenschaft Abt. Org./Personal, Rundschreiben betr. Warthelandeinsatz des Führerinnennachwuchses, 28 Apr. 1942; NSDAP Gau Westfalen-Nord, Gaujugendgruppenführerin an alle Kreisjugendgruppenführerinnen betr. Warthe-landeinsatz der Jugendgruppenführerinnen, 20 May 1942. NWStA Detmold, M15/54; Lisa Keller (Bielefeld), Protokoll: Ernteeinsatzlager der Kreiskindergruppenleiterinnen, 8–31

Aug. 1943 in Scheltz/Kirchdorf, Kreis Wollstein, Warthegau. NWStA Detmold, M15/52.

98. 'Schulungslehrgang der Gaujugendgruppenführerinnen', *Nachrichtendienst der RFF* 10, no. 6 (1941), p. 90; Emmy Poggensee, 'Junge Führerinnen beim Osteinsatz', *NS-Frauenwarte* 10, no. 8 (1941–2), p. 115; Leistungsbericht der NSDAP Gauleitung Wartheland 1940–1, p. 6. Instytut Zachodni, Dokumenty niemieckie, I-377. 'Abschluß des Osteinsatzes', *Nachrichtendienst der RFF* 10, no. 19 (1941), pp. 290–1; 'Führerinnen im Warthegau-Einsatz', *Nachrichtendienst der RFF* 11, no. 10 (1942), p. 146.

99. NSDAP Gau-Westfalen Nord – NS-Frauenschaft, Abt. Org./Personal, Rundschreiben an alle Kreisfrauenschaftsleiterinnen betr. Einarbeitung und Einstellung von haupt-amtlichen Kräften für den deutschen Osten, 26 June 1942. NWStA Detmold, M15/53; Arbeitsbesprechungen mit den Ortsfrauenschaftsleiterinnen (Kreis Herford), 17 und 18 June 1943. NWStA Detmold, M15/52; recruitment advertisement, *Nachrichtendienst der RFF* 9, no. 22 (1940), p. 344.

100. 'Abschluß des Osteinsatzes', *Nachrichtendienst der RFF* 10, no. 19 (1941), pp. 290–1; NSDAP Gau-Westfalen Nord – NS-Frauenschaft, Abt. Org./Personal, Rundschreiben an alle Kreisfrauenschaftsleiterinnen betr. Einarbeitung und Einstellung von haupt-amtlichen Kräften für den deutschen Osten, 26 June 1942. NWStA Detmold, M15/53.

101. 'Ansiedlungsbetreuerinnen auch in Danzig-Westpreußen', *Nachrichtendienst der RFF* 10, no. 19 (1941), pp. 291–2; 'Hilfeleistung für die Rückwanderer', *Danziger Vorposten*, 9 Mar. 1941.

102. Leistungsbericht der NSDAP Gauleitung Wartheland 1940–1, p. 6; Leistungsbericht 1942–3, p. 4.

103. Morgan, *Weiblicher Arbeitsdienst in Deutschland*, p. 385.

104. Willmot, 'National Socialist Organisations', pp. 332–5.

105. Dr Kruse (Deutsches Auslandsinstitut, Büro Berlin), Vermerk: Besuch bei Herrn Dolezalek, VDA, 22 Dec. 1939. BA Koblenz, R57 DAI/748; 'Von der Volkskunde zur Volkspolitik', *Die Bewegung* 8, no. 15 (1940), p. 4; 'Als deutscher Student im ehemaligen Polen', *Die Bewegung* 8, no. 17 (1940), p. 8.

106. Renate Kalb to Luise Fick betr. Facheinsatz der Studentinnen im Warthegau, 7 June 1940. BDC-PK L. Dolezalek. BA Berlin, ehem. BDC.

107. By 1944, the student assignments included areas of occupied Yugoslavia. Hans Streit an das Organisations- und Personalamt, RSF München betr. Volkspolitisches Amt der RSF, 11 Mar. 1944. Archiwum UAM, Reichsuniversität Posen, 143/66.

108. In 1942, 403 women and 333 men were sent to the Wartheland as part of the Facheinsatz Ost: figures for the other eastern territories not found. 'Einsatzstellen und-ziffern im Wartheland', *Rundbrief studentischer Osteinsatz* no. 1, (Aug. 1942), pp. 12–16.

109. Der Reichsstudentenführer/Amt Wissenschaft und Facherziehung, Siedlungs- und Facheinsatz der RSF, Durchführungsbestimmungen zum Siedlungs- und Facheinsatz der Reichsstudentenführung im Sommer 1941, 16 June 1941. Archiwum UAM, Reichs-universität Posen, 78/55.

110. Der komm. Studentenführer, Reichsuniversität Posen, an die RSF, Amt Wissenschaft und Facherziehung, Siedlungs- und Facheinsatz der RSF, betr. Meldungen zum Siedlungs- und Facheinsatz, 19 July 1941. Archiwum UAM, Reichsuniversität Posen, 78/55. For 'threadbare carpet' image, see Gustav Scheel, speech of 26 Jan. 1944 in Erlangen. Archiwum UAM, Reichsuniversität Posen, 78/256.

111. Herwart Vorländer, *Die NSV. Darstellung und Dokumentation einer nationalsozialistischen Organisation* (Boppard am Rhein, 1988), p. 149.

112. Organisation und Leistung der Dienststelle des Sonderbeauftragten für die Umsiedlung, 21 Aug. 1940. BA Berlin, NS37, 1069.

113. Heinze, 'Kindergartenarbeit der NSV in Ostoberschlesien', *Kindergarten* 80, no. 12 (1939), pp. 221–3.

114. Leistungsbericht der NSDAP-Gauleitung Wartheland 1942–3. IfZ Archiv, Fa 88/Fasz. 162, p. 9.

115. NS-Kindergärtnerinnenseminar des Reichsgaues Wartheland an das RErzMin betr. Genehmigung eines Sonderkursus, 13 Dec. 1940. BA Berlin, 49.01, 10575/111.

116. Heinze, 'Kindergartenarbeit der NSV in Ostoberschlesien'; Marie-Therese v. Foelkersam, 'Kindergärten'. Bericht Nr. 5, 21 Jan. 1940. APP, Volksdeutsche Mittelstelle Posen, 115.

117. Schöneborn, Gauamt für Volkswohlfahrt, Westfalen-Nord, an Frl. Finck, NSDAP Reichsleitung, Hauptamt für Volkswohlfahrt, 9 Feb. 1943. NWStA Münster, Gauleitung Westfalen-Nord, Gauamt für Volkswohlfahrt, 542.

118. Reg.präs. Danzig an RErzMin, betr. Sonderlehrgang für Volkspflegerinnen an der NS-Frauenschule für Volkspflege in Danzig-Langfuhr, 19. Aug. 1941. BA Berlin, 49.01, 10749; Herta Jeschonneck, 'Monatsbericht der Kindertagesstätten für den Monat Juli Distrikt Galizien', Lemberg, 13 Aug. 1943. GKW, Bestand 116/4.

119. Schulrat Liegmann, Reg.präs. Litzmannstadt, Abt. für Erziehung und Volksbildung, betr. Abordnung von Lehrkräften, 25 July 1940. APP, RSH im Wartheland, 2397.

120. RErzMin, Schnellbrief an Regierungspräsidenten, Stadtpräsident der Reichshauptstadt Berlin, Unterrichtsverwaltungen der außerpreußischen Länder betr. Abordnung von Volksschullehrkräften in die neuen Ostgebiete zu Beginn des Schuljahres 1940–1, 27 Mar. 1940. APP, RSH im Wartheland, 2397.

121. Dr Ulitz, Abt. Kirchen und Schulen, Bezirksregierung Kattowitz, Der Aufbau des deutschen Schulwesens in dem befreiten Teile des Regierungsbezirks Kattowitz. AP Katowice, OPK, 822.

122. RSH Abt. III/4 in Posen an das RErzMin betr. Lehrerinnen an einklassigen Schulen, 2 Oct. 1940. APP, RSH im Wartheland, 2408. For the number of Volksschulen in autumn 1940, see Georg Hansen, *Ethnische Schulpolitik im besetzten Polen: Der Mustergau Wartheland* (Münster and New York. 1995), pp. 56–9. Around 80% of the Volksschulen were single-class schools: RSH Posen, Abt. III/4, to RErzMin betr. Zuteilung von Volks-schullehrkräften für den Reichsgau Wartheland, 26 Aug. 1940. APP, RSH im Wartheland, 2397.

123. Reg.präs. Litzmannstadt an das RErzMin betr. Einsatz der Schulamtsanwärterinnen, June 1941. APP, RSH im Wartheland, 2409.

124. M. Tiedemann, Landjahrbezirksführerin der Regierungsbezirke Köslin und Schnei-demühl an Landjahrbezirksführerin Ursula Lindner, betr. Einsatz von Führerinnen im Reichsgau Wartheland, 3 Feb. 1940. APP, RSH im Wartheland, 2626.

125. Bericht über die Arbeit des Amtes Studentinnen im II. Trimester 1940. Universität Köln, Siegfriede Pilz, Leiterin des Amtes Studentinnen. StA Würzburg, RSF II, 533.

126. Gertrud Sch. to Ursula Lindner, 23 Apr. 1940. APP, RSH im Wartheland, 2626.

127. Maria Meyer, München-Pasing, an RSH in Posen, ber. Anforderung als Schulamtsbewer-berin im Reichsgau Wartheland, 4 Feb. 1941. APP, RSH im Wartheland, 2389.

128. Elisabeth Hagler (Dachau), an ORR Stegemann, RSH Abt. III in Posen, 4 July 1941. APP, RSH im Wartheland, 2409.

129. Ursula Lindner an Babette Ruprecht, 5 July 1941. APP, RSH im Wartheland, 2626.

130. Hilde Bruchhäuser an Landjahrbezirksführerin Grete Menzel, July 1941; Grete Menzel an Hilde Bruchhäuser, 24 July 1941. APK, Reg. Kattowitz/10038. Erika Heindl an Ursula Lindner, 7 Aug. 1940; Gerda Juhr an Ursula Lindner, 5 Feb. 1941, 10 Apr. 1941; Ursula Lindner an Gerda Juhr, 28 Mar. 1941. APP, RSH im Wartheland, 2626.

131. Ruth Malue an Reg.präs. in Posen, betr. Wiedereinstellung in den Schuldienst, 16 Mar. 1944. APP, RSH im Wartheland, 2389.

132. Lieselotte H., 20 Apr. 1943, *Der Ruf* 2 (June 1943). Copy in: APP, RSH im Wartheland, 2432.

133. Chef der Zivilverwaltung für den Bezirk Bialystok Abt II an den Reichsstatthalter im Wartheland betr. Schulhelferinnen F. und L., 29 Dec. 1943; RSH im Wartheland Abt. III an den Chef der Zivilverwaltung für den Bezirk Bialystok betr. Schulhelferinnen F. und L., 6 Jan. 1944; Gertrud F. an RErzMin betr. Gesuch um Belassung an meinem jetzigen Arbeitsplatz als Schulhelferin an der Volksschule Grodno, 24 Mar. 1944. APP, RSH im Wartheland, 2415.

134. Regierung des Generalgouverneurs, Hauptabteilung Wissenschaft und Unterricht an RErzMin betr. Verwendung der Schulhelferin Inge S. im Schuldienst des Generalgouvernements. APP, 28 Sept. 1943. RSH im Wartheland, 2409.

135. Gertrud Richter an Franz Stanglica, 29 Jan. 1943; Dietlinde Gotz an Stanglica, 25 May 1943. APLub, SSPF Lublin-Fostu, 4.

136. Brunhilde Posch an Stanglica, 4 Mar. 1943. Ibid.

137. Interview with Frau Peters, 14 May 1996.

138. Interview with Frau Bauer, 22 Oct. 1999; see also written report, 'Wie ich dazu kam, Ansiedlerbetreuerin zu werden', in possession of author.

139. Interview with Frau Bauer.

140. Ibid.

141. Ibid.

142. Interview with Frau Holz, 7 Aug. 2001. The colloquial term '*j.w.d.*' stands for 'janz weit draußen' and here conveys the respondent's jokey tone.

143. Interview with Frau Fischer, 25. Oct. 1999.

144. Ibid.

145. Interview with Frau Winter and Frau Mahnke, 27 Oct. 1999.

146. Ibid.

147. Interview with Frau Hagen, 20 Oct. 1999.

148. Interview with Frau Ullmann, 12 Jan. 1999.

149. Interview with Frau Geyer, 21 Apr. 1996.

150. Interview with Frau Andreas, 28 Aug. 1994.

151. Interview with Frau Keller, 8 Jan. 2000.

152. Interview with Frau Eckhard and Frau Vogel, 12 Nov. 1998.

153. Ibid.

154. Interview with Frau Andreas, 28 Aug. 1994.

Chapter 5 'Uncanny Space' or 'German Homeland'? German Women's Constructions of the 'East'

1. Bericht über eine Schulungstagung der Abteilung Grenz-Ausland mit dem Gauamt für Volkstumsfragen in Bad Oeynhausen am 22.–25. Oktober 1942. NWStA Detmold, M15/52.

2. Gauhauptmann im Reichsgau Wartheland, ed., *Der Warthegau: Landschaft und Siedlung in Werken Deutscher Maler: Ein Bildband* (Posen, 1943), preface (unpaginated).

3. 'Fruchtbare BDM-Einsatzarbeit', *Kolonistenbriefe* 3 (Dec. 1943) [= no. 23] , p. 7.

4. Elizabeth Harvey, ' "Die deutsche Frau im Osten": "Rasse", Geschlecht und öffentlicher Raum im besetzten Polen 1940–44', *Archiv für Sozialgeschichte* 38 (1998), pp. 191–214, here, pp. 199–203; Walter Manoscheck, ed., *'Es gibt nur eines für das Judentum: Vernich-*

tung': Das Judenbild in deutschen Soldatenbriefen 1939–1944 (Hamburg, 1995); Klaus Latzel, *Deutsche Soldaten – nationalsozialistischer Krieg? Kriegserlebnis – Kriegserfahrung 1939–1945* (Paderborn, 1998), pp. 187–90.

5. For a definition of the uncanny in terms of the psychology of the unconscious, see Sigmund Freud, 'Das Unheimliche', in *Gesammelte Werke*, vol. 12, *Werke aus den Jahren 1917–1920* (London, 1947), pp. 229–68; on the relationship between the uncanny and the sensation of disgust, see William Ian Miller, *The Anatomy of Disgust* (Cambridge, Mass., 1997), p. 27.

6. Billie Melman, 'Introduction', in Billie Melman, ed., *Borderlines: Genders and Identities in War and Peace, 1880–1930* (New York and London, 1998), pp. 8–11.

7. McClintock, *Imperial Leather*, p. 6.

8. Alison Blunt, *Travel, Gender and Imperialism: Mary Kingsley and West Africa* (New York, 1994), pp. 36–7.

9. Stoler, 'Making Empire Respectable', pp. 634–60.

10. Annette Kolodny, *The Land Before Her. Fantasy and Experience of the American Frontiers, 1630–1860* (Chapel Hill, 1984), esp. pp. 35–54.

11. Felix Lützkendorf, *Völkerwanderung 1940* (Berlin, 1940), pp. 46–7.

12. Ibid., p. 61.

13. Ibid., p. 48.

14. Ibid.

15. Ibid., p. 103.

16. Mary Louise Pratt, *Imperial Eyes: Travel Writing and Transculturation* (London, 1992), pp. 201–8; McClintock, *Imperial Leather*, pp. 30–1; Kolodny, *The Land Before Her*, pp. 4–6.

17. Lützkendorf, *Völkerwanderung 1940*, p. 39.

18. Walter Erdmann, 'Der Osten zeichnet aus', *NS-Volksdienst* 8, no. 7 (1941), p. 134; Hubert Müller, 'Der Osten des Warthelandes. Eine großdeutsche Aufgabe', *Die Bewegung* 9, no. 4 (1941), p. 4.

19. Blunt, *Travel, Gender and Imperialism*, p. 30.

20. Werner Oehlmann, 'Verwandelter Osten. Reise ins Generalgouvernement', *Das Reich*, 2 Nov. 1941, pp. 6–7.

21. S. Holler, introduction, in Hohenstein, *Wartheländisches Tagebuch 1941/2*, p. 11.

22. Oehlmann, 'Verwandelter Osten', pp. 6–7.

23. Carl Ernst Köhne, introduction, in Gauhauptmann im Reichsgau Wartheland, ed., *Der Warthegau* (unpaginated).

24. For instance Eberhard Sauter, 'Die Zäune fehlen. Süd-Ostpreußen im Übergang', *Das Reich*, 5 Oct. 1941, p. 5. On the roads turning to mud, see Anon., 'Als deutscher Student im ehemaligen Polen', *Die Bewegung* 8, no. 17 (1940), p. 8.

25. Heinrich Himmler, 'Allgemeine Anordnung Nr. 20/VI/42 über die Gestaltung der Landschaft in den eingegliederten Ostgebieten vom 21. Dezember 1942', reproduced in Rössler and Schleiermacher, eds, *Der 'Generalplan Ost'*, pp. 136–47.

26. Dr Csaki, 'Das Umsiedlungswerk der Balten', unpublished report, 27 Nov. 1939. BA Koblenz, R57/neu, 25.

27. Gerd Gaiser later achieved fame as a novelist in the Federal Republic.

28. Gerd Gaiser, 'Ob man da leben kann? Ein Landstädtchen im Warthegau', *Das Reich*, 6 Apr. 1941.

29. On 'planning monstrosities' in Posen: Rahn, 'Studenten im "Einsatz Ost"', *Student im Bereich Berlin* 17 (1940), p. 2 [Beilage zu *Die Bewegung* 8 (1940)]; the term 'bestial Satanism' used by an official in the Warthegau propaganda office in: Hubert Müller, 'Der Osten des Warthelandes. Eine großdeutsche Aufgabe', *Die Bewegung* 9, no. 8 (1941), p. 4.

30. Müller, 'Der Osten des Warthelandes', p. 4.

31. Carl Ernst Köhne, introduction, in Gauhauptmann im Reichsgau Wartheland, ed., *Der Warthegau* (unpaginated).

32. Gerd Gaiser, 'Amtskommissar in neuem Land. Begegnung bei einer Fahrt durch den Warthegau', *Das Reich*, 22 June 1941, p. 5.

33. Walter Hebenbrock, *Mit der NSV nach Polen* (Berlin, 1940), p. 23.

34. Hubert Neun, 'Wiedersehen mit Warschau', *Das Reich*, 9 Mar. 1941, pp. 3–4.

35. NSDAP-Kreisleitung Zawiercie-Blachownia an die Gauleitung der NSDAP Oberschlesien, 26 June 1941. BA Berlin, Bestand PL-014, Film 18536.

36. 'Romantischer Osten?', *Die Bewegung* 8, no. 39 (1940), p. 2.

37. Renate Heidner, 'Deutsches Land im Osten: "Der Osten des Warthelandes"', *Die Bewegung* 9, no. 18/19 (1941), p. 16.

38. 'Nach Ostland . . .', *Das Schwarze Korps* 7, no. 8 (1941), p. 5.

39. 'Romantischer Osten?', *Die Bewegung* 8, no. 39 (1940), p. 2.

40. 'Ist das nicht wert . . . ?!', *Das Schwarze Korps* 7, no. 9 (1941), p. 5.

41. Paul Kurbjuhn, 'Zwischen Bug und San', *Das Schwarze Korps*, 7, no. 12 (1941), p. 9.

42. Musial, *Deutsche Zivilverwaltung und Judenverfolgung*, pp. 230–3. For the story of a German Jew who perished in Izbica in 1942, see Mark Roseman, *The Past in Hiding* (London, 2000), pp. 190–255.

43. Theweleit's psychoanalytical reading of texts written by men who joined counter-revolutionary paramilitary units in the wake of the German revolution of 1918 might suggest such an interpretation: see Theweleit, *Männerphantasien vol. 1*, pp. 289–312.

44. Carl Ernst Köhne, untitled introduction: Gauhauptmann im Reichsgau Wartheland, ed., *Der Warthegau*, p. 3.

45. See above, Chapter 3.

46. Gerd Gaiser, 'Ob man da leben kann?' *Das Reich*, 6 Apr. 1941.

47. Richard Czaki, 'Das Umsiedlungswerk der Balten', 27 Nov. 1939. BA Koblenz, R57 neu/25.

48. Hubert Neun, 'Wiedersehen mit Warschau', *Das Reich*, 9 Mar. 1941, p. 4.

49. Dr Heinz Wolff, 'Das Wartheland im Aufbau. Eine Fahrt durch Stadt und Land im deutschen Osten', *Die Bewegung* 8, no. 35 (1940), p. 2.

50. For instance Herta Miedzinski, 'Deutsches Antlitz an der Weichsel', *Die Bewegung* 8, no. 41 (1940), p. 6, on Leslau.

51. H. M., 'Mit der BDM-Reichsreferentin bei den Mädeln Ostoberschlesiens', *Das deutsche Mädel*, June 1940, p. 11.

52. Renate von Stieda, 'Fahrt durch die befreiten Ostgebiete', *NS-Frauenwarte* 9, no. 8 (1940–1), pp. 113–16, here p. 113.

53. Margarete Blasche, 'Studienfahrt in den Reichsgau Danzig-Westpreußen', *Die deutsche Landfrau* 33, no. 24 (1940), pp. 508–9.

54. For other accounts, see for example Klara Hofer, 'Bromberg – Die Stadt der tausend Märtyrer', *Die Frau* 47, no. 2 (1939–40), pp. 39–40; Gertrud Bäumer, 'Das Märtyrium einer deutschen Frauenführerin in Bromberg', ibid., pp. 41–2; Anon., 'Wir fahren durch das Wartheland', *Die deutsche Landfrau* 33, no. 17 (1940), pp. 358–9; von Stieda, 'Fahrt durch die befreiten Ostgebiete'.

55. Jansen and Weckbecker, *Der 'Volksdeutsche Selbstschutz'*, pp. 27–8.

56. Ibid.

57. For example Reichspropagandaamt Danzig-Westpreußen, ed., *Polnischer Blutterror: Dokumente einer Kulturschande* (Danzig, 1940); Fritz Menn, ed., *Auf den Straßen des Todes. Leidensweg der Volksdeutschen in Polen* (Leipzig, 1940).

58. Ruth Krieger, *Deutsche Mädel im Osten* (Berlin, 1940), pp. 116–19.

59. Reichsstatthalter Posen an die Regierungspräsidenten in Posen, Kalisch und Hohensalza

betr. Dokumentensammlung 'Dokumente polnischer Grausamkeit', 16 May 1940. BA Berlin, Bestand PL-116, Film 72636.

60. Blasche, 'Studienfahrt in den Reichsgau Danzig-Westpreußen', pp. 508–9.

61. Dr Suse Harms, 'Ein Land wird wieder deutsch', *Das deutsche Mädel*, March 1940, pp. 3–4.

62. Anon., 'Eine andere Welt', *Das deutsche Mädel*, April 1941, pp. 14–15.

63. Aus den Berichten unserer Kameradinnen (excerpt by Eva Winkler, Berlin-München). BA Berlin, R49, 3052.

64. Lucjan Dobroszycki, ed., *Chronicle of the Lodz Ghetto, 1941–44* (New Haven and London, 1984), p. xxxvii.

65. Alan Adelson and Robert Lapides, eds, *Lodz Ghetto. Inside a Community under Siege* (Harmondsworth, 1989), p. 59.

66. Reproduced in Liselotte Orgel-Purper, *Willst Du meine Witwe werden? Eine deutsche Liebe im Krieg* (Berlin, 1995), p. 28. On Liselotte Purper, see Deutsches Historisches Museum, ed., *'Bildberichterstatterin' im 'Dritten Reich': Fotografien aus den Jahren 1937 bis 1944 von Liselotte Purper* (Berlin, 1997) [= *Magazin: Mitteilungen des Deutschen Historischen Museums* 7, Heft 20].

67. Ilse P., HfL Hamburg, Lehrereinsatz Sommer 1940. BA Berlin, R49, 3052.

68. Abschrift, Brief von Gertrud an Ilse, 10. Oktober 1940. Ibid.

69. Ilse P., HfL Hamburg, Lehrereinsatz Sommer 1940. Ibid.

70. Irene K., Bericht über meine Kindergartenarbeit im Kreise Leslau, Warthegau. BA Berlin, R49, 3051.

71. Orgel-Purper, *Willst Du meine Witwe werden?* pp. 29–30.

72. On the destruction of the ghetto in Lublin, see Dieter Pohl, *Von der 'Judenpolitik' zum Judenmord: Der Distrikt Lublin des Generalgouvernements 1939–1944* (Frankfurt am Main, 1993), pp. 113–17.

73. Ibid., pp. 116–17.

74. Interview with Frau Niemann, 14 Sept. 1996.

75. Ibid.

76. For how a colonial landscape served as a catalyst for a woman traveller's memories of home, see Sara Mills, *Discourses of Difference: An Analysis of Women's Travel Writing and Colonialism* (London, 1991), pp. 182–3.

77. Von Stieda, 'Fahrt durch die befreiten Ostgebiete', p. 114.

78. For instance: Dr Suse Harms, 'Ein Land wird wieder deutsch', *Das deutsche Mädel*, March 1940, pp. 3–4.

79. Abschrift: Brief von Gertrud an Ilse, 10. Oktober 1940. BA Berlin, R49, 3052.

80. Anna G., Dresden, 'Unser Betreuungseinsatz'. Ibid.

81. Marie Luise Schleithoff, 'Aus meiner Arbeit im Warthegau', *Die deutsche Landfrau* 33, no. 26 (1940), p. 547.

82. 'Unsere Spielfahrt durch Sudauen' (no author, undated). BA Berlin, Zsg 145, 22.

83. Frau Peters, letter of 4 July 1942, in author's possession. The quotation is from the first verse of Hans Baumann, 'In den Ostwind hebt die Fahnen': 'Dafür haben viel' geblutet und drum schweigt der Boden nicht': see *Deutsche Musik in der Höheren Schule: Musikbuch I* (Hanover, 1941), p. 145.

84. Blanke, *Orphans of Versailles*, pp. 232–3.

85. Magdalene Pfeiffer, Mein Osteinsatz an der Schule in Dilltal, Trümmerfeld, 12 Sept. 1943. Archiwum UAM, Reichsuniversität Posen 78, 424.

86. Gertrud Kapp, 'Wir beginnen im Wartheland. Bericht über die Aufbauarbeit des Reichsarbeitsdienstes für die weibliche Jugend im Wartheland' (manuscript) [1940]. BA Berlin, Zsg 145, 49.

87. Diary Sept. 1942–Sept. 1944, entry for 27 June 1943.
88. Interview with Frau Ullmann, 12 Jan. 1999.
89. 'Berichte aus dem Einsatz' (Trude Hermann). *Der Ruf* 5 (Oct. 1944). APP, RSH im Wartheland, 2432.
90. Die Hamburger Mädel der LBA an den Oberbürgermeister Litzmannstadt, Hamburg, 22 July 1944. Archiwum Państwowe w Lodzi (APL), Stadtverwaltung Litzmannstadt, 27.
91. Mills, *Discourses of Difference*, pp. 182–3.
92. Maria Emonts an Herta Jeschonneck, 20 June 1943. GKW, 116, 8.
93. Aus Zuschriften von Schulhelferinnen (Anne Weiß, Moltkesruhm), *Der Ruf* 2 (June 1943). APP, RSH im Wartheland, 2432.
94. Diary Sept. 1942–Sept. 1944, entry for 19 June 1943.
95. Volker Rieß, *Die Anfänge der Vernichtung 'lebensunwerten Lebens' in den Reichsgauen Danzig-Westpreußen und Wartheland 1939/40* (Frankfurt am Main, 1995), pp. 28–31, 119–31; see also Götz Aly, *'Endlösung'*, pp. 123–4.
96. Von Stieda, 'Fahrt durch die befreiten Ostgebiete', p. 116.
97. Anon., 'Wir fahren durch das Wartheland', *Die deutsche Landfrau* 33, no. 17 (1940), pp. 338–9.
98. Herta Miedzinski, 'Deutsches Antlitz an der Weichsel', *Die Bewegung* 8, no. 41 (1940), p. 8.
99. Harms, 'Ein Land wird wieder deutsch', pp. 3–4.
100. Ilse Urbach, 'Weibliche Hilfe im Wartheland. Bei den Arbeitsmaiden zwischen Posen und Litzmannstadt', *Das Reich*, 20 Dec. 1940, p. 27.
101. Renate Kalb, 'Fahrt in den Osten', *Die Bewegung* 8, no. 51 (1940), p. 4.
102. Maria Kahle, *Westfälische Bauern im Ostland* (Berlin, 1940), p. 154.
103. Ibid., pp. 35–6.
104. Miedzinski, 'Deutsches Antlitz an der Weichsel', p. 8.
105. Ilse Urbach, 'Weibliche Hilfe im Wartheland', p. 27.
106. Von Stieda, 'Fahrt durch die befreiten Ostgebiete', p. 116.
107. Frau Peters, letters of 4 July 1942 and 10 July 1942, in author's possession.

Chapter 6 Motherliness and Mastery: Making Model Germans in the Annexed Territories

1. Ilse [Behrens], Aktenvermerk, 10 Dec. 1940. BA Berlin, BDC, 'Research' Ordner 'Wartheland' 'Neu', pp. 9–10.
2. 'Studentinneneinsatz Ost', *Die Bewegung* 8, no. 53 (1940), p. 2.
3. Ilse [Behrens], Aktenvermerk, 10 Dec. 1940. BA Berlin, BDC, 'Research' Ordner 'Wartheland' 'Neu', pp. 9–10. On Wilhelm Koppe, see Birn, *Die Höheren SS- und Polizeiführer*, pp. 186–97; brief biographical data in Peter Witte et al., eds, *Der Dienstkalender Heinrich Himmlers 1941/42* (Hamburg, 1999), p. 697.
4. The 'Hauländer' may have been a group of Volhynian German settlers; in 1943 a settlement adviser in Kreis Kempen referred to German settlers from Volhynia as Hauländer: Wilma T., 7 Apr. 1943. BA Berlin, R49, 122.
5. Ilse [Behrens], Aktenvermerk, 10 Dec. 1940. BA Berlin, BDC, 'Research' Ordner 'Wartheland' 'Neu', pp. 9–10.
6. Stephenson, *The Nazi Organisation of Women*, p. 115.
7. 'v. d. L' [= von der Leyen], 'Aus der Arbeit der NS-Frauenschaft im Wartheland' (ms.), 29 Apr. 1942. BA Berlin, R49, 3045.

8. On Josef 'Sepp' Dietrich, founder of the Leibstandarte SS Adolf-Hitler and later SS general, see James J. Weingartner, 'Sepp Dietrich, Heinrich Himmler and the Leibstandarte SS Adolf Hitler, 1933–1938', *Central European History* 1 (1968), pp. 264–84; Witte et al., eds, *Der Dienstkalender Heinrich Himmlers 1941/42*, p. 675.

9. The role of students, BDM leaders and women's Labour Service participants as school assistants in village schools is considered below in Chapter 7.

10. Dr Luise Dolezalek, 'Bericht über die Anfänge der Umsiedlerbetreuung im Warthegau 1940', 21 July 1942. BA Berlin, R49, 3067.

11. Ibid.

12. Hertha Koschowitz, Jahresbericht 1. Dez. 1940–1. Dez. 1941: Ansiedlerbetreuerinnen der NS-Frauenschaft Gau Wartheland. BA Berlin, R49, 3129.

13. Dolezalek, 'Bericht über die Anfänge der Umsiedlerbetreuung im Warthegau 1940'.

14. Steinert, *Hitler's War and the Germans*, pp. 8–72.

15. v. d. L, 'Aus der Arbeit der NS-Frauenschaft im Wartheland'.

16. R.K. [= Renate Kalb], 'Studentinnen im Warthegau: Ihr Anteil am deutschen Aufbauwerk', *Die Bewegung* 8, no. 35 (1940), p. 4.

17. SS-Arbeitsstab für den Kreis Gostynin an den Ansiedlungsstab Litzmannstadt, betr. Bericht über die Generalinspektion, 25 Oct. 1940. BA Berlin, R49, 3072; 'Die Ansiedlung in den einzelnen Kreisen des Warthegaus' [undated = 1940/1]. BA Berlin, R49, 3042. See also the criticisms of resettlers in: Gendarmerie-Kreis Kosten, Lagebericht für die Zeit v. 1.Nov. bis 24. Dez. 1941, an die Gendarmerie-Hauptmannschaft in Lissa, 24 Dec. 1941. BA Berlin, PL-109.

18. On the expulsions and deportations of Poles and Jews from areas to be 'Germanized', see Czesław Łuczak, ed., *Położenie Ludności Polskiej w Tzw. Kraju Warty w Okresie Hitlerowskiej Okupacji [= Dokumenta Occupationis XIII]* (Poznań, 1990), pp. 104–70.

19. Die Ansiedlungstätigkeit im Kreis Leslau/Weichsel im Jahre 1941. Arbeitsbericht des Beauftragten des Reichskommissars f.d.F.d.V. Arbeitsstab für den Kreis Leslau [undated (1942)]. IfZ Archiv, Fb 115. See also Gendarmerie Kreis Ostrowo an den Landrat Ostrowo, betr. Lagebericht, 23 Dec. 1939. BA Berlin, Bestand PL90, Film 72410.

20. Der HSSPF beim Reichsstatthalter in Posen, betr. Betreuung der volksdeutschen Ansiedler, 6 May 1941. BA Berlin, R49, 3050.

21. Irene K., Bericht über meine Kindergartenarbeit im Kreise Leslau, Warthegau. BA Berlin, R49, 3051.

22. See the discussion of this point in relation to the women's Labour Service, and Melita Maschmann's memoirs, in Watzke-Otte, '*Ich war ein einsatzbereites Glied in der Gemeinschaft*', pp. 231–7. Maschmann's memories of expulsions are considered further below.

23. Maschmann, *Fazit*, pp. 126–30.

24. On the contradictions in Maschmann's narrative, see Joanne Sayner, 'An Autobiography of Avoidance: The Construction of Memories about Fascism in Melita Maschmann's Autobiography Taking Stock. My Journey Within the Hitler Youth', unpublished paper given at conference on Women, Gender and the Extreme Right in Europe, 1919–1945, University of Cardiff, July 2001.

25. Hildegard Friese, *Unsere Siedler im Kreis Welun* (Wört über Ellwangen, 1965), footnote p. 47.

26. Helga Thrö to Frau Marianne N., 'Betr. Ihre Fragen betr. Warthegau vom 15.3.1984', 24 June 1984. BA Berlin, NS 44/63.

27. Margarete Gerlach, 'Darf ich nach 30 Jahren sprechen?' BA Berlin, Zsg 145, 24.

28. Stabsführerin Treiber, 'Einsatz des RADwJ im Reichsgau Danzig-Westpreussen', *Jahrbuch des Reichsarbeitsdienstes* 1942, pp. 52–63, here p. 62.

29. Die Ansiedlungstätigkeit im Kreis Leslau/Weichsel im Jahre 1941. IfZ Archiv, Fb 115.

30. Eva P., Betreuungseinsatz Ost 1940. BA Berlin, R49, 3052.

31. Ibid.

32. Ursula N., Bericht über den Einsatz als soziale Betreuerin im Warthegau, BA Berlin, R49, 3051.

33. Renate K., Ein Tag in Vertretung des Hofbetreuers. BA Berlin, R49, 3052.

34. 'Hilfsdienst in Dobberschütz' (ms) and 'Großeinsatz bei der Umsiedlung von 70 buchen-
    länder Familien' describe settlement advisers organizing other women to clean up after
    Poles were evicted. BA Berlin, R49, 3045. See also Sophie W., Erlebnisse einer Ansiedler-
    betreuerin bei der Ansiedlung der Bessarabiendeutschen in Jasiorsko, 4 Nov. 1942. IfZ,
    MA 225/8775.

35. M. M., Slubize, Kreis Waldrode, 6 Sept. 1942. BA Berlin, R49, 3062.

36. Grete St., Ortsgruppe Löwenstadt, Kreis Litzmannstadt, 2 Oct. 1942. Ibid.

37. Meta K., Kreis Konin, 21 July 1942. BA Berlin, R49, 121.

38. It was common for German settlers to be given more than one small Polish farm – hence
    resettlement operations such as the one mentioned above in which 35 Polish families made
    way for 14 German families.

39. Elfriede B., 19 Aug. 1942. Gemeinde Grabow, Kreis Lentschütz. BA Berlin, R49, 3062.

40. Gendarmerie Kreis Krotoschin an den Kommandeur der Gendarmerie des Reg. Bez.
    Posen, betr. Lageberichte, 24. Nov. 1939. APP, Landratsamt in Krotoschin, 33.

41. Gendarmeriekreis Ostrowo, Lagebericht vom 7. August 1940. BA Berlin, Bestand PL
    90-Film 72410.

42. Arbeitsamt-Nebenstelle Krotoschin an das Arbeitsamt Jarotschin, betr. Berichterstattung
    über die Arbeitseinsatzlage, Arbeitseinsatzbericht für den Monat September 1940, 27 Sept.
    1940. APP, Landratsamt Krotoschin, 33.

43. For criticism of the policy of breaking up communities, see Bericht eines Vertrauens-
    mannes, Der Aufbau des deutschen Volkswalles im Osten, pp. 5–6. BA Berlin, R58, 243.

44. Alexander Dolezalek, Planungsabteilung der SS-Ansiedlungsstäbe Litzmannstadt und
    Posen, Vermerk betr: Die kulturelle Aufbauarbeit im Warthegau und die Umsiedlerbe-
    treuung, 17 Feb. 1941. IfZ Archiv, MA 225.

45. Bergen, 'The "Volksdeutschen" of Eastern Europe', p. 82.

46. E. Poggensee, 'Aus dem Tagebuch einer Ansiedlerbetreuerin im Wartheland' (ms) for *NS-
    Frauenwarte*, 28 Mar. 1942. IfZ, MA 225.

47. Bergen, 'The Nazi Concept of "Volksdeutsche"', pp. 575–6.

48. On Nazi policies in the Warthegau towards the Churches, see Bernhard Stasiewski, 'Die
    Kirchenpolitik der Nationalsozialisten im Warthegau 1939–45; *VjZG* 7, no.1 (1959),
    pp. 46–74; Paul Gürtler, *Nationalsozialismus und evangelische Kirchen im Warthegau*
    (Göttingen, 1958).

49. Hübner, Reichsstatthalter Wartheland/Beauftragter RKFDV, an alle Arbeitsstäbe
    im Warthegau betr. Erfassung der Sektenführer, 20 Jan. 1943. BA Berlin, R49, 3038;
    Bericht über das Sektenwesen unter den bisher umgesiedelten Volksgruppen aus
    Nord-Ost- und Südost-Europa [undated], BA Berlin, R49, 3073.

50. Anna G., Dresden, Unser Betreuungseinsatz. BA Berlin, R49, 3052.

51. Lotte H., Arbeitsbuch für die Gemeinde Skrzany, Gostynin. BA Berlin, R49, 3054; Anna
    G., Unser Betreuungseinsatz. BA Berlin, R49, 3052.

52. Margot H., Kreis Kolmar, Ortsgr. Margonin, 29 Nov. 1942. BA Berlin, R49, 3062.

53. Bericht aus Slemien (Oberschlesien), 11 June 1942. Auszüge aus den Berichten der
    Ansiedlerbetreuerinnen (Oberschlesien). BA Berlin, R49, 3133.

54. G. H., Ortsgr. Rennental, Kreis Leslau, 4 Jan. 1943. BA Berlin, R49, 3062.

55. 'K. W.', Thorn, 31 Aug. 1942. BA Berlin, R49, 3084.

56. Ibid.

57. 'R.', Rippin, 1 Apr. 1943. BA Berlin, R49, 120.

58. Wilma T., Kreis Kempen, 7 Apr. 1943. BA Berlin, R 49, 122.

59. Else L., September 1942, Gemeinde Butschek, Kreis Lask; see also report by T. Wibbeke, Dobberschütz, Kreis Krotoschin, 4 May 1943. BA Berlin, R49, 121.

60. 'R.', Rippin, 1 Feb. 1943. BA Berlin, R49, 120.

61. Wilma T., Kempen, 12 Aug. 1942. BA Berlin, R49, 122.

62. Anni P., Praschkau, Kreis Welun. 17 Dec. 1942. BA Berlin, R49, 3062.

63. L. D., Kreis Konin. 26 May 1943. BA Berlin, R49, 121.

64. Sophie W., Kreis Turek, 4 Nov. 1942. IfZ, MA 225/8775.

65. Lisa L., Kreis Samter, 4 Nov. 1942. BA Berlin, R49, 122.

66. Lisa L., Kreis Samter, 5 Mar. 1943. Ibid.

67. Elise Sch., Kreis Wollstein, 1 Aug. 1942. Ibid.

68. M. K., Buchenhain, Bülowstal, Kreis Obornik, Feb. 1943. BA Berlin, R49, 121.

69. Alexander Dolezalek, Planungsabteilung, Ansiedlungstab Posen, an die SS-Arbeitsstäbe im Bereich des SS-Ansiedlungsstabes Posen, 12 Sept. 1940. BA Berlin, R49, 3065.

70. Frau Peters, letter of 4 July 1942, in author's possession.

71. On the 'Reich University of Posen', see Peter Klein, 'Die "Reichsuniversität Posen" 1939–1941: Planung und Aufbau einer Universität in der NS-Zeit', Magisterarbeit, Freie Universität Berlin, 1993.

72. Hildur Jucum, ANSt-Referentin Posen, Bericht über studentisches Einsatzlager Penskowo (1943). Archiwum UAM, Reichsuniversität Posen 78, 16.

73. Kornelia L., Kreis Obornik, 6 July 1942. BA Berlin, R49, 122.

74. Malwine B., Luschwitz, 27 Feb. 1943. Kreis Lissa. Ibid.

75. SS-Arbeitsstab Kutno an den Ansiedlungstab in Litzmannstadt betr. Bericht über die Generalinspektion, 9 Dec. 1940. BA Berlin, R49, 3072.

76. Berichte vom Weihnachtseinsatz der Studentinnen 1940/41: Bericht Kalisch. BA Berlin, R49, 3052.

77. Erika St., Kreis Grätz, 30 July 1942. BA Berlin, R49, 122.

78. Anna W., Kreis Obornik, 7 Dec. 1942. Ibid.

79. M. K., Kreis Obornik, 10 Dec. 1942. BA Berlin, R49, 3062.

80. M. K., Parkdorf, Kreis Obornik, 3 July 1943. Ibid.

81. On Baschkow, see above, Chapter 5.

82. The song, text by Thilo Scheller, is to be found in *Wir Mädel Singen. Liederbuch des Bundes Deutscher Mädel* (Wolfenbüttel, 1941), p. 145.

83. Erna Lundberg, Muttertag im Mai 1942. BA Berlin, Zsg 145, 59.

84. Adelheid K., Bericht über den studentischen Einsatz vom 5. Aug. 1942–25. Sept. 1942 in Kelpin. Archiwum Państwowe w Gdańsku [= APG], HSSPF 265, 4498.

85. Renate K., BA Berlin, R49, 3052.

86. Adelheid K., Bericht über den studentischen Einsatz vom 5. Aug. 1942–25. Sept. 1942 in Kelpin. APG, HSSPF 265, 4498.

87. Anna W., Kreis Obornik, 7 Dec. 1942. BA Berlin, R49, 122.

88. Sophie W., Kreis Turek, 3 Mar. 1943. Ibid.

89. Kornelia L., Kreis Obornik, 10 July 1942. BA Berlin, R49, 121.

90. E. R., Kreis Ostrowo, 5 Apr. 1943. Ibid.

91. 'B', Konitz, 30 Aug. 1941. BA Berlin, R49, 3084.

92. A. Sch., 30 Sept. 1942. Schrimm, Orstgr. Moschin, BA Berlin, R49, 120.

93. Anna B., Feuerstein, Kreis Lissa, 26 Feb. 1943; Sch., Kreis Ostrowo, 3 Mar. 1943. BA Berlin, R49, 121.

94. Sophie W., Kreis Turek, 29 June 1943. BA Berlin, R49, 3062.

95. J. V., Kreis Kalisch, July 1942. BA Berlin, R49, 122.

96. H. D., Gnesen, 7 Sept. 1942; Kr., 10 Apr. 1943. BA Berlin, R49, 121.

97. Karla A., Kreis Kalisch, Nov. 1942. BA Berlin, R49, 122.

98. Olga Sch., Oktoberbericht 1942, Kreis Turek. BA Berlin R49, 3062; for 'unwürdig und gottlos' comment, see 'K. W.', Thorn, 4 Feb. 1943. BA Berlin, R49, 3084.

99. Fred Michaelsohn, 'Neue Heimat im Osten? Aus dem noch unveröffentlichten Roman "Wandlungen"', *Heimatkalender der Bessarabiendeutschen 1965*, pp. 100–9, here p. 107.

100. Abschrift, Brief von Gertrud an Ilse, 10 Oct. 1940. BA Berlin, R49, 3052.

101. Bericht Renate K. Ibid.

102. Ibid.

103. *Die Fachgruppe. Organ des Amtes Wissenschaft und Facherziehung der Reichsstudentenführung*, Folge 4, April 1941, p. 94.

104. Jutta Sch., Lagerbericht vom studentischen Einführungslager am 26.–27. Juni 1943 in Lärchensee, Kreis Birnbaum. Archiwum UAM, Reichsuniversität Posen 78, 16.

105. Frau Peters, letter of 4 July 1942, in author's possession.

106. Anna G., Unser Betreuungseinsatz. BA Berlin, R49, 3052.

107. Gertrud F., betr. Soziale Betreuungsarbeit. Studentischer Einsatz im Warthegau Kreis Warthbrücken, Gemeinde Tonningen, in der Zeit vom 27. July–27. Aug. 1940. Ibid.

108. Gertrud F., Betreuungseinsatz Ost 1940. Ibid.

109. Eva W., Bericht über den Einsatz im Reichsgau Warthe. BA Berlin, R49, 3051; Bericht Renate K., BA Berlin, R49, 3052.

110. Abschrift, Brief von Gertrud an Ilse, 10 Oct. 1940. Ibid.

111. Renate K., Abschied von den Wolhyniern. Ibid.

112. On the Volhynian Germans, see Babette L., Kreis Kutno, Ortsgruppe Kreuzdorf, 31 Mar. 1943. BA Berlin, R49, 121; on the Bukovina Germans, see Gaufrauenschaftsleitung Oberschlesien, Kattowitz, 14 Mar. 1944, Auszüge aus Berichten der Ansiedlerbetreuerinnen für das deutsche Auslandsinstitut Stuttgart. Bericht von Wieprz, 1 July–20 July 1941. BA Berlin, R49, 3133.

113. 'R', Kreis Briesen, 2 Sept. 1941. IfZ, MA 225/8743.

114. Anna Br., Feuerstein, 30 Apr. 1943; Otti D., Kreis Gnesen, 3 Mar. 1943. BA Berlin, R49, 121.

115. 'F'., Kulm, 8 Feb. 1943. BA Berlin, R49, 3084.

116. Lore G., Rozdrazewo, Kreis Krotoschin, 5 Mar. 1943, and 5 May 1943; Marie M., Neusiedeln, Kreis Samter, 28 June 1942. BA Berlin, R49, 122.

117. Ilse H., Ortsgr. Freienstein, Kreis Grätz, 2 Sept. 1942. BA Berlin, R49, 3062.

118. 'Siberia' was how Baltic Germans termed Kreis Altburgund in the northern Warthegau: V. H., Kreis Altburgund, Bartelstein, 2 June 1943. BA Berlin, R49, 121.

119. Reports from Danzig-Westpreußen: 'B', Konitz, 30 Aug. 1941: 3 suicides; 'E. H.', Wirsitz, Feb. 1942: suicide of 24-year-old man; 'E. G.', Zempelburg, 6 July 1942: suicide of young woman. BA Berlin, R49, 3084; reports from Warthegau: Flora Sch., Kreis Lentschütz, 14 July 1942: 2 suicides. BA Berlin, R49, 121.

120. Auszüge aus Berichten der Ansiedlerbetreuerinnen für das dt. Auslandsinstitut Stuttgart, Bericht aus Chocznia vom 1. July bis 20. Jul. 1941. BA Berlin, R49, 3133.

121. 'K.W.', Thorn, 4 Feb. 1943. BA Berlin, R49, 3084.

122. Else R., 3 Mar. 1943, Kreis Ostrowo. BA Berlin, R49, 3062.

123. K. B., Kreis Hermannsbad, 20 June 1942. BA Berlin, R49, 122.

124. Anni W., Ortsgr. Eichstädt, Kreis Warthbrücken. 3 Nov. 1942. Ibid.

125. M. Sch., Kreis Warthbrücken, 5 Nov. 1942. Ibid.

126. O. R., Georgsburg, Kreis Samter, 30 Nov. 1942. Ibid.

127. Kath. Bechtloff, Kreis Hermannsbad, 20 June 1942. Ibid.

128. M. H., Kreis Birnbaum, 31 May 1943. BA Berlin, R49, 121.

129. M. Sch., Kreis Warthbrücken, Oktoberbericht, 5 Nov. 1942. BA Berlin, R49, 3062.

130. 'M. M.', Zempelburg, 1 Mar. 1943. BA Berlin, R49, 3084. Thanks to Mathias Niendorf for this reference.

131. Klara F., Kreis Hohensalza, 8 Mar. 1943. BA Berlin, R49, 3062.

132. Else R., Kreis Ostrowo, Jan. 1943. Ibid.

133. 'E. G.', Zempelburg, 6 July 1942. BA Berlin, R49, 3084; K., Kreis Schrimm, Dec. 1942. BA Berlin, R49, 122.

134. Erna B., Kurovice, Kreis Litzmannstadt, 1 Mar. 1943. BA Berlin, R49, 122.

135. Hanna S., Wiesenstadt, Kreis Kosten, Oct. 1942. Ibid.

136. Anna Br., Feuerstein, Kreis Lissa, Jan. 1943. Ibid.

137. Hanna S., Bericht für Januar–Februar–März 1943. Ibid.

138. M. Sch., Kreis Warthbrücken, 5 Nov. 1942. Ibid.

139. Else R., Kreis Ostrowo, 3 Mar. 1943. Ibid.

140. Erika C., Ortsgr. Mühlental, Warthbrücken, 27 Feb. 1943. Ibid.

141. 'B', Graudenz, 4 Nov. 1942. BA Berlin, R49, 3084.

142. Irmgard B., 1 Mar. 1943, Kreis Altburgund. BA Berlin, R49, 122.

143. 'Flettig', Koschmin, Kreis Krotoschin, 2 Mar. 1943. Ibid.

144. Pospieszalski, ed., *Hitlerowskie 'prawo' okupacyjne w Polsce*, pp. 379–80.

145. Ibid., pp. 376–8.

146. Elis. H., Ortsgr. Pleschen, Kreis Jarotschin, 5 Jan. 1943, 4 Feb. 1943, 2 Mar. 1943; Emma Gerber, Kreis Ostrowo, 4 Dec. 1942 and 5 Mar. 1943. BA Berlin, R49, 122.

147. Friedl H., Kreis Altburgund, 1 Feb. 1943. BA Berlin, R49, 3062.

148. Meta Gr., Kreis Gnesen, 7 Jan. 1943. BA Berlin, R49, 122.

149. L. H., Kreis Wreschen. 11 Aug. 1942. BA Berlin, R49, 3062.

150. M. K., Kreis Obornik, 10 Dec. 1942. Ibid.

151. E. R., Kreis Ostrowo, 5 Apr. 1943. BA Berlin, R49, 121.

152. Paula Sch., Kreis Hohensalza, 9 Feb. 1943. BA Berlin, R49, 122.

153. Emma Sch., Kreis Turek, 1 Oct. 1942. BA Berlin, R49, 3062.

154. G. Br., Kreis Konin, 2 Oct. 1042. BA Berlin, R49, 122.

155. L. H., Wreschen, 8 Dec. 1942. BA Berlin, R49, 121.

156. Gertrud L., Ortsgr. Koschmin, Kreis Krotoschin, 6 July 1942. BA Berlin, R49, 122.

157. Frieda H., Kreis Krotoschin, 7 Oct. 1942. BA Berlin, R49, 121.

158. Frieda H., Altburgund, 31 Aug.[1942]. Ibid.

159. Olga R., Kreis Kosten, 30 Sept. 1942. BA Berlin, R49, 3062.

160. Freyja S., Kreis Krotoschin, June 1942. BA Berlin, R49, 121.

161. N., Kreis Schroda, 7 Oct. 1942. BA Berlin, R49, 3062.

162. A. Sch., 17 Aug. 1942. BA Berlin, R49, 121.

163. 'B', Konitz, 1 Aug. 1941. BA Berlin, R49, 3084.

164. Ibid.

165. G., 1 June 1943, Kreis Birnbaum. BA Berlin, R49, 122.

166. Upper Silesia: Bericht aus Slemien, 11 June 1942. Auszüge aus den Berichten der Ansiedlerbetreuerinnen (Oberschlesien). BA Berlin, R49, 3133; Warthegau: W., Kreis Wreschen, 6 Nov. 1942. BA Berlin, R49, 121; Else R., Jan. 1943, Kreis Ostrowo. BA Berlin, R49, 3062.

167. Bericht aus Saybusch (Oberschlesien), 28 Oct. 1941. BA Berlin, R49, 3133.

168. 'B', Kreis Konitz, 1 Aug. 1941. BA Berlin, R49, 3084.

169. 'R.', Rippin, 1 Aug. 1943. BA Berlin, R49, 120.

170. Rede v. Frl. Koschowitz, Leiterin von Grenz-Ausland, Ansiedlerbetreuerinnen der NS-Frauenschaft Gau Wartheland, II. Jahrestreffen v. 1–3. Dez. 1942. BA Berlin, R49, 3060.

171. Reichsstatthalter im Reichsgau Wartheland, Erlaß an alle Dienststellen des Staates incl. der Sonderverwaltungen, 3 Dec. 1942. IfZ, MA225/9988–9.

172. R. H., 'Die Partei als Betreuerin der Rückwanderer. Das Deutsche Frauenwerk stellte bewährte Helferinnen', *Gau Wartheland, NS-Gaudienst*, 2 Feb. 1940. IfZ, MA 225/8876.

173. Schlepmeier, SS-Ansiedlungsstab Litzmannstadt, Planungsabteilung, 17 Feb. 1942, Vermerk: Der Aufbau der Siedlerbetriebe im östlichen Warthegau im Krieg. BA Berlin, R49, 3068.

174. Richard Rupp, 'Die Hofzuweisung' [undated]. Ibid.

175. M. Brandenburg, 'Nachbarschaftshilfe im Gau Wartheland' (ms), June 1941. IfZ, MA 225/8911.

176. Hildur Jucum, ANSt-Referentin Posen, Bericht über studentisches Einsatzlager vom 2. Aug.–12. Sept. 1943. Archiwum UAM, Reichsuniversität Posen, 78, 16.

177. Meldungen aus dem Reich, Nr. 234 vom 3. Nov. 1941. IfZ, MA 441/4.

178. Gendarmerie Kreis Kosten, 24 Sept. 1942, Lagebericht für die Zeit 7.–25. Sept. 1942, an die Gendarmerie-Hauptmannschaft in Lissa. BA Berlin, Bestand PL-109.

179. Lieselotte Gumpert, 'Die Auswirkungen der Volkstumspolitik auf das Schulwesen im Wartheland' (1956). BA Bayreuth, Ost-Dok 8, 458.

180. Interview with Frau Winter and Frau Mahnke, 27 Oct. 1999.

181. Interview with Frau Fischer, 25 Oct. 1999.

182. Interview with Frau Holz, 7 Aug. 2001.

183. Interview with Frau Bauer, 22 Oct. 1999.

184. Interview with Frau Winter, 27 Oct. 1999.

185. Interview with Frau Bauer, 22 Oct. 1999.

186. Interview with Frau Winter, 27 Oct. 1999.

187. Interview with Frau Danneberg, 8 Jan. 2000.

188. Interview with Frau Fischer, 25 Oct. 1999. This incident is discussed in more detail in Elizabeth Harvey, 'Erinnern und Verdrängen: Deutsche Frauen und der "Volkstumskampf" im besetzten Polen', in Karen Hagemann and Stefanie Schüler-Springorum, eds, *Heimat-Front: Militär und Geschlechterverhältnisse im Zeitalter der Weltkriege* (Frankfurt am Main and New York, 2002), pp. 291–310.

189. Interview with Frau Fischer, 25 Oct. 1999.

190. Interview with Frau Mahnke, 27 Oct. 1999.

191. Interview with Frau Winter, 27 Oct. 1999.

192. Interview with Frau Bauer, 22 Oct. 1999.

193. Interview with Frau Danneberg, 8 Jan. 2000.

194. Interview with Frau Holz, 7 Aug. 2001.

195. For this argument in propaganda targeted at women in the Labour Service, see NSDAP Gauleitung Wartheland, ed., *Arbeitsmaiden helfen im Wartheland* (Posen, 1940), pp. 11–12.

Chapter 7 Moulding the Next Generation: Village Schoolteachers in the 'Reichsgau Wartheland'

1. Rede des Gauleiters und Reichsstatthalters Arthur Greiser bei der Tagung der BDM-Schulhelferinnen am 11.5.1943 in Posen. APP, RSH im Wartheland, 2414.

2. Ibid.

3. 'Denkschrift Himmlers über die Behandlung der Fremdvölkischen im Osten (Mai 1940)', *VjZG* 5 (1957), pp. 194–8.

4. Kershaw, 'Arthur Greiser', p. 116.

5. Dr Böttcher an den Gauleiter und Reichsstatthalter in Posen, betr. Erlaß des Reichserziehungsministeriums vom 16. 7. 1940, 22 July 1940. GKW, 62, 21.

6. Hansen, *Ethnische Schulpolitik* pp. 53–5.

7. RSH Posen, Abt. III/4, Lagebericht über das Volks- und Mittelschulwesen im Warthegau nach dem Stande vom 1. Juli 1941. APP, RSH im Wartheland, 2373.

8. RSH Posen Abt. III/4 an das Sachgebiet I/22 im Hause, 10 Nov. 1941. APP, RSH im Wartheland, 2414.

9. 'Die Schulhelferin: Die Lösung des Lehrerproblems im Wartheland', *Ostdeutscher Beobachter*, 9 Oct. 1943.

10. For statistics on schools and teaching staff, see Georg Hansen, ed., *Schulpolitik als Volkstumspolitik: Quellen zur Schulpolitik der Besatzer in Polen 1939–1945* (Münster and New York, 1994), pp. 140–51.

11. See Chapter 4.

12. Hansen, *Ethnische Schulpolitik*, pp. 68–74.

13. Lieselotte Gumpert, 'Die Auswirkungen der Volkstumspolitik auf das Schulwesen im Wartheland' (1956). BA Bayreuth, Ost-Dok 8, 458.

14. 'Lebensaufgabe im deutschen Osten', *Die Bewegung* 8, no. 39 (1940), p. 3.

15. 'Eine Berliner BDM-Führerin', 'Einsatz im Osten: Pflicht jeder Führerin', *Das deutsche Mädel*, June 1941, pp. 6–7.

16. Reg.präs Litzmannstadt to RSH im Warthegau, Abt. III, betr. Einsatz von BDM-Angehörigen als Hilfskräfte im Schuldienst, 26 Jan. 1942. APP, RSH im Wartheland, 2414.

17. Reg.präs. Posen, Abt. II N, to RSH Abt. III in Posen, betr. Einsatz von BDM-Angehörigen als Hilfskräfte im Schuldienst, 12 Jan. 1942; Reg.präs. Hohensalza, Abt. II 2 D, to RSH Abt. III in Posen, betr. Einsatz von BDM-Angehörigen als Hilfskräfte im Schuldienst, 29 Jan. 1942. Ibid.

18. Der Schulrat Scharnikau, Berichte über die Unterrichtsbesichtigung: Volksschule Gembitz, 28 Apr. 1944; Volksschule Scharnikau, 25 Apr. 1944; Volksschule Staykowo, 31 May 1944; Volksschule Altsorge, 19 May 1942 ('*einseitige Betonung der Leibeserziehung!*'); Volksschule Scharnikau, 14 July 1944 ('*Frl. F ... weiß, worauf es in Unterricht und Erziehung ankommt*'). APP, Landratsamt Scharnikau, 54.

19. Lehrer Arndt, Bericht über den Lehrgang vom 18.–27.1.1943 im Bezirksseminar Hermannsbad, 29 Jan. 1943. APP, RSH im Wartheland, 2414.

20. Gebietsmädelführung Reichsgau Wartheland, BDM-Schulhelferinnen: Erfahrungen und Vorschläge, undated (*c*. March 1942). Ibid.

21. Lieselotte Huber, in 'Berichte aus dem Einsatz', *Der Ruf: Rundbrief der LBA Posen* 4 (Apr. 1944), p. 11. APP, RSH im Wartheland, 2432.

22. Ilse P., HfL Hamburg, 'Lehrereinsatz Sommer 1940'. BA Berlin, R49, 3052. An alternative spelling for Druzbice was Druzbize.

23. Ingrid Nienerza, Mixstadt, in 'Aus Zuschriften von Schulhelferinnen', *Der Ruf: Rundbrief der LBA* 2 (June 1943), p. 3. APP, RSH im Wartheland, 2432.

24. Gabriele Hornung, *Schrimm, Schroda, Bomst: Kein Roman* (Scheinfeld, 1985), p. 18.

25. Interview with Frau Geyer, 21 Apr. 1996.

26. Annelise Schober, in 'Aus Zuschriften von Schulhelferinnen', *Der Ruf* 3 (Oct. 1943), p. 7. APP, RSH im Wartheland, 2432.

27. Marga Wichmann, in 'Berichte aus dem Einsatz', *Der Ruf* 4 (Apr. 1944), p. 9. Ibid.

28. Magdalene Pfeiffer, Mein Osteinsatz an der Schule in Dilltal, 12 Sept. 1943. Archiwum UAM, Reichsuniversität Posen, 78/424.

29. Ilse P., HfL Hamburg, 'Lehrereinsatz Sommer 1940'. BA Berlin, R49, 3052.

30. Hornung, *Schrimm, Schroda, Bomst*, pp. 22–3.

31. Ilse Sasse to Landjahrbezirksführerin U. Lindner, betr.: Besichtigungsfahrt der Land-jahrerzieherinnen Sasse, Lengert, Metzdorf, Mörstedt, Rimpau nach Jägerslust, 15 Feb. 1943; Kottmann to Landjahrbezirksführerin U. Lindner, betr: Besuch der Schule in Rautendorf, 15 Feb. 1943. APP, RSH im Wartheland, 2643.

32. For comments on inadequate premises, see interview with Frau Geyer, 21 Apr. 1996; Lieselotte Grewe, in 'Berichte aus dem Einsatz', *Der Ruf* 4 (Apr. 1944), pp. 8–9. APP, RSH im Wartheland, 2432; Barbara Sch. an RSH Abt. III, Posen, betr. Lehramtsanwärterin Theodora Sch., 22 Feb. 1943. APP, RSH im Wartheland, 2409.

33. Gumpert, 'Die Auswirkungen der Volkstumspolitik auf das Schulwesen im Wartheland'.

34. For comments on pupils' poor German, see Schulrat Scharnikau, reports on Nowina (July 1941) and Dratzig (Oct. 1941). APP, Landratsamt Scharnikau, 54.

35. 'Von unseren Schwarzmeerdeutschen', *Der Ruf* 5 (Oct. 1944), pp. 8–9. APP, RSH im Wartheland, 2432.

36. Hedi K., in '"Ich bin froh wenn ich allen helfen kann": Aus Tagebüchern beim Lehrer-einsatz', *Die Bewegung* 8, no. 35 (1940), p. 4.

37. Ursula Erler, Märzdorf, in 'Aus Zuschriften von Schulhelferinnen', *Der Ruf* 1 (Mar. 1943), p. 3. APP, RSH im Wartheland, 2432.

38. Magdalene Pfeiffer, Mein Osteinsatz an der Schule in Dilltal, 12 Sept. 1943. Archiwum UAM, Reichsuniversität Posen, 78/424.

39. Brunhild Jänicke, Neugrade, 20 Apr. 1943, in 'Aus unserer Gemeinschaft', *Der Ruf* 2 (June 1943). APP, RSH im Wartheland, 2432.

40. 'Lebensaufgabe im deutschen Osten', *Die Bewegung* 8, no. 39 (1940), p. 3.

41. Gertraud von M., in: '"Ich bin froh wenn ich allen helfen kann": Aus Tagebüchern beim Lehrereinsatz', *Die Bewegung* 8, no. 35 (1940), p. 4.

42. Geertien B., ibid.

43. Abschrift, Brief von Gertrud an Ilse, 10 Oct. 1940. BA Berlin, R49, 3052.

44. Lilo Huber to Bühnemann (LBA Posen), 8 July 1943. APP, RSH im Wartheland, 2432.

45. Theda Deters, in 'Aus Zuschriften von Schulhelferinnen', *Der Ruf* 2 (June 1943), p. 2. Ibid.

46. Hildegard Grabe, 'Bericht über Erlebnisse während meiner Tätigkeit als Lehrerin im Warthegau von Ostern 1941 bis Januar 1945'. BA Bayreuth, Ost-Dok 8, 459.

47. Lehrer Arndt, Bezirksseminar Hermannsbad, an Reg.präs. Hohensalza, betr. Bericht über den Lehrgang vom 18.–27.1.1943 im Bezirksseminar Hermannsbad, 29 Jan. 1943. APP, RSH im Wartheland, 2414.

48. Schulrat Scharnikau, Bericht über die Unterrichtsbesichtigung am 30.7.1942 in Grützen-dorf. APP, Landrat Scharnikau, 54.

49. Schulamt Scharnikau, Arbeitsgemeinschaft der Schulamtsanwärterinnen des Kreises Scharnikau am 27.2.1942 in Grützendorf: Tagesordnung, Lehrproben, 21 Feb. 1942. APP, Landrat Scharnikau, 62.

50. Schulrat Scharnikau, Bericht über die Unterrichtsbesichtigung am 4.12.1942 in Lubasch. APP, Landrat Scharnikau, 54.

51. Herta M., Schule Lubasch, Lehrprobe Geschichte (Oberstufe), 30 Oct. 1942. APP, Landrat Scharnikau, 62.

52. Geertien B., in '"Ich bin froh, wenn ich allen helfen kann": Aus Tagebüchern beim Lehrereinsatz', *Die Bewegung* 8, no. 35 (1940), p. 4.

53. Dorothea Klussmann, in 'Berichte aus dem Einsatz', *Der Ruf* 5 (Oct. 1944), p. 7. APP, RSH im Wartheland, 2432.

54. Traute Teufel, 'Berichte aus dem Einsatz', *Der Ruf* 5 (Oct. 1944), p. 7. Ibid.

55. Marga Wichmann, in 'Berichte aus dem Einsatz', *Der Ruf* 4 (Apr. 1944), p. 9. Ibid.

56. Reg.präs. Posen, Vermerk, 25 May 1944; Der Regierungspräsident Posen an die Herren Landräte im Bezirk, 25 May 1944. APP, Landratsamt Scharnikau, 51.

57. Schulrat Liegmann, Reg.präs. Litzmannstadt, Abt. für Erziehung und Volksbildung, betr. Abordnung von Lehrkräften, 25 July 1940. APP, RSH im Wartheland, 2397.

58. The *Volksfortbildungswerk* was the adult education organization of the Deutsche Arbeitsfront.

59. Gebietsmädelführung Wartheland, BDM-Schulhelferinnen: Erfahrungen und Vorschläge. APP, RSH im Wartheland, 2414.

60. BDM Gebietsführung Wartheland, betr. Stellungnahme zu den Vorschlägen für die Zulassung zum Abschlußlehrgang für Schulhelferinnen, 11 Oct and 13 Oct. 1943. APP, RSH im Wartheland, 2416.

61. Schulrat Scharnikau, Bericht über die Unterrichtsbesichtigung am 19. 4.1941 in Briesen (Lehrerin E.); am 18 Oct. 1941 in Dratzig (Lehrerin Marie S.); am 24 Nov. 1942 in Filehne (Lehrerin Marie S.). APP, Landratsamt Scharnikau, 54.

62. Änne Ecker, Patok, 29 Jan. 1943, in 'Aus Zuschriften von Schulhelferinnen', *Der Ruf* 1 (Mar. 1943), pp. 3–4. APP, RSH im Wartheland, 2432.

63. Angela G., in '"Ich bin froh, wenn ich allen helfen kann": Aus Tagebüchern beim Lehrereinsatz', *Der Bewegung* 8, no. 35 (1940), p. 4.

64. Elfriede Janssen, in 'Berichte aus dem Einsatz', *Der Ruf* 5 (Oct. 1944), pp. 6–7. APP, RSH im Wartheland, 2432.

65. Annelise Schober, Krummbach, in 'Aus den Zuschriften von Schulhelferinnen', *Der Ruf* 3 (Oct. 1943), pp. 6–7. Ibid.

66. 'Ilse', 'Vom BDM-Dienst', *Der Ruf* 4 (Apr. 1944), p. 13. Ibid.

67. Liselotte K., in '"Ich bin froh, wenn ich allen helfen kann': Aus Tagebüchern beim Lehrereinsatz', *Die Bewegung* 8, no. 35 (1940), p. 4.

68. Pfeiffer, Mein Osteinsatz an der Schule in Dilltal.

69. Ibid.

70. Elfriede Janssen, in 'Berichte aus dem Einsatz', *Der Ruf* 5 (Oct. 1944), pp. 6–7. APP, RSH im Wartheland, 2432.

71. Pfeiffer, Mein Osteinsatz an der Schule in Dilltal.

72. Kottmann, an die Landjahrbezirksführerin U. Lindner, betr. Besuch der Schule in Rautendorf, 15 Feb. 1943. APP, RSH im Wartheland, 2643.

73. Schulrat Scharnikau, Bericht über die Unterrichtsbesichtigung am 5.6.1942 in Penskowo. APP, Landratsamt Scharnikau, 54.

74. Barbara Sch. an RSH Abt. III, Posen, 22.2.1943, betr. Lehramtsanwärterin Theodora Sch., 22 Feb. 1943. APP, RSH im Wartheland, 2409.

75. Schulrat des Kreises Lentschütz an Reg.präs. Litzmannstadt, Abt. Erziehung und Volks-bildung, betr. Lehramtsanwärterin Theodora Sch., 13 Mar. 1943. Ibid.

76. See Grabe, 'Bericht über Erlebnisse während meiner Tätigkeit als Lehrerin im Warthe-gau'; Mary von Bremen, 'Die Heimoberschule für Mädchen in Wreschen'. BA Bayreuth, Ost-Dok 8, 482; Annelies Regenstein, 'Meine Tätigkeit als Lehrerin in Laningen Krs Kutno 1940–45' (1956). BA Bayreuth, Ost-Dok 8, 467.

77. Reg.präs. Litzmannstadt, II A an RErzM, betr. Bericht des Regierungspräsidenten in Stade vom 31 Dec. 1940, 6 Mar. 1941. APP, RSH im Wartheland, 2397.

78. *Treuhänder* (trustees) were appointed to run farms and businesses that had been expro-priated from their Polish owners.

79. Regenstein, 'Meine Tätigkeit'.

80. Gumpert, 'Die Auswirkungen der Volkstumspolitik auf das Schulwesen im Wartheland'.

81. Anneliese Schober, in 'Aus Zuschriften von Schulhelferinnen', *Der Ruf* 3 (Oct. 1943), pp. 6–7. APP, RSH im Wartheland, 2432.

82. Theda Deters, in 'Aus Zuschriften von Schulhelferinnen', *Der Ruf* 2 (June 1943), p. 2. Ibid.

83. Barbara Sch. an RSH Abt. III, Posen, betr. Lehramtsanwärterin Theodora Sch., 22 Feb. 1943. APP, RSH im Wartheland, 2409.

84. Hornung, *Schrimm, Schroda, Bomst*, p. 12.

85. Schulrat Scharnikau, Bericht über die Unterrichtsbesichtigung am 13 Dec. 1943 in Fitzerie, Kreis Scharnikau. APP, Landratsamt Scharnikau, 54.

86. Hornung, *Schrimm, Schroda, Bomst*, p. 12.

87. Reg.präs. Hohensalza, Bericht betr. Trauthilde S., 13 May 1943. APP, RSH im Wartheland, 2409.

88. Reg.präs. Posen an RErzM, betr. Versetzung der Lehrerin Margot S., 27 Jan. 1944. Ibid.

89. Niederschrift über die Dienstbesprechung der Schulräte am 22. Januar 1944, 8 Uhr, Regierung Posen. APP, Landratsamt Scharnikau, 51.

90. Schulrat Scharnikau an Amtskommissar Filehne-Land, betr. Errichtung einer Schule für polnische Kinder in Penskowo, 27 Aug. 1942. APP, Landrat Scharnikau, 119.

91. A. Hansen, Bericht über den Besuch in der Volksschule Konradsaue, 14 Feb. 1943. Elfriede Waschulewski, Bericht über Besuch der Volksschule in Poppenburg, 15 Feb. 1943. APP, RSH im Wartheland, 2643.

92. See correspondence in APP, RSH im Wartheland, 2401.

93. Abschrift, Brief von Gertrud an Ilse, 10 Oct. 1940. BA Berlin, R49, 3052.

94. Regenstein, 'Meine Tätigkeit'.

95. Grabe, 'Bericht über Erlebnisse'.

96. Hilberg, *Destruction of the European Jews*, vol. 2, pp. 221–3, 266–7: Christopher Browning, *Path to Genocide: Essays on Launching the Final Solution* (Cambridge, 1992), pp. 32–3.

97. Hilberg, *Destruction of the European Jews*, vol. 2, pp. 212–14; Browning, *Path to Genocide*, p. 55.

98. Browning, *Fateful Months* pp. 29–38.

99. Ibid, pp. 30–1, 59, 62–3; Browning, *Path to Genocide*, p. 55; J. Noakes and G. Pridham, eds, *Nazism 1919–45, vol. 3: Foreign Policy, War and Extermination* (Exeter, 1988), pp. 1139–42.

100. Noakes and Pridham, eds, *Foreign Policy, War and Extermination*, pp. 1140–2.

101. Tatiana Berenstein et al., eds, *Faschismus – Getto – Massenmord: Dokumentation über Ausrottung und Widerstand der Juden in Polen während des zweiten Weltkrieges* (Frankfurt am Main, 1962), pp. 285–6.

102. Ibid., pp. 311–13.

103. Noakes and Pridham, eds, *Foreign Policy, War and Extermination*, p. 1143.

104. Regenstein, 'Meine Tätigkeit'.

105. Grabe, 'Bericht über Erlebnisse'.

106. Browning, *Fateful Months*, p. 64.

107. Reg.präs Posen, Abt. IIB, an RErzM, 25 Oct. 1944. APP, RSH im Wartheland, 2409.

108. Schulrat Scharnikau, Bericht über die Unterrichtsbesichtigung am 19 Apr. 1941 in Briesen. APP, Landrat Scharnikau, 54.

109. Schulrat Scharnikau, Bericht über die Unterrichtsbesichtigung am 9. Jul. 1941 in Sokolowo. Ibid.

110. Reg.präs. Litzmannstadt, Abt. IIB an RerzM., betr. Antrag der Schulhelferin Erna Schreyer (Schadek) auf Entlassung aus dem Schuldienst, 5 Jan. 1943. APP, RSH im Wartheland, 2409.

111. Schulrat des Kreises Lentschütz an Reg.präs Litzmannstadt, betr. Lehramtsanwärterin Theodora Sch. in Slugi, 13 Mar. 1943; Reg.präs. Litzmannstadt an RSH Abt. II, betr.

T. Sch. in Slugi, 14 Sept. 1943; RSH Abt. II an Reg.präs. Litzmannstadt, betr. Lehramts-anwärterin T. Sch. in Slugi, 18 Dec. 1944. APP, Ibid.

112. Reg.präs. Posen an RErzM, betr. Gesuch der Lehramtsanwärterin Hedwig Sch. um Versetzung ins Altreich, 19 July 1943. Ibid.

113. RSH Posen, Abt. III/2 an RErzM, 21 Aug. 1943. Ibid.

114. Interview with Frau Vogel, 12 Nov. 1998.

115. Ibid.

116. Interview with Frau Teplitz, 23 Oct. 1999.

117. Interview with Frau Geyer, 21 Apr. 1996.

118. Interview with Frau Ullmann, 12 Jan. 1999.

119. Interview with Frau Eckhard, 12 Nov. 1998.

120. Interview with Frau Ullmann, 12 Jan. 1999.

121. Interview with Frau Geyer, 21 Apr. 1996.

122. 'Tätigkeitsbericht' (ms., 1947), in author's possession.

123. Browning, *Path to Genocide*, p. 43.

124. Inteview with Frau Eckhard, 12 Nov. 1998.

125. Interview with Frau Vogel, 12 Nov. 1998.

126. Interview with Frau Ullmann, 12 Jan. 1999.

127. Interview with Frau Eckhard, 12 Nov. 1998.

128. Interview with Frau Teplitz, 23 Oct. 1999.

129. Interview with Frau Eckhard, 12 Nov. 1998.

130. Interview with Frau Geyer, 21 Apr. 1996.

131. Interview with Frau Vogel, 12 Nov. 1998.

132. Ibid.

133. Interview with Frau Teplitz, 23 Oct. 1999.

134. Frau Teplitz, letter to author, 20 Nov. 1999, in author's possession.

135. Interview with Frau Teplitz, 23 Oct. 1999, and correspondence, in author's possession.

136. Brunhild Jänicke, Neugrade, 20 Apr. 1943, in 'Aus unserer Gemeinschaft', *Der Ruf 2* (June 1943), p. 4. APP, RSH im Wartheland, 2432.

137. Rede des Gauleiters und Reichsstatthalters Arthur Greiser bei der Tagung der BDM-Schulhelferinnen am 11. Mai 1943 in Posen. APP, RSH im Wartheland, 2414.

Chapter 8 Childcare and Colonization: Kindergartens on the Frontiers of the Nazi Empire

1. Walter Erdmann, 'Der Osten zeichnet aus', *NS-Volksdienst* 8, no. 7 (1941), pp. 134–9, here p. 137.

2. For example Frau Andreas, interviewed in 1994.

3. Karol Marian Pospieszalski, *Hitlerowskie 'prawo' okupacyjne w Polsce, Część II: Generalna Gubernia* [= *Documenta Occupationis VI*] (Poznań, 1956), p. 619; Koehl, *RKFDV*, p. 129.

4. Werner Präg and Wolfgang Jacobmeyer, eds, *Das Diensttagebuch des deutschen General-gouverneurs in Polen 1939–45* (Stuttgart, 1975), Einleitung, p. 7; Musial, *Deutsche Zivil-verwaltung und Judenverfolgung*, p. 22.

5. Thomas Sandkühler, *'Endlösung' in Galizien: Der Judenmord in Ostpolen und die Rettungsinitiativen von Berthold Beitz, 1941–1944* (Bonn, 1996), pp. 32–3.

6. SS- und Polizeiführer im Distrikt Lublin to Chef des Distrikts Lublin (Zörner), 15 Oct.

1940; SS-und Polizeiführer Lublin, to Chef des Distrikts Lublin, Abt. Innere Verwaltung, betr. Endzahlen der volksdeutschen Umsiedlung im Distrikt Lublin, 17 Dec. 1940; Chef des Distriktes Lublin Abt. Ernährung und Landwirtschaft an die Abt. Volksfürsorge und Bevölkerungswesen beim Chef des Distrikts, betr. Ansiedlung evakuierter Polen im Distrikt Lublin, 20 Dec. 1940. APLub, Gouverneur des Distrikts Lublin, 134.

7. Auszug aus dem Monatsbericht des Referenten für Bevölkerungswesen und Fürsorge in Hrubieszow, Nov. 1940. APLub, Gouverneur des Distrikts Lublin, 207.

8. Majer, 'Fremdvölkische' im Dritten Reich, pp. 463–5.

9. Ibid., p. 465.

10. Madajczyk, ed., Zamojszczyzna, pp. 12–13.

11. Documenta Occupationis VI, p. 618; Majer, 'Fremdvölkische' im Dritten Reich, p. 465; Sandkühler, 'Endlösung', p. 89.

12. Paul Robert Magocsi, A History of Ukraine (Toronto, 1996), pp. 617–20.

13. Sandkühler, 'Endlösung', p. 63.

14. For recollections by Galician Germans of the resettlement of 1939–40, see for instance Arnold Jaki, 'Werden wir umgesiedelt?', Zeitweiser der Galiziendeutschen 1960, pp. 32–3; Josef Lanz, 'Bei der Umsiedlungskommission in Dornfeld', ibid., pp. 37–40; Schwester Sophie, 'Als Nachhut der Umsiedlung in Stanislau', ibid., pp. 48–54.

15. Krüger an SS Obersturmbannführer Brandt (RFSS, Persönlicher Stab), 20 July 1943. BA Berlin, NS19, 3662.

16. Verordnung über die Einführung eines Ausweises für Deutschstämmige im Generalgouvernement vom 29. Oktober 1941. Documenta Occupationis VI, p. 186.

17. Himmler an Rasse- und Siedlungshauptamt und Volksdeutsche Mittelstelle, 16 Feb. 1943. BA Berlin, NS19, 3662.

18. The Deutschstämmige were placed in one of two categories: the first 'registered for naturalization' ('zur Einwanderung und Einbürgerung angemeldet') and the second 'scheduled for registering for naturalization' ('für die Anmeldung zur Einbürgerung vorgemerkt'). RKF an den Beauftragten des Reichskommissars für die Festigung deutschen Volkstums, Vorgang: Rechtsstellung der aus dem Generalgouvernement in das Reich umgesiedelten Deutschstämmigen, 26 May 1944. Documenta Occupationis VI, pp. 202–3.

19. Greiser an Himmler, 16 Mar. 1943 and 15 Apr. 1943. BA Berlin, NS19, 3662.

20. Kaltenbrunner (Chef der Sicherheitspolizei und des SD) an Himmler, 20 July 1943. BA Berlin, NS19, 3662.

21. On the 'Generalplan Ost', see Rolf-Dieter Müller, Hitlers Ostkrieg und die deutsche Siedlungspolitik (Frankfurt am Main, 1991), pp. 94–110; Madajczyk, ed., Generalplan Ost.

22. W. Gradmann, 'Das Deutschtum im Gebiet von Zamosc. Ergebnisse einer Erkundungsfahrt', 19 Mar. 1942. In Madajczyk, ed., Zamojszczyzna , vol. 1, pp. 53–60.

23. 'Deutsches Leben im Zamoscer Land. Ein Jahr Dorfarbeit', Deutscher Kolonisten-Kalender für die Siedlungen im Distrikt Lublin auf das Jahr 1942/3 (no place, undated), pp. 32–5.

24. SS-Hauptsturmführer H. Müller to SS Rasse- und Siedlungshauptamt, 15 Oct. 1941. Madajczyk, ed., Zamojszczyzna, vol. 1, p. 29.

25. On the expulsions from the villages of Huszczka Duza, Huszczka Mała, Dulnik, Zawada, Wysokie, Bortatycze and Białobrzegi, see Madajczyk, ed., Zamojszczyzna, vol. 1, pp. 33–4; Bruno Wasser, Himmlers Raumplanung im Osten. Der Generalplan Ost in Polen 1940–1944 (Basle, 1993), pp. 133–4; on the influx of ethnic Germans from Distrikt Radom, 'Deutsches Leben im Zamoscer Land', p. 34.

26. This is Müller's characterization of Globocnik's thinking: see note 24 above.

27. Pohl, Von der 'Judenpolitik' zum Judenmord, pp. 99–102; Musial, Deutsche Zivilverwaltung und Judenverfolgung, pp. 193–208.

28. Pohl, *Von der 'Judenpolitik' zum Judenmord*, p. 139. Of the 320,000 Jews living in Distrikt Lublin at the beginning of 1942, only 4,500 were left in January 1946. Musial, *Deutsche Zivilverwaltung und Judenverfolgung*, p. 341.

29. Musial believes that the decision to extend the mass murder to the whole General Government was virtually simultaneous with the decision for Distrikt Lublin: Musial, *Deutsche Zivilverwaltung und Judenverfolgung*, pp. 207–8; Pohl argues that Himmler gave Globocnik the signal to proceed with the mass murder of Jews in Distrikt Lublin as an 'experimental' precedent; meanwhile, however, similar orders seem to have been issued for Distrikt Galizien: Pohl, *Von der 'Judenpolitik' zum Judenmord*, p. 101; idem, *National-sozialistische Judenverfolgung in Ostgalizien*, pp. 139–43.

30. Globocnik to SS Sturmbannführer Brandt, betr. Umsiedlungsbereich Zamosc und Lublin, 31 Aug. 1942. BA Berlin, NS19, 3607.

31. Order of 12 Nov. 1942. Wasser, *Himmlers Raumplanung im Osten*, p. 134.

32. Müller to RFSS, 31 Oct. 1942. Madajczyk, ed., *Zamojszczyzna*, vol. 1, pp. 152–3.

33. Verzeichnis der von den Deutschen besiedelten Dörfer in den Kreisen: Zamość, Hrubieszów, Biłgoraj und Tomaszów, August 1943. Madajczyk, ed., *Zamojszczyzna*, vol. 2, pp. 189–91.

34. Fragment des Lageberichtes des Gouverneurs des Distrikts Lublin über die Aus- und Umsiedlungen im Gebiet von Zamosc, 15 Apr. 1943. Madajczyk, ed., *Zamojszczyzna*, vol. 2, p. 9.

35. Himmler an Frank, 3 July 1943. Madajczyk, ed., *Zamojszczyzna*, vol. 2, pp. 95–7.

36. Ibid., vol. 1, p. 14.

37. Globocnik, 'Einsatzbefehl für die Ansiedlung im Kreise Zamosc', 22 Nov. 1942. Madajczyk, ed., *Zamojszczyzna*, vol. 1, pp. 182–9.

38. 'Deutsches Leben im Zamoscer Land', p. 33.

39. 'Das Deutschtum im Gebiet von Zamosc.' (see note 22).

40. Der Kreishauptmann in Zamosc, Abt. Bevölkerungswesen und Fürsorge, an den Chef des Distrikts, Abt. Innere Verwaltung, Bevölkerungswesen und Fürsorge in Lublin, betr. Bericht über wesentliche Vorgänge auf dem Gebiet des Bevölkerungswesens und der Fürsorge im Mai 1941, 14 June 1941. APLub, Gouverneur des Distrikts Lublin, 207.

41. In autumn 1941, responsibility for provision of welfare facilities for the ethnic German population in the General Government was transferred from the district governments to the NSV. Hauptamt für Volkswohlfahrt an die Gauamtsleiter NSV, betr. Aufgabe und Durchführung der volkspflegerischen Arbeiten für die Reichs- und Volksdeutschen im GG und Zusammenarbeit zwischen den Dienststellen der Staatlichen Fürsorge und der NSDAP, 27 Sept. 1941. NWStA Münster, Gauleitung Westfalen Nord, Gauamt für Volkswohlfahrt, 5 vol. I/2. For Gilgenmann's biographical details: BA Berlin, BDC, Personalakte Gilgenmann.

42. Unterabteilungsleiter Türk an den Beauftragten der Volksdeutschen Mittelstelle bei der Regierung des GG, Gebietsführer Blum, 21 Oct. 1941. APLub, Gouverneur des Distrikts Lublin, 285.

43. For an outline of the purpose of the *Kolonistenbriefe*, see 'Das Deutschtum im Gebiet von Zamosc' (see note 22). I am indebted to Peter Witte for alerting me to the *Kolonistenbriefe* as a source.

44. Dr K., 'Der polnische Jude: Ein Kapitel in der Geschichte volksdeutscher Lebensnot', *Kolonistenbriefe* 12 (Aug. 1942), p. 6.

45. Margrit Niedenzu's account in 'Deutsche Mädel im Einsatz', *Kolonistenbriefe* 2 (May 1941), pp. 4–7, here p. 6.

46. Ibid., p. 7; 'Aus den deutschen Siedlungen', *Kolonistenbriefe* 2 (May 1941), p. 7.

47. On Globocnik's visit to Huszczka, see Marthel Döhrmann's contribution in 'Unsere Frühlingsfeste', *Kolonistenbriefe* 3 (June 1941), pp. 7–8. Himmler's first visit to the Zamość area took place on Sunday, 20 July 1941 in conjunction with his visit to Lublin, although his appointments diary does not mention specifically a visit to a village. His second visit took place on 19 July 1942. See Witte et al., eds, *Der Dienstkalender Heinrich Himmlers 1941/2*, pp. 186, 496. For a description of Himmler's visits: 'Der Reichsführer-SS besucht die deutschstämmigen Kolonisten im Zamoscer Land', *Kolonistenbriefe* 4 (July 1941), pp. 1–2; 'Der Reichsführer-SS im Distrikt Lublin', *Kolonistenbriefe* 12 (Aug. 1942), p. 5.

48. 'Das Dorffest in Brody am 21. März 1941', *Kolonistenbriefe* 1 (Apr. 1941), pp. 4–7; 'Unsere Frühlingsfeste', *Kolonistenbriefe* 3 (June 1941), pp. 2–3; 'Versammlung', *Kolonistenbriefe* 5 (Aug. 1941), p. 8.

49. Hertha Z., Kindergartenbericht vom September 1941, Groß-Brody; Hertha G., Dorbozy, Arbeitsbericht für Monat August, 8 Sept. 1941. APLub, Gouverneur des Distrikts Lublin, 285.

50. Ottilie D., Freifeld, Kindergartenbericht vom 16. Aug.–10. Sept. 1941. Ibid.

51. Elisabeth L./Emma S. an die Dienststelle des SS- und Polizeiführers, Volkspolitisches Referat Lublin, betr. Kindergarten in Dorbozy, 15 Oct. 1941. Ibid., Türk an Kreishauptmann Bilgoraj, Abt. Bevölkerung und Fürsorge, betr. Kindergarten in Dorbozy, 7 Nov. 1941. Ibid.

52. Henriette L., Bericht vom 18. Jul. bis 30. Aug. 1941, 17 Oct. 1941; Bericht vom 1. Sept. 1941 bis 1. Oct. 1941, 2 Oct. 1941, Kolonie Rogozno. Ibid.

53. Hertha Z., Kindergartenbericht vom September 1941, Groß-Brody. Ibid.

54. Mathilde S. an Marie-Luise Gilgenmann, 26 Aug. 1941; Mathilde S. an Chef des Distrikts in Lublin, Abt. Bevölkerung und Fürsorge, 15 Nov. 1941. Ibid.

55. The Sonderdienst was created by Hans Frank in May 1940 as a force of ethnic German armed auxiliary policemen answerable to the civilian authorities in the General Government. In the Zamość area, it was reported that Sonderdienst men were recruited from among the *Volksdeutsche* from Galicia, the Cholm area or from the Warthegau, rather than from among the local *Deutschstämmige*. Peter Black, 'Rehearsal for "Reinhard"?: Odilo Globocnik and the Lublin *Selbstschutz*', *Central European History* 25, no. 2 (1992), pp. 204–26; Gradmann, 'Das Deutschtum im Gebiete von Zamosc' (see note 22).

56. Gilgenmann, Bericht über Freifeld (Zukowo), undated. APLub, Gouverneur des Distrikts Lublin, 285.

57. Ottilie D., Freifeld, Kindergartenbericht vom 16. Aug–10. Sept. 1941 (see note 50).

58. Gilgenmann, Notizen über Antoniowka (undated = autumn 1941). APLub, Gouverneur des Distrikts Lublin, 285.

59. Gilgenmann, Notizen über Sitaniec (undated = autumn 1941). Ibid.

60. Gilgenmann, notes on Białobrzegi, Gemeinde Wysoki, Kreis Zamosc [1941]. Ibid.

61. Reichsbefehl der Reichsjugendführung 1943, 29 Apr. 1943, p. 224; her initial assignment listed in *Kolonistenbriefe* 7 (Oct. 1941), p. 14. The attack on Cieszyn is mentioned in Governor Zörner's memorandum of 23 Feb. 1943. Madajczyk, ed., *Zamojszczyzna*, vol. 1, pp. 415–21.

62. Sandkühler, '*Endlösung*', p. 90; Madajczyk, ed., *Generalplan Ost*, pp. 50–81.

63. Präg and Jacobmeyer, eds, *Diensttagebuch*, pp. 540–1.

64. Sandkühler, '*Endlösung*', pp. 91–2.

65. Koehl, *RKFDV*, p. 188.

66. This point is made by Koehl, ibid., p. 188.

67. Sandkühler, '*Endlösung*', p. 93.

68. Ibid., p. 94.

69. Koehl, *RKFDV*, p. 189.

70. Präg and Jacobmeyer, eds, *Diensttagebuch*, p. 683.

71. List of 36 villages showing dates of expulsions and resettlements: 25 May 1943. GKW, 116, 73.

72. Hans-Wilhelm Tölke an Konrad Meyer, 'Meine Fahrt nach Lemberg', 13 July 1943. Archiwum UAM, Reichsuniversität Posen, 143/145. On Ugartsberg, see Carl Petersen et al., eds, *Handwörterbuch des Grenz- und Auslanddeutschtums*, vol. 3 (Breslau, 1938), p. 28. On Russian Germans' resettlement in Ugartsberg: Ruth A., Monatsbericht des Kindergartens Ugartsberg für Juni 1943. GKW, 116, 41.

73. Sandkühler, *'Endlösung'*, p. 96.

74. 'An alle deutschstämmigen Menschen Galiziens!' *Kolonistenbriefe* 9 (Jan. 1942), p. 6.

75. Befehlshaber der Sicherheitspolizei und des SD im General-Gouvernement, Meldungen aus dem Generalgouvernement für die Zeit vom 1.–30. September 1943. *Documenta Occupationis VI*, pp. 221–8, here p. 226.

76. On 'Durchschleusung' still taking place in Distrikt Galizien in January 1944: Lotte W., Monatsbericht für Januar 1944 vom Kindergarten Gelsendorf. GKW, 116, 3. On 'Durchschleusung' not completed before evacuation of General Government, see RKF, Anordnung Nr. 2/I/44, betr. Überführung von alteingesessenen Deutschen und Deutschstämmigen aus dem GG in das Altreich, 13 June 1944. *Documenta Occupationis VI*, pp. 204–7.

77. This nomenclature did not stop German administrators in the General Government referring in correspondence to 'NSV', 'NSV-kindergarten' and so on. The HAG Volkswohlfahrt claimed responsibility for all welfare measures targeted at ethnic Germans in the General Government: Dr Bühler, Regierung des Generalgouvernements Krakau, an die Distriktchefs, Kreis- und Stadthauptleute, betr. Aufgabe und Durchführung der volkspflegerischen Arbeiten für die Reichs- und Volksdeutschen im Generalgouvernement und Zusammenarbeit zwischen den Dienststellen der Staatlichen Fürsorge und dem NSDAP-Arbeitsbereich Generalgouvernement, Hauptarbeitsgebiet Volkswohlfahrt, 25 Aug. 1941. NWStA Münster, Gauleitung Westfalen-Nord, Gauamt für Volkswohlfahrt, 5 vol.I/2.

78. Hildemann, Obergemeinschaftsleiter, HAG Volkswohlfahrt, Krakau, an NSDAP Arbeitsbereich Generalgouvernement, Amt Hitler-Jugend, z.Hd. Pgn. Irmgard Fischer, 10. Oct. 1941; Hermann, Kreisamtsleiter, HAG Volkswohlfahrt, Lemberg, an die NSDAP, Arbeitsbereich Generalgouvernement, HAG Volkswohlfahrt, Krakau, betr. Einrichtung der Kindergärten, 9 Mar. 1942. GKW, 116, 42.

79. 'An die deutschstämmigen Menschen Galiziens!', *Kolonistenbriefe* 9 (Jan. 1942), p. 6.

80. 'Zolkiew', *Kolonistenbriefe* 10 (Mar. 1942), p. 11; report on kindergarten in Żółkiew, May 1942, and undated note on meeting with BDM-Einsatz in Żółkiew. GKW, 116, 40.

81. File on Herta Jeschonneck. BA Berlin, BDC.

82. Jahresbericht über die Arbeit der Kindertagesstätten. Lemberg, 4 Jan. 1943, unsigned (H. Jeschonneck). GKW, 116, 47.

83. Herta Jeschonneck an die NSDAP Arbeitsbereich Generalgouvernement, HAG Volkswohlfahrt, Krakau, betr. Besetzung der Kindergärten des Distriktes Galizien im Monat September, 1 Oct. 1942. GKW, 116, 42.

84. Herta Jeschonneck, Anforderungen für Kindergärten im Distrikt Galizien, 27 Aug. 1943. Ibid.; Bericht über die Kindergartenleiterinnentagung am 29. und 30 Nov. 1943: Teilnehmerinnenliste, 6 Dec. 1943. GKW, 116, 45.

85. Gerda Hoseur, Sachbearbeiterin für Kindertagesstätten (Lemberg) an die NSDAP Arbeitsbereich Generalgouvernement, HAG Volkswohlfahrt, 27 Apr. 1942. GKW, 116, 42.

86. Jahresbericht über die Arbeit der Kindertagesstätten. Lemberg, 4 Jan. 1943, unsigned (H. Jeschonneck). GKW, 116, 47.

87. Personnel files on kindergarten staff: GKW, 116, 48–68.

88. Edith K., Kindergarten Zolkiew, Monatsbericht für März 1943. GKW, 116, 40.

89. On the overlap in the General Government between the tasks of the *Volksdeutsche Mittelstelle* and those of other agencies responsible for overseeing ethnic German settlers, see Präg and Jacobmeyer, eds, *Diensttagebuch des deutschen Generalgouverneurs*, p. 608.

90. Elfriede I., Kindergarten Dornfeld, Monatsbericht November 1943; Margarete T., Kindergarten Josefsberg, Bericht über den Monat Juni 1943. GKW, 116, 3; Friedel Barg, Bericht über Brigidau (undated). GKW, 116, 13. Maria E. an Herta Jeschonneck, 27 Aug. 1943. GKW, 116, 8.

91. For instance: Steffi G., Kindergarten Grodek, Monatsbericht April 1943, 1 May 1943; Elfriede I., Kindergarten Dornfeld, Monatsbericht Januar, 31 Jan. 1944. GKW, 116, 3.

92. Gerda Hoseur, Monatsbericht Kindergarten Stanislau, Januar 1943. GKW, 116, 38; U. Graefe, Monatsbericht Kindergarten Sambor, Januar 1943. GKW, 116, 36.

93. L. K., Kindergartenleiterin Stryj, Monatsbericht November 1943. GKW, 116, 39.

94. Herta Jeschonneck, Bericht über die Schulung der Kindergartenleiterinnen am 29. und 30. Nov. 1943, Lemberg 7 Dec. 1943. GKW, 116, 45.

95. Ibid.

96. E. Schombert, Leiterin des Referats Kindertagesstätten, Krakau, an den Leiter des HAG Volkswohlfahrt der NSDAP, Distriktstandortführung Galizien, Referat Kindertagesstätten, betr. Weihnachtsfeiern 1942, 23 Jan. 1943. GKW, 116, 42.

97. H. Jeschonneck, Tätigkeitsbericht der Kindertagesstätten über den Monat Dezember 1943. Lemberg, 24 Jan. 1944. GKW, 116, 2.

98. Roswitha R., Monatsbericht für Dezember 1943, 8 Jan. 1944. GKW, 116, 3.

99. Vorweihnachtliche Feierstunde der Eltern im Kindergarten Machliniec 1943 (unsigned, undated); Anni Sch., Kindergartenleiterin Oblisku, 'Bericht über die Weihnachtsfeier mit den Kindern'. The Nazi carol was 'Hohe Nacht der klaren Sterne'. Ibid.

100. Doris L., Bericht über Weihnachtsfeier mit den Müttern, Lubaczow, 3 Jan. 1944. GKW, 116, 41.

101. Elfriede I., Bericht von der Vorweihnachtsfeier mit den Müttern und den Kindern im NSV-Kindergarten Dornfeld, 10 Jan. 1944. GKW, 116, 3.

102. Pohl, *Nationalsozialistische Judenverfolgung in Ostgalizien*, pp. 192–3; Musial, *Deutsche Zivilverwaltung und Judenverfolgung*, pp. 323–7.

103. Pohl, *Nationalsozialistische Judenverfolgung in Ostgalizien*, pp. 185–93.

104. On the creation of ghettos during 1942, see ibid., pp. 193–6.

105. Ibid., p. 245.

106. Ibid., pp. 246–62; Sandkühler, '*Endlösung*', pp. 194–8, here p. 195.

107. 'Zolkiev', *Kolonistenbriefe* 10 (Mar. 1942), p. 11.

108. Pohl, *Nationalsozialistische Judenverfolgung in Ostgalizien*, pp. 189–90.

109. Ursula Graefe an Herta Jeschonneck, 9 Dec. 1942. GKW, 116, 44. Pohl, *Nationalsozialistische Judenverfolgung in Ostgalizien*, pp. 255–7.

110. Steffi G., Bericht vom Monat Januar 1943, Kindergarten Grodek. GKW, 116, 44.

111. Herta Jeschonneck, Monatsbericht für den Monat Mai über die Arbeit der Kindertagesstätten im Distrikt Galizien, Lemberg, 11 June 1943. The original phrase used in relation to Stryj: 'Die Beendigung der Umbauarbeiten geht sehr langsam vorwärts, weil diese immer wieder durch Ausfallen der Arbeiter (Juden) unterbrochen wird.' GKW, 116, 2.

112. Sandkühler, '*Endlösung*', p. 199; Pohl, *Nationalsozialistische Judenverfolgung in Ostgalizien*, pp. 298–9.

113. Standortamtsleiter NSV, Zloczow, 'Bericht über den Monat Oktober 1942', 1 Dec. 1942. GKW, 116, 41.

114. Herta Jeschonneck an die NSDAP, HAG Volkswohlfahrt, Arbeitsbereich Generalgouvernement, Krakau, 15 Sept. 1942. GKW, 116, 42.

115. Gerda Hoseur, Bericht über Zolkiew, 18 Jan. 1944. GKW, 116, 40.

116. Steffi G., Monatsbericht Februar 1943, Kindergarten Grodek. GKW, 116, 3.

117. Maria E., Kindergartenleiterin Machliniec, an Herta Jeschonneck, 27 Aug. 1943; cf. also Kreisreferentin Friedel Barg's report on Maria E. (undated). GKW, 116, 8.

118. Ruth A., Monatsbericht des Kindergartens Ugartsberg, Aug. 1943. GKW, 116, 41.

119. Anni K., Mindorf, Kreis Drohobycz, Aug. 1943. GKW, 116, 4.

120. Elfriede I., Monatsbericht Januar 1944, Kindergarten Dornfeld. GKW, 116, 3.

121. On definitions of 'perpetrator', see Pohl, *Nationalsozialistische Judenverfolgung in Ostgalizien*, p. 300.

122. Emmy H., Kindergarten Boryslaw, monthly report for July 1943, 2 Aug. 1943. GKW, 116, 3; K. Hauber, Kindergarten Sambor, monthly report for September 1943, 3 Oct. 1943. GKW, 116, 36; H. Jeschonneck, Tätigkeitsbericht des Referats Kindertagesstätten für den Monat Januar, 25. Feb. 1944. GKW, 116, 2.

123. Lotte W., Monatsbericht Januar 1944, Kindergarten Gelsendorf. GKW, 116, 3.

124. Emmy H., Kindergarten Boryslaw, Monatsbericht für Juli 1943, 2 Aug. 1943. Ibid.

125. Friedel Barg, report on kindergarten in Nowe Siolo (undated). GKW, 116, 10.

126. Steffi G., Kindergarten Grodek, Bericht vom Januar 1942. GKW, 116, 3.

127. Margo G., Kindergarten Rawa Ruska, Monatsbericht Januar 1944. GKW, 116, 4.

128. Grete H., Bericht über Kindergarten Grodek, Jan. 1944. GKW, 116, 3.

129. Ursula Gräfe an das HAG Volkswohlfahrt Lemberg, Bericht über Gertrud M., 20 May 1943. GKW 116, 50.

130. U. Graefe, Monatsbericht Kindergarten Sambor, Jan. 1943. GKW, 116, 36.

131. Annemarie Sch. an Herta Jeschonneck, 18 Jan. 1943. GKW, 116, 56.

132. Steffi G. an Herta Jeschonneck (undated). GKW, 116, 44.

133. Jeschonneck an Gertrud G., betr. Besuch des Kindergartens, 13 Jan. 1944. Ibid.

134. Gertrud G., Kindergarten Slawitz, an das HAG Volkswohlfahrt, Lemberg, betr. die Antwort auf Ihres Schreiben [*sic*] vom 13. Jan. 1944 'Besuch des Kindergartens', 31 Jan. 1944. GKW, 116, 3.

135. Jeschonneck, Bericht über die Schulung der Kindergartenleiterinnen am 29. und 30. Nov. 1943. GKW, 116, 45.

136. Dora B., Kindergarten Otynin, Monatsbericht Sept. 1943. GKW, 116, 4.

137. Elfriede I., Monatsbericht Feb. 1944, NSV Kindergarten Dornfeld. GKW, 116, 41.

138. Jeschonneck an Emma Metzger, 3 Apr. 1944. GKW, 116, 44.

139. G. Grüschow an die NSDAP HAG Volkswohlfahrt, Lemberg, 2 Dec. 1943. GKW, 116, 32.

140. Martha G., Kindergartenleiterin Rawa Ruska an Distriktstandortführung Galizien, HAG Volkswohlfahrt, betr. Helferin Eugenie P., 13 Mar. 1944. GKW, 116, 34.

141. On the collapse of German rule in Distrikt Galizien, see Pohl, *Nationalsozialistische Judenverfolgung in Ostgalizien*, pp. 381–5.

142. Leiter der Hauptstelle Wohlfahrtspflege und Jugendhilfe, HAG Volkswohlfahrt, NSDAP Distriktstandortführung Galizien, an NSDAP Arbeitsbereich Generalgouvernement, HAG Volkswohlfahrt, Krakau, betr. Kindertagesstätten, 8 June 1944. GKW, 116, 2.

143. Hauptamt für Volkswohlfahrt, Rundschreiben Nr. 115/44. Betr. Maßnahmen des totalen Krieges. Hier: Auswirkung auf das Arbeitsgebiet Kindertagesstätten, 14 Sept. 1944. NWStA Münster, Gauleitung Westfalen-Nord, Gauamt Volkswohlfahrt, 1, Bd. 2.

144. Friedel Barg, Bericht, 26 Jan. 1944. GKW, 116, 2.

145. Standortamtsleiter, NSV Sambor an die NSDAP HAG Volkswohlfahrt Lemberg, 30 Mar. 1944. GKW, 116, 36.

146. Hedwig K., Report (Rückzug von Galizien), (undated). GKW, 116, 30.

147. Elfriede I., Monatsbericht Jan. 1944, Kindergarten Dornfeld. GKW, 116, 3.

Chapter 9 Building on the Volcano: Training Village Advisers in Kreis Zamosc

1. 'Frau Hagen', diary Sept. 1942–Sept. 1944 [hereafter 'Diary'], entry for 5 Dec. 1943.

2. 'Eine Schule für Dorfberaterinnen im Distrikt Lublin für das ganze GG eingerichtet', *Deutsche Gemeinschaft. Wochenschrift für die Siedlungsdeutschen im Generalgouvernement* 2, no. 50 (12 Dec. 1943).

3. Madajczyk, ed., *Zamojszczyzna*, vol. 1, p. 12.

4. Globocnik, Einsatzbefehl für die Ansiedlung im Kreise Zamosc, 22 Nov. 1942. Madajczyk, ed., *Zamojszczyzna*, vol. 1, pp. 182–9.

5. The *Ortsbäuerin* was the female equivalent of the local farmer's leader (*Ortsbauern-führer*); the position was unpaid and represented the lowest rank of officialdom in the Reich Food Estate (*Reichsnährstand*). On women and the Reich Food Estate, see Münkel, ' "Du, Deutsche Landfrau bist verantwortlich." '

6. Letter to parents, 30 May 1943, in author's possession.

7. Diary, entry for 19 June 1943.

8. Ibid., entry for 4 April 1944.

9. Kazimiera Switajowa, 'Pacyfikacja wsi Sochy'. Madajczyk, ed., *Zamojszczyzna*, vol. 2, p. 397.

10. 'Adam', 'Siedliska'. Ibid., pp. 478–80.

11. Zygmunt Klukowski, *Diary from the Years of Occupation 1939–1944*, trans. George Klukowski, ed. Andrew Klukowski and Helen Klukowski May (Urbana and Chicago, 1993), p. 258.

12. Diary, entry for 9 June 1943 [incorrectly dated 19 June 1943].

13. Denkschrift des Gouverneurs des Distrikts Zörner an den Generalgouverneur des GG über die Folgen der Um- und Aussiedlungsaktion im Kreise Zamosc, 23 Feb. 1943; Frank an Hitler, 25 May 1943. Madajczyk, ed., *Zamojszczyzna*, vol. 1, p. 415 and vol. 2, p. 61; Präg and Jacobmeyer, eds, *Diensttagebuch*, pp. 678–83, 700–2.

14. On Moser, see Pohl, *Von der 'Judenpolitik' zum Judenmord*, p. 44; see also Präg and Jacobmeyer, eds, *Diensttagebuch*, p. 678.

15. Diary, entry for 9 June 1943 (see note 12 above).

16. Klukowski, *Diary from the Years of Occupation*, p. 259.

17. Report in Polish underground newspaper *Wieś*, 22 June 1943. Madajczyk, ed., *Zamojsz-czyzna*, vol. 2, p. 82.

18. Pohl, *Von der 'Judenpolitik' zum Judenmord*, p. 156.

19. Ibid., p. 170.

20. Ibid., pp. 168–70.

21. Diary, entry for 29 July 1943.

22. Klukowski, *Diary from the Years of Occupation*, p. 274.

23. Diary, undated entry [September 1943].

24. Reichsführer-SS an das SS-Wirtschafts-Verwaltungs-Hauptamt und an das Hauptamt Volksdeutsche Mittelstelle, Oct. 1942. If Z, MA 331/5139–40.

25. Jan Mirski, 'Wysiedlanie w powiecie zamojskim'. Madajczyk, ed., *Zamojszczyzna*, vol. 2, p. 343; see also pp. 37, 299.

26. RKF, Hauptamt Volksdeutsche Mittelstelle an den Gauverbandsleiter des VDA, betr. Bericht über die Haltung der polnischen Frau im Volkstumskampf, 17 Aug. 1944. BA Berlin, R59, 65.

27. Diary, entry for 19 March 1944 [dated in error '19.3.43'].

28. HSSPF Ost Krakau an SS-Obersturmbannführer R. Brandt betreffend die Evakuierung der Familien der deutschen Siedler aus dem Kreise Zamosc und deren Unterbringung im Lager von Lodz, 21 Mar. 1944. Madajczyk, ed., *Zamojszczyzna*, vol. 2, p. 307.

29. Interview with Frau Hagen, 20 Oct. 1999.

30. Gouverneur Wendler an SSPF Sporrenberg, betr. Lage im Siedlungsgebiet im Kreis Zamosc, 26 Apr. 1944. Madajczyk, ed., *Zamojszczyzna*, vol. 2, pp. 307–9.

31. Klukowski, *Diary from the Years of Occupation*, pp. 319–20 (entry for 2 May 1944).

32. Diary, entry for 26 March 1944.

33. Steinert, *Hitler's War and the Germans*, pp. 259–60.

34. Diary, entry for 19 July 1944, 1.00 a.m.

35. Ibid., entries for 19 July 1944, 1.00 a.m., and 20 July 1944.

36. Klukowski, *Diary from the Years of Occupation*, pp. 347–8.

37. Walter Lippert, 'Wspomnienia z okupacji Zamojszczyzny 1939–1944'. Madajczyk, ed., *Zamojszczyzna*, vol. 2, pp. 350–1.

38. Ibid., pp. 348–9.

39. Diary, entry for 20 July 1944.

40. Ibid., entry for 22 July 1944; on the spectrum of popular reactions to the 20 July plot, see Steinert, *Hitler's War and the Germans*, pp. 264–73; Ian Kershaw, *The 'Hitler Myth'. Image and Reality in the Third Reich* (Oxford, 1987), pp. 215–19.

41. Diary, entry for 'Sonntag. 4. Trecktag' [= 23 July 1944].

42. Ibid., entry for 'Dienstag, V. Trecktag' [= 25 July 1944].

43. Ibid.

44. Ibid., entry for 28 July 1944.

Chapter 10 Leaving the East Behind

1. Konstantin Hierl an Gertrud Kapp, 22 Jan. 1945. BA Berlin, Zsg 145, 49.

2. Lumans, *Himmler's Auxiliaries*, pp. 247–9.

3. These transfers included the resettlement of ethnic Germans from the eastern Ukraine to Distrikt Galizien in spring and summer 1943, from the Nikolayev region of southern Ukraine to Volhynia in late 1943, from the Zhitomir region in December 1943, and the removal of Black Sea Germans to the Warthegau in 1944.

4. Else Reinhardt, NS-Oberschwester, an den Gebietshauptmann des volksdeutschen Siedlungsgebietes Hegewald, betr. Betreuung des volksdeutschen Trecks Hegewald durch die NSV, 26. November 1943. IfZ München, MA 303/9105–6.

5. Inge D., Stimmungsbericht über den volksdeutschen Treck des Kreises Kronau, im besonderen der Dörfer Fürstenfeld, Nikolaital, 29.Oct.–3.Dec. 1943, in author's possession.

6. On this development within National Socialist anti-Bolshevik propaganda in the final years of the war, see Jürgen Förster, 'Zum Rußlandbild der Militärs 1941–45', in Hans-Erich Volkmann, ed., *Das Rußlandbild im Dritten Reich* (Cologne, 1994), pp. 141–63, here p. 160.

7. 'Treck der Dreihundertfünfzigtausend: Volksdeutsche vor dem Bolschewismus gerettet', reprinted without attribution of source in Jutta Rüdiger, ed., *Die Hitler-Jugend und ihr Selbstverständnis im Spiegel ihrer Aufgabengebiete* (Lindhorst, 1983), appendix p. 85.

8. Rückführungsbericht der Bezirksleitung XXVI Posen, geschrieben Ende Januar 1945 v.d. Bezirksführerin Kapp. BA Berlin, Zsg 145,49.

9. See for instance her 1986 account of the women's Labour Service in the Warthegau: Der Arbeitseinsatz im Bezirk XXVI RADwJ im Wartheland: Kurze Übersicht, aufgeschrieben im Juli 1986 von der ehemaligen Führerin des Bezirkes RADwJ XXVI Stbf. Gertrud Kapp; plus note by G. Kapp regarding allegations made by Erich Mende. BA Berlin, Zsg 145, 49.

10. Ute Timm, 'Bericht über meine Arbeit im Kreis Zempelburg/Westpr.', pp. 6–7. BA Bayreuth, Ost-Dok. 8, 15.

11. Frieda Balcerek, 'Aus der Frauenarbeit in Westpreußen von 1939–1945' (1953), BA Bayreuth, Ost-Dok 8, 1.

12. Interview with Frau Geyer, 21 Apr. 1996.

13. Interview with Frau Andreas, 28 Aug. 1994.

14. Ibid.

15. Philipp Ther, *Deutsche und polnische Vertriebene: Gesellschaft und Vertriebenenpolitik in der SBZ/DDR und in Polen 1945–1956* (Göttingen, 1998), p. 54; Bundesministerium für Vertriebene, ed., *Die Vertreibung der deutschen Bevölkerung aus den Gebieten östlich der Oder-Neiße*, Einleitung pp. 12–13.

16. 'Bericht über meine Flucht aus Lupine nach Kassel' [ms. 1999], in author's possession.

17. Hildegard Grabe, 'Bericht über Erlebnisse während meiner Tätigkeit als Lehrerin im Warthegau von Ostern 1941 bis Januar 1945'. BA Bayreuth, Ost-Dok 8, 459.

18. Annelies Regenstein, 'Meine Tätigkeit als Lehrerin in Laningen Krs. Kutno 1940–45'. BA Bayreuth, Ost-Dok 8, 467.

19. Bundesministerium für Vertriebene, ed., *Die Vertreibung der deutschen Bevölkerung aus den Gebieten östlich der Oder-Neiße*, Einleitung p. 79.

20. Mary von Bremen, 'Bericht über die Entstehung, den Aufbau und die Arbeit an der Heimoberschule in Wreschen/Warthegau'. BA Bayreuth, Ost-Dok 8, 482.

21. Hornung, *Schrimm, Schroda, Bomst*, pp. 156–7.

22. 'Tätigkeitsbericht' (ms. 1947), in author's possession.

23. Lieselotte Gumpert, 'Die Auswirkungen der Volkstumspolitik auf das Schulwesen im Wartheland'. BA Bayreuth, Ost-Dok 8, 458.

24. Barbara Besig, 'Meine Erfahrungen in Leipe/Westpr. (Lipno) von August 1940 bis Januar 1945'. Ibid.

25. Regenstein, 'Meine Tätigkeit als Lehrerin in Laningen Krs. Kutno'.

26. Von Bremen, 'Die Heimoberschule in Wreschen/Warthegau'.

27. On the expellee organizations, see Pertti Ahonen, 'Domestic Constraints on West German Ostpolitik: The Role of the Expellee Organizations in the Adenauer Era', *Central European History* 31 (1998), pp. 31–63; on the evolution of public memory of the expulsions in the Federal Republic since the 1970s, see Moeller, *War Stories*, pp. 180–98.

28. Interview with Frau Holz, 7 Aug. 2001.

29. Interview with Frau Vogel, 12 Nov. 1998.

30. Interview with Frau Teplitz, 23 Oct. 1999.

31. Interview with Frau Niemann, 14 Sept. 1996.

32. See the material collected in BA Berlin, Zsg 145 (esp. files 19, 22, 23).

33. Interview with Frau Bauer, 22 Oct. 1999.

34. Hildegard Fritsch, *Land mein Land: Bauerntum und Landdienst. BDM Osteinsatz. Siedlungsgeschichte im Osten* (Preußisch Oldendorf, 1986), pp. 169–70.

35. For example Ute Timm, 'Bericht über meine Arbeit'.

36. Dora Buck, 'Die Verhältnisse in Danzig-Westpreußen, wie wir sie 1940 vorfanden'. BA Bayreuth, Ost-Dok 8, 32.

37. Balcerek, 'Aus der Frauenarbeit in Westpreußen'.

38. Dr Jutta Rüdiger, Stellungnahme der ehemaligen Reichsreferentin fur den Bund Deutscher Mädel zu dem Buch 'Fazit' von Melita Maschmann (22 July 1984); Stellungnahme ehemaliger Arbeitsdienstführerinnen zu dem Buch 'Fazit' von Melita Maschmann (Oct. 1984). IfZ, ZS1609. Jutta Rüdiger, letter to the author, 8 Nov. 1995, in author's possession, recommends her own and various other works on the history of the BDM, including the work of Hildegard Fritsch.

39. Rüdiger, ed., *Die Hitler-Jugend und ihr Selbstverständnis*; idem, *Ein Leben für die Jugend: Mädelführerin im Dritten Reich* (Preußisch Oldendorf, 1999).

40. Reese, 'The BDM generation', pp. 227–46, esp. p. 240.

Bibliography

I. Archival sources

Bundesarchiv (BA)

The following gives the current location of Bundesarchiv records; some of those listed below were originally consulted elsewhere.

Koblenz

Deutsches Auslands-Institut (R57)

Berlin

Reichskommissar für die Festigung deutschen Volkstums (R49)
Reichsfinanzministerium (R2)
Persönlicher Stab Reichsführer SS (NS19)
Reichssicherheitshauptamt (R58)
Reichsministerium für Wissenschaft, Erziehung und Volksbildung (49.01)
Volksdeutsche Mittelstelle (R59)
Reichsministerium für Ernährung und Landwirtschaft (36.01)
Reichsministerium für die besetzten Ostgebiete (R6)
Hitler-Jugend (NS28)
Reichsfrauenführung (NS44)
Hauptamt für Volkswohlfahrt (NS37)
Records of former Berlin Document Center (BDC)
Sammlung zur Geschichte FAD/RAD (Zsg 145)

Bayreuth

Berichte von Persönlichkeiten des öffentlichen Lebens aus den Gebieten östlich von Oder und
    Neiße zum Zeitgeschehen 1919–45 (Ost-Dok 8)

Nordrhein-Westfälisches Staatsarchiv Münster (NWStA Münster)

Gauleitung Westfalen-Nord, NS-Frauenschaft
Gauleitung Westfalen-Nord, Gauamt für Volkswohlfahrt
Gauamt für Volkstumsfragen

Nordrhein-Westfälisches Staatsarchiv Detmold (NWStA Detmold)

NSDAP-Kreisleitung Herford (M15)
NSDAP-Kreisleitung Lippe (L113)

Staatsarchiv Würzburg (StA Würzburg)

Reichsstudentenführung I, II, V/1–2

Institut für Zeitgeschichte, München, Archiv

Microfilm collection:
    Eingegliederte Gebiete – Reichsgau Wartheland (MA–225)
    Reichskommissar für die Festigung deutschen Volkstums (MA–125)
    Umsiedlung von Volksdeutschen (MA–303)
    Meldungen aus dem Reich (CMA 441/4)
Document collection:
Zs 1609   Ms 458   Fb 115   Fa 88   Ms 348.

Archiv des Diakonischen Werkes, Berlin

Evangelischer Siedlungsdienst

Geheimes Staatsarchiv Preußischer Kulturbesitz, Berlin-Dahlem

NSDAP Gauarchiv Ostpreußen (240)

Archiv der deutschen Jugendbewegung, Burg Ludwigstein

Records on Deutsche Freischar (A2–22/3), Freischar junger Nation (A2–55/3)

Landesarchiv Berlin

Helene Lange Archiv, Bestand Bund Deutscher Frauenvereine

Archiwum Pan´stwowe w Poznaniu (APP)

Regierung Schneidemühl (307)
Der Reichsstatthalter im Reichsgau Wartheland (299)
Regierung Posen (300)
Volksdeutsche Mittelstelle, Zweigstelle Posen (800)
Landratsämter Warthegau (449–69)

Archiwum Państwowe w Łodzi (APL)

Regierungspräsident Litzmannstadt 1940–5 (176)
Stadtverwaltung Litzmannstadt 1939–45 (221/VII)
Einwandererzentrale Litzmannstadt (205)

Archiwum Państwowe w Katowicach (APK)

Regierung Kattowitz (119/I)
Provinzialverwaltung Oberschlesien, Kattowitz (118/I)
Oberpräsidium Kattowitz 1941–5 (117/I)
Reichs-Propaganda-Amt Oberschlesien in Kattowitz (122/I)
Kreisleitung der NSDAP Pless (151/I)

Archiwum Państwowe w Gdańsku (APG)

NSDAP-Gauleitung Danzig 1936–45 (266)
Höherer SS und Polizeiführer Danzig-Westpreußen (265)

Archiwum Państwowe w Lublinie (APLub)

Gouverneur des Distrikts Lublin 1939–44 (498)
SS- und Polizeiführer im Distrikt Lublin (510)

Archiwum Głównej Komisji Badania Zbrodni Przeciwko Narodowi Polskiemu, Warsaw (GKW)

Reichsstatthalter im Warthegau (62)
NSDAP Distriktstandortführung Galizien, Hauptarbeitsgebiet Volkswohlfahrt (116)

Uniwersytet im. A. Mickiewicz, Poznań, Archiwum (Archiwum UAM)

Reichsuniversität Posen (78)

Instytut Zachodni, Poznań

Dokumenty niemieckie I-273; I-377.

II. Interview material and other personal documentation

Tapes and transcripts of interviews and copies of respondents' letters: in author's possession. Diary of 'Frau Hagen': deposited with Bibliothek für Zeitgeschichte, Stuttgart: Bestand N 00.7.

III. Periodicals and yearbooks

NB: articles and essays published before 1945 are not listed individually.

Die ANSt-Gruppe

Archiv für innere Kolonisation

Die Bewegung

Deutsche Gemeinschaft: Wochenschrift für die Siedlungsdeutschen im Generalgouvernement

Die deutsche Landfrau

Das deutsche Mädel

Deutsches Frauenschaffen: Jahrbuch der Reichsfrauenführung

Die Erziehung

Die Frau

Frauendienst am Auslanddeutschtum

Gau-Amtsblatt der NSDAP Gau Wartheland

Jahrbuch des Reichsarbeitsdienstes

Das junge Deutschland

Junger Osten: Mitteilungen des studentischen Landdienstes

Kindergarten: Zeitschrift für die Erziehungsarbeit der Kindergärtnerin und Jugendleiterin

Kolonistenbriefe

Land und Frau

Landjahr-Schulungsbriefe

Nachrichtendienst des Bundes Deutscher Frauenvereine

Nachrichtendienst der Reichsfrauenführung

Nationalsozialistischer Volksdienst

Neues Bauerntum

NS-Frauenwarte

NSV: Rundbrief für Kindergärtnerinnen

Ostdeutscher Beobachter

Das Reich

Reich, Volksordnung, Lebensraum: Zeitschrift für völkische Verfassung und Verwaltung

Reichsbefehl der Reichsjugendführung

Der Ruf. Rundbrief der LBA Posen

Das Schwarze Korps

Soziale Berufsarbeit

Studentische Landdienst-Mitteilungen

Wartheland: Zeitschrift für Aufbau und Kultur im deutschen Osten

Wir schaffen: Jahrbuch des BDM

IV. Books (pre-1945)

Anon., *Ostnot Deutschland. Ein Mahnruf von* ** (Berlin, 1930)

Barta, Erwin and Karl Bell, *Geschichte der Schutzarbeit am deutschen Volkstum* (Berlin, 1930)

Brand, Marie Berta Freiin von, et al., *Die Frau in der deutschen Landwirtschaft* (Berlin, 1939)

Fick, Luise, *Die deutsche Jugendbewegung* (Jena, 1939)

Gauhauptmann im Reichsgau Wartheland, ed., *Der Warthegau: Landschaft und Siedlung in Werken deutscher Maler: Ein Bildband* (Posen, 1943)

Geisler, Walter, *Landschaftskunde des Warthelandes: Der physische Raum und seine Gliederung* (Posen, 1941)

Hauptgeschäftsstelle des Oberschlesier-Hilfswerks, ed., *Oberschlesiens Not* (Berlin, undated = 1921)

Hebenbrock, Walter, *Mit der NSV nach Polen* (Berlin, 1940)

Jahresbericht des Deutschen Schutzbundes über Berichtszeit vom 1. Mai 1928 bis 30. April 1929 (Berlin, undated)

[Kapp, Gertrud, ed.], *Arbeitsmaiden schaffen im Wartheland* (Posen, n.d. [1940])

Kahle, Maria, *Westfälische Bauern im Ostland* (Berlin, 1940)

Kleindienst, Alfred and Kurt Lück, *Die Wolhyniendeutschen kehren heim ins Reich* (Leipzig, 1940)

Körber, Wilhelm, *Volkstumsarbeit im Reichsarbeitsdienst* (Berlin, 1943)

Krieger, Ruth, *Deutsche Mädel im Osten* (Berlin, 1940)

Lück, Kurt and Alfred Lattermann, *Die Heimkehr der Galiziendeutschen* (Leipzig, 1940)

Lützkendorf, Felix, *Völkerwanderung 1940* (Berlin, 1940)

Marawske-Birkner, Lilli, *Der weibliche Arbeitsdienst* (Leipzig, 1942)

Menn, Fritz, ed., *Auf den Straßen des Todes. Leidensweg der Volksdeutschen in Polen* (Leipzig, 1940)

Meyer, Konrad, et al., *Landvolk im Werden: Material zum ländlichen Aufbau in den neuen Ostgebieten und zur Gestaltung des dörflichen Lebens*, 2nd edition (Berlin, 1942)

Morrow, Ian F. D. and L. M. Sieveking, *The Peace Settlement in the German-Polish Borderlands. A Study of Conditions Today in the Pre-war Prussian Provinces of East and West Prussia* (Oxford, 1936)

Nitschke, Richard, *Die deutschen Ostgebiete an Warthe und Weichsel* (Breslau, 1940)

NSDAP, Gauleitung Wartheland, ed., *Arbeitsmaiden helfen im Wartheland* (Posen, 1941)

Petersen, Carl, et al., eds, *Handwörterbuch des Grenz- und Auslanddeutschtums*, 3 vols (Breslau, 1938)

Schirmacher, Käthe, *Flammen. Erinnerungen aus meinem Leben* (Leipzig, 1921)

Schirmacher, Käthe, *Grenzmarkgeist* (Berlin and Leipzig, 1929)

Schirmacher, Käthe, *Um Deutschland. Nachgelassene Schriften* (Berlin-Nowawes, 1932)

Sommer, Helmut, *Völkerwanderung im 20. Jahrhundert. Die große Heimkehr der Volksdeutschen ins Reich* (Berlin, 1940)

Tims, Richard Wonser, *Germanizing Prussian Poland: The H-K-T Society and the Struggle for the Eastern Marches in the German Empire, 1894–1919* (New York, 1941)

Der Treck der Volksdeutschen aus Wolhynien, Galizien und dem Narewgebiet. Mit einem Geleitwort von Werner Lorenz und mit einer Einführung von Wilfrid Bade (Berlin, 1943)

Wir Mädel Singen. Liederbuch des Bundes Deutscher Mädel (Wolfenbüttel, 1941)

Zehn Jahre Deutscher Schutzbund (Berlin, 1929)

V. Publications since 1945

Adelson, Alan and Robert Lapides, eds, *Lodz Ghetto. Inside a Community under Siege* (Harmondsworth, 1989)

Ahonen, Pertti, 'Domestic Constraints on West German Ostpolitik: The Role of Expellee Organizations in the Adenauer Era', *Central European History* 31 (1998), pp. 31–63

Aly, Götz, *'Endlösung': Völkerverschiebung und der Mord an den europäischen Juden* (Frankfurt am Main, 1995)

Aly, Götz and Susanne Heim, *Vordenker der Vernichtung: Auschwitz und die deutschen Pläne für eine neue europäische Ordnung* (Frankfurt am Main, 1993)

Arani, Miriam Yegane, 'Aus den Augen, aus dem Sinn? Publizierte Fotografien aus dem besetzten Warschau 1939 bis 1945', Teil 1 & 2, *Fotogeschichte: Beiträge zur Geschichte und Ästhetik der Fotografie* 17 (1997), Heft 65, pp. 33–58, and Heft 66, pp. 33–50.

Baier, Roland, *Der deutsche Osten als soziale Frage. Eine Studie zur preußischen und deutschen Siedlungs- und Polenpolitik in den Ostprovinzen während des Kaiserreichs und der Weimarer Republik* (Cologne and Vienna, 1970)

Bankier, David, *The Germans and the Final Solution: Public Opinion under Nazism* (Oxford, 1992)

Beer, Mathias, 'Im Spannungsfeld von Politik und Zeitgeschichte: Das Großforschungsprojekt "Dokumentation der Vertreibung der Deutschen aus Ost-Mitteleuropa"', *VjZG* 46, no. 3 (1998), pp. 345–89

Berenstein, Tatiana et al., eds, *Faschismus – Getto – Massenmord: Dokumentation über Ausrottung und Widerstand der Juden in Polen während des zweiten Weltkrieges* (Frankfurt am Main, 1962)

Bergen, Doris L., 'The Nazi Concept of "Volksdeutsche" and the Exacerbation of Anti-Semitism in Eastern Europe, 1939–45', *Journal of Contemporary History* 29 (1994), pp. 569–82

Bergen, Doris L., 'The "Volksdeutschen" of Eastern Europe, World War II and the Holocaust: Constructed Ethnicity, Real Genocide', *Yearbook of European Studies* 13 (1999), pp. 70–93

Birkett, Dea, 'The "White Woman's Burden" in the "White Man's Grave": The Introduction of British Nurses in Colonial West Africa', in Nupur Chaudhuri and Margaret Strobel, eds, *Western Women and Imperialism: Complicity and Resistance* (Bloomington and Indianapolis, 1992), pp. 177–88

Birn, Ruth Bettina, *Die Höheren SS- und Polizeiführer: Himmlers Vertreter im Reich und in den besetzten Gebieten* (Düsseldorf, 1986)

Black, Peter R., 'Rehearsal for "Reinhard"?: Odilo Globocnik and the Lublin *Selbstschutz*': *Central European History* 25, no. 2 (1992), pp. 204–26

Blanke, Richard, 'Upper Silesia, 1921: The Case for Subjective Nationality', *Canadian Review of Studies in Nationalism* 2 (1975), pp. 241–60

Blanke, Richard, *Orphans of Versailles: The Germans in Western Poland 1918–1939* (Kentucky, 1993)

Blochmann, Elisabeth, *Herman Nohl in der pädagogischen Bewegung seiner Zeit 1879–1960* (Göttingen, 1969)

Blunt, Alison, *Travel, Gender and Imperialism: Mary Kingsley and West Africa* (New York, 1994)

Bock, Gisela, 'Ordinary Women in Nazi Germany: Perpetrators, Victims, Followers, and Bystanders', in Dalia Ofer and Lenore J. Weitzman, eds, *Women in the Holocaust* (New Haven and London, 1998), pp. 85–100

Böltken, Andrea, *Führerinnen im 'Führerstaat': Gertrud Scholtz-Klink, Trude Mohr, Jutta Rüdiger und Inge Viermetz* (Pfaffenweiler, 1995)

Broszat, Martin, *Nationalsozialistische Polenpolitik 1939–1945* (Stuttgart, 1961)

Broszat, Martin, 'Außen- und innenpolitische Aspekte der preußisch-deutschen Minderheiten-politik in der Ära Stresemann', in Kurt Kluxen and Wolfgang J. Mommsen, eds, *Politische Ideologien und nationalstaatliche Ordnung. Studien zur Geschichte des 19. und 20. Jahrhunderts* (Munich and Vienna, 1968), pp. 393–445

Broszat, Martin, *Zweihundert Jahre deutscher Polenpolitik* (Frankfurt am Main, 1972)

Browning, Christopher, *Fateful Months: Essays on the Emergence of the Final Solution*, revised edition (New York and London, 1991)

Browning, Christopher, *Path to Genocide: Essays on Launching the Final Solution* (Cambridge, 1992)

Bundesministerium für Vertriebene, ed., *Dokumentation der Vertreibung der Deutschen aus Ost-Mitteleuropa, vol. 1/1: Die Vertreibung der deutschen Bevölkerung aus den Gebieten östlich der Oder-Neiße* (Wolfenbüttel, n.d. [1954])

Burleigh, Michael, *Germany Turns Eastwards: A Study of Ostforschung in the Third Reich* (Cambridge, 1988)

Chiari, Bernhard, *Alltag hinter der Front: Besatzung, Kollaboration und Widerstand in Weißrußland 1941–44* (Düsseldorf, 1998)

Chickering, Roger, ' "Casting Their Gaze More Broadly": Women's Patriotic Activism in Imperial Germany', *Past and Present* 118 (1988), pp. 156–85

Comaroff, Jean and John L. Comaroff, 'Home-Made Hegemony: Modernity, Domesticity and Colonialism in South Africa', in Karen Tranberg Hansen, ed., *African Encounters with Domesticity* (New Brunswick, NJ, 1992), pp. 37–74

Connelly, John, 'Nazis and Slavs: From Racial Theory to Racist Practice', *Central European History* 32, no. 1 (1999), pp. 1–33

Corni, Gustavo, *Hitler and the Peasants: Agrarian Policy of the Third Reich, 1930–1939* (New York, Oxford and Munich, 1990)

Cronenberg, Allen, *Volksbund für das Deutschtum im Ausland* (Ann Arbor, Michigan, 1978)

Dallin, Alexander, *German Rule in Russia, 1941–1945: A Study of Occupation Policies*, 2nd edition (London, 1981)

Deutsches Historiches Museum, ed., *'Bildberichterstatterin' im 'Dritten Reich': Fotografien aus den Jahren 1937 bis 1944 von Liselotte Purper* (Berlin, 1997) [= *Magazin: Mitteilungen des Deutschen Historischen Museums* 7, Heft 20]

Dobroszycki, Lucjan, ed., *Chronicle of the Lodz Ghetto, 1941–44* (New Haven and London, 1984)

Domarus, Max, ed., *Hitler: Reden und Proklamationen 1932–1945*, vol. 1 (Würzburg, 1962)

Drummond, Elizabeth, ' "Durch Liebe stark, deutsch bis ins Mark": Weiblicher Kulturimperialismus und der Deutsche Frauenverein für die Ostmarken', in Ute Planert, ed., *Nation, Politik und Geschlecht: Frauenbewegungen und Nationalismus in der Moderne* (Frankfurt am Main and New York, 2000) pp. 147–59

Dudek, Peter, *Erziehung durch Arbeit: Arbeitslagerbewegung und freiwilliger Arbeitsdienst 1920–1935* (Opladen, 1988)

Ebbinghaus, Angelika, ed., *Opfer und Täterinnen: Frauenbiographien des Nationalsozialismus* (Nördlingen, 1987)

Eckert, Elisabeth, *Arbeitsdienst für die weibliche Jugend: Antworten nach 40 Jahren. Befragung ehemaliger Arbeitsdienstführerinnen* (Bad Honnef, 1978)

Eigler, Friederike, 'Engendering German Nationalism: Gender and Race in Frieda von Bülow's Colonial Writings', in Sara Friedrichsmeyer, Sara Lennox and Susanne Zantop, eds, *The Imperialist Imagination: German Colonialism and its Legacy* (Ann Arbor, Michigan, 1998), pp. 69–85

Evans, Richard, *The Feminist Movement in Germany, 1894–1933* (London, 1976)

Evans, Richard J., *In Hitler's Shadow: West German Historians and the Attempt to Escape from the Nazi Past* (London, 1989)

Farquharson, John, *The Plough and the Swastika: The NSDAP and Agriculture in Germany 1928–1945* (London and Beverly Hills, 1976)

Fiedor, Karol, Janusz Sobczak and Wojciech Wrzesinski, 'The Image of the Poles in Germany and of the Germans in Poland in the Inter-war Years and its Role in Shaping the Relations between the Two States', *Polish Western Affairs* 19 (1978), pp. 202–28

Fischer, Peter, *Die deutsche Publizistik als Faktor der deutsch-polnischen Beziehungen 1919–1933* (Wiesbaden, 1991)

Fleischhauer, Ingeborg, ' "Operation Barbarossa" and the Deportations', in Ingeborg Fleischhauer and Benjamin Pinkus, eds, *The Soviet Germans Past and Present* (London, 1986)

Freud, Sigmund, 'Das Unheimliche', in *Gesammelte Werke*, vol. 12, *Werke aus den Jahren 1917–1920* (London, 1947), pp. 229–68

Frevert, Ute, ' "Unser Staat ist männlichen Geschlechts": Zur politischen Topographie der Geschlechter vom 18. bis frühen 20. Jahrhundert', in *'Mann und Weib, und Weib und Mann': Geschlechter-Differenzen in der Moderne* (Munich, 1995), pp. 61–132

Friese, Hildegard, *Unsere Siedler im Kreis Welun* (Wört über Ellwangen, 1965)

Fritsch, Hildegard, *Land mein Land: Bauerntum und Landdienst. BDM Osteinsatz. Siedlungs-geschichte im Osten* (Preußisch Oldendorf, 1986)

Fulbrook, Mary, *German National Identity after the Holocaust* (Cambridge, 1999)

Galos, Adam, F. H. Gentzen and Witold Jakobczyk, *Die Hakatisten. Der deutsche Ostmarken-verein 1894–1933* (Berlin, 1966)

Gehmacher, Johanna, *'Völkische Frauenbewegung': Deutschnationale und nationalsozialistische Geschlechterpolitik in Österreich* (Vienna, 1998)

Gehmacher, Johanna, 'Zukunft, die nicht vergehen will. Jugenderfahrungen in NS-Organisationen und Lebensentwürfe österreichischer Frauen', in Christina Benninghaus und Kerstin Kohtz, eds, *'Sag mir, wo die Mädchen sind': Beiträge zur Geschlechtergeschichte der Jugend* (Cologne, Weimar and Vienna, 1999), pp. 261–74

Gehmacher, Johanna, 'Der andere Ort der Welt. Käthe Schirmachers Auto/Biographie der Nation', in Sophia Kemlein, ed., *Geschlecht und Nationalismus in Mittel- und Osteuropa, 1848–1918* (Osnabrück, 2000)

Gellately, Robert, *Backing Hitler: Consent and Coercion in Nazi Germany* (Oxford, 2001)

Gerke, Wilfried, 'Deutscher Nonkonformismus im Posener Land 1939–1945', *Zeitschrift für Ostforschung* 29 (1980), pp. 385–401

Gerlach, Christian, *Kalkulierte Morde: Die deutsche Wirtschafts- und Vernichtungspolitik in Weißrußland 1941 bis 1944* (Hamburg, 1999)

Giles, Geoffrey J., *Students and National Socialism in Germany* (Princeton, 1985)

Greven-Aschoff, Barbara, *Die bürgerliche Frauenbewegung in Deutschland 1894–1933* (Göttingen, 1981)

Gross, Jan Tomasz, *Polish Society under German Occupation: The Generalgouvernement 1939–1944* (Princeton, 1979)

Grüttner, Michael, *Studenten im Dritten Reich* (Paderborn, 1995)

Gürtler, Paul, *Nationalsozialismus und evangelische Kirchen im Warthegau* (Göttingen, 1958)

Hagen, William W., *Germans, Poles and Jews: The Nationality Conflict in the Prussian East, 1772–1914* (Chicago and London, 1980)

Hagenlücke, Heinz, *Deutsche Vaterlandspartei: Die nationale Rechte am Ende des Kaiserreiches* (Düsseldorf, 1997)

Hansen, Georg, ed., *Schulpolitik als Volkstumspolitik: Quellen zur Schulpolitik der Besatzer in Polen 1939–1945* (Münster and New York, 1994)

Hansen, Georg, *Ethnische Schulpolitik im besetzten Polen: Der Mustergau Wartheland* (Münster and New York, 1995)

Harten, Hans-Christian, *De-Kulturation und Germanisierung: Die nationalsozialistische Rassen- und Erziehungspolitik in Polen 1939–1945* (Frankfurt and New York, 1996)

Harvey, Elizabeth, *Youth and the Welfare State in Weimar Germany* (Oxford, 1993)

Harvey, Elizabeth, 'Gender, Generation and Politics: Young Protestant Women in the Final Years of the Weimar Republic', in Mark Roseman, ed., *Generations in Conflict: Youth Revolt and Generation Formation in Germany 1770–1968* (Cambridge, 1995), pp. 184–209

Harvey, Elizabeth, ' "Die deutsche Frau im Osten": "Rasse", Geschlecht und öffentlicher Raum im besetzten Polen 1940–44', *Archiv für Sozialgeschichte* 38 (1998), pp. 191–214

Harvey, Elizabeth, 'Pilgrimages to the "Bleeding Border": Gender and Rituals of Nationalist Protest in Germany, 1919–1939', *Women's History Review* 9, no. 2 (2000), pp. 201–28

Harvey, Elizabeth, ' "Man muß bloß einen unerschütterlichen Willen haben . . .". Deutsche Kindergärtnerinnen und der nationalsozialistische "Volkstumskampf" im "Distrikt Galizien", 1941–1944', *L'Homme: Zeitschrift für Feministische Geschichtswissenschaft* 12, Heft 1, (2001), pp. 98–123

Harvey, Elizabeth, ' "We forgot all Jews and Poles": German Women and the "Ethnic Struggle" in Nazi-occupied Poland', *Contemporary European History* 10, no. 3 (2001), pp. 447–61

Harvey, Elizabeth, 'Erinnern und verdrängen: deutsche Frauen und der "Volkstumskampf" im besetzten Polen', in Karen Hagemann and Stefanie Schüler-Springorum, eds, *Heimat-Front: Militär und Geschlechterverhältnisse im Zeitalter der Weltkriege* (Frankfurt am Main and New York, 2002), pp. 291–310

Hehn, Jürgen von, *Die Umsiedlung der baltischen Deutschen – das letzte Kapitel baltischdeutscher Geschichte* (Marburg/Lahn, 1982)

Heim, Susanne and Götz Aly, eds, *Bevölkerungsstruktur und Massenmord. Neue Dokumente zur deutschen Politik der Jahre 1938–1945* (Berlin, 1991)

Heimatkalender der Bessarabiendeutschen

Heineman, Elizabeth D., *What Difference Does a Husband Make? Women and Marital Status in Nazi and Postwar Germany* (Berkeley, Los Angeles and London, 1999)

Heinsohn, Kirsten, 'Negotiating Equality and Difference: The Politics of Extreme Right Women in Germany', in Kevin Passmore, ed., *Women and the Extreme Right in Europe* (Oxford, forthcoming)

Herb, Guntram Hendrik, *Under the Map of Germany: Nationalism and Propaganda 1919–1945* (London and New York, 1997)

Herbert, Ulrich, *Fremdarbeiter. Politik und Praxis des 'Ausländer-Einsatzes' in der Kriegswirtschaft des Dritten Reiches* (Bonn, 1985)

Hilberg, Raul, *The Destruction of the European Jews*, 3 vols (New York, 1985)

Hilpert-Fröhlich, Christiana, *'Vorwärts geht es, aber auf den Knien: Die Geschichte der christlichen Studentinnen- und Akademikerinnenbewegung in Deutschland 1905–1938* (Pfaffenweiler, 1996)

Hohenstein, Alexander von, *Wartheländisches Tagebuch 1941/2* (Stuttgart, 1961)

Hornung, Gabriele, *Schrimm, Schroda, Bomst: Kein Roman* (Scheinfeld, 1985)

Jachomowski, Dirk, *Die Umsiedlung der Bessarabien-, Bukowina- und Dobrudschadeutschen: Von der Volksgruppe in Rumänien zur 'Siedlungsbrücke' an der Reichsgrenze* (Munich, 1984)

Jacobsen, Hans-Adolf, *Nationalsozialistische Außenpolitik* (Frankfurt am Main, 1968)

Jahrbuch der Dobrudschadeutschen

Jahrbuch des baltischen Deutschtums

Jahrbuch Weichsel-Warthe

Jansen, Christian and Arno Weckbecker, *Der 'Volksdeutsche Selbstschutz' in Polen 1939/40* (Düsseldorf, 1992)

Jaworski, Rudolf and Marian Wojciechowski, eds, with Mathias Niendorf and Przemyslaw Hauser, *Deutsche und Polen zwischen den Kriegen. Minderheitenstatus und 'Volkstumskampf' im Grenzgebiet. Amtliche Berichterstattung aus beiden Ländern 1920–1939* (Munich, New Providence, London and Paris, 1997)

Judson, Pieter M., 'Inventing Germanness: Class, Ethnicity and Colonial Fantasy at the Margins of the Habsburg Monarchy', *Social Analysis* 33 (1993), pp. 47–67

Judson, Pieter M., 'The Gendered Politics of German Nationalism in Austria, 1880–1990', in David F. Good, Margarete Grandner and Mary Jo Maynes, eds, *Austrian Women in the Nineteenth and Twentieth Centuries: Cross-Disciplinary Perspectives* (Providence and Oxford, 1996), pp. 1–17

Judson, Pieter M., *Exclusive Revolutionaries: Liberal Politics, Social Experience and National Identity in the Austrian Empire, 1848–1914* (Ann Arbor, Michigan, 1996)

Kater, Michael H., 'Die Artamanen – völkische Jugend in der Weimarer Republik', *Historische Zeitschrift* 213 (1971), pp. 577–638

Kaufmann, Doris, *Frauen zwischen Aufbruch und Reaktion. Protestantische Frauenbewegung in der ersten Hälfte des 20. Jahrhunderts* (Munich, 1988), p. 66

Kershaw, Ian, *The 'Hitler Myth': Image and Reality in the Third Reich* (Oxford, 1987)

Kershaw, Ian, 'Arthur Greiser – ein Motor der "Endlösung" ', in Ronald Smelser, E. Syring and Rainer Zitelmann, eds, *Die braune Elite II: 21 weitere biographische Skizzen* (Darmstadt, 1993), pp. 116–27

Kimmich, Christoph, *The Free City: Danzig and German Foreign Policy 1919–1934* (New Haven and London, 1968)

Kindt, Werner, ed., *Die deutsche Jugendbewegung 1920 bis 1933: Die bündische Zeit* (Cologne, 1974)

Klee, Ernst, Willi Dreßen and Volker Rieß, eds, *'Schöne Zeiten': Judenmord aus der Sicht der Täter und Gaffer* (Frankfurt am Main, 1998)

Klein, Peter, 'Die "Reichsuniversität" Posen 1939–1941. Planung und Aufbau einer Universität in der NS-Zeit', Magisterarbeit, Freie Universitat Berlin (1993)

Klessmann, Christoph, ed., *September 1939. Krieg, Besatzung, Widerstand in Polen. Acht Beiträge* (Göttingen, 1989)

Klose-Stiller, Lieselotte, *Arbeitsdienst für die weibliche Jugend in Schlesien* (Garmisch-Partenkirchen, 1978)

Klukowski, Zygmunt, *Diary from the Years of Occupation 1939–1944*, trans. George Klukowski, ed. Andrew Klukowski and Helen Klukowski May (Urbana and Chicago, 1993)

Koch, Angela, 'Von männlichen Tätern und weiblichen Räumen. Geschlechtercodes in antipolnischen Diskursen nach der Ersten Weltkrieg', in Johanna Gehmacher, Elizabeth Harvey and Sophia Kemlein, eds, *Zwischen Kriegen. Nationen, Nationalismen und Geschlechterpolitik in Ost-und Mitteleuropa 1918–1939*, forthcoming

Koehl, Robert L., *RKFDV: German Resettlement and Population Policy 1939–1945* (Cambridge, Mass., 1957)

Kolodny, Annette, *The Land Before Her. Fantasy and Experience of the American Frontiers, 1630–1860* (Chapel Hill, NC, 1984)

Komjathy, Anthony and Rebecca Stockwell, *German Minorities and the Third Reich. Ethnic Germans of East Central Europe between the Wars* (New York and London, 1980)

Koonz, Claudia, *Mothers in the Fatherland: Women, the Family and Nazi Politics* (London, 1987)

Krausnick, Helmut, 'Denkschrift Himmlers über die Behandlung der Fremdvölkischen im Osten (Mai, 1940)', *VjZG* 5 (1957), pp. 194–8

Laqueur, Walter, *Young Germany: A History of the German Youth Movement*, 2nd edition (New Brunswick, NJ, 1984)

Latzel, Klaus, *Deutsche Soldaten – nationalsozialistischer Krieg? Kriegserlebenis – Kriegserfahrung 1939–1945* (Paderborn, 1998)

Lemiesz, Wiktor, *Dąbrówka pod okiem hitlerowskiego żandarma (1935–39)* (Poznań, 1954)

Lemiesz, Wiktor, *Dąbrówka Wielka: przyczynek do dziejów polskiej ludności rodzimej* (Warsaw, 1959)

Lemiesz, Wiktor, *Dąmbrówka Wielka. A Contribution to the History of the Polish Indigenous Population* (Poznań, 1961)

Loesch, K. C. von and Fr. von Unger, 'Zehn Jahre Deutscher Schutzbund', in *Zehn Jahre Deutscher Schutzbund 1919–1929* (Berlin, 1929)

Łuczak, Czesław, ed., *Położenie Ludności Polskiej w Tzw. Kraju Warty w Okresie Hitlerowskiej Okupacji* [= *Dokumenta Occupationis XIII*] (Poznań, 1990)

Lumans, Valdis O., *Himmler's Auxiliaries: the Volksdeutsche Mittelstelle and the German National Minorities of Europe, 1933–1945* (Chapel Hill, NC and London, 1993)

McClintock, Anne, *Imperial Leather: Race, Gender and Sexuality in the Colonial Contest* (New York and London, 1995)

Madajczyk, Czesław, ed., *Zamojszczyzna – Sonderlaboratorium SS: Zbiór dokumentów polskich i niemieckich z okresu okupacji hitlerowskiej*, 2 vols (Warsaw, 1977)

Madajczyk, Czesław, ed., *Vom Generalplan Ost zum Generalsiedlungsplan* (Munich, New Providence, London and Paris, 1994)

Madajczyk, Czeslaw, *Die Okkupationspolitik Nazideutschlands in Polen 1939–1945* (Cologne, 1988)

Majer, Diemut, *'Fremdvölkische' im Dritten Reich. Ein Beitrag zur nationalsozialistischen Rechtsetzung und Rechtspraxis in Verwaltung und Justiz unter besonderer Berücksichtigung der eingegliederten Ostgebiete und des Generalgouvernements* (Boppard am Rhein, 1981)

Manns, Haide, *Frauen für den Nationalsozialismus: Nationalsozialistische Studentinnen und Akademikerinnen in der Weimarer Republik und im Dritten Reich* (Opladen, 1997)

Manoscheck, Walter, ed., *'Es gibt nur eines für das Judentum: Vernichtung': Das Judenbild in deutschen Soldatenbriefen 1939–1944* (Hamburg, 1995)

Marczewski, Jerzy, *Hitlerowska koncepcja polityki kolonizacyjno-wysiedlenczej i jej realizacja w 'Okręgu Warty'* (Poznań, 1979)

Maschmann, Melita, *Fazit: Mein Weg in der Hitler-Jugend* (Munich, 1979)

Melman, Billie, ed., *Borderlines: Genders and Identities in War and Peace, 1880–1930* (New York and London, 1998)

Mendel, Annekatrein, *Zwangsarbeit im Kinderzimmer: 'Ostarbeiterinnen' in deutschen Familien von 1939 bis 1945: Gespräche mit Polinnen und Deutschen* (Frankfurt, 1994)

Michaelsohn, Fred, 'Neue Heimat im Osten? Aus dem noch unveröffentlichten Roman "Wandlungen"', *Heimatkalender der Bessarabiendeutschen 1965*, pp. 100–9

Miegel, Agnes, *Gesammelte Gedichte* (Düsseldorf, 1952)

Miller, William Ian, *The Anatomy of Disgust* (Cambridge, Mass., 1997)

Mills, Sara, *Discourses of Difference: An Analysis of Women's Travel Writing and Colonialism* (London, 1991)

Moeller, Robert G., *War Stories: The Search for a Usable Past in the Federal Republic of Germany* (Berkeley and Los Angeles, 2001)

Morgan, Dagmar, *Weiblicher Arbeitsdienst in Deutschland* (Darmstadt, 1978)

Müller, Rolf-Dieter, *Hitlers Ostkrieg und die deutsche Siedlungspolitik* (Frankfurt am Main, 1991)

Münkel, Daniela, '"Du, Deutsche Landfrau bist verantwortlich!" Bauer und Bäuerin im Nationalsozialismus', *Archiv für Sozialgeschichte* 38 (1998), pp. 141–64

Musial, Bogdan, *Deutsche Zivilverwaltung und Judenverfolgung im Generalgouvernement* (Wiesbaden, 1999)

Nieden, Susanne zur, *Alltag im Ausnahmezustand: Frauentagebücher im zerstörten Deutschland 1943 bis 1945* (Berlin, 1993)

Niehuis, Edith, *Das Landjahr: Eine Jugenderziehungseinrichtung in der Zeit des Nationalsozialismus* (Nörten-Hardenberg, 1984)

Niendorf, Mathias, '"So ein Haß war nicht": Zeitzeugenbefragungen zum deutsch-polnischen Grenzgebiet der Zwischenkriegszeit', *BIOS: Zeitschrift für Biographieforschung und Oral History* 10, no. 1 (1997), pp. 17–33

Niendorf, Mathias, *Minderheiten an der Grenze: Deutsche und Polen in den Kreisen Flatow (Złotów) und Zempelburg (Sępolno Krajenskie), 1900–1939* (Wiesbaden, 1997)

Niethammer, Lutz, ed., *Die volkseigene Erfahrung: Eine Archäologie des Lebens in der Industrieprovinz der DDR* (Berlin, 1991)

Noakes, J. and G. Pridham, eds, *Nazism 1919–45, Vol. 3: Foreign Policy, War and Extermination* (Exeter, 1988)

Orgel-Purper, Liselotte, *Willst Du meine Witwe werden? Eine deutsche Liebe im Krieg* (Berlin, 1995)

Orlowski, Hubert, *'Polnische Wirtschaft': Zum deutschen Polendiskurs der Neuzeit* (Wiesbaden, 1996)

Owings, Alison, *Frauen: German Women Recall the Third Reich* (New Brunswick, NJ, 1993)

Pauwels, Jacques R., *Women, Nazis and Universities: Female University Students in the Third Reich, 1933–1945* (Westport and London, 1984)

Pinkus, Benjamin and Ingeborg Fleischhauer, *Die Deutschen in der Sowjetunion: Geschichte einer nationalen Minderheit im 20. Jahrhundert* (Baden-Baden, 1987)

Piskorski, Jan M., 'The Historiography of the So-called "East Colonization" and the Current State of Research', in Balazs Nagy and Marcell Sebok, eds, . . . *The Man of Many Devices, Who Wandered Full Many Ways. . . . : Festschrift in Honor of Janos M. Bak* (Budapest, 1999), pp. 654–7

Planert, Ute, 'Antifeminismus im Kaiserreich: Indikator einer Gesellschaft in Bewegung', *Archiv für Sozialgeschichte* 38 (1998), pp. 93–118

Planert, Ute, ed., *Nation, Politik und Geschlecht. Frauenbewegungen und Nationalismus in der Moderne* (Frankfurt am Main and New York, 2000)

Pohl, Dieter, *Von der 'Judenpolitik' zum Judenmord: Der Distrikt Lublin des Generalgouvernements 1939–1944* (Frankfurt am Main, 1993), pp. 113–17

Pohl, Dieter, *Nationalsozialistische Judenverfolgung in Ostgalizien 1941–1944: Organisation und Durchführung eines staatlichen Massenverbrechens* (Munich, 1996)

Pospieszalski, Karol Marian, ed., *Hitlerowskie 'prawo' okupacyjne w Polsce, Część I: Ziemie 'Wcielone'* [= *Documenta Occupationis V*] (Poznań, 1952)

Pospieszalski, Karl Marian, ed., *Hitlerowskie 'prawo' okupacyjne w Polsce, Część II: Generalna Gubernia* [= *Documenta Occupationis VI*] (Poznań, 1956)

Präg, Werner, and Wolfgang Jacobmeyer, eds, *Das Diensttagebuch des deutschen Generalgouverneurs in Polen 1939–1945* (Stuttgart, 1975)

Pratt, Mary Louise, *Imperial Eyes: Travel Writing and Transculturation* (London, 1992)

Reagin, Nancy R., *A German Women's Movement: Class and Gender in Hanover, 1880–1933* (Chapel Hill, NC and London, 1995)

Reagin, Nancy, 'The Imagined *Hausfrau*: National Identity, Domesticity and Colonialism in Imperial Germany', *Journal of Modern History* 73 (March 2001), pp. 54–86

Reese, Dagmar, 'Bund Deutscher Mädel – Zur Geschichte der weiblichen deutschen Jugend im Dritten Reich', in Frauengruppe Faschismusforschung, ed., *Mutterkreuz und Arbeitsbuch: Zur Geschichte der Frauen in der Weimarer Republik und im Nationalsozialismus* (Frankfurt am Main, 1981), pp. 163–87

Reese, Dagmar, *Straff, aber nicht stramm; herb, aber nicht derb: Zur Vergesellschaftung der Mädchen durch den Bund Deutscher Mädel im sozialkulturellen Vergleich zweier Milieus* (Weinheim, 1989)

Reese, Dagmar and Carola Sachse, 'Frauenforschung zum Nationalsozialismus: Eine Bilanz', in Lerke Gravenhorst and Carmen Tatschmurat, eds, *Töchter-Fragen: NS-Frauengeschichte* (Freiburg im Breisgau, 1990), pp. 73–106

Reese, Dagmar, 'The BDM Generation: A Female Generation in Transition from Dictatorship to Democracy', in Mark Roseman, ed., *Generations in Conflict: Youth Revolt and Generation Formation in Germany 1770–1968* (Cambridge, 1995), pp. 227–46

Reese, Dagmar, 'Verstrickung und Verantwortung: Weibliche Jugendliche in der Führung des Bundes Deutscher Mädel', in Kirsten Heinsohn, Barbara Vogel and Ulrike Weckel, eds, *Zwischen Karriere und Verfolgung: Handlungsräume von Frauen im nationalsozialistischen Deutschland* (Frankfurt am Main, 1997), pp. 206–22

Rieß, Volker, *Die Anfänge der Vernichtung 'lebensunwerten Lebens' in den Reichsgauen Danzig-Westpreußen und Wartheland 1939/40* (Frankfurt am Main, 1995)

Rimscha, Hans von, 'Zur Umsiedlung der Deutschen aus den Baltischen Staaten während des Zweiten Weltkrieges', *Osteuropa* 11 (1961), pp. 134–6

Roseman, Mark, *The Past in Hiding* (London, 2000)

Rosenhaft, Eve, 'Facing Up to the Past – Again?: "Crimes of the Wehrmacht" ', *Debatte* 5, no. 1 (1997), pp. 105–18

Rössler, Mechthild and Sabine Schleiermacher, eds, *Der 'Generalplan Ost': Hauptlinien der nationalsozialistischen Planungs- und Vernichtungspolitik* (Berlin, 1993)

Rückerl, Adalbert, ed., *NS-Vernichtungslager im Spiegel deutscher Strafprozesse: Belzec, Sobibor, Treblinka, Chelmno* (Munich, 1977)

Rüdiger, Jutta, ed., *Die Hitler-Jugend und ihr Selbstverständnis im Spiegel ihrer Aufgaben-gebiete* (Lindhorst, 1983)

Rüdiger, Jutta, *Ein Leben für die Jugend: Mädelführerin im Dritten Reich* (Preußisch Oldendorf, 1999)

Sandkühler, Thomas, *'Endlösung' in Galizien: Der Judenmord in Ostpolen und die Rettungs-initiativen von Berthold Beitz, 1941–1944* (Bonn, 1996)

Sayner, Joanne, 'Depictions of Fascism in Women's Autobiographies in German', Ph.D. thesis (University of Cardiff, 2002)

Schaser, Angelika, 'Das Engagement des Bundes Deutscher Frauenvereine für das "Auslands-deutschtum": Weibliche "Kulturaufgabe" und nationale Politik vom Ersten Weltkrieg bis 1933', in Ute Planert, ed., *Nation, Politik und Geschlecht: Frauenbewegungen und National-ismus in der Moderne* (Frankfurt and New York, 2000), pp. 254–74

Schechtman, Joseph B., *European Population Transfers 1939–1945* (New York, 1946)

Scheck, Raffael, 'German Conservatives and Female Political Activism in the Early Weimar Republic', *German History* 15, no. 1 (1997), pp. 34–55

Scheck, Raffael, 'Women against Versailles: Maternalism and Nationalism of Female Bourgeois Politicians in the Early Weimar Republic', *German Studies Review* 22 (1999), pp. 21–42

Schenk, Dieter, *Hitlers Mann in Danzig. Albert Forster und die NS-Verbrechen in Danzig-Westpreussen* (Bonn, 2000)

Schmidt-Vanderheyden, H., *Arbeitsmaiden in Pommern. Ein Rückblick* (Göttingen, 1975)

Schneider, Wolfgang, ed., *'Vernichtungspolitik': Eine Debatte über den Zusammenhang von Sozialpolitik und Genozid im nationalsozialistischen Deutschland* (Hamburg, 1991)

Schwarz, Gudrun, 'Verdrängte Täterinnen: Frauen im Apparat der SS (1939–45)', in Therese Wobbe, ed., *Nach Osten: Verdeckte Spuren nationalsozialistischer Verbrechen* (Frankfurt am Main, 1992), pp. 197–223

Schwarz, Gudrun, *Eine Frau an seiner Seite: Ehefrauen in der 'SS-Sippengemeinschaft'* (Hamburg, 1997)

Siegel, Elisabeth *Dafür und dagegen. Ein Leben für die Sozialpädagogik* (Stuttgart, 1981)

Sobczak, Janusz, 'Ethnic Germans as the Subject of the Nazi Resettlement Campaign during the Second World War', *Polish Western Affairs* 8 (1967), pp. 63–95

Spoerer, Mark, 'NS-Zwangsarbeiter im Deutschen Reich: Eine Statistik vom 30. September 1944 nach Arbeitsamtsbezirken', *VjZG* 49, no. 4 (2001), pp. 665–84

Stasiewski, Bernhard, 'Die Kirchenpolitik der Nationalsozialisten im Warthegau 1939–1945', *VjZG* 7 no. 1 (1959), pp. 46–74

Steinert, Marlis G., *Hitler's War and the Germans: Public Mood and Attitude during the Second World War* (Athens, Ohio, 1977)

Stephenson, Jill, *The Nazi Organisation of Women* (London, 1981)

Stephenson, Jill, 'Girls' Higher Education in the 1930s', *Journal of Contemporary History* 10, no. 1 (1975), pp. 41–69

Stephenson, Jill, 'Women's Labor Service in Nazi Germany', *Central European History* 15 (1982), pp. 241–63

Stephenson, Jill, *Women in Nazi Germany* (London, 2001)

Stibbe, Matthew, 'Anti-Feminism, Nationalism and the German Right, 1914–1920', *German History* 20, no. 2 (2002), pp. 185–210

Stoehr, Irene, *Emanzipation zum Staat? Der Allgemeine Deutsche Frauenverein – Deutscher Staatsbürgerinnenverband (1893–1933)* (Pfaffenweiler, 1990)

Stoler, Ann L., 'Making Empire Respectable: The Politics of Race and Sexual Morality in 20th-century Colonial Cultures', *American Ethnologist* 16, no. 4 (Nov. 1989), pp. 634–60

Stoler, Ann L., 'Bourgeois Bodies and Racial Selves', in Catherine Hall, ed., *Cultures of Empire: Colonizers in Britain and the Empire in the Nineteenth and Twentieth Centuries* (Manchester, 2000), pp. 88–119

Stossun, Harry, *Die Umsiedlungen der Deutschen aus Litauen während des Zweiten Weltkrieges: Untersuchungen zum Schicksal einer deutschen Volksgruppe im Osten* (Hamburg, 1990)

Strien, Renate, *Mädchenerziehung und -sozialisation in der Zeit des Nationalsozialismus und ihre lebensgeschichtlichte Bedeutung: Lehrerinnen erinnern sich an ihre Jugend während des Dritten Reiches* (Opladen, 2000)

Süchting-Hänger, Andrea, 'Die Anti-Versailles-Propaganda konservativer Frauen in der Weimarer Republik – Eine weibliche Dankesschuld?', in Gerd Krumeich with Silke Fehlemann, eds, *Versailles 1919 – Ziele – Wirkung – Wahrnehmung* (Cologne, 2001), pp. 302–13

Szefer, Andrzej, 'Die deutschen Umsiedler in der Provinz Oberschlesien in den Jahren 1939–45', in J. Hütter, R. Meyers and D. Papenfuß, eds, *Tradition und Neubeginn. Internationale Forschungen zur deutschen Geschichte im 20. Jahrhundert* (Munich, 1976), pp. 345–54

Szepansky, Gerda, ed., *'Blitzmädel', 'Heldenmutter', 'Kriegerwitwe': Frauenleben im Zweiten Weltkrieg* (Frankfurt am Main, 1986)

Ther, Philipp, *Deutsche und polnische Vertriebene: Gesellschaft und Vertriebenenpolitik in der SBZ/DDR und in Polen 1945–1956* (Göttingen, 1998)

Theweleit, Klaus, *Männerphantasien, Vol.1: Frauen, Fluten, Körper, Geschichte* (Frankfurt am Main, 1977)

Tooley, T. Hunt, *National Identity and Weimar Germany: Upper Silesia and the Eastern Border, 1918–1922* (Lincoln, Nebraska and London, 1997)

Volkmann, Hans-Erich, 'Zur Ansiedlung der Deutschbalten im "Warthegau"', *Zeitschrift für Ostforschung* 30, no. 4 (1981), pp. 527–58

Volkmann, Hans-Erich, ed., *Das Rußlandbild im Dritten Reich* (Cologne, 1994)

Vorländer, Herwart, *Die NSV. Darstellung und Dokumentation einer nationalsozialistischen Organisation* (Boppard am Rhein, 1988)

Walzer, Anke, *Käthe Schirmacher. Eine deutsche Frauenrechtlerin auf dem Wege vom Liberalismus zum konservativen Nationalismus* (Pfaffenweiler, 1991)

Wasser, Bruno, *Himmlers Raumplanung im Osten. Der Generalplan Ost in Polen 1940–1944* (Basle, 1993)

Watzke-Otte, Susanne, *'Ich war ein einsatzbereites Glied in der Gemeinschaft': Vorgehensweise und Wirkungsmechanismen nationalsozialistischer Erziehung am Beispiel des weiblichen Arbeitsdienstes* (Frankfurt am Main, 1999)

Weidenfeller, Gerhard, *VDA: Verein für das Deutschtum im Ausland* (Frankfurt am Main, 1976)

Weindling, Paul, *Epidemics and Genocide in Eastern Europe, 1890–1945* (Oxford, 2000)

Weingartner, James J., 'Sepp Dietrich, Heinrich Himmler and the Leibstandarte SS Adolf Hitler, 1933–1938', *Central European History* 1 (1968), pp. 264–84

Wengst, Udo, 'Schlange-Schöningen, Ostsiedlung und die Demission der Regierung Brüning', *Geschichte in Wissenschaft und Unterricht* 30, no. 9 (1979), pp. 538–51

Wildenthal, Lora, '"When Men Are Weak": The Imperial Feminism of Frieda von Bülow', *Gender and History* 10, no. 1 (1998), pp. 53–77

Wildenthal, Lora, 'Mass-Marketing Colonialism and Nationalism: The Career of Else Frobenius in the "Weimarer Republik" and Nazi Germany', in Ute Planert, ed., *Nation,*

Politik und Geschlecht: Frauenbewegungen und Nationalismus in der Moderne (Frankfurt and New York, 2000), pp. 328–43

Wildenthal, Lora, *German Women for Empire, 1884–1945* (Durham and London, 2001)

Willmot, Louise, 'National Socialist Organisations for Girls: A Contribution to the Social and Political History of the Third Reich', D.Phil. thesis (Oxford, 1980)

Willmot, Louise, 'The Debate on the Introduction of an Auxiliary Military Service Law for Women in the Third Reich and its Consequences', *German History* 2 (1985), pp. 10–20

Winkler, Dörte, *Frauenarbeit im 'Dritten Reich'* (Hamburg, 1977)

Wippermann, Wolfgang, *Der 'deutsche Drang nach Osten': Ideologie und Wirklichkeit eines politischen Schlagwortes* (Darmstadt, 1981)

Witte, Peter, et al., eds, *Der Dienstkalender Heinrich Himmlers 1941/42* (Hamburg, 1999)

Wolff, Larry, *Inventing Eastern Europe* (Stanford, 1994)

Wörner-Heil, Ortrud, *Frauenschulen auf dem Lande. Reifensteiner Verband (1897–1997)* (Kassel, 1997)

Wrzesinski, Wojciech, 'The Union of Poles in Germany and its Attitude to Problems of Consciousness of Nationality (1922–1939)', *Acta Poloniae Historica* 20 (1969), pp. 52–74

Wrzesinski, Wojciech, 'Die Politik der nationalsozialistischen Machthaber gegenüber der polnischen Minderheit in Deutschland (1933–45)', in Ernst Hinrichs, ed., *Deutschland und Polen von der nationalsozialistischen Machtergreifung bis zum Ende des zweiten Weltkriegs* (Braunschweig, 1986), pp. 85–92

Yuval-Davis, Nira, *Gender and Nation* (London, 1997)

Zeitweiser der Galiziendeutschen

Zimmermann, Michael, *Rassenutopie und Genozid: Die nationalsozialistische 'Lösung der Zigeunerfrage'* (Hamburg, 1996)

Index